SHAKESPEARE SURVEY

ADVISORY BOARD

SHAKESPEARE SURVEY

AN ANNUAL SURVEY OF

SHAKESPEARE STUDIES AND PRODUCTION

52

Shakespeare and the Globe

EDITED BY

STANLEY WELLS

CAMBRIDGE
UNIVERSITY PRESS

PUBLISHED BY THE PRESS SYNDICATE OF THE UNIVERSITY OF CAMBRIDGE
The Pitt Building, Trumpington Street, Cambridge CB2 1RP, United Kingdom

CAMBRIDGE UNIVERSITY PRESS
The Edinburgh Building, Cambridge CB2 2RU, United Kingdom   http://www.cup.cam.ac.uk
40 West 20th Street, New York, NY 10011–4211, USA   http://www.cup.org
10 Stamford Road, Oakleigh, Melbourne 3166, Australia

First published 1999

Printed in Great Britain at the University Press, Cambridge

Typeset in Bembo 10/12pt [CE]

A catalogue record for this book is available from the British Library

ISBN 0 521 660742 hardback

Shakespeare Survey was first published in 1948. Its first
eighteen volumes were edited by Allardyce Nicoll.
Kenneth Muir edited volumes 19 to 33.

EDITOR'S NOTE

Future volumes of *Shakespeare Survey* will be edited by Professor Peter Holland.

Volume 53, on 'Shakespeare and Narrative', will be at press by the time this volume appears. The theme of Volume 54, which will include papers from the 2000 International Shakespeare Conference, will be 'Shakespeare and Religions'.

Submissions should be addressed to the Editor at The Shakespeare Institute, Church Street, Stratford-upon-Avon, Warwickshire CV37 6HP, to arrive at the latest by 1 September 2000 for Volume 54. Pressures on space are heavy; priority is given to articles related to the theme of a particular volume. Please either enclose postage (overseas, in International Reply Coupons) or send a copy you do not wish to be returned. All articles submitted are read by the Editor and at least one member of the Editorial Board, whose indispensable assistance the Editor gratefully acknowledges.

Unless otherwise indicated, Shakespeare quotations and references are keyed to the modern-spelling Complete Oxford Shakespeare (1986).

Review copies of books should be addressed to the Editor, as above. In attempting to survey the ever-increasing bulk of Shakespeare publications our reviewers inevitably have to exercise some selection. We are pleased to receive offprints of articles which help to draw our reviewers' attention to relevant material.

S. W. W.

CONTRIBUTORS

JOHN H. ASTINGTON, *University of Toronto in Mississauga*
ANTHONY B. DAWSON, *University of British Columbia*
JANETTE DILLON, *University of Nottingham*
PETER DONALDSON, *Massachusetts Institute of Technology*
CHARLES EDELMAN, *Edith Cowen University, Australia*
GABRIEL EGAN, *De Montfort University, Leicester*
ALISON FINDLAY, *University of Lancaster*
ANDREW GURR, *University of Reading*
BARBARA HODGDON, *Drake University, Iowa*
ANGELA HURWORTH, *Université François-Rabelais, Tours*
YU JIN KO, *Wellesley College, Massachusetts*
BARBARA KREPS, *University of Pisa*
JERZY LIMON, *University of Gdansk*
ANIA LOOMBA, *Jawaharlal Nehru University, New Delhi*
KATE MCLUSKIE, *University of Southampton*
MARION O'CONNOR, *University of Kent at Canterbury*
STEPHEN ORGEL, *Stanford University, California*
RICHARD PROUDFOOT, *King's College, University of London*
ERIC RASMUSSEN, *University of Nevada*
NIKY RATHBONE, *Birmingham Shakespeare Library*
ROBERT SMALLWOOD, *The Shakespeare Birthplace Trust*
W. B. WORTHEN, *University of California, Berkeley*

CONTENTS

CONTENTS

ILLUSTRATIONS

RECONSTRUCTIONS OF THE GLOBE: A RETROSPECTIVE

GABRIEL EGAN

I ought not to have suggested in *The Stage of the Globe*, 356, that the first Globe might have been rectangular.[1]

The Globe playhouse occupies special places in the collective conscious and unconscious of Shakespeare studies and – *where id was, there shall ego be* – the Wanamaker reconstruction has brought important theoretical and practical conflicts into the open. The validity of historical methods and pursuit of authenticity have always been contentious issues, but the act of making a physical reconstruction focuses the minds of supporters and objectors in a way that no hypothetical model can. The Wanamaker project can be credited with the achievement of accelerating research into the design and operation of the Globe so that in the last thirty years the body of published work on the subject has more than doubled. Whether or not the reconstructed building itself aids scholarship, the research underlying its claim to authenticity represents a considerable return on the capital outlay.

The first landmark in the scholarly reconstruction of the Globe is E. K. Chambers's *The Elizabethan Stage* which contained his hypothesized plans for the building.[2] All earlier attempts at reconstruction lacked Chambers's compendious knowledge of early modern drama and cultural history. Chambers argued that the movement of playing companies between different playhouses, especially in the period prior to the construction of the Globe, suggests standardization of design[3] and he found few differences between late sixteenth-century plays and early seventeenth-century plays that might be taken to indicate that the Globe or Fortune differed substantially from their predecessors.[4]

Chambers offered no precise defence of his drawing because it was intended to be schematic rather than architectural, and showed neither the dimensions nor the arrangement of structural members. General features, not unrecoverable particularities, were his concern. It is worth noting that Chambers's octagonal playhouse which was supposed to be Globe-like and typical seems dependent upon J. C. Visscher's engraving of 1616 called *Londinium Florentiss[i]ma Britanniae Urbs*.[5] When Chambers's book was published in 1923 the Visscher engraving was still considered authoritative and of the several pictures which suggest that the Globe had as few as six or eight sides, it enjoyed the highest status. The belief that the Globe was six sided derived from Hester Thrale who, in 1819, recorded having seen its uncovered foundations some fifty years before.[6] Interest in finding corroboration for Thrale's claim has persisted although most scholars disregard her evidence entirely.[7]

---

[1] E. K. Chambers, *The Elizabethan Stage*, 4 vols. (Oxford, 1923), vol. 2, p. 434n2.

[2] Chambers, *The Elizabethan Stage*, vol. 3, p. 85.

[3] Ibid., p. 50.

[4] Ibid., p. 103–104.

[5] R. A. Foakes, *Illustrations of the English Stage 1580–1642* (London, 1985), pp. 18–19.

[6] Chambers, *The Elizabethan Stage*, vol. 2, p. 428.

[7] Martin Clout, 'Hester Thrale and the Globe Theatre', *The New Rambler*, 9 (1993–4), 34–50.

In 1942 John Cranford Adams published his *The Globe Playhouse: Its Design and Equipment* and in 1950 Adams and Irwin Smith completed a beautiful scale model of the First Globe which was immediately incorporated into a public display at the Folger Library in Washington. Following the Visscher engraving, Adams made his Globe octagonal and from the Fortune and Hope construction contracts Adams deduced that the Globe was '84 feet across between outside walls, 34 feet high to the eaves, and 58 feet across the interior yard'.[8] The Fortune contract specified galleries 12 feet 6 inches deep[9] and Adams assumed that this included 6 inches for the outer wall, so the real centre-to-centre spacing of the posts was 12 feet. The Fortune would have been constructed from regularly shaped units, Adams reasoned, and the simplest arrangement would have been to repeat the 12 feet square bays that formed the corners of the auditorium. Six and a half such bays form a structure 78 feet between centres or 80 feet once the thickness of posts and exterior covering is added.[10] The width of the enclosed yard would be that of four and a half bays, 54 feet between centres, or 55 feet to the furthest edges of the posts. Finding that his arrangements led so easily to the 55 feet and 80 feet specifications of the Fortune contract convinced Adams that he had hit upon the ground-plan.

What if the Globe also used 12 feet square bay units? Two such bays could form each of the eight sides of the playhouse. Adams calculated – wrongly, as it happened – that this would give the Globe an external diameter of 84 feet including the six inches of outer covering at either end;[11] the true figure was 83 feet. Adams constructed his Globe's stage from a line connecting 'the middle post of one sector across to the middle post of the next sector but one'[12] which gave a width of 43 feet. The Fortune's stage was 43 feet wide and Adams thought this correspondence could not be coincidence – he must have hit upon the groundplan of the Globe.[13]

Unfortunately, Adams's calculation of the width of his stage was also wrong. The correct figure is the width of one side of the playhouse yard, 24 feet, plus the width of the bases of two right-angled isosceles triangles whose hypotenuses are half the width of one side of the playhouse yard, which comes to very nearly 41 feet. A discrepancy of almost 2 feet – over $4\frac{1}{2}$ per cent – is gross enough to invalidate his postulated correspondence with the Fortune contract and, since this correspondence validated all the assumptions which led to it, the entire reconstruction must be discounted as pure speculation.

Adams spotted the fatal error in his calculations and in 1943 he published a revised text of the book with the offending calculations emended. Although a note was added acknowledging the error,[14] libraries frequently catalogue the 1942 and 1943 printings as a single first edition. Adams excised his insistence that the correspondence between the Fortune stage and his Globe's stage validated the method, but put nothing in its place to substantiate his claim to have discovered the precise dimensions of the Globe. However, it was not the mathematics in Adams's book that drew fire from scholars of original staging, but rather the interior features and facilities of his Globe.

Adams's Globe had a total of six main stage traps and a large recessed alcove discovery space. Suspended above this playing space was a second stage which was fronted with a balustraded balcony ('tarras') and which had another, smaller, recessed alcove discovery space at its rear. At either side of this balcony, and at 45 degrees to it, was a glazed bay

[8] John Cranford Adams, *The Globe Playhouse: Its Design and Equipment* (Cambridge, Mass., 1942), p. 3.

[9] Ibid., pp. 20–1.

[10] Ibid., p. 21.

[11] Ibid., p. 21.

[12] Ibid., pp. 22, 90.

[13] Ibid., p. 22.

[14] Ibid., 2nd printing with corrections (Cambridge, Mass., 1943), p. 90.

window which overhung a correspondingly angled stage door on the platform stage. Extending from the top of the tiring house, and connected to it at the eaves, was a 'heavens' covering the entire stage. At the height of the third auditorium gallery the tiring house had a music room. The upper stage (at the same height as the second auditorium gallery) had a trap door set in its floor which provided communication with the main stage.

Adams's Globe was rich in features to assist theatrical spectacle and to provide a physical referent for almost every scenic structure mentioned in Renaissance drama. If a scene required a 'corner' to hide around, or a 'balcony' from which to be wooed or to be thrown, Adams's Globe could offer a realistic analogue. Supporting his design with dramatic quotations, Adams cared not which playhouse a particular play was written for: the Globe was the finest playhouse and so it must have incorporated at least the major features of all the others.

The history of the scholarship of Globe reconstruction in the fifty years since its publication can broadly be characterized as one of reaction to, and refutation of, Adams's book. Adams shared Chambers's conviction that the playhouses were largely alike and he used a wide range of play texts as evidence for the staging needs which any playhouse might have to satisfy. But as a necessary consequence of this method one is able to reconstruct only an idealized 'typical' playhouse, not any particular playhouse. Chambers implicitly accepted this principle. Adams implicitly rejected it and produced highly detailed plans of the Globe which he misrepresented as reliable scholarly deduction.

Adams's aesthetic judgements were challenged by those who felt that he showed little appreciation of theatrical convention which, contrary to his assumption, would allow a scene set indoors to be played on the front of a thrust stage. But with the mathematical error glossed over, the first part of Adams's Globe to collapse was the octagonal outer wall. In the

first volume of *Shakespeare Survey*, I. A. Shapiro proved that Visscher's engraving was derived from the panorama in John Norden's *Civitas Londini* and was therefore entirely without authority.[15] After considering several other pictures and rejecting their authority, Shapiro concluded that the Hollar engraving of 1647[16] was the most reliable view of the Bankside playhouses. In Hollar's picture the Globe and the Hope appear to be round. A different approach was needed to demolish Adams's interior arrangements.

Before publishing his major work on Elizabethan playhouse design, *The Globe Restored*, C. Walter Hodges published two articles concerning the De Witt drawing of the Swan. In the first Hodges insisted that De Witt showed that the Swan was a polygon with sufficient number of sides that it was virtually round ('This to my mind rules out the notion of an octagonal building in favour of, say, a sixteen-sided polygon') and that the 'inner stage' 'was neither a permanent nor an indispensable part of Elizabethan public stage practice'.[17] The following year Hodges published an article with Richard Southern which argued that De Witt's Swan was essentially a Renaissance rather than a Tudor design. In particular the stage posts being, as De Witt stated, painted to resemble marble, their ornate bases and capitals, and their entasis, all point to classical and continental influence upon the indigenous building tradition.[18] Students of Elizabethan playhouse design can be assigned places along a spectrum of 'faith in De Witt' and the reaction to Adams's Globe was a collective move towards the 'greater faith' end

---

15 I. A. Shapiro, 'The Bankside Theatres: Early Engravings', *Shakespeare Survey 1* (1948), 25–37.
16 Foakes, *Illustrations of the English Stage 1580–1642*, pp. 29–31, 36–38.
17 C. Walter Hodges, 'De Witt again', *Theatre Notebook*, 5 (1951), 32–4, p. 34.
18 Richard Southern and C. Walter Hodges, 'Colour in the Elizabethan Theatre', *Theatre Notebook*, 6 (1952), 57–60.

of this spectrum. The work of Hodges and Southern helped by showing that the sketch does not necessarily contradict anti-theatrical denunciations of playhouse opulence.

Despite its title, Hodges's *The Globe Restored* contained no representation of the first Globe. Instead Hodges offered a typical playhouse of 1595 and the second Globe of 1614[19] for which Hodges had the authority of the Hollar engraving, validated by Shapiro. Hodges's decision not to reconstruct the first Globe appears to have been a reaction to Adams's over-confidence which went 'far beyond the warrant of evidence'.[20] Hodges attempted to reconcile the De Witt drawing with the needs of the plays and with George Kernodle's work on baroque decoration.[21] Hodges's 'typical playhouse' of 1595 added no major features not present in De Witt. To provide a larger upper stage as well as a discovery space Hodges conjectured the use of a stage booth.[22] Hodges rejected the staging principles of Adams's book and with them the need for a permanent upper stage.

In the same vein as Hodges, A. M. Nagler offered a thorough critique of Adams's Globe as an inappropriate venue for the drama. Nagler considered the only reliable evidence to be 'the stage directions in the quartos and the First Folio of Shakespeare's plays' and the documents of Platter and Henslowe[23] and he poured scorn on Adams's theory that many scenes were played on an inner stage and on a large upper stage. Nagler argued for acceptance of the evidence of the De Witt drawing, which shows a flat wall, and for discoveries and concealments achieved using a portable booth.[24] Instead of Adams's large upper stage Nagler, like Hodges, offered the stage balcony shown by De Witt, augmented at need by the solid upper surface of a stage booth placed against the back wall.[25]

Adams's large upper stage had practical drawbacks too. Warren D. Smith noted that it caused a problem in Adams's reconstruction of the original staging of Shakespeare's *King Lear*.[26] The Folio text has a stage direction for

Edgar to come out from his hiding place immediately before Edmund's call 'Brother, a word, discend',[27] which Adams was forced to move down three lines to give Edgar time to descend from the upper stage.[28] Smith argued instead for a booth-like scaffolding serving for 'aloft' scenes. George F. Reynolds concurred and blamed Adams's errors on his misguided convictions about naturalistic staging.[29]

The attack on Adams was sustained in three articles by Richard Hosley.[30] One demolished Adams's upper stage by showing that Shakespeare's use of a raised playing space was less frequent than Adams claimed and that it usually involved engagement with the main stage (for example a conversation or an observation) which kept the players near to the balustraded front of the 'aloft' space. The De Witt drawing of the Swan shows an upper playing space

---

[19] C. Walter Hodges, *The Globe Restored: A Study of the Elizabethan Theatre* (London, 1953), pp. 174, 177.

[20] Ibid., p. 53.

[21] George R. Kernodle, *From Art to Theatre: Form and Convention in the Renaissance* (Chicago, 1944), pp. 130–53.

[22] Hodges, *The Globe Restored: A Study of the Elizabethan Theatre*, pp. 56–60.

[23] A. M. Nagler, *Shakespeare's Stage* (New Haven, 1958), p. 19.

[24] Ibid., pp. 26–32.

[25] Ibid., pp. 47–51.

[26] Warren D. Smith, 'Evidence of Scaffolding on Shakespeare's Stage', *Review of English Studies*, 2 (1951), 22–9, p. 24.

[27] William Shakespeare, *The Norton Facsimile of The First Folio of Shakespeare*, ed. Charlton Hinman (New York, 1968), TLN 948–9.

[28] John Cranford Adams, 'The Original Staging of *King Lear*', in *Joseph Quincy Adams Memorial Studies*, ed. James G. McManaway, Giles E. Dawson and Edwin E. Willoughby (Washington, 1948), pp. 315–35, p. 319.

[29] George F. Reynolds, 'Was There a "Tarras" in Shakespeare's Globe?', *Shakespeare Survey 4* (1951), 97–100.

[30] Richard Hosley, 'Shakespeare's Use of a Gallery Over the Stage', *Shakespeare Survey 10* (1957), 77–89; Richard Hosley, 'The Discovery-Space in Shakespeare's Globe', *Shakespeare Survey 12* (1959), 35–46; Richard Hosley, 'Was There a Music-Room in Shakespeare's Globe?', *Shakespeare Survey 13* (1960), 113–23.

sufficient, Hosley argued, for the staging needs of all of Shakespeare's plays.[31] In 'The Discovery Space in Shakespeare's Globe' Hosley argued against the inner stage by showing that there is no positive evidence to suggest such a space. The term 'study' appears in the stage directions of a few relevant plays, but Hosley argued that these were 'fictional' stage directions referring to the imagined location and not the playhouse fabric.[32] To establish the body of relevant evidence, Hosley produced a list of thirty plays performed by Shakespeare's company between 1599 and 1608 when their only permanent London venue was the Globe. As George F. Reynolds argued in his work on plays at the Red Bull,[33] if a company had only one playhouse for a certain period of time then any play written for the company during that time ought to assume, and to reflect, the features and practices of that venue. Not least of the problems with this method is its potential for logical circularity: the staging of plays is generally inferred from performance conditions, and here the performance conditions are being inferred from the staging. Nonetheless, most people prefer a method that at least aims to be economical with evidence over one that, Adams-like, makes no distinction between public theatre plays of the 1580s and private theatre plays of the 1610s.

Of the thirty 'Globe plays' claimed by Hosley, twenty-one have no scenes using the discovery space and in the remaining ones the uses are 'few and infrequent', are 'essentially "shows"', or disclosures of a player or object invested with some special interest or significance', and 'do not involve any appreciable movement within the discovery-space'.[34] Still, some kind of discovery space is needed and Hosley argued that a discovery 'can be effected without curtains in a tiring-house whose doors open out upon the stage',[35] with perhaps the assistance of a booth-like arrangement of curtains.[36]

In 'Was There a Music-Room in Shakespeare's Globe?' Hosley used his list of Globe plays to show that Adams's third-level music room is contradicted by the evidence of the drama. Most of the Globe plays have stage directions for music, but in only nine of the plays is the location specified. In these nine plays there are a total of seventeen such stage directions and in every case but one the music is described as coming from 'within'. The exception is the direction for 'Musicke of the Hoboyes is vnder the Stage' in *Antony and Cleopatra*.[37] This suggests that there was no elevated music room at the Globe before 1609.

In these three articles Hosley demonstrated by a strict economy of evidence that the De Witt drawing of the Swan shows everything needed to stage all the plays written for the Globe. This was a significant achievement because it placed the subject on what some consider to be the firmest evidential basis available: a contemporary drawing. Later, John B. Gleason provided impressively detailed evidence that we ought to trust the representational skills of De Witt and his copyist Van Buchell and should ignore John Dover Wilson's obscurely racist dismissal of 'one Dutchman's copy of another Dutchman's sketch'.[38]

If the De Witt Swan is capable of staging all the plays written for the Globe then it, together with the Fortune contract, could form the basis of a Globe reconstruction so long as we assume

---

[31] Hosley, 'Shakespeare's Use of a Gallery Over the Stage'.

[32] Hosley, 'The Discovery-Space in Shakespeare's Globe', p. 35.

[33] George F. Reynolds, *The Staging of Elizabethan Plays at the Red Bull Theater 1605–1625*, MLA General Series, 9 (New York, 1940), pp. 1–29.

[34] Hosley, 'The Discovery-Space in Shakespeare's Globe', pp. 44–5.

[35] Ibid., p. 41.

[36] Ibid., pp. 42–3.

[37] Shakespeare, *The Norton Facsimile of The First Folio of Shakespeare*, TLN 2482; Hosley, 'Was There a Music-Room in Shakespeare's Globe?', p. 118.

[38] John B. Gleason, 'The Dutch Humanist Origins of the De Witt Drawing of the Swan Theatre', *Shakespeare Quarterly*, 32 (1981), 324–38, p. 329.

that the outdoor playhouses of London were essentially alike. Two articles published in *Shakespeare Survey 12* (1959) indicated the range of opinion about the homogeneity of the playhouses. W. F. Rothwell argued that playing conditions were far from standardized and that, at least until 1598, players were required to adapt to the exigencies of a variety of venues.[39] Conditions at court were unlike the conditions on tour – it was 'an era of change and experimentations in matters dramatic and theatrical' – and hence standardization of playhouse design is unlikely.[40] By Rothwell's reasoning the De Witt drawing of the Swan and the Fortune contract are good evidence for the Swan and the Fortune, but not for any other playhouses.

Taking the opposite view about typicality, Richard Southern attempted to adjust the dimensions given in the Fortune contract to make them practicable for a 'round' playhouse with reasonable sight-lines.[41] Because Hollar shows what appears to be a smoothly rounded exterior to the Globe, Southern's model had a sixteen-sided polygonal frame which, from a distance, would look almost circular. Southern's stage cover, stage posts, and *frons scenae* were derived from the De Witt drawing of the Swan with the exception of a small discovery space between the stage doors. This was justified, quite ingeniously, by supposing that on the day De Witt happened to attend the theatre the back-wall curtain was never parted and so the visitor 'supposed it a mere decorative hanging against a solid wall'.[42] Southern's reconstruction used the 80 feet width and the gallery heights of the Fortune contract, displaying precisely the confidence about transference of dimensions from one playhouse to another that Rothwell sought to discredit.

In 1975 Hosley published an extended essay which represented his work on the Globe in the form of a single hypothetical model, and it was the first full reconstruction to be published since Adams's assistant, Irwin Smith, had pointlessly re-iterated their discredited arguments.[43] Having shown that the De Witt Swan has

everything necessary to stage the Globe plays, Hosley based his model upon this sketch plus two additions: a trap and a flight machine.[44] From a revised list of twenty-nine Globe plays – one less than before because *A Warning for Fair Women* was inexplicably dropped – Hosley inferred the Globe's fixtures and fittings.[45] Although three stage doors would be convenient for some scenes, Hosley concluded that two would suffice for all the plays. The need for a discovery space of at least 14 square feet could be supplied by one of the stage doors and an arrangement of curtains. The need for an 'aloft' playing space of at least 14 square feet could be satisfied by one or more of the 'boxes' in the gallery over the stage shown by De Witt. There was no need for the music room to be visible or elevated, and hence none is shown by De Witt.

Hosley defended his addition of a trap – De Witt shows none – by reference to four 'Globe plays'. In *A Larum for London* there is a 'vault' into which a character is pushed and then is stoned,[46] and in the graveyard scene in Shakespeare's *Hamlet* a trap seems the logical way to provide a grave into which may descend Ophelia, followed shortly by Laertes and possibly Hamlet.[47] In Shakespeare's *Macbeth*

---

39 W. F. Rothwell, 'Was There a Typical Elizabethan Stage?', *Shakespeare Survey 12* (1959), 15–21.

40 Ibid., p. 20.

41 Richard Southern, 'On Reconstructing a Practicable Elizabethan Public Playhouse', *Shakespeare Survey 12* (1959), 22–34.

42 Ibid., p. 32.

43 Irwin Smith, *Shakespeare's Globe Playhouse: A Modern Reconstruction in Text and Scale Drawings*, Introd. James G. McManaway (New York, 1956).

44 Richard Hosley, 'The Playhouses', in *The Revels History of Drama in English*, ed. Clifford Leech and T. W. Craik (London, 1975), vol. 3: 1576–1613, pp. 119–235, pp. 165, 172.

45 Hosley, 'The Playhouses', pp. 182–95.

46 *A Larum for London, or the Siedge of Antwerpe* (London, 1602), E4v–F1r.

47 S. P. Zitner, 'Four Feet in the Grave: Some Stage Directions in *Hamlet*, v. i', *Text: Transactions of the Society for Textual Scholarship*, 2 (1985), 139–48.

apparitions must rise and fall and likewise in Barnes's *The Devil's Charter* devils 'ascend' and 'discend'.[48] Hosley's trap was a simple horizontally mounted door, but one of Barnes's devils appears to need assistance in rising: 'Fiery exhalations lightning thunder ascend a King, with a red face crowned imperiall riding upon a Lyon, or dragon'.[49] The player's legs must be visible upon the lion/dragon for him to be riding it, so walking up steps would be difficult. Perhaps the lion property was fitted with false human legs so that the player's legs could manage the ascent, although the effect might be considerably more comic than seems appropriate. This evidence seems to imply an elevator mechanism underneath the Globe's stage-floor trap, although Hosley made no mention of it. In his handbook for Italian theatre architects, published in 1638, Nicola Sabbattini claimed to have managed ascent using four strong-armed men lifting a platform by brute force, and, on another occasion, by arranging a see-saw under the stage with one end supporting the platform which rose into the trap.[50] John Astington considered these methods impractical and concluded that the existing technology of elevator machines would have an obvious application in the understage area of a playhouse.[51]

In support of the existence of a flight machine at the Globe, Hosley cited the torturing of the English Factor by strappado and hanging in *A Larum for London*.[52] Since the torture takes place in a street scene it is difficult to understand Hosley's insistence that a rope descended from the stage superstructure. When flight machinery is used for the descent of supernatural characters the rope is the means to a theatrical end and can be ignored by the spectators. In a scene of public torture, however, the rope exists in the world of the play and may be carried on stage by the torturers. Throwing the rope around the balustrades of the stage balcony seems more natural than Hosley's method which brings an undesirable suggestion of supernatural assistance. The only other use of 'suspension gear' in the Globe plays offered by Hosley was the raising of Antony to the top of Cleopatra's monument in Shakespeare's *Antony and Cleopatra* for which Hosley summarized an argument made at length elsewhere.[53] As with the 'suspension' of the English Factor in *A Larum for London*, the raising of Antony is a feat achieved within the world of the play, so the assistance of a flight machine seems unnecessary.

The evidence does not support Hosley's flight machine, so its inclusion makes him as guilty as Adams of scholarly wish-fulfilment. Indeed, we might wonder if Hosley's odd terminology ('suspension equipment') betrays his realization that no Globe play uses flying. Rigorous application of Hosley's minimalist method which takes the De Witt drawing as the highest authority on the design of Elizabethan playhouses has the inevitable consequence of producing a Globe which is functionally identical to the Swan.

Glynne Wickham posited a radical disjunction between the Swan depicted by De Witt and all later playhouses. Wickham argued that the origins of the playhouses lay in multipurpose arenas in which 'play' meant a range of entertainments including animal torture and formalized combat.[54] Drama moved out of

---

[48] Barnabe Barnes, *The Divils Charter; a Tragaedie Conteining the Life and Death of Pope Alexander the Sixt* (London, 1607), A2v.

[49] Ibid., G1v.

[50] Barnard Hewitt, ed., *The Renaissance Stage: Documents of Serlio, Sabbattini and Furttenbach*, trans. Allardyce Nicoll, John H. McDowell, and George R. Kernodle, Books of the Theatre, 1 (Coral Gables, FLA, 1958), pp. 123–4, 177.

[51] John H. Astington, 'Counterweights in Elizabethan Stage Machinery', *Theatre Notebook*, 41 (1987), 18–24.

[52] *A Larum for London, or the Siedge of Antwerpe*, D4r–D4v, E4r–E4v.

[53] Hosley, 'The Playhouses', pp. 192–3; Richard Hosley, 'The Staging of the Monument Scenes in *Antony and Cleopatra*', *Library Chronicle*, 30 (1964), 62–71.

[54] Glynne Wickham, *Early English Stages 1300 to 1660*, 3 vols. (London, 1963), vol. 2: 1576 to 1660, Part I, pp. 153–72.

doors and into these arenas in the second half of the sixteenth century, but the structures retained their multi-use capabilities.[55] The privy council order of 1597 which suppressed playing was intended to put the theatrical companies on a new footing: to serve the monarch.[56] We cannot rely on the De Witt drawing of the Swan for information about the Globe because, Wickham reasoned, the 'new deal' made court performance the aim of public playing and so court conditions became the new template for the public theatres.[57]

The foregoing is, very roughly, where scholarship of Globe reconstruction stood at the commencement of the Wanamaker project. Nothing was achieved by the Wanamaker project during the 1970s, but in 1982 the International Shakespeare Globe Centre (ISGC) Trust was formed and Andrew Gurr and John Orrell became formally responsible for the practical scholarship upon which the reconstruction would be based.[58]

Orrell's first published article on the Globe was concerned with the construction practices of its builder, Peter Street.[59] Orrell argued that since Street was illiterate (he signed the Fortune contract with just his mark) his work should be considered within the tradition of medieval and Tudor practice rather than continental innovation. Street was a surveyor, not an architect, and the primary tool of his trade was the $16\frac{1}{2}$ feet 'rod' and the 'three-rod line' marked off in rod lengths.[60] Orrell noted that the 43 feet width of the Fortune stage is approximately the altitude of an equilateral triangle whose sides are each 3 rods in length. Equilateral triangles are the basic unit of division used by surveyors because their area is conveniently half the base multiplied by the height. Using just the three-rod line and the well-known technique of *ad quadratum* geometry, Street could have constructed a groundplan for the foundations of the Fortune which would provide the external and internal dimensions of 80 feet and 55 feet as specified in the contract.[61] *Ad quadratum* geometric progression works by inscribing a circle around a given square and then producing a further square from four tangents of this circle. The ratio of the widths of the two squares is $1:\sqrt{2}$. The ratio of the areas of the two squares is 1:2, and this is the ratio of the two squares (one 56 feet 1 inch square, the other 79 feet 2 inches square) which formed the yard and outer wall of the Fortune, once the thicknesses of the wall posts had been allowed for.[62] Like Adams before him, Orrell thought he had found a numerical correspondence which was unlikely to be coincidental, and hence *ad quadratum* was Street's working method.

Because the second Globe was built on the same foundation as the first it must have shared the same groundplan. This allowed Orrell to deduce the size of the first Globe from the preliminary sketch made by Hollar for his 'Long View' of London which shows the second Globe and which is apparently free of the artistic distortions fashionable in the period. The sketch shows a Globe whose overall diameter is 1.397 times that of its yard, if we assume that the upper galleries did not project over the lower ones and hence that the inner circuit of the roof is directly above the yard wall. Orrell thought 1:1.397 close enough to $1:\sqrt{2}$ to prove his point about *ad quadratum* construction. Orrell noted that the Hope contract specifies its first gallery as 12 feet high, and that since this is the same as the first gallery at the Fortune, it is reasonable to suppose that the other galleries at the Hope followed those of the Fortune, making the Hope 34 feet high to the plates. In Hollar's sketch the Globe is drawn exactly the same height as the Hope

---

[55] Ibid., pp. 299–323.

[56] Ibid., Part II, pp. 9–29.

[57] Ibid., pp. 29–30.

[58] Barry Day, *This Wooden 'O': Shakespeare's Globe Reborn* (London, 1996), pp. 82–5.

[59] John Orrell, 'Peter Street at the Fortune and the Globe', *Shakespeare Survey 33* (1980), 139–51.

[60] Ibid., pp. 140–1.

[61] Ibid., pp. 143–4.

[62] Ibid., p. 146.

despite being nearer to the vantage point, and hence it must have been a little shorter. From this approximation of the height of the Globe Orrell got the approximate scale of the drawing, and calculated the width to be 100 feet. This yields a centre-to-centre diameter between opposite main posts of 99 feet. The *ad quadratum* principle would give a yard of 70 feet between centres and a stage 49 feet 6 inches wide, which is exactly the length of Street's three-rod line.[63] Again, coincidence seemed an unlikely source of this correspondence.

At a symposium held at Wayne State University in Detroit to discuss physical reconstruction of the second Globe, Orrell revealed an entirely new way to read the Hollar sketch based upon the hunch that Hollar used a drawing frame which yielded almost photographic accuracy.[64] The proper test of this hypothesis required that Orrell locate at least four landmarks whose real-world intervals at the vantage point, St Saviour's church, were in the same ratio as their intervals in the sketch. In the event Orrell was able to line up five landmarks in this way and he emphasized that this indicated an accuracy far beyond the reach of artistic judgement: Hollar *must* have been using an instrument.[65] Moreover, only at a certain angle relative to north – the angle towards which Hollar's instrument pointed – would these particular intervals occur, and so Orrell's method revealed the exact orientation of the instrument. The distance from each landmark to St Saviour's church is known, so the rule of 'similar triangles' told Orrell just how large a given object in the scene would have been to produce the image of itself in the sketch. After an allowance for anamorphosis – a distortion unique to circular objects – Hollar's sketch tells us that the Hope was 99.29 feet wide and the Globe was 103.35 feet wide.[66] This figure was a little too high to reconcile with his theory about *ad quadratum* layout and the three-rod line, but when the work appeared in book form, Orrell had revised the figure down to 102.35 feet – ±2 per cent – helped by the

realization that the sketch is a little wider than he had thought.[67] Now Orrell could say that the Globe and the Hope were probably the same diameter of 'a few inches over a round 100 ft'[68] and that the 'inveterate sightseer' Hollar drew them the same size, despite the Hope being further away, because he wanted to show that they were alike in size.[69]

Knowing the exact angle of Hollar's drawing frame, Orrell was able to deduce that the clearly visible stage-cover fascia board, and hence the Globe stage, faced 48.25 degrees east of north, which is very nearly the bearing on which the sun would have risen at midsummer in Southwark.[70] Whether by design or chance, in the middle of the afternoon the stage would be entirely shaded. With the size, shape, and orientation of the second Globe firmly established, the data were available to design a reconstruction of the first Globe.

Throughout the detailed planning and construction of the Wanamaker Globe, Orrell's arguments held sway despite objections to the size of the building and to the design of the stage cover. Orrell argued that the short cover extending from a chordally ridged stage 'house' shown by De Witt was not copied at the 1599 Globe, which instead had a radially ridged cover projecting from the auditorium roof to the middle of the yard.[71] The first storey of the reconstructed auditorium had to be made at

---

63 Ibid., p. 150.
64 John Orrell, 'Wenceslaus Hollar and the Size of the Globe Theatre', in *The Third Globe: Symposium for the Reconstruction of the Third Globe Playhouse, Wayne State University, 1979*, ed. C. Walter Hodges, S. Schoenbaum and Leonard Leone (Detroit, 1981), pp. 108–16.
65 Ibid., pp. 110–1.
66 Ibid., p. 116.
67 Ibid., 116n9; John Orrell, *The Quest for Shakespeare's Globe* (Cambridge, 1983), pp. 89, 102.
68 Ibid., p. 104.
69 Ibid., p. 106.
70 Ibid., pp. 154–7.
71 John Orrell, 'The Problems', in *'The Shape of the Globe': Report on the Seminar Held at Pentagram Ltd London By ISGC on 29 March 1983*, ed. Andrew Gurr, John Orrell

least twice the height of a person to make room for an entrance tunnel to the yard and a walkway around the back of the lowest gallery, so the Fortune's 13 feet allowance for the lower storey would not do for modern-sized people.[72] Assuming that we are 10 per cent bigger than the Elizabethans pushed the height of the Globe reconstruction to $36\frac{1}{2}$ feet to the plates, which is 2 feet 6 inches taller than the Fortune and considerably taller than Orrell's approximated measurement from the Hollar sketch.[73] This was the first numerical choice which deviated from the known facts of playhouse design in order to meet modern needs and it marks the moment when mere recovery of historical fact became inadequate to the task in hand.

Two stage posts were to support the stage cover and to be placed far enough forward and far enough apart 'to afford clear views of the tiring house doors'. A useful rejoinder to this comment would have been 'from where?', since the positioning of the posts caused controversy later. Specifying its differences from the Globe, the Fortune contract called for pilastered columns, so the stage posts at the Globe would instead be turned and, to keep them slender, proportioned in the Corinthian order.[74] At this first seminar John Ronayne argued that the interior decoration of the Globe must have been something between 'the English tradition of the ornamented facade, low relief decorating flat surfaces, and the innovation of classical sculptural principles'.[75] Ronayne pointed out that in exterior views the Globe appears white with stone walls, although it must have been timber-framed. The Fortune contract specifies 'all the saide fframe and the Staircases thereof to be sufficyently enclosed wthoute wth lathe lyme & haire',[76] and Ronayne remarked that for the Globe 'a magpie black and white half-timbering is not acceptable'.[77] Because De Witt praised the sumptuousness of playhouses his apparently stark sketch cannot alone determine the interior of the Globe, and Ronayne offered contem-porary examples of lavish decoration which might be copied. As well as marbelization effects on the columns and false painted balustrading on the gallery fronts, the *frons* ought not to be considered a visually neutral surface serving only an acoustic function, but should be 'the centrepiece appropriate to a house of fantasy, imagination and illusion'.[78] The project had moved a long way from Hosley's minimalistic approach to reconstruction as articulated in his 1975 paper.

The Wanamaker project was set to proceed with a design based on Orrell's findings when two archaeological discoveries provided a wealth of new evidence to be absorbed. In early February 1989 the foundations of the Rose were unearthed and non-destructively excavated.[79] These foundations showed both the original configuration of the building and the result of the extensive alterations made in 1592, known from the expenses recorded by Henslowe.[80] Upon first glance the remains of the Rose controverted the most basic assumption about playhouse design: the groundplans of both phases were irregular polygons, and so

---

[72] and John Ronayne, The Renaissance Drama Newsletter Supplements, I (Coventry, 1983), pp. 4–11, p. 10.
[72] Ibid., p. 5.
[73] Andrew Gurr, 'The Conclusions', in 'The Shape of the Globe': Report on the Seminar Held at Pentagram Ltd London By ISGC on 29 March 1983, ed. Andrew Gurr, John Orrell and John Ronayne, The Renaissance Drama Newsletter Supplements, I (Coventry, 1983), pp. 14–21, p. 14.
[74] Ibid., p. 16.
[75] John Ronayne, 'Style', in 'The Shape of the Globe': Report on the Seminar Held at Pentagram Ltd London By ISGC on 29 March 1983, ed. Andrew Gurr, John Orrell and John Ronayne, The Renaissance Drama Newsletter Supplements, I (Coventry, 1983), pp. 22–4, p. 22.
[76] R. A. Foakes and R. T. Rickert, eds., Henslowe's Diary, Edited with Supplementary Material, Introduction and Notes (Cambridge, 1961), p. 308.
[77] Ronayne, 'Style', p. 23.
[78] Ibid., p. 24.
[79] Day, This Wooden 'O': Shakespeare's Globe Reborn, pp. 192–201.
[80] Foakes & Rickert, eds., Henslowe's Diary, Edited with Supplementary Material, Introduction and Notes, pp. 9–13.

chaos prevailed where order was expected. The original design appeared to be a 14–sided polygon of about 74 feet across.[81] In both phases the stage was tapered and, unless the stage was remarkably small, the *frons scenae* must have followed the angled wall formed by the fronts of the bays against which the stage stood. Even with this allowance, the original stage was a mere 475 square feet in area.[82] In a study encompassing all the theatres of early modern London Orrell had offered evidence that 'the two Globes, the Rose, the Hope and the Boar's Head all faced northeast, away from the afternoon sun'[83] but the stages of the Rose remains were both 'on the northern side of the polygon'[84] and hence the Rose faced south and its stage received illumination from the afternoon sun. Neither stage reached as far as the middle of the yard, and the earlier stage certainly (and the later possibly) met the yard wall not at a corner but rather in the middle of a bay. The theoretical reconstruction to which the uncovered Rose bore closest resemblance was, to everyone's surprise, the discredited Globe of John Cranford Adams.

Franklin J. Hildy called an academic conference at the University of Georgia in February 1990 to assess the discoveries. While this was being planned a second team from the Museum of London began working on the site of the first Globe and on 12 October 1989 they announced discovery of part of the Globe foundations. At the conference Orrell presented his considered response to the evidence from the Rose and his preliminary examination of the evidence from the Globe.[85] The Globe remains appeared to be part of the foundations of the outer wall and one stair turret. The location of this turret, on a radial about 60 degrees east of north, matched neither of the turrets shown by Hollar, and it was 50 per cent wider than it should have been.[86] Orrell admitted that these anomalies threw doubt on Hollar's representation of the orientation of the Globe, but drew comfort from the fact that the turret was centred on an angle of the main

frame wall, as he expected, and not centred mid-wall as Hosley thought.[87]

Orrell attempted to measure the angles and dimensions suggested by the scant remains, and from them determine the size and shape of the Globe. Assuming that the Globe was a regular polygon – an assumption made less safe by the Rose remains – the few measurable angles and dimensions in the Globe remains suggested a 20-sided polygon with a diameter of very nearly 100 feet.[88] The ground floor galleries were 12½ feet, or 12 feet 8 inches deep if measured radially, which is some 3 feet less than we would expect from the *ad quadratum* method, but nonetheless they could have been constructed using a three-rod line if geometric pre-calculation were used to derive the correct length for each bay's outer wall.

The ISGC decided to build two experimental bays based on Orrell's tentative response to the evidence of the Globe remains, assuming that the original had 20 gallery bays each 12½ feet deep, the overall diameter being 100 feet across points.[89] Orrell had concluded that this was not

---

[81] John Orrell and Andrew Gurr, 'What the Rose Can Tell us', *Times Literary Supplement*, 4497 (1989), 636, 649, p. 636.

[82] Ibid., p. 649.

[83] John Orrell, *The Human Stage: English Theatre Design, 1567–1640* (Cambridge, 1988), p. 92.

[84] Orrell & Gurr, 'What the Rose Can Tell us', p. 636.

[85] John Orrell, 'Beyond the Rose: Design Problems for the Globe Reconstruction', in *New Issues in the Reconstruction of Shakespeare's Theatre: Proceedings of the Conference Held at the University of Georgia, February 16–18, 1990*, ed. Franklin J. Hildy (New York, 1990), pp. 95–118.

[86] Ibid., p. 97.

[87] Richard Hosley, 'The Shape and Size of the Second Globe', in *The Third Globe: Symposium for the Reconstruction of the Third Globe Playhouse, Wayne State University, 1979*, ed. C. Walter Hodges, S. Schoenbaum and Leonard Leone (Detroit, 1981), pp. 82–107, pp. 88–91.

[88] Orrell, 'Beyond the Rose: Design Problems for the Globe Reconstruction', pp. 99–100.

[89] Peter McCurdy, 'Shakespeare's Globe Theatre: The Construction of Two Experimental Bays in June 1992', in *The Timber Frame – From Preservation to Reconstruction:*

an *ad quadratum* design since the diameters of the circles within which are inscribed the inner and outer polygons of the groundplan are not in a $1:\sqrt{2}$ relation. But the workshop experience of the project's timber-framing expert, Peter McCurdy, suggested that the wall plate frame would be fabricated at the same time as the ground sill frame, and that Peter Street would have considered the proportions of the former, which defined the dimensions of the uppermost gallery bay, to be just as important as those of the ground sill frame. If there was a jetty (the 'Juttey-forwards' of the Fortune contract) of 12 inches in each of the two elevated bays, the uppermost gallery bay would be in an *ad quadratum* relationship with the overall diameter. McCurdy noted that the possibility of converting the Theatre into tenements, discussed by Allen and Burbage,[90] indicates that the rakers which supported the seating were not structurally integrated into the frame since such conversion would require their removal. Only a playhouse constructed floor-on-floor, and hence with an overhanging jetty and without integrated rakers for bracing, could be converted to tenements.[91]

When more of the Globe's foundations were unearthed, Orrell measured the most intact angle in what appeared to be part of the inner gallery wall as 162 degrees, which indicated a 20-sided playhouse.[92] If the playhouse was about 100 feet across, as Orrell had long believed, a 20-sided configuration could be made to fit extremely well with the uncovered remains.[93] In an article describing the construction of the experimental bays, Hildy argued that Orrell had not used the most accurate drawings of the uncovered Globe remains – the ones made on the site – and that these showed the one measurable angle to be 160 degrees rather than 162. This small difference would reduce the extrapolated playhouse to 90 feet diameter and 18 sides.[94]

The discovery of the Globe remains gave the best indication yet of the precise geographical site of the playhouse and Orrell fed into his formulae derived from Hollar's sketch to produce a revised diameter of 97.6 feet ± 2 per cent.[95] Orrell accepted that the published plans of the remains were inaccurate, but showed that Hildy's 'originals' too were distorted. At a meeting to determine how the project should proceed, plans of competing configurations were laid over a diagram of the Globe remains to see which would best fit. Apart from Orrell's proposed configuration, the closest fit was an 18–sided 90 feet diameter configuration offered by Hildy. All sides accepted that they were working with inaccurate drawings, and Hildy argued that the only proper method was to count the grid squares on the original drawings and to derive the angles by trigonometry, as he had done.[96] Gurr, as chair of the meeting, called for delegates to vote on whether the project should adopt Orrell's or Hildy's plan. Orrell's design won by 14 votes to 6.[97]

The Wanamaker Globe is 100 feet across because of this vote, apparently taken in a hurry and with ambiguous and distorted evidence placed before the voters. With two Globe bays

---

Papers Presented at the International Council on Monuments and Sites UK Timber Seminar Held at Haydock Park on 26 April 1993, ed. F. W. B. Charles (London, 1993), pp. 1–20.

90 C. W. Wallace, *The First London Theatre: Materials for a History* (Lincoln, 1913), p. 216.

91 McCurdy, 'Shakespeare's Globe Theatre: The Construction of Two Experimental Bays in June 1992', pp. 11–12.

92 Simon Blatherwick and Andrew Gurr, 'Shakespeare's Factory: Archaeological Evaluations on the Site of the Globe Theatre at 1/15 Anchor Terrace, Southwark Bridge Road, Southwark', *Antiquity*, 66 (1992), 315–33, p. 331.

93 Ibid., pp. 332–3.

94 Franklin J. Hildy, '"If You Build it They Will Come": The Reconstruction of Shakespeare's Globe Gets Underway on the Bankside in London', *Shakespeare Bulletin*, 10.3 (1992), 5–9, p. 7.

95 Andrew Gurr, 'Evidence for the Design of the Globe: The Report of a One-day Seminar Held on 10 October 1992 at Pentagram in London', in *The Design of the Globe*, ed. Andrew Gurr, Ronnie Mulryne and Margaret Shewring (London, 1993), pp. 1–19, p. 5.

96 Ibid., p. 10.

97 Ibid., pp. 11–14.

completed, perhaps the pressing need to get started on the remaining bays rather than dismantle what had already been accomplished – as Hildy's plans would have required – was uppermost in committee members' minds. Objections to the vastness of the Globe reconstruction – the entire Rose playhouse could be placed within its yard – were received from all quarters and the disagreement continues.[98]

Of course, a 100 feet diameter is about 11 per cent greater than a 90 feet diameter, and modern humans are about 10 per cent larger than Elizabethans, so it could be argued that our Globe feels about as large to us as their Globe felt to them. However, it is not clear that our voices are commensurately louder and actors know that adding a little to the diameter of a circular auditorium adds a lot to the volume of air to be moved. The significance of the decision to make the Globe reconstruction taller than the original to allow for a two-person clearance in the lowest gallery has been overlooked in arguments about the size of the building. If the original was about 100 feet across then the extra height of the reconstruction throws the building out of proportion, a fact not publicly acknowledged by the project. If the proportions are right, then the building's overall size may be defended as an attempt to recreate the 'feel' – in relation to human body-size – of the original.

The three-quarters-complete Wanamaker Globe opened for a workshop season in the autumn of 1995 and, as has been extensively reported, the proposed location of the stage posts was rejected by a number of theatre practitioners.[99] Moving the posts necessitated redesigning the stage cover, but the chosen solution involving a pentice apron 'skirt' to the cover was defended as the kind of thing Street could have made if his clients had objected to the posts being near the corners of the stage.

As the Wanamaker Globe reached completion a book was published which provided justification for its least well-documented feature: the decoration. Ronayne's position on the external rendering of the building had altered since his comment that 'a magpie black and white half-timbering is not acceptable'.[100] Now he argued the opposite:

As our reconstruction is the first major timber-framed building in the capital since the Fire, our decision, on balance, was to expose the structure of what is a rare sight in London, rather than cover it up as the Elizabethans may have done, taking for granted the frameworked appearance. For them, outer rendering was grander. For us, half timbering is more generally evocative.[101]

---

98 The progression of the arguments can be traced through John Orrell, 'The Roof of the Globe', Richard Hosley, 'The Stage Superstructures of the First Globe and the Swan', Andrew Gurr, 'The Discussion', John Orrell, 'Afterword', in 'The Shape of the Globe' and 'The Interior of the Globe': Reports on Seminars Held on 29 March 1983 and 12 April 1986, ed. Ronnie Mulryne and Margaret Shewring, The Renaissance Drama Newsletter Supplements, 8 (Coventry, 1987), pp. 33–41; 42–78; 81–9; 96–107; Orrell, 'Beyond the Rose: Design Problems for the Globe Reconstruction'; Blatherwick & Gurr, 'Shakespeare's Factory: Archaeological Evaluations on the Site of the Globe Theatre at 1/15 Anchor Terrace, Southwark Bridge Road, Southwark'; Hildy, '"If You Build it They Will Come": The Reconstruction of Shakespeare's Globe Gets Underway on the Bankside in London'; Gurr, 'Evidence for the Design of the Globe: The Report of a One-day Seminar Held on 10 October 1992 at Pentagram in London'; Paul Nelsen, 'Reinventing Shakespeare's Globe? A Report of Design Choices for the ISGC Globe', Shakespeare Bulletin, 10.4 (1992), 5–8; Franklin J. Hildy, 'A Minority Report on the Decisions of the Pentagram Conference', Shakespeare Bulletin, 10.4 (1992), 9–12; John Orrell, 'The Accuracy of Hollar's Sketch of the Globe', Shakespeare Bulletin, 11.2 (1993), 5–9; Tim Fitzpatrick, 'The Fortune Contract and Hollar's Original Drawing of Southwark: Some Indications of a Smaller First Globe', Shakespeare Bulletin, 14.4 (1996), 5–10; and John Orrell, 'The Size and Shape of the First Globe: Interpreting the Archaeological and Mathematical Evidence', Shakespeare Bulletin, 16.3 (1998), 5–8.

99 Paul Nelsen, 'Positing Pillars at the Globe', Shakespeare Quarterly, 48 (1997), 324–35.

100 Ronayne, 'Style', p. 23.

101 John Ronayne, 'Totus Mundus Agit Histrionem [The Whole World Moves the Actor]: The Interior Decorative Scheme of the Bankside Globe', in Shakespeare's Globe Rebuilt, ed. J. R. Mulryne,

This is a surprising shift in the theoretical underpinning of the project, since the stated aim was always recovery of 'what had been' in the Elizabethan period and not 'what is evocative' of the period.

Ronayne cited contemporary accounts of the sumptuousness of playhouses to defend the brightly painted interior of the Wanamaker Globe, and the 'carved proporcions Called Satiers'[102] from the Fortune contract to defend the statues in the *frons scenae*.[103] Triumphal arches made of wood but painted to look like stone were another source of information, made relevant by De Witt's statement that the Swan stage posts were cunningly painted like marble. The interior decoration of the Globe was based upon analogues from the late 1590s and early 1600s rather than the 1570s when the Theatre was built because in the hurried dismantling and move to Southwark only the main timbers would have been preserved; the decoration would have been remade in 1599 at the new site.[104] The iconographical scheme at the Wanamaker Globe, which relates the name of the playhouse to its function, was chosen because early modern English design combined 'Northern continental "classicism" with the grotesques, strapwork, cartouches and feigned architectural patterns of Flemish Mannerism' and '. . . it was conventional for Early Modern decorative schemes to make some statement about their use, purpose or patrons'.[105]

There is no possibility of recreating Elizabethan London, its politics, its relations with a rapidly expanding world of commerce, and its inhabitants who visited its theatres. New Historicist and Cultural Materialist scholars have pointed out that, detached from its cultural milieu, a reconstructed playhouse is vulnerable to anachronistic ideas about the drama. This theoretical objection has practical correlations. From the mid 1590s spectators sat on the stage at outdoor theatres,[106] and this provided opportunities for characters to 'hide' from others on stage by sitting amongst the onstage audience. If a character were dressed in everyday clothes similar to those worn by members of the audience this trick might be reasonably realistic, but in a modern performance this would require the character to wear modern dress. Authentic original dress would be a barrier to the recreation of the authentic original trick.

A similar dilemma relates to the playhouse fabric: as Ronayne noted, a building with an exposed timber frame is as unusual in late twentieth-century London as one with exterior rendering would have been in early modern London. But to use this as a justification for not covering the timber frame of the Wanamaker Globe is to privilege historical effect over historical cause and amounts to a prejudgement of a result of the experiment. The true historicist value of an authentic reconstruction can be measured by the number and detail of apparently insignificant features which are recreated.

New Historicist and Cultural Materialist attacks upon the Wanamaker Globe have concentrated upon the struggle between Southwark Council and ISGC and on the support the project has received from right-wing elements of the academic, theatrical and political establishment. Two typical studies are John Drakakis's 'Theatre, Ideology, and Institution: Shakespeare and the Roadsweepers',[107] and Terence Hawkes's chapter 'Bardbiz' in his

Margaret Shewring and Andrew Gurr (Cambridge, 1997), pp. 121–46, p. 122.

[102] Foakes & Rickert, eds., *Henslowe's Diary, Edited with Supplementary Material, Introduction and Notes*, p. 308.

[103] Ronayne, 'Totus Mundus Agit Histrionem [The Whole World Moves the Actor]: The Interior Decorative Scheme of the Bankside Globe', p. 124.

[104] Siobhan Keenan and Peter Davidson, 'The Iconography of the Globe', in *Shakespeare's Globe Rebuilt*, ed. J. R. Mulryne, Margaret Shewring and Andrew Gurr (Cambridge, 1997), pp. 147–56, 155n2.

[105] Keenan & Davidson, 'The Iconography of the Globe', p. 148.

[106] Orrell, *The Human Stage: English Theatre Design, 1567–1640*, p. 90; Gabriel Egan, 'The Situation of the 'Lords Room': A Revaluation', *Review of English Studies*, 48 (1997), 297–309.

[107] John Drakakis, 'Theatre, Ideology, and Institution: Shakespeare and the Roadsweepers', in *The Shakespeare*

Meaning By Shakespeare.[108] Drakakis and Hawkes rightly claim that many supporters of the project are motivated by an urge not to historicize Shakespeare but to glorify him. But this objection is poor historicism if it glosses over the remarkable tensions between and contradictions within the various groups and forces which aligned to make Wanamaker's intentions viable. Hawkes raised a theoretical objection to the project, but it was not serious:

If the first Globe is the 'original one', then a central problem must be that the timbers from which it was built were themselves 'originally' used to construct Burbage's first playhouse, called The Theatre, situated on the north bank of the Thames and dismantled in December 1598. . . . The dizzying prospect of a third remove enters with the fact that the best physical picture of the Globe is the one afforded by Wenceslas Hollar's 'Long View' of London. But this gives a view of the second Globe, which is of course a reconstruction on the same site of the first Globe. Finally, as if in mockery of all such reaching after authenticity, it happens that Hollar's engraving reverses the captions on the two buildings, with the result that the one it clearly nominates as 'The Globe' is no such thing.[109]

Leaving aside the error concerning Hollar's work (it is the preliminary sketch, not the labelled engraving, that constitutes 'the best physical picture of the Globe'), this apparent objection is in fact a good example of the relative freedom from theoretical difficulty which certain aspects of the project enjoy as a consequence of evidential plenitude. We possess an exterior view of the Theatre (Abram Booth's 'Utrecht' engraving), plus details of court cases arising from the transformation of the Theatre into the Globe and from the renegotiation of the lease for the Bankside land on which the second Globe was built, and also a deposition swearing that the second Globe re-used the foundations of the first Globe. There are grave problems concerning the notion of authenticity but the 'third remove' identified by Hawkes is not among them and the fact that he can so easily trace the history of the

Burbages' outdoor playhouses is testament to early twentieth-century scholarship of historical recovery within relatively unproblematic conceptual parameters.

Hawkes quoted from Joseph Quincy Adams's speech upon the opening of the Washington Folger Library which described 'the forces of immigration' as 'a menace to the preservation of our long-established English civilization'.[110] Such bigotries are worth recording, but it must be remembered that the resources of the Folger Library are as available to New Historicist and Cultural Materialist scholars as they are to their opponents. It is a delicious irony that Karl Marx minutely dissected the economic instability of capitalism from within one of its greatest expressions of confidence, the British Library, and likewise an edifice built to the glorification of a transcendent bard must, if it is meticulous, undermine that very transcendence by rendering Shakespeare's world strange to us.

Historical materialism aims to create intellectual models of the cultural and political milieu of early modern London which necessarily presuppose that worthwhile knowledge about the past is recoverable. No further theoretical justification for the Wanamaker project is needed if it is accepted that the experiment may as likely fail as succeed. That is to say, it may be discovered that playhouse design has no important bearing on the meaning of, and methods of signification used within, early modern drama. If it is found that playhouse design is an important determinant of the drama then the reconstructed Globe may be defended as a historicist tool which undermines the claim that Shakespeare's work transcends historical and cultural difference. The constituency of, and the class antagonisms within, the original

---

Myth, ed. Graham Holderness, Cultural Politics (Manchester, 1988), pp. 24–41.

[108] Terence Hawkes, *Meaning By Shakespeare* (London, 1992), pp. 141–53.

[109] Ibid., p. 142.

[110] Ibid., p. 152.

audience cannot be recovered, but this is equally true of intellectual and physical models of the past: our partial, anachronistic, twentieth-century minds are all we have to start with. As Leah Marcus pointed out, E. K. Chambers's motivation for his monumental studies was essentially anti-historicist: he 'advocated the study of history in order to discount it'.[111] That is to say, Chambers attended to the minute details of material influence in order to subtract this from the drama of the period in the hope of revealing the transcendent 'art'. Even if, as Hawkes claimed, the Wanamaker project 'packages' historical difference and smoothes over historical tensions and contradictions, the scholarship of the project is equally available to materialists and idealists and, as with Chambers's work, the former are likely to make full use of it.

---

[111] Leah S. Marcus, *Unediting the Renaissance: Shakespeare, Marlowe, Milton* (London, 1996), p. 21.

'USEFUL IN THE YEAR 1999': WILLIAM POEL AND SHAKESPEARE'S 'BUILD OF STAGE'

MARION O'CONNOR

'When you have finished this letter', William Poel wrote in postscript to a correspondent at Trinity College, Cambridge, early in 1909, 'send it on to the British Museum! It will come in useful in the year 1999.' Poel as usual got the details wrong but the main drift quite right. The letter was not sent on to the British Museum: instead, it survives in the Theatre Museum, part of a huge collection there of Poel's papers, photographs, programmes, promptbooks and other memorabilia[1] which was amassed by Poel himself, his widow, and others, including the family of his correspondent.[2] Nor is the letter, taken in isolation, especially useful for readers of *Shakespeare Survey*: it presents developments in Poel's plans to stage a new English translation of the *Alcestis* of Euripides and reports on a recent performance, at the Manchester Corn Exchange, of Poel's production of Milton's *Samson Agonistes*. Yet as those readers will be well aware, in the year 1999, a century after Poel started campaigning for the erection in London of a purpose-built reconstruction of the first (1599–1613) Globe, a building such as that which he sought is a permanent feature of the Bankside in Southwark. Poel's career as a whole contains extensive and impressive evidence of both the possibilities but also, and even more, the limits of theatrical reconstructions. Those limits tell against – indeed, they preclude – any claims for theatrical reconstruction as experimental science. Reconsideration of Poel's record is indeed useful in the year 1999.

These possibilities and limits can be mapped around a pair of policy statements by Poel. The programme for the Elizabethan Stage Society's first production (*Twelfth Night* at Burlington Hall on 21 and 22 June 1895) gave clear statement of the society's raison d'être:

The ELIZABETHAN STAGE SOCIETY is founded to give practical effect to the principle that Shakspere should be accorded *the build of stage* for which he designed his plays.

Six months later, the programme for the society's second production (*The Comedy of Errors* in Gray's Inn Hall on 6, 7 and 9 December 1895) gave a somewhat different statement of the society's guiding principle:

The ELIZABETHAN STAGE SOCIETY is founded to illustrate and advance the principle that Shakspere's

---

plays should be accorded *the conditions of playing* for which they were designed.

It could be said that these principles were to be Poel's theatrical legacy. Certainly the principles outlived the society founded to further them.[3] Long after its dissolution in 1905, Poel continued to invoke the italicized formulations. Using them pretty well interchangeably over the years, he does not appear to have discriminated between them. Yet although these desiderata – (1) 'build of stage' and (2) 'conditions of playing' – are associated, they are not identical. The first desideratum was variously conceived, and partially secured, by Poel. The second desideratum was more elusive. One seemingly paradoxical contention of this article may be stated as an inverse proportion: the fuller Poel's realization of his understanding of the build of stage for which Shakespeare designed his plays, the further he was from the conditions of playing for which they were designed.

Poel's attempt to reconstitute the build of stage for which Shakespeare wrote was driven by his understanding of Shakespearian dramaturgy. He did not assert any absolute superiority for an Elizabethan stage over the stages for which Victorian and Edwardian playwrights wrote – merely the suitability of such a stage for the presentation of plays by Shakespeare and his contemporaries.[4] Across his long career modifications to his idea of the build of stage for which Shakespeare wrote were concomitant with changes in emphasis within his understanding of Shakespearian dramaturgy. His eventual notion of the build of stage for which Shakespeare designed his plays was given uncharacteristically crisp summary in a late-in-life letter:

For a Shakespearian representation, I am myself content with a balcony, a recess, two doors and the forward platform which must be the same size as that in use in the Fortune theatre![5]

The relative clause specifying the dimensions of the platform presents a requirement which Poel introduced fairly late in his long theatrical day. As he laid ever greater emphasis upon the importance of a forward platform as the stage for which Shakespeare wrote his plays, Poel's preoccupation with stage pictures became a preoccupation with theatrical space. His understanding of Shakespearian dramaturgy went from two-dimensional to three-dimensional analysis. Turning his attention away from the absence of scenery and towards the theatrical presence of audiences and the dramatic ubiquity of characters, he moved from the playwriting consequences of the relative bareness of the Shakespearian stage to the consequences of its projection. A typical pronouncement of the 1880s and nineties:

Shakspere's method of dramatic composition, that of uniting a series of short scenes with each other in one dramatic movement, will not bear the elaboration of heavy stage sets, and with the demand for carpentry comes in the necessity for mutilation.[6]

Two decades later, having turned from the

---

3 See Jill L. Levenson, 'The Recovery of the Elizabethan Stage', in *The Elizabethan Theatre IX*, ed. G. R. Hibbard (Port Credit, Ont.: P.D.Meany, 1986), 205–29; Cary M. Mazer, *Shakespeare Refashioned: Elizabethan Plays on Edwardian Stages* (Ann Arbor: UMI Research Press, 1981); and J. L. Styan, *The Shakespeare Revolution: Criticism and Performance in the Twentieth Century* (Cambridge University Press, 1977).

4 The point is reported – more crisply than it is likely to have been uttered in Poel's prolix and contorted prose – in a newspaper account of a lecture which Poel gave at the University of Toronto late in 1905: 'The Elizabethan playhouse, said Mr. Poel, was not ideally the best form of stage, and we see to-day the form of theatre Shakespeare hoped for . . .' (*The Globe*, 11 December 1905, 3). See also Poel's opinions as evinced at a meeting held in the Guildhall on 24 October 1905 and eventually published as London Shakespeare League Pamphlet No. 1, *Report of a Public Discussion on the Best Method of Presenting Shakespeare's Plays* (1915).

5 1927 letter to W. J. Lawrence, quoted in Speaight, *William Poel . . .* , 85.

6 'The Stage-Version of *Romeo and Juliet*', paper read to the New Shakspere Society on 12 April 1889, published in *Transactions of the New Shakspere Society 1887–1892*, 227–246. This quotation, p. 240.

flexibility of the Shakespearian stage to the indeterminacy of the Shakespearian scene (and having abandoned the orthographical affectations of F. J. Furnivall's New Shakspere Society), he would enquire:

How many realise that the art of Shakespeare's dramatic construction differs fundamentally from that of the modern dramatist? . . . . Even the erudite do not seem to have grasped how Shakespeare conducts his story on the open platform, or they would not contend that it be settled by a compromise between the old and the modern stage. No revolving stage or other invention to abolish "waits" between changes of scene abolishes the fact that Shakespeare does not wish his audience to think about localities, except when his characters refer to them, and then only to the extent to which they affect the characters themselves and not the spectators.[7]

It is not just the difference in spelling conventions that dates these quotations to their respective times (1889 and 1911). Each quotation, it will have been noted, opposes Shakespearian dramaturgy to theatrical resources widely used at the time of writing – 'heavy stage sets' in 1889 and 'revolve[s and] other invention[s] to abolish "waits"' in 1911. Both pronouncements, that is, are reactive, but they react against different things. Both, moreover, are informed by assumptions which are less axiomatic now than they were then. Poel's understanding of Shakespearian dramaturgy was not that of a professional man of letters nor that of an amateur antiquarian. It was, rather, shaped by his own professional experience as (in effect although not in name) an itinerant actor-manager, mainly of amateurs, who got through more than fifty years of low-budget staging with minimal resources in places more or less ill-suited to his theatrical purposes. Articulated in reaction to the changing theatrical praxis of his own time (1852–1934), Poel's understanding of Shakespearian dramaturgy was also shaped by the dramatic canons of that time. Taking aim at moving targets, he sometimes shot himself in the foot.

Poel himself never found bricks and mortar in which to fix any phase in his developing notion of the build of stage for which Shakespeare designed his plays. He did, however, translate versions of that notion into wood and canvas. The first of Poel's successive simulacra of a Shakespearian stage was the so-called Fortune fit-up, built for a production of *Measure for Measure* at the Royalty Theatre in November 1893[8] and used for some (but by no means all) Elizabethan Stage Society productions until 1905, when the society was wound up. The Fortune fit-up is the best known of Poel's Shakespearian stages, probably because it is so fully documented. Photographs and drawings survive from at least seven of the Elizabethan Stage Society productions on it; its novelty ensured that reviewers took note of it; and Poel left some instructive records of its specifications. A month after the Elizabethan Stage Society presented its final production (*Romeo and Juliet*, again on the Fortune fit-up and at the Royalty Theatre) on 5 May 1905, Poel wrote to William Salt Brassington, Librarian and Chief Curator of the Shakespeare Memorial Theatre to put a proposal:

I have been offered by one of the members of our Society £100 for the purchase of the Elizabethan Stage with its Tapestry Curtains and furniture provided some public Institution is willing to accept the gift on the understanding that the stage is either erected for exhibition in a Museum or else is put up not less than once a year for a dramatic performance of one of Shakespeare's Plays, or one of his contemporaries, to be given in the Elizabethan manner.

The Stage requires, for its erection, a space on the

---

7 From a symposium of views on the representation of Shakespeare collected by Huntly Carter and published in *The New Age*, n.s. vol. VII, no. 11 (12 January 1911), 249–250.

8 See Arthur Harris, 'William Poel's Elizabethan Stage: The First Experiment', *Theatre Notebook*, 17 (1963), 111–114; and my *William Poel and the Elizabethan Stage Society* (Cambridge & Alexandria, Va.: Chadwyck-Healey, 1987), pp. 26–32.

1 *Measure for Measure* at the Royalty Theatre, 9–11 and 18 November 1893, Act 2, scene 2.

floor of thirty feet in length and twenty four feet indepth and a height of not less than twenty three feet.

The stage will all take to pieces and then consists only of lengths of timber and rolled cloths with one or two small flat pieces and takes very little room to store.

Poel had made the Shakespeare Memorial Theatre an offer which it could refuse. In a letter postmarked three days later, 8 June 1905, he enquired 'if the Merchant Taylors School would care to have the Elizabethan Stage'. Apparently the school did not care to have Poel's simulacrum stage either, for the catalogue of the Elizabethan Stage Society auction on 5 July 1905 begins with a precisely detailed description of the Fortune fit-up:

LOT 1 THE UNIQUE MODEL STAGE OF THE OLD FORTUNE PLAYHOUSE, having a frontage of 30 feet with a depth of 24 feet. The entire height is 21 feet. This is the original stage with working equipment,

designed by Mr William Poel, and used at the performances of the Elizabethan Stage Society. It was copied in actual dimensions from a contemporary Builder's Contract and is correct in historical and other details. It comprises a substantial stained oak frame stage, constructed to easily fit up, with bolt and nuts complete. There is a practical rostrum and balcony and canvas painted cloths, representing galleries, boxes and amphitheatre, two entrances to Stage under balcony, a centre entrance, closed by pair [*sic*] of painted oak doors, two pillar supports, 18 feet high, to carry the roof or 'Heaven' to centre of stage, with facsimile ceiling piece of blue ground and gilt stars and covered by a lean-to tile painted roof joining on to tyring house, roof and wall, a pair of reproduction curtains, each 18 feet high by 9 feet, suspended on brass rods between the pillars, with ropes, pullies, etc.; also the back curtain in similar material of different design, each 8 feet square with ropes and pullies. There are also tapestry curtains for doors under balcony, matting for floor of Stage, painted canvas palisade for front of platform. The whole in excellent order and condition and in

2 *Hamlet* at Carpenters' Hall, 21 February 1900, Act 1, scene 2

perfect working order, together with the whole of the equipment, including two Jacobean chairs, carved table and other moveable furniture.[9]

Illustration 1 reproduces a photograph of the Fortune fit-up in its initial use, for Poel's 1893 production of *Measure for Measure* at the Royalty Theatre, while Illustration 2 reproduces a photograph of it as used for his 1900 production of *Hamlet* in Carpenters' Hall. From these it is clear that the 1905 catalogue entry flatters: even by 1900, the fit-up was looking worn as well as tawdry. The entry also grossly overstates the resemblance of William Poel's Fortune fit-up to Peter Street's Fortune contract: although there was some similarity in decorative detail, the dimensions of the late Victorian fit-up had been determined, not so much by the Elizabethan builder's specifications, as by the dimensions of the mid-Victorian theatre building for which it was initially designed. That design, moreover, owes more to the so-called De Witt drawing of the amphitheatrical Swan Theatre (a document which had surfaced only five years before the Fortune fit-up was built) than it does to the contract for the rectangular Fortune Theatre. Still, after generous allowance has been made for the overstatements of advertising, it is clear from both the visual and the verbal evidence that with the Fortune fit-up Poel had secured 'a balcony, a recess, two doors' – and a considerable quantity of tapestry hangings with which to curtain off all of these and thereby divide the fit-up into zones. However, any 'forward platform' was but an optional adjunct of this, Poel's first simulacrum of a Shakespearian stage: for his initial use of the Fortune fit-up in 1893,

---

[9] There is a copy of the 5 July 1905 Elizabethan Stage Society sale catalogue in the Shakespeare Centre Library, Stratford-upon-Avon.

3 *The Alchemist* at Apothecaries' Hall, 24–5 February 1899, Act 5, scene 4.

the apron of the Royalty was carried out over the orchestra pit, but it is not clear whether, let alone how far, the aprons of other venues may have been extended when the fit-up was used elsewhere over the next dozen years. Other features of the Fortune fit-up which may have been used only for the 1893 *Measure for Measure* include: the canopy, its blue painted roof fretted with golden fire (in fact, gilt stars); the tiring house roof with its painted tiles; and the 'canvas painted cloths, representing galleries, boxes and amphitheatre' which in 1893 Poel populated with a simulacrum of an Elizabethan audience – Elizabethan Stage Society members in period costume.

Poel's second realization of his notion of 'the build of stage for which Shakspere designed his plays' is discernible in the six photographs which survive from Poel's production of *The Alchemist* in the Hall of the Society of Apothecaries on 24 and 25 February 1899[10]: see Illustration 3. This shows another fit-up. Smaller and shallower than the Fortune one, it evidently consisted of five flats framed at either side by narrow wing pieces, effectively a proscenium. Another entry in the 1905 sale

---

[10] Severely cropped reproductions of five of these photographs were published in *The Sketch* for 8 March 1899, from which Laurence J. Raw took his illustrations for 'William Poel's Staging of *The Alchemist*', *Theatre Notebook*, 44 (1990), 74–80. See my '"William Poel's Staging of *The Alchemist*" Some Corrections', *Theatre Notebook*, 46 (1992), 95–104.

4 *The Two Gentlemen of Verona* at His Majesty's Theatre, 20 April 1910, newspaper photograph of Poel (standing third from left, figure indicated by white cross) supervising stage construction. Published in *The Daily Mirror*, 21 April 1910.

catalogue appears to be describing this second fit-up:

No. 258. A WELL-MADE PORTABLE PLAIN DEAL STAGE, constructed to carry fit-up, 24 feet long and 12 feet deep, on 6 framed supports, with bolts and nuts, together with proscenium, fascia board, with [$\frac{1}{2}$]-inch rake to the foot, deal top[11]

This second fit-up, which did not attract reviewers' comment, gave Poel even fewer of his final requirements 'for a Shakespearian representation, [*viz*,] ... a balcony, a recess, two doors and a forward platform'. The flats which constitute the surround could provide two doors and a recess. However, the shallow stage is no platform: raked, fronted by footlights and contained behind the wing piece frame, it is effectively a proscenium stage. Moreover, the second fit-up contained neither an inner stage

nor a balcony: thus, whenever a separate acting area was required for a production on this second fit-up, such an area had to be built into the venue in which the fit-up was being used. For the February 1899 production of Jonson's *The Alchemist* in the Apothecaries' Hall, for example, the second fit-up was placed against a wall which contains a small balcony: on this Face appeared in Act 5. (Invisible behind the top of the central flat in the photographs, the balcony is immediately below the heraldic

---

[11] Square brackets enclose my emendation from '2', which would produce an implausibly steep rake on a gradient of 1 in 6. Another description of this stage is given in Poel's leaflet, *Acting Shakespeare in Schools* (1912), which advertised the availability for hire of 'a platform stage, 24 feet long by 12 feet deep, 3 feet 6 inches high in front and 4 feet high at back'.

beasts at the upper margin of the photograph which is reproduced as Illustration 3.) A similar architectural feature of the Mansion House served for the first scene of *The Tempest* when Poel staged the play there in November 1897.

Poel's third and last realization of his notion of the build of stage for which Shakespeare designed his plays was a succession of temporary adaptations of the stages of West End theatres, beginning with his production of *The Two Gentlemen of Verona* at His Majesty's Theatre for the London Shakespeare Birthday festival in 1910[12]. For this production, a structure representing the facade of an Elizabethan tiring house – a balcony with two doors and a recess below – was set up on the stage, the apron of which was extended eighteen feet out over the stalls. The tiring house facade gave him the requisite balcony, doors and recess, while the extension of the apron gave him a 'forward platform'. The verbal record gives some indication of the dimensions of the platform and of the difficulties it presented. The only visual record is a single, probably surreptitious, newspaper photograph of the stage under construction (see Illustration 4). From reviews and promptscripts it is evident that Poel worked variations on this arrangement in productions across the 1910s and 1920s. Finally, in the last five productions of his career, he was able to build a 'forward platform ... the same size as that in use in the Fortune theatre'. For the first of these, a production of Samuel Rowley's *When You See Me You Know Me* at the Holborn Empire in July 1927, Poel added a platform 45 feet wide by 27 feet deep to the permanent stage of his venue.[13]

For all that he realized something of his notions of the build of stage for which Shakespeare designed his plays, Poel cannot be said to have presented any of those plays under the conditions of playing for which they were designed. On all of the three simulacra – the Fortune fit-up, the simpler fit-up, and the platform extensions – it was notionally possible to play full texts, without interruption for

changes of scenery and without cuts or re-arrangements to minimize the number of such changes. And yet Poel never took full advantage of this possibility. The promptbooks testify to the scale of Poel's textual interventions – not just excisions but also transpositions. Some of these were made in deference to then-current standards of sexual discourse and behaviour. Others were undertaken in service to 'dramatic interest' as Poel understood it, which was as a man accustomed to the rhythms of the nineteenth-century 'well-made play' – exposition, complication, crisis, denouement. On the basis of such an understanding, he could justify the labours of his directorial blue pencil in terms worthy of Shakespearian adapters from Nahum Tate to Charles Marowitz. In response to questioning about his text for a production of *Hamlet* in 1914, for example, he protested:

But I only did what I needed to do to cut out the tiresome meaningless scenes and to bring out the drama of the play. I used my own liberty, and my own judgment in giving what I thought was a good play.[14]

And though he frequently and firmly proclaimed that the act-divisions in printed texts since the First Folio were distortions of Elizabethan theatrical practice, Poel did not often abandon the Victorian use of intervals. Programmes from his productions often include an oxymoronic announcement along the lines of the following, from the November 1893 production of *Measure for Measure* which introduced the Fortune fit-up:

The Plays of Shakespeare that were published in his life-time and which are known as the Quartos, are

---

12 See Michael Booth, *Victorian Spectacular Theatre 1850–1910* (London, 1981) pp. 138–9; Mazer, *Shakespeare Refashioned*, p. 113; and O'Connor, *William Poel and the Elizabethan Stage Society*, pp. 89–93.

13 See J. A. B. Somerset, 'William Poel's First Full Platform Stage', *Theatre Notebook*, 20 (1966), 118–21.

14 Florence May Warner, 'William Poel and the Shakespearean Revolution', *Vassar Quarterly*, February 1931, 19–28. This quotation, 27.

5 *The Coxcomb*, at the Inner Temple Hall, 10–11 February 1898. Original pencil drawing by Ralph Cleaver, published in *The Illustrated London News*, 19 February 1898.

not divided into Scenes and Acts, and it is possible that in Shakespeare's time no pause was made in acting his plays from beginning to end.

At 9.45 o'clock the action of the Play will be stopped for ten minutes, during which interval the Stage Orchestra will play music of the Elizabethan period, Composed by William S. Vinning, Mus.Bac.Cantab. [typography *sic*]

Poel did dispense with an interval for performances of *Twelfth Night* on the Fortune fit-up in Middle Temple Hall on 10, 11 and 12 February 1897. For this production, moreover, his editorial blue pencil did less damage than it usually did: just under one hundred lines in the prompt-book are marked for excision or emendation (for example, 'page' for 'eunuch'!). Yet the mere fact that Poel took the Fortune fit-up into that venue is another marker of distance from the conditions for which Shakespeare wrote his plays. After all, *Twelfth Night* had been played,

presumably by Shakespeare's company, in Middle Temple Hall on 2 February 1602: the entry in John Manningham's diary which records that performance gives no hint of the players having imported or improvised any stage from their purpose-built theatre;[15] and analysis

---

[15] 'At our feast wee had a play called "Twelve night, or what you will"; much like the commedy of errores, or Menechmi in Plautus, but most like and neere to that in Italian called Inganni. A good practise in it to make the steward beleeve his Lady widdowe was in Love with him, by counterfayting a letter, as from his Lady, in generall termes, telling him what shee liked best in him, and prescribing his gesture in smiling, his apparraile, &c., and then when he came to practise, making him beleeve they tooke him to be mad,' *The Diary of John Manningham of the Middle Temple, 1602–3*, ed. Robert Parker Sorlien (Hanover, New Hampshire: University Press of New England, 1976), 48.

of the script shows the architectural features of the hall to have been adequate unto the occasion.[16] Producing the same Shakespearian play in the same Elizabethan hall, Poel brought in the Fortune fit-up! Illustration 5, which reproduces a graphic artist's record of Poel's 1899 production of Beaumont and Fletcher's *The Coxcomb* on the Fortune fit-up in Inner Temple Hall, gives some sense of what that stage looked like when it was set up in such non-theatrical spaces as the halls of the inns of court and of the city companies. It should perhaps be noted that this illustration shows a conjunction of facsimiles: the Inner Temple Hall of Poel's time was the Victorian Gothic work of Robert Smirke.

Poel's manner of blocking performances on the stage of the Fortune fit-up was as profoundly Victorian as that simulacrum was. From the promptbook for the 1897 performances of *Twelfth Night* in Middle Temple Hall, for example, it is clear that Poel staged the play in accordance with 'alternation theory', playing its eighteen scenes as alternately 'front' scenes before the 18 foot traverse curtains drawn between the satyr-topped columns of the fit-up, and 'full' or 'open' scenes discovered behind the line of those curtains. The alternation was insistently regular, the traverse curtains opening or closing fully a dozen times in the course of the performance. Only between 2.1 and 2.2 (both 'front' scenes), 2.4 and 2.5 (also both 'front' scenes), and 3.4 and 4.1 (both 'full' scenes) were they left unadjusted. Thus replacing intervals and 'waits' for scene changes with interruptions and pauses for curtain changes, Poel merely accelerated Victorian stage practices. He could not abandon such practices as long as he assumed that every scene signified some specific place, and even that the places generally alternated between indoors and outdoors. The second fit-up afforded him a less satisfactory theatrical grid onto which to map out dramatic terrains: as contrasted with the Fortune fit-up, it had no balcony, a shallow central recess, and far less tapestry to swish

about in punctuation. Nevertheless, Poel still managed to signal dramatic geography on this second fit-up. For the 1899 production of *The Alchemist*, for example, the door at the right of the photograph reproduced as Illustration 3 was understood, in Acts 1 to 4, as leading from an onstage interior to the offstage exterior, but *vice versa* for most of Act 5, when the situation of Face, appearing on the balcony in the wall above, was understood to be indoors looking out.

Occasionally Poel used no fit-up at all but simply the space and architectural features in the hall of one of the city companies and inns of court. In these venues Poel was as close as he ever would or could get to the build of stage for which Shakespeare wrote his plays: they provided neutral and undivided acting areas in front of galleried and elaborately carved hall screens containing at least two doors. See Illustration 6, one of eight photographs which survive from the 1895 Elizabethan Stage Society production of *The Comedy of Errors* before the screen in Gray's Inn Hall (which had seen a performance of that play four centuries earlier). To these halls, however, Poel brought assumptions which were geared to the scenic conventions of the proscenium theatres of his time. The hall screen in Gray's Inn Hall provided a musicians' gallery above and at floor level a pair of doors, between and to either side of which were shallow recesses. The doors contained fan-shaped lights to which paint or soap was applied, apparently to block sight of players offstage. More importantly, Poel's use of these doors imposed a fictional geography upon the theatrical space and thereby both contained the fluidity of that space and required him to find another entrance/exit. The left-hand door in the photograph reproduced as Illustration 6 was used for access to the house of Antipholus of Ephesus, while the right-hand one gave access to the market and to the house (upstairs

---

16 T. J. King, *Shakespearean Staging 1599–1642* (Cambridge, Mass.: Harvard University Press, 1971), 97–115.

6 *The Comedy of Errors* at Gray's Inn Hall, 7 December 1895, Act 5, scene 1.

in the gallery) of the Abbess. Playing without an interval, Poel found it necessary to use a third door, which stands in a wall at right angles to the hall screen, for traffic to and from other parts of Ephesus. Similarly, when in the following year Poel staged *The Two Gentlemen of Verona* before the screen in Merchant Taylors' Hall, the use of one door indicated that the scene was in Milan and the other that it was in Verona, while the forest near Mantua was signalled by the entrance of banditti through the audience. Such dramatic geographies confused reviewers, particularly those from the theatrical trade press:

In and out of these exits the performers came and went in a way quite subversive of illusion. No further attempt was made to mark changes of scene, which are rather marked in the play and have no little bearing on the ingenious action. Upon this plan was the comedy given, line after line. To the antiquary a representation on this would-be Elizabethan method has ... its interest ... to the nineteenth-century eyes of the theatre [it is] so much incongruity and disillusion.[17]

To the late twentieth-century eyes of the theatre, however, Poel's method, for all that it would be Elizabethan, looks Victorian.

Reviewers of Poel's productions objected to other points of his stagecraft as abandonments

---

[17] *The Stage*, 12 December 1895, 12.

27

of Elizabethan methods. In *An Account of the Elizabethan Stage Society*, a booklet published in June 1898, half-way through that society's lifespan, Poel countered criticism on two frequently remarked points:

It has been asserted that our performances have not been archaeologically consistent, that we have used footlights of the electric light, and that the women's parts have not been played by boys ... With regard to the lighting of our stage ... the object has been to give a diffused and subdued light ... Whether this be done by candle or electric light is not much to the moment, if the visible effect is the same. So also in regard to the acting of the women's parts by boys. The boy who in Shakespeare's time acted Desdemona wore the farthingale; in appearance he was a girl ... However this may be, the fact remains that boy-actors are no longer available for our stage because neither the schoolmaster nor the choirmaster will give the necessary permission.

The explanation for Poel's virtual abandonment of one important condition of the Elizabethan theatre, then, lies in Victorian social circumstances. The same explanation probably accounts for his regular reversal of the direction of Elizabethan theatrical cross-dressing: not only did he almost never assign female roles to boys, but he frequently gave adult male roles to women.[18] Poel himself claimed to find women's voices better suited to speaking Shakespearian verse as he instructed, but study of his correspondence and the cast lists for his productions suggests that this claim made virtue of necessity. Poel's performers were recruited as amateurs; and with some conspicuous exceptions,[19] they remained amateurs. Poel seems to have had greater difficulty recruiting amateur actors than amateur actresses,[20] probably on account of the relative leisure of the (mostly middle-class) ladies' lives. However, his actors stayed with him longer than his actresses did, presumably because the patterns of those same ladies' lives were more subject to variable demands, notably those attendant upon marriage and childbearing.

Poel's work had no place in the commercial theatre of his time but existed in a curious relationship to it. The Elizabethan Stage Society was a play-producing society, one of those late-nineteenth and early-twentieth-century groups which sponsored productions of non-commercial drama. Even by the membership standards of such groups, the Elizabethan Stage Society was a very small organization, with fewer than forty members at its inauguration in 1895 and fewer than fifty in 1899, halfway through its lifespan. Their annual subscription fee of a guinea (that is, £1.05) went towards the costs of productions, of which there were never more than five per year and in some years only one or two. Although productions were sometimes revived, they usually played only once or twice in the first instance.

---

[18] A very incomplete list of productions for which Poel cast women in male roles would include: *Much Ado About Nothing* (1890), *Measure for Measure* (1891), *The Two Gentlemen of Verona* (1892), and *Julius Caesar* (1896) for the Shakespeare Reading Circle; *King Richard II* (1899), *The Coxcomb* (1899), and *Twelfth Night* (1903) for the Elizabethan Stage Society; *The Two Gentlemen of Verona* (1910), *Troilus and Cressida* (1912/3), *Hamlet* (1914), *When You See Me You Know Me* (1927), and *Coriolanus* (1930). Only very rarely, as for *Hamlet* in 1900 and *Poetaster* in 1916, did Poel cast boys or men in female roles. A note on a programme for Ben Greet's 1928 production of *Hamlet* (Q_1) reads rather like a retrospective sneer: 'An attempt was made to act the female parts by boys, but a singing Ofelia with a cockney voice was found unsuitable, so the plan this year had to go.'

[19] Among the most conspicuous exceptions to this rule were: Lewis Casson, Elsie Fogarty, Harley Granville-Barker, Lillah McCarthy, Esmé Percy, and later, after the demise of the Elizabethan Stage Society, Edith Evans and Andrew Leigh.

[20] On 8 October 1898 Alfred J. Wareing, president of the Elizabethan Society, wrote to Poel with names of seven men whom he might approach to play in his production of *The Merchant of Venice*, performed at St George's Hall on 29 November, 3 and 10 December of that year. On 3 July 1925 Poel wrote to Alan Edmiston: 'I forgot to tell you I am very hard up for four or five young men, or if not girls to read small parts and who have light voices that modulate well and will tell easily in the hall ... Tell anyone you think suitable to write to me. I do hope I shall get [Hubert] Carter.'

Thus, the Elizabethan Stage Society never presented more than ten performances in any given year of its decade of existence – at which time, the achievement of one hundred performances was the mark of a successful production in the commercial theatre. Poel's productions went on, fleetingly, in the interstices and at the margins of that theatre. They were presented in buildings which were more or less peripheral to the West End (such as, during the life of the Elizabethan Stage Society, the Royalty in Soho, or later, various of the suburban theatres in Robert Arthur's network), or which catered to the market in amateur theatricals (such as St George's Hall), or which normally had no theatrical function (such as the halls of the inns of court and the city companies). The only production by Poel to play more than a week's consecutive performances in a single place was *Everyman*, which played at the Imperial from 11 June to 9 July 1902.[21] Those twenty-seven performances were further unusual within Poel's career in that they took place in a West End theatre. All but two of the twenty-seven, however, were matinées, long the provenance of non-commercial productions.

The very fact that so much is known about Poel's productions is another sign of his time and marker of distance from the conditions of playing for which Shakespeare wrote his plays. The purposes served by these productions were those of propaganda, not profit. From, at latest, his 1881 production of the first quarto of *Hamlet*, Poel staged Shakespearian and other Elizabethan and Jacobean plays in order to demonstrate his understanding of how they had been written and to discredit the ways in which they were being presented in the commercial theatre of his time. In order both to communicate his ideas and opinions as widely as possible and also to generate some income, Poel gave lectures which he illustrated with lantern slides. In direct consequence of this practice, the photographs which are extant from Poel's productions between 1893 and 1901 are unique as records of theatrical performance at the time.

Made at photo calls, they show players posed, in costume and as if enacting a particular moment in production, on whichever stage was being used for it. By contrast, most theatrical photography through the 1890s is studio work, sometimes using scenery or furniture imported from the theatre for the occasion but more often with the photographer's stock items: before 1901, the technology of the time did not allow photographs to be taken of productions in actual performance onstage.[22] Just when it became possible to do so, Poel, convinced that he had been cheated of his due in the Elizabethan Stage Society revival of *Everyman*, that sole financial success of his career, became paranoid about publicity and forbade further photographs showing his stages. Up until that point, however, the visual record of early productions by the Elizabethan Stage Society is unrivalled in quantity and quality alike.

The same compound of missionary zeal with protection of self-interest also motivated Poel's retention of documents, which survive in extraordinary abundance. They record, among many other narratives, Poel's campaign for a simulacrum building – a full, working reconstruction of an Elizabethan theatre. He pursued this project even while he built and used his successive stage simulacra. Late in 1894, within a year of his first use of the Fortune fit-up, the gossip in the theatrical trade press was

that Mr Poel ... proposes erecting an Elizabethan playhouse, where Mr Poel will continue his efforts to convince the British public that Shakespeare's plays are independent of scenic effects.[23]

Poel promoted this proposal through various channels (most of which went nowhere in next to no time) and by various means. It was advertised on programmes for Elizabethan Stage Society productions, the inaugural one pre-

---

[21] See J. P. Wearing, *The London Stage 1900–1910* (Metuchen, New Jersey, 1981), p. 168

[22] See H. Snowden Ward, 'Photography and the Footlights', *The Playgoer*, 1.4 (January 1902), 195–200.

[23] 'ChitChat', *The Stage*, 13 December 1894, 12.

senting the project as an extremely (and implausibly) easy option:

A theatre specially built on the plan of the 16th century would not be an expensive building; besides, with no scenery, and with no necessity to renew the costumes for every play, the bill can be changed at little cost.

Poel's photographic records of Elizabethan Stage Society productions saw service in the campaign for 'a theatre specially built on the plan of the 16th century', as did a pair of scale (1:24) models of the Fortune and Globe Theatres. The former was built by 1894 and promptly went on display at Poel's lectures. He also used a photograph of this Fortune model on various publicity materials, most notably, a petition asking the London County Council to grant land as a site for the reconstruction of a Shakespearian playhouse:

In the event of such a building being erected it should be used as a Shakespearian Library and Museum. Elizabethan plays might also sometimes be acted there under the conditions that attended their original production, thus furthering the knowledge of Shakespeare's time, while the interest attaching to such a building to visitors from America and the colonies will be obvious.

The scale model of the Globe was built in 1897. The plans which Poel drew for it in April of that year have recently been rediscovered and studied.[24] The Globe model itself can be traced from its construction by one of Poel's supporters, Frieda Loewenthal (Mrs Ludwig) Mond, to its display at a succession of lectures and meetings in the late 1890s, at the British Museum by 1905, at a theatrical exhibition in the Whitechapel Art Gallery in 1910, and then in the loan collection of the 'Shakespeare's England' exhibition at Earl's Court in 1912. Most of the 1912 exhibition consisted of fake Elizabethan buildings, late-Tudor-style facades and facsimiles designed by the fashionable architect Edwin Lutyens.[25] There was also a full-size replica of Sir Francis Drake's ship, 'The Revenge': this was designed by Sir John Seymour Lucas, RA, on whose expertise in historical costume Poel had drawn for some productions. And there was a full, working replica of the Globe Theatre. This, the first Elizabethan playhouse to be erected in post-Restoration England, appears to have been derived from Poel's 1897 plans, probably via the scale model which had been built from those plans. The ancestry of the Earl's Court Globe of 1912 is strongly suggested by comparison of, on the one hand, the 1897 plans and the photographs of the Globe model, with, on the other hand, the photographs of the 1912 building, one of which is reproduced as Illustration 7.[26] Scrutiny of this visual evidence, however, also turns up points of difference between Poel's work and the 1912 Globe, above all in the relative shallowness of the stage of the Earl's Court replica. Fifteen years later, when a 'forward platform ... the same size as that in use in the Fortune theatre' had become for Poel the *sine qua non* of Shakespearian staging, he

---

[24] By Martin White, whose article about Poel's 1897 plans for a scale model of the Globe Theatre appear in *Theatre Notebook* Vol. 53, No. 3. One of the (three) plans was reproduced – 'from the original in the possession of Mr O. D. Savage' – in *Drama* n.s. 35 (Winter 1954), 40. Much of the Poel memorabilia amassed by Savage went to the Theatre Museum, but these plans went elsewhere, vanishing from scholarly sight until Professor White's recent rediscovery of them.

[25] See my 'Theatre of the Empire: "Shakespeare's England" at Earl's Court, 1912', in Jean E. Howard and Marion F. O'Connor, eds., *Shakespeare Reproduced: The Text in History and Ideology* (London, 1987), pp. 68–98; and Franklin J. Hildy, 'Reconstructing Shakespeare's Theatre', in Franklin J. Hildy, ed., *New Issues in the Reconstruction of Shakespeare's Theatre* (New York: Peter Lang, 1990), pp. 1–37, and especially pp. 18–25.

[26] There is also some less direct evidence. Lutyens' correspondence includes a letter dated 17 August 1907 in which his wife, née Emily Lytton, reports on her visit to Little Thakeham (a Lutyens house built in 1902) with Mrs (by now Lady) Mond, who is reported as being enamoured of one of Lutyens' furniture designs and enquiring about his house prices (LUE/26/3/1–42 in Lutyens correspondence, British Architectural Library, Royal Institute of British Architects, Portland Place, London).

7 Ye Olde Globe reconstruction at 'Shakespeare's
England' Exhibition, Earl's Court, May–October 1912.
Photograph of the stage.

reminded the readers of the correspondence columns in *The Times* about the lack of such a platform in the Globe reconstruction at 'Shakespeare's England':

Although the building erected in 1912 at Earl's Court, in the enclosure known as 'Shakespeare's England', was advertised on the programme as being a copy of the Globe Theatre, yet the dimensions and proportions of the building were not the same. Moreover, it lacked the essential feature of an Elizabethan playhouse – that is, the projection of the platform into the middle of the arena. At Earl's Court these differences were due to economic reasons – namely, want of space together with a desire to add to the seating capacity within the playhouse. Perhaps I ought to add that if a replica of the original Globe Theatre were erected at Stratford-upon-Avon, then the residents might with

justice regard the building, from the outside at least, as being both 'huge' and 'ugly'.[27]

Writing nearer the time of the 'Shakespeare's England' exhibition (indeed, before it had closed!), Poel had had a longer list of objections to the 1912 reconstruction of the Globe:

There are some merits attached to the design, but also several errors, notably, on the stage, in the position of the traverse, in that of the staircases, and in the use made of the side boxes as approaches to the stage ... exception might [also] be taken to the movement of the costumed figures who are supposed to impersonate the 'groundlings'.[28]

Poel's objection to the groundlings at the 1912 Globe reconstruction was that they were too rowdy. William Archer's objection to the onstage audience at Poel's 1893 introduction of the Fortune fit-up had been that they were too sedate:

The gallants, smoking their Elizabethan clay pipes on their sixpenny stools on the stage, certainly contributed to the illusion; but I fear it was very seldom that the ruffling blades of the Court and the Inns of Court conducted themselves with such propriety. To make the realism perfect they should have called for and consumed burnt sack in the midst of the performance, exchanged banter with the citizens in the 'yard', and between-whiles quarrelled among themselves. It would not have been amiss if one of them had casually run another through the body.[29]

The mere presence of groundlings in 1912 and/ or gallants in 1893, whatever their behaviour, betrays a problem fundamental to theatrical reconstructions: unreconstructed audiences. A dramatic revival on the stage of a theatrical reconstruction is a play-within-a-play. The outer dramatic fiction is the one afforded by the reconstruction itself. As one reviewer noted of

---

27 Poel, 'Shakespeare Memorial Theatre' [points from letter], *The Times*, 7 November 1927, 10.
28 'Shakespeare at Earl's Court', *New Age*, 22 September 1912, reprinted in Poel's *Shakespeare in the Theatre* (London, 1912), pp. 208–12. This quotation, p. 208.
29 Review published in *The World* for 15 November 1893, reprinted in Archer's *The Theatrical 'World' for 1893* (London, 1894), pp. 266–70. This quotation, p. 268.

Poel's inaugural use of the Fortune fit-up: 'The old-fashioned stage with its surroundings is, of course, as good as a play to the modern spectators.'[30] Another wrote of the occasion:

It was an attempt to stage Shakespeare's *Measure for Measure* on a stage arranged after a sixteenth-century model, the members of the [Shakespeare Reading] Society ... appearing on the stage as spectators dressed in the costumes of the period. The aim of the Society was to test the dramatic effect of the comedy played under the conditions originally associated with the performance, but to have carried out this idea completely would also have involved the rearrangement of the audience.[31]

Rearrangement of the audience is the advantage held by the Globe reconstructions of 1912 and of 1996/7/8 over the Fortune fit-up of 1893–1905. Rearrangement of spatial relations between auditorium/stage does not suffice, however, to secure 'the conditions originally associated with the performance'. The insufficiency is evident from the adoption – both at the Earl's Court 'Shakespeare's England' Globe before World War I and now at the Southwark 'Shakespeare's Globe' – of assorted strategies to bring audiences into the outer fiction, turning everybody into Queen Elizabeth for a Day: the placement of costumed actors among the audience; the musical processions and dances paced by almost irresistible thumping of staffs; the benches without supports for backs or cushions for bottoms; the sale of period comestibles alongside the usual interval snacks. The pursuit of authenticity may not always end in theme parks, but it does generally seem at least to skirt very close to them.

Such devices finally preclude even the notional possibility of testing anything in theatrical reconstructions, for all that the rhetoric around them is riddled with talk of tests. From the rhetorical stable of quasi-scientific terminology around 'Shakespeare's Globe' on Southwark, the pair of tropes which get trotted out particularly often are those of theatrical reconstruction as laboratory and of dramatic revival therein as experiment.[32] This verbal tic, like so much else, can be traced back to Poel. After her husband's death, Ella Poel recalled: 'Through all he "experimented", as he put it, with his "dress rehearsals", as he called many of his necessarily *single* performances.'[33] That may have been how Poel put it, but his successors should, thanks to him, know better. Close examination of Poel's record points to the impossibility of his project to reconstitute the conditions of playing for which Shakespeare wrote and the consequent inappropriateness of presenting such a project as experimental science. If experiments are to determine the effect of variable factors, they must establish constant factors. Between Shakespeare's theatres and Poel's, as likewise between the Globe reconstructed from the Theatre for Shakespeare's company in 1599 and the 'Shakepeare's Globe' reconstruction in 1999, there are only variables.

---

[30] *The St James's Gazette*, 10 November 1893, quoted in Harris, 'William Poel's Elizabethan Stage', p. 114.

[31] *The Morning Post*, 13 November 1893, 3.

[32] For some egregious examples in a single volume see, in Hildy, ed., *New Issues*: Walter Hodges, seeking 'a stage on which the many problems of Elizabethan stagecraft still eluding us can at last be properly tested, and the answers found' (40–1); Alan Dessen, listing canny caveats 'to ensure that the new Globe will indeed be a meaningful testing ground or laboratory' (136) and warning lest 'with our evidence and our questions already tainted by sanitized playscripts and by post-Elizabethan theatrical thinking, both the laboratory and the experiments to be conducted therein will be contaminated from the outset' (139); and J. L. Styan, offering 'speculations about what discoveries we may make about the plays when the first [*sic*] authentic [*ditto*] replica of the Globe Theatre is built on the South Bank in London, and is in use for experimental performance in 1993' (p. 185–6).

[33] 'Personal Notes' added to Allan Gomme's typescript bibliography, p. 19.

RECONSTRUCTING THE GLOBE
CONSTRUCTING OURSELVES

W. B. WORTHEN

1. THE HOLE AND ITS HISTORICITY

I want to begin this discussion of performance and the past by looking briefly at Suzan-Lori Parks's recent play *The America Play* (1994), a theatrical meditation on the relationship between history and the space of performance. The play opens in '*A great hole. In the middle of nowhere. The hole is an exact replica of the Great Hole of History*'.[1] The main character, 'The Foundling Father' (a former gravedigger, now known by his stage name, 'The Lesser Known') describes how he travelled west, and built this replica of 'the Great Hole', an eastern 'theme park. With historical parades . . . The Hole and its Historicity and the part he played in it all gave a shape to the life and posterity of the Lesser Known that he could never shake' (p. 162); 'Amerigo Vespucci hisself made regular appearances' in the Great Hole of History, as well as 'Marcus Garvey. Ferdinand and Isabella. Mary Queen of thuh Scots! Tarzan King of thuh Apes! Washington Jefferson Harding and Millard Fillmore. Mistufer Columbus even. Oh they saw all thuh greats' (p. 180). The Foundling Father – played by an African American actor – 'bore a strong resemblance to Abraham Lincoln' ('He was tall and thinly built just like the Great Man. His legs were the longer part just like the Great Man's legs' (p. 159)), and so devised a 'Great Man' living-history performance. Choosing a beard from his extensive collection – 'as authentic as

he was, so to speak' (p. 160) – his act consisted 'of a single chair, a rocker, in a dark box. The public was invited to pay a penny, choose from the selection of provided pistols, enter the darkened box and "Shoot Mr Lincoln." The Lesser Known became famous overnight' (p. 164).

In the course of Act 1, the Foundling Father re-enacts the scene of Lincoln's assassination with a variety of customers; each shoots Lincoln, shouts some 'historical' catchphrase – two are attributed to John Wilkes Booth as he fled the stage of the Ford Theater, others to Robert E. Lee, Edwin Stanton, and Mary Todd Lincoln – as '*Lincoln "slumps in his chair"*' (p. 165). In the second half of the play, the Foundling Father's wife Lucy and son Brazil appear on stage; a gravedigger, the Foundling Father had once planned a mourning business with his family, using Lucy's talents for 'Confidence work' and hiring Brazil as a professional 'weeper' (p. 162). As Una Chaudhuri remarks in her subtle reading of the play, Lucy and Brazil epitomize 'the historian and archaeologist, the one listening for echoes from the past, the other digging for its remains'.[2] Lucy listens through an ear trumpet for the echoes of gunshots, while

---

[1] Suzan-Lori Parks, *The America Play*, in *The America Play and Other Works* (New York, 1995), p. 159. Further references to *The America Play* are to this edition, and are incorporated in the text.

[2] Una Chaudhuri, *Staging Place: The Geography of Modern Drama* (Ann Arbor, 1995), p. 265.

Brazil digs, unearthing the detritus of the Great Hole for a new museum onstage. Brazil turns up various documents ('peace pacts, writs, bills of sale, treaties, notices . . .' (p. 186)), and displays a bust of Lincoln, the Foundling Father's beard box ('A Jewel Box made of cherry wood, lined in velvet, letters "A. L." carved in gold on thuh lid'), and 'Over here one of Mr Washington's bones, right pointer so they say; here is his likeness and here: his wooden teeth. Yes, uh top and bottom pair of nibblers: nibblers, lookin for uh meal' (p. 185). He also unearths a television, which plays the Foundling Father's 'Lincoln Act'.

Parks describes her playwriting as formally modelled on the 'Rep & Rev' of jazz, the repetition and revision 'in which the composer or performer will write or play a musical phrase once and again and again; etc. – with each revisit the phrase is slightly revised'.[3] Staging and restaging the Lincoln assassination, re-playing scenes from *Our American Cousin*, and improvising over the structure of progressive African American theatre – the theme park recalls the design of Adrienne Kennedy's *Funnyhouse of a Negro* and of George C. Wolfe's *The Colored Museum* – *The America Play* reprises the American past as Rep & Rev, staging history as fully complicit with the dynamics of performance; as Lucy remarks, 'Fakin was your Daddy's callin but diggin was his livelihood' (p. 181).

The Great Hole of History is the stage of fakin and diggin, where history is enacted as an encounter with its signifiers, indeed 'with its signifiers *as* signifiers'.[4] In the metonymic logic of popular history, Lincoln becomes the charade props of beard and rocker, and Booth's ill-remembered cry; Washington is the cherry tree, crossing the Delaware, the wooden nibblers, much as Henry VIII is his many wives, or Churchill is his 'cigar', as Joe Orton pointed out in *What the Butler Saw*. 'The size of the hole itself was enough to impress any Digger but it was the historicity of the place the order and beauty of the pageants which marched by them'

(p. 162): The Great Hole is a replica both of the fullness (whole) of history, and of its undoing, its absence (hole) in representation. Materializing the past as object and as echo, it enacts – like that other Great Hole, the Globe theatre – an anxious performance of the past in the present.

II. FAKIN AND DIGGIN

The building of Shakespeare's Globe is in many ways a concrete – or lath and plaster – encounter with the problematics of performance and history, fakin and diggin. As rhetoric, the performances at Shakespeare's Globe appear to cite the original circumstances of Shakespearian dramatic production, and possibly even to cite those original productions themselves; the new Globe's performances claim to be *of* 'Shakespeare' in new, perhaps unique ways, because they restore the means by which Shakespeare's plays had their original force. Yet as everyone connected with the project is well aware, the Globe can only be a complex *contemporary* undertaking, one which evinces an understanding of the working of history that is fully our own. Straddling a commitment to an 'origin' that it at once invokes, creates, and displaces, Shakespeare's Globe dramatizes the conditions of authority animating (some would say enervating) dramatic performance today.

In his now-classic essay 'Collective Reflexivity: Restoration of Behavior', Richard Schechner uses a range of performance forms – from ritual, to conventional theatrical modes, to 'Renaissance Pleasure Faires, restored villages' and other themed amusements – to instigate a comprehensive theory of performance; placing the dynamics of Western

---

[3] Suzan-Lori Parks, 'From "Elements of Style"', in *The America Play and Other Works*, pp. 8–9.

[4] Alice Rayner and Harry J. Elam, Jr, 'Unfinished Business: Reconfiguring History in Suzan-Lori Parks's *The Death of the Last Black Man in the Whole Entire World*', *Theatre Journal*, 46 (1994), 447–61; p. 459.

dramatic theatre within a wider understanding of performance behaviour, Schechner offers an incisive way into the theatrical, and extra-theatrical character of Globe performativity. Arguing that 'Performance means: never for the first time', Schechner suggests that whether the performance is shaped as conventional theatre, religious ritual, or even a staging of traditional performance forms for modern tourists (at the Polynesian Cultural Center in Hawai'i, for instance), what performance reproduces is not an origin, but the illusion of originary behaviour: 'the event to be restored is either forgotten, never was, or is overlaid with other material, so much so that its historicity is irrelevant. What is recalled are earlier performances: history not being what happened but what is encoded and transmitted. Performance is not merely a selection from data arranged and interpreted; it is behavior itself and carries with it a kernel of originality, making it the subject for further interpretation'.[5]

Performance at the Globe depends on 're-storation' of this kind; the meanings of Globe performance emerge through the performative citationality of its characteristic behaviours – offstage and on – and on what (and how) they claim to 'restore'. Although it is in many ways a unique performance – and performative – space, the Globe participates in a continuum of familiar history-performance venues, ranging from reconstructed historical performance environments like Plimoth Plantation and Colonial Williamsburg, to constructed 'histor-ical' sites like the Ironbridge Gorge Museum, the Open-Air Museum at Beamish and Green-field Village (new villages built of old build-ings), to efforts to rejuvenate moribund industrial or agricultural towns as picturesque historical/commercial centres (on the model of the Wigan Pier Historical Centre, or indeed any number of towns in New England), to their controversial – demonic, to some – avatars in the historically 'themed' sections of Disney-land and Disney World; the Globe is, of course, also explicitly a theatre.[6] What these sites share

is what they sell: a participatory *experience* of the past in a mode of performance designed to be pervasive, incorporating the audience in a virtual society, a landscape, an engulfing atmo-sphere (the authentic aromas of the Jorvik Viking Centre in York). At the same time, the specific activities that constitute performance in these places are quite divergent, and so con-struct different experiences and different visions of history as well. The Globe is a unique structure, true enough; but Globe performance works at just this juncture, at the intersection between the early-modern experience of theatre it labours to restore, and the modern regimes of theatrical performance and history-performance that are its means of production.

Environmental history-performance sites, such as Plimoth Plantation in Plymouth, Massa-chusetts, deploy a range of typical performance strategies that are engaged by both actors and audiences, strategies that shape the visitor's experience and so his or her access to history. Like the Globe, Plimoth Plantation is a monu-ment to the persistence of mimetic desire; re-enacting the Pilgrims can be traced to the Pilgrim tableaux performed at historical festivals in Plymouth in the 1890s, through the more elaborately staged pageants of the 1920s,

---

5 Richard Schechner, 'Collective Reflexivity: Restoration of Behavior', in *A Crack in the Mirror: Reflexive Perspectives in Anthropology*, ed. Jay Ruby (Philadelphia, 1982), pp. 40, 43.
6 There is a large, often polemical literature on the heritage industry and on the National Trust; although I am indebted to this literature in many ways, it is not my intention here to enter into the two main thrusts of controversy, which have to do with the ultimate purposes of preservation and restoration, and with how the historical function of a wide variety of sites should best be communicated, and to what audience. For a range of views, see Robert Hewison, *The Heritage Industry: Britain in a Climate of Decline* (London, 1987); Peter J. Fowler, *The Past in Contemporary Society: Then, Now* (London, 1992); Michael Hunter, ed., *Preserving the Past: The Rise of Heritage in Modern Britain* (Stroud, 1996); Raphael Samuel, *Theatres of Memory. Volume 1: Past and Present in Contemporary Culture* (London, 1994).

through the annual Pilgrims' Progress of costumed townspeople (each portraying an actual member of the colony) of the 1930s and 1940s. The current plantation was first imagined by Henry Hornblower II, an amateur archaeologist who encouraged his father to donate $20,000 as seed money to build a Pilgrim Village in the late 1940s. Initially conceived on the model of Greenfield Village (built outside Detroit by Henry Ford, Jr in the 1920s), Colonial Williamsburg (built by John D. Rockefeller, Jr in the 1930s), or Old Sturbridge Village (a working nineteenth-century farm in central Massachusetts that opened in 1946), the Pilgrim village was to be a reconstructed version of the original settlement, and several buildings were constructed in the early 1950s on the waterfront in downtown Plymouth, on ground that had been cleared for the Tercentenary pageants of 1921. In 1956, however, Hornblower acquired fifty acres from his grandmother, an open site on the Eel River overlooking Plymouth harbour where he began to reconstruct the homes of prominent colonists. When Plimoth Plantation opened in 1957 (like the Globe, near-but-not-on the site of the original settlement), it was accompanied by a second venue: the Mayflower II. Built with some early-modern shipbuilding methods, the Mayflower sailed to Plymouth (using some seventeenth-century seamanship as well), arriving in June.[7]

From its opening until the late 1960s, the Plantation consisted of charming cottages filled with period antiques. The buildings housed wax Pilgrims, while costumed interpreters lectured, demonstrated various activities, and answered visitors' questions. Although these guides wore costumes, the clothing was inauthentic both in design (buckled shoes and hats traditionally, but inaccurately, ascribed to the Pilgrims) and in construction (polyester), and the guides assumed neither Pilgrim roles nor early-modern English accents. In his vivid account of Plimoth Plantation, Stephen Eddy Snow – a descendant of the Plymouth colony

who spent two summers acting as an 'interpreter' on the Plantation in the 1980s – reports a momentous change in educational philosophy and historiographic practice that took place at the Plantation in 1969. Not only were 'the antiques . . . removed from the restored village', but in succeeding years, the village was rebuilt to resemble more accurately a struggling agricultural community rather than a tidy pastoral folly.

Under the direction of Harvard-educated anthropologist James Deetz, Plimoth was put on course to become a 'living museum,' in which the material culture of the period would be reproduced and the mental and behavioral culture of the people (the *ethnoi*) would be re-created . . . The third-person narrative presentation of the 'Pilgrim Fathers' (mythic figures) by museum guides who were frequently dressed in inauthentic period attire was replaced by a format in which the cultural life of the Pilgrims was re-created by 'interpreters' dressed in well-researched historical costumes and giving, as Deetz said, 'the appearance of seventeenth-century Pilgrims'.

The next phase of this metaphrasis came in the early 1970s, when interpreters began to experiment with speaking in period dialect and in the first person . . . By 1978, this living history method was the modus operandi in the re-creation of Pilgrim life at Plimoth. Interpreters were trained to embody fully the ethnohistorical roles, to act as if they truly were seventeenth-century Pilgrims.[8]

Over the past two decades, Plimoth Plantation and the Mayflower have come to exemplify the work of living-history performance. At Plimoth Plantation, the actors attempt to capture, 'restore' (in Schechner's sense) the language, the dialect, the behaviour, and even the *episteme* of seventeenth-century farmers; Plimoth labours to provide a seamless perfor-

---

[7] On the history of Plimoth Plantation, see Stephen Eddy Snow, *Performing the Pilgrims: A Study of Ethnohistorical Role-Playing at Plimoth Plantation* (Jackson, Mississippi, 1993), pp. 18–27. I am generally indebted to this fine study of performance at the Plantation.

[8] Snow, *Performing the Pilgrims*, pp. xix–xx.

mance of the plantation in the year 1627, and as visitors move through it, they encounter the villagers in that lost lifeworld.[9] Visitors eager to learn about Pilgrim life must engage Plimoth's denizens in conversation, a dialogue across the centuries. For at Plimoth, the actors no longer work as modern guides. They perform fictional Pilgrim roles, and diligently avoid mentioning – or even recognizing – aspects of post-seventeenth-century life. Visitors no longer meet modern 'instructors in Pilgrim attire, but "informants" portraying William Bradford, John Billington, John and Priscilla Alden and others.'[10] The performers are 'acting', of course, but the boundary between their offstage and onstage behaviour is difficult to locate: they are always signifying the past, 'acting' it, even when they're merely 'behaving'. In this sense, performance at Plimoth, and on the nearby Mayflower, is different from the performances of the Young National Trust Theatre at various heritage sites in the United Kingdom, where the actors' performance is more clearly bound to the quasi-historical 'drama' they invent, script, and perform for the spectators (although there are several festivities held throughout the summer season at Plimoth that follow a generalized scenario, in which the interpreters improvise action and dialogue consistent with their individual roles and function in the event). It is also different from the widespread use of costumed guides or craft-demonstrators, who don't assume a first-person 'role' in the past, but instead provide information about their craft from a third-person perspective that they share with the contemporary audience. At Plimoth, the 'restoration' extends from the landscape to the architecture to the performers' 'performance' of carpentry or candle-making to their mere behaviour, their being in the world. Their immersion in seventeenth-century mannerisms 'onstage' tends to make their 'offstage' behaviour also appear to restore the past – even if they're just walking across the plantation to the concealed modern toilets, or to the break-room where they have lunch and punch their time-

clocks.[11] The characteristic 'subjunctive mood' of Plimoth Plantation creates the impression that everything addresses the participant/spectator from the seventeenth century.[12]

Yet while the boundary between performer and audience at sites like Plimoth is less visible than in a proscenium theatre, it is no less marked, especially where issues of liability, entertainment value, or cultural politics are at stake (I am thinking of the controversial slave auction at Colonial Williamsburg, Virginia, which was structured in such a way as to prevent 'bidding' by anyone who was *not* an actor, as a way both to reinforce the 'pastness' of this performance, and to prohibit an unsavoury enactment of slavery's continuity with contemporary racial tensions).[13] In this sense, participatory venues like Plimoth, or the Blitz

---

9 As Anthony R. Jackson noted recently, Plimoth's engagement of its ambulatory spectators is more formal than it at first appears; encounters with performers become more complex as one proceeds through the village, and increasingly depend on knowledge gleaned from previous conversations and demonstrations. Jackson has also developed an interesting typology of the kinds of performance undertaken at heritage sites: actors can be dressed in period costume, and perform as historical figures who principally interpret and explain the past to the modern spectators (i.e., functioning as guides); they can perform invented roles – blacksmith, publican – in which they attempt to reproduce historical behaviour for an audience addressed as historical 'contemporaries' in the past; or they can construct full-dress 'dramas', addressing the spectators as moderns across an implied proscenium. See Anthony R. Jackson, 'Interacting with the Past: The Uses (and Abuses) of Participatory Theatre at "Heritage" Sites', unpublished paper, International Federation for Theatre Research World Congress, Canterbury, July 1998.
10 Snow quotes from the 1983 Plimoth Plantation Annual Report, in *Performing the Pilgrims*, pp. 40–1.
11 Snow, *Performing the Pilgrims*, pp. 115, 74.
12 Schechner, 'Collective Reflexivity', p. 40.
13 See Bruce McConachie, 'Slavery and Authenticity: Performing a Slave Auction at Colonial Williamsburg', unpublished paper, Institute for the Humanities, University of California at Santa Barbara, February 1998. I am grateful to Professor McConachie for providing me with a copy of this fine paper.

Experience at the Imperial War Museum, provide a more conventionally 'theatrical' kind of entertainment than experiential immersion of battle re-enactors like the Sealed Knot (which enacts battles between Roundheads and Royalists), or various Roman Army groups in the United Kingdom, or the 'period rush' sought by 'hardcore' enthusiasts of the American Civil War, 'living historians' as they call themselves.[14] This subculture of men – a subculture of a subculture, really, since 'hardcores' comprise a tiny minority of the estimated 40,000 Civil War re-enactors in the United States – use period dyes to make their uniforms (which, of course, are never washed), meticulously probe photographs (and specialist merchandise catalogues directed to them) for uniform-fashion details, soak their brass buttons in urine, sleep rough in the field holding one another for warmth ('spooning'), sometimes march barefoot, and even follow extreme, low-calorie diets (for that hauntingly emaciated, hollow-eyed, Matthew Brady-esque physique), all in pursuit of what they call 'Wargasm'.

Places like Plimoth Plantation transform the past into something with 'exhibition value', 'Pastness'.[15] For all their vitality, these sites involve their visitors in the performance of 'culture as dead practice'; building their characters by imaginatively blending biographical and historical information with the given circumstances of Plimoth, the interpreters' routine use of the performance practices of stage realism makes the Plantation 'a kind of museum of theatre practice' as well.[16] As performed history, the animated 'virtual pilgrim world' involves a museum aesthetic far removed from the display-case of artifacts (or indeed from the site of Plymouth Rock, sunk several feet below street level in a kind of classical portico), which objectifies the material past in a mute dialogue with the present.[17] Nonetheless – unlike the battlefield re-enactments in this regard – Plimoth is a strangely haunted place for its contemporary visitors.[18] For although the past is voluble –

carrying on in several regional accents of reconstructed seventeenth-century English – we are mute, at least to the extent that the actors are allowed to engage the audience only in seventeenth-century terms (hence the typical sport of Plimoth and other such sites, 'Pilgrim-baiting': trying to get the actors to break frame and allude to your sneakers, sunglasses, wristwatch, cell-phone). Much as it is periodically torn down and rebuilt, so as continually to resemble, despite the Massachusetts weather, the colony in the year 1627, Plimoth Plantation resembles another living town locked in the past, occasionally visited by strangely ignorant, kindly spectres of a time yet to come: Brigadoon.

Much of the controversy surrounding the Globe – whether it's a 'Disneyland' or not; whether this comparison is pejorative or not – concerns the 'subjunctive mood' of the performances it frames, the kind of restoration, or 'surrogation' to use Joseph Roach's term, it

---

14 Tony Horwitz, *Confederates in the Attic: Dispatches from the Unfinished Civil War* (New York, 1998), p. 10. Horwitz describes 'hardcore' behaviour pp. 6–13, and again in his chapter on 'The Civil Wargasm', pp. 209–81; he provides the statistics on Civil War re-enactment p. 126. Raphael Samuel discusses re-enactment in the United Kingdom – Roman marching groups, the Sealed Knot – and mentions the National Association of Re-enactment Societies and the Jousting Federation of Great Britain in *Theatres of Memory*, pp. 169, 174, 191–2.

15 Barbara Kirshenblatt-Gimblett, 'Afterlives', *Performance Research*, 2.2 (Summer, 1997), p. 5.

16 Kirshenblatt-Gimblett, 'Afterlives', p. 5. On the Stanislavskian dimensions of the interpreters' work, see Snow, *Performing the Pilgrims*, passim.

17 Kirshenblatt-Gimblett, 'Afterlives', p. 7.

18 The battlefield and the plantation do share a disquieting lexicon; as the Plimoth interpreters are having their morning meeting in the centre of the village, 'David Hobbs, at six feet six inches the tallest Pilgrim, yells out: "In coming!" All heads turn toward the top of the hill. The first visitors of the day have entered the top portal, about one hundred yards away'; Snow, *Performing the Pilgrims*, p. 61. Snow also discusses the use of dialect at Plimoth and on the Mayflower (p. 127), and 'Pilgrim-baiting' (p. 71).

promises.[19] Like Plimoth Plantation, the Globe is deeply textured by efforts toward architectural and historical accuracy, as well as by the necessity to commodify a vision of the past to finance the project. The Globe's construction is a landmark in contemporary architecture. It at once memorializes and recovers lost architectural practices – such as *ad quadratum* laying out of the design – and brings an English cottage-industry in Tudor construction methods into the public eye; in the minutiae of its construction, it implicitly demonstrates the transformation of English culture and economy over the past four centuries (the plastering is done with goat hair, because cow hair today is too short); it teaches new lessons about early-modern building practices (how effective lath and plaster is as a fire break), and indeed about how those methods could be adapted to modern requirements (the Globe is the first thatched building in London since the great fire; the thatching is treated with retardant and the roof is protected from fire by a sprinkler system).[20]

Much as the Globe is a testament to the survival or reanimation of traditional crafts, it is also enabled by the explosion of a retrofit aesthetic in the 1970s and 1980s and its attendant technologies, an aesthetic that 'depends as much on concealing the evidence of modernity as in multiplying period effects'.[21] For while Shakespeare's Globe restores the past, it also operates as a living theatre. The requirement that it function *as* a living theatre, with living audiences, has perhaps been the signal challenge to authentic reconstruction, running afoul of fire laws, maximum theatre occupancy rules, conventions of modern theatre design (toilets), as well as of modern Tudor aesthetics, which may require anachronistic or inauthentic period effects (exposed rather than whitewashed exterior timbers, for instance). Although there is an ongoing controversy about doing 'experimental' productions involving Elizabethan accents or reconstructed rehearsal and performance practices (Patrick Tucker's Original Shakespeare Company has conducted such

experiments, but not as part of the Globe season), the Globe is intended not merely as a place for the performance of the past, a place for its audiences to conjure an imagined experience of Shakespeare's theatre. For the Globe to achieve its experimental mission, the performances taking place there have to be contemporary as well, using the structure of the Globe as a springboard to the ongoing dialogue between Shakespeare's plays and contemporary audiences. Unlike at Plimoth Plantation, the Globe's actors must, some of the time, speak to *us, now*.

The specific contours of Globe performance emerge with greater clarity against the backdrop of environments like Plimoth Plantation; so too it is important to consider the Globe's relation to the other end of the performing-history spectrum, the theme park. From its inception, the creators of the Globe have resisted the obvious linkages between the Globe and Renaissance Pleasure Faires, theme parks, or Disneyland and Walt Disney World. Although some of this resistance may spring from marketing savvy, high-cultural pretension, or a scholarly sense that theme parks are 'doubly offensive because they seem to come to us from America, and because they link history to the holiday industry', theme parks do provide an index to some aspects of Globe performativity.[22] Dean MacCannell describes theme parks as 'decoys' – a decoy is a 'restricted-access, large-scale (though usually not full-scale) architectural copy of an authentic attraction' in

---

[19] Schechner, 'Collective Reflexivity', p. 40; Joseph Roach, *Cities of the Dead: Circum-Atlantic Performance* (New York, 1996), pp. 2–3.

[20] On building practices, see Jon Greenfield, 'Timber Framing, The Two Bays and After', in *Shakespeare's Globe Rebuilt*, ed. J. R. Mulryne and Margaret Shewring (Cambridge, 1997), pp. 97–120; John Orrell, 'Designing the Globe', *Shakespeare's Globe Rebuilt*, pp. 51–65; on plaster composition, see *Shakespeare's Globe: The Guidebook* (Reading, 1996), p. 27.

[21] Samuel, *Theatres of Memory*, p. 77.

[22] Ibid., p. 268.

which the 'tourists are the "ducks"'.[23] Since theme parks offer the commodified experience of a place's theme or essence, it is generally easier to build a successful theme-location around a place that is not very specific or familiar, or that can be made to represent a larger and more complex culture whole (in the way Renaissance Pleasure Faires do not refer to specific historical events, but to a generalized sense of 'Renaissance' festivity). As the Project on Disney remarks, 'Although the design of the Canadian pavilion [at Disney World] is based upon actual structures – a chateau in Ottawa, for example – these structures are not nearly as recognizable [to Americans] as the Eiffel Tower in the French pavilion. One is free, therefore, to imagine Disney's "Canada" as somehow the "essence" of the country without being reminded of an actual place' – confirming, it hardly needs to be said, how many Americans tend to imagine Canada anyway.[24] Yet historical sites also require 'theming' of this kind. The interpreters of Plimoth Plantation, for example, often improvise narratives that are thematically consistent with Plimoth's portrayal of Pilgrim life, stories that circulate among the characters and visitors in the course of a given day, and so help to create the gossipy texture of daily life.[25]

Theming tends to generalize and essentialize, and the principal source for thematic imagery at theme parks is typically the media, mainly film and television. The Disney World Prime Time Café, for instance, places patrons in a 'set', a diner derived less from the 1950s than from television images of fifties culture, images which are replayed on television sets in the restaurant (as of course much of Disneyland and Disney World are predicated on the animated characters and their film stories).[26] Like theming, though, mediatization is not confined to theme parks, but also sustains more 'authentic' historical re-enactment. Robert Lee Hodge, a 'hardcore' Civil War player, and the 'Marlon Brando of battlefield bloating', not only studies photographs for the details of living (and dead) soldiers, but also yearns to see his hardcore squad of Southern Guardsmen assemble to reproduce the photograph of Confederate soldiers on the march displayed in the Antietam battlefield visitors' centre.[27] To some extent, theme parks are simpler – 'Disneyfied' – versions of sites like Greenfield Village (mainly eighteenth-century American buildings) or Ironbridge (mainly nineteenth-century structures), which assemble period buildings from a variety of locations to form a typical, 'themed' town, 'what Barrie Trinder, a moving spirit at Ironbridge, calls "a hypothetical industrial community"' framed by 'assembling historical artefacts on a greenfield site and threading them with narrative'.[28] We play these sites differently, and they do have different kinds of meaning for us: living-history and open-air museums arose in Scandinavia as part of late nineteenth-century romantic nationalism; Ford's Greenfield and Rockefeller's Williamsburg were built as memorials to a way of life modern industry was helping to destroy, and to

---

23 Dean MacCannell, 'Virtual Reality's Place', *Performance Research*, 2.2 (Summer 1997), p. 17.

24 Project on Disney, *Inside the Mouse: Work and Play at Disney World* (Durham, North Carolina, 1995), pp. 204–5.

25 As Snow reports, sometimes these narratives are used to cover a gap in the historical texture of Plimoth, as when a visitor asks an interpreter (playing Edward Winslow) where he might find his ancestor Richard Warren. Winslow replies that 'he is "off wi' the' fishin' partie, to Cape Anne, for a fortnight"' (in reality, the role of Richard Warren has not been cast for this season)'. On other occasions, 'the interpreters get inspired and want to do a little historical playwrighting of their own', by starting a story – say, about a fight between two of the Pilgrim girls – that will be elaborated 'in character' by the various interpreters throughout the day. Snow, *Performing the Pilgrims*, pp. 63, 75.

26 Project on Disney, *Inside the Mouse*, p. 46.

27 Horwitz, *Confederates in the Attic*, pp. 8, 228.

28 Samuel, *Theatres of Memory*, p. 169. The Project on Disney notes that while 'Disneyfication' is 'not yet in the dictionary', it is 'understood to refer to the application of simplified aesthetic, intellectual, or moral standards to a thing that has the potential for more complex and thought-provoking expression'; *Inside the Mouse*, p. 103.

instil a conveniently capitalist ideology of 'American' identity through the rhetoric of historical recovery; Ironbridge is a United Nations World Heritage Site. For all their differences, what these sites share is the aesthetics of theming.[29]

The Globe is a tourist destination, and there are T-shirts and postcards and film and books in the giftshop (there *is* a giftshop). Yet the Globe most resembles theme parks in what it sells: a mediated experience of the past in the present. As Dennis Kennedy argues, it may well be that the form of experience it offers is so defined by the logic of theme-park tourism – 'Ancient sites are mediated through intellectual effort and imply that the visitor is obligated; theme parks build in whatever is needed and construct the visitor as already knowing' – that its authenticity is largely irrelevant: 'It is both authentic and inauthentic: it is carefully built using reconstructed Tudor oak carpentry and hair-and-lime plaster; yet it is as counterfeit and synthetic as any theme park.'[30] Yet, performance at Disney usually evokes the totalitarian dimension of theming, for which Disney has become notorious. Theme parks choreograph and commodify all aspects of experience (where to take photographs, where to stay, what to do), regimenting their visitors as much as their famously regimented employees. For all their 'themed' similarity, sites like Plimoth Plantation (let alone battle re-enactments) require the visitor's active participation. The Pilgrim interpreters assimilate historical and biographical information, but do not play a scripted role; their highly improvisational performance of Pilgrim life depends on the active agency of the visitors, their questions and comments, their desire to speak with the dead – often about seventeenth-century religion and politics. Theme parks tend to construct their visitors more passively, as *consumers* rather than producers of experience. It is not surprising that visitors preferring forms of recreation in which their agency matters find theme parks disenchanting; in the words of one bored visitor to

Disney World, 'I don't like to go somewhere where they chew the food for you.'[31] In this sense, the explicitly theatrical function of the Globe marks a remove from the total-institution of the theme park: though the performance of the Globe is clearly 'themed', onstage Globe performances presumably work to avoid the pre-chewed pastiche of theme-park enactment, the performance of 'performance' so to speak.

The effort to stage the performances as *contemporary* theatre both characterizes the 'restored behaviour' of Globe performance, and distinguishes the work of Shakespeare's Globe from sites like Plimoth, and from that much-feared evil twin, 'Bard World'.[32] As living theatre, the plays at the Globe should be different from Renaissance Pleasure Faire antics, and from reconstructed museum-performance as well; unlike the performances of eighteenth-century drama in the theatre at Colonial Williamsburg, the Globe actors *act* like contemporary actors: they usually don't speak to us 'from' the past, a Mark-Rylance-as-Dick-Burbage-as-Hamlet performance. The performances – even the 1997 *Henry V*, which 'restored' authentic staging practices and costumes made with period technology and

29 Michael Stratton, 'Open-Air and Industrial Museums: Windows onto a Lost World or Graveyards for Unloved Buildings', in Hunter, *Preserving the Past*, 156–76; pp. 157–8.

30 Dennis Kennedy, 'Shakespeare and Cultural Tourism', *Theatre Journal*, 50 (1998), p. 185. Indeed, as Kennedy notes in this probing discussion, the claims to 'authenticity' of the final project were not really part of Sam Wanamaker's original plans, which were to build 'a modern design that contained only the external features of the original' (p. 181). I am very much indebted to Kennedy's groundbreaking work here and elsewhere on the commodification of spectatorial experience in a range of contemporary performance venues; see also Dennis Kennedy, 'Shakespeare and the Global Spectator', *Shakespeare Jahrbuch*, 131 (1995), 50–64.

31 Project on Disney, *Inside the Mouse*, p. 109; on employment conditions, see pp. 110–62.

32 David Patrick Stearns, 'Reconstructed Globe Provides Theater in the Real', *USA Today*, 13 June 1997, 11A.

dyes (and, of course, the underwear) – are not meant to be performances *then* that we overlook like the village idiots watching the Plimoth blacksmith ('duh, what's that for, Miles?'), or the faux-Georgians of the Williamsburg theatre. The notion is that 'The reconstruction of the Globe is as faithful to the original as scholarship, construction and craftsmanship can make it', and that by constructing this frame, modern performers and modern audiences will have (in Andrew Gurr's phrase) 'a working theatre, Shakespeare's factory, to see how his plays were originally intended to work'.[33] While this may sound like the craftsman-performer aesthetic at work (we can watch someone shoeing a horse, we can watch early-modern acting), the performances typically strike a distance from reconstructed 'Elizabethan' acting. In an important sense, 'acting' at Plimoth consists of the demonstration of labour, of work; indeed, while these performances sometimes fail to convey the 'drudgery, danger, or squalor' of early-modern agricultural labour, much of what the actors/characters *do* is in fact *real* work in the world (several women, for example, demonstrate Pilgrim cooking by making a meal that the 'Pilgrims' eat later in the day).[34] The Globe actors' acting, on the other hand, *is* their performance. Rather than demonstrating Elizabethan acting (as though their performance were like the Pilgrim cooking class, or perhaps a product like Pilgrim food), the Globe actors *act* like modern actors acting Shakespeare; while whatever work the characters perform is purely fictive, the real-world labour of the actors is the performance itself, and whatever drudgery or danger it overcomes or excitement it creates is part of its character *as* work in the here-and-now. The audience, too, is both addressed and performs as a contemporary theatregoing public; despite the hissing and booing, we are hardly re-enactors: remember those urine-soaked buttons (Michael Holden once promised to eject any patrons arriving at the Globe in hose and doublet).[35] While Plimoth uses acting to restore the life-ways of the past, acting at Shakespeare's Globe seems directed toward something else, toward using the physical frame to make the persistent properties of Shakespeare's plays visible as contemporary performance. Rather than the 'period rush' sought by the American Civil War players, the Globe 'restores' the medium of Shakespeare's theatre to the present, in order to demonstrate that we – behaviour today, onstage and off – can still 'discover' what has been there, in the text, all along.

The work of 'restoration' really takes place in the relationship between performers, between actors and audiences. The wooden O is, of course, not hollow at all; like all space – built or unbuilt, constructed or natural – the Globe space is saturated with meanings. To many audiences, the Globe appears to cite not merely the conditions of Shakespeare's theatre, but an entire vision of the past. Writing in *The Sunday Times*, John Peter describes the 'serious, entertaining, commercially viable and classless' theatre that he thinks was destroyed when 'Cromwell closed the theatres in 1642', a theatre whose 'excitement, its vigorous, classless appeal, and . . . stylistic and political audacity' the new Globe seems to recapture.[36] Unlike what passes for political and populist theatre today – 'a working-class knees-up aggressively lowbrow, and flourishing its moral and social membership card by rejecting serious argument, long words and uncomfortable ideas' – Shake-

---

[33] *Shakespeare's Globe: The Guidebook*, p. 41; Andrew Gurr, 'Shakespeare's Globe: A History of Reconstructions and Some Reasons for Trying', in *Shakespeare's Globe Rebuilt*, p. 34. Andrew Gurr, here and elsewhere, is quite aware that it's impossible to 'go the whole hog' as far as authenticity of performance circumstances is concerned, while nonetheless trying to find out as much as possible about how 'the Globe worked as a theatre in its own time' (p. 46).

[34] Stratton, 'Open-Air and Industrial Museums', p. 171.

[35] Michael Holden made this remark in a discussion at the Institute for the Humanities, University of California at Santa Barbara, March 1997.

[36] John Peter, 'Where the Audience is King', *The Sunday Times*, 15 June 1997, 16–17.

speare's Globe appears to restore a mythic vision of a classless, vibrant past as the ideal image of post-Thatcher British culture, a vision that Peter can only articulate by simultaneously enacting the persistent privileges and prejudices of class. While the Globe may work to restore the workaday practice of Shakespearian playing, to its audiences the present practice of performing (in) the Globe resembles what Joseph Roach calls surrogation, in which performance re-produces 'an elusive entity that it is not but that it must vainly aspire both to embody and to replace'.[37]

Peter's fantasy of the energetic classless vigour of the original Globe smacks a bit of the roast-beef-and-wenches imagery of Renaissance Pleasure Faires, a nostalgic citation of absent origins that animates the audience's engagement in Globe performance as well. Perhaps I should point out that it *is* a richly interesting experience to stand in the pit, and I suppose when the hazelnuts are laid in, a more authentic one, too. This performance has quickly become conventionalized; the 'groundling groupies' have developed a kind of ritualized behaviour, which is readily 'played' by the actors onstage.[38] 'The prommers stand merrily for three hours at a time; stand there beaming merrily up at the stage; stand like patience on a monument, smiling at grief — smiling indeed at everything, and laughing wherever possible.'[39] Globe performance strikes its distance from conventional contemporary Shakespeare by involving the audience energetically in a participatory engagement with the space and with the performance; characteristic of theme parks, of theme events (Renaissance Pleasure Faires), and of heritage performance, this aspect of Globe performance requires the audience to bring its own notions of appropriate behaviour to bear, in ways that are at once democratic and potentially disruptive of claims to authenticity. For like Peter's review, this behaviour typically cites a recognizably Victorian vision of Merrie Olde England; our performance — like the retrofit aesthetic, concealing 'the evidence of moder-

nity' while multiplying 'period effects' — has at least as much in common with the chemically-treated thatch than with the incendiary social realities of behaviour in the early-modern house.[40] (In the 1998 *As You Like It*, for example, the actors — anachronistically, of course — cleared a space in the pit for the wrestling match, in part by drawing their swords on the audience, clearly a much less volatile act than it would have been four centuries ago: presumably Renaissance actors could 'carry' only while acting; what would it have meant for an actor to leave the stage armed, let alone to draw upon a gentleman?)

One complex version of the transformation of convention has to do with the lively hissing

---

[37] Roach, *Cities of the Dead*, p. 3. In some ways, this 'inclusive' dimension of Globe performance has now been internationalized in ways that point out the ideological closure of Shakespearian universalism. Sam Wanamaker's sense that 'The Globe will make the *theatre* (not only Shakespeare) once again popular, public and accessible: the working-class man will feel less constrained and inhibited there than in the plush, enclosed space of a bourgeois theatre' is reflected in his sense that Shakespeare will be one of the 'forces to bring people together whatever their language, social status, culture, educational level', a purpose evoked in the Globe's current mission to use international casts; see Graham Holderness, 'Sam Wanamaker, Interviewed by Graham Holderness', in *The Shakespeare Myth*, ed. Graham Holderness (Manchester, 1988), pp. 21, 19.

[38] Penny Wark, review of *The Maid's Tragedy*, by Francis Beaumont and John Fletcher, and *A Chaste Maid in Cheapside*, by Thomas Middleton, *The Sunday Times*, 31 August 1997; rpt. *Theatre Record*, 17.17 (August 1997), 1084–5.

[39] Alastair Macaulay, review of *The Maid's Tragedy*, by Francis Beaumont and John Fletcher, and *A Chaste Maid in Cheapside*, by Thomas Middleton, *The Financial Times*, 30 August 1997; rpt. in *Theatre Record*, 17.17 (August 1997), 1087. Macaulay continues, 'The Globe players have discovered how to play this audience to perfection, if not the plays they happen to be performing. The method is simple: deliver everything like Christmas pantomime. Play broadly for laughs; wait for each laugh; invite the audience to boo or hiss the baddies; have cast members rush comically through the audience. The recipe works, only too well.'

[40] Samuel, *Theatres of Memory*, p. 77.

and booing of the villains, first widely noted during the 1997 *Henry V*, and now *de rigueur* at the Globe. It's difficult to register the force of this behaviour, for like all behaviour it registers several kinds of meaning at once; the audience seems not quite to indulge itself in 'Pleasure Faire' antics and yet to behave in ways – booing, hissing, etc. – that are clearly constituted as an increasingly large dimension of 'Globe' performativity. The conventionality of this behaviour is recognized by the Globe producers, who regard the performances as 'licensing' such behaviour as a necessary element in the investigation of Shakespeare's factory. The limits of this 'licence' are enacted everywhere in the theatre: in the actors' performances, in what the audiences are asked to do and not to do, in the distinctly modern behaviour of those distinctly modern performers, the ushers. For all its genteel rowdiness, the Globe is a visibly policed space; fire laws, ticket pricing, and the easy access to the gallery from the pit call for unusually active ushers, who keep people from standing or sitting on the steps in the gallery aisles, as well as occasionally preventing fatigued groundlings from sitting on the ground, which is said to disrupt the actors' concentration much as it breaks the illusion of the happy, united audience. Performing in Shakespeare's Globe involves being given a kind of 'freedom' while seeing that it's not 'abused': 'There is a need to strike a balance between liberating the audience and telling them how far it is admissible to go.'[41] To the producers, what 'licenses' the audience's performance, and indeed authorizes the project as a whole, is an understanding of the proper present regard for Shakespeare.

The Globe is a hugely interesting 'decoy', much like any other experimental laboratory; rather than sneering at the ironies of 'deconstructive postmodernists,' we should recognize that the Globe can only work as 'an extraordinary laboratory for analysing Shakespeare's drama and his age' (if that is its goal) to the extent that it can accomplish what – in their

very different ways – Plimoth Plantation and the Prime Time Cafe do as well: open a space where the past is engaged as present performance.[42] What distinguishes the Globe is not its use as a laboratory for investigating Shakespeare's age, but the extent to which it uses theatrical performance – the audience's as well as the actors' – to imply that this specifically theatrical form of historical recovery is 'a social form of knowledge', an 'ensemble of activities and practices in which ideas of history are embedded or a dialectic of past-present relations is rehearsed'.[43] The regimes of Globe performativity are evocative of a wide range of contemporary performance; touristical, recreational, historical, everyday-life, and theatrical genres of behaviour all frame its occasion of Shakespearian drama. The Globe's performers – actors and audiences – bring these significant, signifying behaviours to bear, behaviours trained on historical sites, Renaissance Pleasure

---

41 Chantal Miller-Schütz, *Shakespeare's Globe Research Bulletin*, 1 (November 1997), p. 5. In the second Research Bulletin, Pauline Kiernan reports, 'There was a need, it was felt, for the actors to be able to "front them out", speak more clearly, and learn ways of dealing with the audience, so that "we don't lose a sense of the 'whole', of the story; so we don't let a moment get pulled apart. We have to learn to control that"'; see Pauline Kiernan, *Shakespeare's Globe Research Bulletin*, 2 (January 1998), p. 22.

42 Richard Hornby, 'The Globe Restored', *Hudson Review*, 50 (1998), 617–24; p. 617. Having been one of the 'deconstructive postmodernists' at the University of California, Santa Barbara conference on the Globe that Hornby discusses, I can only say that I remember a much different event than he describes: while the Globe was indeed considered in relation to tourism (Dennis Kennedy spoke at this conference) and to Disneyland, I had the sense that these were earnest efforts to come to terms with the complex and refractory cultural work taking place at the Globe. Rather than being 'downright vicious when it comes to physical reconstruction', the speakers – including both Andrew Gurr and Michael Holden – struck me as quite fascinated by the project, and by both the conceptual and practical problems and consequences of Globe performance.

43 Raphael Samuel, *Theatres of Memory*, p. 8.

Faires, sporting events, and theme parks, as well as on a familiarity with Shakespeare plays, with summer Shakespeare festivals, with theatregoing, with Shakespearian and non-Shakespearian acting, and perhaps with the 'experimental' cast of mind evoked by the project's animators. It's sort of authentic, sort of theme park, tourist dependent, mediated, a Polonian early-modern-modernist-postmodern event. In other words, it's *our* Globe, necessarily part of how we imagine the great (w)hole of history.

The Globe provides a salient metaphor for our understanding – or misunderstanding – of the relationship between history and performance. Like the 'wargasm', which involves driving frantically between Civil War sites (now usually ringed by suburban development) in order to march through thickets in the dark and sleep in the rain, Shakespeare's Globe enacts what Barbara Kirshenblatt-Gimblett has described as the 'hallmark of heritage productions – perhaps their defining feature . . . the foreignness of the "tradition" to its context of presentation'.[44] As a mode of contemporary performance, Shakespeare's Globe offers audiences live theatre performed in the here and now, actors using contemporary ideas about actor training, physical movement, the character's journey and so on, to make the plays meaningful, perhaps experimenting with the closeness and visibility of the audience and the specific (Renaissance Faire?) licence to volubility that the Globe performances labour to liberate and to control. What the experience is said to restore is how Shakespeare's plays 'worked' – that is, the ability to visualize, through the alienating lens of our own performance, what it was like, what features of the plays are *there*, in them, that come into visibility only in this kind of space, in this kind of relationship, even if that relationship is only with 'groundling groupies'. Of course, we

don't need Tudor timbers to frame this relationship; surely reinforced concrete would work just as well (though it would be difficult to reproduce the surprisingly clear yet rich acoustics of the Globe with harder materials). Yet the much-heralded commitment to accuracy of building practices and materials is critical to the rhetoric of the Globe; it appears to substantiate the practices and materials of the performance, ours as well as the actors' – even despite alterations in location (it's down the street), building materials (goat hair), performance practices (staging scenes in the pit), the size, disposition, gender, and behaviour of actors and audiences. Performance is always in the present; ideologies of restoration are always rhetorical, a frictionless disciplining of the past through its embodiment in the present. Barbara Hodgdon argues in her reading of another spatial materialization of 'Shakespeare', that 'At the Birthplace as at the other properties, Shakespeare is everywhere but is also invisible'; Stratford and its collections offer 'a metaphor about the past' which is 'also a cultural argument in the present' (203).[45] Shakespeare's Globe incarnates an attitude animating many productions of classic drama today, an attitude it shares with theme parks and living-history museums from Anaheim to York: if we build the structure right, and put ourselves into it, the past – Shakespeare's 'work' – will be 'restored', both to the theatre and to us. Not to put too fine a point on it, like Plimoth Plantation, the battlefields of Gettysburg and Antietam, perhaps even like the Magic Kingdom itself, Shakespeare's Globe is a field of dreams. If we build it, he will come.

---

[44] Barbara Kirshenblatt-Gimblett, *Destination Culture: Tourism, Museums, and Heritage* (Berkeley, 1998), p. 157.
[45] Barbara Hodgdon, *The Shakespeare Trade: Performances and Appropriations* (Philadelphia, 1998), pp. 202, 203.

FROM LITURGY TO THE GLOBE: THE CHANGING CONCEPT OF SPACE

JERZY LIMON

The starting point of my argument is the assumption that spatial and temporal structures and relationships are basic to the way in which societies both shape and comprehend the world around them. These structures and relationships may be of dual natures: physical, belonging to the empirical world, and mental, belonging to imaginary, fictional or metaphysical realms. Thus, among other creations of the human mind and technical skills, theatre and drama may be seen as reflections of particular cognitive models of the universe, created in given periods. One of the peculiar features of theatre is the division, which may generally be defined as one between two times and two spaces, that of the performers and that of the spectators. This division lies at the very roots of the rise of theatre and drama and their further evolution and the whole history of theatre may in fact be depicted as a constantly changing relationship between the two spaces and between the two times, the spatio-temporal continuum of the auditorium and that belonging to the artistic realm created on the stage during a spectacle.[1]

For archaeologists or architectural historians space belongs to empirical reality and can be measured and related to other measurable spaces. However, in theatres this physical space is only one of the spaces present there and the fictional or artistic space that is being created during the actual performance seems far more important and interesting for theatre studies. Consequently, while there are many similarities between the two areas of investigation, one is bound to accept the differences and the fact that architectural historians and theatre historians will ask different questions and focus on different problems. Theatre historians, or theatrologists, will be predominantly interested in those aspects of purely architectural studies which will be helpful in describing the complex network of signs through which the artistic space is created during dramatic performances. What exactly is the relationship between the auditorium and the stage? What is the artistic or ideological programme of the interior or exterior of a theatre? In what way will that programme be corroborated, neutralized or even negated by the spectacle? In what way will it influence our perception? The basic distinction is linked not only to space itself, but also to time. An architectural historian will focus on permanent features of the building, such as the structural elements and the relationships between them, the characteristics of the interior design, ornamentation, displayed works of art,

---

[1] An additional relationship will be between the two spheres and the world outside. It is important to remember that it is not only the stage that provides a spectacle that can be related to the outer world: an equally interesting, although much less obvious relationship may be established between the auditorium and the outer world (the auditorium in the Banqueting Hall, London, is a conspicuous example). The two spheres of interior space may relate similarly to the outer world (the staging of the masques at early Stuart courts), but sometimes differently (a production of, say, *King Lear*, in the same venue before, say, King James I).

affinity to other buildings of the same kind and so on; the theatre historian will take account of all this but will also focus on the temporary significance of all those elements during the actual performance, that is during the time when the theatre interior may become part of the fictional artistic reality created by the spectacle. A theatre historian will also be interested in the fictional time created on stage and the possible relationship of that time to the time of the theatre interior or of the empirical reality.

In an attempt to bring some order into the area of theatre history called Elizabethan theatre studies, which as such has always had problems in deciding whether it is a part of the history of architecture or a part of theatrology, we should first distinguish at least four theatre spaces: first is the space of the theatre as a building or, more generally, an architectural edifice; second is the space of the stage in its physical appearance; the third is the fictitious space that is created by multi-medial theatre signs, such as the stage set, lighting, music, acting, and, of course, the spoken word; and the fourth is the space of the auditorium, often neglected in scholarship. The particular techniques of creating fictional space, called theatre conventions, will vary from one period to another, and it is not by any means impossible to look at theatre history from this particular perspective asking how fictional space and time are created and what is their relationship to the time and space of the auditorium and to the world outside. The opposition created is between the fictional reality and the empirical one. From this perspective, it is totally irrelevant whether the Globe was 99 or 106 feet in diameter; the problem which seems crucial to architectural historians (or reconstructors) does not even appear unless we can prove that the actual dimensions are part of a code that contributes to the interpretation of the meaning of the entire building or of the artistic space created during a performance.[2] Since we watch the play through the prism of the meaningful text of the theatre interior, even the same

production will generate different meanings when staged in different spaces. Stuart masques, for instance, meant something specific when staged in Inigo Jones's Banqueting Hall, where the ceiling, painted by Rubens, presented an iconographic image of Stuart ideology which the masques corroborated. *Macbeth*, if staged in the Banqueting Hall, would mean something different from the same production presented at the Globe, since Shakespeare's text would be understood in conjunction with and through the prism of the iconographic text of the theatre's interior.

There have always existed theatres of two kinds (with a multitude of variants in between): those with interiors that in themselves carry a 'message', or even a whole ideological programme independent of whatever performance is staged within their space, and those which do not, in themselves, carry a specific meaning, except for being a permanent or temporary acting area. Our basic concern in this context is whether and to what extent the interior – especially the space of the auditorium – becomes part of the performance. Most contemporary theatre interiors do not reveal the tendency of acquiring text-significance during the performance: lights are faded out just before the performance, other lights are lit when the curtain is drawn aside, so that it becomes clear what the director wants us to see, and what he or she wants us to neglect. In other words lights strengthen the division of the fictitious reality and empirical reality, which is blackened and does not imply its continuity or extension anywhere (in other words, the reality of the

---

[2] For instance, in a very influential work, John Orrell was at pains to prove that the Globe had a diameter of about 100 feet and its inner yard a diameter of 70 feet; neither of these figures was confirmed by the findings of the 1989 *Globe* excavations. For the discussion see Andrew Gurr and John Orrell, *Rebuilding Shakespeare's Globe* (London, 1989), p. 113. For a recent discussion of various aspects of Elizabethan theatre architecture see Martin White, *Renaissance Drama in Action* (London and New York, 1998), chapter 4: *Palaces of Pleasure*, pp. 109–29.

auditorium is faded out into non-existence). Moreover, we, the spectators, also find ourselves in the blackened area: this limits our ability to watch others who are not figures on stage, and in addition brings a relief from being watched by fellow-spectators (it does not really matter whether or not the latter is comfortable to us: the visible presence of other people creates a crowd, and, consequently, evokes the feeling of a confined space). Psychologically that means that once the auditorium is darkened, the crowd disappears and our perception of the space opens to greater dimensions, not limited by the presence and sight of others. In this way, the materiality of theatre space is partly suspended for the time of performance (not completely, of course, because we are still able to see something in the dark, and all sorts of noises, like coughing, laughter, whispering and so on remind us of the existence of other members of the audience). Furthermore, the dematerialized non-dimensional auditorium is contrasted with the world outside which retains its dimensions and materiality. Thus, the darkened auditorium, along with perspective scenery, creates better conditions for an individual, or egocentric, perception of the spectacle and marks a clear-cut division between the artistic and empirical realities.

However, the history of indoor theatres with artificial lighting is relatively short, and in most of their history, as we all know, theatrical performances took place during day time and the density of light did not divide the stage from the auditorium. Even today, we have all sorts of outdoor or street theatres, not to mention the reconstructed Globe, where hardly any artificial lighting is used. What this means, of course, is not only that artificial lights were not used on the stage, but there were no technical means to darken the auditorium. Instead of dematerialized space, we have a clearly visible and measurable space of the interior, which never ceases to be recognizably a theatre and also a part of the world outside, with the possible exception, of course, of theatre interiors which are programmed to be treated as spaces separated from the outer world as, for instance, was often the case with royal palaces. Instead of egocentric, individual perception of the performance, we remain part of the crowd and we retain the continuous sensation of communal perception of whatever is presented to us, which among other things is caused by our ability to observe other spectators freely, along with their reactions which – with no regard to whether we find them appropriate or inappropriate – influence our own perception and reactions. Characteristically, in theatres of that kind, of which the Globe is a conspicuous example, perspective scenery is never used, which strengthens the sensation of communal perception of the spectacle (there is practically no division into better and worse seats). Moreover, spectators seated in the galleries of the Globe view the stage through a kind of 'proscenium', composed of the groundlings' heads and bodies, which – along with the visible and audible reactions of the latter – never allows them to forget that they too are a part of the audience.

What separates any theatre space from the world outside is its functionality: this is a place for gatherings of people who, owing to mutual agreement, watch another group perform. However, it has to be a special kind of performance, for its essential feature is the creation of a fictional reality, of a spatio-temporal continuum which exists as an imaginary construct rather than a physical entity. Without that fictional reality no theatre is possible. The one essential convention which marks the appearance of fictional space is the so-called rule of accessibility. Basically, what that means is that the spectators have full access to the world created by performers, whereas the latter do not have that power and simply pretend not to notice anyone else's presence. There are of course numerous examples known of ways in which actors break the invisible boundary separating the stage from the auditorium by means of asides, songs, and other direct addresses to the spectators; and the epic theatre of Bertholt Brecht obsessively reminded us of the conventionality of theatre. We also have reasons to believe that a lot of interaction between the players and the spectators took place at the Globe and other Elizabethan playhouses. However, a careful balance has to be preserved, because the rule of accessibility is what differentiates theatre from any other type of spectacles even though the division of performers and spectators is preserved in them, as in rock concerts or academic conferences.

Another aspect that cannot be neglected is the relationship of the space of the theatre to the space outside. As mentioned above, there are theatre interiors which are meaningful in themselves, that is independent of the performance. This is often the case with temporary theatres arranged *ad hoc* in buildings that originally had not been constructed and designed to house theatrical activity. Early Renaissance Tudor halls or Inns-of-courts served theatrical functions for at least a century; similarly, Romanesque and Gothic churches were used as theatres. All of these spaces are significant in themselves. The iconography of royal or ducal palaces is often incorporated into the current ideological programme of a given house, and the aim of the programme is often to mark a rigid boundary between the semi-divine and super-human world of the interior and the ordinary human world outside. Thus, the space and time of these interiors are often separated from the space and time that govern the lives of ordinary humans. Thus, a performance staged in a space meaningful in itself is bound to create meanings peculiar to that space and the circumstances or the 'present occasion' of the actual spectacle. In other words, the fictitious reality created during the performance will inevitably be related to both the space of the theatre and the world outside it. Consequently, one may distinguish theatres in which triple relatedness may be observed (fictitious reality versus ideology or programme of the interior versus the empirical reality outside) and theatres with

dual relatedness only (fictitious reality versus empirical reality). The first of these will characterize those theatres which originally had not been designed as free-standing theatre buildings, but were either occasionally used for theatrical purposes, like Romanesque and Gothic churches, or were part of a more complex architectural structure, like all sorts of banqueting halls and temporary theatres in royal or ducal palaces. In all of these interiors, the space of the auditorium is separated from the physical space outside. The second type of relatedness, that of a dual nature, will characterize all those theatres which had originally been designed to serve a specifically theatrical function and do not dissociate themselves from the outer reality. In those theatres the time and space of the auditorium is part of a larger whole, of empirical reality.

In what follows, I shall argue that the Globe, as one of many London theatres of the period that shared common features (spatial relationships in particular), may be treated as an extreme example of theatre space that is separated from the outer world by its functionality only. In other words, the space of the Globe does not mean anything apart from conveying the following message to us: I am a space where plays are performed and watched. Moreover, this space is not blackened into non-existence during the performance, and reminds us constantly that we are not in an illusionary world, but in a theatre: illusion is never complete. From this perspective, Shakespeare's image of the 'wooden O' would not only mark the circularity of the frame of the theatre, but could also mean 'zero', the 'crooked figure' that denotes a space that before and after performance signifies 'nothing' – an empty space that awaits to be filled with meaning. It is only during a performance that certain structural elements of the building begin, through a layer of fictionality, to mean something and for this reason may contribute to the infinite varieties of meanings generated by the performance. It is the fictional reality created during the actual performance that makes the otherwise semantically neutral interior of the theatre mean something. Thus the 'cock-pit' becomes a theatre sign and turns into the 'vasty fields of France', and the 'unworthy scaffold' into the globe. The gallery in the tiring-house facade may become a balcony or the crenellations of a castle. The 'heavens' above the stage may become astronomical heavens, by which the stage becomes the earth or the globe, creating thus a model of the universe. However, all of this happens during the performance only: before and after, the stage has only one meaning, that of a wooden, raised platform which is used for dramatic presentations. The frame means three storeys of galleries for spectators, made of timber and very simple in their construction. However, since both the exterior and the interior of that type of theatre have no meaning except as an area for performing plays, during the actual performance of a play any physical element of the theatre may become literally anything, depending on the artistic demands and the actual wording of the script. Covered with a layer of fictionality, the visible wooden structure, filled with spectators, will also remind us constantly of the spectacle's conventionality. And exactly for this reason it will invite all sorts of metaphoric interpretations, in which human life, fate, the world itself will be seen as a theatre. To see this theatre as a philosophical construct and a permanent sophisticated model of the universe would impose a meaning that may occur during a brief scene in a play, but does not exist at all before and after the performance.

I have already labelled this type of spatial organization of the theatre extreme, because it is opposite to the other extreme known in history, in which the theatre interior is so rich in its iconography that it generates meanings that are independent of the fictional worlds created on stage. Moreover, the space of this second type of interior is rigidly separated from the space outside and reveals a tendency to dominate totally over the meanings generated

by performances. In this second extreme type of theatre the subject matter and ideology of the latter are usually limited and predominantly serve to elucidate the ideology, or to corroborate the existing 'text' of the theatre itself. Thus, we may distinguish two extremes of theatre spaces. One — my second type — is oriented towards itself, and allows for a limited variety of performances which will tend to contribute to and complement the meanings of the interior, and, in this sense, this introvert theatre might be labelled autotelic: the primary function of performances staged in this kind of the theatre will be to corroborate or elucidate (or both) the meanings generated by the theatre interior. Because the other extreme — my first type — is semantically neutral, without significance (apart from its being a theatre), it is extrovert in character and oriented towards the outer world and towards an infinite variety of plots and meanings. As Shakespeare put it, 'a crooked figure may / Attest in little place a million'. The autotelic type may be exemplified by some historical cases of court theatre, but above all is manifested by Christian church-as-theatre, the extroverted type by all kinds of 'poor' theatres, of which the London theatres of the period between 1576 and 1642 are perhaps the best-known manifestations.

It is the spatial arrangement of the stage and the auditorium that makes these theatres unique. As is well known, the semi-circular (or square) frame incorporated three galleries for spectators and surrounded an inner yard which was sometimes used as an acting area; the stage proper is a raised platform, surrounded on the three sides by spectators and backed by a tiring-house facade. This spatial arrangement of the stage determined certain characteristics of Elizabethan staging and acting: perspective scenery is not possible there at all, for it would obstruct the view for approximately two thirds of the spectators, and in fact there is no place there for any elaborate stage set; secondly, the style of acting may be labelled as circular, for the actors must move around the rectangular stage in order to avoid neglecting any of the three sides of the stage directly facing the auditorium. If we assume that the 'Lords' Room' was over and behind the stage, then the actors would inevitably have an additional awareness of the audience behind.

Without going into any further detailed discussion of Elizabethan theatres' architectural details, it may be noted that it is predominantly the roundness of the theatres' frame that has attracted the attention of scholars and stirred their imagination: the cylindrical shape in conjunction with the name Globe has invited astronomical, metaphysical and even geographical interpretations, by which the 'wooden O' has been seen in allegorical or symbolic terms, as a model, for instance, of the universe or the earthly globe or both. According to these interpretations, carpenters who were responsible for building the London playhouses had a deep knowledge of neoplatonism, astronomy, alchemy, astrology, emblems and other areas of human knowledge and art, which makes these skilled craftsmen intellectually comparable to the leading architects and thinkers of the age. For Frances Yates, to give an often-quoted example, 'The Globe Theatre was a magical theatre, a cosmic theatre, a religious theatre, an actors' theatre, designed to give the fullest support to the voices and gestures of the players as they enacted the drama of the life of man within the Theatre of the World . . . His theatre would have been for Shakespeare the pattern of the universe, the idea of the Macrocosm, the world stage on which the Microcosm acted his parts.'[3] In a recent book, John Gillies goes even further than Yates and claims that 'There is every suggestion that the Elizabethan theatre was a "theatre of the world" in specifically geographic and ethnographic senses as well as in the cosmic sense'.[4] Again, this is a very stimulating thought, but I think it is wrong and totally unnecessary to adorn Elizabethan theatres with meanings they did not have. It is redundant, because, among other things, their major attraction lies in the fact that they did not have any meaning of their own. This quality enabled them to acquire an infinite number of possible meanings during a performance.

Another way scholarship is trying to show the deep significance of Elizabethan theatre architecture is through analogy and through the ways in which theatre metaphors were used in contemporary writing, fine arts and cartography. And all in spite of the fact that in most cases images, metaphors and similes do not allude specifically to any of the Elizabethan playhouses, but to the generic concept of a theatre. Ironically, pictorial and written evidence used by modern scholarship seems more appropriate to explain the other extreme type of theatre – the celestial one inside Christian churches. For instance, Gillies has drawn our attention[5] to the dual relevance of the *theatrum mundi* metaphor in the Renaissance: on the one hand, *theatrum* becomes a stock metaphor in cartography, and, indeed, maps and atlases in particular were treated as imaginative theatres of the world; on the other, the London theatres themselves became architectural metaphors of the world. Thus, Gillies persuades us to see a clear analogy between cartography and theatres. In order to prove this, an analogy method is applied. Thus we are informed that Ortelius who not only produced the first Renaissance atlas but invented the very idea of the atlas, enriched the purely cartographical value of his maps with a narrative-theatrical function performed by various verbal and pictorial devices. 'Pictures appear either on the body of the map itself or framed by cartouches or set within ornamental frames', Gillies explains. 'Textual legends appear before or within or beneath maps, in order to convey the historical dimension of the geographic image.'[6] In one of the more elaborate of these

---

3 *Theatre of the World* (London, 1987), p. 189.
4 *Shakespeare and the Geography of Difference* (Cambridge, 1994), p. 92.
5 Ibid., pp. 70–98.
6 Ibid., p. 72.

we find no less than twenty-two narrative paintings of episodes from Abraham's life. Thus, the map becomes much more than an image of a place: it also deals with people and history, it tells a story. Since the Ortelian atlas presents itself in the image of theatre, a question may be raised whether, and to what extent, Elizabethan theatre proposes itself in an image that may be analysed and explained in geographic and cosmographic terms. Again, Gillies says yes, and goes on explaining the 'geography' of Elizabethan theatre, the Globe in particular. The name of the theatre has an obvious, though not very clear geographic or cosmographic resonance. Its ambiguity derives from the fact that the 'globe' could either mean the entire universe or the earthly globe alone. Whether or not the alleged motto of this theatre (*Totus Mundus Agit Histrionem*) physically existed at all is not really important; what counts, scholars will argue, is the fact that contemporaries interpreted the Globe (and other theatres too) in terms of the *theatrum mundi*, and Shakespeare translated the motto as 'All the world's a stage'. However, this ancient metaphor often presents the celestial spheres as encircling the earth in the form of a classical temple. Thus, it is from within the temple, which is the auditorium, that the human comedy is watched, enacted on the earthly globe which is the stage. This is exactly the same type of relationship that existed not at the Globe, but in the liturgical theatre: we watch human actions from the divine perspective. The space of heavenly Jerusalem gives authority and validity to the human story; the latter cannot be interpreted outside that space. Moreover, the divine space and time are juxtaposed with the human, or worldly, spatio-temporal continuum.

Does the same relationship exist in the Elizabethan theatre? Does the stage of the Globe represent the 'mundus'? And consequently, does the frame of the theatre represent the celestial sphere rather than the earthly globe? First of all, quite contrary to church drama, in Elizabethan theatres there is no discrepancy between the time and space of the auditorium and the time and space of the human world outside. This means that the two spheres are in fact part of one human sphere and are separated by their functionality rather than anything else. Only those who find themselves within the frame of the theatre are able to watch whatever is presented on the stage; people outside are deprived of that privilege. Even though the metaphysical sphere is frequently hinted at in Elizabethan drama, no one can actually experience it physically. The supposedly painted heavens above the stage is an icon,[7] but it is not transparent; it does not offer us any insight into the invisible and impenetrable celestial sphere which remains an 'undiscovered country'. In other words, the rule of accessibility is fully applied here: in our human theatre, we can watch the actors freely, whereas they do not notice our presence. In the macro metaphor of *theatrum mundi*, however, in the divine theatre of the world, we are not only spectators, but indeed actors as well, who are not capable of 'seeing' the heavenly spectators; however, this inability is not a theatre convention but it stems from a different ontological status of the two spheres, the different time and space they respectively belong to. In this theatre of the world, the other side, that is the divine spectators, whoever they are, have a full and unobstructed view of our comedy. And the two spheres are separated by their different times and spaces, which to non-believers are and to believers are not illusionary. Thus, the basic difference is that in the human world, the actors, following the fundamental theatre convention (the rule of accessibility), only pretend not to see the spectators, whereas in the implicated celestial theatre, we, the humans, can only create a metaphor by analogy, but are never capable of seeing who our spectators are,

---

[7] That the heaven was decorated with symbolic representations of heavenly bodies is by no means certain; see Peter Thomson, *Shakespeare's Theatre*, 2nd edn (London and New York, 1992), p. 44.

unless through a divinely inspired vision. Thus, the cosmic dimension of Elizabethan theatres is at best a metaphor only, and not an intrinsic meaning of the simple wooden structure that did not even require an architect to design it.

Thus, what the Elizabethan theatre offers us is basically a model of a human world, where in two hours' traffic of the stage, we – the poor players – 'strut and fret' our time and then are heard no more, lost in a world that, because we are human, seems to be out of joint, knocking in despair at heaven's doors, expecting at least a sign that would negate the fear of nothingness and life's absurdity. The circularity of the theatre itself may or may not be a reflection of the globe's roundness; seeing celestial spheres in the frame of what used to be animal-baiting houses is an interesting thought, but cannot be verified by substantial evidence.[8] During a performance at the Globe the empty space of the theatre is covered with a layer of fictional meaning that may convert it into practically any other space. And this infinite variety of possible spaces created by the unrestricted imagination of playwrights is what made these theatres almost ideal locations for the staging of plays. Thus, any attempt to read into these wooden structures a richness of meaning characterizing sophisticated interiors of the times, would inevitably lead to the creation of boundaries in this unlimited potential of the theatres. However, owing to the physical conditions in Elizabethan theatres, and particularly to the fact that the auditorium was not darkened for the time of performance, it constantly reminded the spectators of the conventionality of theatre art and for this reason became a perfect metaphor for the whole world and human life seen as a

theatre. This meaning is not contrasted with or related to any permanent meaning of the theatre interior. Thus, the evolution from church-as-theatre to the Globe would mark the two extreme models of two extreme types of spatial relationships between the stage and the auditorium: the totally divine one and the totally human one. Through the abundant use of allegory and symbol, the first reveals text-significance in its own right, the second is a *carta blanca* that may become significant only during the performance. The first type may be treated as a text that elucidates and brings order, knows exactly what was in the beginning and what is to be expected at the end, does not question anything; the second one, created during the performance, often strives to understand what is inscrutable, does not know its beginning and does not foresee the end, falls into chaos and despair, asks questions, many of which remain unanswered. Owing to the richness of meaning the first type of theatre interior does not invite metaphoric interpretations, whereas the second one does. Similarly, the first type will be open to predominantly allegorical meanings, the second to symbolic ones. Between these two extremes all other types of theatres may be found.

---

[8] One must not forget that at least one of the Elizabethan and Jacobean theatres, the Hope, was used for both purposes – animal baiting and the staging of plays. Shakespeare himself did not have much respect for the wooden structure, calling it a 'cock-pit'. All of this should make us more cautious when applying lofty theories to those basically very simple, if not 'primitive', wooden structures, which were not designed by architects, but were in fact constructed by carpenters.

THE ARITHMETIC OF MEMORY: SHAKESPEARE'S THEATRE AND THE NATIONAL PAST

ANTHONY B. DAWSON

I want to begin with two exemplary memorial moments. The first is from *Henry V*, in the lull before the battle at Agincourt. It is a famous moment of social remembering, framed as reminiscence in the future tense:

> Old men forget; yet all shall be forgot,
> But he'll remember, with advantages,
> What feats he did that day. Then shall our names,
> Familiar in his mouth as household words [. . .]
> Be in their flowing cups freshly remembered.
> This story shall the good man teach his son.
> And Crispin Crispian shall ne'er go by
> From this day to the ending of the world
> But we in it shall be rememberèd,
> We few, we happy few, we band of brothers.
> For he today that sheds his blood with me
> Shall be my brother; be he ne'er so vile,
> This day shall gentle his condition.   (4.3.49–63)

As Harry presents it, the source of social cohesion is the potential for future re-telling offered by the events that are about to take place. Both the soldiers clustered around Henry and the audience in the theatre are projected forward, into a narrative moment that will give the present (or, more precisely, the near-future) retrospective meaning. The story will be passed on, and embellished ('with advantages'), gaining a momentum of its own, a fictional reality that will allow it, among other things, to be staged at the Globe theatre almost two hundred years later. The performance curls around on itself: within the fiction, the triumphs that will be memorialized in narrative have not yet happened, but in order to engage

with the scene, the Globe auditors are required to remember them. At the same time those auditors, in order to experience the pleasure of identifying themselves with Henry's onstage audience, have to 'forget' the future that the moment evokes (that is, the present moment in the theatre). Engaging with the scene thus requires participating in the projection into the future of the narrative delights, but also involves recognizing that that future has arrived and is being nostalgically played out, 'with advantages' and, at least figuratively, 'in flowing cups'.

My second example is from *Julius Caesar*, when, following the blood-bath of the assassination, the conspirators kneel over the felled Caesar and literally wash themselves in his quasi-sacred blood. Having succeeded in erasing the man but not his memory, they represent themselves briefly as the actors they actually are, casting their minds and those of the audience forward to endless re-enactments, both political and theatrical:

> CASSIUS   How many ages hence
>   Shall this our lofty scene be acted over,
>   In states unborn and accents yet unknown!
> BRUTUS How many times shall Caesar bleed in
>   sport,
>   That now on Pompey's basis lies along,
>   No worthier than the dust!   (3.1.112–17)

As in the *Henry V* passage, the play's performance stands as a memorial of an originary event, one that is strangely both present and absent. (And, incidentally, in both plays, memorial power is linked to a shedding and sharing of blood.) The assassination is the model for a potentially infinite series of future re-enactments, in both the actual world and on the stage, of which the Globe performance is one example, even while it represents itself as the original. Such future performances will remind their viewers that these were 'the men that gave their country liberty' (3.1.119). Despite the revolutionary optimism of the characters, the scene's uncertain position between past and future, between the event remembered and the prophecy of its replays, gives this performative moment a ghostly presence that hovers over the play the way Caesar's spirit comes to haunt his assassins.

In both these passages, a strange kind of historical consciousness is produced as part of the performance. The audience in the theatre is not only a witness to a re-enactment of a singular historical event, but is also encouraged to see the performance as part of a re-telling that was implicit in that originating event. Witnessing the process of re-telling in the performance before them, the audience recognizes that what connects them to the past is precisely that that past contained in it the seed of this future. The past *is* its future narratives. In moments such as these, the theatre is helping to shape historical consciousness, but in a complex way. The past is being remembered – represented or re-enacted – but at the same time the very act of re-telling, of making history, is foregrounded by being made part of what purportedly happened. Narrative and performance are represented as co-extensive with historical understanding, including even the participants' understanding that history is being made at Agincourt or the Roman Capitol. Meta-theatrical awareness, in other words, is a constituent of historical memory, even as it de-stabilizes the 'truth' of memory by underlining its constructedness.

In what follows I want to trace some of the affiliations of these memorial moments. My trajectory will take me through a number of distinct, but bordering, territories. I want first to consider the relation of memory and the construction of a national community in *Henry V*, and then, leading out of the passage from *Julius Caesar*, connect the iconographic controversy of the sixteenth century (in particular the reformers' zeal against images) to both social memory and the framing of theatrical ritual. I will finish with a discussion of *Hamlet* as a text that self-consciously links memory and performance, and in so doing foregrounds the uses of memory as they are articulated in the other two plays.

WHAT *HENRY V* FORGETS

Theatrical performance is a conduit for what historians call 'social memory',[1] and one of the purposes of social memory is to configure a national past. Harry the King and the other participants at Agincourt seem only to exist because of the narratives that will follow, pre-eminent among which is the narrative within the Globe. But as Peter Burke reminds us, forgetting (what Burke calls 'social amnesia') plays as crucial a role in the establishment of national genealogies as remembering.[2] Benedict Anderson suggests that, in fact, the two are dialectically inseparable.[3] We might therefore want to ask of the passage from *Henry V*, what is being forgotten in this hymn to remembrance? In his examination of the origins of nationalism, Anderson argues that a sense of nation can only emerge under certain conditions, among which is a levelling of hierarchical 'high centres' within a 'dynastic realm' – that is when horizontal connections among members

---

[1] The term is drawn from social historians such as Peter Burke, Paul Connerton, James Fentress and Chris Wickham. See notes 2, 24, and 27 below.

[2] Peter Burke, *Varieties of Cultural History* (Ithaca, 1997), pp. 56–9.

[3] Benedict Anderson, *Imagined Communities: Reflections on the Origin and Spread of Nationalism*, rev. edn (London, 1991), pp. 187ff.

of a polity come to predominate over vertical ones.[4] In the Crispin speech, Henry goes to some pains to insist on such a horizontal connection. And note that it is remembering that will confer that sense of continuing brotherhood, begun with the shedding of blood but maintained through narrative recall: 'we in *it* (the story) shall be remembered' and specifically, that this day will 'gentle' the condition of even the meanest soldier, whose future tales will fix that gentility. Of course, as Richard Helgerson would no doubt object, that isn't strictly what is happening.[5] The king is not only still at the top, but is the focus of what is to be remembered. So one thing that is forgotten in Henry's vision of national community is hierarchy, even as his phrase 'be he ne'er so vile' vividly recalls it. We are still a long historical distance from the period when nation and nationalism, as described by Anderson, became the dominant feature of political organization.

If differences of rank are occluded by social amnesia, so too is an inconvenient similarity between brother and enemy. In the oddly lopsided opening of the play, the Archbishop explains at painful length to Henry and the audience the genealogical basis for the attack on France. For all its murkiness, one thing is clear: Henry is as much French as he is English (or Welsh). In fact, the category 'French' is a vexed one, merging with German (the 'Salic land') and various Frankish and Saxon kingdoms and duchies, such as that of Lorraine, that were not in any sense 'French' during the period being described. And as the presence of Burgundy in the play might remind some of its audience, Burgundy, far from being part of 'France', was a rival principality, with a powerful Duke in league with England, a point that casts a certain irony over the Duke's evocation, in Act 5, of the disordered countryside of fertile France. Add to such considerations the fact that Henry's claim rests on his actually being 'French', descended in the female line as he is from the daughter of Philip IV of France.[6] And so what

is forgotten in Henry's stirring lines is precisely that the brotherhood which he invokes and which future narratives, including Shakespeare's play, will generate, should by rights include the 'enemy' from which the English must necessarily differentiate themselves.

Thus, despite the play's numerous insistences, 'gentle' and 'English' are both vexed categories, constructed out of social memory and historical narrative. Not only that, but the text puts before us the process by which that construction is effected. Consider the little touch of Harry in the night before Agincourt. Harry may have the common touch, but the fellowship he mimics is fictional: it is the product of theatrical performance not only because it arises out of disguise and is thus consistent with a range of other Henrician performances, but also because it is part of the theatrical narrative constructed at the Globe for the delectation of spectators and the establishment of a certain version of national memory. Richard Helgerson argues that Shakespeare wrote the history plays in order to purge himself and his company of the baseness of their plebeian roots; it was a campaign of deliberate 'withdrawal', specifically excluding the concerns of the ruled and designed to celebrate 'the power and mystery of the crown'. I find Helgerson's view rather too narrow; while I acknowledge the general desire to gentle one's condition, among players and audience alike (expressed, for example, in the Chorus's opening address to his diverse audience, 'But pardon *gentles* all ...'), the plays seem to me to treat social conflicts in

---

4 See Anderson, *Communities*, pp. 19–22.
5 See Richard Helgerson, *Forms of Nationhood: The Elizabethan Writing of England* (Chicago, 1992), chapter 5, pp. 193–240.
6 Phyllis Rackin, in *Stages of History: Shakespeare's English Chronicles* (Ithaca, 1990), pp. 167–9, stresses the importance of French women to Henry's claim to and eventual acquisition of the French crown; and she notes as well the exclusion from the play of any mention of the Yorkist claim to the throne, itself based on inheritance through the female line.

various and often contradictory ways, rather than foreclose them. The commoners in *Henry V* are not, as Helgerson claims, 'subjected to a steady stream of abuse'.[7] To take just one example among many: Williams is given a strong voice in the night before Agincourt, and is later able to confront the King with a legitimate claim about being treated unjustly (4.8).[8] But more important than this, I want to suggest that the actors and the theatre are making a bid for legitimacy *not* in order to join the aristocracy against the commons, but to establish a place from which to speak as custodians of memory and social meaning. The meta-theatrical highlighting of performance is a kind of space-clearing. In framing the narrative commemoratively, the players, as Enobarbus puts it, earn 'a place i'th' story' (*Antony* 3.13.44). The dynamic in the scene before Agincourt, and throughout the play, is thus more complicated than Helgerson allows. The balancing act between fellowship and hierarchy, memory and forgetting, 'nation' and 'dynastic realm', is a response to real tensions in the culture and, as such, a part of the process by which the players define themselves as makers of social memory.

In response to the common soldiers, whose probing critique of the ethics of making war haunts the subsequent battle, Henry argues cogently for the king's ordinary personhood, a moral levelling in which every man is responsible only for the salvation of his own soul. A little later, he confronts directly the superficiality of status difference, and meditates on the sustaining power of iconic performance:

And what have kings that privates have not too,
Save ceremony, save general ceremony?
And what art thou, thou idol ceremony?
What kind of god art thou, that suffer'st more
Of mortal griefs than do thy worshippers?

(4.1.235–9)

The language here was familiar to sixteenth-century audiences – it echoes radical Protestant reformers and their zeal against idols, though its

sympathy with the false god it attacks is uncharacteristic. Throughout the sixteenth century in England, as Margaret Aston has made clear,[9] the whole matter of the externals of worship had loomed even larger than it did on the continent. It was precisely *performance* that was both suspect and absolutely necessary for the sustaining of religious observance.[10] As William Cecil (later Lord Burleigh and Elizabeth's chief minister) put it in 1562, 'The question is not of doctrine, but of rites and ceremonies.'[11] For *Henry V* to invoke such theological debate at this moment is both bold and dangerous. Though he is, of course, talking of royal, not religious, panoply, it is well known that the pageantry of royal power was an important staple of Elizabethan government. The monarchy, as has been often pointed out, sustained itself partly by performance: the queen, and later the king, saw themselves as highly visible, much watched actors, set upon a scaffold. When Henry here takes an iconoclastic swipe at the externals of power, his gesture serves both to align him with the ordinary men with whom he has just been debating royal responsibility, and robs him of a crucial prop. For does monarchy not rest on a pillar of ceremony? And, from the point of view of the platform from which this player-king speaks, Henry's dilemma extends reflexively to the matter of

---

7 Helgerson, *Forms*, pp. 239–44.
8 See Rackin, *Stages*, for an eloquent evocation of Williams' challenge to the king's official version of events, in which she notes the echo of Shakespeare's own name in this invented character and suggests how his silencing marks the exclusions by which history is constructed.
9 Margaret Aston, *England's Iconoclasts*, vol. 1: *Laws Against Images* (Oxford, 1988).
10 This paradox has been explored by Bryan Crockett in *The Play of Paradox: Stage and Sermon in Renaissance England* (Philadelphia, 1995). He argues that sermons, for all their insistence on the value of hearing the word, were also performances, and sometimes accompanied by visual or ritual spectacle calculated to convince the wayward.
11 Quoted in Aston, *Iconoclasts*, p. 12.

theatrical spectacle — what gives *it* legitimacy or moral weight? The iconoclastic element in the speech about ceremony may thus be said to apply uncomfortably to the very show that the audience is watching, but the speech also reminds us paradoxically of the *power* of ceremony, theatrical as well as political and religious.

In his next speech, Henry addresses not the idol, but God himself, seeking to bribe Him with the payment of five hundred poor who daily raise their withered arms to plead for divine pardon for the shedding of Richard's blood. He has even built 'two chantries, where the sad and solemn priests / Sing still for Richard's soul' (4.1.298–9). It should be noted that 'chantries', in the more common sense of a lay endowment for the singing of masses for the dead, were one of the great targets of reform in the 1540s and the subject of the Chantries Act of 1547, which abolished these ceremonies all over England and confiscated the funds.[12] For Henry to evoke them here is thus a bit peculiar, especially given the fact that Holinshed, in detailing the reverential treatment accorded Richard's body, says nothing about them. The tension in the scene as a whole between the iconoclasm directed at royal ritual in the king's attack on ceremony, and the positive spin given to the deeply popish practice of chantries (which, considering the English success in the ensuing battle of Agincourt, seem to be marvellously efficacious), allows us to peer into the recesses of a cultural conflict with which the theatre, because of its professional commitment to image and spectacle, was necessarily concerned.

REMEMBERING ICONIC STRUGGLE IN *JULIUS CAESAR*

That concern may be seen in the multiple echoes of the passage from *Julius Caesar* quoted earlier. As the conspirators stoop to partake symbolically of Caesar's blood, the decisive historical event is given a Eucharistic valence, and linked to a theatrical process of memoriali-zation. The ritual is of course not 'real' — it is invented on the spot, as part of a political strategy. It is hence a performance, its Eucharistic overtones a construction. (It is significant that Plutarch gives no hint of any such ritual, concentrating instead on the panic of the senators and the conspirators' vain attempts to calm their fears.) Such self-conscious memorialization does not, however, make the moment any less potent as a focus of memory. Quite the opposite — my argument is that the theatre establishes social memory by highlighting performance. The scene evokes the sacred without being so, suggesting a correspondence between sacred and secular ceremony while simultaneously exposing such a correspondence as a convenient fiction. (Of course, in the eyes of the Reformers, traditional Eucharistic ritual was itself a false performance that generated a phony presence, while Protestants saw what they called the 'Lord's Supper' as strictly memorial.) Cassius and Brutus, intent on constructing a certain reading of the events in which they have taken centre stage, are as yet unaware that the interpretation of such memorial images is far from stable. To produce such an image and send it out into the interpreting world is to lose control of it — memories and meanings are malleable, the act of interpretation potentially dangerous.

One aspect of the play about which most recent commentators agree is its concern with the making and reading of images. From the first scene, when Flavius instructs his fellow tribune to 'disrobe the images / If you do find them decked with ceremonies' (1.1.64–5), to the last, when Antony holds up Brutus as an icon of Roman manliness and Octavius quietly insists on guarding Brutus' bones as a trophy for himself, the play returns obsessively to the question of how images are produced and interpreted. Whether it is the superstitious

---

12 See Eamon Duffy, *The Stripping of the Altars: Traditional Religion in England c. 1400–c. 1580* (New Haven, 1992), pp. 454ff.

Casca finding portentous signs in the storm only to be brought up short by the hermeneutically suspicious Cicero ('men may construe things after their fashion, / Clean from the purpose of the things themselves' – 1.3.34–5); Brutus 'fashioning' an image of Caesar as a gestating serpent or reminding his fellow conspirators to construct the assassination as a sacrifice; Decius re-reading Calphurnia's dream; Brutus and Antony promoting competing versions of the assassination after the fact – these, and many similar sequences, keep before us the deeply divisive issue, for Elizabethans, of the value of images. Iconic power and the spirit of iconoclasm (the latter arising out of an acknowledgement of the former) are locked in conflict throughout the play, just as they had been in England for seventy odd years before the play was written.

In the often bitter theological debates that characterized the controversy, moderates argued that the dangers of images could be offset by the word, while radicals condemned all images as idolatrous. For most, images were acceptable as commemoration, just as the efficacy of the Lord's Supper was seen as memorial. The Edwardian Injunctions of 1547 permitted images as objects of 'remembraunce, whereby men may be admonished of the holy lives ... of them that the said images represent'.[13] Images as 'memorials' were also approved by Luther, though Calvin was deeply ambivalent about them. The debate about images was not simply an esoteric theological scrum – its effects reached everyone in every parish of the realm. Elizabethan people had lived through a prolonged period of iconoclasm during which they witnessed massive changes in the iconic landscape that they inhabited. Eamon Duffy calls iconoclasm a 'sacrament of forgetfulness',[14] a paradoxical formulation since sacramental rituals are typically designed to generate remembrance. But the phrase aptly suggests the dialectic between cultural remembering and forgetting which was generated by iconoclasm.

Shakespeare's own family offers us a glimpse of this complex interplay: in 1564, the year of his famous son's birth, John Shakespeare was chamberlain of Stratford. Acting in his administrative capacity, he oversaw the whitewashing of the wall paintings in the Guild Chapel, which included a 'curiously paynted' dance of death, and the dismantling of the rood-loft, actions in conformity with the decrees of the ecclesiastical authorities, who were bent on stamping out idolatry.[15] What exact pressures were brought to bear on him, what his personal investments were in the situation, is not known. Whatever they were, his son grew up in an environment of conflict concerning the value of iconic objects, and of course turned out to have a knack for reproducing their power onstage. Did he, in writing *King Lear*, symbolically remember what had been officially forgotten – that 'curiously paynted' fresco of the dance of death? But of course I am not speaking here only of Shakespeare – Elizabethan playgoers in general carried with them the cultural baggage inherited from the generation or two of iconoclastic fervour that they had experienced or that was part of their recent history. The pleasure that playgoers took in the theatrical spectacle was thus deeply coloured by their ambivalent sense of the power of images.

Throughout most of the sixteenth century, this cultural ambivalence persisted; it is evident in the repeated attempts from the 1530s on to police, through legislation and injunction, the various practices associated with images. Although the period from the 1530s to the 1550s witnessed the most rapid and confusing shifts between Protestant and Catholic perspectives,

---

[13] Quoted in Duffy, *Stripping*, p. 450; see also Ernest B. Gilman, *Iconoclasm and Poetry in the English Reformation* (Chicago, 1986), p. 35.

[14] Duffy, *Stripping*, p. 480.

[15] S. Schoenbaum, *William Shakespeare: A Documentary Life* (New York, 1975), pp. 7 and 30–1, who quotes John Leland's description of the painting; see also Clifford Davidson, 'The Anti-Visual Prejudice' in *Iconoclasm vs. Art and Drama*, ed. Clifford Davidson and Ann E. Nichols (Kalamazoo, 1988), pp. 33–5.

and the bitterest struggles between radicals and conservatives within Protestantism, the accession of Elizabeth did not put the issue to rest.[16] The queen's characteristic skill at playing both ends against the middle produced an intermixture of radical and conservative attitudes, a shifting movement that reflected her own ambivalence as well as, undoubtedly, her acute sense of the mixed attitudes of her people. Her well-documented, Protestant reverence for the English Bible (celebrated, for example, in Heywood's *If You Know Not Me You Know Nobody* [1605?]) was joined uneasily to her fondness for a little silver cross and other accoutrements of her private chapel; such popish decorations drove her spiritual advisers wild with godly consternation – from Bishop Jewel in 1559 to William Fuller in 1586, the latter reproaching the queen, Ananias-wise, because of her reverence for 'that foul idol, the cross' on its 'altar of abomination'.[17] The chapel was actually attacked twice during the 1560s and the idols broken and burnt, much to the delight of Bishop John Parkhurst of Norwich who wrote to Zurich: 'A good riddance of such a cross as that! It has continued there too long already, to the great grief of the godly, and the cherishing of I know not what expectations to the papists.'[18] Elizabeth, not to be outdone by her inferiors, refurbished her chapel with similar 'idols', while at the same time going along with the policy of eliminating church images, thus sending a double message to her people (as Parkhurst's comment about the papists suggests). But men such as Fuller and Parkhurst were no doubt more zealous than most of their compatriots, to whom the queen's double message might not have been wholly unwelcome. The widespread cultural uncertainty, which Elizabeth's adroit politics both perceived and abetted, allowed for doubt, and fostered an interpretive latitude that was endemic and at the same time subject to harsh surveillance and regulation. I am suggesting that this mixed attitude was embedded in the theatre's understanding of its own representational potential.[19]

Another way of putting the issue would be to say that, during the struggles over what Patrick Collinson calls 'iconophobia',[20] the nation had experienced a kind of trauma and, on the analogy of personal trauma, makers and consumers of narrative returned again and again to the issues the nation had confronted. Thus the consuming interest in *Julius Caesar* and so many other plays of the period, in the construction, meaning and value of images, may be read as a (perhaps unconscious) reminiscence of similar struggles in a related and painful cultural sphere. The pseudo-sacred ritual that I have taken to represent the ambivalent production of spectacle is a performance which, escaping the control of its participants, generates a multiplicity of meanings. The initial purpose is to bind together the participants in a ritual of violent community ('Stoop, then, and wash' (3.1.112)). There are evident analogies to the Catholic mass. But the precise meaning of what is being performed is up for grabs. As Antony's later response, and that of Octavius' servant, make abundantly clear, Cassius' interpretation is far from stable. Further, an analogy to the Catholic mass is not necessarily calculated to win unambiguous affirmation on a late

---

16 See Aston, *Iconoclasts*, chapter 6 (pp. 220–342), for a detailed account of the many shifts in policy and approach during the whole period.

17 Aston, *Iconoclasts*, p. 314. See also M. N. Knappen, *Tudor Puritanism* (Chicago, 1970), pp. 283–4.

18 Aston, *Iconoclasts*, pp. 313–14.

19 My point here has benefited from James Siemon's powerful account of the controversy and its effect on the drama, but I am not persuaded by Siemon's argument that *Julius Caesar* espouses a kind of iconoclasm which arises from a Protestant distrust of fixed, or 'national', interpretations of images. See James R. Siemon, *Shakespearean Iconoclasm* (Berkeley, 1985).

20 Patrick Collinson, *From Iconoclasm to Iconophobia: the Cultural Impact of the Second English Reformation* (Reading, 1993).

Elizabethan platform.[21] The scene recalls the antitheatricalist charge that the stage trades in idolatrous shows and seems to invite the suspicion of spectacle characteristic of both the reformed view of church ceremony and antitheatricalism. Hence the moment's ritual analogies, its status as performance, its reminiscence of iconoclastic controversy, and its lodgement within a larger performance all complicate its reception – it is both iconic and iconoclastic. The anti-theatrical undercurrent is the more apparent since the construction of the performative moment is as fraudulent (that is, politically motivated) as it is expressive. The sacred ritual is framed with irony, implicit in the complex motivation and public relations campaign constructed by Brutus before and after the actual event, and voiced sardonically by Antony when he enters a minute later to shake each conspirator by his 'bloody hand'. The play's meta-theatrical resonances, that is, serve an iconoclastic narrative, even as this, the play's most intense moment, vividly proclaims the power of spectacle.

The particular configuration of the English church, the so-called Elizabethan settlement, was a product of conflict and compromise, a theology that was dominantly Calvinist linked to a liturgy that retained ceremonial features not found in the stricter Reformed churches on the continent. The struggle to define a theology and a church government that were unique, and strategically placed in relation to both Catholic and Protestant Europe, contributed to a developing sense of a specifically English identity during the period. The iconoclastic movement was a key element of that struggle. In connecting the strife over images to theatrical spectacle, *Julius Caesar* not only recalls that history, but extends its resonance into a different cultural field.

There is a curious passage in *Titus Andronicus* that may throw some oblique light on this matter. An unnamed 'lusty Goth' comes triumphantly forward leading as prisoner Aaron, the transgressive Moor:

> Renownèd Lucius, from our troops I strayed
> To gaze upon a ruinous monastery,
> And as I earnestly did fix mine eye
> Upon the wasted building, suddenly
> I heard a child cry underneath a wall. (5.1.20–4)

How strange that in late antique Rome an early German tourist should be fixing his wayward eye on a sight new to the English countryside of Shakespeare's England: a ruined monastery! Gratuitous as it is, the reference recalls the painful strife of the recent past, and signals how theatrical allusion can evoke a brief nostalgia. The alien nature of Aaron is framed within a landscape that is both foreign and domestic, 'Roman' (Catholic) and English, suggesting perhaps that Aaron's 'otherness' masks a hidden sameness. And it is a singular feature of cultural history that, as Margaret Aston has shown, the dissolution of the monasteries, and the destruction and/or dissemination of a vast array of antiquities that had been housed therein, led to a self-conscious awareness of the past in England, which in turn prepared the historical ground for an enriched national consciousness. Paradoxically, then, iconoclasm, the sacrament of forgetfulness, had a direct, material effect on the development of social memory and, in consequence, national identity.[22]

THEORETICAL INTERLUDE

It might be helpful at this point to reflect on the term at the centre of my discussion – 'social

---

21 Hence, like Huston Diehl, I do not share the view of C. L. Barber, Louis Montrose and others that theatrical spectacle compensates for its loss in the religious sphere. See Huston Diehl, *Staging Reform, Reforming the Stage: Protestantism and Popular Theater in Early Modern England* (Ithaca, 1997), pp. 94–8; C. L. Barber, *Creating Elizabethan Tragedy* (Chicago, 1988), especially chapter 1; and Louis Montrose, 'The Purpose of Playing: Reflections on a Shakespearean Anthropology', *Helios* n.s. 8 (1980), 51–74.

22 Margaret Aston, 'English Ruins and English History: the Dissolution and the Sense of the Past', *Journal of the Warburg and Courtauld Institutes* 36 (1973), 231–55.

memory'. I am adopting it from historians who, since Maurice Halbwachs broached the problem seventy years ago, have tried to understand the relation between individual memory and how societies may be said to remember the social past.[23] Two aspects of this investigation are particularly germane to my discussion – the body and the word. Paul Connerton describes social memory in terms of 'incorporation' rather than inscription – that is bodily practices rather than documents, especially commemorative ceremonies (a subset of rituals) and *habits* in the sense of culturally incorporated practices, bodily remembering that is not just a code or sign.[24] While images of the past may work to legitimate the social order, such knowledge is 'sedimented in the body' through repeated performances. Even in times of revolutionary change, social memory creates a 'deposit' in such commemorative acts – culturally specific bodily practices that have a socially cohesive, rhetorical force. Thus collective memories are passed on through ritual performances. Clearly, ceremonial religion both played a commemorative role and worked as an example of what Connerton calls 'exemplary recurrence',[25] a way of repossessing the past and assuring continuity. This is the precise charge that the reformers levelled at the old religion – that it was performative and theatrical (but perhaps for just that reason, more memorially effective and hence in need of surveillance and repression). If the theatre can be said to do something analogous, it does so at one remove, not being itself a ritual. In theatre, the physical memorial, the 'habit' is absent; it is gestured toward, represented. Or rather a different habit is put into play, an institutional one specific to theatre in which we might say that social ritual is 'remembered' and a temporary community nostalgically configured. Hence social memory as transmitted by theatre works differently than it would in ordinary social practice. Abstracted from 'real' physical presence, it is linked to awareness of the doubleness of the actors – as persons in their own right and as the figures

they personate[26] – and made inseparable from performance itself. As in the example from *Julius Caesar*, it is the meta-theatrical element, the awareness of the actorly and the staged, that produces the memorial effect. What might be called an institutional 'habit' is foregrounded in scenes like those I have been discussing.

Protestants of course stressed the Word over representational practices. And the importance of the word in drama picks up on that concern and relates to the other aspect of social memory that I want to emphasize, its link to language and representation. James Fentress and Chris Wickham argue that, among other things, social memory must be 'articulate memory' since it depends on transmission; it is both semantic and sensory, and tends to be more conventionalized and more conceptual than personal memory. They stress the importance of interpretive acts in forming memories and suggest that the culture provides 'avenues of interpretation'.[27] Theatre is just such a cultural avenue; in combining word and material image, it brings together the semantic and sensory aspects of social memory, and underlines the importance of performance in the process of transmission. In my two exemplary passages, the historical events are identified with their future re-enactment; they become history by being made part of a self-consciously constructed performance, analogous to a play within a play, which the audience is invited both to celebrate and scrutinize. Memorial effect and historical distance are both generated via meta-theatre.

---

23 Maurice Halbwachs, *Les cadres sociaux de la mémoire* (Paris, 1925).
24 Connerton, Paul, *How Societies Remember* (Cambridge, 1989), pp. 7–40.
25 Ibid., p. 65.
26 See Anthony B. Dawson, 'Performance and Participation: Desdemona, Foucault, and the Actor's Body', *Shakespeare, Theory, and Performance*, ed. James C. Bulman (London, 1996).
27 James Fentress and Chris Wickham, *Social Memory* (Oxford, 1992), pp. 20–35.

So, I would argue that the theatre had its own way of dealing with the national trauma experienced by English people over the previous seventy years or so, when the struggle raged over what could count as memory, what should be erased, how the nation should be configured in relation to, among other things, an English religion. Elizabethan theatrical culture made the production and interpretation of images self-conscious and meta-theatrical, and so highlighted performance as a way of making and maintaining a national historical consciousness. Such a formulation, however, makes the effort seem too controlled; better perhaps to suggest that there is an element of obsessive return to the trauma of broken images, a staging and re-staging of the struggle for control of meaning. Performance in this reading becomes a form of cultural re-play, akin to the belated, but still sometimes cathartic, return of the victim of severe trauma to the scene of pain. In the latter case, as Mary Jacobus, Cathy Caruth and others have claimed, it is precisely narration, the organizing of pain into coherence, that can generate relief.[28] Perhaps Shakespeare's drama, with its ingenious deployment of the meta-theatrical, was engaged in something similar, though certainly at a far greater distance from the original trauma than is the case with individuals. And because of that distance, the irony that theatre typically puts into play makes an enormous difference.

Even when nationhood and comradeship are evoked as eloquently as they are in *Henry V*, and made explicitly part of social memory, or when the quasi-religious ritual of social togetherness is constructed as assiduously as it is in *Julius Caesar*, the theatre contrives ironies that complicate the ideological issues. This is not simply because of Shakespeare's characteristic complexity of attitude, though that undoubtedly plays a part. More generally, Shakespeare's theatre occupies an institutional position as a repository of memory, a kind of *midden* in which the rags and bones of culture

could be taken up and examined. And this position allows for a perspective on a culture in which memory is contested and threatened with erasure, and in which iconoclasm and anti-theatricalism have entered into theatrical consciousness. Thus the very energies which give the theatre its power are themselves deeply suspect; such factors make the commemorative process both vexed and necessary.

HAMLET, TRAUMA AND PERFORMANCE

In *Hamlet*, the necessity and the vexation take centre stage. The play explores the way in which personal and social memory intersect, and represents theatrical performance itself as a strategy of reconfiguration, a way of transforming a personal struggle between forgetting and remembering, figured in the play as trauma, into a narrative of cultural commemoration.

Rather self-consciously, the play makes the intersection of memory and performance a subject in itself. One way it does so is through a proliferation of memories of performance. Here is one of them:

HAMLET My lord, you played once i'th' university, you say.
POLONIUS That I did, my lord, and was accounted a good actor.
HAMLET And what did you enact?
POLONIUS I did enact Julius Caesar. I was killed i'th' Capitol. Brutus killed me.
HAMLET It was a brute part of him to kill so capital a calf there. (3.2.94–100)

Nostalgically recalling his student days, Polonius remembers a performance of the sort predicted by Cassius in the scene quoted earlier. What was there represented as a memorial ritual, with wide ranging cultural implications,

---

[28] See Cathy Caruth, *Unclaimed Experience* (Baltimore, 1996); and Mary Jacobus, 'Border Crossings: Traumatic Reading and Holocaust Memory', unpublished lecture given at the Social Sciences and Humanities Congress (Ottawa, May 1998).

is now reduced to something much smaller – an old man's personal recollection. But Hamlet's brutal joke turns the recollection into something comically prophetic – a harbinger of Polonius' own violent death, coming later that very night. The glance backwards at an old enactment of Caesar and his death in the Capitol, parallel and opposite to Cassius' look forward, is a joking reference to the excess of performance, its tendency to mean more and mean differently from its apparent intentions. As such, it extends the perception underlying the casting forward to future remembrances presented in *Julius Caesar* – that is, the difficulty of controlling interpretation. Polonius' harmless memory of his student acting days, a garrulous nostalgia, actually means miching mallecho. His remembered performance serves as a prefiguring of 'The Mousetrap' itself, a far more intent reminder of a murder remembered – and one which dramatizes a struggle over the control of meaning.

'The Murder of Gonzago' re-enacts a crime remembered in different ways by Claudius, a ghost, and Hamlet; it is part of a strategy of remembering, one that has a social as well as a personal dimension. At the same time it cannot help but be a forgetting – in that it falsifies, or at least displaces, the originary event, the murder in the garden, even as it makes it live again. As a performance, it both recreates and mis-remembers. The players, we are told, are to be the abstract and brief chroniclers of the time, but the inexactness of performance, what it misses, is put before us as emphatically as its power to present – not just by the play within the play, but by the many other performances within *Hamlet*. Of these, the most prominent are forms of madness: Hamlet's antic disposition is a direct result of his determination, as he scratches on his tables, to remember; and it is a performance which not only puzzles his courtly companions, but has vexed commentators ever since. Ophelia's madness is a result of trauma, and is represented as a vain remembering splintered into a compulsion to repeat: 'There's

rosemary, that's for remembrance. Pray, love, remember' (4.5.175–6). In each case, the performance of madness both speaks the traumatic memory and misrepresents it. To generalize from such instances, we might then say that, while performance may be radically forgetful, like the future narratives promised to Henry's hearers on the eve of Agincourt, its life as performance also enables an assertion of presence and continuity.

The issue of performance as memory-making and interpretation enters into the play when the ghost, in bidding his son 'Adieu', voices his initiating command: 'Remember me' (1.5.91). Hamlet vows to do so, while 'memory holds a seat / In this distracted globe' (96–7). He seeks to keep that memory alive by staging a performance, his antic disposition, which, in turn, leads to a follow-up memorialization – 'The Murder of Gonzago'. But at the same time, remembering entails forgetting: 'Remember thee? Yea, from the table of my memory / I'll wipe away all trivial fond records, / All saws of books, all forms, all pressures past ...' (97–100). In the mnemonic economy suggested here, there is always a loss when something is remembered. Recollection, according to Michael Roth, is always 'about the confrontation with absence and forgetting'.[29] The confrontation with absence involved in personal recollection is reactivated in performance inside the 'distracted *Globe*' – the skull and the theatre. The pun is germane, since it suggests a connection between the personal, subjective dimension of memory – which gives Hamlet both interiority and substance – and the cultural one – the theatre in which memory and forgetting hold a privileged place.

The task of theatre as Hamlet develops it when he advises the players – to show the 'very age and body of the time his form and pressure' (3.2.23–4) – suggests a responsibility to *preserve*, to memorialize, and the metaphors of im-

---

[29] Michael S. Roth, *The Ironist's Cage: Memory, Trauma, and the Construction of History* (New York, 1995), p. 204.

pressing a form on the body link memory to the scars of trauma (where there is a deep link, at least in Freud's thought, between bodily harm and psychic trauma[30]). But the phrase also recalls the 'forms' and 'pressures past' that he had earlier resolved to forget in order to remember his father. Then, Hamlet had explicitly rejected all written records, all such forms and pressures, and yet in his version of the purpose of theatrical representation, they occupy a central metaphorical position. The books which he rejects earlier are themselves stockpiles of memory, items that encroach upon the consciousness that seeks to forget them.

Hamlet, vowing to remember the ghost, both cuts himself off from cultural memory (the trivial fond records) and attempts to reconstitute it. He commits himself to memorializing that ghostly presence – not just his father, but the past that haunts. He does so paradoxically by *writing*: the tables of his memory become the tables he literally writes upon. He even turns to writing for the theatre. His writing is clearly an attempt to record, to fix a newly discovered past. And it is also a step into narrative – to tell the story that remains unfinished but promised at the close of the play. Thus he writes that 'one may smile and smile and be a villain' (1.5.109), producing a character and a theme that he can insert into the narrative of Gonzago's murder. But as both history and performance, the move into narrative is, again in Roth's words, inescapably 'to confront the past with the forces of forgetting'.[31] This is so because narrative is precisely a relief from trauma, a way of writing, and dispelling, grief.[32] Hence the very promise to remember, to keep the trauma of his father's murder before him above all other records, is, as soon as it moves towards story and enactment, a move also towards forgetting, a kind of mourning whose purpose is to assuage by means of an act of commemorative reconfiguration.

We are reminded explicitly of the problem of reproducing the past when Hamlet asks the player for a speech, and then goes about to remember it himself: 'If it live in your memory, begin at this line – let me see, let me see ...' (2.2.450–1) and we proceed to Hamlet's 'memorial reconstruction' of the speech, more accurate it seems than that of the often-accused makers of the First Quarto.[33] And then, when the Player recalls the speech, we are given an object lesson in trauma remembered: Hecuba and her story are made present before us in a narrative enactment which transforms grief into reparation. After all, the fall of Troy was the beginning of Rome and, so Tudor mythology would have it, of England as well. All this is framed explicitly as a performance, and an enormously affecting one at that, a point of which Hamlet is acutely aware – 'For Hecuba! / What's Hecuba to him or he to Hecuba / That he should weep for her?' (2.2.560–2). The answer is that Hecuba is a figure for trauma, a memorial within the play for Hamlet and Ophelia's grief. More speculatively, let me suggest that she can stand too as a 'record' of *national* trauma – a 'form' and 'past pressure' that is neither 'trivial' nor 'fond' nor susceptible to being 'wiped away'. In the Player's performance, the memory is created and maintained. It becomes part of the larger project of remembrance which the ghost has set Hamlet, and which, as his acting theory reminds us, is a task of cultural representation – holding a mirror up to 'the time'. It is also an opportunity for an unstable, but not unreal, bliss, an achievement of narrative, theatrical, coherence.

---

[30] Caruth, *Experience*, passim.

[31] Roth, *Cage*, p. 208.

[32] This is a point made by some modern theorists of trauma, e.g. Jacobus, 'Border'.

[33] The problem of accuracy in the act of memory – not to mention the mnemonic strategies so dear to Renaissance occultists, rhetoricians and the like (on this point see Frances Yates, *The Art of Memory* (London, 1966)) – is neatly symbolized by the textual puzzles surrounding *Hamlet* and their relation to the nostalgia for what Hamlet, after the play scene, calls 'a whole history' (3.2.285).

Hecuba, in mourning Priam, weeps too for a national loss, the fall of Troy. The player weeps for Hecuba. Hamlet wonders at the spectacle, but knows that his own mourning is social as well as personal, for a king as well as a father. Mourning the dead, of course, is a recurrent, almost obsessive, motif in the play, epitomized in Hamlet's contemplation of Yorick's skull. In the subsequent squabble over the appropriate rites for Ophelia's funeral, the question of how one properly goes about remembering the dead becomes a subject of controversy. Behind the raised voices of Laertes and Hamlet may be heard echoes of the transformation in attitudes toward the liturgical commemoration of the dead which had taken place over the previous century.[34] The sense that rituals are inadequate means of addressing or containing memory, that remembrance is an interior, individual matter, not a social one, that the truth of memory is ineluctably private – these are beliefs that flow from the reformed ways of thinking that had transformed English cultural life in the previous fifty years. But the power of the rituals themselves, their links with performance and their being embedded within a drama that depends on spectacle and sensuous appreciation, even the very materiality of Yorick's skull as a stage object, such things speak of an older, less austere aesthetic. The play bears the scars of Tudor cultural conflicts, not only about religious doctrine, but about the value of visual and performative representation and the role of memory in cultural continuity.

At the very end of the play, after Hamlet has called for his own memorial narrative ('in this harsh world draw thy breath in pain / To tell my story' (5.2.300–1)), and after Horatio has offered a confused preview of that narrative, with its 'purposes mistook / Fall'n on th'inventors' heads' (5.2.338–9), Fortinbras reminds his shocked audience that he has 'some *rights of memory* in this kingdom, / Which now to claim my vantage doth invite me' (5.2.343–4). This returns us to the issue of nationhood and dynasty, as the kingdom of Denmark gets folded into an expanding Norwegian empire, only recently enlarged (or so we are led to believe) through the conquest of chunks of Poland. Memory is here invoked to legitimate a political claim, just as it had been, though more elaborately, at the beginning of *Henry V*. Fortinbras' exact 'rights' are debatable, but the fact that he claims them on the basis of what can be remembered adds one further twist to the play's skein of memory. We are reminded of the beginning, when the hovering exit of the memorable and memorial ghost provides a prologue for Claudius' diplomatic speech about mourning his dear brother's death 'Together with remembrance of ourselves' (1.2.7). At the end, Prince Hamlet's ghost, with its promise of a narrative performance designed to assuage the national trauma, hovers over Fortinbras as he seeks adroitly to put that ghost to rest with appropriate military honours. But by now we are aware of how easily the performance of memory can falsify as well as revive, how it ignites a struggle for control of interpretation. Fortinbras' performance of mourning merges with that of the play in a meta-theatrical coda which quietly draws attention to the varied ways theatre can construct social memory – that is, in terms that can align the personal and political or set them at odds. It is clear that the project of social commemoration can fly in the face of individual personal memory – what Horatio remembers is not what will be socially inscribed.

It is thus apparent that what Hamlet mockingly calls the 'arithmetic of memory' is 'dozied' not only by an inventory of Laertes' virtues,[35] but more broadly and significantly by the commemorative affiliations of the theatre

---

[34] On the shifts in the ways the dead were remembered see Duffy, *Stripping*, pp. 474–5; Gail McMurray Gibson, *The Theater of Devotion: East Anglian Drama and Society in the Late Middle Ages* (Chicago, 1989), pp. 90–6; and Diehl, *Staging*, pp. 122–4.

[35] See 5.2.112–14 in the Riverside edition (the Oxford edition prints this as part of an additional passage).

with both personal and cultural histories. The two evocatively nostalgic figures who appear, one at each end of the play, ghostly king and chop-fall'n jester, bespeak both a need for memory and an awareness of the pain it costs: 'Heaven and earth, / Must I remember?' (1.2.142–3). The answer simply is yes. Hamlet's theatre had the task of delivering some sense of community, through memory, though it was always a riven and conflicted thing. As a maker of social ritual it was in the end no doubt a failure; but insofar as it generated both a sense of the past and a form of personhood that grew in the cracks between social and personal memory, the Globe, distracted or no, earned a place in the story.

MAXIMAL AND MINIMAL TEXTS: SHAKESPEARE V. THE GLOBE

ANDREW GURR

In the Induction to *Bartholomew Fair*, staged at the new Hope in 1614, Jonson set up a mock covenant by which the '*Spectators*, and *Hearers*' waiting for the play would accept the performance and 'agree to remain in the places, their money or friends have put them in, with patience, for the space of two houres and an halfe, and somewhat more'. Such a specific timing for a mock-legal contract probably reflects the likelihood that Jonson, unlike most of his contemporaries, owned a watch.[1] More likely it reflects his selfconscious awareness of the length of time the performance was expected to take, and possibly some discomfort at its likely duration. Two hours was the standard time for a performance. For *The Alchemist* with the King's Men his prologue boasted that it took only 'two short houres'.[2] The distinctly apologetic tone with which he proclaimed the extra half-hour, and the reluctant admission that it might be even longer, is as explicit an apology for excessive length as the convoluted Jonson would ever allow himself to make. Since *Bartholomew Fair* has as many words as the Folio text of *Hamlet*, making them the longest plays of the time, his proclamation that the performance would run to less than two and three-quarter hours must have been defensive. Jonson knew what he was saying, however little he may have expected it to be swallowed whole. His play was much longer than the norm. His other notorious apology in the same Induction, for staging the play at the new Hope, a dual-purpose playhouse and bear

garden, which called for regret because its other users made it as smelly as the Smithfield cattle market, was a different matter. It was the duration of the smells, not the audience's knowledge that the normal traffic of the stage was only two hours, that prompted this apology. Evidently, though, the abnormality of both features of the first performance demanded acknowledgement.

The real oddity of Jonson's claim is the discrepancy between how long he timed the original performance at and how long the full text needs when performed today. Modern performances of an uncut *Hamlet* run to four hours, and even a shortened *Bartholomew Fair* takes close to four. This discrepancy invites reconsideration of the principles that lie behind staging Shakespeare then and now, and particularly the two kinds of early text, those that came from the press and those actually performed. The inheritance we live with, centuries of concern for edited texts that give the play in its most full form, may have misled us over the

---

[1] Jonson's characters, especially Face in *The Alchemist*, tend to count the hours with some precision. Pennyboy Junior shows his pretensions to affluence by buying a watch in *A Staple of News*, 1626. Watches were still a rarity in the early seventeenth century, most people relying on the church clocks in each parish to tell the hours, and at a few of them the quarter-hours.

[2] For *Bartholomew Fair*, see *Ben Jonson, Works*, eds. C. H. Herford and P. and E. Simpson, 11 vols. (Oxford, 1925–52), vol. 6, p. 15; for *The Alchemist*, see vol. 5, p. 294.

content and duration of the early performance texts.

It has frequently been argued that any Renaissance drama text, brought into its modern form through the work of centuries of editors, is an ideal version, and that the text as originally performed at the Globe or the Fortune or the Blackfriars was likely to have been quite different from what the modern reader is offered. The New Bibliography took the view that performed texts were always likely to be shrunken or 'corrupted' versions of the ideal text which the company held in the form of the playhouse manuscript. The exact nature of their publishable ideal, though, and the ways it differed from the texts originally performed at the Globe or the Blackfriars, are not what the older generations of editors took them to be. The early playing companies followed different practices from those of the nineteenth century which influenced McKerrow and Greg. Reassessing those early bibliographers' assumptions suggests not so much a new kind of approach to editing the plays (though that might help), as a different concept of the relations between the printed text and whatever written text may be used either when trying to characterize its early performances or when designing a new one.

It is a truism that the written word as a means of recording spoken and visual scripts leaves a great deal to be desired. Television can show nuances of speech and gesture that writing can only record by pages of painstaking description. So if we are curious about the only form of publication that Shakespeare sought for his plays, in performance, we need to look with caution at just what the surviving records have to give us. In written form words are accessible and easy to make rich intellectual games of, but unless the performed text is examined, we will not even know the other riches that we might have lost. So-called performance texts have rightly gained in priority in recent years. The Oxford edition in 1986, for instance, announced that its target was not the old hunt for the text that first left the author's hand, unsullied by alterations introduced by the players and their book-keepers. Instead, the Oxford's ideal was 'a text presenting the play as it appeared when performed by the company of which Shakespeare was a principal shareholder in the theatres that he helped to control and on whose success his livelihood depended'.[3] Like most ideals, that seems a little remote from reality. Given what a high-speed process the business of producing the plays for early performance was, how irregular the original performances themselves were, how liable to change were the conditions of playing, and how flexible the text as performed had to be in its steps from page to stage, it is a fairly desperate hope to retrieve much of the original performance conditions from the written records, let alone any settled 'performance text'.

The editorial team who produced the first volume of the new Cambridge Webster make what might be a useful distinction between what Webster called the 'poem', his own composition, and the 'play', the text performed by the play's owners, the players.[4] The differences between the 'poem' and the 'play' in performance are complex, and are made particularly difficult to identify because of the inherently static nature of the one and the inescapably fluid character of the other. Peter Blayney's view, shared with several hundreds of theatre directors, that 'the author's final draft is essentially only the raw material for performance',[5] has a potency that distances the two versions even further from each other than the removal of the author's draft from the theatre copy that the New Bibliographers used to call, anachronistically, the 'promptbook'. In this lengthy and

3 William Shakespeare, *The Complete Works*, eds. Stanley Wells and Gary Taylor (Oxford, 1986), p. xxxv.
4 *The Works of John Webster*, eds. David Gunby, David Carnegie and Antony Hammond (Cambridge, 1995), 1.35–9.
5 *The First Folio of Shakespeare: The Norton Facsimile, Second Edition* (New York and London, 1996), p. xxx.

fluid collaborative process, no single moment ever existed when a written script, a uniquely authoritative record of the 'performance text', could be established.

There are several ways in which this new ideal of a performance text, however unattainable, might reward fresh scrutiny. One feature of the early texts in particular, a characteristic of playing company practices through the whole period from the 1580s to 1642, needs better recognition than it has been given even in the intense debates of recent years. That is the inherent difference between the original company's own written playbook and the text the players performed. The essential qualification that needs to be applied to the ideal of an immutable written text from the Shakespeare period is recognition that the authoritative written text was designed from the outset to be an idealized text, and that every one of the early performances altered it into more realistic or realisable shapes, often at a quite drastic remove from the ideal. This polarization between the ideal and the staged text, the opposing impulses separating what I prefer to call the maximal text from the minimal, is my basic proposition, although like all polarizing labels the problem of essentialism intrudes, and we must step warily around the pitfalls of oversimplification. Calling the two kinds of text 'maximal' and 'minimal' at least has the advantage of identifying a tendency, rather than a precise condition.

My argument is, first, that the standard practices of the early companies did require them to possess an 'ideal' text of their plays. It was not quite what modern editors seek to retrieve, but it was what the players themselves saw as their maximal version of the text. Secondly I would argue that its representation in modern printed texts of the plays of Shakespeare and his fellow writers is in a form that is unlikely to have been presented in full on any of the original stages. Every early playing company's ideal was a 'maximal' text. It had a highly specific identity, and an absolutely authorizing function. It was

the players' manuscript that the Master of the Revels had read and 'allowed' for playing, and to which his signature was appended. Today we might call it the 'playscript', the unique manuscript held by the players as their authorization for whatever version they might perform. It was from the basis of that ideal text that the more minimal reality was drawn out for performance. The minimal versions changed according to the local and immediate conditions of performance. Given the chronic constraints imposed on every company's activities, whether performing in London or in the country, performance almost always meant a text trimmed and modified, in varying degrees of substantiality, out of the maximal playscript. The 'allowed' book and its comprehensive text, the target of the most recent modern editors, was maximal. The conditions that determined the performed text always pushed it in the direction of the minimal. When Shakespeare's fellow-players composed their preface to the First Folio, their praise of his facility was based on their own lengthy experience of having constantly to cut and trim his over-supply of words. The absence of the six famous choruses from the 1600 quarto of *Henry V*, a text much nearer the play as performed than the author's first manuscript on which the Folio text is based, probably indicates that the original players never actually did ask their audiences to piece out the play's imperfections with their thoughts.

Some of the shift of focus by the Oxford and other recent editors of Shakespeare, replacing the priority of the authorial manuscript with the idea of a theatre 'promptbook', is anachronistic because it is based on nineteenth-century theatre practices. To use the term 'promptbook' for any of the early play manuscripts is seriously misleading. As William Long has concluded,

Elizabethan-Jacobean-Caroline bookkeepers seem to have functioned much differently from modern 'prompters'. More recent practice is concerned with an intense watch on minutiae: word-for-word prompting and exact timing for entrances and exits as well as a seeming infinitude of other small details. The older bookkeepers were concerned chiefly with synchronizing backstage happenings with those onstage. Their principle [*sic*] concern seems to have been the proper timing of off-stage noises. Once a player is on stage, there seems to have been little worry that he could perform without assistance from backstage. This situation is the outgrowth both of professionalism and of a repertory system where members of the company regularly worked with and depended upon each other.[6]

Historical misconceptions aside, evidence from the initial trials [*sic*] at the new Globe in Southwark support this denial of the idea that a playtext usable by an in-house prompter ever existed. The oak and plaster structure of the Globe's *frons scenae* makes it quite difficult to hear offstage what is being said onstage, and vice versa. The physical shape of the large, square stage, and the proximity of audience all around it makes offstage prompting of the onstage players quite impractical. Offstage prompting was a tradition that developed with proscenium-arch stages. An onstage prompter, like the stool-sitter at the Globe in Olivier's film of *Henry V*, would not fit the evidence of the markings in the surviving 'prompt-books' either, since they all show, as Long has demonstrated, that the book-keeper's concern was solely with what happened backstage, and that once a player was on stage he was on his own. The few early play manuscripts surviving and the occasional printed playbook marked by a book-keeper appear to use the text principally to mark the times when offstage noises were needed, and to anticipate by a few lines when a player must be made ready to enter.[7] These were duties undertaken inside the tiring-house. None of the markings indicate that such 'playbooks' were used to check the lines spoken on stage.

Figures in Henslowe's *Diary* show the value the companies placed on their 'playbooks': rather less in strictly financial terms than they paid for costumes and properties, but still their second most valuable asset. Henslowe's

accounts in fact understate the real value of the 'allowed book'. The case for re-conceiving the early 'ideal' that these maximal playscripts represented is their peculiar identity and authority as the unique documents they were. They were the papers that authorized the company to perform the play they recorded anywhere in England. Their value lay not in playhouse use as prompt copy but as play manuscripts carrying the signature of the Master of the Revels. That signature was the only thing that allowed the company to perform the play in London or anywhere else in England. As such, the 'allowed book' became the source for every performance based on it, and it was treasured for the financial resource that provided. Hardly any of the playtexts surviving in manuscript have the Master's signature on their last page. Most of the surviving play manuscripts are either scribal transcripts made for presentation by the authors, or revised versions taken from their source in the licensed copy, sometimes composed as memory-aids for the book-keeper and players, containing their cuts, abbreviations, staging changes and other adjustments designed for the actual performances. Most of the surviving Henslowe play-scripts,

---

6 William B. Long, 'Perspective on Provenance: The Context of Varying Speech-heads', in *Shakespeare's Speech-Headings*, ed. George Walton Williams (Newark, NJ, 1997), p. 24. See also Long, 'Stage-Directions: A Misunderstood Factor in Determining Textual Provenance', *Text*, 2 (1985), 121–37. Marion Trousdale, 'A Second Look at Critical Bibliography and the Acting of Plays', *Shakespeare Quarterly*, 41 (1990), 87–96, makes the related point that the markings on surviving play manuscripts are far too variable to indicate any standard practices with playbooks. Paul Werstine, 'Plays in Manuscript', *A New History of Early English Drama*, eds. John D. Cox and David Scott Kastan (New York, 1997), pp. 481–97, gives an account of the mistakes made by New Bibliographers in identifying the origins of the extant manuscripts.

7 G. E. Bentley, *The Profession of Player in Shakespeare's Time, 1590–1642* (Princeton, 1984), pp. 80–6, supplies evidence for the existence of a functionary called the 'prompter' or 'Book-holder' from about 1615 on. There is little evidence about his precise duties.

including *Sir Thomas More*, along with the seven surviving 'plots', are rough working papers from the theatre, not the precious 'allowed' playbooks.

Conjectures about the source manuscripts for Shakespeare's own plays range from the manuscript or 'foul papers' that the author first delivered to the company, to the company's own 'playbook' (usually called by editors the 'prompt copy'), thought to be a manuscript transcribed from the author's copy and modified for performance. Some, conceivably though implausibly, might have been the authorized copy. Others are defective scripts assembled by a group of players who made up their text by writing out the lines they remembered from the original performances. Within that wide range, varying from the author's own hand telling what he hoped would be enacted to copies made after a run of performances by some of the players out of their memories, either as an alternative record of the performed text or as a more fanciful text for the reader, lie a whole series of likely transcriptions, any or all of which might have modified the original authorial intention.

Within that range, the company's chief concern, their 'ideal' text, was a single manuscript which they owned, usually a transcript of the 'foul papers', made sacred by the licensing signature on its last page. After that 'ideal text' was established, scribes made their versions, because the 'allowed book' itself had to be kept with the players. Authors often did their own rewrites. Professional scribes were paid to transcribe the 'parts' for individual players to learn, and to make transcripts that were more readily legible than rough drafts – Henry Herbert, the last Master of the Revels, once insisted on receiving 'a fairer Copy' of a play whose manuscript he had mauled.[8] Company book-keepers like Thomas Vincent (also described as a 'prompter') and Edward Knight, working for the King's Men in the 1620s and 1630s, routinely made adjustments and rewrites on the orders of the censor or the company sharers.[9]

All but one of these forms of record for the text might have been allowed out to a printer, and hence to modern editors as their 'copy text'. The exception was the licensed text, the players' 'ideal', the company's maximal 'playscript'. Manuscripts given to the press were not expected to survive the experience undamaged, so no play manuscript that was used to set plays in the press was likely to be the company's ideal text, dignified and made precious as it was by the Master's signature. That was far too valuable an asset to be allowed out of the company's possession.

The unique value of the authorized playing text or 'playscript' to any company cannot be overstated. Company patents and Revels licences were nothing without the licensed playbooks. Even the oldest and most worn of playscripts were essential to their owners for the unique signature they carried. In a rapidly evolving and changing set of practices, that was one need that never altered after Edmund Tilney established himself in the Revels Office in 1578. Henry Herbert, the last of the Masters of the Revels in this period, and the only one whose notes have survived, spent a good part of his time through his first years in office re-reading the manuscripts of plays previously licensed by his predecessors. On 19 August 1623, for instance, he made a note about one of the plays that was printed in the Shakespeare First Folio from a Ralph Crane transcript: 'An olde playe called Winter's Tale, formerly allowed of by Sir

---

8 On 27 June 1633 he noted that he told Knight of the King's Men 'I commande your Bookeeper to present mee with a fairer Copy hereafter and to leave out all Oathes, prophanes, & publick Ribaldry . . .' *The Control and Censorship of Caroline Drama. The Records of Sir Henry Herbert, Master of the Revels 1623–73*, edited, with an Introduction, by N. W. Bawcutt (Oxford, 1996), p. 180.
9 Henslowe has left no name for any book-keeper in the companies he managed, though he does identify his 'tireman', Steven Magett, and his property man, William White. *Henslowe's Diary*, eds. R. A. Foakes and R. T. Rickert (Cambridge, 1961), pp. 37, 178.

George Bucke, and likewyse by mee on Mr. Hemmings his worde that there was nothing profane added or reformed, thogh the allowed booke was missinge; and therefore I returned it without fee.'[10] It is possible that by 1623 the version that Herbert called the 'allowed book' may have suffered from being used to prepare the texts for printing in the Folio. It is now generally assumed that the Folio text of *The Winter's Tale* was set from a manuscript copy made by the scribe Ralph Crane. We might well conclude that it was nearly as risky giving the licensed playhouse book to a scribe as to a printer.

The playing companies did not often take that risk. Amongst the long lists of Admiral's company possessions that Henslowe and Alleyn drew up in 1598 and after, the most precious assets made the shortest lists. Malone's transcript of the 1598 inventories includes one list totalling twenty-nine playbooks. Not one of these has survived. The more valuable the asset, the more likely it was to be worn out by regular use in the playhouse. Licensed playscripts underwrote everything a company did, and the manuscript of a popular play would be subjected to heavy use. It had to be transported with them whenever the company wanted to take the play on tour into the country. Such a commodity would not readily be released to a printer unless the company truly had no more use for it and could not sell it to another company. Precious commodities as they were for the unique signature they carried, it is not surprising that hardly any examples have survived.

The job of Master of the Revels depended on the care with which he controlled plays, both because of the troubles that followed any complaint, and because it gave him his income. That alone was enough to keep him exercising his function thoroughly. Mostly he worked with the London companies, but his word was law throughout the country. In his first years, Herbert noted five 'old' plays which he read in 1623, and two others in February 1625. In later years he read and licensed a number of revised versions of old plays. In 1633 he reprimanded the King's Men for restaging Fletcher's sequel to *The Taming of the Shrew*, called *The Woman's Prize, or The Tamer Tamed*, without asking him to re-read it first. He ordered the players to cancel their performance on receipt of complaints about the 'foul and offensive matters' in it,[11] took the playhouse manuscript away to read, and later gave it back to the company duly 'purgd of oaths, prophaness, and ribaldrye'. His main concern as censor was for, or rather against, what he considered to be profanities. His predecessors, Sir Edward Buck and before him Tilney, so far as the few of their markings on play manuscripts that have survived indicate, were more relaxed about oaths and more concerned for what might be heard as political allusions. These varying degrees of censorship were the prelude to any playscript being authorized with the Master's signature.

After the 1570s, once the government had set up its new office to control professional playing and Tilney as the first Master of the Revels began to license all plays for performance, the playhouse manuscript became uniquely vital to the company for the authorizing signature it carried.[12] Tilney and his successors, with the aid of their informers, kept direct watch over the London playhouses. Outside the immediate environs of the city and the court, whenever a company went on its travels, the mayors of the towns the companies visited played their part as

---

[10] *The Control and Censorship of Caroline Drama*, ed. N. W. Bawcutt, p. 142.

[11] *Ibid.*, pp. 182–3, 143, 146, 160, 174, 181, 185, 189. Like many others of Fletcher's unpublished playtexts, *The Woman's Prize* was eventually printed in the 1647 Folio from the censored manuscript. That was done when Parliament's closure of the theatres had reduced the value of the 'allowed' playscripts, and made publication the only ready version of performance.

[12] For a full account of the history and functions of the Revels Office, see Richard Dutton, *Mastering the Revels. The Regulation and Censorship of English Renaissance Drama* (Basingstoke, 1991).

authorizers. In her Proclamation of 1559 Elizabeth had required mayors or local magistrates to censor plays before they could be performed. Once Tilney took that work over, they or their clerks were expected to check that his signature was on the text proposed for performance before they would agree to anything being staged in their territory. The manuscript with its signature was an intractable fixity. It could not be duplicated or changed, for all the variants that the players might be tempted to introduce in performance. The company had to pretend to use the same playscript everywhere they went, regardless of what cuts might be made for individual performances. Nothing in Herbert's papers or elsewhere suggests that the Master was ever asked to approve a version of a playbook that had been specifically made or modified for touring. The maximal text was the heart of the company's operations, and it went with them everywhere.

For all the major companies' fixation on the custom-built playhouses in London's suburbs, the knowledge that they would have to travel with their playscripts was never far from their minds. Touring remained a habit with most London companies throughout the period to 1642, and onsets of plague might drive them out of London at any time. A playing company's life was so precarious that any difficulty, financial, political or managerial, made travelling the first of the very few fallback positions they could use. Even in the years when the London companies were first licensed by the Privy Council to perform at assigned London playhouses, after 1594, they continued to go on their travels through the country. Whether they did so willingly, as a traditional practice, or on compulsion when there was an inhibition against playing in London, we cannot be sure. The only period with no record of touring by Shakespeare's company is between 1598 and 1601, when first they had no playhouse in London and then they were busy building and settling into a new one. The only year when Henslowe did not record the Lord Admiral's /

Prince's Men travelling is 1598, which does not mean that they did not tour in that year.[13] Henslowe's records through 1598 are more spasmodic than those for earlier years, after a change in his managerial relationship with his players.[14] Evidence about the leading London companies suggests that touring was irregular but by no means infrequent.[15] Many of the provincial records of visits by London companies seem to belong to the summer period, but by no means all. Plague was most active when the weather was warmest, but the records show visits especially in East Anglia and Kent through autumn and into the Christmas season. Most outsiders made the cynical assumption that whenever a company left London for the country it was either because of the plague closures or it was evidence of their declining fortunes. Against that is the clear notation in the *Records of Early English Drama* volumes[16] that even the best London companies could be found playing outside London in almost every year up to 1642.

On the travel circuit the local authorities always checked a visiting company's authority to play, although usually, once Tilney had circulated copies of his patent to them, they left the censoring of playscripts to him. A Leicester clerk in 1583 understandably questioned the credentials of Worcester's company when they

---

[13] See Gurr, *The Shakespearian Playing Companies* (Oxford, 1996), pp. 254–6, 303–4.

[14] See Neil Carson, *A Companion to Henslowe's Diary* (Cambridge, 1988), pp. 19–21; and Carol Chillington Rutter, ed. *Documents of the Rose Playhouse* (Manchester, 1984), pp. 110–11, 121–4, 138–9, 146–7, 151–2.

[15] J. Leeds Barroll, in *Politics, Plague and Shakespeare's Theater: The Stuart Years* (New York, 1991), has challenged the view accepted by the Oxford editors and others that summer tours were the standard practice (p. 227).

[16] So far twelve multi-volume works, covering nine counties and six major towns, have been published by the *Records of Early English Drama* project. They provide records of performance across about half of the regions of England. Further publications, including Wales, Ireland and Scotland, are in preparation.

arrived just three days after another group with a forged licence claiming to be Worcester's had visited the city. He noted along with his concern about the forged credentials that 'No play is to bee played, but such as is allowed by the sayd Edmond [Tilney], & his hand at the latter end of the saide booke they doe play.'[17] This was quoted directly from Tilney's patent dated 24 December 1581, a copy of which was sent to all local authorities.[18] Similarly worded patents were made out for Tilney's successors as Master. Under the same imperative the Common Council at Bristol laid down in June 1585 that the mayor was responsible for approving all plays performed in the city. In effect this meant that the mayor or his deputy had to check that Tilney's signature was in the books of any plays the visitors proposed for performance.[19] Control of playtexts was important to the authorities, and the maximal written text was the company's chief defence against the imposition of local prohibitions against them playing.

The form of the Master's licence appears in the manuscript of a play, possibly by Middleton, that belonged to the King's Men. On 31 October 1611 Sir George Buck censored the playbook, which survives in the form of a neat and professionally-made transcript. It is certainly not a perfect script for performance, since it contains several mistranscriptions of text, some inadequate stage directions, additions inserted on slips stuck onto the manuscript, and inconsistent names for the characters, once even a player's name. But it stands as the only surviving authorized playhouse version of the maximal text out of the three thousand or more plays performed between 1580 and 1642. Having read and marked the changes he required, Buck wrote after the word 'finis' on the final page,

> This second Maydens tragedy (for it hath no name inscribed) may with the reformations bee acted publikely. 31 october. 1611.   /.   G. Buc.[20]

This allowance, with the Master's signature, was the most valuable feature of any play manuscript. With it, the company was authorized to perform the play anywhere in England. Without it, or if they performed anything not contained and licensed in it, they could suffer whatever punishment the authorities chose to apply, from imprisonment in the local jail to loss of their patent to play.

The licensed playscript provided the key defence for the King's Men in 1624, in the enquiry over their run with A Game at Chesse. The Privy Councillors studying the evidence insisted on seeing the licensed copy that they used for the performances. On 21 August they reported that 'touching the suppressing of a scandalous comedie acted by the King's players we have called before us some of the principall actors and demanded of them by what lycence and authorities they have presumed to act the same, in answere whereunto they produced a booke being an originall and perfect coppie thereof (as they affirmed) seene and allowed by sir Henry Herbert, knight, master of the revelles, under his owne hand and subscribed in the last page of the said booke.' This was the key piece of evidence. They sent the manuscript with its licence from Herbert to the king, noting 'we have thought it our duties for his Majesties clearer informacion to send herewithall the booke itself subscribed as aforesaid by the master of the revelles that soe ither yourself or some other whom his Majestie shall

---

[17] J. T. Murray, English Dramatic Companies, 1558–1642, 2 vols. (London, 1910), vol. 2, p. 320.

[18] E. K. Chambers, The Elizabethan Stage, 4 vols. (Oxford, 1923), vol. 4, pp. 285–7. See also Dutton, Mastering the Revels, pp. 47–50.

[19] Ordinances of the Common Council, 21 June 1585. The order seems to reflect a dispute within the Council over whether to allow players to perform in the Guildhall. See REED Bristol, ed. Mark C. Pilkinton (Toronto, 1997), p. 129.

[20] The manuscript is well described by Anne Lancashire, in her edition. See The Second Maiden's Tragedy, ed. Anne Lancashire (Manchester, 1978), pp. 1–13.

appoint to peruse the same may see the passages themselves out of the orriginall and call Sir Henry Herbert before you to know the reason of his lycensing thereof . . ."[21] The players claimed that they had performed nothing that was not in the playtext they supplied in their defence. They said nothing about using the suit of Gondomar's clothes and his litter that visitors to the play had noted. The written playscript conveniently told the inquisitors nothing about this and the other visual features of the staging that incited a direct and personal 'application' of the chess-game to the current surge of anti-Spanish feeling.

The play manuscript with the signature of the Master of the Revels, the 'allowed booke', was the sole form of playtext which might be counted as the fully authoritative text in playing company terms. It was thus the one copy least likely ever to leave the players' possession. Keeping the authorized play manuscript in their hands was their chief protection not only against governmental questioning but against its misuse by other companies. The same protectiveness kept these 'ideal' texts from use by a printer. Most of the King's Men's manuscripts delivered to the First Folio's printers, if they were not marked-up copies of earlier quarto printings, were transcripts of one sort or another, or at best the 'foul papers' that had themselves been superseded by the manuscript copies sent to the Revels Office for licensing. Foul-paper copy or a transcript of the original papers the author sold to the company is usually thought to lie behind for instance *The Taming of the Shrew, King John, 3 Henry VI, The Comedy of Errors, Henry V, Q2 Hamlet, All's Well That Ends Well, Timon,* and *Antony and Cleopatra*.[22] Even these authorial copies were a secondary resource. The first four plays in the Folio, *The Tempest, The Two Gentlemen of Verona, The Merry Wives of Windsor*, and *Measure for Measure*, and very likely at least one other (*The Winter's Tale*), were set from copies made by the King's Men's scribe of the 1620s, Ralph Crane. Only

when the time and perhaps the cost of making such transcripts dawned on Heminges and Condell did they fall back on sending to the press the author's original manuscripts from which the licensed playbooks had been transcribed. Such rough copies were seen, at least by the compositors, as not very satisfactory versions of the text. Where possible, the players supplied the printers with a quarto text already in print instead. This printed text they were prepared to edit and correct by reference to the authoritative playhouse manuscripts, notably for *Titus Andronicus, Richard III, Love's Labour's Lost, A Midsummer Night's Dream, Romeo and Juliet, Richard II, The Merchant of Venice, 1* and possibly *2 Henry IV, Much Ado About Nothing, Troilus and Cressida*, and *King Lear*. The licensed playscript itself they never allowed to go to the printer.

For practical reasons, to protect themselves against the censor, the players needed their licensed playscripts to contain the fullest possible text that the company might perform. From such a maximal text the players could make any number of cuts, but they could not readily add anything new to what had been 'allowed'. How often the ideal and maximal text was realized on stage is anybody's guess. I have noted elsewhere the anomaly in the heavy demands for staging resources laid down in early plays like *Titus Andronicus* and *Romeo and Juliet*, both of which were written at a time when travelling was likely to fill a greater part of the year than performing in the London theatres.[23] That signals the quick development of the habit of creating 'ideal' texts, since at the beginning of the 1590s the author well knew

---

21 *Acts of the Privy Council of England 1623–1625*, 305.
22 In a few cases, such as *Julius Caesar, As You Like It*, and *Macbeth*, editors have identified playhouse influence in an otherwise authorial manuscript used to print the F text. The absence of Shakespearian spellings in *Julius Caesar* may indicate that the source manuscript was a scribal copy, not Ralph Crane's.
23 See Gurr, 'The Date and Expected Venue of *Romeo and Juliet*', *Shakespeare Survey* 49 (1996), 15–26.

how unlikely it was that the full text could be performed. Only those companies renting playing time at London's three open-air playhouses could expect to stage plays which demanded special features in full. Scenes written with demands for a trapdoor or a stage balcony when the venue could not provide one had to be altered whenever the stage to be used that day had inadequate resources. Almost any venue other than the London playhouses would have required such changes. That was one of the major reasons for keeping the real expectations of how to stage a play fairly plastic. If in doubt, or in difficulty with the staging or the doubling of parts, cut the text.

It has long been argued that the maximal written texts are too long to be staged in the limited time usually ascribed to Elizabethan performances. The likely reasons for making cuts in the 'allowed' text, however, if indeed they were made, have to be identified in the circumstances of the companies and their playing practices. That is the only way to explain and conceivably identify the kind of cuts that would have been made. Asking whether the playhouse manuscript was routinely cut in performance is a much broader question than the common assumption that speeches would have been trimmed simply because the full script seemed overlong or because a stand-in player had to perform one of the parts. It is partly a question of how easy it was for the players or the book-keeper to find sections of text to cut. The book-keeper would have to intervene while a play was in rehearsal if, for instance, the need for doubling the parts created problems and episodes had to be cut because the participants had too little time to make their role-changes.

The chief measure of the impetus to cut the maximal texts is the question whether the players had any fixed idea of the length of time that a performance should take. Was it in human nature at that time, as it tends to be now, to prefer something like the average of two interval-free hours for a film over the three

hours and more with social intervals entailed in the performance even of a modern play? Would any such prejudice in the audiences have influenced the players when they rehearsed and modified a play for performance?

We should begin that enquiry with the basic question whether, how much, and in what ways the plays could possibly have been cut in performance. Any modern director of a Shakespeare play knows how difficult it is to make a cut without losing some of the story. It is usually easier to shorten speeches than to delete whole scenes or sub-plots, even in the clumsier non-Shakespeare plays. We may think the notes added to Alleyn's 'part' for Orlando in Greene's *Orlando Furioso*, claiming that it was 'scurvy poetry' and 'a litell to long'[24] might have been nineteenth-century forgeries. The sentiment, though, is not at all surprising, and might support the idea that the players were in the habit of shortening their more orotund speeches. What is unsure is how far such marginalia might express an Elizabethan sentiment or whether they reflect a nineteenth-century prejudice. The habit manifested in several of the so-called 'memorial texts', where lines from other plays were used to fill gaps in the copyist's memory of the original text, suggests that with long speeches the players were often happy to allow the sound to weigh more heavily than the sense. But that hardly indicates that they were equally happy to drop many of their more resonant lines. Marlowe's and Greene's enthusiasm for long lists of exotic names might well have been shared by the players. And yet the shortening of long speeches and even scenes was likely to be necessary, whatever the justification might have been for any one performance. The Master's licence gave no allowance for adding to a text, but cutting it was easy, and it was legal.

Reasons to shorten texts for the early perfor-

---

[24] W. W. Greg, *Dramatic Documents from the Elizabethan Playhouses*, 2 vols. (Oxford, 1931), vol. 2, C, strip 9.

mances in addition to the excessive verbosity of single speeches are not far to seek. Plays on tour had to be adjusted to fit the limitations of local venues. We know that *Hamlet* was performed from its earliest years across the country, at the universities and even on a ship at sea.[25] Needing a trapdoor for the ghost and the grave-digger, it posed special staging problems for the company on tour. Guildhalls never had trap-doors, and could only very rarely offer anything like a stage balcony. The inns that became indoor playhouses early in James's reign, at Bristol and at York, may have been equipped with such features as part of their conversion.[26] But even such specially adapted venues could not easily have supplied the trapdoors needed for *Hamlet* and the murder of Bassiano in *Titus*. The main room at guildhalls and inns was always on the upper floor, and the installation of a trapdoor, besides seriously weakening the floor, would only give access to the taproom or the marketplace underneath.[27] While it is unlikely that the gravedigger's scene would have been cut altogether, it would have had to be adjusted. Expectation of such shifts and adjustments in performance was an automatic part of the players' mindset.

Nor could such internal spaces provide a stage balcony. The innyards could, but the seventeenth-century inns used by the travelling companies seem more often to have provided their upper rooms for playing than their yards.[28] What the basic travelling venues offered for staging and what the playwrights in London, even in the early 1590s, seem to have expected to be available for the staging of the new plays they were writing, are widely diver-gent. The King's Men evidently had a bed available to them at Oxford in 1610 for the finale of *Othello*,[29] and whatever the same company did on their travels for the monument in *Antony and Cleopatra*, they should have had what Caesar identifies as a bed for the queen to die on. A travelling company might expect to be able to find such portable properties locally. But even without taking into account the

special demands that arose when they had to transport a play to be performed at court or in the halls of one of the great estate houses that opened their doors to the travelling companies, the variety of venues made it inevitable that any play which required a special feature like a balcony or a hell's mouth had to be adapted to whatever the venue could provide. One of the more likely ways of identifying texts prepared for touring or made while on tour is their lack of elaborate staging devices. It is quite con-ceivable that the recurrence of *The Jew of Malta* in the repertory of every company that played at Henslowe's Rose, a unique distinction, was because the complexity of the device which Barabbas has to set up before he falls into his cauldron was too integral to the play's ending

[25] The first Quarto (1603) claimed that it had been played at Cambridge and Oxford. The captain of The Dragon, an East India Company ship, staged it on board off the coast of West Africa, along with *Richard II*, in 1607. Presumably he used Quarto copies of the texts. A company called Lord Cholmley's Men used the printed quartos of *Pericles*, *King Lear* and *The Travels of the Three English Brothers* in 1609 for their Christmas perfor-mances at Gowthwaite Hall in Yorkshire. See Barbara A. Mowat, 'The Theatre and Literary Culture', in *A New History of Early English Drama*, pp. 213–30.

[26] See Pilkinton, Mark C., 'The Playhouse in Wine Street, Bristol', *TN,* 37 (1983), 14–21, and *Records of Early English Drama: York*, eds. Alexandra F. Johnston and Margaret Rogerson, 2 vols. (Toronto, 1979), vol. I, pp. 530–1.

[27] See Robert Tittler, *Architecture and Power: The Town Hall and the English Urban Community, c.1500–1640* (Oxford, 1991).

[28] Tittler, *Architecture and Power*, lists all the Tudor guild-halls and town halls, with notes about those surviving, either in some version of their original form or in pictures (pp. 162–8). None of the 31 surviving guild-halls out of the original 202, nor the 27 in illustrations, could have had a trapdoor in its flooring. Nor does any of them have enough space for a balcony or gallery in their main hall.

[29] The famous comment on the King's Men's visit to Oxford in 1610, and Desdemona's face alone moving the audience while she lay on her bed, confirms the availability of a bed there. The letter is quoted and translated by G. Tillotson, *Times Literary Supplement*, 20 July 1933, p. 494.

to be cut, and made too many demands for the play to work well on tour. Its peers *Tamburlaine* and *Faustus*, both easier to stage although still pretty demanding of resources, certainly spent a lot of time out of London between 1591 and 1594.[30] The versions of the 'allowed booke' staged around the country had to be thoroughly plastic.

How much that plasticity was exercised in London is another matter that has to be left to educated guesswork. The King's Men adopted the practice of adjusting their performances each year from 1609, when they switched from the Globe's ample stage to the confines of the Blackfriars, with its stool-sitting gallants cluttering up the acting space. The Blackfriars stage had no stage posts, but its dimensions still gave it less than a third of the square footage of the Globe. The Globe stage is thought to have been 44 feet across and 27 deep. So far as we know the one at the Blackfriars was not much more than 20 feet across and 16 deep,[31] making the spatial difference 1,188 square feet against 320. Since the stage of the Blackfriars was further hampered in its already shrunken dimensions by the extra space needed for the fifteen or so gallants who saw the play from stools on the stage itself, in front of the flanking boxes, it needed quite different configurations for stage movement, and very likely a rather different repertory.[32] If we allow a minimum of three square feet per well-dressed sprig, not to mention his obtrusive sword, ideal for tripping up any players striding by, there was less than a third of the acting space on the hall theatre stage compared with the open-air stage. The two stage posts at the Globe each took up a little more than the stage area occupied by one gallant, leaving a net difference between the two spaces for playing of at least 807 square feet. That certainly called for plasticity in movement if not in the speeches.

The largest question about this plasticity is of course the likelihood that sections of the words as well as the more ambitious staging devices

might have been cut. Whether the four thousand lines of the Folio *Hamlet* were ever spoken even at the Globe is a question to which we can give no confident answer. Precisely for the reasons given above about the maximalization of the written and printed playtexts, the texts themselves say little about what might have been taken out for any specific performance. Cutting the script, whether to eliminate sections that had not worked well in previous performances, or to censor dubious pieces of dialogue which might give offence or had become irrelevant, or to limit parts to cover for a missing player, must have been routine practice. The weight of such conditioning, however circumstantial, is difficult to ignore. The other and even more weighty question which this evidence leaves dangling is whether the 'ideal' text was also likely to be cut to suit any external constraints about the length of time that performances were normally expected to take.

The idea that the companies regularly shortened their scripts largely depends, like most of the rest of this argument, on a body of circumstantial evidence. But it is consistent, and it is fairly potent. The surviving texts of plays written for staging on special occasions, and Lyly's boy company plays, do tend to be shorter than most of the published texts from the

---

[30] See Gurr, 'The Chimera of Amalgamation', *Theatre Research International*, 18 (1993), 85–93, p. 90.

[31] The stage in Inigo Jones's drawing, thought to be for the Cockpit, measures 20 feet by 16, in a theatre with an outside width of 38 feet. The dimensions of the Blackfriars stage were probably also about 20 by 16. Irwin Smith, *Shakespeare's Blackfriars Playhouse* (New York), 1964, calculates it at a minimum of 28 feet across and 22 in depth, but when this calculation was made it had not been established that the boxes were on the flanks of the stage. Smith also included an inner stage as part of his dimensions.

[32] For some speculations about differences in the staging of plays at the Globe and the Blackfriars and likely differences in the choice of plays for each type of venue, see Gurr, 'Playing in Amphitheatres and Playing in Hall Theatres', *Elizabethan Theatre*, 13 (1994), 27–62.

professional repertory. Some of the playtexts that got into print did advertise that they were longer than the performed versions. Jonson claimed on the titlepage of *Every Man Out of His Humour* that his printed text had the advantage for the reader of '*Containing more than hath been Publickely Spoken or Acted*'. Webster's *Duchess of Malfi* was printed in 1623 with a note on its titlepage claiming that it was 'The perfect and exact Coppy, with diverse things Printed, that the length of the play would not beare in the Presentment'. That claim was copied by most of the other playwrights who chose to print their texts as originally written.

The main reason why writers published their texts may itself have something to do with the length of the official texts compared with their abbreviation in performance. Richard Brome complained of the difference between the curtailed text that was performed and his 'allowed' playscript on the titlepage of his *Antipodes*, printed in 1640. He justified printing his text by claiming that '*You shal find in this Booke more then was presented upon the Stage, and left out of the* Presentation, *for superfluous length (as some of the* Players *pretended) I thogt good al should be inserted according to the allowed* Original'. Such claims were the result of authors taking pride in their products. They emphasized that it was the company who bought the author's full text and made it the 'allowed original' but chose to trim its 'superfluous length' for performance. Given the extreme length of Jonson's plays in comparison with those of almost all of his contemporaries, that may not seem surprising, but the supporting evidence from authors of shorter plays such as Webster and Brome does reinforce the point that the licensed playhouse scripts usually had more words for speaking than were heard in what was performed. Unfortunately, this does not help us to determine just what the average length of a performance was expected to be.

As owners of the playbooks the players could do with the texts what they pleased. Cutting local allusions that had passed their sell-by date

must have been the practice in every company. *Hamlet*'s 'little eyases', the boy companies who took audience from the Globe, for instance (2.2.319–46),[33] need not have survived in the acting text after 1608. The reference by the Chorus in *Henry V* (5.0.29–32) to the Queen's 'General' returning to London with the Irish rebellion impaled on his sword, a likelihood in the summer of 1599, would have had to be cut once the Earl of Essex had returned in disgrace that September and was sent to the Tower. That embarrassing reference may have been one of the reasons for omitting the Choruses altogether in the quarto text, printed in 1600. Scottish Jamy with his culpable accent would probably have been cut from the same play once King James came to the throne, at least in time for the play's royal performance in January 1605. When audiences expected immediacy and current newsworthiness, local allusions must have been discarded when their application died.

Like the staging, the scripts varied according to their occasions. The difficulty for us is that the 'allowed' maximal playscripts are precisely the texts where such cuts would not have been recorded. The tradition of editors insisting on reproducing these maximal texts, as close to the author's and perhaps the licensed playscript as possible, is its own guarantee that they differ from the texts that were originally performed.

We know from Henslowe's records that the repertory itself ran as a high-speed operation. Such conditions meant that even if the constraints of the licensing system had made additions possible it was always going to be easier to cut text than to add new lines. The fact that a different play had to be mounted each day meant, if nothing else, that not much

---

[33] Line references are to the Oxford edition. For the probable date and transitory existence of the eyases reference, see Roslyn L. Knutson, 'Falconer to the Little Eyases: A New Date and Commercial Agenda for the "Little Eyases" Passage in *Hamlet*', *Shakespeare Quarterly*, 46 (1995), 1–31.

time could be allocated to rehearsal. A careful study of the evidence for rehearsal practices can be found in Peter Thomson's essay on early acting, where Henslowe's and other evidence seems to indicate that it would normally take not much more than three weeks to bring a text from page to stage.[34] In repertory, companies could rehearse and substitute one play for another at only a few hours' notice. Whether a comparable celerity was applied to the actual performances we cannot be sure, but again the circumstantial evidence is persuasive. The playscripts were not wrapped in the esteem they have acquired subsequently, and the players' irreverent attitude to the texts suggests that speed was as much a feature of early staging as the readiness to trim the texts for performance. Herbert's records show that even in the settled years under Charles it proved possible for the King's Men to change the play they expected to perform in the course of a single morning. When told by the Master of the Revels early on Friday 18 October, 1633, that their performance of The Tamer Tamed, planned for that afternoon at the Blackfriars, would have to be cancelled because of its ribaldry (another case of an old play subject to new censorship), they managed to play The Scornful Lady that afternoon instead. This means that they could manage such a switch at less than five hours' notice, however little they enjoyed the experience, and however little the boys who posted the playbills around town would have enjoyed their extra labour.[35] Herbert returned the playbook of The Tamer Tamed to them on the Monday, with its profanities purged. The company staged his expurgated text a few days later.

The other body of circumstantial evidence for the practice of shortening the texts comes from the fairly consistent testimony about the expected two-hour period of time that a performance should take. This raises the cutting-both-ways spectre of Procrustes, and all the other factors that might have come into operation if we conclude that all the plays had to be squeezed into a performance time of little more than two hours. In practice the implication that there was an expected or average performance time has to be measured on not one but a pair of Procrustean beds. The first entails averaging the length of the surviving printed playtexts, maximal as most of them are, the other calculating the consistency of the claims about how much time a performance was expected to take. Both of these procedures need to be treated cautiously if we are to make allowance for what Procrustes might have done to his guests.

Almost all of the contemporary claims about the length of performances assume they required little more than the 'two hours traffic of the stage' claimed in Romeo and Juliet's prologue. Such claims were made early and late in the period, and apart from Jonson's defiant declaration about Bartholomew Fair they always rounded it up or down to the full hours. The maximum time that anyone ever claimed for a performance in Shakespeare's day was three hours.[36] Two was the customary claim, with just a few suggesting as many as three. Even though the number of lines in the average playtext gradually lengthened, the claim that plays lasted only two hours was sustained all through the fifty years from the 1590s until the closure in 1642. Fletcher and Shakespeare in The Two Noble Kinsmen specified 'two hours travel', and Middleton asked for 'two poor hours' for Hengist, also a King's Men's play.[37] As late as 1636 Shirley wrote that his 3,000-line The Duke's Mistress also took 'but two howers'.

---

[34] 'Rogues and Rhetoricians: Acting Styles in Early English Drama', in A New History of Early English Drama, eds. John D. Cox and David Scott Kastan, pp. 321–55, esp. 324–5.

[35] See The Control and Censorship of Caroline Drama, ed. N. W. Bawcutt, p. 46.

[36] For a more exhaustive survey of the evidence for the expected length and timing of early performances, see Gurr, The Shakespearian Playing Companies, pp. 78–83.

[37] A. Hart, 'The Time allotted for Representation of Elizabethan and Jacobean Plays', RES, 8 (1932), 395–413, p. 397.

Dekker, for all his qualifications as a Henslowe playwright and a spectator, was almost unique in writing of 'three houres for two pence', in *The Raven's Almanack* (1608). He also specified 'three howres of mirth' by the Queen's Men at the Red Bull for *If It Be Not Good, the Devil Is In It* (1611).[38] On the other hand Christopher Beeston, who was then leader of the Queen's Men, wrote at about the same time in his prefatory note for Heywood's *Apology for Actors* that playgoing was no more than 'two hours well spent'. Two hours was the convention, a cliché about a play's expected duration. Conventions tend to develop a force of their own as standards, and the evidence indicates that this expectation of performance length did not vary throughout the period.

Playgoing crowds were claimed in the 1619 petition to throng the narrow streets of the Blackfriars precinct in winter 'from one or twoe of the clock till sixe att night'.[39] Allowing for the additional time it took the hundreds of playgoers and their coaches to get to the playhouse and a similar time for them to disperse, that gives a maximum of three hours for a performance, and quite a lot less if we include the music that was said to be offered by the Blackfriars consort for up to an hour as an overture before the play. Internal references to the time of day in *The Tempest* seem to have been keyed to a three-hour performance time, from 2 to 5 o'clock. This stretches the two hours of the normative claim more than a little, but it does not discount the specification Shirley gave for his play's time at an indoor playhouse.

The first question which the standard prescription of two hours raises is how far it was just a convenient or conventional average, possibly set as a convenient fiction because officials wanted to reduce the length of playing time, and whether any official or officious constraints did exist on the time the performances had to conclude. The case for the latter is slight. Almost no records have survived about external restrictions on performance times that

might have determined their length, or that indicate much concern by the authorities for their duration. In London the Lord Chamberlain promised the Lord Mayor in October 1594 that his new company would 'begin at two and have done betwene fower and five'.[40] William Percy noted that the Paul's Boys had an even shorter performance time, since they were constrained by the hours of canonical services, which made them 'not ... begin before foure, after prayers, and the gates of Powles shutting at six'.[41] That may explain the relative brevity of Lyly's plays for Paul's Boys. There is no other evidence for any external restrictions on the length of the performances at any venue.

The best testimony to the idea that plays were expected to last for a standard amount of time comes from the Induction that was written, probably by Webster, to preface Marston's *Malcontent*, and printed in the play's third edition in 1604. The play was originally written for a boy company at the Blackfriars indoor playhouse, with its singing and dancing boys and its consort of musicians. The Chamberlain's Men subsequently 'found' it and played it at the Globe. The Induction written for this new production plays games with the differences between the two kinds of theatre. It starts with Will Sly and John Sinklo coming on stage pretending to be gallants, and expecting to sit on stools on the stage as they used to do at the Blackfriars. Sly calls for the actors, including Burbage and 'Will Sly', to come out and speak to them. Richard Burbage, Henry Condell and John Lowin enter, and the game that follows

---

38 The extreme case is a satirical German poem of 1615, quoted by Jerzy Limon, *Gentlemen of a Company. English Players in Central and Eastern Europe, 1590–1660* (Cambridge, 1985), p. 29. It speaks of people preferring to stand and hear an English play for four hours rather than spend one hour in a church. A little exaggeration to strengthen the case seems likely here.
39 G. E. Bentley, *The Jacobean and Caroline Stage*, 7 vols (Oxford, 1941–68), vol. 1, p. 4.
40 *The Elizabethan Stage*, vol. 4, p. 316.
41 A. Hart, 'The Time allotted', p. 400.

includes Burbage, fresh from playing Hamlet, confronting Will Sly holding a feathered hat like Osric's in his hand. Sly refuses Burbage's request to put it back on his head, using Osric's phrase: 'No, in good faith, for mine ease'.

Burbage subsequently comes to the point, explaining that the Induction they are playing consists of 'additions' made

only as your sallet to your great feast, to entertain a little more time, and to abridge the not-received custom of music in our theater.[42]

His claim is that it was designed to be an appetiser, and to fill in the time lost by the absence of the Blackfriars consort and their music. Whether it really was written as a time-filler is open to question. The play when stripped of its boy company trappings may have proved to be too short, but more likely the Induction was simply designed to do what prologues and inductions normally did, prepare the audience with a 'sallet' for the main feast. Allowing for most of the text being in prose, and the consequent uncertainty of its line-lengths when measured against verse, *The Malcontent* in its original form for the Blackfriars boys came to 2,228 lines of prose and verse. That included a 14-line prologue and 18-line epilogue in verse, three songs, two of them probably functioning as act breaks, a dance and two musical measures. The Induction for the later version at the Globe consists of 134 lines of prose, giving the Globe version a total of 2,362 lines. That compares well with the average through this period of a little over 2,500 lines per play. 'To entertain a little more time', therefore, can hardly have been the chief motive for adding the Induction. It certainly would not have been intended to make the play satisfy any pre-ordained standard period of time. The Induction's wording suggests that its value lay in compensating for the absence of the formal overture and the musical ambience which the play enjoyed in the boy company performances. In all, the Induction could have added barely ten minutes of time for the adult

players, which certainly would not have done much to lengthen the total performance time at the Globe over the boys' version of the play, with its act breaks, music, dances and singing. Neither version would have run beyond two hours. If any sort of official Procrustean bed existed to predetermine the performance times in London, its intention would have been much more often to cut them short than to make them longer. *The Malcontent*'s Induction may have set out an 'adult' replacement for the boys' music, but it did not significantly alter the length of the performance.

The general need of the working population to complete the day's work by dusk must have constrained the London performance times to some extent, along with the need for daylight in the open-air venues. Plays, like work, had to end at dusk. It may be that the country was rather less restrictive in this than in London, particularly when the players used not the open yards of town inns to perform in but their upper rooms, where it was customary for the occupants to eat and drink by lamplight till well into the night. The times of performance in country towns could be varied more easily than in London, and sometimes they may not have started till the working day was over. The mayor of Canterbury complained in 1636 of a company visiting in Lent and running performances that lasted till 'neere midnight'.[43] Allowing for a little exaggeration, and the horrified and not very specific closing time alleged in the complaint, this would have meant total performance times of about four hours, if we assume that the plays started some time after the day had ended, which in Lent would have been at nightfall, about seven p.m. The

[42] I have used the edition of M. L. Wine in the Regent's Renaissance Drama Texts series (New York, 1965) for my line count, on the grounds that its line-lengths are consistent.

[43] See *REED Kent*, ed. James M. Gibson, forthcoming. The letter is quoted in full on page 9 of his article, 'Stuart players in Kent: fact or fiction?', *REED Bulletin* (1995), 20.2.

likelihood of this mayor exaggerating a little, especially in the context of a complaint about how the plays were encouraging drunkenness and the seduction of the town's girls, is quite high. He seems to have taken no account of the possibility that the inn where the plays were staged reverted to its more usual activities once the performance was over.

Procrustes helped the New Bibliographers to condemn the briefer playtexts through the averaging process, since averages lead to the assumption that any text much shorter than the average must be defective in some way. The hundreds of playtexts that survive are thoroughly variable in length. Counting by verse lines or their equivalents, they vary from less than one thousand to more than four thousand lines. That is a huge span. Some of it may be accountable for in the different origins of different texts, although there is a circular argument inherent even in the otherwise plausible assumption that texts derived from performance must always have been shorter than the author's originals. Without a close analysis of the character of the manuscripts behind the texts of all the plays from the period, and identification of their origins, no conclusions based on the length of texts can be very reliable. Identifying the average lengths, as Alfred Hart did,[44] draws us straight into the Procrustean exercise. Hart's figures indicate that between 1590 and 1616 the average length of a play, measured by the number of lines in all the plays staged by five major companies, was 2,532 lines.[45] Few texts ran to more than 3,000 lines except for some of Jonson's, which were published with the claim that they included more than was set down for performance, and some of Shakespeare's plays, particularly the earlier histories. By this accounting Jonson's plays average 3,580 lines. Without the ten English history plays, Shakespeare's average 2,671 lines. Sixty-two plays of the King's Men, Shakespeare's and Jonson's included, altogether average 2,644 lines. From my own less-than-

comprehensive checks it seems that Caroline plays averaged rather more, getting towards a norm of nearer three thousand lines, as with Shirley's *The Duke's Mistress*.

Taking them all together, the average length of the six hundred or so playtexts surviving today cannot be used as a very reliable guide to the length of performance. The available playtexts range from the 757 lines of *A Yorkshire Tragedy* (which may have been written to provide only part of an afternoon's performance) or the twelve hundred of *The Massacre at Paris* and *The Old Wives' Tale* to the four thousand of *Hamlet* and *Bartholomew Fair*. The old assumption, strongly propagated by Greg and widely accepted until recently, was that all of the conspicuously short texts must have been mangled in order to cut them down to make a text convenient for travelling with. This is a neatly circular and quite fallacious argument. David Bradley[46] and others have shown how weak the evidence for it is. What such short texts are much more likely to represent are the minimality of the performed text, in contrast to the maximal written text which has been the target of all editors.

Like Procrustes, averages are hard on the extremities. Plays like *The Old Wives' Tale* should perhaps get more attention in this

---

44 A. Hart, 'The Length of Elizabethan and Jacobean Plays', *RES*, 8 (1932), 139–54.

45 'The Length of Elizabethan and Jacobean Plays', pp. 153–4. Line-counts tend to vary according to whether stage directions are included and according to which editions used. Spevack's Concordance is useful for the spoken lines in the Shakespeare texts, but other line-counts are too variable for really exact comparisons. Through-line numberings, in for instance the Norton facsimile of the First Folio and some of the Malone Society Reprints, always include stage directions in their count. The best basis for comparison is a count of the spoken lines, although some allowance occasionally has to be made for the time taken when elaborate stage directions call for extended mute action.

46 David Bradley, *From Text to Performance in the Elizabethan Theatre: Preparing the Play for the Stage* (Cambridge, 1992), pp. 58–74.

regard. Its brevity at 1,170 lines long,[47] compared with the average of 2,500 lines, led Greg to assume that it was a mutilated text, probably of the kind shortened for performance on tour. This assumes, dangerously, that the standard length of a play and of a performance was established early in the 1580s. The truth is likely to be rather less subject to such uniform patterning. Near the beginning of the play Fantastic speaks of 'a tale of an howre / long' (107). Conceivably it was written as a shorter piece for a more flexible kind of staging than the mode of longer large-cast plays which started in about 1587 and ran till 1594.[48] It may possibly have formed one of the groupings found in the Queen's Men's play-lists under the omnibus heading 'Five Plays in One', or 'Three Plays in One', both in 1584–5, close to the time when *The Old Wives' Tale* was written, or *A Yorkshire Tragedy*.[49] On the whole, plays seem to have grown longer once playing in London became established. That may have made the duration of a performance grow too, although the claims about length remained constant throughout the whole period.

It seems, then, that the only playtexts which might have a substantial claim to be based on the performed minimum rather than the authorial or licensed maximum are what Laurie E. Maguire calls the 'suspect' texts, those versions that the New Bibliographers notoriously used to isolate and downgrade as 'bad' quartos.[50] Recent attempts to redefine the origins of such distinctive copies of the plays have disabled the value-judgement implied in the label 'bad', but have not removed the likelihood of memorial transmission, a record of the text made subsequent to performance and dependent on it in one form or another. Written texts do not make it easy to distinguish between memorial errors such as mishearings that come from transcribing spoken lines onto the page and mishearings that are a consequence of dictation from a written script.[51] The ways that errors could creep into texts are legion. The question of precisely what produced those

shorter texts of Shakespeare that seem to be at least partly memorized versions of their longer forebears probably has no single answer.

While we may have reason to question the indiscriminate nature of Maguire's sweep and the effectiveness of her technique of microsurgery by grand gestures, which lump together texts as divergent as Q1 *Hamlet* and Q1 *The Maid's Tragedy*, her line-count for each of her thirty 'suspect' candidates does set all of their lengths well below the Hart average. Excluding those plays which have only a single scene that may have been reported, like Q4 *Richard II*'s deposition, the major candidates include *A Yorkshire Tragedy*, with its 757 lines of speech, *Jack Straw* with 970 (1,207 if you include stage directions), *The Fair Maid of Bristow* at 1,334, and the manuscript of *John of Bordeaux* at about 1,474 lines. The longest of them all is *Pericles* at 2,271. Prime candidates for being based on a performed text when more 'maximal' texts exist in much longer versions include Q1 *Faustus* at 1,450, Q1 *Merry Wives of Windsor* at 1,502, Q1 *Henry V* at 1,640, and Q1 *Hamlet* at 2,155. It could be argued that chicken-and-egg thinking makes some of these plays candidates for performed texts merely because they are shorter than Hart's average, but it is certain that many of them do have substantial claims to be based on something much closer to what went

---

[47] Laurie E. Maguire, using speech only and not counting stage directions, makes it 1,081 lines. See *Shakespeare's Suspect Texts. The 'Bad' Quartos and their Contexts* (Cambridge, 1996), p. 290.

[48] For the phenomenon of the writing of 'large' plays for the new size of playing company in this period, see Gurr, 'The Chimera of Amalgamation'.

[49] I am grateful for this conjecture to Michela Calore. She also suggested that when it was written the duration of plays may not yet have been standardized.

[50] Maguire, *Shakespeare's Suspect Texts*. See especially pp. 146–8. The Tables, pp. 230–322, list 41 plays containing possible memorially reconstructed texts or sections of text.

[51] See for instance Paul Werstine, 'Narratives About Printed Shakespeare Texts: "Foul Papers" and "Bad" Quartos', *Shakespeare Quarterly*, 41 (1990), 65–86.

through performance than the full text of the 'allowed' book. Regardless of what shortages of memory or imagination might do to affect these texts (inventing summary versions where memory of the words failed, for instance), the average length of the thirty plays runs to barely 1,500 lines. The full text for any of them could easily be delivered in less than two hours. Their genesis is, to say the least, disputable, but their likely provenance as versions of the performed texts gives them a peculiarly distinctive authority.

The fluid conditions of early playing do supply a little direct evidence to suggest that Elizabethan performances might have run faster than modern ones, but not much. There were no sets to change, and no scene or act breaks to create any pauses in the action, except in the boy plays and those of the King's Men and the indoor playhouse companies after 1609. Less easily determined is whether the players spoke their lines very much faster than modern actors. Elizabethan culture, especially in the theatres, was certainly more speech-related than visual, so faster speaking was a possibility. The enthusiasm for quick and intricate witplay as the mind's equivalent to swordplay, when matched with the modern mind's capacity to absorb the quick and intense speech of rap or comic monologue, makes it very possible that the Globe's playgoers were used to the kind of high-speed delivery characteristic of modern rap. In 1932 Hart[52] claimed that for modern listeners the optimum speaking rate for blank verse is 22 lines or 176 words per minute. This, represented for instance by the old Marlowe Society recordings, whose *King Lear* and *Twelfth Night* both take three hours, is rather slower than current speaking rates now, as radio and other media for speech have rejected middle-class ponderousness. Faster speaking, entries and exits overlapping on the huge stages, no pauses for scene-changes, and an interval-free performance aimed at an audience standing through the whole show, with food and drink sold by peddlers from the yard while the play was

running, could easily reduce the time needed for speaking nearly three thousand lines to less than three hours. At an average speaking-rate even of twenty lines per minute, the two hours of *Romeo and Juliet*'s posited traffic could deliver 2,400 lines. That is almost nine minutes more than is needed for the 2,225 lines of dialogue in the Q1 text. The extra time spent breathlessly brawling or duelling and the addition of a jig as postlude to such a performance would not have pushed the total out far beyond the two hours of its total traffic that the Prologue so confidently claims.

Acting as a profession is ruled by conservative traditions. Small companies of players working as a team and performing in constantly changing conditions have to sustain themselves by operating under well-understood and therefore long-running working practices. The habits that grew through the first decades when the large professional companies were developing their standard practices lasted all through the Stuart years. Their readiness to fall back on travelling when under stress of any kind and the regularity of their tours gives ample confirmation of that. Performances had to be inherently portable, and the staging traditions reflected that need more than any other. With very few exceptions the players had neither expectation nor experience of playing in any one venue for any length of time, and when they did they had to change their plays daily. Even among the prized membership of the London companies every player's training-ground must have been the travelling venues: market-places, guildhalls, inns and inn-yards, church halls and the halls of great houses.[53] When travelling, no one venue could be used more than two or three times, and the same play could not be staged in the same venue more than once. Mobility demanded plasticity.

---

[52] A. Hart, 'Time Allotted', p. 404.
[53] For an overview of the practices of the professional companies on their travels, see Gurr, *The Shakespearian Playing Companies*, ch. 3.

Plays had to be staged at short notice under whatever conditions could be found on the day of or immediately following the company's arrival in a new place. Since the best form of transport a company could expect was a covered cart and a few horses for the ten or a dozen players, their boys and their equipment, everything had to be light, portable, and easily adapted to the alien circumstances. The players rarely stayed more than a few days in any one place, and the few plays they travelled with had to be fitted into a wide range of venues and resources. The essence of the traditionally flexible practices they brought to the new venues in London was versatility and adaptability, familiar acting practices, minimal staging, and a plastic playing text. Under such free circumstances, playing before audiences who were unlikely to have seen any of the plays before, the temptation to cut or otherwise modify the text was always an easy one to fall for. The full bloom of Blayney's 'raw material', the maximal text, could never have been an ideal they strove after with much devotion.

It used to be claimed that there is little evidence of serious cutting in the surviving playbooks and printed texts. Even the First Folio (or 'playhouse') text of *Hamlet* is less than three hundred lines shorter than the authorial second quarto, and much of that cutting is due to the removal of the fourth soliloquy and its attendant speeches. So, the argument goes, if the playhouse text was left largely uncut it testifies to the general reluctance of the players to make any cuts in what they always per-formed. This is part of the assumption that the maximal or 'ideal' text did correspond exactly to the text the company performed. That is inconceivable, as is the idea that the ideal performance which the two quarto texts of *Romeo and Juliet* reflect could have been done in any of the guildhalls or inns outside London, or indeed anywhere but a few of the custom-built playhouses of suburban London.

Through the last twenty years most of us have come round to the idea that Shakespeare revised at least some of his texts. To that concept we ought to add the idea of more transient revisions introduced by his playing company for performance. On the principle that if it is Shakespeare it must be in, every edition prepared for the reader is likely to incorporate more of the text than was heard in the early performances. Editorial reasoning is different from that of the early scribes and book-keepers, but the effect is similar.

The catch-all character of the original play-books, and the pursuit of a similar maximal ambition in their descendants in the early printed texts and the subsequent centuries of new editions, means that the texts derived from them for performance were likely to have been shortened, even when they were staged at the playhouses for which they might have been written. Too much of the evidence for this is circumstantial, but if nothing else it does offer a serious explanation for the drastic discrepancy between the length of most of the printed playtexts and the volume of claims that the early performances were short.

WILLIAM SHAKESPEARE'S ROMEO + JULIET: EVERYTHING'S NICE IN AMERICA?

BARBARA HODGDON

I want to begin with an anecdote. When I proposed writing about Leonardo DiCaprio – and titling my essay, 'Was This The Face that Launched a Thousand Clips' – one colleague, taking me somewhat seriously, mentioned the best-selling Leo books, and another sent me a Hong Kong action comic in which 'Leon' single-handedly foils an evil gang and gets the girl. A third, addressing my penchant for reading Shakespearian and popular bodies, glanced at how the Shakespeare myth insists on the physical spectre of the Bard with the Forehead and at the delicious possibility that someone like DiCaprio might have played Cleopatra. A fourth was decidedly visceral: 'The most watery Romeo in film history? His acting is appalling, his affect minimal, and his intelligence – well, why go on? I can understand why teenage girls fall all over themselves for him. But you? Tell me it isn't so'![1] Such concerns about my 'low' taste and possible adolescent regression point to the lack of critical distance and loss of rational control associated with an intense engagement with the popular; but then, such over-involvement and over-identification, traits traditionally ascribed to women, do mark the popular (and especially its emphasis on the body) as a feminine realm.[2]

These fraught notions trope what I take to be the competing, contradictory horizons of reception surrounding Baz Luhrmann's 1996 *William Shakespeare's Romeo + Juliet*. How, I want to ask, does that film resonate within both 'Shakespeare-culture' and global popular culture? And how are those echoes linked to DiCaprio, the film's 'beautiful boy' star and 'modern-day Romeo', for whom Prince William has recently emerged as a royal twin?[3] Although I am especially interested in looking at how diverse audiences refunction Luhrmann's film and DiCaprio's presence to serve their own uses and pleasures,[4] I also want to look at the relations among text, image and music in the film itself and at how citations from those economies escape and are caught up in a cultural narrative that offers to renegotiate

---

[1] In order, these colleagues are Bill Worthen, Joseph Schneider, Peter Donaldson and Jim Bulman, whose e-mail communication I cite. The mass market DiCaprio books are Grace Catalano, *Leonardo: A Scrapbook in Words and Pictures* (New York, 1998); Catalano, *Leonardo DiCaprio: Modern-Day Romeo* (New York, 1997); and Brian J. Robb, *The Leonardo DiCaprio Album* (London, 1997). For the filmscript, see *William Shakespeare's Romeo + Juliet: The Contemporary Film, The Classic Play* (New York, 1996).

[2] See, for instance, Mary Ann Doane, *The Desire to Desire: The Woman's Film of the 1940s* (Bloomington, 1987), pp. 2–16.

[3] See *Life*, 'Special Royals Issue: A Guide to the 28 Monarchies of the World' (Summer 1998). The cover features 'The Boy who WILL be King'. Remarks Prince William: 'I think [DiCaprio will] find it easier being king of Hollywood than I shall being king of England', pp. 58–9.

[4] My framework derives from Paul Smith, *Clint Eastwood: A Cultural Production* (Minneapolis, 1993). As I turn to reception, I am indebted to Janet Staiger, *Interpreting Films: Studies in the Historical Reception of American Cinema* (Princeton, 1992).

the fictions of and frictions between the academic study of filmed Shakespeare and the 'popular' – what Internet discourse calls DiCaprio ideology or, alternatively, DiCapri-orgasm.

Among recent Shakespeare films, Luhrmann's not only most stridently advertises itself as a product of global capitalism but also knowingly flaunts how that culture consumes 'Shake-speare'. In an America where Wendy's Dave, wearing a silly floppy hat, holds up a burger and intones 'To be or not to be'; where 'Something wicked this way comes' promotes the newest black Lexus; and where a clip of Kenneth Branagh's St Crispin's Day speech, equated with a football coach's locker-room pep talk, climaxes a (1997) Superbowl pre-game show[5], seeing Shakespeare's words appear on billboards for loans or massage parlours – The Merchant of Verona Beach, Mistress Quickly's – as product slogans for Phoenix gasoline or ammunition – 'Add more fuel to your fire', 'Shoot forth thunder' – and brand names – Romeo drives a silver Eclipse – comes as no surprise. The logical Madison Avenue descendants of Matthew Arnold's touchstones and of New Criticism's emphasis on language as glowing artifact, these sound bites sign Shakespeare in and on the film's surface in flashes, confirming that he is indeed the universal brand name and, as W. B. Worthen writes, extending beyond Romeo + Juliet to embrace Shakespeare the Author and cultural icon, marking how the film traces and re-places signs of its origins.[6]

The film's opening, where a grainy image of an African American TV anchorwoman speaking the prologue grounds Shakespeare's language in the familiar discourse of popular news-speak, stages that replacement: nearly half the speech turns into print headlines or graphic poster art, further fragmented through flash edits and slammed at viewers. Elsewhere, espe-cially but not exclusively in the ball sequence, the film restyles textual culture as fashion or fetish and writes it onto actors' bodies or their props, as with Montague's 'Longsword' rifle,

Tybalt's Madonna-engraved pistol, or Mantua's 'Post-post haste' dispatch van. At times, this traffic between verbal and visual imagery reads as hyped-up anti-Shakespeare-culture panache; at others, it appears curiously literal. Although Romeo + Juliet is clearly a film with an attitude, its tone ricochets between Wall-and-Moonshine tongue-in-cheekiness and playing it straight, between selling Shakespeare as one-off visual in-jokes and tying its scenography, almost over-explicitly, to the word. Voguing in a white Afro, silver bra and garter belt that evoke Mab's 'moonshine's wat'ry beams', Mercutio not only punningly embodies the fairy Queen but out-masquerades Lady Capulet's Cleopatra, marking the power of his own extravagant artifice in terms of her even more parodic bodily display. Juliet's white dress and wings literalize her as Romeo's 'bright angel'; he becomes her 'true knight', a Boy King Arthur in shining armour – guises that situate the lovers within medieval Christian romance even as they send up that myth. Although Dave Paris's astronaut get-up connects him metony-mically to the heavenly Juliet, it just as clearly spaces him out to the story's margins, together with those like Capulet's gold-bespangled, purple toga-ed Nero/Antony, the Trimalchian host of this feast of poses and corruptions.[7] Equally saturated with signs, Tybalt's pointed face, neat moustache and black disco outfit, complemented by red-sequined devil's horns and vest, code him as a macho Prince of Cats

---

[5] Dave is the owner and 'advertising star' of Wendy's (a chain restaurant) TV commercials; the Lexus is a luxury car; and the Superbowl is an annual US title football game – a media-constructed 'holiday' occasion.

[6] W. B. Worthen, 'Drama, Performativity, and Perfor-mance', PMLA 113.5 (October 1998), 1103. My thanks to Worthen for providing me with a copy of his essay before publication and for comments on an earlier version of this essay entitled 'Totally DiCaptivated: Shakespeare's Boys Meet the Chick Flick'.

[7] As in Luhrmann's debut film, Strictly Ballroom (1992), it is parents, not children, who are the 'unnatural' – or parodically perverse – gender performers.

whose two cronies dressed as white-faced skeletons foreshadow his violent end. And when, after the balcony-pool sequence, Romeo meets Mercutio, his shirt blazons a heart circled by a wreath of roses, capped with a 'very flame of love', and emanating rays of golden light – the Dante-esque symbol that, glossed by 'My only love sprung from my only hate', serves as the signature logo for the film, the CDs and the official web site.[8]

Sensing an obligation to speak for Shakespeare (especially given his perceived demotion within the American academy), most mainstream critics balked at such over-determined commodifications of his text. Mourning the cuts, they produced resistant readings tied to notions about verse-speaking protocols (singling out Pete Postlethwaite's properly British Friar and Miriam Margolyes's Latina Nurse for praise) and focused on those aspects of the film – notably, how the storm sequence following Mercutio's death mirrors 'the characters' ageless passions'[9] – which fit within traditional knowledge-making frames. This is hardly an unfamiliar story: critics once attacked Zeffirelli's *cinéma vérité* documentary of Renaissance Verona, now ensconced in the educational pantheon, on precisely these grounds. But rehearsing it seems curious, given *West Side Story* and, more recently, the Bologna-Taylor film, *Love Is All There Is*, and the Oscar-winning *Titanic*, or *Romeo and Juliet* with three hours of water (and a remodelled close). Certainly the slasher-porn *Tromeo and Juliet*, an evil twin poised between nineteenth-century burlesques and Luhrmann's film, where 'She hangs upon the cheek of night / Like some barbell in a thrasher's ear' describes a Shirley Temple-curled Juliet whose sleeping potion transforms her into a pig, offers a stronger case for devalued Shakespeare.[10] Still, even those who, like the *New Yorker*'s Anthony Lane, preferred 'John Gielgud filling the aisles with noises',[11] acknowledged the appeal of Luhrmann's bizarre parallel universe comprised of twentieth-century icons and inventive raids on the cinematic canon, from *Rebel Without a Cause* to Busby Berkeley musicals, Clint Eastwood-Sergio Leone spaghetti westerns, and Ken Russell's or Fellini's surreal spectaculars. Freeze-frames identifying characters recall *Trainspotting*; in the high-voltage Capulet–Montague shoot-out, Shakespeare meets cultist John Woo (a Hong Kong action film director now working in Hollywood); John Leguizamo's Tybalt sailing through a frame and then appearing in slow motion quotes a device characteristic of contemporary action-spectacles, introduced in *Bonnie and Clyde*; and when, backed by chorus boys in purple sequins, Mercutio performs before a triptych of Madonnas, Shakespeare moves into music video by way of *To Wong Foo, With Love* and *Priscilla, Queen of the Desert*.[12]

If this be postmodernism, give me excess of it: that impulse seems to propel what might be dubbed a semiotician's dream or, as Peter Matthews writes, 'the most radical reinvention of a classic text since [Kurosawa's] *Throne of Blood*'.[13] To say that subscribes to a particular take on postmodernism as well as on viewing pleasure, one that derives a sense of identification from dissonance and disjuncture: from hearing early modern language through the flat affect of American speech (which at best works productively to remind spectators of the play's provenance at the same time as they see it made contemporary); and from seeing the story set in a decaying and decadent city over which, à *La Dolce Vita*, a colossal statue of Christ looms,

---

8 As for Zeffirelli's film, two CDs were released, one with and one without dialogue. For the official web site, see http://geocities.com/MotorCity/4147/romeo.html.

9 Janet Maslin, 'Soft! What light? It's flash, Romeo', *New York Times*, 1 November 1996.

10 See *Tromeo and Juliet*, dir. Lloyd Kaufman; Troma Video Entertainment, 1997; 107 minutes.

11 Anthony Lane, 'Tights! Camera! Action!' *New Yorker*, 25 November 1996, p. 66.

12 Most mainstream reviews cite several of these 'classic' filmtexts. I am indebted to seminar students for some of the references to cult films.

13 Peter Matthews, review of *William Shakespeare's Romeo + Juliet*, *Sight and Sound* (April 1997), 55.

separating the skyscrapers erected by warring corporate owners – a world that comments on our own and renders understandable the importance of 'filial duty, religious devotion, family honour, and the institution of marriage [and] emphasizes the ritual performance of ancient hates'.[14] That angle of vision aligns more with the film's target market, youth, than with the adult critical community, who constructed that audience as 'other' – attuned to a culture of cars, guns, fashion and music but not to Shakespeare – and, with few exceptions, either disassociated from or condescended to it. 'So enslaved by its worship of Energy that you want to slip it a Valium', wrote *Newsweek*; 'Watching it simulates having a teenager in the house', said the *Los Angeles Times*.[15] Teenagers, however, embraced Luhrmann's move to drag High-Culture Will over to the neighbourhood: mounting a still-active Internet discourse (in January 1998 alone, some two years after the film's release, hits on the official web site reached 8 million),[16] they made *Romeo + Juliet* their cultural property and took into their own hands knowledge-making and its attendant power.

Michel de Certeau's distinction between *strategies* – interpretive modes performed from positions of strength and tradition and employing property and authority belonging to literary 'landowners' – and *tactics* – moves belonging to relatively dispossessed and powerless reader-spectators – offers a useful framework for placing the claims of both communities.[17] Whereas those who seek to monitor and manage youth culture and uphold the Shakespeare industry have access to an existing public forum, the young speak freely only in the marginal spaces they themselves create, absent of parental control and of educational protocols – circumstances which trope the power relations of the play.[18] Yet however socially peripheral, this conversation the young hold with themselves remains symbolically central to a wider conversation that implicates *Romeo + Juliet* within a network of cultural

meanings by which and through which we – as agents in that culture – live.

Simultaneously commercial teaser and memory archive, the film's official web site invites viewers to look at image files and video clips from late-night star interviews, listen to sound bites, meet 'Bill' Shakespeare, download a *Romeo + Juliet* screensaver, play a 'Do You Bite Your Thumb at Me' game, and explore a Verona Beach Visitors' Guide: What to Wear, Getting There (glossed by 'Go forth with swift

---

14 Speaking of the team's search for a location, Catherine Martin, the film's designer, remarks on how Mexico had many of the elements necessary to make a contemporary version work. 'Religion still has a very strong presence there, culturally and visually; marriage is still big, and sex before marriage is frowned on. There are whole streets in Mexico City which are only bridal shops. And the social structure is closer to that of Elizabethan times than anywhere else in the modern world: a few very rich people with guns, and the vast majority poor'. See Jo Litson, '*Romeo and Juliet*', *TCI: The Business of Entertainment Technology and Design*, vol. 30 (November 1996), 46.

15 See David Ansen, 'It's the '90s, so the Bard is Back', *Newsweek*, 4 November 1996: 73; Kenneth Turan, 'A Full-Tilt Romeo', *Los Angeles Times*, 1 November 1996, F1.

16 Overall, forty web sites are devoted to the film; 500 to Leonardo DiCaprio. I am indebted to Erik Steven Fisk, 'Professor Shakespeare, Director Shakespeare: Examining the Role of the Bard on the Way into 2000 à la *Romeo + Juliet*', unpublished seminar paper.

17 Michel de Certeau, *The Practice of Everyday Life* (Berkeley: University of California Press, 1984; cited in Henry Jenkins, *Textual Poachers: Television Fans and Participatory Culture* (New York and London, 1992), pp. 44–5. These distinctions point to the boundaries separating elitist and popular texts, marking cultural space as a contested territory. The reviewers' comments also point to what Jenkins identifies as a frequent mistake: treating popular culture productions as though they were the materials of elite culture. See Jenkins, *Textual Poachers*, p. 60.

18 Zeffirelli's *Romeo and Juliet* had a similarly divided reception history. See, for example, Jill L. Levenson, *Shakespeare in Performance: 'Romeo and Juliet'* (Manchester, 1987), p. 123; and my 'Absent Bodies, Present Voices: Performance Work and the Close of *Romeo and Juliet*'s Golden Story', *Theatre Journal* (October 1989), 341–59.

wheels'), Night Life (clubs called Midnite Hags, Pound of Flesh, and Shining Nights) and a list of Sponsors. The site's epigraph image – Romeo and Juliet kissing, framed by boys with guns, all pointing at the couple – perfectly condenses one of the film's central tropes: the desire for a private, utopian space within a threatening social world. The film also rehearses other aspects of this sub-cultural imaginary: a sense of adult indifference and betrayal, of loss, fragmentation, and despair. As one fan writer put it, 'Complete with death, hate, love, feuds and the hopelessness of the inner city, *William Shakespeare's Romeo + Juliet* is a true look at how we live and think today'.[19] In such a world, these viewers perceive Romeo and Juliet's love as an anchor – an 'image of something better' that teaches what utopia would *feel* like; writes one, 'I'm in love with a fictional tragic romance because I don't like tragic reality'.[20] Such longings find their fullest expression on 'Totally Decapitated: World Headquarters of the DiCaprio Cult', a web fanzine (similar to Shaksper) whose contributors 'share Leonardo DiCaprio as a common source of inspiration'; using film and star as experiential resources, they integrate the meanings attached to both into their lives.[21]

Unlike those devoted to 'flaming' or 'foaming' – 'the closest I've ever come to understanding the play ... the only thing missing is SUBTITLES'! or 'I'd die for Leo ... he is such a hot babe'! – this site offers a space for activity and agency where participants can immerse themselves in the film's world, scribble in its margins and create their own texts. A Palace Chat Room, for instance, 'takes you right inside the vibrant and dramatic world of *Romeo + Juliet*, where you can see yourself and others as graphical "heads"', handle and even create props, move from room to room, and talk with other fans. Each issue prints poetry (in French as well as English): inspired by the film's images, some incorporate Shakespeare's lines; others, such as 'Révicide' and 'Génération virtuelle', link the play's themes to contem-

porary anomie; still others (future Oxfordians?) play out anagrams of Leonardo. Reproducing Shakespeare's balcony scene, one issue invites readers to compare text to film; in another, one can listen to a piano rendition of Tchaikovsky's fantasy-overture. All suggest fans who have moved beyond their pre-assigned roles as cult consumers to collaborate with Shakespeare, using his texts (much as scholar-critics do) to stage their own performances.

Yet if the 'zine forges an alternative community through Shakespeare, it concentrates primarily on his surrogate, DiCaprio's Romeo – the 'boy-poet [who] embodies the perfect lover'.[22] As Dennis Kennedy writes, the actor's body is not only the object of the most intense and profound gaze in the culture but, at times when notions of the body undergo change, it becomes a site where that cultural crisis is represented.[23] Appealing to the precarious liminality of early to late adolescents, DiCaprio functions as a tabula rasa on which fans project the romance of identity and, using tactics of personalization and emotional intensification, voice their desire for 'truth' instead of lies, for transparency instead of manipulation, for a 'real' hero in a world without them. As fanwriter Sonia Belasco says: 'When our president is cheating on his wife, when the mayor of the city I live in gets caught doing crack, when

---

[19] Comment from fan writer on http://www.Asu.edu.

[20] From 'The Diaries of Joshua Runner', a regular feature of 'Totally Decapitated'; the cite is from Issue Four and is dated 25 November 1996. The web site address is http://www.com/leo/issuefour/html. For the idea of using stars as resources, see Richard Dyer, *Stars* (London, 1979), pp. 59–60.

[21] Jenkins argues that, by blurring the boundaries between producers and consumers, spectators and participants, both web discourses and fanzines constitute a cultural and social network that spans the globe. See *Textual Poachers*, esp. pp. 45, 279.

[22] Quote from 'The Diaries of Joshua Runner', 10 November, 1996.

[23] See Dennis Kennedy, 'Shakespeare Played Small: Three Speculations About the Body', *Shakespeare Survey 47* (1994), p. 10.

everything is about money and hate and violence ... [Leo] mirrors us ... what we want to be, what we are, what we'll never be'.[24] Taking on idealized – and ideological – contours on and off the web, DiCaprio's body morphs into other texts, especially *Titanic* – and especially for girls. My fifteen-year old niece, who disavows 'loving Leo', nonetheless has seen most of his films, including *Titanic*, three times – but only once with her boyfriend. What threatens him with loss tells her a different story, a 'romantic feminism' found only at the movies.[25]

In a culture fascinated by youth and in a subculture where one is most interesting if one's sexuality cannot be defined, DiCaprio's pale androgynous beauty – sharp Aryan looks and hint of exotic heritage, a quintessential Greek boy god – makes him a polysexual figure, equally attractive to young women and to gay and straight men. Just as *Romeo + Juliet* is not precisely a chick flick – one where more tears than blood are shed – but, given its coterie of boys who crash cars and carry big guns, can be 're-branded' within a masculine discursive space, DiCaprio's Romeo straddles several cultural masculinities. On the one hand, he figures the vulnerable 'new man' (romancing Juliet and spending the last half of the film in tears); on the other, by gunning down Tybalt, he conforms to contemporary fictions of violent masculinity and subscribes to its homosocial honour codes. Moreover, because he is embedded in a fiction that fetishizes his body as well as those of other men, one premised on a forbidden, secret love in which Juliet can substitute for Mercutio, his presence yields to a queer reading.[26] As Joshua Runner, author of regularly featured web diaries, puts it, 'Romeo, Romeo whyfore art thou Romeo? Tending to girls' fantasies, leaving nothing for the boys who exist. Juliet, divine perfection, you may be his sun, but the pale moon needs love too.'[27] Indeed, it is precisely because Leo disrupts dominant fictions of masculinity that his transitional, differently eroticized body can be read as

exemplary, as providing a safe harbour for sexual awakening; and by offering fan writers opportunities to externalize and work through their anxieties about sexuality, the site serves a therapeutic function.[28]

Although mainstream critics read his body from a greater distance, even the most conservative found DiCaprio riveting; comparing him

24 Sonia Belasco, 'Totally Decapitated', Issue Ten: prose.
25 See Katha Pollitt, 'Women and Children First', *The Nation*, 30 March 1998, 9.
26 See, for instance, Jonathan Goldberg, '*Romeo and Juliet*'s Open Rs', in *Queering the Renaissance*, ed. Jonathan Goldberg (Durham and London, 1994), pp. 218–35. See also Robert Appelbaum, '"Standing to the Wall": The Pressures of Masculinity in *Romeo and Juliet*', *Shakespeare Quarterly*, 48.3 (1997), 251–72; and Paul Smith's notions of hysterical or wounded masculinity in Smith, *Clint Eastwood*. See also Ellen Goodman, 'Romancing a New Generation of Women', *Des Moines Register*, 12 May 1998, 7A; and Pollitt, 'Women and Children First'.
27 'The Diaries of Joshua Runner', 8 November 1996. Wolf, another frequent contributor, writes, 'He is the embodyment [sic] of what we need, someone like us to hide with ... someplace far away'; responding to a fan calling himself 'Like Minded' who had rented the film and found himself desiring Leo, Wolf urges him to read Shakespeare's sonnets addressed to the young man, saying that he himself had found comfort in them. 'Totally Decapitated', Issue Five: prose.
28 On fan writers, see Jenkins, *Textual Poachers*, pp. 152–84. On internet discourse and therapy, see Sherry Turkle, *Life on the Screen: Identity in the Age of the Internet* (New York, 1995). See also Janet H. Murray, *Hamlet on the Holodeck: The Future of Narrative in Cyberspace* (New York, 1997). Significantly, the fan writers I cite do not represent all cultures: Joseph Schneider's students (women as well as men) at the University of Hong Kong, for instance, prefer Bruce Willis or Jet Li, the Hong Kong action film star, to Leo, who is 'too boyish' for their tastes – 'not a real man'. Harold Bloom puts such opportunities for meaning-making into a wider context. Shakespeare, he writes, 'teach[es] us how to overhear ourselves when we talk to ourselves'; the true use of Shakespeare, he goes on to say, is 'to augment one's own growing inner self', a process that will bring about 'the proper use of one's own solitude, that solitude whose final form is one's confrontation with one's own mortality'. See Harold Bloom, *The Western Canon* (New York and London, 1994), pp. 30–1.

to James Dean, the cult figure of their generation, many decoded his affect in terms of
intensity and authenticity, citing his 'passionate
conviction', 'an ardour you can't buy in acting
class', a performance that is 'all raw emotion'.[29]
Favouring him with 'brooding rock-star close-
ups',[30] the film urges a near-oneiric encounter
with Leo's face. Writes José Arroyo, 'He . . .
bears the brunt of the feeling . . . It's his face in
close-up . . . indicating how he wants, longs,
feels, and suffers. [But] it's [also] the way he
moves in the Mantuan desert when he hears of
Juliet's death, not just that the camera lifts up
suddenly to crush him that expresses his grief
but the way he falls on his pigeon-toed heels.
It's a superb performance'.[31] Or, more specifically, a superb *physical* performance, for even
the friendly *Rolling Stone* was hearing echoes of
another Romeo: '[Leo] doesn't round out
vowels or enunciate in dulcet tones, but when
he speaks, you believe him.'[32] In short, the idea
that both DiCaprio and Claire Danes are 'doing
Shakespeare' lends a kind of pseudo-Brechtian
distantiation to their performances, marking off
Danes's Valley-speak – 'I was about to do the
famous balcony scene, and I was thinking, like,
this is a joke, right? How am I going to do this
in a fresh way'? – from iambic pentameter.[33]
Yet because she handles the unfamiliar verse
better than the more awkward DiCaprio, it
feels culturally 'authentic' – at least in relation
to gendered adolescent stereotypes about linguistic facility – especially when, in the balcony
scene, as the pair seem to discover words and
ways of thinking, viewers can *see* that
happening: he learns from her how to talk the
talk, she from him how to act like a natural
born lover.[34]

A witty send-up of the play's hallmark scene,
Luhrmann's balcony-pool sequence under-
scores the film's distinctions between the carnivalesque, associated with Verona Beach, where
prostitutes solicit older men beneath a billboard
advertising 'Shoot forth thunder', or with the
Capulets' masquerade ball, and the natural
world inhabited by the lovers. First seen

silhouetted in pale orange light, Romeo gazes
out to sea in a deliberately painterly 'still' that
not only sets him apart from the frenzied pyro-
technics of the opening gang war but links him
metonymically to Juliet, introduced as she surfaces, like a mermaid rising from the sea, from
her bath. At the ball, when Romeo douses his
face in water to clear his head, a cut from his
face beneath the water to his mirrored reflection
suggests a return to self and keys his glance at
Juliet through a fishtank, as, in slow motion, to
the opening strains of Des'ree's 'Kissing You',
exotic tropical fish glide over their faces, already
side by side even though separated. These
images culminate in the pool where the pair
appear first as bodiless heads floating on its
surface, their desire condensed into an exchange
of looks.[35] But once they take the plunge, the
water joins them as one body, out of their
depth in love and immersed in a private space,
simultaneously enclosed within the social and
remote from it. On the one hand, representing
the lovers as at one with life-giving nature –
and naturalized within it – situates their rebellion within heterosexual norms; on the other, it
plays into a conventional opposition between
eros and *thanatos* which confuses those assumptions. For another image chain – Romeo
submerging in the pool to avoid the guard;

[29] In order, quotations are from David Horspool, 'Tabs and Traffic Jams', *Times Literary Supplement*, 11 April 1997, 19; Peter Travers, 'Just Two Kids in Love', *Rolling Stone*, 14 November 1996, 124; José Arroyo, 'Kiss Kiss Bang Bang', *Sight and Sound* (March 1997), 9.

[30] Kuran, 'It's the' 90s', F1.

[31] Arroyo, 'Kiss Kiss', 9.

[32] Travers, 'Just Two Kids', 124.

[33] Claire Danes quoted in Christine Spines, 'I Would Die 4U', *Premiere*, v. 10 (October 1996): 137.

[34] I appropriate 'natural born lovers' from Joe Morgen-stern, 'Mod Bard; Muted Vonnegut', *Wall Street Journal*, 1 November 1996, A11. Morgenstern, however, in alluding to Quentin Tarantino's *Natural Born Killers*, gives the phrase a different sense from mine.

[35] Just before they fall into the pool together, they are posed on either side of a statue of Pan, another marker of this 'natural' though man-made setting.

Mercutio dying in the same space where Romeo was introduced; Tybalt falling backward into a fountain, a shot reprised as nightmare when Romeo wakes from his tryst with Juliet; and her last sight of Romeo, an extreme close-up of his face under the water – not only places both lovers in jeopardy but catches them up within a widening circle of homoerotic and homosocial relations.

Those relations are most clearly marked when an extended close-up of Romeo embracing the dead Mercutio, framed by the crumbling seaside proscenium arch, dissolves to a shot of Juliet on her bed, reframing her briefly with the fading image to link Mercutio's death and the possibility of her fulfilled desire. Yet meditating on gender is not the only way Luhrmann's film hits the hotspots of current conversations, both within Shakespeare studies and in the culture as a whole. Because it takes place, not in a Eurocentric culture, but in a multicultural borderland – a mythic geographical space open to variant readings (Miami, California, Mexico) – the film not only accentuates the performative possibilities for 'othering' but ties its representation of gender to somewhat slippery markers of ethnicity and class. Capulet figures the Mediterranean Old World and a nouveau-riche status which set him apart from the white Montague's tacit, if not precisely represented, affiliation with old money; though inflected with old-world codes, Tybalt and the Capulet boys inhabit a new-generation, New World Latino culture. In this multi-ethnic mix, Mercutio and Juliet are the two most liminal, most transgressive figures. As the white Romeo's 'double', Mercutio shares his gender-bent androgyny but is marked off from him by a flagrant racial 'exoticism'. From the outset, but especially during the Tybalt-Romeo fight, a series of triangulated shots consistently places Mercutio in the middle, a position he shares with the Chief of Police-Prince figure, also a black actor. Apart from the Friar (differently marked by his RSC-trained voice), coding blackness as the sign of media-tion works, somewhat uncomfortably, to attribute the failures of mediation as much to skin colour as to the law's – or religion's – impotence and delay.

Yet by insisting on the significance of black voices – especially those of women (the African American news anchor, Des'ree's ballad, 'Kissing You' [the film's 'love theme'] and Leontyne Price's rendition of Wagner's *liebestod*) but also that of the choirboy who sings Prince's 'When Doves Cry' – to frame *Romeo + Juliet* and to articulate two crucial events in the lovers' story (their meeting and their death), the film not only gestures toward embracing African-American experience but also acknowledges the contributions of that culture to both popular- and high-culture art forms.[36] Moreover, although the film's overall narrating position differs substantively from that of the TV anchorwoman, that position can be read as a figure for Luhrmann's own marginal status as an Australian national who observes and anatomizes a 'foreign' American culture. Simultaneously, however, *Romeo + Juliet* seems unable to register most 'other' identities except in terms of stereotypes – Margolyes' highly exaggerated vocal performance – or drag – Diane Venora's non-Latina Lady Capulet staggering like an Egyptian; Harold Perrineau's Mercutio queening his role. That inability becomes especially slippery in terms of Claire Danes's Juliet, who, much like *West Side Story*'s Maria, does not need to pass to become a Montague: in spite of being a young Hispanic woman whose father is depicted as a 'minority', her white skin already 'places' her. Because of this, her ethnicity appears as a kind of drag impersonation which, in equating her with Mercutio, not only adds an erotic frisson to her attraction for Romeo but also makes his love a promise of integration into some idealized

---

36 My thanks to Margo Hendricks for pointing out how the film works to situate black women's voices at its centre.

realm of 'whiteness' associated with purity, virginity and perfection.[37]

Even if these dislocations and slippages of ethnicity operate merely as another instance of the film's postmodern aesthetic, they nonetheless produce potential sociopolitical resonances. Yet *Romeo + Juliet* makes no overtly tactical alignment with melting-pot ideologies. In decoding it, however, mainstream critics called its ethnic politics into question and gestured toward restoring classical paradigms and privileging 'whiteness'. How, they wondered, could Governor Paris permit his son to woo a Mafia Don's daughter? How could the police chief banish a killer instead of locking him up? And how was it possible that 'the milky-skinned Juliet [could be] daughter to the thuggish Capulet, or that prep-school handsome Romeo's best friend was the black disco-diva Mercutio [and that he hung out] with a crew of boys from the hood via Mad Max'?[38] Coming from the right (*Commonweal*) as well as the left (*Village Voice*), such queries suggest critics who imagine they reside somewhere other than an America where such blurrings and crossings of ethnic, racial, gender and class boundaries occur daily. Yet even more troubling is how they attest to an ideological failure, offering evidence that the promise of an integrated social fabric ordained by public discourse about constructing nationality is just that – a conversation, not a cultural reality.

As the film negotiates its closing moves, these tropes of failed mediation and integration are remapped in terms of voices and bodies and pushed into a contemporary performative space ideally attuned to the play's imaginative repertoire, music video.[39] For just as the set speech and the soliloquy functioned as verbal icons of interiority for the early modern drama, music video, which expresses emotions and interior states of mind through lyrics and collaged images, represents a late twentieth-century equivalent. After all, it shares characteristic modes – stylistic jumbling, dependence on fragmentation and pastiche, rapid accumulation

of images, blurring of internal and external realities – with Shakespeare's early verse, especially that of this play, which, as Anthony Lane notes, exhibits the ' "just-you-look-at-this" quality of a young playwright' who, like the film's young director, is simply showing off.[40] Heightening the film's strategy of putting text-as-image on commercial display and cutting it to the beat of a non-Shakespearian sound, several mini-music-video inserts refunction the play's ending, unmooring its traditional narrative designs and simultaneously preserving, though reinflecting, its meanings.

Two of these – one keyed by Romeo, the other by Juliet – map their desires onto the Friar, who envisions a happy ending. Interweaving his words with Prince's 'When Doves Cry', the first reprises the opening headline, 'Ancient Grudge', but adds a news photo of Montague and Capulet shaking hands; linked by flash cuts of flames, these yield to a grainy image of Juliet and Romeo kissing, across

---

[37] See Arroyo, 'Kiss Kiss', 8; and Richard Dyer, *White* (London and New York, 1997), esp. pp. 70–2.

[38] These objections, as well as the citations, are from Richard Alleva, 'The Bard in America', *Commonweal*, 6 December 1996, 19; and Amy Taubin, 'Live Fast, Die Young', *Village Voice*, 12 November 1996, 80. The problematics of reading the film's multiculturalism also embraces how casting invites blending actors' performances in *Romeo + Juliet* with their most recent roles: for instance, American viewers might well connect Brian Dennehy (Montague) to his most recent appearances as a hawker of antacids on TV rather than to his film roles or to stage performances at New York's Public Theater.

[39] *Romeo and Juliet*'s focus on adolescent rebellion and narcissistic love and its obsession with sexuality and violence pre-tailors it for MTV, which addresses the desires, fantasies and anxieties of the young. See E. Ann Kaplan, *Rocking Around the Clock: Music Television, Postmodernism, and Consumer Culture* (New York and London, 1987), esp. pp. 5–7, 31. On MTV, see also Jenkins, *Textual Poachers*, pp. 233–40; Richard Dyer, 'Entertainment and Utopia', in *Movies and Methods, Volume II*, ed. Bill Nichols (Berkeley, 1985); and John Fiske, 'MTV: Post-Structural Post-Modern', *Journal of Communication Inquiry* 10. 1 (Winter 1986), 74–9.

[40] Lane, 'Tights!', 75.

which a dove flies in slow motion, and then to the radiant heart. Yet, although this vision confirms the Friar's decision to marry the lovers, a cut to Mercutio's and Benvolio's parodic gun-play picks up a billboard ad for recliners – 'Such stuff as dreams are made on' – undermining his hopes of peace and union. Later, when Juliet seeks his advice, the Friar appears in left screen as a talking head, his narrative of the effects and consequences of the sleeping potion glossing an image chain that concludes with an extreme close-up of Juliet's eyes, which key shots of Romeo and her exchanging smiles and, then, of the fatally mis-sent letter. On the videocassette, this segment is letter-boxed, not scanned, deliberately calling attention to its special status and to what its X-ray vision diagnoses: the most improbable gimmicks that mark the play's early modern heritage – the potion and the letter. Framed up within the Friar's imaginary, made hyper-real and morphed into MTV's contemporary gimmickry, those devices appear indeed the very stuff of dreams. Nonetheless, his visions construct two spaces of ending: one recirculates the religious iconography of divine union, the other anticipates a resolution for the lovers' dilemma. Cutting off the latter's more fully 'real-ized' space, the film draws on the former to generate another, even more breathtakingly surreal, dream space of ending.

That space condenses and intensifies the lovers' desire for a private universe, a utopian room of their own. Visually as well as metaphorically interior, it takes place inside the church but travels beyond Shakespeare's implied setting and his text into a knowing, aesthetically satisfying, cinematic plenitude addressed to and complicit with a spectatorial imaginary that idealizes and mystifies the lovers' experience as their own. After Romeo dies, an extreme close-up of the gun pointed at Juliet's temple articulates her own death; as the gun's report bleeds over the cut, a high-angle long shot reveals her body falling beside Romeo's onto the bier, flanked by hundreds of candles

that illuminate the church aisle lined with banked flowers and blue neon crosses. The shot holds in silence until Leontyne Price's voice, singing the *liebestod* from *Tristan and Isolde*, keys a cut that shifts the perspective, so that the lovers float above the candles, transforming bier to altar.[41] Images reprising their shared moments – catching sight of one another through the fish tank; laughing together at the ball; the ring, inscribed 'I love thee' – link bier with wedding bed where, beneath a fluttering white sheet, they again exchange smiles across a cut. When the image of the bier returns, the camera angle further inverts and disorients point of view, so that instead of looking down at them, we seem to be looking up at a Tiepolo-like ceiling fresco, and the candle-flames have become radiant catherine-wheels that evoke the exploding fireworks at the ball, as if to visualize Juliet's fantasy of 'cut[ting Romeo] out in little stars'. At the centre of their own jewelled orrery, they appear as a treasured artifact, a pair of saintly pilgrims joined in eternal embrace. Exalting their love-death, the sequence offers a sensual experience in which subject identity is lost in the image: read by the body and through the body, its affect is further enhanced by a visual and aural saturation that makes it appear, not as a sign of absence but of an intensely pleasurable present.[42]

In locating the lovers' mythic union inside rather than outside the narrative design, the film offers to rewrite the traditional reading formations associated with the play, those which, as Jonathan Goldberg notes, not only privilege heterosexual love but, by giving value

---

41 Sung by a black soprano, this aria not only connects the lovers to the most famous of all love-deaths but also represents an instance of how the film's soundtrack, much like its casting (which blends stage and film traditions) mixes opera, classical music (phrases from Mozart's Symphony 25 introduce Romeo) and pop culture, especially music from groups that mix white, black and latino/latina or hispanic voices.

42 I adapt these terms from Fiske, 'MTV', pp. 74–9.

to the lovers' private experience, disconnect the personal from the political.[43] Although the thousand-candle tableau may suggest that love is all there is, its garish MTV excess also clearly marks it as an imported fantasy, something cooked up when an old play confronts a new medium. And that is precisely the point: highlighting the tension between the two, Luhrmann's film juxtaposes medium and message, has it both ways. As the candle-flames dissolve into bubbles to freeze frame the lovers' underwater kiss, a long fade to white, accompanied by the *liebestod*'s final strains, dissolves in turn to the 'social real' – a white-sheeted body on a hospital trolley. Chastizing Montague and Capulet – 'All are punished' – the Police Chief passes their silent figures, looking at the second white-sheeted body being loaded into an ambulance.[44] Glossed by the voice of the newswoman who spoke the opening prologue, these images then turn to grainy video; reframed within a TV monitor, that image fades, finally, to video snow.

Michael Bogdanov's 1986 RSC production, of course, anticipated this ending: there, the unveiling of the golden statues became a photo op that enhanced the Prince's public image, and it was Benvolio who, after all had left, rose from a nearby café table to mourn his friend's death.[45] Ten years later, Luhrmann's film denies, or suspends, any promise of securing the social through either the heterosexual or the homosocial. That points, all too knowingly, to how, in our present cultural moment – at least in America – there seem to be no answers, fictional or real, religious or legal, to gender, ethnic and class differences and conflicts, to generational strife, or boys with guns. If, as the web discourse on Leo tells us, chick flicks do matter, then *William Shakespeare's Romeo + Juliet* matters even more: it bears watching precisely because it has been watching us.

---

43 See Goldberg, '*Romeo and Juliet*'s Open Rs', esp. pp. 219–20.

44 Peter Holland suggests a pertinent analogue: the moment in Bob Fosse's 1979 film, *All That Jazz*, where a cut from Ben Vereen's final production number (celebrating the Fosse-character's death) yields to an image of a body bag being zipped shut.

45 See my 'Absent Bodies, Present Voices', especially p. 358, n. 47.

WHICH IS THE JEW THAT SHAKESPEARE KNEW?: SHYLOCK ON THE ELIZABETHAN STAGE

CHARLES EDELMAN

As John Gross remarks in *Shylock: Four Hundred Years in the Life of a Legend*, 'everyone who writes about the stage history of *The Merchant of Venice* is doomed to quote, sooner or later', the couplet supposedly spoken by Alexander Pope upon seeing Charles Macklin's portrayal in 1741:

> This is the Jew
> That Shakespeare drew.[1]

Pope's comment shows that he considered Macklin's hard and bitterly malevolent interpretation to be a welcome corrective to the Shylock of Thomas Doggett and his successors in George Granville's adaptation, *The Jew of Venice*,[2] a lurid burlesque of the role that had held the stage since 1701. It also shows a yearning, shared by all students of the play, to reconstruct somehow the first Shylock, about whom there is no reliable contemporary information whatsoever – the actor Thomas Jordan's doggerel description,

> His beard was red . . .
> His habit was a Jewish gown,
> That would defend all weather;
> His chin turned up, his nose hung down,
> And both ends met together

dates from 1664, when the theatre was not, contrary to the view of E. E. Stoll, 'still swayed by the tradition of Alleyn and Burbage'.[3]

Given that any role is going to be significantly altered from its conception in the dramatist's imagination once it is in the hands of an actor and an audience, this essay is not concerned with the Jew that Shakespeare 'drew' – that Shylock was forever lost the moment the play was performed. My topic is the Jew that Shakespeare 'knew', the Shylock whom he, Francis Meres, and other spectators saw some time before September of 1598, when the role was reinvented by Richard Burbage or another actor of the 'Lord Chamberlaine his Servants'.[4]

In all that has been written about *The Merchant of Venice*, one point has remained virtually constant: however sympathetic the portrayals of Edmund Kean, Henry Irving, Laurence Olivier, or any number of others may have been, the original Shylock would have conformed to the so-called Elizabethan stereotype of the villainous stage Jew. Gross writes

. . . to an Elizabethan audience, the fiery red wig that he almost certainly wore spelled out his ancestry even more insistently than anything that was actually said. It was the same kind of wig that had been worn

[1] John Gross, *Shylock: Four Hundred Years in the Life of a Legend* (New York, 1994), p. 105.

[2] Gross, *Shylock*, 91–105; John Russell Brown, introd., *The Merchant of Venice* (London, 1955), pp. xxxii–xxxiii; M. M. Mahood, introd., *The Merchant of Venice* (Cambridge, 1987), pp. 42–3; Jay L. Halio, introd., *The Merchant of Venice* (Oxford, 1993), pp. 61–5.

[3] Jordan's poem and Stoll's comment in E. E. Stoll, *Shakespeare Studies* (New York, 1942), p. 255.

[4] Francis Meres, *Palladis Tamia* (entered 7 September 1598), in *The Riverside Shakespeare*, ed. G. Blakemore Evans (Boston, 1974), p. 1844; the title page of Q1 (1600) claims that the play is printed 'as it hath been divers times acted by the Lord Chamberlaine his Servants'.

by Marlowe's Barabas, and before that by both Judas and Satan in the old mystery plays.[5]

Similarly, Jay L. Halio, in the introduction to his Oxford edition, notes that 'Shakespeare's initial conception of him was essentially a comic villain, most likely adorned with a red wig and bottle nose.' Halio is at pains to point out, however, that 'the evidence for Shylock as a comic villain' is not to be found in the play, but 'partly in the literary and dramatic traditions which Shakespeare followed, that lie behind the character, and partly in certain generic and other considerations'.[6] He then provides a lucid account of the qualities held in common by such fictional Jews as Zadoch and Zachary in Thomas Nashe's *The Unfortunate Traveller*, and Abraham, the Jewish poisoner in Greene's *Selimus* (both 1594), these three characters probably having been influenced by the notoriety of Dr Roderigo Lopez, tried and executed in the same year, and above all by the popularity of Marlowe's extraordinary creation, Barabas, first seen *c.* 1589.

As cogent as the views of Gross and Halio are, there is a troubling premise behind them: a portrayal possible in 1814, when Kean stunned Drury Lane, and obviously possible, even obligatory nowadays, could not have been done four hundred years ago; one would be hard pressed to think of any other Shakespearian character who is thought to have changed so completely as to be unrecognizable from Elizabethan to modern performance. In questioning this premise, I am not arguing for a 'tragic' Shylock as the correct one, or arguing that the play is pro- or anti-Semitic; my sole object is to challenge the *a priori* assumption that Shylock must have conformed to a particular theatrical tradition, or that he must have been played in a certain way to satisfy the expectations of that wonderfully malleable group, who always think and believe whatever we want them to, Shakespeare's audience.

Assuming that the text remains the same (a point I will take up later), what are the variables that might separate the 1590s *Merchant* from those of the nineteenth century onwards? They might be divided into three categories: (1) limitations imposed by literary or theatrical tradition; (2) limitations imposed by audience beliefs, attitudes, or expectations; and (3) theatrical limitations imposed upon the range of performance options by acting style, costume, the shape of the stage, or any of the many other historically discrete theatrical conventions and technical considerations associated with Elizabethan performance practice.

Earlier I referred to the 'so-called' stereotype of the Elizabethan stage Jew, for it is far from certain that there ever was such a thing. When considering Jews in the early modern drama, we are struck first by how few of them there are, and then by how different these few are from each other. In the twelve years leading up to *The Merchant of Venice*, there are exactly three Jews in extant plays: one of them is a tiny part, the aforementioned Abraham in Greene's *Selimus*. The others are, of course, Barabas in *The Jew of Malta*, and Gerontus in Wilson's *Three Ladies of London* (1584).

Barabas' villainous attributes are too well known to require description here, but Gerontus is by far the most honest and admirable, one might even say 'Christian', character in his play. E. E. Stoll, in his oft-cited argument for the 'traditional' Shylock, summarily dismisses Gerontus as 'the single instance in the Elizabethan drama of an honourable Jew',[7] which is easy for Stoll to do since he has already established that 'to get at Shakespeare's intention (after a fashion) is, after all, not hard', and that 'Shakespeare, more than any other poet, reflected the settled prejudices and passions of his race'.[8] But whatever Stoll may think about *Three Ladies of London*, Gerontus shows that single instance or not, even if there

---

[5] Gross, *Shylock*, pp. 16–17.
[6] Halio, *Merchant of Venice*, p. 10.
[7] Stoll, *Shakespeare Studies*, p. 273.
[8] Ibid., p. 262, 280.

was a stereotypical stage Jew, the Elizabethan theatre was capable of accommodating alternative portrayals.

This leads us away from Jews on the stage and in literature to the far more controversial topic of how Jews were seen in Elizabethan England. Is it true, as James C. Bulman writes in his valuable contribution to the *Shakespeare in Performance* series, that 'some knowledge of the history of anti-Semitism in England is critical to an understanding of the stereotype with which Shakespeare appealed to his audience's prejudices'?[9] Here I am indebted to Laurence Lerner, who in his essay 'Wilhelm S and Shylock',[10] suggests in a most engaging way that the perceived anti-Semitism of the play could be more a product of audience appropriation than anything in the text itself. Had the Elizabethans, all of whom were predisposed to think of Jews as devils and ritual murderers, read enough Terence Hawkes to know that the meaning of the play resided not in the author or actors, but entirely in themselves?

If they had, then it is not hard, as so many have done, to construct a picture of the first Shylock as the archetypical villain, for it is all too true that along with the execution of Dr Lopez (although it should be noted that Lopez's religion was hardly mentioned at his trial),[11] there was pamphlet after pamphlet, sermon after sermon, and story after story, from Chaucer's *Prioress' Tale* to Nashe's *Unfortunate Traveller*, encouraging people to see Jews in the worst possible light. If that is the picture we want, though, we have again gone outside *The Merchant of Venice* to see it, since, as Gross reminds us, however ubiquitous stories about Hugh of Lincoln and well-poisoners might have been, none of the traditional charges are alluded to in the play: nothing about Christ-killers, sorcerers, ritual murderers, crucifiers of children, or host-desecrators.[12]

This brings me to one of the central points of my argument: that it is simply not true that everyone in Elizabethan England, and hence everyone on the stage and in the audience at

The Merchant of Venice, was an anti-Semite. As James Shapiro shows in *Shakespeare and the Jews*, by the late 1590s a significant number of Jews lived in or visited England, exactly how many depending on how one defined the group. Many were, of course, Marranos, Jews who had to some degree converted to Christianity, including Lopez, and there were others who were considered at least in some respects to have retained their Jewish identity, such as the descendants of the Jewish musicians brought to England from Italy by Henry VIII.[13] There were also the many contacts that merchants, ambassadors, and other English travellers had with Jews – Laurence Aldersey's description of a service he attended at the Venice synagogue in 1581 is one of total respect:

For my further knowledge of these people, I went into their Sinagogue upon a Saturday, which is their Sabbath day : and I found them in their service or prayers, very devoute : they receive the five bookes of Moses, and honour them by carying them about their Church, as the Papists doe their crosse. Their Synagogue is in forme round, and the people sit round about it, and in the midst, there is a place for him that readeth to the rest: as for their apparell, all of them weare a large white lawne over their garments, which reacheth from their head, downe to the ground, The Psalmes they sing as we doe, having no image, nor using any maner of idolatrie: their error is, that they beleeve not in Christ, nor yet receive the New Testament.[14]

---

9 James C. Bulman, *Shakespeare in Performance: The Merchant of Venice* (Manchester, 1991), p. 18.

10 Laurence Lerner, 'Wilhelm S and Shylock', *Shakespeare Survey 48* (1995), 61–8; p. 64.

11 Peter Berek, 'The Jew as Renaissance Man', *Renaissance Quarterly*, 51 (1998), 128–62; p. 151.

12 Gross, *Shylock*, p. 17.

13 James Shapiro, *Shakespeare and the Jews* (New York, Columbia University Press, 1996), pp. 55–88; Roger Prior, 'A second Jewish Community in Tudor London', *Jewish Historical Studies* 31 (1990), 137–52; see also Gross, *Shylock*, p. 23; Berek, 'The Jew', pp. 131–6.

14 'The first voyage or journey, made by Master Laurence Aldersey, Marchant of London, to the Cities of Jerusalem, and Tripolis, &c. In the yeere 1581. Penned and set downe by himself', in Richard Hakluyt, *The*

Documents such as this one encourage us to conclude that no matter how pervasive anti-Semitic literature may have been, the idea that a universal 'Elizabethan horror of Jews' must have informed the reception of *The Merchant of Venice* is simply one more Tudor myth, similar not only to the supposed Elizabethan horror of rebellion said to have dictated the reception of the history plays, but also, as I will argue, to the equally mythical Elizabethan horror of usury.

Virtually everything, and worse, that was said about Jews in Elizabethan England was said about Moslems, and yet throughout her reign Elizabeth was busy establishing trade relations with whoever would deal with her, from Morocco to Constantinople, buying saltpetre for gunpowder from the Emperor of Morocco and selling him munitions in return, munitions that were used to annihilate the Portuguese and their fellow Christians at the Battle of Alcazar.[15] And, as most editions of *Othello* point out, in 1600 she received an embassy of sixteen Moors, the portrait of their leader now hanging in the Shakespeare Institute, Stratford-upon-Avon.

How could this have been possible if Islam was, in the words of the Reverend Joseph Hall, 'a rude ignorance and a palpable imposture . . . their laws, full of license, full of impiety: in which revenge is encouraged, multitudes of wives allowed, theft tolerated . . . a monster of many seeds, and all accursed'?[16] Whatever one's private feelings might be, the history of international commerce shows that overt prejudice flies out of the window when there is money to be made.

But what if there is money to be lost? If Shylock's religion, in itself, is not enough to give him automatically the attributes of a Herod or a Barabas, there is still the matter of Shylock as usurer to be considered. Even if most, or at least some, Elizabethans did not in fact feel all that strongly about Jews, perhaps they all, along with Philip Stubbes, thought that 'he that killeth a man, riddeth him out of his paines at once, but he that taketh usury is long in butchering his pacient, suffering him by little

and little to anguish, and sucking out his hart blood . . . an Usurer is worse than a Jew, for they to this daye, will not take any usurie of their Brethren, according to the lawe of God'.[17]

Stubbes has done us a favour by distinguishing between Christian and Jewish usurers, since there are actually very few Jews amongst the many usurers in early modern drama. As Garry Wills has noted,

some who discuss this play believe that only Shylock and his coreligionists are the usurers in Venice. There would be no reason for Elizabethans, so familiar with their own Christian usurers, to assume that. In fact, the usurer, a common figure in the drama of Shakespeare's age, is normally a Christian.[18]

Still, Lawrence Danson writes of 'the Elizabethan horror of the idea of taking interest for the loan of money', going on to say that writers, 'depending for their view of economics upon the most venerable of classical and medieval sources, were unanimous in their condemnation of the practice of usury'.[19]

This might be true, but whether or not Shylock is, in fact, a usurer requires far more careful interrogation than has so far been given

---

Principal Navigations Voyages, Traffiques, and Discoveries of the English Nation, vol. 5 (Glasgow, 1903), pp. 204–5. Brown (pp. xxxvii–xxxviii) discounts anti-Semitism as a large part of the Elizabethans' day to day lives.

[15] 'The Amassage of M. Edmund Hogan, one of the sworne Esquires of her Majesties person, from her Highnesse to Mully Abdelmelech Emperour of Marocco, and king of Fes and Sus: on the yeere 1577, written by himselfe', in Hakluyt, vol. 6, pp. 285–93; Eldred D. Jones, *The Elizabethan Image of Africa* (Washington, 1971), p. 35.

[16] Samuel C. Chew, *The Crescent and the Rose* (New York, Oxford University Press, 1937), p. 445.

[17] Philip Stubbes, *Anatomy of Abuses* (London, 1583), sig. K7ʳ, K8ᵛ.

[18] Garry Wills, 'Shylock Without Usury', *New York Review of Books*, 18 January 1990, 22–5; p. 24, citing A. B. Stonex, 'The Usurer in Elizabethan Drama', *PMLA*, 31 (1919), 190–210; p. 191.

[19] Lawrence Danson, 'The Problem of Shylock', in Harold Bloom, ed., *Major Literary Characters: Shylock* (New York, 1991), p. 273.

to the point. The word 'usury' does not occur in *The Merchant of Venice*, while 'usance' is heard three times: Shylock hates Antonio most of all for bringing down the 'rate of usance' (1.3.43) in Venice, and for having 'rated' him for his 'moneys and [his] usances' (1.3.106). In the third and last use of the word, Shylock is prepared to take

> . . . no doit
> Of usance
>
> (1.3.138–9)

for his loan to Antonio. The only person to use the word 'usurer' is, by report, Antonio:

He was wont to call me usurer: let him look to his bond. He was wont to lend money for a Christian courtesy: let him look to his bond.

> (3.1.43–6)

To Shylock, then, 'usance' is a straightforward synonym for 'interest', which Shylock freely admits he takes – Shakespeare's choice of one term or the other in each case could be purely for metrical reasons. 'Usury', however, is an epithet delivered by the same man who called Shylock 'misbeliever' and 'cut-throat, dog' (1.3.110), after he spat on him, and openly states his willingness to do the same again (1.3.128–9).

The way Shakespeare employs the words 'usance' and 'usurer' in *The Merchant of Venice* epitomizes what was a major public debate of Elizabethan England, for although Elizabethan writers were, as Danson says, 'unanimous in their condemnation of the practice of usury'[20] they were anything but unanimous in defining it. As Norman Jones writes in his endlessly fascinating book, *God and the Moneylenders*, 'all good Christians agreed that usury was wrong, but they could not agree on what it was and when it occurred'.[21]

Until 1545, any charging of interest was considered usury, and hence illegal, with the obvious effect of keeping interest rates extremely high. In response, Henry VIII's 1545 statute defined the offence as interest in excess of 10 per cent, although most loans were for periods much shorter than a year, so the nominal annual interest was actually far higher. Enforcement proved very difficult, however, and rates remained high, so the lawmakers did what they always do when they cannot regulate something – they outlaw it again. In 1552 Henry VIII's statute was repealed and replaced by total prohibition, with the same effect as that other well-known prohibition, so in 1571, a year after one John Shakespeare of Stratford was fined 40 shillings for charging an astonishing £20 interest for a *one-month* £80 loan,[22] Elizabeth's parliament, after extensive debate, restored the legal limit at 10%, whatever the term of the loan was. (If there was a *New York Daily News* in those days, it would have reported that 'Johnny Gloves' was busted for nailing his customers on a 'vig' of six points a week.)[23]

In reading *God and the Moneylenders* and Laura Caroline Stevenson's *Praise and Paradox: Merchants and Craftsmen in Elizabethan Popular Literature*, one learns that writers such as Miles Mosse, who saw usury as the charging of any interest, rather than excessive interest, were what we would call today the extreme right wing, or even a 'lunatic fringe'.[24] Still, interest rates, like taxes, are always too high, so we

---

20 Danson, 'The problem of Shylock', p. 273.

21 Norman Jones, *God and the Moneylenders* (London, 1989), p. 24.

22 S. Schoenbaum, *Shakespeare's Lives*, new edn. (Oxford, 1991), 562–3; E. A. J. Honigmann, ' "There is a World Elsewhere", William Shakespeare, Businessman', in *Images of Shakespeare: Proceedings of the Third Congress of the International Shakespeare Association, 1986*, ed. Werner Habicht, D. J. Palmer, Roger Pringle (Newark, 1986), p. 40; see also D. L. Thomas and N. E. Evans, 'John Shakespeare in The Exchequer', *Shakespeare Quarterly*, 35 (1984), 314–18.

23 According to the *Wall Street Journal*, as cited in *The New Dictionary of American Slang*, ed. Robert L. Chapman (London, 1986), 'vig' or 'vigorish' – the extortionate interest charged by criminal loan sharks – would be about 180 per cent per year, or 15 per cent per month. John Shakespeare charged double that.

24 Laura Caroline Stevenson, *Praise and Paradox: Merchants and Craftsmen in Elizabethan Popular Literature* (Cambridge, 1984). Mosse's *Arraignment and Conviction of*

might easily assume that many in Shakespeare's audience would have known the difficulty of repaying a loan, and would have seen Shylock as a usurer. But for every borrower there is a lender, and there were no banks or credit unions then – ordinary people who needed money borrowed from a neighbour or acquaintance, or found an acquaintance to act as broker to negotiate the loan with someone else. Given the diverse social makeup of the Elizabethan theatre-going public, it is quite probable that some in the audience, since they were engaged in the practice themselves, believed that lending money at the going market rate, or receiving a commission for arranging a loan, was a socially useful and even honourable thing to do. *One member of the original audience at The Merchant of Venice* would surely have thought so, presuming he was not acting a part on stage – the play's author.

It has been established beyond doubt that like his father, William Shakespeare loaned out, at interest, what were sizable sums of money, and he was prepared to sue when he was not paid back. He also, as the Quiney correspondence shows, acted as a broker on occasion, arranging loans of what would be, as E. A. J. Honigmann notes, 'five-figure' sums today.[25] When Antonio says

> Shylock, albeit I neither lend nor borrow
> By taking nor by giving of excess
>
> (1.3.59–60)

would not the play's author have expected, even wanted, at least someone in the audience, in those very inflationary times, to ask what Antonio was doing with a shirt on his back?

It is ironic that Stubbes is so often cited as speaking on behalf of the Elizabethans and their horror of charging interest, since his eleven pages on the evils of interest are closely followed by ten pages on the evils of plays and playing, a reminder that moral tracts tell us far more about what audience preconceptions were not, rather than what they were. If we are looking for books to tell us about prevailing

social values of early modern England, we might consult those containing tables of interest rates, freely available by the early 1600s, rather than *The Anatomy of Abuses* or *The Arraignment and Conviction of Usurie*.[26]

My last category, theatrical limitations imposed upon the range of performance options, requires discussion of another argument that has been offered for the traditionally villainous Shylock – perhaps the most potent argument in that it relies, to a degree, on the text itself rather than things external to it. I refer to Shylock's famous 'aside', labelled as such in every modern edition of the play I have seen:

> How like a fawning publican he looks.
> I hate him for he is a Christian . . .
>
> (1.3.39–40)

In *Understanding Shakespeare's Plays in Performance*, Halio writes that

omission of this passage is usually a clear indication of how the director has conceived Shylock's role – and with it, much else in the play. The script is then tailored accordingly, so that Shylock can emerge, as in Henry Irving's famous portrayal, as a tragic hero.[27]

Specifically referring to both Olivier and Irving, he adds that cutting this speech 'is of course essential for this interpretation'.[28]

Unfortunately, neither Irving, nor Kean, nor Booth, cut a single word of the speech – indeed it was the centrepiece of Irving's portrayal, as described by his grandson:

His anger grew keener and more savage at the beginning of the aside, 'How like a fawning publican he looks . . .' For a moment he recovered his self-

---

Usurie, 1595, receives ample discussion in N. Jones, pp. 144 ff.

25 Honigmann, 'World Elsewhere', pp. 41–5; see also his *Shakespeare's Impact on his Contemporaries* (London, 1982), pp. 8–14.

26 N. Jones, *God and the Moneylenders*, p. 78.

27 Halio, *Understanding Shakespeare's Plays in Performance* (Manchester, 1988), p. 12.

28 Halio, *Merchant of Venice*, p. 10.

control, and then, on the words, 'If I can catch him . . .' his spleen once more got the better of him.[29]

How did these great 'tragic' Shylocks leave the 'aside' intact, and still manage to stun audiences with their sympathetic portrayals? The answer, I believe, is that the speech is not an 'aside' at all, as the word is usually defined by editors and critics. As is well known, the first quarto of *The Jew of Malta* shows many asides, labelled as such, for Barabas, but this stage direction is used indiscriminately for what are actually two separate conventions.[30] When Barabas is feigning distress over Abigail's entry into the convent, the asides are secret 'whispers to her':

> Wilt thou forsake mee too in my distresse,
> Seduced Daughter, *Goe forget [not].*　　*aside to her.*
> Becomes it Jewes to be so credulous,
> *To morrow early Il'e be at the doore.*　　*aside to her.*
> No come not at me, if thou wilt be damn'd,
> Forget me, see me not, and so be gone.
> *Farewell, Remember to morrow morning.*　　*aside.*
> 　　　　　(DI[r], lines 18–19, 28–32)

Other asides, however, invite Barabas to speak directly to the audience, conspiring with them, as it were, with a series of 'one-liners' (in both senses of the term) such as:

> I, like enough, why then let every man
> Provide him, and be there for fashion-sake.
> If any thing shall there concerne our state
> Assure your selves I'le looke unto my selfe.　　*aside*
> 　　　　　(B4[r] lines 6–9)

and

> I must make this villaine away: please you dine
> With me, Sir, & you shal be most hartily
> 　　　poyson'd.　　　　　　　　　　*aside*
> 　　　　　(H3r lines 28–9)

Must Shylock imitate Barabas and speak directly to the audience in his twelve-line speech? Can he not, in what we would call a soliloquy if he were alone, think aloud to himself? The one-word stage direction 'aside' appears exactly once in the Folio, in *Titus Andronicus*, when Tamora addresses Titus in her imagination while musing,

> Why thus it shall become
> High witted *Tamora* to glose with all:　　*aside*
> But *Titus*, I haue touch'd thee to the quicke,
> Thy life blood out: If *Aaron* now be wise,
> Then is all safe, the Anchor's in the Port.
> 　　　　　(TLN 2027–31)

There are only two such directions in the various Quartos, both within one speech in *Pericles* Q1, as Simonides addresses Thaisa, the first 'aside' sitting one line below where it should be:

> Yea, Mistris, are you so peremptorie?
> I am glad on't with all my heart,
> Ile tame you; Ile bring you in subjection.　　*Aside.*
> Will you not, having my consent,
> Bestowe your love and your affections,
> Upon a Stranger? who for ought I know
> May be (nor can I thinke the contrary)
> As great in blood as I my selfe:　　　　*Aside.*
> 　　　　　(D4[v], lines 2–9)

As in *Titus*, the context implies thinking aloud rather than addressing the audience.[31]

While the very word 'soliloquy' indicates that only the speaker is on stage, there are countless examples in Shakespeare, unmarked by any stage direction, of this other convention for which we have no convenient label – thinking aloud while others are present. It is hard to imagine any Claudius saying

> How smart a lash that speech doth give my
> 　　conscience.
> The harlot's cheek, beautied with plast'ring art,
> Is not more ugly to the thing that helps it
> Than is my deed to my most painted word.
> O heavy burden!
> 　　　　　(3.1.52–6)

directly to the audience.

It is all too easy to confuse Shylock with the great Elizabethan villains such as Barabas,

---

[29] Lawrence Irving, *Henry Irving: the Actor and his World, by his Grandson, Lawrence Irving* (London, 1951), p. 40.

[30] On the aside, see Alan Dessen, *Recovering Shakespeare's Theatrical Vocabulary* (Cambridge, 1995), pp. 51 ff.

[31] There is also an 'aside' in the 'bad' Quarto of *Merry Wives of Windsor* – see Dessen, *Recovering Shakespeare's Theatrical Vocabulary*, p. 51.

Richard III, and Iago by assuming that in the theatre, he, as they almost certainly did, spoke directly to the spectators. While such generalizations about performance practice are admittedly dangerous, I would suggest that one major limitation of the proscenium arch theatre is that the long aside is most difficult to manage. Further to this point, in the nineteenth century direct address to the audience would have carried with it strong associations of that nineteenth-century descendant of Barabas, the stock villain – 'curses! foiled again!' – of the melodrama.

For Kean, Booth, or Irving to turn to the audience and secretly whisper his hatred while Bassanio and Antonio sit there feigning conversation would have been most inimical to a sympathetic portrayal, so they changed the aside into a soliloquy by having Bassanio leave the stage before 'How like a fawning publican' was spoken.[32] This, however, would not have been necessary in the far larger, more flexible, and multi-dimensional space of the Shakespearian theatre, where thinking aloud in a serious mode, at some length, while others are on stage, was common.

If Kean, or indeed Olivier, had played Shylock at the Globe, he would have been able, as the Folio text indicates, to have Antonio and Bassanio on stage while he spoke 'How like a fawning publican he looks . . .' without automatic association of villainy. Indeed, the lines denied Olivier at the National could easily have been restored for the television production through the simple device of the voice-over, television's equivalent of this Elizabethan theatrical convention. 'Fawning publican' and all, he might still have been, as I believe Kean might have been, very much like 'the Jew that Shakespeare knew'.

---

[32] Mahood, introd., *Merchant of Venice*, p. 44.

A LITTLE TOUCH OF HARRY IN THE LIGHT: *HENRY V* AT THE NEW GLOBE

YU JIN KO

With the play's many direct appeals to audience members to piece out its imperfections with their thoughts, Shakespeare's *Henry V* was a fitting choice to open the inaugural season at the new Globe, the meticulous replica of the original built with the primary goal of re-creating the active dynamic that seems to have existed between the players and audiences in Shakespeare's time.[1] In the afternoon performance I attended (29 August 1997), the spectators were indeed, as Artistic Director Mark Rylance wrote, 'recognized and empowered in their creative role as imaginers of the drama',[2] and a large portion of them responded with enthusiasm. When the Chorus asked at the outset, 'Can this cock-pit hold / The vasty fields of France?' (1 Cho. 11–12), a rousing swell of 'Yeahs!' came in answer. In this the audience was affirming not only its role as participants in the imaginative recreation of past military glory – which is the role in which the original audiences were cast – but also a parallel role of recreating the past glory of Shakespeare's Globe from what the Chorus would call 'mock'ries' (4 Cho. 53), and which, to critics of the new Globe project, reek of amusement park cheesiness. The vocal members of the audience were affirming, that is to say, their intention of overcoming the various strains involved in the imaginative labour demanded of them by the play itself and the particular circumstances of its current performance. Notwithstanding the enormous differences that separate us from Elizabethan audiences, I believe much can be learned about the play and its possible initial reception by exploring this imaginative labour in today's Globe audiences.

Since the publication of Stephen Greenblatt's 'Invisible Bullets', discussion of *Henry V* and audience response has been dominated by his quasi-Foucauldian model of contained, or re-cuperated, subversion. In his reading (which I beg indulgence to rehearse), the play aligns the actions of participating in theatrical illusion-making and investing kings (onstage and off) with authority and charisma. Both actions are said to become severely strained, however, on the one hand, by continual reminders of the 'unworthy scaffold['s]' (1 Cho. 10) inadequacy in representing the most glorious of England's battles, and on the other, by the play's continual effort to subvert the heroic stature of this legendary king. Nonetheless, Greenblatt continues in a turn that has become familiar, the strains only work to enhance both aesthetic

---

[1] The play's presence in the 1599 repertory of the Globe's first season also seems to have played a part in the choice. Though the reference to Essex in the Act 5 Chorus dates the composition of the play to early 1599 when the Globe was still under construction, and thus rules out the play's having been written for the Globe, it certainly seems to have received a performance at the new site later that year. See Andrew Gurr, 'Introduction', *King Henry V* (Cambridge, 1992), p. 1, and *The Shakespearian Playing Companies* (New York, 1996), p. 291.

[2] 'Playing the Globe: Artistic Policy and Practice', in *Shakespeare's Globe Rebuilt*, ed. J. R. Mulryne and Margaret Shewring (Cambridge, 1997), p. 171.

pleasure and royal power: just as a 'sense of the limitations of [...] theatre only excites a more compelling exercise' of what the play calls 'imaginary forces' (1 Cho. 18), 'the very doubts that Shakespeare raises serve not to rob the king of his charisma but to heighten it'. This latter point in turn further informs the aesthetic pleasure associated with the play insofar as complexity and tension are valued above 'unequivocal, unambiguous celebrations of royal power'. In sum, the 'apparent production of subversion' in *Henry V* constitutes 'the very condition of power'.[3]

So dominant has this reading become that discussions of the play and its performances tend to fall into two categories. On one side, one finds those that openly subscribe to its vocabulary and thus become rather predictable; for example, Dympna Callaghan's review of Kenneth Branagh's film of the play concludes that it 'presents doubts and resistances only to incorporate them and enhance Henry's sovereign power' and thus ultimately 'corroborates Stephen Greenblatt's prescient observations'.[4] On the other, one finds those that attempt to refute Greenblatt but end up only reinscribing his vocabulary by making subversion the primary marker of artistic merit (which makes Greenblatt seem the very embodiment of the power he writes of). An example striking for its penetrating intelligence and insight is Graham Bradshaw's chapter on *Henry V* in his *Misrepresentations: Shakespeare and the Materialists*. In an effort to get beyond both the older question of 'whether Henry V is an ideal king or a Machiavellian hypocrite' and its more recent and more ideologically shaped counterpart of whether the 'one Authorized Version' is the 'Right Story' or the 'Left Story', Bradshaw focuses on the play's 'powerfully generative matrix of multiple meanings', ultimately arguing that 'we find ourselves *simultaneously* apprehending opposed potentialities of meaning'.[5] However, faced with Greenblatt's argument that the Left Story is a ruse of power, Bradshaw, his disclaimers to the contrary notwithstanding, essentially tells a

sophisticated Left Story that authenticates subversion. So relentless is his insistence on the many ways that the play undermines the 'Chorus's hagiographic account' (p. 47) of Henry and the war that one wonders how a divided response is possible. After being told that 'Henry loot[s] on a truly regal scale' (p. 41), that his 'Ceremony' speech, 'like a well-oiled machine ... delivers [a] slick, envious but self-protecting contrast with the "happy low" and the vile who can sleep well' (p. 43), that the play's imagery 'repeatedly associates war with rape' (p. 41), that 'there is a sharp descent from the grand quarrel about vast amounts of money and who should possess France to a sordid quarrel about petty cash and who should possess Mistress Quickly' (p. 67), it becomes hard to imagine a 'continuously unfolding counterpoint' that 'admits no simple, harmonious resolution', nor 'any reassuringly single or simple' (p. 109) response. If there is a divided response, the division exists *between* more and less perceptive members of the audience: 'not everybody does see, or would have seen, what is there to be seen. Yet we can be perfectly sure that the play's (various) subversive implications were not lost on some members of the original audience' (pp. 55–6). As a result, while criticizing the fact that new-historicist theory preemptively 'ensures that the concept of the "subversive" is only allowed to function as one term within a duality that already privileges state and institutional authority' (p. 87), Bradshaw goes so far in shifting the balance that he

---

[3] *Shakespearean Negotiations* (Berkeley and Los Angeles, 1988), pp. 63–5.

[4] 'Resistance and Recuperation: Branagh's *Henry V*', *Shakespeare on Film Newsletter* 15.2 (April 1991), 5–6; pp. 6, 5.

[5] (Ithaca, 1993), pp. 39, 22, 37, 33, 38. Here Bradshaw is also arguing against Norman Rabkin's famous either/or model for responding to the play that draws on the gestaltist's drawing of the rabbit-duck and asserts 'that we cannot experience alternative readings at the same time' (*Shakespeare and the Problem of Meaning* (Chicago, 1981), p. 35).

reinstates and privileges subversion. This brings to mind Gerald Graff's thoughts on how 'subversion' is used in critical evaluation today: '"Subversive" has become little more than a plus-mark, a gold star awarded to whatever a critic happens to approve of, rather the way an earlier generation of critics used words like "beautiful" and "noble"'.[6]

Indeed, critical misgivings about Branagh's *Henry V* among many who contest Greenblatt's conclusions primarily stem from their sense that Branagh ultimately squandered his opportunity to show fully the subversive potential of the play. Perhaps the most baldly stated view comes from Chris Fitter, who concludes his essay on the film this way: 'What Shakespeare had demystified, Branagh, persuasively, affably, immorally, has resanctified.'[7] In a far more qualified and sympathetic assessment, Peter Donaldson suggests that the film's initial revisionist impulse becomes diverted because of parallels Branagh is conjectured to have seen between his rise from an Irish working-class background and Henry's 'personal growth':

Branagh begins as an avant-garde film artist, unmasking the cinematic apparatus in a move that parallels Shakespeare's disjunctive treatment of the relation between epic and history and its theatrical representation. But this critical stance undergoes a gradual *aphanisis*, or fading, in the course of the narrative, as Branagh moves from Brechtian counter-cinema to an affirmation of cinema's traditional claim to present real people with authentic feelings; from cynicism about the war to something like acceptance of its tragic necessities [...] Reading *Henry V* partly as an analogue to his own remarkable rise to a position in English theatre rivalling that of Olivier, Branagh questions – but ultimately affirms – those aspects of the play that coincide with the values of professional competition and success.[8]

Even the guarded unease with celebrating success visible in Donaldson's final sentence tellingly reveals the widely felt desire to see a film or stage production that exposes the fraudulence and brutality of Henry's success. Such a desire among Branagh's critics, along with the suggestion that the only truly successful performance of the play is a subversive one, seems a counter-response engendered by Greenblatt's famously doubting 'that *Henry V* can be successfully performed as subversive'.[9] One should first note the tautology operating in Greenblatt's assertion. That is, a 'successful' performance is understood as one in which, for instance, spectators feel hot tingles rushing down their spines to such a degree upon hearing the 'Crispin's Day' speech that all doubts are dispelled in favour of a jingoistic 'celebration of the charismatic ruler' (p. 64). *Of course* the play cannot be successfully performed as subversive if success is defined *a priori* as having these particular political inflections. More to the point, the two extremes envisioned by Greenblatt and his critics need not preclude other possibilities, and a closer examination of the elisions in Greenblatt's argument as well as the audience's response at the new Globe will suggest different ways in which a performance of *Henry V* can be successful.

Greenblatt's reading is founded on parallels he draws between Shakespeare's play and Thomas Harriot's *Brief and True Report of the New Found Land of Virginia*. Greenblatt begins by looking in the latter work for a possible, if indirect, basis for the 'persistent rumors' (p. 23) and 'charges of atheism' (p. 21) that dogged Harriot his entire life, which is to say that he wants to understand the accusations as reader responses. He finds grist for the rumour mill in those sections of Harriot's account that come dangerously close to confirming the 'Machiavellian hypothesis' (p. 31) that the origin and function of religion lay in the need to impose socially coercive doctrines. However, locating

---

[6] 'Co-optation', in *The New Historicism*, ed. H. Aram Veeser (New York and London, 1989), pp. 173–4.

[7] 'A Tale of Two Branaghs: *Henry V*, Ideology, and the Mekong Agincourt', in *Shakespeare Left and Right*, ed. Ivo Kamps (New York and London, 1991), p. 275.

[8] 'Taking on Shakespeare: Kenneth Branagh's *Henry V*', *Shakespeare Quarterly*, 42.1 (1991), 60–71; pp. 61, 71.

[9] *Shakespearean Negotiations*, p. 63.

here the model of recuperation to be used later, Greenblatt argues that if 'subversive religious doubt' (p. 23) is entertained, it is ultimately 'contained by the power it would threaten' insofar as the 'project of evangelical colonialism is not set over against the skeptical critique of religious coercion, but battens on the very confirmation of that critique' (p. 30). Thus it is that he can conclude, 'Like Harriot in the New World, the Henry plays confirm the Machiavellian hypothesis that princely power originates in force and fraud even as they draw their audience toward an acceptance of that power' (p. 65).

However, through a number of critical slip-pages, the argument confuses three variables separately subject to power: the text, the author, and the reader. Since Graham Bradshaw has already shown the confusions bedevilling the depictions of the author, the text, and their relation to power, I will focus on the reader.[10] Although Greenblatt begins with readers who do not stop at using 'smear tactics' with 'reck-less abandon' (p. 21) against anyone even remo-tely suspected of heterodoxy, when he goes on to draw parallels between responses to Harriot's *Report* and *Henry V*, he focuses exclusively on the counterparts to the seemingly great majority ('most') of readers to whom the 'potential subversiveness' of Harriot 'is invisible' (p. 31). The problem here is twofold. First, if indeed the enduring charges of atheism make it im-possible to conclude that 'the radical doubt implicit in Harriot's account is *entirely* con-tained' (p. 34, his emphasis), then the blandly monolithic picture Greenblatt provides of Shakespeare's audience drawn towards a cele-bration of power must be revised to include those scandalized by the play.[11] These specta-tors would, of course, ultimately reaffirm royal power, though not by suffering reincorporation but in the act of rejecting the play. Secondly, the model of a power that builds upon a self-produced subversion cannot operate on that part of the audience to whom subversion is invisible – for there would be nothing to

recuperate. Simply put, the mechanism must have failed with the persistently scandalized, and could have had no effect on the blind.

What is most instructive here is that while Greenblatt's model requires a reader who is just perceptive enough to become vulnerable to containment, much as sophisticated magic tricks rely on spectators just knowledgeable

---

[10] It is indeed unclear whether Shakespeare is a fool, a court knave, or a frustrated radical in Greenblatt's account (*Misrepresentations*, pp. 87–9, et passim). Brad-shaw notes that, on the one hand, Shakespeare seems very much a helpless toady in passages such as the following: 'The ideological strategies that fashion Shakespeare's history plays help in turn to fashion the conflicting readings of the plays' politics. And these strategies are no more Shakespeare's invention than the historical narratives on which he based his plots.' (*Shakespearean Negotiations*, p. 23). Here Shakespeare is merely a medium through which the 'powerful logic [that] governs the relation between orthodoxy and subversion' (ibid., p. 23) finds itself onto the text. On the other hand, Shakespeare is also seen as engaged in 'an effort to intensify the power of the king and his war' (ibid., pp. 62–3), suggesting that there is calculation in the 'doubts that Shakespeare raises' (ibid., p. 63) and making 'Shakespeare's own effort' ... wholly in accord with the 'carefully plotted official strategy' (*Misrepresen-tations*, p. 88). And yet, the subversive doubt is also characterized as 'genuine and radical', though ultimately 'contained by the power it would appear to threaten' (*Shakespearean Negotiations*, p. 30), which suggests that despite Shakespeare's best efforts to write a subversive play, 'power' trumped his will. The mechanism by which power contains subversion is fundamentally different for each of these 'alternative Shakespeares'.

[11] Throughout the sections on *Henry V*, Greenblatt uses 'audience', 'we', or 'spectators' in the collective sense seen in his introduction: '[T]he theater manifestly addresses its audience as a collectivity ... The Shake-spearean theater depends upon a felt community: there is no dimming of lights, no attempt to isolate and awaken the sensibilities of each individual member of the audience' (p. 5). Such absolute characterizations, along with the absoluteness of his rhetoric ('There is subversion, no end of subversion, only not for us', p. 65), are surely behind charges against Greenblatt in particular and new historicists in general that their world picture represents a demonically hegemonic one in which no resistance is of any avail. For Greenblatt's rebuttal, see his *Learning to Curse* (New York and London, 1990), p. 166.

enough to be always one step behind, by his own account the majority of readers perceive too much or too little. This ultimately suggests that responses of actual historical persons are not so uniform and thus resist easy formulation. No doubt the 'model' response did exist, but because at least two other responses to Harriot's work are discernible, the analogy to *Henry V* would minimally require the following: certainly, affirmation that strangely issues from and even gets intensified by the recognition of subversive doubt, but also untroubled affirmation of the nation's purpose and its leaders, and most importantly, outrage at the potential subversion (in much the same way that Elizabeth was alarmed by the incendiary potential of *Richard II*). To this list of analogous possible responses, one could add a fourth, though this by no means exhausts the possibilities. For this I turn to George Chapman's response to Harriot.

In his panegyric to Harriot that accompanies his *Achilles Shield*, George Chapman figures Harriot as a visionary whose work, when known to those 'in staring ignorance' on 'this lumpe of blindness', will bring light to 'errors Night' (line 89) and lead to his vindication, if not total understanding:

> your self shall shine
> Aboue all this in knowledge most diuine,
> And all shall homage to your true-worth owe,
> You comprehending all, that all, not you. (lines 85–8)[12]

Though the 'knowledge' clearly refers primarily to unpublished scientific work, Chapman's characterization of Harriot here resembles Harriot's self-presentation in *A Brief and True Report* as the colonizer of superior knowledge and skill 'giuen and taught [. . .] of the gods',[13] while his general audience recalls the Algonquins who became infected by contact with Harriot but were able to account for the illness only by recourse to theories of invisible bullets. Indeed, the unsettling nature of the knowledge to be bestowed is indicated in

Chapman's assertion that the enlightened will perceive, though imperfectly, 'What true man is, and how like gnats appeare' (line 98). Greenblatt, while considering *A Brief and True Report*, had entertained the notion that Harriot was 'demonically conscious' (p. 31) of the dangerously subversive potential of his observations, but ultimately dismissed it. To Chapman at least, Harriot was indeed demonically conscious of the earth-shattering potential of his vision; and the particular delight Chapman derived from reading Harriot's works seems to have consisted in sharing this demonic consciousness. The analogous response to *Henry V* might be for one to suppose himself having privileged access to the hidden intentions of the author and to delight demonically in thinking that a befuddled audience is being subtly manipulated by the play's hero and the play.

The reception history of the play is certainly littered with instances of the four responses adduced above, and the text, as read, could be said to validate all of them. The portrayal of ecclesiastical realpolitik that begins the play and colours the motive for going to war, or the much commented-upon foregrounding of the strategies by which Henry tries to evade responsibility, can easily be imagined to rankle devoted royalists.[14] Indeed, the lament of a disappointed royalist – though it is hard to say he in fact was one – can be heard in Tillyard's assertion that because the Tudors lacked the 'steady belief in the missionary and civilizing destiny of Rome that animated' Virgil, Shakespeare's Henry 'could at best stand for Elizabethan *political* principle [and] could only fail when great weight was put on him' (my

---

12 *The Poems of George Chapman*, ed. Phyllis Brooks Bartlett (New York, 1941).

13 *A briefe and true report of the new found land of Virginia* (London, 1588, n.p.), E4.

14 From Hazlitt's assessment of Henry's character to W. L. Godshalk's 'Henry V's Politics of Non-responsibility', *Cahiers Elisabéthains* 17 (April 1980), 11–20, hardly a piece of anti-Henry criticism gets written that does not mention Henry's evasion of responsibility.

emphasis).[15] To an untroubled patriot like Dover Wilson, who admiringly compares 'Henry's words before Agincourt' to 'Churchill's after the Battle of Britain', the Archbishop's manoeuvrings are 'perfectly legitimate', and only sanction further the English 'triumph which, under God, was due to the heroic spirit of the great King'.[16] Olivier did not need to cut troubling scenes for Dover Wilson. To still others, doubts raised by the seemingly Machiavellian behaviour of the leaders and the choric apologies for the theatre's inadequacy have become merely fertile materials for a renewed faith in royal power and its destiny. After registering the many ways, dramatically and metadramatically, by which the play 'indicate[s] to us that it may be the speeches of the Chorus whitewashing the war which are to be taken as mockeries', Anthony Brennan concludes that 'the cumulative effect is to give the play a much broader range than was available in the chronicles, humanizing the king in a presentation of war from a variety of viewpoints'.[17] And finally, to a large number that has steadily been growing in the twentieth century, the play has been read with a kind of demonic consciousness that appreciates, as Gerald Gould has asserted, the 'irony . . . meant to "take in" the groundlings'.[18] It is worth remembering here that Greenblatt concludes his essay by asserting that 'we are free to locate and pay homage to the play's doubts only because they no longer threaten us',[19] suggesting that history itself has been complicit in containing subversion when it all mattered. But Gould offered his ironic reading in 1913, with England on the cusp of war and the fate of the monarchy far from resolved.

The response I wish to focus on now, however, is the one that was most prominent at the afternoon performance I attended at the new Globe. For the fullest understanding of this response, it would be useful first to think about the effects of platform staging in Shakespeare's time and today, and about the corollary issue of how responses in the theatre and the study might differ. If, as is generally agreed, the Chorus's appeal to the audience for active interaction to complete the play carried practical immediacy in Shakespeare's 'Wooden O', a concomitant effect would have been to confer significant authority onto the audience, thus partially releasing the meaning of the play from authorized interpretation. This is not an argument about the inevitable lacunae in signification that are supplied in the act of interpretation (though it is related). Rather, it concerns what Robert Weimann has called the 'division of authority' on Shakespeare's stage that stems from the 'divisive agencies of authority' within 'the representational process itself'.[20] If one finds a mimetically represented 'authority' on the conceptual space of 'verisimilitude, decorum, aloofness from the audience, and representational closure' (p. 409) that Weimann calls locus, the 'authority of misrule' embedded in the participatory and 'indecorous mimesis' (p. 402) of the platea-dimension bestows authority on 'the signifying capacities of a good many ordinary people' and 'expand[s] the margin of indeterminacy' (p. 412).[21] Put another way, in opening up the 'place' of performance so that the boundary between stage illusion and audience becomes permeable, the royal power residing in mimetically represented authority becomes subject to the power of a group that could appear from the perspective of authority as 'the many-headed multitude' (2.3.16–17)[22] of Coriolanus'

---

[15] *Shakespeare's History Plays* (London, 1944), pp. 305–6.

[16] 'Introduction', *King Henry V* (Cambridge, 1947), pp. xxxi, xxii, xxx–xxxi.

[17] *Onstage and Offstage Worlds in Shakespeare's Plays* (London and New York, 1989), pp. 204, 196.

[18] 'A New Reading of *Henry V*', *The English Review* (1919), 42–55; p. 42.

[19] *Shakespearean Negotiations*, p. 65.

[20] 'Bifold Authority in Shakespeare's Theatre', *Shakespeare Quarterly*, 39.4 (1988), 401–17; p. 402.

[21] For more on the distinction between *platea* and *locus*, see his *Shakespeare and the Popular Tradition in the Theater* (Baltimore and London, 1978), especially chapter III.4.

[22] The phrase is reported by the First Citizen to have been used by Coriolanus.

description. Indeed, in relation to the play at hand, the dramaturgy insistently promotes what Coriolanus most fears and what Henry IV had warned Prince Hal against in *1 Henry IV*: losing 'princely privilege / With vile participation' (3.2.86–7).

Joel Altman has brilliantly shown how being subject to 'participation' by audiences on and offstage – being partly created by, but also being 'partaken of' in a sense with 'sacramental overtones' – becomes the key strategy and 'distinguishing feature of Harry's princely career as Shakespeare represents it'.[23] That is, figuring participation as ennobling the participants, the play draws a parallel between the Chorus's constant 'gentling' of the audience ('gentles all' are implored 'Gently to hear ... our play' (1 Cho. 8, 34)) and the gentling promised by Henry to his soldiers at Agincourt ('[H]e today that sheds his blood with me/ Shall be my brother [...] / This day shall gentle his condition' (4.3.61–3)). Accordingly, 'by means of an embracing ritual gesture, Shakespeare [...] join[s] past to present, audience to soldiery, in an honorable fellowship transcending time and space' (p. 16). However, Altman also recognizes very clearly the dangers of a figurative strategy that links audience to soldiery; if engaging in actual violence gentles the soldiers, 'this audience that does no work today finds itself inducted into combat duty' to 'engage in a series of assaults upon the spectacle, violently wresting and re-shaping it' (p. 19). Once empowered, the audience can work its own will on the spectacle, leaving its imprint, or little touch, on Harry himself. In assessing the relation of the play to contemporary historical circumstances, it has become a commonplace since Greenblatt's 'Invisible Bullets' to think of Elizabeth I's remark, 'we princes, I tell you, are set on stages, in the sight and view of all the world dulie obserued',[24] as a programmatic slogan for strategically engaging in theatrical displays of power. But surely apprehension about autonomy in her audiences, or subjects, is much more behind Elizabeth I's

remark, as her words immediately following it make clear; especially in the context of her answering Parliament's petition for a quick execution of Mary, Queen of Scots, they show her continually wary of public opinion in the manner of beleaguered politicians today who are forced to advertise their efforts to avoid even the 'appearance of impropriety':

[T]he eies of manie behold our actions; a spot is soone spied in our garments; a blemish quicklie noted in our dooings. It behooueth vs therefore to be carefull that our proceedings be iust and honorable. (p. 934)

To be sure, Elizabeth was an adept and vigorous practitioner of image control, most literally so in her proscribing unauthorized visual representations of herself, but the continual concern with image control also betrays deep anxieties about the uncontrolled remaking of the proffered image. Indeed, in her second answer to Parliament regarding Mary, Queen of Scots, she laments that her delay in deciding the fate of her cousin – which historians attribute in no small measure to Elizabeth's bouts of conscience[25] – might be misconstrued as an act of image control: 'But if anie there liue so wicked of nature, to suppose, that I prolonged this time onelie, Pro forma, to the intent to make a shew of clemencie, thereby to set my praises to the wierdrawers to lengthen them the more: they doo me so great a wrong, as they can hardlie recompense' (p. 938). Elizabeth continues in this vein for an entire paragraph, before alluding in the next paragraph to the 'manie opprobrious books and pamphlets against me, my realme and state, accusing me to be a tyrant' (pp. 938–9). If these words and thoughts reveal anything, it is how close Elizabeth is to Bill

---

23 "Vile participation": The Amplification of Violence in the Theater of *Henry V*', *Shakespeare Quarterly*, 42.1 (1991), 1–32; pp. 5, 7.
24 *Holinshed's Chronicles of England, Scotland and Ireland* (London, 1808), p. 934.
25 See J. E. Neale, *Queen Elizabeth* (New York, 1934), especially ch. 16.

Clinton, that master *and* hapless prey of the media; today's media-feeding frenzies are continuous with 'partaking of' royalty.

Again, I do not doubt at all that Elizabeth's self-professed vulnerability to bad publicity resulted from her strategy of manipulating self-display. It is critical to recognize, however, the particular dangers of self-display to a ruler for whom, to paraphrase Annabel Patterson, replacing obedience with popularity was an urgent political need.[26] The much-noted rhetoric of Petrarchism that Elizabeth encouraged and tried to enact (in the court especially) was clearly, if only partly, a means by which she maintained popularity without being 'so lavish of [her] presence' or 'common-hackney'd in the eyes of men' (*1 Henry IV* 3.2.39–40). That is, she encouraged representations that figured her as the object of widespread erotic and political desire who remained remote, elusive, and unsullied – and therefore continually desirable.[27] However, as Susan Frye in particular has argued, the discourse of politicized Petrarchism had its own risks for Elizabeth insofar as the subject position of the traditionally male poet carried with it significant authority and power to anatomize and reshape the person represented; in the case of Spenser and his *Faerie Queene*, Frye suggests, if Busirane's relationship to Amoret is defined by the 'siege principle' visible in his 'textualization' of her (III.xii.), that relationship merely mirrors Spenser's desired one to Elizabeth.[28] The act of writing, in other words, was for Spenser an aggressive attempt to transform himself from subject of the Queen to an autonomous subject laying siege to and re-making the royal object. More extreme examples of the apparatus of Petrarchism becoming aggressive weapons can be found among pornographic blazons from the 1590s that parodied the cataloguing of the royal body native to the genre of erotic encomia and which directly and indirectly 'implicated', in Hannah Betts's words, 'the nation's most famous virgin'.[29]

I would argue that audiences in Shakespeare's theatre occupied relative to the stage spectacle the dual subject position of poets responding to Elizabeth as both the Queen's obedient subjects and her remakers. While the act of reading has always been a subjective act of remaking, the act of assisting at a performance, as the French term it (and as Peter Brook delights in pointing out[30]), would have been considerably more active given both the openness of the stage and what Michael Bristol has called the 'heteroglot condition of the theatre' that promoted 'the dispersion of authority'.[31] A mere shout from the groundlings' pit could have visibly altered the performance. Accordingly, in drawing parallels between theatrical spectacle and royal display, we need to understand how precarious and contingent such performances are. As a broad cultural matter in today's England, respect for authority, royal and otherwise, has probably diminished since Elizabethan times, but the respect for the inviolability of stage illusion, especially Shakespearian, has undoubtedly increased in the darkness of the pervasive proscenium theatre; indeed, given the cultural status of the *Royal* Shakespeare Company in England, it is almost as though Shakespeare has become a displaced repository for lost royal authority. An editorial poem (in doggerel) in *The Times* in anticipation of the new Globe's opening made the displaced substitution of

---

26 'Back by Popular Demand: The Two Versions of *Henry V*', *Renaissance Drama*, New Series XIX (1988): 29–62; p. 46.

27 For a fuller account of the complex and continual ways in which Elizabeth responded to pressures originating in discomfort with female authority, see Carole Levin, *The Heart and Stomach of a King: Elizabeth I and the Politics of Sex and Power* (Philadelphia, 1994).

28 *Elizabeth I: The Competition for Representation* (New York and Oxford, 1993), p. 133.

29 'The Pornographic Blazon 1588–1603', in *Dissing Elizabeth*, ed. Julia M. Walker (Durham and London, 1998), p. 166.

30 See *The Empty Space* (New York, 1968), pp. 138–9.

31 *Carnival and Theater* (London and New York, 1985), pp. 123, 115.

Shakespeare for royalty quite explicit, ending the tortured attempt at verse with the line, 'A little touch of Shakespeare at the Globe'.[32] If the various reviews of the early performances of *Henry V* at the new Globe are any indication, however, renewed vitality and risk seem to have been injected into the relationship between audience and Shakespearian spectacle. Hardly a review goes by without explicit mention of 'the rapport between actor and spectator',[33] often to point out similarities to 'the buzz of a football match',[34] and the 'collusions and challenges'[35] that are made possible. At a post-production talk I attended, one of the actors (David Fielder, who played Fluellen and Monsieur Le Fer) stated that 'sixty per cent' of the energy during the performance came from the audience, by which he also meant that he ceded an equal percentage of authority to the audience. When asked if this upset him, he responded that he 'accepted' this economy as the premise of this theatre and found it, among other things, 'exhilarating'.[36] I would like, however, to understand more deeply the effect this exhilarating negotiation might have had on the audience's imagination of royal power on the afternoon I attended the new Globe.

It is not unimaginable that individual members of the audience had one or more of the responses found in the reception history of the play outlined some pages ago, though by what signs one could gauge them remains a difficult question. Strikingly, a sizable majority responded with such unencumbered enthusiasm that their intentions and thoughts became readily readable. Those who began by vociferously answering the Chorus's call to use their imaginary forces to 'cram / Within [the] wooden O the very casques / That did affright the air at Agincourt' (1 Cho. 13–15) had clearly come to see a good fight. Indeed, the very mention of the French brought out catcalls and hisses, which were redoubled each time the French actually entered.[37] So ready was this group to relive war glory that it deliciously

chuckled throughout Canterbury's tortuous explanation of the Salic Law, as if the flimsy grounds of the war provided more to savour with hearty bravado, and then gave a triumphant cheer when Canterbury finally urged Henry, 'Stand for your own' (1.2.101). What could be thought subversive became a joke that only a special band of brothers could share. This was a group that understood when the action went against what critics call the Chorus's hagiographic account of Henry, but retained its cheerful and self-consciously jingoistic optimism. Perhaps the most remarkable thing was how sustained the participatory energy was. The first words of Henry's 'Once more unto the breach' speech were met with thunderous applause that drowned the actor's voice, as though the first bars of a signature aria had been sung; at the end of the speech, moreover, the audience helped finish it, shouting in unison, 'God for Harry! England and Saint George!' (3.1.1, 34). With this group in charge, something remarkable and magical happened: in self-consciously participating in the creation of stage illusion, this audience invested the actor with reality, kingship with charisma, the country's past with glory, and the new Globe with renewed life.

The intimacy and sturdy magnificence of the architecture that John Peter called 'both heroic

---

32 'Ring of Triumph', 21 May 1997.

33 Richard Hornby, 'The Globe Restored', *The Hudson Review* 1.4 (1998), 617–24, p. 618.

34 'Velvet Touch', *Times Educational Supplement*, 13 June 1997, sec. 2, p. 10.

35 'Harry's great but why the cod cockneys?', *The Observer*, 15 June 1997, Review, p. 9.

36 The talk took place at the Globe Education Centre on 27 August 1997.

37 Nearly every review I have read mentioned this response, which suggests the dominant response to this production was uniform in certain respects. The Globe website (www.rdg.uk /globe/OpeningReport/Summary.html) notes that exit polls showed that 83 per cent of the spectators were English, which partly accounts for the expressions of nationalistic fervour.

and humanly proportioned'[38] clearly helped to charge the audience, but the effective use the actors made of the platform stage to engage the audience directly seemed to me the most responsible for the collective intensity of response. Mark Rylance as Henry was perhaps the most insistently presentational, and therefore solicitous, in his playing, beginning with his delivery of the opening Chorus.[39] In the scene with the French Ambassador (1.2), he began his speech in response to the Dauphin's gift by picking up the tennis balls, doing a take to the audience as if to say, 'Now watch this', and briefly juggling. This little piece of stage business captured well the gamesmanship and game-metaphor prevalent throughout the ensuing speech (and the play), even if the light-heartedness deflected too easily the ferocity found there. Most importantly, the audience was again reminded that it shared a privileged part in this game that Henry was leading it in. This *platea*-gamesmanship, as it were, became most prominent in the speech before Harfleur that often becomes 'Exhibit A' in ironic or anti-Henry readings of the play. Taking a tack suggested by Dover Wilson, Rylance's Henry played the speech as a calculated bluff, throwing knowing glances to the audience before the most egregious of threats, such as:

The gates of mercy shall be all shut up
And the fleshed soldier, rough and hard of heart,
In liberty of bloody hand shall range
With conscience wide as hell, mowing like grass
Your fresh fair virgins and your flow'ring infants.
(3.3.93–7)

By this time in the play audience members were directly sharing field strategies with the King, and deservedly so if they had included themselves among the 'dear friends' (3.1.1) whom Henry had implored earlier to the breach. Resisting the call had in point of fact been quite hard since, again, the actor addressed the crowd directly as surely those working on the stage in 1599 would have done with such lines as the following:

On, on, you noblest English,
Whose blood is fet from fathers of war-proof.
[...] And you, good yeomen,
Whose limbs were made in England, show us here
The mettle of your pasture. (3.1.17–27)

The sense of participation in a collective enterprise became most apparent in arguably the most famous speech in the play – the Saint Crispin's Day speech – which, delivered *sotto voce* by Rylance, had the effect of raising collective concentration to an intensity even higher than in the more vociferous scenes:

And Crispin Crispian shall ne'er go by
From this day to the ending of the world
But we in it shall be rememberèd.
We few, we happy few, we band of brothers.
(4.3.57–60)

Undoubtedly John Peter had scenes like this one in his mind when he wrote, 'In tense moments [...] a silence descends, an almost palpable silence of hundreds of attentive people close together, such as I have not experienced before.'[40]

With such audience reactions, it is no wonder that many reviewers used the term 'jingoistic' to describe the play, with Paul Taylor even wondering, given the 'amazing sense of audience solidarity' the theatrical space promotes, whether 'the production does enough to put such atavistic jingoism into perspective'.[41] Clearly he is mindful that today's English audiences can share easily in nostalgic communing, especially with the added memories of a lost empire and of fine hours in history that include victories over not only Hitler but Napoleon. All this further means that many at the new Globe engaged in various forms of imagined violence. However, I would question some reviewers'

---

[38] 'Where audience is king', *The Sunday Times*, 15 June 1997, Culture, p. 16.
[39] Different members of the company spoke the other Choruses.
[40] 'Where audience is king', p. 16.
[41] 'Theatre: *Henry V/ The Winter's Tale*', *The Independent*, 9 June 1997, p. 4.

implicit suggestion that the production realized rather too well what Joel Altman sees as the play's intention to 'gratify the passion for violence that [. . .] aches to be released in foreign quarrels'.[42] Indeed, a most remarkable turn in the new Globe performance took place when the director (Laurence Olivier's son Richard) chose to stage, as one critical tradition has it, no other fighting at Agincourt than the 'brawl ridiculous' (4 Cho. 51) between Pistol and Le Fer. That is to say, the audience did not get the culminating battle whose mere name is talismanic and towards which expectation had steadily been building. For the Folio stage direction of '*Excursions*' at 4.4, only a group cross by four or five men took place that recalled the Chorus's apology for 'four or five most vile and ragged foils' (4 Cho. 50). To make matters even worse, Richard Olivier, unlike both his father and Branagh in their films, included a line from 4.6 that left many in the audience visibly and audibly at a loss: Henry's chilling order to his men, 'every soldier kill his prisoners' (4.6.37). As the Act progressed with one wordy interlude after another, and it became clear that no battle would be staged, the loss of energy and the deflation of defeated expectations became palpable. The atmosphere was not unlike that in a basketball arena when the home team goes through a scoreless stretch and gives the crowd nothing to cheer about.

It is impossible to know precisely what went through the minds of the various audience members who started out cheering but were left unfulfilled. Perhaps some shrugged it off and immediately became engaged in the next Act, and consciously or unconsciously, saw Henry's courtship of Katherine as a mere sexual extension of military conquest, and thus left the theatre feeling satisfied anyway.[43] The effect of defeated expectations seems to have lingered for many, however, if one can judge from the large number of otherwise highly positive reviews that recorded some sense of disappointment, though some of the connections misleadingly made or left incompletely explored seem

to me the most telling. Benedict Nightingale, for instance, points to a presumed lack of resources, and not directorial intention, while lamenting that the 'small English army look[ed] like a slightly expanded version of the Famous Five' and that 'the smoke of war was a cigarette puff'.[44] Clearly Nightingale saw the problem as one of execution. Similarly, while marvelling at the 'intoxicating' space and granting the appropriateness of Richard Olivier's allegedly 'return[ing] to the exuberant approach of his father' in it, Richard Hornby concludes that, 'in the end', the show suffered from Mark Rylance's lacking the heroic bearing of more 'charismatic stars'.[45] More interestingly, Hornby approvingly quotes 'a nearby groundling' snickering 'in the spirit of the show' about Rylance, '"He is a bit of a runt, isn't he"' (p. 420), but never quite explores the relation between the perceived lack of charisma in Rylance and the unruly control the crowd seems to have maintained on that particular afternoon. The *Guardian*'s reviewer, along with a number of others, expressed his dissatisfaction by remarking at some length on the distractions at the theatre, such as 'the dreary sound of plastic beakers crunched underfoot' and the meddling of 'officious ushers', suggesting that he found himself rather too often reminded of his presence at a performance; however, his grievances are registered in the context of praising the 'excellent production' for how self-consciously it demands 'our imaginative participation', especially in its use of 'refreshing humour' to 'acknowledge we too are part of the experience'.[46] To be sure, an annoying

---

42 '"Vile Participation"', p. 30.
43 For the relation between Henry's military conquest and his wooing of Katherine, see Lance Wilcox, 'Katherine of France as Victim and Bride', *Shakespeare Studies*, 7 (1985), 61–76.
44 'Summon up the bloodless', *The Sunday Times*, 7 June 1997, p. 20.
45 'The Globe Restored', p. 617.
46 'Epic victory amid crunch of plastic beakers', 9 June 1997, p. 2.

outside distraction is not the same thing as an internal mechanism that induces a kind of Brechtian alienation, but in the context of this play in this space, the difference effectively collapses; to recognize the inadequately representational nature of the 'brawl ridiculous' is to be aware of one's presence in a material space that includes nearby groundlings and crinkly drinking cups. Indeed, it is no coincidence, I believe, that the *Guardian*'s reviewer mentions not only extraneous noise but the French 'cries of agony when Henry instructs his soldiers to kill their prisoners' in a review that praises the production's 'aware[ness] of [its] own rhetoric'.

To varying degrees, then, the three immediately preceding reviewers seem to have been unwillingly taken out of the moment more frequently than is usual even for reviewers, and, again to varying degrees and with different spins, drew some connection between that experience and disappointment of epic expectations. Curiously, all three seem to believe that on the whole the audiences enjoyed the shows more than they themselves did, or at least experienced far fewer problems and distractions, as indicated in Benedict Nightingale's patrician quip that 'the audience entered into such spirit as there was'. If shuffling and looking about are any indication, the audience I was a part of not only felt disappointment but also underwent that disconcerting experience of being taken out of the moment during the Agincourt sequence. I would speculate that the audience covered at least the range of experiences articulated by the three reviewers above, from disappointment with the director to some degree of self-consciousness about participating in theatrical illusion. Indeed, I would venture to say that the consciousness of being in an ersatz space – a mere replica of the original wooden O – became more acute for many there, and not only for the likes of other sophisticated reviewers who duly made note of Japanese tourists with 'camera trained on the production throughout' and remarked on how much the audience relished the 'dull' produc-

tion.[47] For those who are especially reflective, perhaps the self-consciousness extended to the thought that for this play the fun of suspending disbelief and the desire to see exciting violence had become inseparable, and that the result was an uncritical mythologizing of a king with a Machiavellian streak on a deeply compromised enterprise. I cannot believe, again, that only reviewers had misgivings about 'the moral ambiguity of [Henry's] campaign'.[48]

In the event, whatever complexly or simply deflated desire to witness war glory was felt, it seemed to have become coaxed for many into a desire for comic reconciliation in the next scene. Judging by the complete absence of jeering at the French in Act 5, and the goodwill extended to Henry's wooing of Katherine, a new desire to enlarge the band of brothers to include the French emerged. In this respect, though the element of male imperial fantasy in it cannot be denied, especially as the comic sprezzatura in Mark Rylance's performance must have rekindled the imaginations of many, the final scene seemed to have been witnessed as not merely an extension of but an alternative to military aggression. Though Henry's form of love could well be understood as war by other means, the wooing was cheered in the spirit of making love not war.

Is this containment or subversion? I am not sure that either of the terms popularized by Greenblatt adequately captures the journey of the audience I have outlined. The wooing, because of its dynastic importance and Katherine's need of a translator, is a public scene of private intimacy, a paradox that Rylance caught beautifully with more takes to the audience at laugh lines (Henry's 'Can any of your neighbours tell, Kate?' [5.2.194] in response to her profession of not being able to tell whether she can love him). Such sharing and participation,

---

47 Taylor, 'Theatre', p. 4. It is rather ironic that Taylor should decry the 'atavistic jingoism' on display even as he holds up the Japanese tourist for ridicule.

48 Hornby, 'The Globe Restored', p. 618.

or 'indecorous mimesis' as Weimann would term it, can, however, democratize and dilute the mimetically represented authority on stage in a way that is not unrelated to how Prince Hal was feared to have been degraded by being 'so lavish of [...] presence' and 'common-hackneyed in the eyes of men' (*1 Henry IV*, 3.1.39–40). It is also worth noting here that the attempt at 'authenticity' in this production extended to all-male casting, which was something not lost on either the reviewers or the audience. Hence, what one reviewer heard as a 'teasing sigh'[49] when Henry finally won his kiss included knowing titters of laughter when I saw the play. Indeed, as noted in the *Guardian*, the all-male casting 'add[ed] to the sense of audience engagement'[50] in heightening the consciousness of attending a theatre. One must take seriously H. N. Hillebrand's caution not to underestimate the 'familiarizing effect'[51] of custom when pondering original audience reactions to cross-dressed playing, particularly in a play that lacks potentially self-referential devices like cross-sexual disguise plots. Accordingly, though the mistakenly racy catalogue of body parts in Katherine's English lesson might have brought attention to the physical body of the boy actor for Elizabethan audiences, it would be difficult to postulate reactions at the original Globe as being similar to today's. Nonetheless,

as I have been arguing, elements specific to the present that induce forms of self-consciousness can be regarded as continuous with the play's references to the materiality of the original performance space that foreground the audience's participation in a performance. The self-consciousness induced is, perhaps, the most significant and volatile effect of equating participatory spectatorship with hero-worship, for part of what the audience becomes conscious of is its power as makers of kings and queens. If Henry's romantic success at the play's close helps to reconstitute royal power, the handling of this power by the audience with such intimacy and self-consciousness leaves Henry's 'imaginary puissance' indeed 'piece[d]' out' and divided 'into a thousand parts' (1 Cho. 23–5). One might more usefully conclude from this that there is no end to either subversion or containment; the play experience in the theatre as I witnessed it neither reaffirms the utopia asserted by royal power nor points to the utopia born of subversion coveted by the left, but re-enacts the circling of rule and resistance that has characterized so much of English history.

---

49 Clapp, 'Harry's great', p. 9.
50 'Epic victory', p. 2.
51 *The Child Actors* (Urbana, 1926), p. 275.

GULLS, CONY-CATCHERS AND COZENERS: *TWELFTH NIGHT* AND THE ELIZABETHAN UNDERWORLD

ANGELA HURWORTH

The age-old ploy of practising deception upon one's fellow for material profit and/or vindictive amusement, known as gulling, cozenage or cony-catching in the rogue literature of the Elizabethan period, figures prominently in the contemporary drama where its principal exponent is, of course, Ben Jonson. In *Volpone* and *The Alchemist* deception is treated as an art-form in itself. This is gulling on a grand scale, where the theatricality of deceiving and the deception inherent in the theatrical illusion find their finest expression. In Shakespeare's plays, gulling rarely occupies centre-stage as in Jonson (*Othello* may be the one exception to this), although it frequently surfaces as an incident in the main plot, for example, the double gulling of Beatrice and Benedick in *Much Ado About Nothing*, or the cozening of Falstaff by Hal after the Gadshill episode in *1 Henry IV*. The term itself, however, occurs infrequently in Shakespeare's plays. Unusually, in *Twelfth Night* the text designates two characters, Malvolio and Sir Andrew Aguecheek, as 'gulls', the instigator of the trap set for the steward, Maria, is addressed as 'my noble gull-catcher' by Fabian (2. 5. 180), and there may be an implicit reference to 'gulling' in the title of the play, since the prologue of *Gl'Ingannati*, a likely source, has a reference to *la notte di beffana*,[1] a phrase usually rendered as 'Epiphany' or 'Twelfth Night' in English but which, literally translated, may be understood as *The Night of Gullings*.

The gulling of Malvolio which results in his transformation from dour Puritan to ridiculous suitor is the comic highlight, if not the centre, of the play.[2] In fact Malvolio's comment that he is the 'most notorious geck and gull / That e'er in vention played on' (5. 1. 340–1) may be read as a meta-theatrical prophecy of his box-office popularity,[3] initially commented upon by Digges:

---

[1] G. Bullough, *Narrative and Dramatic Sources of Shakespeare*, vol. 2 (1958), p. 287, says :'If we believe that Shakespeare used *Gl'Ingannati* as a source we may also believe that he took his title from a phrase in its prologue.' However, he fails to make the connection between the sense of *beffana* and the comic gullings which figure in *Twelfth Night*: 'Yet even if Shakespeare had read the passage and had recognized "la notte di beffana" as meaning "Twelfth Night", there is nothing in the context of that prologue to lead him towards choosing this title for his comedy.'

[2] In 1602 John Manningham's comments record his impression of the gulling of Malvolio being the play's most memorable feature; see *The Diary of John Manningham of the Middle Temple (1602–3)*, edited by Robert Parker Sorlien (1976), p. 48. Many modern critics have concurred with the view that Malvolio is the play's central attraction, for example, Mark Van Doren, 'The center is Malvolio', *Shakespeare* (1939), p. 169 and Milton Crane, '*Twelfth Night* and Shakespearean Comedy', *Shakespeare Quarterly*, 6 (1955). For a counter-view, see Harold Jenkins, *Shakespeare's 'Twelfth Night'* (Rice Institute Pamphlet 45, 1958–9), pp. 19–42. All references to *Twelfth Night* are taken from *The Complete Oxford Shakespeare*, edited by Stanley Wells and Gary Taylor (Oxford, 1986).

[3] For an account of the theatrical history of Malvolio's success, see *Twelfth Night*, The Cambridge Shakespeare, edited by Elizabeth Story Donno (Cambridge, 1985), pp. 28–33.

loe in a trice
The Cockpit Galleries, Boxes, all are full
To hear Malvoglio, the cross-garter'd gull.[4]

And the propensity of the comic sub-plot to upstage the main plot has characterized the play ever since Charles I wrote 'Malvolio' against the title in his copy of the Second Folio. Indeed we may note that the term 'gull' in its ornithological sense is interchangeable with 'cuckoo' in Shakespeare's usage: 'As that ungentle gull, the cuckoo's bird, / Useth the sparrow' (*I Henry IV*, 5. 1. 60–1), so that there is a semantic association between the cuckoo-like sub-plot in *Twelfth Night* and gulling.[5] The secondary intrigue's appropriation of the place normally accorded to the main plot functions as a metatextual paradigm of the patterns of deception, substitution and metamorphosis in the play.

I wish to compare the representation of gulling in *Twelfth Night* with the narratives of underworld literature where such deception, known as cony-catching, cozenage or gulling, receives its fullest treatment. In his study of the Elizabethan underworld, G. Salgādo noted the affinities between the deception practised in the narratives of rogue literature and the Elizabethan stage:

The paraphernalia used in this form of cheating had all the imagination, energy, sense of timing and understanding of character that we find in the Elizabethan drama itself . . .[6]

However it should be remembered that these narratives are every bit as fictive as their onstage representation and should not be read as documentary evidence of criminal activity in Elizabethan London.[7] My aim therefore is not to establish a relationship between Shakespeare's play and criminality in Elizabethan London but to draw attention to the contact between the two different representational modes. Firstly I shall relate the dramatic syntax and lexis of gulling in Shakespeare's play to the lexis and syntax of gulling in the underworld literature; I shall then show how the definition of gulling as a game with rules influences the

configuration of the gulling in *Twelfth Night*, and note the theatricality of gulling, as presented in these pamphlets.

Malvolio may be the play's most 'notorious geck and gull', but he is certainly not alone in the part. *Twelfth Night* is replete with gullings, albeit of different degrees and durations. Andrew Aguecheek is by nature a gull[8] (as he virtually admits[9]), and he is gulled from first to last. It is no secret that he is fleeced financially throughout, that he is deceived into 'supposing that Toby's dry gullet is the way to Olivia's heart',[10] and then cozened into challenging Viola/Cesario by Sir Toby, as the latter's boast, 'Marry, I'll ride your horse as well as I ride you' (3. 4. 281), proclaims for all to hear.

But gulling is not merely exemplified by those designated as 'gulls' nor is its functioning simple. The dynamics of gulling is centripetal and draws many of the characters into its force field. For instance, we observe a spiral of

---

4 Leonard Digges' much quoted commendatory verses in the Preface to *Poems: Written by Wil. Shakespeare. Gent* (London, 1640).

5 Quoted by E. Story Donno, *Twelfth Night*, p. 8. The play was performed before Charles I at Whitehall on 2 February, 1631.

6 Gāmini Salgādo, *The Elizabethan Underworld*, repr. Alan Sutton Publishing Company (Gloucestershire, 1995), p. 26.

7 On the problem of the Elizabethan representation of the underworld, see A. L. Beier, *Masterless Men: The Vagrancy Problem in England 1560–1640* (London, 1985).

8 Bertrand Evans, 'The Fruits of the Sport' in *Shakespeare's Comedies* (Oxford, 1960), p. 130: 'Of the race of Bottom, Sir Andrew would be at a disadvantage if he were not being gulled; being gulled, he is doubly "out".'

9 Nashe, in *The Terrors of the Night* (1594), qualifies the gull in the following terms: 'Lives there anie such slowe yce-brained, beefe-witted gull' (*OED*, *sb.* 3, 1., quoted from Grosart, III, 257) and we note that Andrew Aguecheek inadvertently advertises his own gullibility by applying the epithet 'beef-witted' to himself: 'I am a great eater of beef, and I believe that does harm to my wit'; to which Sir Toby replies: 'No question' (1. 3. 80–1).

10 Evans, 'The Fruits of the Sport', in *Shakespeare's Comedies*, p. 135.

gulling in the activities of Sir Toby Belch. He gulls Andrew into providing him with money, and inveigles Viola/Cesario into a farcical duel, but his control of its energy falters when Sebastian appears, and his duping backfires on him. Indeed, gulling shows itself to be a reversible game since Toby himself is gulled most effectively by Maria. Such is the implication of Fabian's comment when Sir Toby, carried away by his delight in the spectacle of Malvolio's humiliation, says:

> SIR TOBY I could marry the wench for this device
> [...] *Enter Maria ...*
> FABIAN Here comes my noble gull-catcher.
> SIR TOBY (*to Maria*) Wilt thou set thy foot o' my neck?
>
> (2. 5. 175–81)

This moment is an example of the intersection of two trajectories of gulling: that of Malvolio by Maria and of Toby by Maria. This mistress of the game is also expert enough to synchronize two moments of gulling when, immediately prior to Malvolio's appearance before his mistress in yellow stockings, she represents him to Olivia as unhinged: 'Your ladyship were best to have some guard about you if he come, for sure the man is tainted in's wits.' (3. 4. 11–13), thereby tricking Olivia, just as she has duped her steward. It should be noted however that there are different varieties of gulling. The trick played on Malvolio is of the savage, vengeful kind (known in the *commedia dell'arte* as a *beffa*) whereas Maria's gulling of Olivia and Sir Toby is essentially harmless (thus, in Italian terms, a *burla*).[11]

Although as a 'waiting gentlewoman' Maria is socially and dramatically marginal to the play, her part in concocting the plot and stage-managing the gulling game in its opening stages reveals her to be at the centre of the secondary intrigue, the mainspring of the action. She is responsible for unleashing forces which bring about hugely comic situations before spinning out of control. In spite of J. W. Draper's exhaustive and perceptive character sketch of Mistress Mary, she nevertheless remains something of an enigma.[12] She never makes any comment on her role as a gull-catcher: all we are shown is her evident enjoyment in devising and executing her own schemes, and her apparent desire to please Sir Toby. Draper's conjectures regarding Maria's reasons for wanting to marry Sir Toby are plausible enough in terms of the social ambitions of Elizabethan waiting-women, for him the play's main theme is 'the Elizabethan pursuit of social security',[13] but Maria is as much a dramatic construct as a representative of Elizabethan society. Her role is steeped in comic tradition: adept at the classic techniques of duping associated with the *commedia dell'arte*, she is also

---

[11] According to B. Rey-Flaud, *La Farce ou la Machine à rire. Théorie d'un genre dramatique 1450–1550*. Droz (Geneva, 1984), the former is 'un bon tour pour rire' (a good-natured trick to arouse laughter), and the latter 'un mauvais tour' . . . 'pièce au déroulement complexe, articulée sur une tromperie fondée sur le jeu d'un mécanisme déterminant strictement les rapports entre les personnages' (a nasty trick ... whose progression is complex, involving a deception based on the action of a mechanism determining the relations between characters); p. 218, n. 50. The *beffa* is typically used to obtain reparation for insult or injury, as D. Boillet notes in 'L'usage circonspect de la beffa dans le *Novelino* de Masuccio Salernitano', *Formes et significations de la 'Beffa' dans la littérature italienne de la Renaissance*, 2 vols. (Paris, 1972–5) vol. 2, p. 101. See also K. M. Lea, *Italian Popular Comedy. A Study in the Commedia dell'arte 1560–1620 with special reference to the English Stage*, 2 vols. (New York, 1962).

[12] J. W. Draper, *The 'Twelfth Night' of Shakespeare's Audience* (Stanford and London, 1950), see the chapter on 'Mistress Mary', pp. 70–85.

[13] Draper, *The 'Twelfth Night' of Shakespeare's Audience*: '*Twelfth Night* is rather the comedy of the social struggles of the time. Orsino wishes to fulfill his duty as head of the house and prolong his family line by a suitable marriage; Maria wants the security and dignity of marriage to a gentleman – a difficult accomplishment in view of her lack of dowry. Feste and Sir Toby want the security of future food and lodging; Viola and Sebastian hope to reassume their doffed coronets; and Sir Andrew and Malvolio are arrant social climbers ... In short, this is Shakespeare's play of social security', pp. 249–50.

the trickster figure of classical comedy, the clever slave figure found in Plautus.[14]

Early in the play, the object of her desire, Sir Toby, apparently sees her in terms of sexual opportunity rather than wedlock. Feste comments on Sir Toby's failure to appreciate Maria: 'If Sir Toby would leave drinking, thou wert as witty a piece of Eve's flesh as any in Illyria' (1. 5. 24–6). This reveals to her the need to curb Sir Toby's carousing if she is to succeed in capturing his attention, hence her readiness to devise a scheme to be revenged on Malvolio for his disapproval of their drunken antics. The knight has to be brought to a realization of her worth as a wife. To use Leo Salingar's phrase, it is the experience of 'the pleasure of contrivance' that awakens Sir Toby to Maria's eligibility: 'She's a beagle true bred and one that adores me' (2. 4. 173–4). This appreciation of the pleasure of intrigue leads Sir Toby to want to emulate his better half, to become a master of the game himself, but forces beyond his control make his gulling misfire, whereas Maria not only emerges unharmed, but is rewarded, as Fabian reminds us: 'Maria writ / The letter, at Sir Toby's great importance, / In recompense whereof he hath married her' (5. 1. 359–61).

The case of Malvolio demonstrates how a gulling trajectory may be subject to inversion, for not only is the steward gulled by the plotters, but he is also in the grip of 'self-gulling'. In his egoism, Malvolio unwittingly appropriates the discourse of gulling. After reading the forged letter, he believes that he has in fact become a gull-catcher, having snared Olivia like a bird on a branch:[15] 'I have limed her' (3. 4. 75). This reveals the steward at the centre of a web of real and imagined gullings: 'self-gulled', about to be gulled, he believes himself to be the gull-catcher. To complicate matters, Olivia is, of course, ironically enough, the victim of a gulling, but not by Malvolio, by Viola/Cesario instead (an unwilling and unwitting gull-catcher). Thus various instances of gulling may coincide or intersect, spiral or reverse one another.[16]

But gulling may also be linear and sporadic, in contrast to the density of gulling trajectories enmeshing Malvolio. Thus in the course of the gulling of Malvolio, the cozening of Sir Andrew surfaces from time to time in the text, as when Toby tells Andrew baldly:

SIR TOBY Thou hadst need send for more money.
SIR ANDREW If I cannot recover your niece, I am a foul way out.
SIR TOBY Send for money, knight. If thou hast not her i' th' end, call me cut.

(2. 3. 176–81)

Likewise, later, Sir Toby refers unabashedly to his fleecing of Sir Andrew:

FABIAN This is a dear manikin to you, Sir Toby.
SIR TOBY I have been dear to him, lad, some two thousand strong or so.

(3. 2. 51–3)

This follows the broad outlines of the typical relationship between the would-be gallant and his gull described in Dekker's *The Guls Horne-book*[17] (1609). The author claims to write as the arbiter of advice to the man-about-town – as opposed to his opposite, a gull – but the syntax

---

14 Leo Salingar, *Shakespeare and the Traditions of Comedy* (Cambridge, 1974), p. 84: 'The lesson of classical "art" for the comic playwright was the pleasure of contrivance. And the other leading motif Roman comedy, readopted and constantly diversified by Shakespeare and his renaissance predecessors, was deception – the irony of the trickster.'

15 See *The Black Book's Messenger* by Dekker where Ned Browne designates 'the fool that is caught, the bird', in A. V. Judges, *The Elizabethan Underworld* (London, 1930, repr. 1965), p. 250.

16 This may be another example of what L. G. Salingar calls 'points of contact between characters' which is a constant theme in the play; 'The Design of *Twelfth Night*', *Shakespeare Quarterly*, 9 (1958), 117–39.

17 I have reproduced the title as found in the original printing. In *The Gull's Hornbook*, edited by E. D. Pendry , in *Thomas Dekker: 'The Wonderful Year', 'The Gull's Hornbook', 'Penny-Wise, Pound-Foolish', 'English Villanies Discovered by Lantern and Candlelight' and Selected Writings* (London, 1967), the title-page gives 'The Gvls Horne-book' (p. 67) showing that the editor's normalizing techniques have operated a grammatical choice.

of the title *The Guls Horne-book* is ambiguous, since 'gulls' may function as either a possessive plural or a genitive plural here. The choice of construction determines the meaning. Is it a manual of instruction for the gull-catcher or the gull? If the title has the sense of the possessive plural, then it is a manual destined for use by gulls, in order to avoid being gulled. Conversely, if the genitive plural construction is intended, then it is a work describing gulls, a manual for the would-be gallant whereby he may identify a gull (and take advantage of him). Furthermore, the grammatical ambiguity of the title is never elucidated by the hornbook's content, which implicitly ridicules the activities of the would-be gallant, so that there is only a difference of degree between his foolishness and that of his victim, the gull.

Sir Toby and Sir Andrew fit the categories of the would-be gallant and his gull to a nicety. Sir Toby is a 'kinsman' of Olivia's, apparently dependent on her hospitality. Salgādo suggests that part of the underworld society was composed of precisely this kind of rootless person, probably knighted in the wars and discharged from the army after some expedition against Spain[18] (the gallants in *The Guls Horne-book* are frequently posited as soldiers[19]). Demographically the lesser gentry were increasing in numbers in the second half of the sixteenth century, but decreasing in wealth;[20] enclosures, the abolition of the monasteries had swollen the ranks of vagrants; court faction also meant that today's great man (and his retinue) could be down on their luck tomorrow. If Sir Toby Belch conforms to the portrait of the gallant in Dekker's manual, and Sir Andrew Aguecheek is a perfect example of a gull,[21] then their association may be no accident, for Dekker recommends that every gallant should find a foil to accompany him:

Select some friend . . . to walk up and down the room with you. Let him be suited if you can worse by far than yourself: he will be a foil to you, and this will be a means to publish your clothes better than Paul's, a tennis-court or a playhouse.[22]

To be a successful gallant, it is desirable to practise a perfectly hedonist life-style, adopting revelling and drinking as primary occupations: 'your noblest gallants consecrate their hours to their mistresses and to revelling'.[23] And as in *Twelfth Night*, life consists not of the four elements but of eating and drinking, so Dekker advocates joining forces with a fellow roisterer and getting drunk in public:

And if any of your endeared friends be in the house and beat the same ivy-bush that yourself does, you may join companies, and be drunk together most publicly.[24]

Moreover the gallant lives by his wits, never paying for his drink if he can avoid it,[25] and the advice given by the hornbook is that gallants with empty purses should have recourse to gulling:

and, no question, if he be poor he shall now and then light upon some gull or other whom, he may skedler, after the genteel fashion, of money.[26]

Even though *The Guls Horne-book* was written in the decade following Shakespeare's play, it is possible to see it as an intertext to *Twelfth Night*, for it describes a category of person well known in Elizabethan London (or at least, in its fiction). Dekker's syntax of gulling has much in common with Shakespeare's: we see Sir Toby's strategies mimic the behaviour of the would-be gallant in the *Horne-*

---

[18] Salgādo, *The Elizabethan Underworld*, p. 111.
[19] See Draper, *The 'Twelfth Night' of Shakespeare's Audience*, the chapter 'Sir Toby Belch', pp. 26–7.
[20] S. T. Bindoff, *Tudor England* (Harmondsworth, 1950, repr. 1967), pp. 34–8.
[21] Draper in *The 'Twelfth Night' of Shakespeare's Audience*, chapter on 'Sir Andrew Aguecheek', comments on the 'fellowship between Sir Toby and this foolish knight, the archetype of the contemporary dupe': 'Such gulls as Sir Andrew feathered the nests of many a rare bird in Elizabethan London', p. 61.
[22] *The Gull's Hornbook*, p. 93.
[23] Ibid., p. 86.
[24] Ibid., p. 105.
[25] Ibid., p.105–6.
[26] Ibid., p. 97.

book. The reversibility of gulling is also suggested by Dekker, both in the title and in his advice to impecunious gulls that they should 'skedler' other gulls of money. In *Twelfth Night* the gulling game is reversed in the case of Sir Toby Belch, as we have noted. Equally, the term denoting his relationship to Olivia contains a certain semantic ambivalence, an inversion of its apparent meaning. At first Sir Toby is known as 'kinsman' to Olivia, but she later calls him 'Cousin' (1. 5. 113, 119) and subsequently 'my coz' (1. 5. 130), terms which may indicate a closer degree of relationship as well as suggesting that she is aware of his taking advantage of her hospitality, since the terms 'cousin' and 'cozen' were considered cognate by Cotgrave (1611): 'to clayme kindred for advantage, or particular ends; as he, who to save charges in travelling, goes from house to house, as cosin to the owner of every one'.[27] Toby is therefore acknowledged by Olivia as the swindler in their midst, but as we have already seen the word 'cousin' can equally well designate the victim of a cozenage, the 'practice or habit of [...] cheating, deception',[28] and this reversibility is replicated in his portrayal as both guller and gull.

Gulling, as represented in the literature of the underworld, is an essentially ludic activity, and, as such, rule-bound. A survey of early rogue pamphlets reveals its division into two main sub-genres: beggar-books such as the anonymous *Fraternity of Vagabonds* (1561) or Thomas Harman's *A Caveat or warning for Common Cursitors* (1566), and cony-catching tracts which were ostensibly written to expose underworld activities whereby the unwary were deprived of their worldly goods. One of the earliest exponents of this sub-genre was Robert Greene. His pamphlets span the early 1590s, and the first, *A Notable Discovery of Cozenage* (1591), contains narratives describing elaborate methods of cheating at cards. This is based on *A Manifest Detection of Dice Play* (1552), a tract attributed to Gilbert Walker. This narrative sets out a paradigm for cheating at cards which is subsequently expanded by Greene to provide formulaic accounts of other forms of cozening in *The Second Part of Cony-Catching* (1591), and *The Third and Last Part of Cony-Catching* (1592). There are also plays directly drawn from the rogue narratives of the pamphlets, such as the anonymous *A Knack to Know a Knave* (1592) where the protagonist is the arch cony-catcher Cutbert Cutpurse.

A Manifest Detection demonstrates the organization and codification of card-sharping crime, which functions according to specific rules just like an inverse form of law:

And thereof it riseth that, like as law, when the term is truly considered, signifieth an ordinance of good men established for the commonwealth to repress all vicious living, so these cheaters turned the cat in the pan, giving to divers vile patching shifts an honest and goodly title, calling it by the name of a law; because by a multitude of hateful rules, a multitude of dregs and draff (as it were good learning) govern and rules their idle bodies, to the destruction of good labouring people.[29]

There are many kinds of the 'art', but cheating is the common ground of them all and this is based on the cozener's capacity to dissemble effectively:

the first and original ground of cheating is a counterfeit countenance in all things, a study to seem to be, and not to be indeed.[30]

---

27 *OED*, v.

28 Ibid., 1.

29 *A Manifest Detection of the most vile and detestable use of Dice-play, and other practices like the same; A Mirror very necessary for all young gentlemen suddenly enabled by worldly abundance to look in. Newly set forth for their behoof*, by Gilbert Walker (1552), in A. V. Judges, p. 35. For comprehensive accounts of underworld literature see E. D. Pendry, *Four Pamphlets*, Stratford-upon-Avon Library (London, 1967), the collections of Frank W. Chandler, *The Literature of Roguery*, 2 vols. (Boston, 1907); and Frank Aydelotte, *Elizabethan Rogues and Vagabonds* (Oxford, 1913).

30 Judges, *A Manifest Detection*, in *The Elizabethan Underworld*, p. 36.

– a phrase which evidently evokes Viola's 'I am not what I am' (3. 1. 139). The rules for cheating with dice are set out in detail, and a frequent configuration described by Walker is that four accomplices lure a victim to participate in an elaborate game:

a jolly shift, and for the subtle invention and fineness of wit exceedeth all the rest, is the barnard's law which. . . asketh four persons at the least, each of them to play a long several part by himself.[31]

Greene takes up the same distribution of roles:

There be requisite effectually to act the art of cony-catching three several parties, the setter, the verser, and the barnacle [the fourth element being the cony himself].[32]

The narrative describes the complex interaction of the three rogues in extracting money from their prey: the plot is set in motion as soon as a suitable prey comes into view, typically:

a plain country fellow, well and cleanly apparelled, either in a coat of homespun russet or of a frieze, and a side-pouch at his side.[33]

and then the victim is duped into taking wine with the rogues:

then ere they part, they make a cony and so ferret-claw him at cards, that they leave him as bare of money as an ape of a tail.[34]

The ingenuity of such rogues is stressed: 'they do employ all their wits to overthrow such as with their handy thrift satisfy their hearty thirst'.[35] This same configuration surfaces in the gulling of Malvolio; there are three main gullers: Maria, Toby and Feste or Fabian (this may explain the mutual exclusivity of the last two in the gulling scenes), but Maria plays the most elaborate role, like the 'barnard' or the 'barnacle',[36] and she is careful to observe the tripartite pattern of the game:

I will plant you two – and let the fool make a third – where he shall find the letter.

(2. 3. 167–68)

Indeed the ludic dimension of the tricking of Malvolio is underlined by its designation as 'Sport royal' (2. 3. 166), and it is alluded to as 'sport' several times (2. 5. 173; 2. 5. 191). In the last scene, when the Duke is about to pass judgement on the affair, Fabian pleads for this view of gulling as essentially ludic to be upheld:

How with a sportful malice it was followed
May rather pluck on laughter than revenge
If that the injuries be justly weighed
That have on both sides passed.   (5. 1. 362–65).

We may equally question whether the inversion of values in the underplot of *Twelfth Night* where Sir Toby Belch functions as the Lord of Misrule, and honest everyday activity is absent, does not replicate the inversion of the rules of honest society demonstrated by the description of the cheating 'laws' in the underworld pamphlets.[37]

Nevertheless 'justice' is not always done, for as the authors of rogue literature recognize, the game can sometimes turn against its instigator, and biters can also be bit:

Thus we may see, *fallere fallentem non est fraus*: every deceit hath his due: he that maketh a trap falleth into the snare himself, and such as covet to cozen all are crossed themselves oftentimes almost to the

---

[31] Ibid., p. 47.

[32] Greene, *The Art of Cony-Catching* in Judges, *The Elizabethan Underworld*, p. 123.

[33] Ibid., p. 124.

[34] Ibid., p. 125.

[35] Ibid., p. 125.

[36] *A Manifest Detection*: 'the barnard go so far beyond him in cunning (i.e the taker-up), as doth the sun's summer brightness exceed the glimmering light of the winter stars' (in Judges, *The Elizabethan Underworld*, p. 47). This is an apt description of Maria's mastery of the game. A barnacle is, of course, a species of wild goose, but it seems probable that both expressions for this virtuoso role in the game are derived from the French verb, *berner*, to dupe.

[37] Greene, *A Notable Discovery of Cosenage*: 'High law is robbing by the highway side; sacking law is lechery; cheating law is play at false dice, cross-biting law is cozenage by whores; cony-catching law is cozenage by cards; figging law is cutting of purses and picking of pockets, etc.' in Judges, *The Elizabethan Underworld*, p. 135.

cross, and that is the next neighbour to the gallows.[38]

This mutability of fortune can be seen to apply to Sir Toby: his gulling Sir Andrew into a duel results in a bleeding head, and, as already demonstrated, he is comically 'caught' by Maria as a consequence of her success with Malvolio.

If gulling is a game, this implies performance, and, as such, it constitutes a spectacle. For example, the metamorphosis is verbally and visually an essential characteristic of the gulling process. In the table of words published in the *Notable Discovery of Cozenage* (1591), Greene informs us that in highway robbery the victim is called 'a martin'; in cony-catching law, the victim received the designation of 'cony'. In *The Black Book's Messenger* (1591), the same Greene lists the terminology used by Ned Browne, 'one of the most notable Cutpurses, Crossbiters and Cony-catchers that ever lived in England', which emphasizes the cynegetic transformation of all involved in the gulling process:

> He that draws the fish to the bait, the beater.
> The tavern where they go, the bush.
> The fool that is caught, the bird.[39]

Dekker, in *Lantern and Candlelight* (1608) appends a list of those necessary to execute a swindle in a game of cards where all the participants are designated as varieties of birds:

> In this battle of cards and dice are several regiments and several officers: . . .
>
> He that wins all is the 'Eagle'.
> He that stands by and ventures is the 'Woodpecker'.
> The fresh gallant that is fetched in is the 'Gull'.
> He that stands by and lends is the 'Gull Groper'.[40]

The *OED* records 'to grope a gull' as being synonymous in 1536 with the expression 'to pluck a pigeon'.[41] Thus the lexis of rogue literature represents gulling as the transformation of a human victim into an animal species, often into birds.

Similarly the representation of gulling in *Twelfth Night* recognizes that transformation is, by definition, inherent in cozening; Maria expresses her intention to transform Malvolio into his very opposite: to 'gull him into a nayword' (2. 3. 130); later she notes the success of her ambition, saying 'Yon gull Malvolio is turned heathen, a very renegado' (3. 2. 65–6). To be revenged on the steward for his reproval of their revelry, the plotters seek to change Malvolio into a creature of farce; like Bottom in *A Midsummer Night's Dream*, he is to be transformed into an ass, as indicated by Maria's comment 'Go shake your ears' (2. 3. 121). Sir Andrew, for once, manages a real witticism in this respect, for when Maria says: 'My purpose is indeed a horse of that colour', he replies: 'And your horse now would make him an ass' (2. 3. 161–3).

When Malvolio takes up the forged letter, this process of transformation is marked by his metamorphosis into a whole range of native woodland animals. Already, in anticipation he has been designated 'the niggardly rascally sheep-biter' (2. 5. 4–5), 'the trout that must be caught with tickling' (2. 5. 20–1)[42], and, as the extent of his self-delusions is revealed, the tricksters turn him into 'a rare turkeycock' (2. 5. 29). Then, just as he approaches the letter he is seen as a game bird (of a proverbially stupid nature): 'Now is the woodcock near the gin' (2. 5. 81); immediately after opening the letter he becomes a badger – 'Marry, hang thee, brock' (2. 5. 102) – then a bird of prey – 'And with what a wing the staniel checks at it!' (2. 5. 112) – then a hound sniffing at a scent

---

[38] Greene, *The Second Part of Cony-Catching*, in Judges, *The Elizabethan Underworld*, pp. 161–2.

[39] Greene, *The Black Book's Messenger*, in Judges, *The Elizabethan Underworld*, p. 250.

[40] Dekker, Thomas, *English Villanies Discovered by Lantern and Candlelight*, ed. by E. D. Pendry, Stratford-upon-Avon Library (London, 1967) p. 205.

[41] *OED*: 3. fig. b. slang: 'one who lets himself be swindled'.

[42] Cf. Dekker, *The Black Book's Messenger*: 'He that draws the fish to the bait [is] the beater', in Judges, *The Elizabethan Underworld*, p. 250.

while he wrestles with the conundrum of MOAI:

SIR TOBY . . . he is now at a cold scent.

FABIAN Sowter will cry upon't for all this, though it be as rank as a fox.

(2. 5. 119–21).

This process of metamorphosis (of the *basse-cour*) echoes that of the real court (i.e. the *haute-cour*)[43] where Orsino is changed into Actæon, the stag devoured by his own hounds, and Olivia compares herself to a bear chained to the stake, attacked by her own desires (3. 1. 117–19).[44] Malvolio too is transformed into a bear, as Sir Toby says:

To anger him we'll have the bear again, and we'll fool him black and blue, shall we not, Sir Andrew?

(2. 5. 8–10).

What is more, in his comic transformation, Malvolio may well change himself into a grotesque bird before our very eyes, when he says to Olivia: 'Not black in my mind, though yellow in my legs' (3. 4. 24–5). This kind of grotesque transformation intersects with the disguises adopted as part of Carnival, where the sober black and white garb of the Puritan is transformed into motley, the garb of the Fool, by the garish addition of yellow; his identity is inverted and subverted by the force of comedy. The imposition of a symbolic animal identity on an individual, as E. Le Roy Ladurie notes, was characteristic of late sixteenth and seventeenth-century Carnival and the person thus disguised was king of his *reynage* or faction: thus in Romans in 1580, the representative of the upper classes adopted the identity of an Eagle, that of the lower classes, a capon, a castrated cock. There are references to Malvolio's provisional castration in the constriction imposed by cross-gartering; and by exposing him to the force of satire, *via* visual and mental metaphormosis into a gull, we recognize one of the typical forces unleashed by Carnival, that of seeking to purge society of evil[45] – indeed Maria refers to her gulling as *physic* (2. 3. 166). Such evil is formulated in *Twelfth Night* as self-

love, hypocrisy, social ambition, elements united, for the gullers and for the play-goers too, in the guise of Puritanism. Indeed in this play deliberate trickery exposes hidden truth, evidence of a dialectic between truth and untruth noted elsewhere by Shakespeare, for instance when Polonius says: 'Your bait of falsehood takes this carp of truth' (*Hamlet*, 2. 1. 62).

It is possible that this visual transformation of Malvolio also contains a reference to the iconography of melancholy since the *OED* records as late as 1600 the adjective 'gull', meaning yellow:[46] 'Thou was full blyth and light of late . . . / And art now both gool and green': thus yellow stockings may also be the symbolic markings of a melancholic. Malvolio has therefore been metamorphosed into the comic double of Orsino, whose narcissism he reflects and comically amplifies.

Nevertheless metamorphosis is not the only element borrowed from the performance aspect of gulling as presented in the narratives of underworld literature. Other characteristics include putting on an entertainment for the sake of others – this is what Maria achieves by making Malvolio into 'a common recreation'. A typical cony-catching story demonstrates how the enjoyment of the spectacle of a victim's discomfiture constitutes an integral part of the action:

A kind of foist performed in St Paul's:

There walked in the middle walk a plain country farmer, a man of good wealth, who had a well-lined purse, which a crew of foists having perceived, their

---

43 See the analogy with the Carnival of Romans where social rank was replicated by the variety of birds adopted as disguises: the bourgeoisie assumes the identity of birds capable of flight, whereas the vulgar elements are earth-bound animals: Le Roy Ladurie, *Le Carnaval de Romans: De la Chandeleur au mercredi des Cendres 1579–1580* (Paris, 1979), p. 240.

44 Stephen Dickey, 'Shakespeare's Mastiff Comedy', *Shakespeare Quarterly*, 42 (1991), 225–75.

45 See Le Roy Ladurie, *Le Carnaval de Romans*, p. 345.

46 *OED*, 'gull', A. Obs.

hearts were set on fire to have it, and every one had a fling at him, but all in vain, for he kept his hand close in his pocket, and his purse fast in his fist like a subtle churl. Well, however, it was impossible to do any good with him he was so wary. . . . At last one of the crew . . . spoke to fellows . . . went to the farmer and walked directly before him . . . swooned . . . the poor farmer, seeing a proper young gentleman, as he thought, fall dead afore him, held him in his arms . . . the foist drew the farmer's purse and away . . . coming to himself, staggered out of St Paul's to join his crew and there boasted of his wit and experience.[47]

The ingenuity required to devise a plan to rob this particular farmer of his money commands the admiration of the co-plotters: a similar concern for and delight in plotting is evident in the play, as Sir Toby says, gleefully: 'Excellent, I smell a device . . . ' (2. 3. 156)

The 'play-acting' in St Paul's with the elaborate charade of the mock fainting emphasizes the incident's status as a dramatic interlude, and in *The Guls Horne-book*, Dekker describes how 'plotting' is one of the activities which occupy the gallant's leisure hours:

The Duke's Tomb is a sanctuary . . . There you may spend your legs in winter a whole afternoon: converse, plot, laugh and talk any thing.[48]

In *Twelfth Night* the plot to gull Malvolio introduces a theatrical *mise en abŷme*, the intradramatic doubling of all the aspects of performance. It is an additional layer of reflexivity in a play whose plot turns upon the confusion engendered by the existence of twins, where narcissism creates its own double(s), and where disguise inverts notions of sameness and difference.

In the sub-plot of Shakespeare's comedy, energy and appetite – characteristics of gulling[49] – are meshed with farce. Although the origins of farce are ancient, it was an essential component of Mystery and Morality plays and flourished in medieval France as a dramatic genre in its own right. In *La Farce ou la Machine à rire*, Bernadette Rey-Flaud argues that medieval farce was not an intrigue following a linear scheme but a tripartite mechanism, comparable to a syntactic group centred on a verb.[50] In her view, whatever the specificity of the verb according to the individual farce, its essential significance must be 'to dupe'. One of the expressions for 'to dupe' in Middle French farces, especially *La Farce de Maistre Pathelin*, was '*manger de l'oie*'.[51] It is striking that the paradigmatic image of the goose contains the same elements as we have seen in 'gull', i.e. a bird and the victim of a stratagem. Moreover, 'gull' in the dialect of Warwickshire and Worcestershire could, until relatively recently, have the meaning of 'an unfledged bird, especially a gosling': a sense found in Shakespeare: 'for I do fear / When every feather sticks in his own wing / Lord Timon will be left a naked gull, / Which flashes now a phoenix.' (*Timon*, 2. 1. 29–32); the word 'gull' here is cognate with 'goose'. In medieval fabliaux, the goose is an object of desire, thus an object of theft, an easy prey and a silly victim. These characteristics are codified in 1597 in a game entered by John Wolfe in the Stationers' Register as *A new and most pleasant Game of the Goose* (sometimes also known as *Fox and Geese*).

The association of duping with the image of

---

47 *The Second Part of Cony-Catching*, in Judges, *The Elizabethan Underworld*, pp. 167–8. This is a condensed quotation of the incident as indicated.

48 *The Gull's Hornbook*, p. 90.

49 In *Figures théâtrales: spectacle et société*, edited by F. Decroisette and Elie Konigson (Paris, 1970), B. Faure considers that the dynamic of farce is determined by the will for money, food and sex.

50 B. Rey-Flaud, *La Farce ou la Machine à rire*: 'on voit que le seul moment dynamique, celui qui engendre l'action, est constitué par la farce, qui fonctionne comme un verbe, porteur de l'action' (one notes that the only dynamic moment, which starts up the action, is constituted by farce, which functions like a verb, the part of speech which signifies action), p. 231.

51 Mario Roques, 'Notes sur Maistre Pathelin', *Romania*, 57 (1931) 548–60, sees the meaning of *manger de l'oie* to be *de faire moquer de soi* (to be an object of derision), p. 554.

a bird is therefore common to both gulling literature and farce. If we examine the lexical ramifications of the term 'gull' in detail, a further clue to the dramatic syntax of the sub-plot may emerge. There are earlier attestations of the word where the seabird – a prominent meaning of the term here – figures allusively as an image of appetite. Crowley in *A Way to Wealth* in 1550 has it that: 'Men that would have all in their own handes . . . Comerauntes, gredye gulls, yea men that would eate up mene, women and children'.[52] This meaning can be extrapolated to include the other sense of 'gull', i.e. throat or mouth, and which occurs as a verb, from the French *engouler*. Palsgrave (1530) glosses 'I gulle in drinke as great drinkers do', as 'je engoule'. There exists a further attestation (1607): 'O you that gull up the poysoned cup of pleasure'. In the seventeenth century, this sense is apparently always associated with revelry and indulgence in drink: 'They are roystering and gulling in wine with a dear felicity'[53] (a phrase which admirably describes the knights' activities in this play). On a semantic level Sir Toby and Sir Andrew inscribe themselves as 'gulls', so that the dramatic and linguistic ramifications of 'gulling' reinforce one another in the play.

In the last Act, the limit of comedy is attained with the denunciation of gulling. Of the tricking of Malvolio, Orsino remarks: 'This savours not much of distraction' (5. 1. 311), the pun on *distraction* indicating that he finds not only that the steward is sane but that as Duke and ultimate authority, he fails to appreciate the humour of gulling. Here the designation of the various victims as 'gulls' can be seen as the final stage in the dramatic syntax, since for Malvolio and Sir Andrew the term 'gull' is the culmination of previous insults: Malvolio refers to himself as the 'most notorious geck and gull'; and Sir Toby turns on Sir Andrew, stripping away any pretence of friendship, calling him 'an ass-head, and a coxcomb, and a knave; a thin-faced knave, a gull' (5. 1. 203–4). The ultimate metamorphosis bears no face, and as such it is the *ne plus ultra* of grotesque metamorphosis which marks the limit of carnivalesque transformation.

Examination of the context, or of the inter-texts, of gulling in *Twelfth Night* might reveal an instance of what Stephen Greenblatt calls 'the circulation of social energy',[54] when he argues that the theatre appropriates the energy of other kinds of discourse and adapts them for dramatic purposes. I would argue instead that the gulling game has affinities with theatrical representation since the simple narratives of the pamphlet literature enact fictive deceptions, in which comedy is often latent. To use Feste's expression (5. 1. 292) we observe how drama allows *vox*[55] to the potential of these narratives, the result being an amplification of the dramatic dimension of gulling and a release of comic energy, as palpable on the twentieth-century stage as in the seventeenth-century playhouse.

But this is not to say that the loss of the Elizabethan context does not, in some sense, weaken the impact of the gulling on the spectator. The playhouse itself was the site of much nefarious activity: cut-purses, pickpockets and prostitutes thrived in the vicinity, if not on the premises themselves. Leah Scragg goes as far as reading into *Twelfth Night* a meta-textual warning against pickpockets: she argues that Malvolio's reference to Olivia's Cs, Us, Ts and her great Ps spells out the beginning of the word *CUTP* –, that is, cutpurse.[56] The bear-

---

52 *OED* 'gull' n.[1] b.

53 *OED* 'gull' v.[1] Obs. 1. *trans.*

54 Stephen Greenblatt, *Shakespearean Negotiations: The Circulation of Social Energy in Renaissance England* (Oxford, 1988). Although Greenblatt states that 'in a *Caveat for Common Cursitors* (and in much of the cony-catching literature of the period in England and France) printing is represented in the text itself as a force for social order and the detection of criminal fraud', pp. 50–1.

55 In the Arden edition of *Twelfth Night*, 'allow vox' is glossed by J. M. Lothian and T. W. Craik as 'permit me to use the appropriate voice' (London), 1975.

56 L. Scragg, '"Her Cs, her Us and her Ts": Why's That? A New Reply', *Review of English Studies*, 42 (1991), 1–16.

baiting imagery associated with the treatment meted out to Malvolio may also allude to the proximity of the Elizabethan playhouse to the Bear Garden. 'Yon gull Malvolio' may then be designated as the most notorious of gulls, but certain of those looking on are gulled too, so the text reflexively implies that being a spectator to a gulling is to run the risk of becoming a gull oneself. Indeed the onstage gulling may have held a mirror up to cozenings in progress within the confines of the playhouse. Moreover, if the spectator has been led to believe in the innocuousness of gulling on account of its place in the comic underplot, the final moments of the play when Malvolio departs vowing 'I'll be revenged on the whole pack of you' (5. 1. 374) demonstrate that gulling takes comedy to its limit, and that in fact the playgoer may have been gulled into an assumption of its inoffensiveness.

In *Twelfth Night* gulling is allied with farce, but is also a means of exposing the truth. Malvolio, the pious Puritan, is revealed as an abominable hypocrite and a libidinous *arriviste*. But Maria is replaced by Feste as the master of the game, and the 'sportful malice' turns its perpetrators into sadistic persecutors in its latter stages, and demonstrates that gulling may unleash evil impulses in apparently good-natured characters. Malvolio has committed no crime, he is appreciated by Olivia for the quality of his stewardship and, if his humiliation may appear as poetic justice, his imprisonment and virtual torture cannot be justified; as Hazlitt remarks, 'poor Malvolio's treatment is a little hard'.[57] It has often been observed that Malvolio's refusal to participate in the festive ending points to the tragic potential of gulling, but the corrupting influence of the 'sport' on its agents passes without comment.

The darker implications of this ostensibly ludic activity may anticipate the Machiavellian appropriation of the sport by Iago in *Othello* (1604). Here there is but a single player, an infinitely more sinister master of the game than Maria, who nevertheless acquires diabolic associations by setting events in motion, being apostrophized as 'thou most excellent devil of wit' (2. 5. 199–200). But in *Othello*, the pleasure of contrivance is a private, perverted pleasure experienced only by Iago, whose gullings exceed the force of the *beffa* in their savagery. Like his counterparts, Iago takes delight in gulling, but unlike them, he revels in evil for its own sake; there is no satisfactory explanation for his obsessive desire to destroy, whereas we understand, and even sympathize with, the plotters' desire for revenge on Malvolio. Iago's prey, Othello, although not without failings, does not deserve to be cozened into murdering his wife, forfeiting his self-respect and taking his own life; thus the balance of sympathy is wholly on the side of the victims in this play, and the consequences of cozening result in the deaths of most protagonists. In *Twelfth Night* Malvolio's predicament awakens only tardy and partial sympathy and his refusal to join in the general celebration does not have any incidence on the comic *dénouement*; he emerges unscathed and unchanged from the gulling game. But the gulling of Malvolio (and even of Sir Andrew Aguecheek) has revealed that this is potentially, if not necessarily, a cruel game. Othello undergoes tragic metamorphosis, the efficient soldier being transformed into a jealous monster, and the moment of anagnorisis is reached when (as in *Twelfth Night*) the victim is called a 'gull' to his face. Emilia says to Othello:

> O gull, O dolt,
> As ignorant as dirt!. . . (*Othello*, 5. 2. 170–1)

The depiction of gulling in *Twelfth Night* progressively reveals its latent forces, for the game's centripetal energy corrupts the players: Feste's sadistic treatment of Malvolio in the dark contrasts with Maria's innocent enjoyment of a ridiculous spectacle. In *Othello*, the latent

---

[57] W. Hazlitt, *Characters of Shakespeare's Plays*, 1817, quoted in *Twelfe Night, or What You Will*, edited by Horace Howard Furness, A New Variorum Edition of Shakespeare (Philadelphia and London, 1901), pp. 378–9.

energy of gulling is unleashed and we witness the extent of its capacity for destruction. But the game's forces, multiple trajectories and dramatic syntax are identifiably the same in both plays. Hence the difference between 'comic' and 'tragic' gulling as exemplified by *Twelfth Night* and *Othello* is one of emphasis and not of essence.

THE GLOBE, THE COURT AND
MEASURE FOR MEASURE

JOHN H. ASTINGTON

Measure for Measure was written within the first twenty-one months of King James's reign, and probably first was seen on the stage when the Globe re-opened in the later summer of 1604, prior to the play's recorded performance before the king at Whitehall Palace on St Stephen's Day, 26 December. The long closure of the Globe, first for the death of Queen Elizabeth and then for the serious plague which immediately followed in 1603 and 1604, suggests on the one hand that Shakespeare would have had more leisure to write; on the other, that there would have been no compelling need for him to provide new plays when his company was largely inactive and had the prospect of remaining so. Court patronage provided welcome oases within this stretch of theatrical desert, and it has understandably fed suppositions that the grandly named King's Men had a rather closer relationship with their monarch than did any players in the old queen's reign. The payment of thirty pounds to Burbage on behalf of his fellows in February 1604 'for the mayntenance and releife of himselfe and the rest of his company being prohibited to p^{r}sente any playes publiquelie in or neere London', 'by way of his Maties free gifte',[1] particularly in the absence of similar payments to the other companies, may be taken as a sign of special favour. And if the company as a whole was favoured, their leading dramatist, 'the King's Playwright' as he has been dubbed by Alvin Kernan,[2] is quite likely to have responded with entertainment which reflected the new ruler's theoretical interests in the properties of government and the procedures of the law. Josephine Waters Bennett's notion that the Duke in *Measure for Measure* was a portrait of King James and was first played by Shakespeare himself is an extreme version of such fancies, but its implausibility need not lead to our entirely dismissing the likelihood that the actors made calculations about the taste of the new court audience.[3] The players' own suggestions about repertory would have been fed through the habitual conduit of approval by the Master of the Revels, and perhaps also by the Lord Chamberlain; on occasion the king himself made his own choice plain. It may be that *The Merchant of Venice*, presented before him at Shrovetide in 1605, had been chosen particularly to appeal to his interest in the issues of justice and mercy, but whether for that reason or for others it was a pronounced success, and the king called for a repeat performance two days later.[4] A piece nearly ten years old could hardly have been *written* with these occasions in mind, and the Shrove performances of Shakespeare's earlier play should warn us against reading too much into the

---

[1] Malone Society, *Collections Volume VI* (Oxford, 1961 (1962)), p. 39.

[2] Alvin B. Kernan, *Shakespeare, the King's Playwright: Theater in the Stuart Court, 1603–1613* (New Haven, 1995).

[3] Josephine Waters Bennett, *Measure for Measure as Royal Entertainment* (New York, 1966), chapter 9.

[4] Malone Society, *Collections Volume XIII* (Oxford, 1986), p. 9.

process of composition of *Measure for Measure*. The tension and the rhetoric of the courtroom, hairsbreadth escapes from the rigorous law, thrilling last-moment confessions and revelations of truth may all have suited King James's taste, but in that respect he concurred with most of his theatre-going subjects. Such material was a staple of dramatized stories in the sixteenth and seventeenth centuries, and it remains so today, although the stories are now more frequently watched on the screen than on the stage.

For all that, *Measure for Measure* had a literary genesis during the period I defined at the start of the preceding paragraph. The same space of time also saw the writing of a very different piece – *Othello* – yet the two plays share a common source in the stories of Giraldi Cinthio's *Ecatommiti*, some version of which Shakespeare must have been consulting in 1603–1604. But what led him at precisely this time to read or to reread George Whetstone's *Promos and Cassandra*, for example? It seems hardly likely that the old play, published in a single edition in 1578, received any theatrical revival in the late Elizabethan or early Jacobean years. Brian Gibbons has suggested that the royal entry by King James into the City of London in March 1604, in which Shakespeare took part as a liveried Groom of the Chamber, walking in procession, stirred the playwright's memory about an episode in Whetstone's play, and led to the writing of the corresponding part of *Measure for Measure* – the end of Act 4 and the start of Act 5.[5] And if James's ceremonial activities rekindled Shakespeare's interest in the dramatic episode of a ruler entering his city, the king's own writing – *Basilikon Doron* – seems equally likely to have influenced *Measure for Measure* in respect of the theoretical and speculative side of the Duke, and of his sententious tendencies.

Although all the evidence suggests Shakespeare's reading was wide, eclectic, and conducted in several languages, I want to concentrate attention in this paper on the influence of the medium in which Shakespeare worked as an actor and sharer in a playing company, the English theatre of the early 1600s, and more specifically on the repertory of the King's Men in the years preceding and contemporary with *Measure for Measure*. In the introduction to his Cambridge edition of the play Brian Gibbons puts forward a number of other dramas more recent than *Promos and Cassandra* from which Shakespeare may have drawn suggestions in writing his own piece.[6] Two of them he would have known at first-hand: Marston's *The Malcontent*, in its second theatrical version, and Jonson's *Sejanus* were King's Men's plays; while the third, Middleton's *The Phoenix*, was acted by Paul's Boys. But the dating of all three is problematic. On the testimony of the 1616 Folio edition of *Sejanus* Shakespeare had acted in the play at some time in 1603, although quite when and where remain obscure. Yet unless Jonson's own retrospective dating is out by a year – an unlikely proposition, I think – we can take it that Shakespeare certainly knew *Sejanus* before *Measure for Measure* was written. The other two plays are harder to date – they may have preceded *Measure* or they may not, and their influence is consequently moot. Since *The Phoenix* was not published until 1607 any awareness Shakespeare may have had of it did not come from reading printed text. There is, however, a fourth play which Shakespeare certainly knew by early 1604 at the latest, and which has a distinct claim to be a source for certain theatrical features of *Measure for Measure*.

This leads me to the question of what was acted by the King's Men at court in the first Jacobean English Christmas and Shrove festival seasons of late 1603 and early 1604, in the year before the St Stephen's night performance of *Measure for Measure*. The nine performances presented by the King's Men between early

---

[5] *Measure for Measure*, ed. Brian Gibbons (Cambridge, 1991), pp. 12–13.
[6] Ibid., pp. 15–24.

December and the third week of February are of considerable significance. Given the gravity of the plague in London and throughout England they must constitute a large proportion of the shows by Shakespeare's troupe during the long period – some sixteen months – when the Globe remained closed, opening only, so far as we can tell, for a few days in the spring of 1603 and for a week or two at the same time in the following year.[7] The plague of 1603 even left the keeping of Christmas court in some doubt. James held himself at some distance from London until the very last minute, when he was persuaded to travel to Hampton Court, the most remote from the city of the large palaces in the greater London area, and which was again to serve as a retreat for the Christmas court in the subsequent bad plague outbreaks of 1625 and 1636. There the King's Men presented six plays at Christmas 1603–4; when the court moved to Whitehall for Candlemas and Shrovetide they performed twice more at that palace.

For none of these occasions is the title of a play recorded. This is not an unusual omission from the court accounts: for most Jacobean court seasons we have little precise information about repertory; rather the season of 1604–5 is unusual in having been fairly thoroughly documented. One hint concerning the plays of 1603–4 is provided by Dudley Carleton, who was present at Hampton Court, in a letter to his friend John Chamberlain. He confirms that many of the plays were staged in the Great Hall, which survives today, and that on the evening of New Year's Day 1604 'we had a play of Robin Goodfellow'.[8] It is not unlikely that this was Shakespeare's *A Midsummer Night's Dream*, although the identification is not unanimously accepted by modern commentators. We can guess that among the nine plays in 1603–4 at least one more is likely to have been by Shakespeare – the relatively new *Hamlet*, *Twelfth Night*, or *Julius Caesar*, perhaps, none of which was presented in the following year. There is a tradition that the play performed by

the company for the King at Wilton House near Salisbury on 2 December 1603 was *As You Like It*; this seems perfectly plausible, if unverifiable.[9] The plays offered at Hampton Court would have been drawn from the King's Men's repertory at the Globe during the four years prior to its closing for the plague epidemic. Apart from those mentioned above and those shown at court in 1604–5 other Shakespeare plays staged at the Globe between 1599 and 1603 probably included *Much Ado About Nothing*, *Troilus and Cressida*, and *All's Well That Ends Well*. A dozen more plays by other authors may have been first staged during the same period, and might have been drawn on for showing at court in 1603–4.[10] Yet the modern legend that *Sejanus* was performed at Hampton Court is unsupported by any direct evidence. Jonson's preface to the 1605 edition of his play makes no mention of a court performance, which one might expect him to have proclaimed, given his rueful allusions to the play's failure 'on the publike Stage' – at the Globe, where I think the brief theatrical life of *Sejanus* is likely to have been entirely contained.[11] When this could have been at any time in 1603 is hard to guess, and hence the modern

---

7 See Leeds Barroll, *Politics, Plague, and Shakespeare's Theater. The Stuart Years* (Ithaca, 1991), pp. 101–16; 173.

8 Ibid., p. 120.

9 See E. K. Chambers, *William Shakespeare. A Study of Facts and Problems*, 2 vols. (Oxford, 1930), vol. 2, p. 329.

10 See Roslyn Knutson, *The Repertory of Shakespeare's Company 1594–1613* (Fayetteville, 1991), pp. 79–101.

11 Jonson's 1616 dedication of *Sejanus* to Esmé Stuart, Lord Aubigny, recounts that the performance 'suffer'd . . . violence from our people here', and that Aubigny was present '(if I well remember)'. The address to the readers advises that the text as printed 'is not the same with that which was acted on the publike Stage, wherein a second Pen had good share' (C. H. Herford and P. Simpson, ed., *Ben Jonson*, 11 vols. (Oxford, 1925–52); vol. 4, pp. 349, 351). It seems quite likely that by the early seventeenth century men of Aubigny's rank were attending the Globe: see Andrew Gurr, *Playgoing in Shakespeare's London*, 2nd edn. (Cambridge, 1996), pp. 71, 225. Aubigny appears to have taken up residence in London early in 1603.

inference that *Sejanus* was first performed at court, with its public failure to follow in 1604. The relationship between the published text and the stage history of Jonson's later play *Bartholomew Fair* suggests to me, however, that if there had there been an early court performance of *Sejanus* it is surely very odd that neither edition of the play should mention it.

The related matters of the dating and stage history of *Sejanus*, then, remain a puzzle. Shakespeare was a participant in its brief hour upon the stage, but as far as I can see this did not include acting in the play at court in 1603–4. But he would have taken a part in a second play also published, like *Sejanus*, in 1605, yet which clearly announced on its title-page that a court performance had been part of its history. The printed text of *The Fair Maid of Bristow* claims to represent the play 'As it was plaide at Hampton, before the King and Queenes most excellent Maiesties', and the preceding entry in the Stationers' Register of 8 February 1605 records that it was 'played at Hampton Court by his Maiesties players'. This relatively obscure anonymous play, then, is the only part we can now reliably identify of the King's Men's repertory at the Christmas court of 1603. And Shakespeare the player performed in it.

The Fair Maid has the air of an older piece which has been dusted off to serve the occasion, perhaps rather apologetically in the absence of anything better. The rather clumsily printed black-letter text, sold by Thomas Pavier, shows signs of prior theatrical use. At twelve hundred and twenty-five lines it is on the short side, and has probably been cut somewhat:[12] there are moments when the development of the plot seems rather abrupt, even allowing for its thoroughly conventional nature, and in need of rather more explanatory connective material, which a putative earlier version might have supplied.[13] The scenes, of which there are fourteen, rely on the audience's familiarity with staple situations and dramatic tropes rather than on presenting an entirely plausible and connected development, and to that extent the anonymous play seems very thoroughly a product of the commercial theatre; the unknown hand or hands which wrote it were not attempting anything striking or original. It takes the shortcuts only highly conventionalized drama can, when both players and audiences are familiar with a supporting framework of expectations and assumptions: hence the abruptness of the written form of much nineteenth-century melodrama, for example. The theatrical nature of the hypothetical cutting of the text of *The Fair Maid* shows itself in the retention of striking stage action where longer speeches may have been trimmed; several stage directions give full descriptions of gesture and movement. The entire play is an eminently practicable piece for the contemporary theatre, fairly simple in its physical demands; there are nineteen named roles, and it could have been played – as it was played – by a troupe of thirteen to fifteen actors, including four boys for the female roles, two of which are prominent. It could be asked whether Shakespeare's connections with the piece may have included his doctoring it into the shape of the 1605 imprint, and hence having given the kind of attention to its structure his responsibility as a player would not have called for. If so, the signs are he did a rapid but effective job, leaving a few stitches showing.

The play tells the story of a group of friends and lovers, and its themes might broadly be said to be constancy and betrayal. It begins with

---

[12] I use the lineation of the edition by Arthur Hobson Quinn, *Publications of the University of Pennsylvania. Series in Philology and Literature*, 8, 1 (Philadelphia, 1902).

[13] Quinn suggests that the play has been cut at the close of the third scene, where the marriage agreement between Vallenger and Annabel is very summarily concluded. On signature C3r there occurs the marginal direction 'The drunken mirth', between the exit of Sentlo and the entry heading for the following scene (9). This is presumably a fragmentary survival of a longer comic episode between the servants Frog and Douce, who betrothe themselves in the extant seventh scene.

dialogue between a pair of friends, Challener and Vallenger, who shortly quarrel over the eponymous fair maid, Annabel. Pairing is a structural motif in the play. There is a second pair of male friends, who also quarrel and are subsequently reconciled. Annabel, who becomes the patient and long-suffering wife of Vallenger, is set against the whore Florence, who seduces him from the straight and narrow. There are also two matched *senex* characters, both rather comically exuberant, the fathers of the married pair. The play is constructed in a manner common and conventional for its period, in short.

The first scene relies fairly heavily on *Romeo and Juliet*, both in situation and in language: the opening twenty-five lines of dialogue, in which Challener tells of his love and Vallenger professes indifference, end with the couplet 'then prethee peace here will we keepe our stand: / For by the Drum the Maskers are at hand.'[14] Romeo watches for Juliet's 'place of stand' (1.5.49) in the scene following that which opens with masquers preceded by a drummer (see 1.4.114–15). Before the dance begins, as in *Romeo and Juliet*, the paterfamilias greets his guests:

> Now gentlemen, your welcome to my house,
> Good maister Challener and your honest frend,
> So are you all young gallants every one,
> But we forget ourselves, boddy of me,
> Where be these Ladds, what shall we have
> No dauncing after dinner? Ho, up with the tables,
> If they have dined within, and come
> Yong Ladds now to your dance againe.

Sir Godfrey is clearly cast from the mould of Capulet.[15] The parallels continue: 'Here they dance' reads the stage direction, 'and Vallenger speaks.'

> VAL. False tong that spoke such blasphemy before,
>   That I dispraised, now doth my soule adore.
> CHAL. How dost thou like my love now Vallenger.
> VAL. O shees devine and I become her thrall.

This Romeo-like conversion leads shortly to a fight, so that the two theatrical excitements of the first act of *Romeo and Juliet* are both reversed and compressed into a breathless episode of rather more than fifty lines before 'Sir Godfrey, his wife, and his Daughter(s) comes forth with lights', as Challener flees and the match between Annabel and the wounded Vallenger is left to develop, as it does, like so much else in the play, with considerable speed.[16]

Although I characterized *The Fair Maid* as an older piece, then, it evidently postdates *Romeo and Juliet*, and hence was less than a decade old when performed at Hampton Court – perhaps it was of a similar age to *The Merchant of Venice*, the hit at the Shrove court of 1605.[17] And the likelihood is that *The Fair Maid* had been in repertory at the Globe before the break in playing in 1603 – there would have been a limit to the amount of dust the players would have been prepared to blow off their scripts. Even though it may have been some years old, then, the play had held the stage.

The second scene introduces another pair of close friends, Herbert and Sentlo, also disagreeing over a woman, but a woman of quite a different character: 'Florence a Courtizan'. Sentlo dismisses Herbert's warnings about his girl, and leaves with her, but Herbert follows, as he tells us, 'to prove a friend and not a foe'. The proving of character, we begin to realise, is to be a moral theme of the play. The following scene returns us to Sir Godfrey's household, to the business of marriage between Annabel and her new admirer, and briefly to echoes of *Romeo and Juliet*. In recommending her new suitor Annabel's father rephrases a line from the

---

14 All quotations follow the Tudor Facsimile Text of *The Fair Maid of Bristow*, ed. J. S. Farmer (London, 1912).

15 Cf. *Romeo*, 1.5.16–28.

16 *Romeo* is also imitated in a play which may be roughly contemporary with *The Fair Maid of Bristow*, the anonymous *How a Man May Choose a Good Wife from a Bad*, printed in 1602, and acted by Worcester's Men.

17 Roslyn Knutson assigns *The Fair Maid* to the Globe as a new play in 1603; see *Repertory*, pp. 115–18. For reasons stated in this paper I take the play to have been rather older.

mouth of Juliet's nurse: 'Looke yonder what saist thou to yong Vallenger,/ He is a man as twere compleat of waxe'.[18] Thereafter the play picks up the careers of the two estranged friends; first Challener, who announces his intent to return to Bristol disguised, in 'a Docters weed', and Herbert, who simply turns up in the fifth scene 'disguised like a Servingman', the aptly named Blunt, a kind of down-market Kent, under which cover he continues to act as critic of and counsellor to Sentlo. Disguise will remain a prominent feature of the play until its end – once again, entirely in accord with the conventions of contemporary theatrical entertainment.

Vallenger is no sooner married to Annabel than he falls for her antithesis, Florence (the two plots now connect), and seeks the help of 'an Italian docter' now under his roof – none other than Challener – in disposing, first, of the inconvenient Sentlo by poison, with Annabel to follow him later. Left alone, Challener declares that his project, born of dubious motives, has been a fortunate one, and that certain kinds of deviousness have good ends:

> Blessed be the time I tooke a Docters Shape,
> For by this meanes Sentloe his death shall scape,
> And lovely Anabell her life set free,
> False Vallenger shall be deceived by me,
> And that deceit is lawfull kind and iust,
> That doth prevent his murder and his lust

The false doctor will circumvent the false husband: he reveals the scheme to Vallenger's family. Annabel meanwhile is subjected to humiliation at the hands of Vallenger and Florence, which she endures meekly in the manner of Patient Grissell, subsequently defending her erring husband against the outraged denunciations of her father and father-in-law.

As the plots join, so does the plotting. Florence independently schemes to do away with her current partner, since she has assessed Vallenger as the more profitable target of her business skills, and she enlists Blunt – the disguised Herbert – to poison Sentlo, in a scene which concludes with further moralizing lines from the concealed friend. Once she discovers Vallenger has been cut off from his patrimony for abandoning Annabel and that it is too late to reverse her first scheme she adds him to Blunt's list: he is to be framed with murdering Sentlo. In an episode of extremely creaky theatre the drugged Sentlo staggers on stage to collapse, followed by a conveniently exhausted Vallenger, who lies down to sleep off his troubles. Blunt follows him, and, to quote the stage direction, 'stabs his arme, and blodies Senloes face, and pluckes out vallingers sword and blodies it, and laies it by him'. Blunt runs off to call the watch and an understandably confused Vallenger is arrested for murder; Herbert re-enters, out of his Blunt disguise, to claim the supposedly dead body of his friend, and as the arrested prisoner leaves announces:

> So this goes well, once
> Ile be blont again.
> For now the time(s) drawes on of his awake.

Re-entering he feigns surprise that his master has survived the evil Florence's plots, and then reveals his identity and his mission; like Hermia's on another occasion, Sentlo's reaction line is 'I am a masd, and knowe not what to say'.

We are now at the conclusion of the eleventh scene, and roughly at the three-quarter point of the play. Three scenes remain, and they deal chiefly with the workings of justice: a long scene of trial, a relatively brief prison scene, and a long final scene of threatened execution prevented by a string of revelations of the truth, as the discrepant awareness of the characters is brought into line with that of the audience, who theoretically know all, if they haven't become confused. My description of the final three scenes may offer some kind of answer to where this description of *The Fair Maid* may be going, and reassurance that I have not forgotten *Measure for Measure*. It may also suggest why *The*

---

[18] Cf. *Romeo* 1.3.77–8.

Fair Maid of Bristow was felt to be suitable for a court performance: the play concludes with the spectacle of justice dispensed by a fictional monarch, nominally King Richard the Lionheart, whose return from the Crusades opens the twelfth scene. As the two fathers call for justice on Vallenger, and Richard promises to provide it, Annabel steps forward:

> Have mercy, Richard, mercy in a king,
> Is like the peerles Diamond set in gold,
> He [*pointing at her father*] out of envy and of fury speaks,
> I out of love and passion plead for him.

'What pleasing advocate' asks the king, 'hath pitty rais'd,/ To plead the prisoners cause, himselfe not there.'

But Annabel's advocacy has to undergo considerable adversity before it prevails, and in spinning out suspense the plot rather sacrifices coherent motivation. So Herbert, still committed to kind deceit, reminds everyone of Sentlo's murder. More interestingly, Vallenger is overwhelmed with guilt and self-accusation: 'I do imbrace the law, as pleased to die' he says on being condemned; like Angelo in Shakespeare's play he has to be saved not only from the law but from himself. And Herbert's postponement of the truth catches him in the toils of the law; as Blunt, he denounces Florence, but is himself condemned to die as an accessory. The moral point of his silence, which otherwise makes little sense, is made clear in the following scene by the emblematic appearance of the friend he has saved now come in disguise to save him:

> Enter Sentloe like a frier.

> SENT. Thus like a frier I have disguised my selfe,
> To see my deere friend, that hath saved my life,
> And that same strumpet that
> Would have caused my death.

His approach to the prison appears to have been remembered by Shakespeare as he wrote 2.3 of *Measure for Measure*:

> But stay: I am at the prison gate, [*knock*]
> Where are you keeper, let me speake with you?

> KEEP. [*within*] Who knocks there?
> SENT. A fryer come to confesse your prisoners.
> KEEP. Stay ile bring them to you presently.
> Enter Vallenger, Florence, and Blunt, and the keeper.
> SENT. Health to this place: [*to* Vallenger] sir, let me speake with you.

And the disguised friar in *The Fair Maid* does indeed proceed to confess the prisoners: Vallenger, whom he cautions against despair, and Florence, who is garrulous, unrepentant, and flip, much as Lucio also is. The episode is short, however, and the final scene, dominated by the gallows platform, begins. The expected revelation is further deferred by an episode rather in the manner of Beaumont and Fletcher: two men step forward to offer themselves for execution in Vallenger's place, and engage in a contest of honour over which should be privileged to die. One is Challener, now dressed as himself, offering his life for Annabel's sake; the second is Annabel herself, in man's clothes. Her father recognizes her, however:

> Why my ledge, this is my child, my anabell
> Came in this disguyse,
> to save his life, that was the spoile of hers

In a further Fletcherian turn the annoyed king now announces that the suit for mercy is successful in that Vallenger is pardoned, but Annabel is condemned to death for her presumption, to be beheaded only by her husband himself. While absurd, this sadistic tyranny is a theatrical gambit to raise the stakes of pathos, and Challener responds once again with an impassioned offer to die in the place of the condemned prisoner, 'Should mercy pardon now what law doth threaten.' The mounting anguish is finally dispelled by the expected speech from Herbert, still the condemned Blunt:

> . . . now Soveraine hear me speak,
> If he that is supposèd slaine doth live,
> Then friendly may we reconsile these iars

The acts of the disguised Herbert and Challener are recounted before the final ace is played:

And Sentloe which by me should have bin slaine,
I saved him by an honest policie.
And now aliue present him to your sight,
To make a pleasing end of these sad sightes.

The stage direction reads 'Heere Sentloe putteth off his whod and kneeles downe.' The unhooding of an apparent friar puts everyone's understanding into a new frame, and the play moves quickly to its conclusion.

For all the factitious and flimsy qualities apparent as we read it there is no reason to think the play would not have worked quite satisfactorily in the theatre: it has a clear moral line, suspense, pathos, and a strong conclusion which satisfies an audience's expectations. Compared with many other second-rank plays it looks remarkably coherent, and it is quite likely to have drawn applause from the royal pair and the courtiers watching it at Hampton Court. What stayed with Shakespeare, it seems, was the theatrical force of the final episode of discovery, which combines, as it were, Lucio's unhooding of the mysterious friar with the Duke's revelation of the supposedly dead Claudio. What stayed with the company was the disguise costume which featured in both *The Fair Maid of Bristow* and *Measure for Measure*. The friar's robe carried to Hampton Court in 1603–4 was taken again to Whitehall the following Christmas.[19]

The questions of sources for and influences on Shakespeare are complex, but it may be readily agreed that *The Fair Maid of Bristow* is not a major source for the plot of *Measure for Measure*. Its story is quite different, and it does not make any use of Shakespeare's chief motifs, as Gibbons defines them, of the disguised ruler and the corrupt judge. There is no bed-trick substitution in *The Fair Maid*, although there is a debate, conducted in open court, about substitution first for a man and then for a woman condemned to death. But one would be guilty of Fluellenism to say that the two plays are alike because there is disguises in both. A larger but more diffuse question is how Shakespeare may have drawn on the very large bank of words

and dramatic situations he had stored up over a career of professional memorization, and of listening, on stage and from the tiring house, to many thousands more lines of dramatic writing. If a substantial proportion of these were tosh, he had a practical commitment to making the best of them as they were spoken on the stage. He knew the lines for at least one of the parts in *The Fair Maid*, and he had to support his fellows in making the play work before a very important audience. In any event the play's performance was a relatively recent part of Shakespeare's memory as he was writing *Measure for Measure*, in a period when theatrical performances were few.

Knowing this, what might we conclude? The most telling effect of the older play on Shakespeare's imagination may have been visual – the final moment of dénouement through unmasking. And the Duke's disguise as a friar occurs in none of the long-recognized sources of *Measure for Measure*; his arrival at the prison in Act 2 might well be Shakespeare's development of a sketch provided by the twelfth scene of *The Fair Maid*. The characters of that play also may have suggested certain aspects of his own, particularly the self-enclosed and gloomy Vallenger of the later scenes, and the faithful wife who is patient, entirely devoted, and passionate in her defence of her imperfect husband. It is Annabel's lines that have most claim to have had some impact on Shakespeare's, although on the face of it the possibility of verbal influence in that direction would seem to be absurd. But while pedestrian reworkings of *Romeo and Juliet* are easy to spot, Shakespeare's elaborations of verbal suggestions from external sources may not be so. The generally terse, unremarkable, off-the-peg

---

[19] This costume was used fairly frequently in the plays of the King's Men. There are friars in both *Romeo* and *Much Ado*, and a further disguise as a friar in the anonymous *The Merry Devil of Edmonton*, dated by Knutson as belonging to the Globe repertory of early 1603: *Repertory*, p. 195.

rhetoric in which *The Fair Maid* is written is entirely forgettable, but its language might, for example, have revived an earlier Shakespearian vocabulary. Across his entire works Shakespeare uses the verb 'remit' – in the sense of to forgive a forfeiture, debt, or punishment – only four times. Two of these occurrences are early – once in *Titus* and once in *Love's Labour's Lost* – and the other two are in *Measure for Measure*; once in Angelo's mouth, to Isabella, and once in the Duke's, to Lucio at the end of the play: 'Thy slanders I forgive, and therewithal / Remit thy other forfeits' (5.1.518–19). The word is used in precisely the same sense in the twelfth scene of *The Fair Maid of Bristow*, when the king initially seeks mercy for Vallenger: 'Sir Godfrey since your daughter doth / Remit his fault, methinks you should forgive him.'

Annabel's determined constancy to her erring husband and her passionate pleas for mercy in his defence appear to have been remembered not only in certain aspects of Mariana but also in the otherwise quite different Isabella. Annabel's lines may have percolated through Shakespeare's re-inventing imagination. One such moment comes in the ninth scene, where the abandoned and humiliated Annabel warmly defends the disloyal Vallenger against the curses and threats of her family:

> O say not so, deere father heele repent,
> And I shall have a husband of new birth.

The new birth arising from repentance and from accepting forgiveness – which Vallenger subsequently experiences – has a corresponding state in the reciprocal act of showing mercy. Isabella urges Angelo to think of the divine forgiveness shown to him by God, and to temper his justice accordingly.

> O, think on that,
> And mercy then will breathe within your lips
> Like man new made.
>
> (2.2.79–81)

Angelo's 'new birth' through repentance is more ambiguous than that of Vallenger; his 'penitent heart' craves 'death more willingly than mercy' (5.1.475–6), and he is given no lines after the revelation of the living Claudio. Whereas Shakespeare allows Angelo only 'a quick'ning in his eye' following the production of his supposedly dead victim (5.1.494), *The Fair Maid of Bristow* more typically underlines the point by having Vallenger exclaim immediately after Sentlo's revelation, 'This breaths new life into my hated hart.'

Following the shocking announcement that Angelo is condemned to death immediately after their marriage, Mariana pleads for mercy on the grounds that though imperfect her husband is redeemable: 'I crave no other, nor no better man' (5.1.423). And urging Isabella to join her, she repeats the point:

> They say best men are moulded out of faults,
> And, for the most, become much more the better
> For being a little bad. So may my husband.
>
> (5.1.436–8)

In defending Vallenger Annabel insists that if she can forgive him then so should the law, and in the final reconciliation she greets him as having actually been improved by his failure.

> Thou art more deere, more pleasing to my mind,
> then at the first: before thou prove[d]st unkind,
> tis insident for yong men to offend,
> And wives must stay their leasures to amend.

As Isabella heeds Mariana's request, and kneels to plead for mercy for the man she believes has compromised and betrayed her, her famous lines are:

> For Angelo,
> His act did not o'ertake his bad intent,
> And must be buried but as an intent
> That perished by the way. Thoughts are no
> subjects,
> Intents but merely thoughts.
>
> (5.1.447–51)

How far behind this complex construction of simple words, we may ask, lies the simpler line of Annabel as she defends her husband in the twelfth scene of *The Fair Maid*? 'Intents are nothing till they come to acts' she cries, as the Doctor gives his testimony about Vallenger's crimes.

And we may choose to answer that the verbal correspondence is simply coincidence – certainly the matter cannot be proved either way. But we are unlikely to argue over the proposition that Shakespeare's professional memory, made up of material from plays he had read, seen, and performed in, fed his own writing. *The Fair Maid of Bristow*, we know, was a fresh item in that memory at the beginning of the year in which he wrote *Measure for Measure*, and it should be admitted, I think, as one of the tints which produced the complex coloration of that great play.

MACBETH AND THE ANTIC ROUND

STEPHEN ORGEL

I begin my consideration of *Macbeth* some years before the Folio, for what seem to me good historical reasons: while it is certainly true, as historians of the book from Stanley Morison to Donald McKenzie and Randall McLeod have insisted, that works of literature do not exist independent of their material embodiment in texts, the printing of Shakespeare's plays is, nevertheless, really incidental. In their inception, in their conception, they are not books but scripts, designed to be realized in performance; and in this form they are not at all fixed by their material embodiment, whether Quarto or Folio (to say nothing of Riverside, Oxford or Norton), but fluid and open-ended. To realize them requires an infinite number of collaborative, often non-authorial, decisions, both textual and interpretive, which in turn eventuate in continual, increasingly non-authorial, revisions, excisions, additions. In this respect, Shakespeare plays have always been the free-floating signifiers of postmodern theory, standing for an infinitely variable range of signifieds. The play, that is, even in print, is always a process.

In the case of *Macbeth*, we are well into the process from the outset, since the earliest surviving version of the play, that included in the Folio, is demonstrably a revision. It includes songs for the witches, given in the text only as incipits ('Come away, come away, etc.'; 'Black spirits, etc.'). These are songs from Middleton's play *The Witch*. In performance they would have been accompanied by dances, which means that in the theatre these scenes took a good deal longer than they do on the page. The manuscript of Davenant's version of the play, prepared around 1664, includes the whole text of the witches' songs from Middleton – these are really musical dialogues, short scenes. The fact that Davenant did not supply his own witches' material at these points, as he did elsewhere, suggests that the Middleton material was already a standard feature of the play (Stanley Wells and Gary Taylor, in the Oxford Shakespeare, assume that the inclusion of all the Middleton material dates from the revision printed in the Folio, and include the complete text of the songs in their edition).

The elaboration of the witches' roles could have taken place anywhere up to about fifteen years after the play was first performed, but the presence of the Middleton songs suggests that Shakespeare was no longer around to do the revising, which presumes a date after 1614. Why, only a decade after the play was written, would augmenting the witches' roles have seemed a good idea? To begin with, by 1610 or so witchcraft, magic and the diabolical were good theatre business – Barnabe Barnes' *The Devil's Charter* was at the Globe in the same season as *Macbeth*, and Marston's *The Wonder of Women*, with its sorcery scenes, was at the Blackfriars. Jonson's *Masque of Queens*, performed at court in 1609, inaugurated a decade of sorcery plays and masques, including *The Tempest*, *The Alchemist*, *The Witch*, *The Witch of Edmonton*, *The Devil is an Ass*, and the revived and rewritten *Doctor Faustus*.

The ubiquitousness of theatrical magic is perhaps sufficient reason for the elaboration of the witches in *Macbeth*, but for me, it does not account for everything. When Macbeth, after the murder of Banquo, goes to consult the witches, and they show him a terrifying vision of Banquo's heirs, Hecate proposes a little entertainment to cheer him up:

> I'll charm the air to give a sound
> While you perform your antic round,
> That this great king may kindly say
> Our duties did his welcome pay.　(4.1.145–8)

The tone of the scene here changes significantly: the witches are not professional and peremptory any more, they are lighthearted, gracious and deferential. We may choose to treat this as a moment of heavy irony, though Macbeth does not seem to respond to it as such; but if it is not ironic, the change of tone suggests that the 'great king' addressed in this passage is not the king on stage, but instead a real king in the audience, Banquo's descendant and the king of both Scotland and England.

The editors of both the recent Oxford and Cambridge editions have resisted the suggestion that this moment in *Macbeth* reflects the local conditions of a court performance, observing that nothing in the scene positively requires such an assumption. This is true enough, but I also see nothing implausible about it, and though there is no record of a court performance, King James surely must have wanted to see a play that included both witches and his ancestors. What are the implications if we assume that the text we have is a revision to take into account the presence of the king, and that his interest in witchcraft also accounts for the augmentation of the witches' scenes, so that the 'filthy', 'black and midnight hags' become graciously entertaining after they have finished being ominously informative? Such a play would be significantly less author-centred than our familiar text: first because it is reviser-centred – and the presence of the Middleton scenes implies that Shakespeare was not the

reviser – and second, because it is patron-centred, taking a particular audience into account. To this extent Shakespeare's *Macbeth* is already, in the Folio version, a significantly collaborative enterprise. But if this is correct, it also means that this version of *Macbeth* is a special case, devised for a single occasion, a performance at court, not the play in repertory, the play for the public.

This leads us to another question: how did this text become the 'standard' version – why was it the right version to include in the Folio? It needs to be emphasized that this is a question whether we assume that a performance before the king is involved or not: there is no denying that this is a revised text with non-Shakespearian material. Most attempts to deal with this issue beg the question, assuming that what we have is indeed the wrong text, and that Shakespeare's first editors would never have included it if they had had any alternative. The right text, the text we want (the prompt-book, or even better, Shakespeare's holograph) must have been unavailable, lost – burned, perhaps, in the destruction of the Globe in 1613, as if only a conflagration could explain the refusal of Hemminge and Condell (who promise, after all, 'the true original copies,) to give us what we want. But perhaps it was included precisely because it was the right text – whether because by 1620 this, quite simply, was the play, or, more interestingly, because the best version of the play was the one that included the king.

This would make it an anomaly in the Folio, a version of the play prepared for a single, special occasion, rather than the standard public theatre version. In fact, the play as it stands in the Folio is anomalous in a number of respects. It is a very unusual play textually: it is very short, the shortest of the tragedies (half the length of *Hamlet*, a third shorter than the average), shorter, too than all the comedies except *The Comedy of Errors*. It looks, moreover, as if the version we have has not only been augmented with witches' business, but has also been cut and rearranged, producing some real muddles in the narrative: for example, the scene between Lenox and the Lord, 3.6, reporting action that has not happened yet, or the notorious syntactic puzzles of the account of the battle in the opening scenes, or the confusion of the final battle, in which Macbeth is slain onstage, and twenty lines later Macduff re-enters with his head. Revision and cutting were, of course, standard and necessary procedures in a theatre where the normal playing time was two hours; but if theatrical cuts are to explain the peculiarities of this text, why was it cut so peculiarly, not to say ineptly? Arguments that make the muddles not the result of cutting but an experiment in surreal and expressionistic dramaturgy only produce more questions, rendering the play a total anomaly, both in Shakespeare's work and in the drama of the period.

The very presence of the witches is unusual. Shakespeare makes use of the supernatural from time to time – ghosts in *Richard III*, *Julius Caesar*, and most notably in *Hamlet*, fairies and their magic in *A Midsummer Night's Dream*, Prospero's sorcery in *The Tempest*, Joan of Arc's and Marjory Jordan's in the *Henry VI* plays, and Rosalind's claim to be a magician at the end of *As You Like It* – but there is no other play in which witches and witchcraft are such an integral element of the plot. Indeed, whether or not King James was in the audience, the fact that it is the witches who provide the royal entertainment can hardly be accidental. The king was intensely interested in witchcraft; his dialogue on the subject, *Dæmonology*, first published in Edinburgh in 1597, was reissued (three times) upon his accession to the English throne in 1603. This and the *Basilicon Doron*, his philosophy of kingship, were the two works that he chose to introduce himself to his English subjects, and as I have argued elsewhere, witchcraft and kingship have an intimate relationship in the Jacobean royal ideology.[1] This is a culture in which the supernatural and witchcraft, even for sceptics, are as much part of reality as religious truth is. Like

the ghost in *Hamlet*, the reality of the witches in *Macbeth* is not in question; the question, as in *Hamlet*, is why they are present and how far to believe them.

Like the ghost, too, the witches are quintessential theatrical devices: they dance and sing, perform wonders, appear and disappear, fly, produce visions – do, in short, all the things that, historically, we have gone to the theatre to see. They open the play and set the tone for it. On Shakespeare's stage they would simply have materialized through a trap door, but Shakespeare's audience believed in magic already. Our rationalistic theatre requires something more theatrically elaborate – not necessarily machinery, but some serious mystification. For Shakespeare's audience, the mystification is built into their physical appearance, which defies the categories: they look like men and are women. The indeterminacy of their gender is the first thing Banquo calls attention to. This is a defining element of their nature, a paradox that identifies them as witches: a specifically female propensity to evil – being a witch – is defined by its apparent masculinity. This also is, of course, one of the central charges levelled at Shakespeare's theatre itself, the ambiguity of its gender roles – the fact that on Shakespeare's stage the women are really male. But the gender ambiguity relates as well to roles within the play – Lady Macbeth unsexes herself, and accuses her husband of being afraid to act like a man. What constitutes acting like a man in this play: what other than killing? Lady Macbeth unsexing herself, after all, renders herself, unexpectedly, not a man but a child, and thus incapable of murder: 'Had he not resembled / My father as he slept, I had done't' (2.2.12–13). Indeed, the definitive relation between murder and manhood applies to heroes as well as villains. When Macduff is told of the murder of his wife and children and is urged to 'Dispute it

---

[1] 'Jonson and the Amazons', in Elizabeth D. Harvey and Katharine Eisaman Maus, eds., *Soliciting Interpretation* (Chicago, 1990), pp. 119–39.

like a man', he replies that he must first 'feel it as a man' (4.3.221–3). Whatever this says about his sensitivity and family feeling, it also says that murder is what makes you feel like a man.

The unsettling quality of the witches goes beyond gender. Their language is paradoxical; fair is foul and foul is fair; when the battle's lost and won. One way of looking at this is to say that it constitutes no paradox at all: any battle that is lost has also been won, but by somebody else. The person who describes a battle as lost and won is either on both sides or on neither; what is fair for one side is bound to be foul for the other. In a brilliantly subversive essay about twenty years ago, Harry Berger, Jr, suggested that the witches are in fact right, and are telling the truth about the world of the play – that there really are no ethical standards in it, no right and wrong sides.[2] Duncan certainly starts out sounding like a good king: the rhetoric of his monarchy is full of claims about its sacredness, about the deference that is due to it, how it is part of a natural hierarchy descending from God, how the king is divinely anointed, and so forth. But in fact none of this is borne out by the play: Duncan's rule is utterly chaotic, and maintaining it depends on constant warfare – the battle that opens the play, after all, is not an invasion, but a rebellion. Duncan's rule has never commanded the deference it claims for itself – deference is not natural to it. In upsetting that sense of the deference Macbeth feels he owes to Duncan, maybe the witches are releasing into the play something the play both overtly denies and implicitly articulates: that there is no basis whatever for the values asserted on Duncan's behalf; that the primary characteristic of his rule, perhaps of any rule in the world of the play, is not order but rebellion.

Whether or not this is correct, it must be to the point that women are the ones who prompt this dangerous realization in Macbeth. The witches live outside the social order, but they embody its contradictions: beneath the woman's exterior is also a man; beneath the man's exterior is also a woman; nature is anarchic, full of competing claims, not ordered and hierarchical; and to acknowledge that is to acknowledge the reality and force and validity of the individual will – to acknowledge that all of us have claims that conflict with the claims about deference and hierarchy. This is the same recognition that Edmund brings into *King Lear* when he invokes Nature as his goddess. It is a Nature that is not the image of divine order, but one in which the strongest and craftiest survive – and when they survive, they then go on to devise claims about Nature that justify their success, claims about hierarchies, natural law and order, the divine right of kings. Edmund is a villain, but if he were ultimately successful he would be indistinguishable from the Duncans and Malcolms (and James I's of) Shakespeare's world.

Here is a little history: the real Macbeth was, like Richard III, the victim of a gigantic and very effective publicity campaign. Historically, Duncan was the usurper – that is what the rebellion at the beginning of the play is about, though there is no way of knowing it from Shakespeare. Macbeth had a claim to the throne (Shakespeare does know this: Duncan at one point in the play refers to him as 'cousin' (1.4.14) – they were first cousins, both grandsons of King Malcolm II). Macbeth's murder of Duncan was a political assassination, and Macbeth was a popular hero because of it. The legitimate heir to the throne, whose rights have been displaced by the usurping Duncan, was Lady Macbeth. When Macbeth ascended the throne, he was ruling as Protector or Regent until Lady Macbeth's son came of age (she did have children – it is Shakespeare who deprives her and Macbeth of those heirs). Macbeth's defeat at the end of the play, by Malcolm and Macduff, constituted essentially an English invasion – the long-term fight was between native Scottish Celts and Anglo-Norman

---

[2] 'The Early Scenes of *Macbeth*: Preface to a New Interpretation', in his collection *Making Trifles of Terrors* (Stanford, 1997), pp. 70–97.

invaders, with continental allies (such as the Norwegian king) on both sides. One way of looking at the action is to say that it is about the enforced anglicization of Scotland, which Macbeth is resisting.

Shakespeare knows some of this. In Holinshed, Macbeth not only has a claim to the throne, he also has a legitimate grievance against Duncan. Moreover, in Shakespeare's source, Banquo is fully Macbeth's accomplice, and the murder of Duncan has a good deal of political justification. All this would be very touchy for Shakespeare, because Banquo is King James's ancestor, and if Duncan is a saint, then Banquo is a real problem, the ancestor one wants to forget. Shakespeare's way of handling Banquo fudges a lot of issues. Should he not, as a loyal thane, be pressing the claim of Malcolm, the designated heir, after the murder? Should he remain loyal to Macbeth as long as he does? In fact, this is precisely the sort of question that shows how close the play is to *Hamlet*: in both plays, the issue of legitimacy remains crucially ambiguous. Nobody in *Macbeth* presses the claim of Malcolm until Malcolm reappears with an army to support him, any more than anyone in *Hamlet* presses the claim of Hamlet. In both plays, there is deep uncertainty about the relation between power and legitimacy – about whether legitimacy constitutes anything more than the rhetoric of power backed by the size of its army. Duncan tries to legitimize his son's succession by creating Malcolm Prince of Cumberland on the analogy of the Prince of Wales, thus declaring him heir to the throne. But this is not the way the succession works in Scotland – Cumberland is an *English* county, which was briefly ceded to the Scottish crown, and Malcolm's new title is the thin edge of the English invasion. James I himself became king of England not because he was the legitimate heir (he was one of a number of people with a distant claim to the throne), but because he was *designated* the successor by Queen Elizabeth; or at least several attendants at her death claimed that he was, and the people in control sup-

ported him. This is much closer to the situation in *Hamlet* and *Macbeth* than it is to any system of hereditary succession. And Macbeth is, even in the play, a fully legitimate king, as legitimate as Duncan: like Hamlet's Denmark, this is not a hereditary monarchy; Macbeth is *elected* king by the thanes, and duly anointed. The fact that he turns out to be a bad king does not make him any less the king, any more than the rebellion that opens the play casts doubt on Duncan's right to the throne.

Let us return to the witches' royal entertainment, with its songs and dances from Middleton. *The Witch* was written between 1610 and 1615; so by that time there was felt to be a need for more variety in the play, of a specifically theatrical kind, singing and dancing. I have suggested that witchcraft was good theatrical capital, but this does not really account for the revisions. Witchcraft was good theatre no matter what the witches did – spells, incantations, visions, appearances and disappearances, diabolical music were their stock in trade. It would not have been at all necessary to transform them into the vaudevillians they become for Macbeth's entertainment. If variety was required, Duncan's hosts could have entertained him at dinner as the King of Navarre entertains the Princess of France, with dances and a disguising; or Banquo's ghost, like Puck or Hamlet, could have interrupted a play within the play; or like Prospero, Duncan could have presented a royal masque to celebrate his son's investiture as Prince of Cumberland. Why bring the witches into it? But, to judge from the play's stage history, the vaudevillian witches constituted a stroke of theatrical genius.

Or did they? Consider the play's stage history. How successful, in fact, was *Macbeth* in its own time? Though it seems inconceivable that King James would not have been interested in the play, there is, as I have said, no record of a court performance – nor is there, in fact, any record of *any* pre-Restoration performance other than the one Simon Forman saw at the Globe in 1611, and reported in his diary. The

Shakespeare Allusion Book records only seven other references to the play before 1649; of these, only three, all before 1611, seem to me allusions to performances. A fourth, from 1642, is quoting it as a classic text. The remaining examples merely refer to the historical figure of Macbeth.[3] This, it must be emphasized, is a very small number of allusions: for comparison, there are fifty-eight to *Hamlet*, thirty-six to *Romeo and Juliet*, twenty-nine to the *Henry IV* plays, twenty-three to *Richard III*, nineteen to *Othello*.

This is all we know of the stage history of the play up to the Restoration. So perhaps re-inventing the witches was not a stroke of theatrical genius after all; perhaps all it did was undertake, with uncertain success, to liven up an unpopular play. When Davenant revised *Macbeth* for the new stage, he inserted the whole of the singing and dancing scenes from Middleton – this is, as I have indicated, at least arguably how the play had been performed on the public stage for two decades or more before the closing of the theatres in 1642, and it would thus have been this version of the play that Davenant saw throughout his youth. (Davenant was born in 1606, so he was going to the theatre in the 1620s and thirties). Indeed, since *The Witch* remained unpublished until 1778, it is likely that Davenant took his text not from Middleton at all, but directly from the King's Men's performing text of *Macbeth*. Pepys provides a good testimony to the success of these and Davenant's other additions. Between 1664 and 1669 he went to the play nine times. The first time he found it only 'a pretty good play, but admirably acted' – the admirable Macbeth was Betterton at the outset of his career. What Pepys saw on this occasion was certainly the folio text, with its Middleton additions. There-after he saw the play as Davenant refurbished it, and his response changed dramatically. It was, at various times, 'a most excellent play for variety'; 'a most excellent play in all respects, but especially in divertisement, though it be a deep tragedy; which is a strange perfection in a

tragedy, it being most proper here and suitable'; and finally, 'one of the best plays for a stage, and a variety of dancing and music, that I ever saw'.[4]

The interesting point here is the relation between 'deep tragedy' and 'divertisement', which clearly for Pepys is a critical one. It is what he likes best about the play – indeed, it is what makes him revise his opinion of the play from 'pretty good' to 'most excellent'. And what Davenant added to the play – songs, dances, spectacle – is not simply something to appeal to Restoration taste. He expanded and elaborated elements that were already being added even before the folio text was published in 1623. So that is something to pause over: the really striking theatricality of the tragedy, its emphasis not just on visions and hallucinations, but on spectacle of all kinds, and even overtly – in scenes like the witches' dances – on enter-tainment, and its move toward the court masque. We see *Macbeth* as the most intensely inward of Shakespeare's plays, in which much of the action seems to take place within Macbeth's head, or as a projection of his fears and fantasies. But if we look again at the text we have, and fill in the blanks, we see that, as far back as our evidence goes, a great deal of the play's character was always determined by what Pepys called 'variety' and 'divertisement'. Perhaps for early audiences, then, these elements were not antithetical to psychological depth after all. In this respect *Macbeth* resembles

3 The book tabulates seven allusions, but in fact includes eight. *The Knight of the Burning Pestle* and a play called *The Puritan* refer pretty clearly to Banquo's ghost, and *The Two Maids of Mortlake*, a parodic play by Robert Armin, the principal clown in Shakespeare's company, recalls Macbeth's 'Will all great Neptune's ocean wash this blood / Clean from my hands?' Since Armin's play was published in 1609, this must be a recollection of *Macbeth* on the stage. Sir Thomas Browne in 1642 saying that he begins 'to be weary of the sun' is more likely a recollection of the printed text.
4 For a fuller discussion of Pepys's response to the play, see my essay 'Shakespeare and the Kinds of Drama', *Critical Inquiry* 6:1 (Autumn, 1979), 107–23.

The Tempest more than it does the other tragedies.

The play's 'divertisement' is a quality that is largely lost to us, partly because it is only hinted at in the folio text, which merely indicates that the songs are to be sung, but does not print them, and partly because it is so difficult to imagine doing the full-scale grotesque ballet they imply in a modern production. Pepys thought divertisement should have seemed radically indecorous too; but, to his surprise, he did not find it so. What is the relation between tragedy and the antic quality of the witches? Why does that antic quality keep increasing in size and importance in the stage history of the play from the seventeenth through the nineteenth century? Addison, for example, recalls his attention being distracted at a Betterton performance by a woman loudly asking 'When will the dear witches enter?';[5] Garrick, despite his claim to have returned to the text as originally written by Shakespeare, kept all Davenant's witch scenes; and in 1793, when Mrs Siddons was the Lady Macbeth, Hecate and her spirits descended and ascended on clouds, and the cauldron scene constituted a long interpolated pantomime.[6] Clearly Mrs Siddons did not think she was being upstaged. Can we imagine similar elements playing a similarly crucial role in the stage history of *Lear* or *Hamlet*?

In fact, we can: in *Lear*, if it is the antic quality we are concerned with, there are Lear's mad scenes and the fool's zany speeches, which we find so hard to understand and pare down to a minimum, but which must have been popular in Shakespeare's time because new ones were added between the 1608 quarto and the 1623 folio. As for *Hamlet*, perhaps the witches externalize that anarchic quality that makes the prince so dangerous an adversary to the guilty king.

Suppose we try to imagine a *Hamlet* written from Claudius' point of view, in the way that *Macbeth* is written from Macbeth's. Look at it this way: the murder Claudius commits is the perfect crime; but the hero-villain quickly finds that his actions have unimagined implications, and that the world of politics is not all he has to contend with. Even as it stands, *Hamlet* is a very political play, and does not really need the ghost at all: Hamlet has his suspicions already; Claudius tries to buy him off by promising him the succession, but this is not good enough. It turns out that the problem is not really conscience or revenge, it is Hamlet's own ambitions – he wanted to succeed his father on the throne; Claudius, Hamlet says, 'Lept in between the election and my hopes'. The ghost is really, literally, a deus ex machina. But in a *Hamlet* that did not centre on Hamlet, Claudius' guilty conscience, which is not much in evidence in the play, would have a great deal more work to do. So would the ghost – who should, after all, logically be haunting Claudius, not Hamlet. This play would be not about politics but about how the dead do not disappear, they return to embody our crimes, so that we have to keep repeating them – just like *Macbeth*. In this version of *Hamlet*, Hamlet is hardly necessary, any more than in *Macbeth*, Malcolm and Macduff are necessary – the drama of Macbeth is really a matter between Macbeth and his ambition, Macbeth and the witches and his wife and his hallucinations and his own tortured soul, the drama of prophecies and riddles, and how he understands them, and what he decides to do about them, and how they, in themselves, constitute retribution.

What, then, about the riddles, those verbal incarnations of the imperfect speakers the witches? Macbeth is told that he will never be conquered till Birnam Wood comes to Dunsinane; and that no man of woman born will harm him. Are these paradoxical impossibilities realized? Not at all, really: the Birnam Wood prophecy does not come true, it just appears to Macbeth that it does – the wood is not moving, it merely looks as if it is. Or alternatively, we

---

[5] *Spectator* 45 (1711).
[6] *The Dramatic Mirror*, quoted in Gāmini Salgādo, *Eyewitnesses of Shakespeare* (Sussex, 1975), p. 299.

could say that 'Birnam Wood' is a quibble: Macbeth assumes it means the forest, but it could mean merely wood from the forest, the branches the soldiers are using for camouflage – it comes true merely as a stage device. As for 'no man of woman born', maybe the problem is that Macbeth is not a close enough reader: he takes the operative word to be 'woman', – 'No man of *woman* born shall harm Macbeth' – but the key word turns out to be 'born' – 'No man of woman *born* shall harm Macbeth.' If this is right, we must go on to consider the implications of the assumption that a Caesarian section does not constitute birth. This is really, historically, quite significant: a vaginal birth would have been handled by women, the midwife, maids, attendants, with no men present. But surgery was a male prerogative – the surgeon was always a man; midwives were not allowed to use surgical instruments – and the surgical birth thus means, in Renaissance terms, that Macduff was brought to life by men, not women: carried by a woman, but made viable only through masculine intervention. Such a birth, all but invariably, involved the mother's death.

Macbeth himself sees it this way, when he defies Macduff and says,

> ... though Birnam Wood be come to Dunsinane,
> And thou opposed being of no woman born,
>
> (5.10.30–1)

where logically it should be 'being not of woman born': the key concept is not 'no woman', but 'not born'. But Shakespeare seems to be conceiving of a masculine equivalent to the immaculate conception, a birth uncontaminated by women, as the Virgin's was uncontaminated by man.

So this riddle bears on the whole issue of the place of women in the play's world, how very disruptive they seem to be, even when, like Lady Macduff, they are loving and nurturing. Why is it so important, for example, at the end of the play, that Malcolm is a virgin? Malcolm insists to Macduff that he is utterly pure, 'as

yet / Unknown to woman' (4.3.126–7), uncontaminated by heterosexuality – this is offered as the first of his qualifications for displacing and succeeding Macbeth. Perhaps this bears too on the really big unanswered question about Macduff: why he left his family unprotected when he went to seek Malcolm in England – this is what makes Malcolm mistrust him so deeply. Why would you leave your wife and children unprotected, to face the tyrant's rage, unless you knew they were really in no danger?

But somehow the question goes unanswered, does not need to be answered, perhaps because Lady Macduff in some way is the problem, just as, more obviously, Lady Macbeth and the witches are. Those claims on Macduff that tie him to his wife and children, that would keep him at home, that purport to be higher than the claims of masculine solidarity, are in fact rejected quite decisively by the play. In Holinshed, Macduff flees only *after* his wife and children have been murdered, and therefore for the best of reasons. Macduff's desertion of his family is Shakespeare's addition to the story. Maybe, the play keeps saying, if it weren't for all those women ... ? It really is an astonishingly male-oriented and misogynistic play, especially at the end, when there are simply no women left, not even the witches, and the restored commonwealth is a world of heroic soldiers. Is the answer to Malcolm's question about why Macduff left his family, 'Because it's *you* I really love'?

So, to return to the increasingly elaborate witches' scenes, the first thing they do for this claustrophobic play is to open up a space for women; and it is a subversive and paradoxical space. This is a play in which paradoxes abound, and for Shakespeare's audience, Lady Macbeth would have embodied those paradoxes as powerfully as the witches do: in her proclaimed ability to 'unsex' herself, in her willingness to dash her own infant's brains out, but most of all, in the kind of control she exercises over her husband. The marriage at the centre of the play is one of the scariest things about it, but it is worth observing that, as Shakespearian marriages go, this is a good one: intense, intimate, loving. The notion that your wife is your friend and your comfort is not a Shakespearian one. The relaxed, easygoing, happy time men and women have together in Shakespeare all takes place before marriage, as part of the wooing process – this is the subject of comedy. What happens after marriage is the subject of tragedy – Goneril and Regan are only extreme versions of perfectly normative Shakespearian wives. The only Shakespearian marriage of any duration that is represented as specifically sexually happy is the marriage of Claudius and Gertrude, a murderer and an adulteress; and it is probably to the point that even they stop sleeping together after only four months – not, to be sure, by choice.

In this context, Macbeth and Lady Macbeth are really quite well matched. They care for each other and understand each other deeply, exhibiting a genuine intimacy and trust of a sort one does not find, for example, in the marriage of the Capulets, or in Iago and Emilia (to say nothing of Othello and Desdemona), or in Coriolanus and Virgilia, or in Cymbeline and his villainous queen (who is not even provided with a name), or in Leontes and Hermione. The prospects for life after marriage in Shakespeare really are pretty grim. And in this respect, probably the most frightening thing in the play is the genuine power of Lady Macbeth's mind – not just her powers of analysis and persuasion, but her intimate apprehension of her husband's deepest desires, her perfect understanding of what combination of arguments will prove irresistible to the masculine ego: 'Be a man', and 'If you really loved me you'd do it.'

But can the play's action really be accounted for simply by the addition of yet another witch? Macbeth's marriage is a version of the Adam and Eve story, the woman persuading the man to commit the primal sin against the father. But the case is loaded: surely Lady Macbeth is not the culprit, any more than Eve is – or than the

witches are. What she does is give voice to Macbeth's inner life, release in him the same forbidden desire that the witches have called forth. To act on this desire is what it means in the play to be a man. But having evoked her husband's murderous ambition, having dared him to stop being a child, she suddenly finds that when he *is* a man she is powerless. Her own power was only her power over the child, the child she was willing to destroy to gain the power of a man.

Davenant, redoing the play, does some really interesting thinking about such issues. His version has had a bad press from critics since the nineteenth century, but like all his adaptations, it starts from a shrewd sense not merely of theatrical realities, but of genuine critical problems with the play – problems of the sort that editors and commentators lavish minute attention on, but directors and performers simply gloss over or cut. Many of his changes have to do with elucidation, clarifying obscurities in Shakespeare's text, especially in the opening scenes. There is also a move toward theatrical efficiency in casting. In the opening, for example, Macduff becomes Lenox, Seyton becomes the Captain – it is difficult to see why these are not improvements. Davenant also worries a lot, to our minds unnecessarily, about the location of scenes and the topography of the action, matters Shakespeare is resolutely vague about. Thus when Lady Macduff fears that she is lost, her servant is able to reassure her that 'this is the entrance o' the heath' (2.5.3)[7] – do heaths even have entrances? Such moments are the price of adapting the play to a stage where topography is realized, location materialized in scenery.

The most interesting aspects of the revision involve the women. It has often been observed that since the Restoration theatre employed

---

[7] Davenant's *Macbeth* is quoted from Christopher Spencer's edition, *Davenant's* Macbeth *from the Yale Manuscript* (New Haven, 1961).

actresses, it made sense to increase the women's parts; but this is hardly adequate to account for Davenant's additions: for one thing, the witches continued to be played by men. It is the moral dimension of the woman's role that Davenant rethinks. Thus in a domestic scene that has no parallel in the folio, Lady Macduff sharply questions Macduff's motives, accusing him of ambition: 'I am affraid you have some other end / Than meerely ScottLand's freedom to defend' (3.2.18–19) – doesn't he really want the throne himself? Lady Macduff here articulates the same critique of her husband that Hecate does of Macbeth, that he is out for himself alone. Her fear articulates that perennial problem in the play, Malcolm's question about Macduff that never gets answered – where are your real loyalties; why is coming to England to join my army more important than the lives of your wife and children? The problem remains in Davenant, but is mitigated by the fact that Lady Macduff encourages Macduff to flee after the murder of Banquo. If it was a mistake, it was her mistake as well as his. Davenant's Lady Macduff also expresses a conservative royalist line, insisting that the only thing that can justify Macduff's rebellion will be for him to place the true heir, Malcolm, on the throne, rather than claiming it himself – the women, for Davenant, consistently articulate the moral position. Even Lady Macbeth, in a scene of love and recrimination inserted before the sleepwalking scene, accuses Macbeth of being like Adam, following her when he should have led her. But as Davenant's women are more important, they are also less dangerous: the Restoration Malcolm does not claim to be a virgin.

Revisers and performers have never been happy with the way Lady Macbeth simply fades out, and Macbeth is perfunctorily killed. The play does not even provide its hero with a final speech, let alone a eulogy for Shakespeare's most complex and brilliant studies in villainy. Malcolm dismisses the pair succinctly as 'this dead butcher and his fiend-like queen'. Davenant added a rather awkward dying line for

Macbeth ('Farewell vain world, and what's most vain in it, ambition', 5.7.83), and tastefully resolved the problem of Macbeth's double death by leaving the body on stage and having Macduff re-enter with Macbeth's sword, instead of his head. By the mid-eighteenth century, Garrick – who was claiming to be performing the play 'as written by Shakespeare' – had inserted an extended death speech for the hero:

'Tis done! The scene of life will quickly close.
Ambition's vain, delusive dreams are fled,
And now I wake to darkness, guilt and horror;
I cannot bear it! Let me shake it off –
'Twill not be; my soul is clogged with blood –
I cannot rise! I dare not ask for mercy –
It is too late, hell drags me down; I sink,
I sink – Oh! – my soul is lost forever!
Oh!

This Faustian peroration went on being used until well into the nineteenth century.

The editors of Bell's Shakespeare in 1774 declared themselves pleased with the play's ending, observing, with characteristic condescension, that Shakespeare, 'contrary to his common practice ... has wound up the plot, punished the guilty, and established the innocent, in such a regular progression of important events, that nothing was wanting but very slight alterations ...'[8] But there is a puzzling element in Shakespeare's conclusion, which is less symmetrical and more open-ended than this suggests. Why, in a play so clearly organized around ideas of good and evil, is it not Malcolm who defeats Macbeth – the incarnation of virtue, the man who has never told a lie or slept with a woman, overcoming the monster of vice? In fact, historically, this is what happened: Macbeth was killed in battle by Malcolm, not Macduff. Shakespeare is following Holinshed here, but why, especially in a play that revises so much else in its source material? Davenant recognizes this as a problem, and, followed by Garrick, gives Macduff a few lines of justifica-

---

8 *Bell's Edition of Shakespeare's Plays* (London, 1774), vol. 1, p. 71.

tion as he kills Macbeth: 'This for thy Royall Master Duncan/ This for my Dearest freind my wife,/ This for those pledges of our Loves; my Children/ … Ile as a Trophy bear away his sword/ To wittness my revenge' (5.7.76–82). The addition is significant, and revealing: in Shakespeare, Macduff, fulfilling the prophecy, is simply acting as Malcolm's agent, the man not born of woman acting for the king uncontaminated by women. But why does virtue need an agent, while vice can act for itself? And what about the agent: does the unanswered question about Macduff abandoning his family not linger in the back of our minds? Does his willingness to condone the vices Malcolm invents for himself not say something disturbing about the quality of Macduff as a hero? Is he not, in fact, the pragmatic soldier who does what needs to be done so that the saintly king can stay clear of the complexities and paradoxes of politics and war? Davenant does not quite succeed in disarming the ambiguities of the ending. What happens next, with a saintly king of Scotland, and an ambitious soldier as his right hand man, and those threatening offspring the heirs of Banquo still waiting in the wings?

MACBETH / UMABATHA: GLOBAL SHAKESPEARE IN A POST-COLONIAL MARKET

KATE McLUSKIE

Umabatha was presented in 1997 as part of the first season's repertory at the Globe theatre on London's Bankside. It was a curious piece, most memorable for the huge cast of astonishingly agile dancing extras and its energetic, but deafeningly loud, drumming. It was performed in Zulu with English sur-titles taken from text provided by Welcome Msomi and the programme included a scene by scene synopsis of the action. Yet, the play was recognizably *Macbeth*. It included all the play's familiar elements, including the witches, the bloody sergeant, the dagger scene, the ghost of Banquo, the murder of Lady Macduff and her son, the sleepwalking scene, and the final battle in which Macbeth is defeated.

The narrative came from Shakespeare but the setting and the style signalled the play's African origins. The witches who opened the action were young women with beaded hair who performed their magic by casting stones (or were they bones?) in a calabash. The cast was dressed in leather skirts and furry leggings, the men were armed with short stabbing-spears. The drunken porter drank liberally from a gourd and when Macbeth saw the witches' vision of the procession of kings, he induced the spectacle by snorting a powder. There was a splendid ceremony of dance and spear shaking for Duncan's funeral and the transfer of power from Duncan to Macbeth was signalled by Duncan's leopard-skin cloak ceremonially placed over the new king's shoulders in a gesture accompanied by further dancing and drumming.

Dancing and drumming provided the energy for the whole show. The dancers, though often huge men and women, were astonishingly agile and light of foot and the drumming, if somewhat repetitious in its rhythms, filled the open-air space, insisting on the shared physical relationship between audience and stage. The dancing and drumming also inflected the rhythms of the action, drawing out the battle scenes, giving a communal, celebratory quality to the key moments in the narrative. When Lady Macbeth, called Kamadonsela, received the news of Macbeth's imminent arrival, she was accompanied by her women 'stamping corn and preparing *tshwala*'.[1] The 'cry of women' noted as an offstage scream in the Folio text – the trigger for Macbeth's anguished contemplation of tomorrow and tomorrow – was fully dramatized in a long, keening lament. The witches, too, were part of this community of women. They performed their magic with giggling insouciance, a sort of girlish trick on the heroic men. Lady Macbeth was a large and equally cheerful woman whose early encounters with Macbeth were more comic harangue than evil insinuation. The women were not the evil, immoral opposites to the tragic hero: they,

My thanks go to Ken Parker and Shula Marks who generously shared with me their knowledge of South African theatre and South African historiography and to David Turley who lent me the books.

[1] Welcome Msomi, *Umabatha*, 2.1. SD (Pretoria, 1997), p. 21.

including the witches, were an alternative community, destroyed by the warriors' conflict.

The physical theatre of dancing and drumming, of course, diminished the dialogue and the soliloquies. The spoken parts seemed extraneous to the performance, requiring an attention to the text, retranslated from Zulu into modern English sur-titles. The sudden shift of focus from a noisy full stage to a quiet, empty one was disorientating. The spectacle of an actor, speaking an unknown language, by turns stroking his chin or furrowing his brow, turned Mabatha's (Macbeth's) performance into a series of mimed set pieces representing 'anxiety', 'guilt' and 'despair'.

In some ways, this production of a Zulu *Macbeth* was a commonplace enough event. Adaptations of *Macbeth*, including many with African settings, recur in every annual list of Shakespeare performances. The show's production values which substituted dynamic physical theatricality for the traditions of interiorized character interpretation can also be easily mapped onto and read against the protocols of contemporary performance theory. The performance of *Umabatha* was definitely Shakespeare without his language (as Dennis Kennedy puts it)[2] but Welcome Msomi's text which substituted African proverbs for Shakespeare's poetry offered no easy route into more abstract or resonant meaning. And though the production could have been configured in terms of what Dennis Salter calls 'tradaptation',[3] its style of performance was too firmly tied to Zulu drumming and dancing to demystify the social relations of Shakespeare performance in the post-colonial world.

Part of the problem was the style. Bare-breasted women with beaded hair and dancing warriors in furry leggings are a slightly embarrassing image of Africa for the sophisticated consumer of post-colonial Shakespeare, though the young, mostly (but not exclusively) white audience at the Globe lapped it up. As the *Guardian* reviewer put it, this was 'a form of tourist theatre which invites us to celebrate the

exotic and treat it as a photo opportunity'.[4] The implication of this review was that there could be an African Shakespeare which would not attract tourists and would offer a more discerning audience an insight into the real social and political relations of contemporary South Africa. The production, nevertheless, came with an endorsement from none other than Nelson Mandela. Unembarrassed by academic critical theory or a knowing appreciation of the witty paradoxes of global commercialization, he praised the production for its dramatization of 'the universality of ambition, greed and fear'.[5] The programme notes also told the story of the play's origins in a 1970 production at the University of Natal and then at Peter Daubeny's World Theatre Season at the Aldwych in 1972. An old product, in other words, had been repackaged, a process which began with the first Folio text and continued through rewritings, travesty and pastiche from Davenant's Restoration adaptation to the present day.

THE RHETORIC OF RECEPTION

In the endless game of pass the parcel which Shakespeare production has become, the packaging often seems as interesting as the product. This particular show, both a repeat and a revival and a tribute to Shakespeare, offers a way of understanding the process by which theatre practice is connected to political and aesthetic discourse, the way one culture connects to another, whether those connections are historical or geographical, Zulu or English, pre or post imperial, pre or post modern.

The *Guardian* reviewer's anxieties about

---

[2] Dennis Kennedy, 'Shakespeare Without his Language', in *Foreign Shakespeare* (Cambridge, 1994), pp. 1–19.
[3] Dennis Salter, 'Acting Shakespeare in Post Colonial Space', in James Bulman, ed., *Shakespeare, Theory and Performance* (London and New York, 1996), pp. 113–32.
[4] *Guardian*, 5 August 1997.
[5] Letter from Nelson Mandela to Welcome Msomi. Included in the press release for reviewers of the Globe production in August 1997.

'tourist theatre' which nevertheless offered what she called the 'irresistible toe-tapping hand-clapping appeal of traditional African rhythm and dance'[6] was also reflected in the reviews of the 1972 World Theatre season version of the show. In *Plays and Players*, Jonathan Hammond noted the 'professional performance standards' of the Natal Theatre Workshop company in spite of its University origins. Hammond also commented on the company's repertory which included Shakespeare and Brecht and Athol Fugard as well as following a policy of 'the promotion and fostering of indigenous drama'. The juxtaposition of names from the canon of European theatre with the concept 'indigenous drama' begged the question of how 'indigenous' was to be defined in the multiracial culture of modern South Africa and how the diverse traditions of dramatic performance associated with different ethnic groups might be assimilated by such cultural production. In the context of the 1965 Equity boycott of South African theatre, Hammond described the 'mixed feelings among those firmly against apartheid'. He connected the London production to contemporary politics, noting that the cast had been invited to a reception at South Africa House but that the South African government had provided no funding for the tour.[7]

A similar mixture of politics, economics and aesthetics was evident in critiques of the early productions in South Africa. Msomi's play was associated with other so-called 'black musicals' such as *Ipi Tombi* and *Kwa Zulu*. These shows sentimentalized and celebrated the life of the rural 'native'. Antony Akerman has suggested that this form of theatre in South Africa 'confirms white attitudes and prejudices and is blatantly paternalistic in the long colonial tradition' The Shakespeaian origins of *Umabatha* differentiated the play from the 'black musical' genre but Akerman still found it 'a bit of a bore – the result of Black art being diluted and marketed by commercial adventurers'.[8]

Akerman's and others' critique of the black musical genre focused both on the deformation of indigenous culture by modern theatre productions and on the exploitation of black theatre workers. The two objections were fused in his opposition between 'commercial adventurers' and his sense of the possibility of a politically acceptable authentic and unexploitative African theatre art. However, in the complex political and artistic situation of South Africa in the 1970s, there could be no simple polarization between progressive politics and commerce. Radical Black cultural activity was sponsored, in some cases, by finance from mining companies and commercial interests were often set against the reactionary censorship legislation of the apartheid regime which reduced theatre managements' access to overseas material and their ability to attract a larger, mixed race audience.

The black musical, too, had a complex political history. The form had first been developed in the Union of South African Artists' production of *King Kong*, a show about the tragic exploitation of a black boxer. It provided a showcase for the potent mix of American jazz and African music which created the idiosyncratic 'township sound' and it ensured the commercial success of that musical style by introducing it to more affluent white and international audiences. It launched the career of the singer, Miriam Makeba, and made township music internationally known. In the purely economic sense, *King Kong* was a 'commercial product' but it had been sponsored by a group of white progressives who had set up the Union

---

[6] *Guardian*, 5 August 1997.

[7] Jonathan Hammond, 'World Theatre Season 72', *Plays and Players*, 19, 7 (1972), p. 24.

[8] Antony Akerman, 'Why must these shows go on? A critique of Black Musicals made for White Audiences', *Theatre Quarterly*, 7, 28, (1997–8), 67–9; p. 67. Robert Mshengu Kavanagh, *Theatre and Cultural Struggle in South Africa* (London, 1985), p. 119, also notes that by 'being acted in Zulu and sited in the traditional culture' *Umabatha* had no base in the urban, Sotho speaking audiences of Johannesburg.

of South African Artists expressly to protect theatre workers from exploitation by record companies. The Union of South African Artists then used the profits from *King Kong* to found The African Music and Drama Association which was devoted to training and organizing Black theatre and musical workers. As Robert Mshengu Kavanagh has shown, the tensions between English and Afrikaans speaking whites and between different political and ethnic groups among blacks cut across any simple opposition between 'indigenous' and 'commercial' theatre. The politics and economics of 'Black theatre' constituted a site of considerable contest in the cultural production of the apartheid era.[9]

Umabatha's place in this cultural contest was extremely problematic. The play did not purport to be illustrating the lives of contemporary black South Africans but the fact that it was presented by a white management to a segregated audience linked it to the more thematically exploitative work. Its London tour also created economic problems. The review in *The Sunday Times* noted, possibly tongue in cheek, that the cast 'will stay, for community's sake, six to a room in a Bayswater hotel'.[10] However after meeting actors in London, the cast 'made demands for a fair working wage' and Peter Daubeny, the sponsor of the World Theatre season, 'had to raise £30,000 from private sources for the show to go on'.[11]

The principal impact of international success on *Umabatha* meant it could be reproduced. Its initial use-value as a show created in and for a particular theatrical occasion was transformed by its commercial success into a potential exchange value as the performance was repeated in different national contexts. After its success at the World Theatre Season, the show toured in the United States where it both received rave reviews and was picketed by anti-apartheid groups 'who believed [Msomi] had the support of the apartheid government'. The reproduction of the show also created a new career for Msomi himself. In an interview for the Durban

Mercury Showtime Msomi described how he 'opened a school of African dance and later formed an African dance group of black Americans'. His work in television brought about the meeting with Mandela when, he claims, Mandela asked him 'when he was coming home to stage *Umabatha* for a whole new audience'.[12]

In the post apartheid context, the reception of *Umabatha* was changed by the changing conditions of its production. Reviewing the 1995 Johannesburg revival, Lynne Goodman again referred to the discredited 'black musical' tradition but excluded *Umabatha* from the critique: 'Unlike the *Ipi Tombis* and *Sarafinas*, this is essentially a drama. If it drums up a storm with its dancing, it is not out to exploit ethnic spectacle.' Cleared of its association with reactionary politics, the commercial repetition of the show is now differently described: 'When this all-black theatrical venture was first presented, the audience was predominantly white. Now it includes many black watchers, waving their approval for a production that turns out to be as ever-green as the Shakespearian tragedy is universal.'[13]

The production, of course, remained commercial. The 1997 London production was managed by Columbia Artists and the *Wall Street Journal* review of the Johannesburg revival described 'a preview audience of business men' to whom Msomi was directing a bid for future funding. The review also notes 'Mr Msomi, a communications adviser to the African National Congress during last year's election . . . now

---

[9] Kavanagh, *Theatre*, pp. 19, 29–30, 88; see also Russell Vandenbrouke, 'Chiaroscuro: A Portrait of the South African Theatre', *Theatre Quarterly*, 7, 28 (1997–8), 48–57.

[10] *The Sunday Times*, 23 January, 1972.

[11] See Akerman, 'Black Musicals', p. 68

[12] David Coleman, 'Welcome return for playwright', Durban *Mercury Showtime*, 5 July 1995.

[13] Lynne Goodman, 'Shakespeare with a Zulu flavour', *Theatre Review*, 5 July 1995.

also heads an event management company in South Africa.'[14]

It is tempting, but I think impossible, to draw quick conclusions from this information. All it demonstrates, at this stage in the argument, is that the production of theatre is similar to that of other products in a mixed economy. As with other products, the rhetorics and discourses of its description and evaluation pay scant attention to its conditions of production. They circulate in a relation to other discourses, including, in this case, the discourse of the universality of Shakespeare.

The rhetorical polarization between authentic art and inauthentic commerce was further complicated by the role of Shakespeare in Msomi's play. In South Africa, as elsewhere, 'Shakespeare' was overdetermined as an emblem of human universality but in South Africa, in particular, 'Shakespeare' was also associated with the cultural pretensions of the settler community. In the emergent South African theatre, however, Shakespeare's plays provided safe (no censorship) and cheap (no royalties) production materials. Both black and white theatre groups produced the plays in a variety of conditions which included, as in other industrialized societies, a mixture of commercial production, state funding and semi-amateur fringe activities.[15] In all of these contexts, the 'universality' of Shakespeare could be quite casually invoked as a positive marker of value. Equally the concept could be used as the negative marker of traditionalism and *arrière garde*. The Durban *Daily News,* for example, contrasted the 'incredibly fresh' performance of *Umabatha* with the 'traditional, terribly British renditions of Shakespeare'. *The Star* contrasted the 'new naked brilliant theatre' of *Umabatha* with the 'safe English theatre' and the reviewer of Johannesburg *Sunday Times* considered that 'In *Macbeth*, the ghosts seem silly: in *Umabatha* they are entirely credible and potent. The ancestors are always with us, and that is the crux of Msomi's version.'

The reviewer for *The Sowetan,* on the other hand, deplored the fact that township audiences should 'form a beeline to the Standard Bank Arena to see Phil Collins and not do the same with our own products'.[16] In the new South Africa, Shakespeare, as adapted by Msomi, could be celebrated as a local product in opposition to 'British Shakespeare' but Shakespeare was also invoked as the bearer of the values of serious culture, set in opposition to imported mass culture in a commercial venue.

THE POST-COLONIAL SPIN

In the world-market of international cultural production, individual products have to be validated by invoking notions so embedded in cultural assumptions as to seem unchallengeable, however much they are contested and deconstructed by intellectuals. In the particular post colonial context, however, those assumptions also intersect with rhetorics of anti-colonialism. The familiar opposition between commerce and art is articulated through an alternative opposition between the colonizing power and a purposefully homogenized indigenous culture. When *Umabatha* was re-imported onto the Bankside Globe, the press release and programme notes which accompanied it managed those intersecting lines of opposition in intriguing ways. They told the story of how Msomi was encouraged by Elizabeth Sneddon, professor of Drama at the University of Natal, to 'write a play about the

---

[14] Philip Revzin, 'A Zuluized Macbeth', *The Wall Street Journal,* 14 June 1995.

[15] See Kavanagh, *Theatre,* p. 53; Vandenbrouke, 'Chiaroscuro', p. 45, David Johnson, *Shakespeare and South Africa,* (Oxford, 1996) and Martin Orkin, *Shakespeare Against Apartheid* (Johannesburg, 1987), passim.

[16] See Suzy Bell, 'Msomi's Macbeth fresh and energetic', *Durban Daily News,* 10 June 1996; Richard Lawton, 'Reasons to love Umabatha', *The Star,* 24 May 1995; Charlotte Bauer, 'Viva Macbeth (and Umabatha)', *The Sunday Times* (Johannesburg), 21 May 1995; Elliot Makhaya, 'Take Pride in African Soul Brew', *The Sowetan,* 12 June 1995.

great African nations, based on universal epics so that the world at large would be able to understand and follow the intended play'.

Elizabeth Sneddon's interest in 'the great African nations, based on universal epics' betrayed assumptions about the most appropriate subject matter and style for an African dramatist in 1969, but the end product was interestingly at odds with her Africanist project. Msomi describes how

To be honest, I never took Professor Sneddon's suggestion seriously, and when, after six months, she asked me if I had completed the Zulu epic (which at the time I hadn't given much thought), to avoid embarrassing myself, I told her it was almost completed. The Professor smiled and asked me the title of the play, without hesitation I told her – Umabatha ... I also told her how I had incorporated the traditional symbols which became part of a Zulu story ... In three nights I completed the script which I then submitted to Professor Sneddon, and in two weeks the cast of 55 performers was assembled.

With a deadline to meet, the author could re-use Shakespeare's narrative, taking the disconnected raw materials of culture and assimilating them to a new work, the performance at the University of Natal of Umabatha.

This process of re-assimilation, however, required a discursive as well as a stylistic connection between Shakespeare and African culture. In the repackaging of the play in the 1990s, a connection was suggested between Shakespeare's Macbeth and the famous story of the great Zulu warrior Shaka. Msomi wrote

What inspired me to choose Macbeth is that the intrigue, plots and counterplots of the Scottish clans were almost a carbon copy of the drama that took place with the early nations of Africa ... As in Macbeth, Shaka the great warrior king was also murdered by those close to him.[17]

Msomi's account of the connection between Shakespeare and Shaka makes a generalized claim for a new synthesis, building on buried assumptions both about the continuing relevance of Shakespeare and about the capacity of a post-colonial culture to enact similarly universal themes. The Shakespearian history and the Zulu history are equally available for cultural recycling. A narrative of witchcraft and murder among the primitive Scots is presented as a synecdoche of Shakespeare's play: an anecdote from the Shaka myth can stand in for the whole of South Africa's pre-colonial history.

In linking Shakespeare to Shaka, Msomi connected two of the most potent and contradictory names in Southern African culture. Shaka was the revolutionary founder of the Zulu nation, organizing the disparate peoples of the Nguni into a fighting machine, conducting a series of wars with the surrounding population which significantly increased the territories of the Zulu people. His story became one of the most contested arenas of Southern African history and politics, not least because the events which it retold took place at the time of the Boer and English migration into the Transvaal.[18] The sources for that history layered oral narratives, the memoirs of white traders, imperial apologetics and the data of treaties, all of which were used by subsequent historians with a variety of more or less explicit political agendas.[19] The historiography of the Shaka revolution (and that term in South African historiography is as contentious as 'the English revolution' in early modern historiography) involved struggles between the disciplines of history and anthropology and complex resistances between a liberal Africanizing history exemplified by Elizabeth Sneddon's interest and the equally energetically Africanizing impulses of the exponents of a transhistorical 'Bantu mentality'.[20] Most recently Shaka has been written out of the story and the mfecane which he initiated has been interpreted as a response to an ecological crisis

---

[17] Programme notes for the Globe Theatre production August 1997.
[18] See Christopher Saunders, The Making of the South African Past (Capetown, SA, 1988)
[19] See Carolyn Hamilton, Terrific Majesty: Powers of Shaka Zulu and the Limits of Historical Invention (Boston, 1998).
[20] See Saunders, South African Past, p. 155.

which quite overshadowed the arrival of white settlers.[21]

These cross currents in historiography were also embodied in a huge range of fictionalized versions from a large number of writers from all over Africa.[22] Each version, like each adaptation of a Shakespeare play, signals the ideological versatility of the story. The Zulu leader's outcast origins have allowed him to be presented as a champion of the free individual spirit, his commitment to discipline and triumph over hardship have provided a message for socialist African politicians of the post-independence generation and his fusion of the disparate Nguni peoples into the powerful Zulu nation has been presented as an allegory of both pan-Africanism and the aspiration for a modern independent Zulu nation of Chief Buthelezi.[23] In more recent times, the story of Shaka was also used as the first home-produced drama series for South African television and the location sets for that series were used to furnish and equip an upmarket theme park where multi-ethnic and international visitors can view a 'traditional way of life' and be instructed in Zulu ritual and life-style by Zulu people.[24]

These many different literary and entrepreneurial strands which make up the Shaka myth suggest that it is just as complex and just as culturally useful as the Shakespeare myth. Msomi used his version of the Shaka-myth to provide a pseudo-historical commentary which would validate his play as an intervention in a cultural exchange between South Africa and the rest of the world. A similar commentary was required to inflect the significance of Shakespeare and *Macbeth* to the same end. The 'plots and counter plots' of the Scottish clans, which Msomi invoked to connect *Macbeth* to Shaka, have no more part in the narrative of Shakespeare's tragedy than the myth of Shaka in the action of Msomi's play. Nevertheless, by invoking a primitive Scotland, Msomi brought together the history of the two nations, the English and the Zulu, connecting both of them to a pre-modern moment before the differences

imposed by imperialism took effect. One of the most important strands in the Shaka myth was the Zulu warrior's efforts to forge a unified modern nation. In Masizi Kunene's introduction to *Emperor Shaka the Great, A Zulu Epic*, for example, he asserts that

in Britain (before unification) there were regions often referred to as kingdoms, even though some were no more than a third of what would amount to a princedom in the early Nguni and Sotho states of the pre-Shakan period,

and in F. M. Mulikita's, *Shaka Zulu a Play*, he emphasizes Shaka's importance as a modernizer, introducing the institutions of 'monarchy, government, cleanliness and discipline and social security'.[25] The reminder that Britain had not always been a unified imperial power carried a political resonance which was reinforced by the link between Shaka and Macbeth. Pre-modern Scotland was equated with pre-modern South Africa as a way of validating the use of Zulu dancing as an appropriate form for the re-enactment of the Scottish play.

The resulting spectacle bore only a mediated relationship to the traditional dances and drumming of Zulu culture: the conditions of their performance, the separation of a paying, spectating audience from the performers, the transformation from dance as ritual to dance as performance all contribute to the changed effect. However, the discursive link between Shaka and Macbeth and by implication between Msomi and Shakespeare, both validated the play and attempted to shield it from the negative

[21] See Jeff Guy, 'Ecological Factors in the rise of Shaka and the Zulu kingdom', in *Economy and Society in Pre-Industrial South Africa*, edited by Shula Marks and Antony Atmore (London, 1980) pp. 102–19.

[22] See Donald Burness, *Shaka King of the Zulus in African Literature* (Boston, 1976).

[23] See Jordan Kush Ngubane, 'Shaka's social, political and military ideas' in Burness, *Shaka King*, pp. 127–64.

[24] See Hamilton, *Terrific Majesty*.

[25] Masizi Kunene, *Emperor Shaka the Great, A Zulu Epic* (London, 1979), p. 15; F. M. Mulikita, *Shaka Zulu a Play* (Lusaka, 1967), p. 65.

political associations which had affected its original performances.

CULTURAL CONCLUSIONS

Welcome Msomi's commentary on his play, his claim to represent a history shared by both Shakespeare's play and the traditions of Zulu culture, offered a set of claims for the production's cultural value. The history *of* the play (the story of the Drama professor and the African playwright) and the history *in* the play (the story of the Zulus and the Scottish clans) claimed an attention which would transcend the mere exchange-value of the play's commercial success and increase the use-value of shared aesthetic experience by extending its significance to the contemporary political moment.

Msomi was able to effect this connection because of the terms of value which had become attached to Shakespeare since the modernist moment. As Richard Halpern has shown, 'Shakespeare's "universal" quality, his presumed ability to embody a world culture, were tied, in the early twentieth century to "the empire on which the sun never sets".'[26] Writers from the same 'empire' however, could also co-opt Shakespeare for their own forms of cultural resistance. Sol Plaatje, the first translator of Shakespeare into Tswana, admired Shakespeare's ability to show that virtue transcends colour and

hoped that with the maturity of African literature, now still in its infancy, writers and translators, will consider giving to Africans the benefit of some at least of Shakespeare's work. That this could be done is suggested by the probability that some of the stories on which his dramas are based find equivalents in African folk-lore.[27]

The perceived thematic connection between Shakespeare and world culture, moreover was invoked in a wider context of changes in theatrical practice. In the modernist avant-garde theatre, designers and directors searched for new forms which would provide an antidote to what was perceived as the moribund repetitiveness of the commercial stage. Those forms were variously found in William Poel's and Nugent Monck's experiments with a historical Shakespearian stage,[28] and Yeats's attempts to locate a more valuable theatrical experience in the ancient peasant cultures of Ireland, or Artaud's fascination with the theatrical potential of Balinese cultural forms.[29]

All of these experiments were validated in terms of a rhetoric of authenticity and immediacy but they articulated a desire for a theatrical experience which would transcend the uneasy relationship between art and commerce. They came at a time when the technologies of theatrical production, the footlights and proscenium arch of the realist stage, were making the break between scene and spectator the more acute.[30] Artaud's crazy denunciation of all the conventions of the contemporary stage made him especially receptive to the alien forms of Balinese theatre which seemed to him to communicate with an immediacy which transcended mere language.[31] However, Artaud's most important innovation lay not in the coherence of his theatrical theory but in his suggestive observations about the need for changes in costume and lighting and design, a simplification of theatre technology which would release it from the economies of buildings and sets which were stultifying the

---

[26] Richard Halpern, *Shakespeare Among the Moderns* (Ithaca, 1997), p. 19.

[27] Sol Plaatje, 'A South African's Homage', in Israel Gollancz, ed., *A Book of Homage to Shakespeare* (Oxford, 1916), p. 339, discussed in Johnson, pp. 74–80 (see note 15).

[28] See Dennis Kennedy, *Looking at Shakespeare* (Cambridge, 1993), pp. 34–42 and Halpern, *Shakespeare*, p. 6.

[29] See James W. Flannery, *W. B. Yeats and the Idea of a Theatre* (London, 1976), pp. 58–100 and Antonin Artaud, 'On the Balinese Theatre', *The Theatre and its Double*, translated by Victor Corti (London, 1970), pp. 36–49.

[30] See Kennedy, *Looking*, p. 29.

[31] See Artaud, 'The Theatre of Cruelty First Manifesto', pp. 74–6.

contemporary stage, not least because of the expensive infrastructure which the commercial theatre required. For avant-garde modernist theatre critics, the theatre could be both saved from commercialism and renewed by a return to an authenticity. This new return could be historical, like Elizabethanist *mise-en-scène*, primitive, and therefore outside commercial culture, like the Balinese or the Irish peasants and it would also avoid commercialism by being simple and cheap.[32]

In the case of avant-garde Shakespeare productions, the theatrical shifts away from realism, the repudiation of the picture frame stage in favour of more abstract design intersected with a criticism which stressed the inherent meaning of imagery and denied the psychological focus on character. Together they emptied the plays of their specific historical applications and offered instead a range of abstract oppositions which could readily be adapted into different styles of *mise-en-scène*. This abstraction of the historical and psychological into universal themes turned *Macbeth* into an abstract encounter between good and evil and reinforced the centrality of the witches as the embodiment of primitive evil at the heart of the play.

The inheritors of this tradition were those postwar cosmopolitan theatre directors of whom Peter Brook or Ariane Mnouchkine or Eugenio Barba are only the most famous. These directors have integrated the Shakespeare text with images and performance styles taken from the colonized cultures of India, Africa and Indonesia. Their aim in this was to reanimate old texts with new images, drawing on new cultural resources much as global commerce drew on new markets and producers in the formerly colonized world. As David Williams has noted,

Brook's relativism [. . .] is a product of a professionalism, always on the look-out for new performance techniques [. . .] here is a Western director who sustains a dialogue with a range of 'other' cultures, as if to consolidate his own place in the universe.[33]

Brook's ability to effect this dialogue, however, depends both upon a global economy which had brought these cultures within reach and on the modernist move towards abstraction which empties Shakespeare's works of their historical particularity, leaving an echoing but undefined significance at their heart. In terms which echo Artaud's search for the 'fragile fluctuating centre which forms never reach', Brook has asserted

Even though Shakespeare's worlds are inevitably coloured by their period, the fine richness of their writing lies at a deeper level beneath the words, where there is no form, nothing but the vibration of a great potential force.[34]

The search for the essence of theatre is also applied to the images and forms taken from other cultures, turning them into what Pavis has called 'aestheticising phantasmagoria'.[35] In a cultural move similar to that of modernism on Shakespeare, international directors aestheticize cultural forms into images of beauty and pathos and fear, suitable for the avant garde *mise en scène*, to be attached to whatever narrative Shakespeare or Faust or Iphigenia or any of the familiar texts of the European repertory can provide. In the process, they release the arts of colonial cultures from their originating relation-

---

[32] See, for example, Yeats' denunciation of Beerbohm Tree as 'the chief representative of the commercial theatre we are exposed to', discussed in Flannery, *W. B. Yeats*, pp. 136–7. Compare Edward Gordon Craig's infuriating vagueness about the material process required to make his innovative screens which would act as the substitutes for scenery. See Flannery, *W. B. Yeats*, pp. 269–70.

[33] David Williams, 'Remembering the others that are us: Transculturalism and Myth in the Theatre of Peter Brook', in *The Intercultural Performance Reader* edited by Patrice Pavis (London, 1996) pp. 67–79, p. 67. See also Dennis Kennedy, 'Shakespeare and the Global Spectator', *Shakespeare Jahrbuch* 131 (1995), 50–64.

[34] Quoted in Williams, 'Remembering the others' pp. 71–2.

[35] Patrice Pavis, *Theatre at the Crossroads of Culture* (London, 1992), p. 195. Compare Kennedy, 'Global Spectator', p. 55: 'to the spectator the style dominated, and substituted an aesthetic experience for a social one'.

ship to the cultures which produced them and reinvest them with both the symbolic value and the exchange value of the metropolis.

Patrice Pavis has described the activities of these cosmopolitan companies as 'cultural exchange'.[36] The sense of reciprocity involved in his use of the term is misleading: nothing is returned to the cultures whose forms are appropriated for Western art. The term 'cultural exchange', moreover suggests that similar activity would be available to artists from the colonized world. It might seem that Welcome Msomi in linking Shakespeare to the Zulus was effecting a similar cultural process to Brook and Mnouchkine and Barba. However the effect of Msomi's production was different and that difference is to do with the history and economics of cultural exchange in colonized cultures.

This cultural appropriation is intrinsically connected to the superior economic power of the colonizing metropolis. Theatrical primitivism celebrates the simple and the spontaneous but it depends on high levels of state funding and commercial sponsorship which obfuscates its economic relationship to the means of cultural production. This funding provides for the long rehearsal periods required to train performers in new cultural forms, international travel for research and performance, and the ability to employ an international cast of performers.[37] More importantly, it removes the need for the number of repetitions which would provide a return on investment but which would also make the productions over-familiar and reduce their claims to carry the aura of unique works of art.

It was paradoxically harder, too, for Msomi to transcend his relationship to Zulu culture. Post-colonial artists and intellectuals had insisted on the continuity of African cultural forms, surviving against the odds, ready to flower again in the moment of liberation. But as Fanon described in *The Wretched of the Earth*, the nativist intellectuals 'set a high value on the customs, traditions and appearances of his

people but his inevitably painful experience only seems to be a banal search for exoticism.'[38]

Those failures were particularly poignant in the case of theatre productions in post-independence Africa. Michael Etherton has described, for example, how the Chikwakwa theatre established in the University in Zambia in the 1970s sent out

teams of University staff and students go out with drums, instruments, masks and artefacts [. . .] to the Provinces and work with groups of local residents from all walks of life in specific performance projects, or theatre writing projects, or dance workshops.[39]

The 'drums, instruments, masks and artefacts' represented the artistic version of African culture, extrapolated from their ritual function and returned to that rural culture in order to make a new artistic form, the post-colonial theatre. Even in cases when particular performances manifested a formal continuity with dance and ritual and other mimetic forms in indigenous culture, the legacy of colonialism, like the legacy of modernization in other cultures, remained in the separation of theatrical events from the functional role of ritual in culture. Patterns of funding also deformed the process as British Council-funded co-productions between University theatre departments from England and post-colonial African Universities were replaced by an instrumental support for Theatre in Education projects which brought messages about clean water and infant vaccination to rural populations.[40]

Unlike Brook and Mnouchkine, Msomi

---

36 Pavis, *Theatre*, pp. 6–7.

37 See Kennedy, 'Shakespeare and the Global Spectator', p. 63. See also the worries about the difficulty of funding a production of *Macbeth* based on work with aboriginal Australians, in Geraldine Cousin, 'Footsbarn: from a tribal *Macbeth* to an Intercultural *Dream*', *New Theatre Quarterly* 9, 33 (1993), 16–30.

38 Quoted in Antony Appiah, *In My Father's House: Africa in the Philosophy of Culture* (London, 1992), p. 97.

39 Michael Etherton, 'Indigenous Performance in Zambia', *Theatre Quarterly*, 3, 10 (1973), p. 48.

40 See Tim Prentki, 'Theatre for Development: Strategies

cannot simply celebrate primitivism or re-enact indigenous cultural forms because the relationship of African artists to contemporary culture has already been deformed by colonialism. In the theme parks of international tourism the artefacts for sale and the dancing and drumming which illustrate Zulu culture are as much the product of the Bantu education policy of the apartheid period as of the continuities of traditional culture.[41] As Antony Appiah has described, the artefacts of traditional culture are so overlaid with the history of their appropriation, and so implicated in the global art market, that they have become 'neo-traditional'. Their celebration involves a denial of modernity, an obfuscation of the real cultural and economic relations of the contemporary African world.[42]

While visiting South Africa with a new production of *Titus Andronicus* which modernized the play and connected it to the politics of post-apartheid, Greg Doran saw the revived *Umabatha* and another production of *Macbeth*. Doran admired *Umabatha* because of seeing it 'in this context, in a society with a *real* [his italics] relationship to witchcraft', a relationship whose absence, in his view, made 'ninety-nine per cent of modern British *Macbeth*'s fail.' The other production, by the Performing Arts Council of the Transvaal, on the other hand, was not apparently informed by the culture of witchcraft. Doran wrote 'I get the sense that *Macbeth* has been scheduled from a set text mentality.'[43] For the purposes of the aestheticized international Shakespeare, African witchcraft is real and can generate a productive relationship between the play and its cultural moment; African education, apparently, is not.

As Doran's reaction, and that of the reviewers discussed earlier, suggests, where Msomi's play gained cultural recognition it did so by virtue of unexamined assumptions about the authenticity with which it represented its originating culture. These connections, however, had to be reinforced discursively as well as in the performance itself, partly because of the artistic resources at Msomi's disposal. Some of the metropolitan

reviewers in 1972 displayed their own cultural sophistication by sneering at the inauthenticity of the dancing. Writing from London, Charles Marowitz, in the *New York Times*, described the dance sequences as having 'the drill-like precision of the Rockettes' and dismissed them as 'in the style one might call Busby Berkeley Primitive'.[44] The reviewer of the *New York Daily News* offered a more considered awareness of cultural politics by asking 'Can it be that Western show business has exerted a worldwide corrupting influence on native art?' Nonetheless he did not refrain from the cultural sneer, commenting 'If that's honest to goodness Zulu wear, then I'm Fred Astaire.'[45]

In the economic conditions of its original production, when Msomi was working full-time for a pharmaceutical company, he did not have the economic resources to perform the expensive alchemy of cultural exchange which would create a new and autonomous aesthetic form. His achievement was rather to exploit existing assumptions about Zulu culture, to release it into the post-colonial market. In the first version of the play he attached Zulu dancing to the brand name of Shakespeare to insulate it against the charge of ethnic exploitation. He then recognized its potential for revival in the post-apartheid desire for cultural cohesion and turned the new hybrid product into a commercial success.

The repeated versions of Msomi's *Umabatha* across twenty-five years of political, economic and artistic change provide a particular insight into modern institutions of the cultural repro-

---

for Self Reliance', *New Theatre Quarterly*, 11, 44 (1995), 391–4.
[41] See Hamilton, *Terrific Majesty*.
[42] See Appiah, *In My Father's House*, chapter 7, 'The Postcolonial and the Postmodern'.
[43] Antony Sher and Greg Doran, *Woza Shakespeare! Titus Andronicus in South Africa* (London, 1996), pp. 237, 211. Compare Makhaya, 'African Soul Brew', whose review notes that 'schools can benefit from reduced block bookings. *Macbeth (Umabatha)* is their set work.'
[44] Charles Marowitz, *New York Times*, 7 May 1972.
[45] *New York Daily News*, 10 April 1979.

duction of Shakespeare. The relationships between the performance, its reception and the surrounding commentary, illustrate the discourses which articulate the intersection between performances of Shakespeare in the theatre and successive movements of cultural politics. Those discourses include the opposition between art and commerce, between the authentic and the fake and, in this case, between the metropolitan and the third world. These discourses manage the process by which a Shakespeare play is transformed into a theatrical commodity, and they articulate the ways in which the continuity of the theatrical production beyond the text is reproduced and through which it takes its place in culture.

WHEN ALL IS TRUE: LAW, HISTORY AND PROBLEMS OF KNOWLEDGE IN *HENRY VIII*

BARBARA KREPS

In the last scene of *The Famous History of the Life of King Henry the Eight*,[1] Cranmer's prophecy provides Elizabeth's father with knowledge of the future not available at the play's ostensible chronological cut-off point in 1533; nor, because of the legal arrangements Henry left, was this future imaginable when Henry died in 1547. The panegyric delivered from the perspective of 1613 is a utopian evaluation of the Elizabethan past and the Jacobean present which the stage Henry receives as an 'oracle of comfort' (5.4.66), and the obvious flattery requires Cranmer's prefatory affirmation that the words he utters are all 'truth' (15–16); less obvious in this context of apparently uncomplicated praise is that the prophecy builds on a series of real historical ironies and legal reversals that represented major defeats for Henry and his plans for the future. Henry learns here that Elizabeth will reign, but that she will die childless (thus extinguishing the direct line of succession with which he was obsessed); the second major piece of information Cranmer provides is buffered by linguistic evasions that neatly sidestep the problem of revealing the name of Elizabeth's Stuart successor and the ultimate triumph of the Scottish line that Henry had passed over when he laid out his dispositions for succession in his last will and testament. That Cranmer is presenting Henry with knowledge that later historical developments would turn out to defeat his will is a situation of de facto irony, but though the audience knew quite well before entering the theatre that Henry had

laid out very different plans for ruling from the grave, it seems doubtful to me that this irony could have been easily recognized in performance. This raises a question pertinent to the domain of literary theory about the relationship between an audience's extra-theatrical

---

[1] The play's title in the First Folio. Henry Wotton's reference to the play as *All is True* in his letter describing the fire at the Globe has given rise to perplexity about the title; the title reported by Wotton has taken firm root as a result of the decision made by the 1986 Oxford Shakespeare editorial team (Stanley Wells, Gary Taylor, John Jowett, William Montgomery) to use it in place of the Folio title in their *William Shakespeare: The Complete Works* (Oxford, 1986). References in this essay are to the Arden *King Henry VIII*, ed. R. A. Foakes (London and New York 1964; reprinted 1991).

The last scene may have been written by Fletcher rather than Shakespeare: 5.4 is one of the six scenes (scenes 3 and 4 of Act 1; 3.1; scenes 2,3,4 of Act 5) about which Cyrus Hoy produces the most convincing arguments to date concerning the possibility of Fletcher's part in the play's authorship. (See his 'The Shares of Fletcher and his Collaborators in the Beaumont and Fletcher Canon', *Studies in Bibliography*, 15 (1962), 71–88.) There is still no clear consensus among Shakespeare scholars about either single authorship or collaboration, however, and my own essay has nothing to add to that debate. The point I wish to make here is that, if Fletcher did indeed write the final scene, the prophecy represents an epistemological manoeuvre on history that I shall be considering along with others in the play where Shakespeare's authorship is considered much surer. Given the lingering uncertainties of authorship and my own emphasis here on legal history and audience reception, I usually refer to 'the play' rather than to its author (or authors).

knowledge and textual manipulation of that knowledge, but I will address this question only very briefly, and only insofar as I wish to point out links or analogies between the epistemology of performance and the issues of time, discrepant levels of knowledge, and problematized perceptions of 'truth' embedded within the script. These I see as coming not only from the specific questions of history and law that furnished plot material for the four 'trials' dramatized in the play, but also as influenced by other legal and historical examples that, after 1529, made for numerous areas of uncertainty in England. Henry VIII had intended to provide a non-contestable succession and hence a clear and – at least inside England's borders – peaceful future for his subjects, but his matrimonial politics left a record of historical ironies that created in turn a series of legal crises – some, but not all, of which were later rectified by the hindsight of awkward and quasi-apologetic statutory revisions.

Henry VIII is enormously preoccupied with time. Cranmer's prophecy is not the only point at which the future is either projected or hinted at, but I will come back to this later on; for the moment, I would like to consider *Henry VIII*'s relation to the past. In addition to itself *being* a depiction of the past, the play is also very often *about* depicting the past: recounting, examining, interpreting it. And though the past is commonly considered a known or knowable fact, the play reveals again and again that the past is unsure, subject to different interpretations, and holds unknowable secrets.[2] The opening conversation between Norfolk and Buckingham about the Field of the Cloth of Gold begins innocently enough as an admiring account of its regal marvels and the 'Order [that] gave each thing view' (1.1.44), but gives way at half point to criticism of the violation of the old order represented by the upstart butcher's son Wolsey ('a keech'(55), 'not propp'd by ancestry' (59)) and his role in arranging the meeting between the courts of England and France. Within six lines the word 'order' thus turns into a heated

linguistic fulcrum as it takes on its other English meaning for those nobles who resent being 'order'd' by 'this butcher's cur' (120): 'All this was order'd by the good discretion / Of the right reverend Cardinal of York' (50–1). Norfolk describes the glitter of the kings' encounter, 'All was royal; / To the disposing of it nought rebell'd' (42–3), but this is shortly revealed to be untrue: Buckingham contests it indeed since Wolsey, rather than Henry, was the organizer. Buckingham's outrage at the economic strain the nobles have been obliged to bear for the display of 'these fierce vanities' (54) is exacerbated by its political pointlessness since, even as they speak, the pact between France and England has already been violated. Buckingham reveals too that Charles V's recent trip to England, ostensibly to visit his aunt, in reality veiled his purpose of bribing Wolsey to undermine the Anglo-French peace treaty. This revelation of animosity between Buckingham and Wolsey quickly sketches in the picture of factionalism historically true of court circles under all the Tudors, but Buckingham's loyalty to Henry himself would seem proved by the rhetoric with which he expresses his indignation at Wolsey's 'corrupt and treasonous' (155) behaviour and its insult to the honour of 'the king our master' (164). None of the chronicles claims that Buckingham intended to denounce Wolsey for treason, so that the invention of such intent here adds decided irony to the arrival of the guards who have come to arrest the Duke for that very crime. But this show of loyalty to the King's interests is also theatrically perplexing since – *if* Buckingham is guilty[3] – the total lack of conspiratorial talk

---

2 Pierre Sahel calls attention to the frequency of indirect discourse and the importance of rumour and reporting in the play. See his 'The Strangeness of a Dramatic Style: Rumour in *Henry VIII*', *Shakespeare Survey 38* (1985), 145–51.

3 On this and other uncertainties and contradictions, see Lee Bliss, 'The Wheel of Fortune and the Maiden Phoenix of Shakespeare's *King Henry the Eighth*', *ELH*, 42 (1975), 1–25.

breaks the early modern stage convention that, either through soliloquy or through privileged fourth-wall eaves-dropping as plots were hatched and motivations explained, gave audiences access to fuller information than that available to most of the characters on stage. On the other hand, Buckingham's reaction contains the play's strongest indication that the accusations against him, which are later made to seem so weak, may indeed be founded, since the Duke already knows – without having been told – that the accusation has been made by his surveyor.

Metonymically linking the so-called 'Amicable' Grant with the question of Buckingham's treason, the second scene also recounts the recent past and makes clear that though someone knows the facts, a single version of them remains elusive. The metonymy also points to Henry's inconsistency in dealing with the question of treason, a consideration I will return to later. Buckingham's trial and execution took place in 1521, but Shakespeare went to Holinshed's entries for 1525 to retrieve the tax issue. The tax question has no plot significance after this scene; neither, obviously, did it have to be included from simple chronological necessity. Extracted from its historical sequence and having in the plot economy no consequence, Shakespeare's insertion of the Amicable Grant thus exposes the difficulties of arriving at supposedly objective facts or discovering truth in public forums, particularly when political questions are mediated by political experts. Henry does not seem at first to be one of these experts. If true, Henry's claims of complete ignorance about the tax are an admission of his administrative ineptitude, but the appearance of ignorance clears him from willing responsibility in a fiscal procedure which was without Parliamentary approval and therefore was not legal, shifting that responsibility squarely to the cardinal.[4] Wolsey's defence that 'others tell steps with me' may or may not vaguely glance at Henry, but it elicits Katherine's heated retort which focuses entirely on Wolsey's culpable knowledge, without addressing that of the king:

> No, my lord,
> You know no more than others; but you frame
> Things that are known alike, which are not
>   wholesome
> To those which would not know them, and yet
>   must
> Perforce be their acquaintance.
>
> (1.2.43–7)

After Henry orders that the tax be rescinded and pardon be sent to those who had not paid it, Wolsey's aside that the pardon should be 'nois'd' as coming through the cardinal's intercession is a theatrical demonstration of how knowledge of political truths can be distorted for the public's consumption, and through it the audience has been sent an obvious sign of Wolsey's deviousness; but though this is an unmistakable signal about Wolsey, it does not automatically exculpate Henry or dispel doubts about how much he really knows. If Henry is telling the truth, this scene shows through the interventions of Katherine, Norfolk, and Wolsey that the King is the only major figure at court who knows nothing of the tax. It is possible, but it strains credulity.

The play starts therefore with two consecutive scenes in which the possibilities of multivocal evaluations of 'facts' are revealed. From here on it is largely constructed on the process, implications and/or results of trials of major figures of Henry's time; but, though trials exist to establish an official version of truth, the play begins by exposing in non-judicial contexts

---

[4] For varying interpretations of Henry's part in the Amicable Grant, see G. R. Elton, *Reform and Reformation* (London and Melbourne, 1977), pp. 90–1; J. J. Scarisbrick, *Henry VIII* (Berkeley and Los Angeles), pp. 138–9; Neville Williams, *Henry VIII and his Court* (New York, 1971), p. 97; D. M. Loades, *Politics and the Nation*, 4th edn. (London, 1992), pp. 158–60; John A. F. Thomson, *The Transformation of Medieval England* (London and New York, 1983), pp. 38, 249–51; John Guy, *Tudor England* (Oxford, 1990), pp. 86–8.

how difficult it can be to arrive at ideas of truth about the past untinged by ambiguity or multiple interpretations.

Henry VIII's imaginative rescripting of the past leaves many critics uncomfortable with its status as a history play. Certainly the play challenges the idea that history can recover a reliable, unequivocal, or totally truthful narrative about the past. One reason for this, as Cranmer's prophecy partially illustrates, is that time removes closure from the narrative: subsequent events can alter the interpretation of earlier ones. In 1533 the birth of a girl, rather than a boy, represented personal disaster for her parents, and a political crisis for the country; by 1613, Elizabeth's birth had acquired a different significance. One of the points I wish to make in this essay is that the narrative distortions that have disturbed the play's position in the history genre seem to me to stem from the historical example of rethinking and rewriting the certainties of the past that was set by Henry himself, who – as long as he was alive – was quickly seconded by the legal acrobatics of Parliament as it passed the legislation necessary to accommodate his changes in heart and mind and turn his will into law. But it is also relevant that the play was written long after his death and after the death of the last direct heir of his body, ten years into the reign of a king whose line had been ignored by the provisions of Henry's will.

Henry VIII's determination to rewrite the history of his marriage to Katherine was made possible by passage of the Act of Appeals (March–April, 1533), which – at least in England – cleared the obstacle of Katherine's appeal to Rome from the legal path that finally led to the annulment decreed, in May 1533, by Cranmer's ecclesiastical court. Henry's marriage to Anne had already taken place before this annulment was procured, although exactly how long before was adjusted in the chronicles. In reality Henry and Anne were secretly married on 25 January 1533, but Holinshed discreetly fixed an earlier date:

And herewith vpon his returne, he married priuilie the ladie Anne Bullongne the same daie, being the fourteenth daie of November, and the feast daie of saint Erkenwald; which marriage was kept so secret, that verie few knew it till Easter next insuing, when it was perceiued that she was with child.   (p. 777)[5]

Given Elizabeth's birth in September 1533, the tactic served to make the legitimacy of the baby's conception a matter of historic record, in addition to making an honest woman of Anne. Whether in the months that passed between marriage to Anne and annulment from Katherine Henry was legally a bigamist or – since he claimed that the marriage had never been valid – a newly married bachelor is a point that passed in official silence. Parliament's role was to address the legitimacy of children from the Boleyn marriage and assure their right to succession, which it did in the First Act of Succession (1534):

And also be it enacted by auctoritie aforseid that all the issue hade and procreate, or hereafter to be had and p[ro]create, bytwene your Highnes and your seid moost dere and entyerly beloved wyfe Quene Anne, shalbe your lawfull childerne, and be inheritable and enherit accordyng to the course of inheritaunce and lawes of this Realme the ymperiall Crowne of the same.   (25 Henry VIII. c.22)[6]

Two years later, Henry's 'moost dere and entyerly beloved wyfe Quene Anne' was found guilty of adultery and beheaded for treason. The law's sentence against her was, like a great deal of Parliament's most important legislation after 1530, an act of compliance with Henry's determined will. Anne had failed to produce the inheriting son expected of her, and Henry's passion for her had, after so many years of ardent desire and courtship, quickly burnt itself out once the legitimation of marriage was achieved. On 17 May 1536, Cranmer, in his

---

[5] Raphael Holinshed, *The Third Volume of Chronicles . . . Now Newlie Recognised, Augmented, and Continued . . .*, reprint 1807–8 edn. (New York, 1965).

[6] *Statutes of the Realm* (1817), vol. 3, p. 473. Hereafter referred to as *SR*.

ecclesiastical court, pronounced the nullity of the marriage, based on the impediment deriving from Henry's earlier liaison with Anne's sister Mary. As G. R. Elton points out, 'Thus the stories, so hotly denied when they were used by Catherine's supporters to argue against the Boleyn marriage, were in the end allowed to serve the new situation' (*Reform and Reformation*, p. 252). Elton also points out that the legal inconsistency of the charge of adultery, in a marriage adjudicated never to have been legal, disturbed no one. Thus Anne – judged in one court to be an adulteress and in another never to have been a legal wife – was beheaded on 19 May. Within twenty-four hours of her death Henry and Jane Seymour were formally betrothed, and their marriage was celebrated on 30 May. These developments in Henry's matrimonial history obviously changed the significance of the First Act of Succession: the act meant to assure England's future had become a potential danger, but to undo its earlier legislation Parliament apparently felt that it needed to find and put on record a legitimizing rationale. The rationale was perhaps that found by Cranmer's ecclesiastical court – the invalidity of the marriage on the basis of affinity caused by Henry's earlier liaison with Mary Boleyn – but the statute does not specify the logic at its base. The first paragraph of the statute 28 Henry VIII c. 7 simply finds objectionable 'c[er]tayne articles and clauses concernyng the ratification of your said unlawfull mariage betwene your Highnes and the said Lady Anne and the lymitacion of your Succession to the issues of your body had by the said Lady Anne . . . which clauses and articles be nowe become of late so dishonorable and so far distaunte from the due course of your com[m]on lawes of your Realme, and also so moche ayenst good reason equitie and good consciens, that they cannot be tollerated to contynue and endure without great perill and dyvysion hereafter . . .' (*SR*, III. 656). The same clause had already established that, in view of the 'unlawfull mariage', Elizabeth's succession would clearly be 'ayenste all honour equite reason and good consciens if remedye shulde not be p[ro]vyded for the same'. Rewriting the legal past was a necessary step for smoothing over the present and mapping out the legal future. Parliament expressed its gratitude that Henry, 'notwithstandyng the great and intollerable perilles and occasions which your Highnes hath suffred and susteyend', had acquiesced in marrying again 'at the moste humble peticion and intercession of us your Nobles of this Realme' (p. 657). Jane, unlike Anne, was not pregnant at the time of her marriage to Henry, but 'for her convenient yeres excellente beautie and pureness of flesh and blode is apte (God willyng) to conceyve issue by your Highnes'. This likelihood necessitated that neither Elizabeth nor Mary should be Henry's legal issue, so that the 'remedye' Parliament enacted was the bastardization of both. Mary's illegitimacy was not specifically addressed, though it was implicit in the Act of 1534, but in the Act of 1536 both she and Elizabeth were explicitly declared, in separate paragraphs but in parallel formulae, 'illegittymate'. This act also conferred on Henry the right to name his successors 'by your letters patentes under your great seale or ells by your laste Will made in wrytynge and signed with your moste gracious hande' (p. 659).

In the Third Act of Succession (1543/4), Elizabeth was restored to a place in the line of succession after Edward and Mary, though the statutory illegitimacy of both of Henry's daughters remained. In paragraph 7 this act also excluded 'forreyne Powers' from succeeding (*SR*, III. 957), a provision that technically excluded Henry's Scottish relatives – who, in any case, remained unmentioned in Henry's last will and testament.[7] Of the many ironies in

---

[7] For a series of reasons, Henry's relations with Scotland deteriorated throughout the early 1540s; war between the two countries was declared in 1542, with the Scots being routed at Solway Moss in November. The English made brutal incursions again in 1544 and 1545 – partially

Henry's personal and political life, certainly one of the major ones is that Henry, who was so anxious in the last twenty years of his life to ensure the legitimacy of his successors, should have been responsible for legal measures that, in different ways, clouded the legitimacy of three of them.[8]

Henry's pre-marital passion for Anne was intense and determined, but his purpose in seeking annulment from Katherine was beyond anything else dictated by his concern for England's political future based on his knowledge of England's recent political past. His own Lancastrian father had consolidated his claim to the throne through his marriage with Elizabeth of York, but the two separate challenges to the legitimacy of the first Tudor king mounted by Lambert Simnel and Perkin Warbeck had demonstrated that fifteenth-century uncertainties over succession were not terminated either by Henry VII's accession or by his political marriage. Henry VIII meant to avert the renewal of such internal divisions in the country by providing England with a son. Henry eventually got his son, though not by Anne. But by then the Defender of the Faith had broken with the faith he had defended, and the split in the country the desired son presumably ought to have avoided was instead assured through religious differences that outlived all the Tudors.

Perhaps uniquely among Shakespeare's English history plays, *Henry VIII* was not likely to have been, even for the most illiterate member of the audience, anyone's sole source of information about Henry's wilful temperament or many of the events during and after his reign – including, among other things, the variety of legal difficulties and ironic developments that, even before Henry died, complicated the history of the succession that Henry so fervently wished to direct. And thanks to the audience's knowledge and memory, *Henry VIII* occasionally suggests more than it strictly says. There are several points in which the play reminds the audience that the future would bring ironic surprises and tragic reversals. (Consider, for example, Anne's

fearfulness at the end of 2.3 ('it faints me / To think what follows') and the repeated dangers felt for Anne's life in Act 5 as she is giving birth to the child that turns out to be a girl. There are a number of such arch reminders in 3.2: the repeated emphasis on Thomas Cromwell's future 'safety' as Henry's servant; the reminder of the importance of Thomas More's 'conscience', and the obvious double meaning in Henry's reproof of Wolsey: 'I deem you an ill husband, and am glad / To have you therein my companion' (142–3).) About religion, though, the play is noticeably circumspect. In Cranmer's prophecy eighty years of tumultuous religious change are quietly addressed in only half a line: 'God shall be truly known' (5.4.36). By changing the Privy Council's actions against Cranmer in the 1540s to 1533, and thereby ostensibly cutting

---

because of Scottish resistance to Henry's plans to marry his son Edward with the infant Mary, Queen of Scots. The marriage plans thwarted, Henry avoided any mention of the Stuarts in his will, skipping over their precedence by representative primogeniture, naming instead his younger sister Mary's descendants as next after his three children, should these die without heirs of their body. See Mortimer Levine, *Tudor Dynastic Problems 1460–1571* (London, 1973), pp. 72–5.

8 One result was the muddle created at the death of Edward VI with the Dudleys' attempt to place Lady Jane Grey on the throne. From the pulpit of Paul's Cross, Nicholas Ridley preached on 9 July 1553, that neither Mary nor Elizabeth could succeed, since the Acts of Parliament that had bastardized them had never been repealed. Though the Protestant congregation heard him out without enthusiasm, Lady Jane was not without support, and as Loades points out, 'research has only recently uncovered the tracks which they were so quickly forced to hide' (see Loades, *Politics*, pp.239–40). One of the first Acts of Mary's Parliament in 1553 was to repeal the Henrician legislation that had denied the lawfulness of her parents' marriage (*SR* IV.201). Unlike Mary, Elizabeth never addressed the question of bastardy. On various problematic aspects of the will's legitimacy and its implications for the Stuarts, see Loades, *Politics*, pp. 204–34, 287–91; Scarisbrick, *Henry VIII*, pp. 488–94; Guy, *Tudor England*, pp. 196–9; Elton, *Reform*, pp. 331–2, and also his *England Under the Tudors* (London, 1955, rev. 1965), pp. 269–70, 280–4, 370–1, 474; Mortimer Levine, *The Early Elizabethan Succession Question 1558–1568* (Stanford, 1966), pp. 99–162.

off at Elizabeth's birth, the play operates in a selective time frame which theoretically blocks from view the historical bloodshed – much, though not all of it, for religious causes – that came later. I would suggest, though, that by choosing at all to dramatize Gardiner's plot against Cranmer the play manages to remind the audience, without apparently saying so, that Cranmer's difficulties with his Catholic enemies were not over. With Henry's dramatically drawn-out actions to save Cranmer the play officially demonstrates the power of Henry's will, as well as a unique instance of his mercy; but since Cranmer's martyrdom under Mary was one of the better known stories in Foxe's *Actes and Monuments*, the play also reminds the audience of Cranmer's on-going historical difficulties with his Catholic enemies – difficulties only temporarily laid to rest here by the force of Henry's will. The audience with access to the whole of Cranmer's story knew what awaited him in Mary's reign: liminally, then, the very act that dramatizes the overriding effect of Henry's will also suggests its legal and chronological limits.

Cranmer's 'trial' in the Privy Council only barely gets under way before it is truncated by Henry's partisanship for his useful friend, but the episode recalls the play's earlier depiction of the legal procedures against Buckingham in several ways. One of these is the obvious contrast between Henry's interest in Cranmer in Act V and his refusal, at the conclusion of his examination of Buckingham's surveyor in 1.2, to exercise the mercy of his royal prerogative in the Duke's favour:

> he is attach'd,
> Call him to present trial; if he may
> Find mercy in the law, 'tis his; if none,
> Let him not seek't of us. By day and night,
> He's traitor to th' height.

> (1.2.210–14)

This scene alters the pre-trial process recorded in Holinshed – who got his details from Polydore Vergil – where it is Wolsey alone

who, 'boiling in hatred against the duke of Buckingham, & thirsting for his bloud' (p. 657), both procures the witness and examines him: 'This Kneuet being had in examination before the cardinall, disclosed all the dukes life . . . The cardinall hauing thus taken the examination of Kneuet, went vnto the king, and declared vnto him, that his person was in danger by such traitorous purpose, as the duke of Buckingham had conceiued in his heart, and shewed how that now there is manifest tokens of his wicked pretense; wherefore, he exhorted the king to prouide for his owne suertie with speed. The king hearing the accusation, inforced to the vttermost by the cardinall, made this answer; If the duke haue deserued to be punished, let him haue according to his deserts' (pp. 657–8). On stage, as in historical fact, it was normal praxis for a king to examine informants, so the public would see nothing strange in Henry's role here. But Holinshed stresses Wolsey's maliciousness as well as Henry's reluctance in proceeding against the Duke ('inforced to the vttermost by the cardinall'), so that the substitution of Henry for Wolsey alters the dynamics of the inquisition as it appears in Holinshed, and this choice is problematized by two other choices: (1) omission of Buckingham's incriminating letters and (2) the contrast between Henry's leniency in dealing with the rebellion in Kent and his harshness with Buckingham. In the chronicles, part of the numerous accusations contained in the indictment read against Buckingham involved letters the Duke had written to the monk, and these were produced as evidence against him at the trial: 'Maister Ihon Delacourt . . . his owne hand writyng layde before hym to the accusement of the duke.'[9] What remains of the chronicles in the play are unverifiable 'words' and 'speech'

---

[9] Edward Hall, *The Vnion of the two noble and illustre Famelies of Lancastre & Yorke . . .* (London, 1550), fol. lxxxvi. John Bellamy refers to the role of Buckingham's letters at his trial in *The Tudor Law of Treason* (London, 1979), p. 149.

the surveyor claims to have overheard between the Duke and his son-in-law:

> First, it was usual with him, every day
> It would infect his speech, that if the king
> Should without issue die, he'll carry it so
> To make the sceptre his. These very words
> I've heard him utter to his son-in-law,
> Lord Aberga'nny.   (1.2.132–7)

Shakespeare emphasizes throughout that the evidence against Buckingham consists entirely of reported words: 'words of sovereignty', 'the duke said', 'certain words / Spoke by a holy monk', 'says he', 'what he spoke / My chaplain to no living creature but / To me should utter'.

Treason for words was a shadowy area when Buckingham was tried, and had a varied legal history throughout the 1500s. That words alone could constitute treason did not achieve statutory status until 1534, a provision repealed after Henry's death. But 'words' came and went and came again into the numerous treason statutes Parliament passed throughout the sixteenth century. The legal concept that words alone, without an overt deed, could constitute treason was unstable, and the legislation that at various times throughout the sixteenth century ratified this concept stands as a barometer of the government's fears of the political climate in the country each time it passed. Buckingham's trial preceded this series of changing treason statutes, however; he was tried under the 1352 act of treason (25 Edward III), and apparently argued in his defence that no overt act of treason stood in the charges against him (Bellamy, *Tudor Law of Treason*, p. 151). That act provided, among other things, that 'to compass or imagine the death of the king, his queen or the royal heir' was treason (Bellamy, *Tudor Law of Treason*, p. 9), and 'imagine' proved to be a slippery concept in the context of a treason charge. The nobles who comprised Stafford's jury were perplexed about how to act on evidence that was both reported and written but that did not point to an active plot against the king's life, and they asked Chief Justice Fineux for legal advice on the difference between felony and treason. His answer was that felony required an act, 'but merely to intend the king's death was high treason and such intention was sufficiently proven by words alone. In such cases no overt deed was needed beyond . . . the traitorous statement which revealed the intent in the mind' (Bellamy, *Tudor Law of Treason*, p. 32). Once the peers have decided that Knevet's allegations are true, therefore, Shakespeare's Duke is simply referring realistically to the law: 'The law [. . .] has done upon the premises but justice' (2.1.62–3).

The justice thus historically reserved for Buckingham through Fineaux's construction of the terminology of the 1352 treason statute is contrasted in 1.2 with Henry's treatment of the tax protest in Kent, which the text itself insists must be treated with the legally loaded word 'rebellion'. Katherine states, with the mildness typical of her, that the protest of the clothiers 'almost appears / In loud rebellion', but Norfolk corrects her, calling a spade a spade: 'Not almost appears, / It doth appear' (28–30). Popular disorders were another area in which definitions could be a matter of life and death, since the linguistic difference between 'rebellion' on the one hand and 'riot' on the other marked out for the government the boundaries between actions to be considered treasonable and those which were not. Bringing the charge of treason against the tax rebels was in fact debated in 1525 – Wolsey apparently favouring the treason charge – but in the end the king's counsel and judges concurred that the insurrection was to be dealt with as 'only riot and unlawful assembly' (Bellamy, *Tudor Law of Treason*, p. 21). By the time *Henry VIII* was written, however, legal interpretation of popular protest was decidedly less lenient. In 1595 the London apprentices rioted against the Lord Mayor, and in 1596 there was an abortive insurrection against enclosure in Oxfordshire,[10] and though neither

---

[10] See John Walter, 'A "Rising of the People"? The Oxfordshire Rising of 1596', *Past and Present*, 107 (May 1985), 90–143.

action was directed against the queen's person, the leaders of both were charged with compassing to levy war and tried for treason: 'Rebellion of all types was thenceforth a traitorous act and that very word which in earlier times had been associated with the withdrawal by peasants from their legal obligations and with assemblies of a riotous nature became synonymous with treason' (Bellamy, *Tudor Law of Treason*, p. 81).

The writings deleted from the chronicle sources and the contrast with the rebellious masses in Kent are part of the design favouring Buckingham that finds its most obvious expression and most immediate theatrical impact in Katherine's generous defence of the Duke. This is not found in Holinshed; what *is* found there is the difficulty of accepting the surveyor's charges which lies behind Katherine's arguments in the play. It was not Katherine, however, but the chronicler who made this point. In Holinshed, the narrating voice of the historian departed (copying Vergil) from an external account of the fact of accusation to an internal account of its motivation, entering the informer's mind, and interpreting for the reader Knevet's action against Buckingham as inspired by two base motives that had nothing to do with loyalty to the king: he was 'partlie prouoked with desire to be reuenged and partlie mooued with hope of reward' (p. 658).[11] Katherine appropriates Holinshed's omniscient narrative in her addresses to Wolsey and the surveyor: interrupting the cardinal, she ironically reminds him that it would become his religious role better to 'Deliver all with charity' (1.2.143), while to Buckingham's former servant she delivers the solemn warning that with his dubious accusations he risks eternal damnation: 'You were the duke's surveyor, and lost your office / On the complaint o'th' tenants; take good heed / You charge not in your spleen a noble person / And spoil your nobler soul' (1.2.172–5). Henry ignores this observation of the surveyor's unsavoury reputation in Act 1, but in Act 5 he recalls how

corrupt knaves can serve corrupt masters, and here Shakespeare ironically assigns to the king himself the play's most cynical evaluation of the fallibility always possible in legal procedures ideally meant to discover and guarantee the truth:

> not ever
> The justice and the truth o'th'question carries
> The due o'th' verdict with it: at what ease
> Might corrupt minds procure knaves as corrupt
> To swear against you? Such things have been
>   done.   (5.1.129–33)

Katherine's partisanship plays an important role in the text's recovery of Buckingham from history's official opprobrium, since both her

---

11 The phrase originates with Vergil: 'Tum ille partim ulciscendi se cupiditate incensus, partim praemio ductus . . .' which Denys Hay translates 'Partly fired by a desire for revenge, partly led on by bribes'. See Polydore Vergil, *The Anglica Historia of Polydore Vergil: A. D. 1485–1537*, ed. and trans. Denys Hay, Camden Series, vol. 74 (London, 1950), p. 271. Hall and Stow, unlike Vergil and Holinshed, did not mention Wolsey as having any role in bringing Buckingham to trial, and in their simpler versions they expressed no doubts that Buckingham was guilty. Vergil, however, had been imprisoned in the Tower, thanks to Wolsey, and his resulting hatred of the cardinal everywhere colours his reportage. His *Anglica Historia* was published during Henry's reign, so of course Buckingham's guilt was not to be questioned but, because of his own experience, Vergil could not avoid leaving an ambiguous account which accuses Wolsey of malice and personal vindictiveness in setting a trap for Buckingham by suborning Knevet to testify against the duke. Holinshed relied heavily on Vergil as he wrote his section on Buckingham, and calls attention to his own addition:
These were the speciall articles and points comprised in the indictment, and laid to his charge: but how trulie, or in what sort prooued, I haue not further to say, either in accusing him or excusing him, other than I find in Hall and Polydor, whose words in effect, I haue thought to impart to the reader, and without anie parciall wresting of the same either to or fro.
    Sauing that (I trust) I maie without offense saie, that (as the rumour then went) the cardinall chieflie procured the death of this noble man, no lesse fauoured of the people of this realm in that season, than the cardinall himselfe was hated and enuied. Which thing caused the dukes fall to be pitied and lamented, sith he was the man of all other, that chieflie went about to crosse the cardinall in his lordlie demeanor, & headie proceedings (p. 661).

character and her arguments operate strongly in his favour; and though the two never meet on stage, the link established between them in this scene is a recurring textual association that carries mutual reflexes on their legal situations. In 2.1, Buckingham's plight explicitly suggests to the Second Gentleman comparison with that awaiting Katherine:

> If the duke be guiltless,
> 'Tis full of woe: yet I can give you inkling
> Of an ensuing evil, if it fall,
> Greater than this. [. . .]
> [. . .] a separation
> Between the king and Katherine.   (2.1.139–49)

2.1 thus links Buckingham's fate, already decided, with gossip of the uncertainties now gathering around Katherine, and the following scene shows that the gossip is true. The association made between Buckingham and Katherine in these scenes is reinforced by the echoes in the descriptions of their trials. Buckingham concedes that, in having a trial at all, he is 'A little happier than my wretched father' (2.1.120), who had been attainted in Parliament and so 'without trial fell' (2.1.111); but he avoids pronouncement on the justice of his trial by granting simply that it was formally correct: 'I had my trial, / And must needs say a noble one' (2.1.118–19). Wolsey, projecting the clerical trial in England (where Katherine's defeat seems more probable than in Rome), repeats Buckingham's adjective 'noble', adding as well the adjective 'just' which the Duke had refrained from using, when he points to the importance of observing legal form: 'The Spaniard tied by blood and favour to her / Must now confess, if they have any goodness, / The trial just and noble' (2.2.89–91) – though Katherine herself will shortly disappoint Wolsey's expectations, when she contests the possibility of getting a fair trial in England. As in Act 2, the first two scenes of Act 3 also juxtapose the two plot interests. Following the cardinals' visit to Katherine in 3.1, the next scene opens (eight years after Buckingham's death) with the nobles' complaints about Wolsey and with Surrey's 'Remembrance of my father-in-law, the duke' (3.2.8) which gives him personal reasons to seek revenge against the cardinal, and memory of Buckingham's trial returns at greater length in the argument between Wolsey and Surrey in lines 254–69. The intersection of the fates of Katherine and Buckingham also appears in two crossed metaphors: proclaiming his innocence to the end, Buckingham goes to a death which for him is 'that long divorce of steel' (2.1.76), while the divorced Katherine receives the news of Henry's belated solicitousness for her welfare as appropriate to one who has already been condemned and executed: 'O my good lord, that comfort comes too late: / 'Tis like a pardon after execution' (4.2.120–1).

Despite the passage of time, the play refuses to forget Buckingham, and he is explicitly named again in 4.1, this time in connection with Anne, as the two Gentlemen who meet to describe her coronation (in 1533) recall for the audience that 'At our last encounter / The Duke of Buckingham came from his trial' (4.1.4–5). Harking back self-consciously to 1521, this appears to be simply fatuous court gossip, but the chronological dislocation – together with that of the third Gentleman's reference to 'York Place' rather than 'Whitehall' (as if Wolsey's fall from power in 1529 were too recent to avoid the linguistic confusion ('tis so lately altered that the old name / Is fresh about me') – is a reminder of changing legal and political fortunes in Henry's reign, and it is strategically inserted into this high-point of Anne's career. The play avoids showing Anne's subsequent fall, but the audiences of 1613 already knew the trajectory of her story, and some at least must have reflected, even as they watched the splendour of the coronation ceremony, that her moment of glory would not last long, and perceived the ironies of imminent change that placed her in the same lengthening list with Wolsey, Buckingham, Katherine, and others.

Six years separated Buckingham's death for

treason in 1521 from the first rumours (which Henry angrily denied as untrue) of problems in the marriage between Katherine and the king, reported in the chronicles for 1527. The chronological gap obscures – and contemporary historical narratives did not point out – the common causality behind Henry's antagonism to Buckingham and Katherine. Modern historians have long agreed that by the early 1520s Henry had come to see in each of them a major threat to the continuation of his dynasty: Katherine's non-production of a male heir was linked to Henry's fear of any of Edward III's male descendants who might contest the succession of Mary, whose sex weakened her claim to rule. But this is an evaluation that, even had they wanted to, Elizabethan chroniclers could hardly make, and between the temporally disjunctive fates of Buckingham and Katherine they wove no such political thread. In their accounts they chronicled events that stayed within the boundaries of the regime's official truths, and in this version Henry systematically eliminated potential problem-makers descending from Edward III because they were traitors and he sought annulment from Katherine because the marriage was against God's law. By choosing to start with Buckingham's trial for treason and linking him to Katherine, Shakespeare makes an association not easily visible in his chronicle sources. And yet, despite the various artistic means by which their two fates are so evidently joined, the play backs away from underlining the dynastic logic that historians now find so easily identifiable. In 1.2 Henry puts an obvious question to Buckingham's Surveyor: 'How grounded he his title to the crown / Upon our fail? To this point hast thou heard him / At any time speak aught?' (1.2.144–6). But the Surveyor's answer points to necromancy, not ancestry: 'He was brought to this / By a vain prophecy of Nicholas Henton' (146–7). Holinshed did not call attention to the dynastic logic that linked Katherine to Buckingham, but he did report the Duke's dangerous closeness to the throne,

through the surveyor's account of Buckingham's treasonous statement that 'if ought but good come to the king, the duke of Buckingham should be next in bloud to succeed to the crowne' (p. 659). Shakespeare suppresses this: about Buckingham's royal blood the play remains completely silent. Not present either is Buckingham's trial which occupies several pages in the chronicles. Henry has already publicly pronounced his own certainty of the duke's guilt, however, so that the verdict surprises no one:

SECOND GENTLEMAN
    Pray speak what has happen'd.
FIRST GENTLEMAN
    You may guess quickly what.
SECOND GENTLEMAN   Is he found guilty?
FIRST GENTLEMAN
    Yes truly is he, and condemn'd upon't.

                        (2.1.6–8)

This is the only instance in any of the history plays in which conspiracy and the guilt of treason are left in doubt. In place of the gallows confession which would justify the state's version of truth are Buckingham's obstinate affirmations of loyalty, his equivocal evaluation of the course of justice, and his pardon for those responsible for his death:

> I have this day receiv'd a traitor's judgment,
> And by that name must die; yet heaven bear witness,
> And if I have a conscience, let it sink me,
> Even as the axe falls, if I be not faithful.
> The law I bear no malice for my death,
> 'T has done upon the premises but justice:
> But those that sought it I could wish more Christians:
> Be what they will, I heartily forgive 'em.

                      (2.1.58–65)

The theory of the law's verdicts, as the word's two Latin roots suggest, is that they pronounce truth, but the audience has been supplied with none of the usual theatrical evidence that nails down guilt, and Buckingham is sent to his death, in a text which signals various reasons to doubt that justice has been wrought. Having

Katherine as his chief defender is an enormous boost to Buckingham's reputation; but the doubts Shakespeare creates in his case also have reflexes that are pertinent to Katherine – in part by illustrating how non-conflicting evidence and uniformity of opinion about the events of the past are difficult to achieve, but principally by suggesting that – despite ideal theories of the law's independence – the reality of law in Henry's reign made both of them victims of partisan injustice serving Henry's obvious power to bend legal process in the direction determined by his will.

If Shakespeare made the questions surrounding Buckingham more opaque than he found them, he greatly simplified the welter of legal problems that followed the belated awakening of Henry's conscience about his marriage to his brother's widow. Contradictions in the jurisdictions of law, in the legal past, and in legal procedure (not to mention the contradictions in Henry's professed beliefs about the Pope's power to dispense) emerged at every stage of the historical struggle between Henry and Katherine, and though Henry persistently opposed the Pope's ecclesiastical power to dispense his marriage to Katherine with the superior authority of God's law enunciated in Leviticus, the Bible itself contained conflicting laws about marriage to a dead brother's wife. (Leviticus xx, 21 affirms that 'If a man shall take his brother's wife, it is an impurity: he hath uncovered his brother's nakedness; they shall be childless', but Deuteronomy xxv, 5, enjoins a deceased man's brother to marry the widow. Anne Boleyn's sister Mary had been Henry's mistress, thus creating impediment for marriage with Anne – for which Henry asked the Pope for dispensation – but Henry opted for Leviticus and a strictly to-the-letter construction of 'brother's wife' that ignored any problems of affinity in 'wife's sister' when he decided to challenge the 1503 bull of dispensation that had permitted Katherine and Henry to marry in 1509.) The legal moves and countermoves over seven years of litigation were intricate, but in the end both Henry and Katherine averred, though from different sides, that the basic question was whether or not the marriage between Katherine and Arthur had been consummated. And this is precisely the question that *Henry VIII* ignores.

Katherine always maintained that she had been a virgin when she married Henry; in 1527–8, Henry began to gather witnesses he would later use to affirm that she was not.[12] The bull of dispensation which had permitted them to marry did not clarify this point for either side, since it had slipped the strange word 'perhaps' into the preamble: '*forsan consummatum*'.[13] After this uncertain opening description of marital relations between Katherine and Arthur, Julius's bull goes on to dispense the impediment of affinity between Henry and Katherine. But affinity depended on consummation. Without affinity, the impediment was that incurred by the act of formal betrothal, 'the justice of public honesty', which – precisely because there was no affinity produced by coitus – required specific dispensation. If the marriage with Arthur had not been consummated, therefore, Julius had dispensed the wrong impediment. Henry's awareness of the legal loophole open to him through public honesty is clear from the letter that was part of the documents dispatched to his agents in Rome in 1532: 'For in the bull is expressed that the pope dispensed [upon affinity], which springeth not without carnal [copulation], and no mention is made of . . . justice of public

---

[12] Scarisbrick, *Henry VIII*, p. 189.

[13] Though Bishop Fisher argued that the doubt had been added by Henry VII, Henry Ansgar Kelly suggests that '*forsan*' had been inserted at the insistence of Katherine's mother Isabella, 'because in her view the statement of consummation was not true'. See his *The Matrimonial Trials of Henry VIII* (Stanford, 1976), p. 97. Scarisbrick discusses the importance of '*forsan*' in the argument about the impediment of public honesty incurred by the promise to marry, as opposed to the carnal affinity of marriage, on pp. 187–96, and Kelly responds to this on pp. 30–7 and *passim*.

honesty . . . And so his bull was nothing worth, and consequently for lack of a sufficient dispensation, the marriage was not good, the impediment of justice and of public honesty letting the same' (quoted in Kelly, *Matrimonial Trials*, p. 154). But for Henry to avail himself of the defect of public honesty perforce necessitated his admission of the queen's virginity at marriage. Unwilling to give up his argument that in divine law non-dispensable affinity existed between him and Katherine and gamble on the less heinous irregularity committed in ecclesiastical law, Henry relinquished the argument of public honesty that did in fact technically impugn the legality of his marriage, and to the end encouraged the public belief that Katherine's relationship with Arthur had been consummated.[14]

The comparison of two texts which are nearly identical except for the crucial question of Katherine's virginity illuminates the sensitivity of Tudor chroniclers to political issues and exposes the weight of censorship (whether official or self-imposed) to which their texts were exposed.[15] Here is an excerpt from Katherine's self-defence at Blackfriars in the version John Stow published in 1592:[16]

I haue beene your wife these twentie yeeres or mo, and you haue had by me diuers children, *and when yee had me at the first, I take God to be my iudge, that I was a verie maid, and whether it be true or no, I put it to your conscience.* If there be anie iust cause that you can alledge against me either of dishonestie or in matter lawfull to put me from you, I am content to depart to my shame and rebuke: and if there be none, then I praie you to let me haue iustice at your hand.[17]

Holinshed's version is almost identical – except for the absence of the line I have emphasized above:

I haue beene your wife these twentie yeares and more & you haue had by me diuerse children. If there be anie iust cause that you can alleage against me, either of dishonestie, or matter lawfull to put me from you; I am content to depart to my shame and rebuke: and if there be none, then I praie you to let me haue iustice at your hand.   (p. 737)

The missing line would have been, after all, an inconvenient statement in a history that so often affirmed as historical fact that Katherine's marriage to Arthur had been consummated.

Like Holinshed, the play also suppresses any mention of Katherine's virginity; unlike Holinshed, however, it takes no stand at all regarding the consummation of her first marriage. Henry's 'conscience' is frequently – and by people out of Henry's ear-shot, ironically – alluded to, but even in Henry's longest public explanation, the real nature of the legal problem behind his 'scruple' is kept vague:

My conscience first receiv'd a tenderness,

---

[14] Chapuys wrote to Charles V in 1529 of Henry's taunting Katherine in private that her virginity did not matter, 'You are not my wife for all that, since the bull did not dispense *super impedimento publicae honestatis*'. As Kelly points out, once the trial was under way, 'This is the closest that Henry would come to admitting the queen's virginity' (pp. 129–30).

[15] Betty Travitsky's excellent article 'Reprinting Tudor History: The Case of Catherine of Aragon', *Renaissance Quarterly*, 50 (1997), 164–72, compares the textual changes that throughout the sixteenth century overtook the frequent reprintings of Vives's *Instruction of a Christen Woman*; she shows how these reflect the dangers felt in dealing with Katherine's political fortunes after the divorce, and then demonstrates how textual alterations and re-admissions at the end of the century rehabilitate Katherine, signalling that she was no longer felt to be a dangerous topic.

Phyllis Rackin's observations on the relationship between 'historiographic writing' and truth are pertinent: 'Historiographic writing no longer had a direct, unequivocal relation with historical truth. Alternative accounts of historical events and opposed interpretations of their causes and significance now threatened each other's credibility . . .' (*Stages of History: Shakespeare's English Chronicles* (Ithaca, 1990), p. 13).

[16] Judith Anderson presents evidence in *Biographical Truth: The Representation of Historical Persons in Tudor-Stuart Writing* (New Haven and London, 1984) that Shakespeare seems to have read the 1592 edition of Stow (see pp. 136–42).

[17] John Stow, *The Annales of England faithfully collected . . .* (London, 1592), p. 913 (emphasis mine). Cavendish's account slightly differs from Stow in wording, but not about Katherine's clear assertion of her virginity prior to marriage with Henry.

Scruple and prick, on certain speeches utter'd
By th' Bishop of Bayonne, then French
　　ambassador,
Who had been hither sent on the debating
A marriage 'twixt the Duke of Orleans and
Our daughter Mary: i'th' progress of this business,
Ere a determinate resolution, he
(I mean the Bishop) did require a respite,
Wherein he might the king his lord advertise
Whether our daughter were legitimate
Respecting this our marriage with the dowager,
Sometimes our brother's wife.　　(2.4.168–79)

And so it is with Katherine at Blackfriars in 2.4. In her defence she recalls her obedience as a wife, and fidelity in 'My bond to wedlock' ever since marriage to Henry. She has been sexually faithful to Henry, but the real issue, which concerned her sex life with Arthur, is skirted.

The delicacy about consummation with Arthur is noteworthy, particularly since her sexual activity with Arthur had been turned into such public material – a matter of prolonged international scrutiny, legislated on by Parliament and inscribed in the rolls of public statute, a subject for jokes in the chronicles about Arthur's thirst when he rose in the morning after spending a hot night in the middle of Spain. But Shakespeare maintains silence about what happened privately between Katherine and Arthur, while he is not so delicate about Anne. Sands' sexual badinage and his immediate physical familiarity with Anne in 1.4 create a problematic introduction to her, and the tone set there continues. In addition to the scabrous dialogue in 2.3 in which Anne and the Old Lady argue the economics of maidenhead (e.g., 'for little England / You'd venture an emballing'), we also hear that Henry's conscience 'Has crept too near another lady' (2.2.18); 'Our king has all the Indies in his arms, / And more and richer, when he strains that lady / I cannot blame his conscience' (4.1.45–7); 'Believe me sir, she is the goodliest woman / That ever lay by man' (4.1.69–70); it is 'not wholesome to / Our cause, that she should lie i'th' bosom of / Our

hard-rul'd king'(3.2.99–101) – with a double meaning of 'hard-rul'd' certainly intended; at her coronation procession 'Great-bellied women, / That had not a week to go, like rams / In the old time of war, would shake the press' (4.1.76–8). In short, Katherine's sexual conduct – which Henry, Parliament, and the Tudor chronicles turned into the central issue of debate in the litigation – is muted in the play, whereas Anne's sexuality clearly is not.

Neither Henry nor Katherine was present when the legatine court first met on 31 May 1529, and received from Henry's confessor, the Bishop of Lincoln, the pope's commission to the legates. On the next day the royal couple received their summonses to appear on 18 June, the day on which the public trial opened at Blackfriars (Kelly, *Matrimonial Trials*, pp. 75–8). Henry was represented by proxy, but Katherine appeared together with her legal counsel to announce her intention of appealing to Rome. On 21 June, the court reconvened. It is this session which is reported in such detail by Hall, Holinshed, Cavendish, and Stow, and dramatized by Shakespeare in 2.4.

The stage directions of the First Folio name four bishops – Lincoln, Ely, Rochester, St Asaph – as among those crowding the stage in the trial scene, but of these only one – the Bishop of Lincoln – gets to speak. Lincoln was, as indicated above, of the king's party; the silent bishops of Ely, Rochester, and St. Asaph were of the queen's. In historical fact, John Fisher, the Bishop of Rochester, was known to have been courageously outspoken in the queen's defence, and in Cavendish's account of the events after Katherine's departure from court on 21 June, Fisher publicly contradicted Henry's public announcement (compliantly backed by the Archbishop of Canterbury) that all the bishops had subscribed a document allowing their doubt of the marriage, and his protest contains a clear accusation of forgery:

'No, Sir, not I', quoth the Bishop of Rochester, 'ye have not my consent thereto.' 'No! Ha'the!'quoth the king, 'look here upon this, is not this your hand and seal?' and showed him the instrument with seals. "No forsooth, Sire', quoth the Bishop of Rochester, 'it is not my hand nor seal!' To that quoth the king to my Lord of Canterbury: 'Sir, how say ye, is it not his hand and seal?' 'Yes, Sir' quoth my Lord of Canterbury. 'That is not so', quoth the Bishop of Rochester, 'for you were in hand with me to have both my hand and seal, as other lords had already done; but then I said to you, that I would never consent to no such act, for it were much against my conscience; nor my hand and seal should never be seen at any such instrument, God willing, with much more matter touching the same communication between us.' 'You say truth', quoth the Bishop of Canterbury, 'such words ye said unto me; but at the last ye were fully persuaded that I should for you subscribe your name, and put to a seal myself, and ye would allow the same.' 'All which words and matter', quoth the Bishop of Rochester, 'under your correction, my lord, and supportation of this noble audience, there is no thing more untrue.'[18]

Rochester's was a highly visible role in Katherine's defence; in the years after Blackfriars, until he was executed for treason in 1535, he published seven tracts in defence of the marriage, was convicted of misprision in connection with the Holy Maid of Kent affair (see Hall, *The Vnion*, fol. ccxxiii[v] and Holinshed, *Third Volume of Chronicles*, p. 791), defied the terms of the First Act of Succession, and refused to subscribe to the oath of the Act of Supremacy (see Holinshed, *Third Volume of Chronicles*, p. 792). In view of Fisher's defence of her cause, Katherine's protest to Wolsey that she is 'Shipwrack'd upon a kingdom where no pity, / No friends, no hope, no kindred weep for me' (3.1.149–50) is not accurate; but without naming names, Shakespeare accommodated the truth elsewhere in the understanding of realpolitik expressed in Katherine's rhetorical question:

> can you think lords,
> That any Englishman dare give me counsel?
> Or be a known friend 'gainst his highness'
>   pleasure
> (Though he be grown so desperate to be honest)

And live a subject? (3.1.83–7)

The elderly bishop who appeared on the scaffold erected on Tower Hill in 1535 was neither the first nor the last of Katherine's defenders who provided the obvious answer to what it meant to operate "gainst his highness' pleasure'.

Katherine's majestic exit from the tribunal at Blackfriars was not entirely the dramatic surprise it appears in the chronicles and in the play. By the end of April 1529 agents for Katherine's nephew Charles V had already lodged a petition that the cause be revoked to Rome, and in her appearance at Blackfriars on 18 June Katherine had requested that her refusal of the papal legation's jurisdiction in England, together with her intention of appealing directly to the Pope, be recorded and notarized. The tribunal of 21 June began with the announcement that her request was overruled,[19] and it is after this point of order that Hall and Holinshed begin their descriptions of the day's events – a beginning altered in turn by the play, with Henry's order to dispense with the reading of the commission from Rome:

> What's the need?
> It hath already publicly been read,
> And on all sides th' authority allow'd;
> You may then spare that time. (2.4.2–5)

This is a brief, but remarkable, addition to the sources. It is certainly a sign of Henry's eroded patience, but it is also a sign immediately readable in the theatre that Henry is directing proceedings in this ecclesiastical court. I would also suggest that the addition holds somewhat more subtle criticisms of Henry's legal position as well, since two points are to be noted in the king's affirmation that the commission's authority is 'on all sides . . . allow'd': one is the historically known untruth of that affirmation

---

18 George Cavendish, *The Life of Cardinal Wolsey*, ed. Henry Morley (London, n.d.), pp. 101–2.
19 On these events see Kelly, *Matrimonial Trials*, pp. 59–86; Scarisbrick, pp. 222–5.

as far as Katherine's 'side' is concerned, a repudiation the court's of authority she repeats twice in this scene; the other is the ironic postscript added to the trial a few months later, when on 9 October the charge of praemunire – the illegal exercise of foreign jurisdiction on English soil – was brought against Wolsey in the King's Bench. The legal pretext was furnished by Wolsey's operating in England as Rome's legate *a latere*, an office he had exercised in England – obviously with Henry's consent – since 1521. But the real reason underlying this charge was his loss of Henry's support when he failed to procure Henry's divorce either in Rome or through the legatine court over which he had presided in England – a court whose 'authority', only a few months earlier, had clearly been 'allow'd'. The play tinkers with the sources making graft and corruption, rather than failure to free Henry from Katherine, appear as the principal reason for Wolsey's fall, but the historical importance of praemunire is recalled two scenes after the divorce trial:

> Lord cardinal, the king's further pleasure is,
> Because all those things you have done of late
> By your power legative within this kingdom
> Fall into th' compass of a praemunire;
> That therefore such a writ be sued against you,
> To forfeit all your goods, lands, tenements,
> Chattels and whatsoever, and to be
> Out of the king's protection. This is my charge.
>
> (3.2.336–44)

Praemunire was a legal weapon of uncertain scope and definition, which was part of its terror and efficacy, and Henry used it to cow not only Wolsey. With legal actions initiated in 1530, Henry found in praemunire the legal instrument by which he forced the entire English clergy into submission, an action that was an important preliminary to the revolutionary legislation that separated the church in England from that of Rome in 1534. The accusation started out as an indictment of the church for having accepted Wolsey's 'illegal' legateship, but by 1531, when Parliament

enacted its Pardon of the Clergy, the charge had become more comprehensive: the church was – after paying a hefty price – being pardoned for having exercised the Pope's jurisdiction in the ecclesiastical courts. Giving Henry the affirmation that Rome's commission to the legatine court is 'on all sides . . . allow'd' strikes me therefore as another of the play's telegraphic reminders of Henry's talent for adjusting legal 'facts' to his convenience.

Katherine never meant her cause to become what it did become, a case testing the legal limits of international church versus national state authority. But Katherine stymied Henry and Wolsey by pushing her right to have her cause heard under international ecclesiastical law. So Henry shed his chancellor and blocked Katherine's possibility of defence by changing England's relation to the internationalism of ecclesiastical law. It was a revolution, but the king and Parliament declared that they were simply resuscitating old rights that had lain buried under centuries of Rome's oppressive yoke: England had always been sovereign – it was Rome that had introduced novelty, and England was now only reasserting what had always been its ancient right.

Because of its chronological limits on Henry's reign and its final flattering leap forward into James's, *Henry VIII* eliminates from view decades of traumatic change and uncertainty in English history, delicate material that might have had difficulty getting past the censor; yet if the play thereby avoids any direct dealing with the most terrifying aspects of Henry's reign, it nonetheless holds out brief reminders that what happened later was already known. And it is through this area of the 'already known' that the text suggests ironic comparison with the version of history being represented, inviting at times a double vision of events through the different optics of the past being represented on stage and the future extending beyond it – a future known, when the play was first presented in 1613, to have held unsuspected reversals for many: Anne

Boleyn, Thomas More, Thomas Cromwell, Thomas Cranmer – and in the end, Henry himself. Henry removed a number of long-standing certainties from his subjects, but he did so within the forms of law: Henry waited years for his divorce before he seized on the fact that the laws which bound him to the past and dictated the present could not only be interpreted, but could also be – less expensively and more immediately – re-written or invented. Henry used the law to redefine the past and to attempt to direct the future: his operations on the past were largely successful, but it was the future – and the intensity of his interest in the future was, after all, the principal reason Henry struggled so tenaciously against the past – that time and again escaped Henry's script. By 1613 it was obvious that Henry's reign had brought important legal and religious change to England; but it was also obvious that his personal dynastic hopes and plans, which were largely responsible for these coming into being, had failed. Henry's complicated matrimonial history, though referred to by politicians and law-makers at the time of his divorce from Katherine as the king's 'private matter', produced numerous areas of uncertainty for the nation at large. Elizabeth's very different brand of marital politics also created national uncertainty: almost all of the spectators watching *Henry VIII* in 1613 were old enough to re-member the anxiety caused by the old Queen's refusal to name her successor until she lay dying, and although James was not an unex-pected choice once the death of his Catholic mother obviated the religious problem, his accession was, as Alan G. R. Smith points out, 'an explicit breach of Henry VIII's will and thus, by implication of the statute on which it was founded'.[20] Like the relationship between church and state, or Katherine's virginity, or

the number of months perceived to elapse between Anne's marriage to Henry and the birth of Elizabeth, or the validity of Henry's marriages and the legitimacy of his children, Henry's will proved to be yet another 'fact' of legal history subject to second thoughts and revision. Cran-mer's prophecy over Elizabeth in the play's final scene constructs the theatrical illusion of a non-problematic – and patriarchally sponsored – genealogy that, however James privately felt about Henry's memory, was politically useful to the first Stuart King of England. But if the genealogical links between Henry and James are made to seem smoother than they were in fact, other aspects of Henry's relationship to the law are shown for much of the play to be ambiguous, unstable, or untrustworthy. While he lived, the historical Henry found the law a useful instru-ment for implementing his will, and the play mirrors this truth. With the help of his coopera-tive Parliaments, Henry succeeded in covering the changes in his private thoughts and affections by rewriting the legal interpretation of the past, but his attempt to write the future failed: and the accession of the Stuart line was – literally – the crowning irony in the history of Henry's dynastic obsession. Only later history, well beyond the knowledge available to the audi-ences of 1613, would reveal the unsuspected failure of the males in the Stuart line as well.

---

[20] *The Emergence of a Nation State* (London and New York, 1984), p. 380. On the legality / illegality of the succes-sion see F. W. Maitland, *The Constitutional History of England* (Cambridge, 1968): 'if statutes on such a matter had any validity, the succession was probably illegal' (pp. 281–2); and Sir David Lindsay Keir, *The Constitu-tional History of Modern Britain Since 1485* (London, 9th edn. 1969): 'Henry VIII's will, statutory though its force was, had little effect either on the governmental system of Edward VI or on the succession to the throne' (p. 103).

'ALL WHICH IT INHERIT': SHAKESPEARE, GLOBES AND GLOBAL MEDIA

PETER DONALDSON

Shakespeare's association with something called 'the Globe' began in the late 1590s, when the first playhouse of that name was built in South-wark. Shakespeare's plays had been and would be performed in other locations, but the Globe has held a near-monopoly on the imaginations of later generations. There have been Globe theatres in England, Germany, Japan, New Zealand, Canada and the United States and no doubt elsewhere.[1] In 1997 'Shakespeare's Globe', reconstructed with assiduous scholarly care, opened near the original site on the South Bank of the Thames. Scale drawings, physical models, cinematic representations, editions of the plays, virtual reality tours[2] and countless references in scholarly and popular literature sustain the almost automatic pairing of play-wright and playhouse. 'The Globe' has become a near synonym for Shakespeare's work in the theatre.

This would not have been the case if the playhouse had been given a different name such as the Rose or the Curtain, for the local and historical embeddedness of the Globe is balanced by its being at the same time a reference to the world as a whole. Such a name helps reinforce the frequent claims that Shakespeare's plays are universal either in their appeal or in the accuracy and completeness of their representation of the human world. Before such a contemporary expression was ever uttered, Shakespeare had become a 'global' author.

Shakespeare's association with the electronic means of communication now known as global media began much later than his connection with the Globe. On 14 September 1876, Sir William Thomson (later Lord Kelvin) reported to the British Association in Glasgow on a new invention he had seen in North America: 'I heard "to be or not to be ... there's the rub" through an electric telegraph wire.'[3] Though there were as yet no intercontinental calls, telegraph cables linked Europe, America and Asia, and the telephone was thought of as an improved telegraph; it was the 'wonder of

---

[1] The original playhouse was rebuilt after fire in 1613 and retained the name; modern theatres which continue this tradition (some are replicas or reconstructions) include the Tokyo Globe, the Dunedin (NZ) Globe, the Neuss Globe in Germany, the Regina, Saskatchewan Globe, the San Diego Old Globe, the New York Globe (renamed the Lunt-Fontanne Theatre in 1958), the Norwalk, Connecticut Globe and the Globe of the Great Southwest in Odessa, Texas.

[2] Irwin Smith, *Shakespeare's Globe Playhouse: A Modern Reconstruction in Text and Scale Drawings* (New York, 1956); the C. Walter Hodges model in the Harvard Theatre Collection is described in *Shakespeare's First Globe Playhouse: the Harvard Theatre Collection Model* (Cambridge, Mass., 1984). Editions include The Globe Shakespeare (*The Works of William Shakespeare*, ed. William George Clark and William Aldis Wright (London, 1861) and the Shakespeare's Globe Acting Editions, ed. Patrick Turner (London, 1990–). The website of the reconstructed Globe is at *http://www.rdg.ac.uk/globe*; follow links to models of the New Globe in various stages of construction.

[3] Avital Ronel, *The Telephone Book* (Lincoln, Nebraska, 1989), p. 283.

8 Martin Behaim's Erdglob, 1492.

wonders of electric telegraphy'.[4] The new possibility that not merely coded messages but the subtle and evocative cadences of human voice could be transmitted electronically made the choice of Shakespeare appropriate as matter for the first demonstrations. So did the prospect that such messages would soon circle the planet, for Shakespeare was deemed a universal author, his works not 'of an age,' but for 'all time', not for one playhouse alone, but for the world, the 'great globe' to which the name of the playhouse alluded.

Since 1876 Shakespeare has provided early

---

[4] Ronel, *Telephone*, p. 285.

demo or launch content for many other modern media, including silent film, television, laserdisc, the expanded book on CD-ROM, and the World Wide Web.[5] Today, full productions continue to appear on film, radio and television, and there are sound recordings, videotapes, laserdiscs and digital video discs, Shakespeare websites, electronic Shakespeare discussion groups, interactive CD-ROMs and experiments in virtual reality production.[6] Shakespeare even appears as a cartoon figure in the 1997 version of Microsoft Word, a tiny bald figure in a ruff who pops up on screen when help is needed. Just as a web of artistic practices, resonances and connotations connected Shakespeare and the Globe at the turn of the seventeenth century, so, at the turn of the millennium, Shakespeare seems to have an ever more natural, self-evident role to play as a symbol of the successful transition from the era of print and live theatre to that of digital media and world-wide networks.

In this essay I reflect on several of the ways in which 'global Shakespeare' inherits and transforms the associations and resonances of 'Shakespeare and The Globe', emphasizing lexical shifts, changing images of the earth, and the appearance of the Globe in several Shakespeare films. This will not be a comprehensive treatment of 'global Shakespeare' but a traversal of a fragmentary and partly imaginary mapping, a set of *ad hoc* navigational aids.

GLOBUS, ERDGLOB, 'THE' GLOBE

In classical Latin, globes are often more humble and domestic than the 'great globe' evoked in *The Tempest*, less exciting and more provincial than the 'global' economies, global warming, and global cuisine of today. *Globare* means to compress into a ball, and *globus* is that ball. It can be a heavenly body, as it often is, for example, in Apuleius and Cicero, or, much more rarely, a model of the heavens, as when Ovid describes the orrery of Archimedes, 'made by Sicilian art and suspended in air'. It also *can*

be the earth (*globus terrae*) but only when specified as such (*globus* alone does not mean earth).[7] The word can equally well refer to a

5 Herbert Beerbohm Tree's *King John* and the Meliès *Antony and Cleopatra* were produced in 1899, and Sarah Bernhardt performed the 'duel scene' from *Hamlet* for the Paris Exposition of 1900. See Kenneth Rothwell and Annabelle Henkin Melzer, *Shakespeare on Screen: An International Filmography* (New York, 1990), pp. 6, 74, 238 and Olwen Terris and Luke McKernan, *Walking Shadows: Shakespeare in the National Film and Television Archive* (London, 1994), pp. 81–2. The Sarah Bernhardt sequence is now available as part of the Shakespeare Electronic Archive at the Folger Shakespeare Library and at MIT. Television production of Shakespeare began in 1937 with the BBC Television Service productions of several scenes, followed by a full production of *Julius Caesar* (see Rothwell, *Shakespeare on Screen*, p. 114). Among the first laserdisc titles was the Criterion editions of *Hamlet*. The first CD-ROM expanded book edition of a Shakespeare play was the Voyager *Macbeth* (Irvington, NY, 1994), incorporating the text of the New Cambridge *Macbeth*, ed. A. R. Braunmuller. The earliest 'complete works' on the World Wide Web was Jeremy Hylton's site at *http://the-tech.mit.edu/Shakespeare*.

6 A 'virtual reality' version of *A Midsummer Night's Dream* produced by Stphen N. Matsuba and Bernie Roehl was multicast on the World Wide Web on April 26, 1998, using animated puppets. See *http://www.shoc.com/vrmldream*.

7 I summarize the references in the sixteenth-century Latin dictionaries of Thomas Elyot, *The Dictionary of syr Thomas Eliot* (London, 1538) and Thomas Thomas, *Dictionarium Linguae Latinae et Anglicanae* (Cambridge, 1587), as well as Charlton T. Lewis and Charles Short, *A Latin Dictionary* (Oxford, 1879, repr. 1966) and P. G. W. Glare, *Oxford Latin Dictionary* (Oxford: Clarendon, 1986), supplemented by a word search on Pandora, which yielded 256 instances of the string 'glob . . .'. These references suggest that the word had an astronomical sense far more often than one might expect on the basis of the printed dictionaries, but the more general meanings of the word and especially the military one predominate. For *globus* as a heavenly body see Apuleius: *De mundo* 2.7, 2.17,21.8,29.5; only the last refers to earth, where it is *globus terrae*; Cicero: *De republica* 6.15.9,6.15.12,6.16.15,6.17.4,6.17.10; *Tusculanae disputationes* 1.68.12,2.47.15; *De divinatione* 1.97.7. When, in these instances, *globus* means the earth it is *globus terrae*. Ovid: *Fasti* 6.278–280 refers to the globe of Archimedes, brought to Rome by Marcellus in 212 BC The whole model of the heavens is *globus*, while the model of earth (*terra*) is a part of it. J. G. Frazer, trans., *Ovid's Fasti*

child's toy or anything vaguely spherical and pushed together – small spheres (*globi farinae* are dumplings; *globi lanae*, balls of wool) or large roughly round masses, including fireballs, groups of people standing together or soldiers in close formation. In fact, this last meaning is the most common one in classical and late Latin.

Medieval Latin has a similar range of meanings. D. R. Howlett's *Dictionary of Medieval Latin from British Sources*, for example, lists meaning (1) as 'A compact mass of more or less spherical shape', and instances 'globes' of thread, of water, of fire and clots of blood as examples. Meanings (2), (4), (5), and (6) continue classical usage: ball, mass, group, throng or pack (of dogs). Meaning (3) is 'sphere of heavenly body' and (3b) specifies 'of earth', citing John of Salisbury: 'de singulis que in sublunari globo proveniunt' (*Policraticus* 440a), where the 'globe' has to be specified as 'beneath the moon' for the word to refer unambiguously to earth.[8] As in classical Latin, *globus* can refer to the sphere of the planet earth, but there are no instances in which *globus* alone is a synonym for the earth, as 'globe' is in English today.

This use of 'globe' to mean a large mass or mass of people is the main one in Middle English, where 'globbe' or 'glubbe' is used by Wycliff to translate both *moles* ('the water that been nethermore sholyn rennyn and faylyn: tho forsothe that comyn from aboue sholyn stonde to gedere in o globbe', Josh. 3:13) and *globus* ('Al thi glubbe stoonde agen the Lord', cf. Vulgate 'Et omnis globus tuus stet contra Dominum?', Num. 16:11). The Michigan *Middle English Dictionary*[9] has a separate entry for 'globe' as distinct from 'glob' or 'globbe', and defines it as 'a sphere, globe': 'As he [St Martin] was at mes, a byrning globe aperid aboun his head.' But this example is very late in the Middle English period (1450) and does not in any case require that one understand 'globe' in its Modern English sense of sphere or globe, since 'byrning globe' corresponds to the common Latin meaning of fireball (*globus ignis*). Neither the Michigan dictionary nor the older Middle English dictionaries of Stratmann and Mayhew have examples of globe in the sense of the globe of earth or a model of the earthly or heavenly spheres.[10]

In Modern English, the *Oxford English Dictionary*'s first citation is from 1551, where globe means 'a body round as a bowl'. For globe meaning 'the earth' *OED* cites Richard Eden's *Treatise of New India*, 1553 where the context is circumnavigation: 'the whole globe of the earth has been sailed about'. *OED* also cites Shakespeare: 'We the globe can compass soon, / Swifter than the wandring moone'. (*Midsummer Night's Dream* 4.1.97). This reference is actually the first listed in which 'the globe', used without specification, means 'the earth', though the *OED*'s heavy reliance on Shakespeare should make one hesitate to declare this usage a Shakespearian first. Both Eden and Shakespeare present the globe of earth as wholly traversible. The third meaning in the sixteenth century is a spherical map of the earth or the celestial spheres, and Eden again provides the first instance. The *Midsummer Night's Dream* passage alludes to this third meaning as the second since the conjunction of 'compass' and 'globe' could refer as appropriately to cartographic measurement as well as to actual travel (the fairies in the play are sometimes referred to as if they themselves were miniature beings).

Among early dictionaries in English, Florio's Italian dictionary defines *globo* as 'A globe. Also

(Cambridge MA, 1909), pp. 340–1. I am grateful to Jon E. Lendon of the University of Virginia for advice and on-line searches of Latin sources.

8 D. R. Howlett, *Dictionary of Medieval Latin from British Sources* (Oxford, 1989).

9 Sherman Kuhn and John Reidy, *Middle English Dictionary* (Ann Arbor (in progress), 1963–).

10 Francis Henry Stratmann, *Middle English Dictionary*, rev. Henry Bradley (Oxford, 1891; repr. 1978); A. L. Mayhew and Walter W. Skeat, *A Concise Dictionary of Middle English from A.D. 1150 to 1580* (Oxford, 1888; repr. Folcroft, PA, 1972).

a type of the whole world' (1598),[11] and Bullokar and Cockeram's 'hard-word' English dictionaries of 1616 and 1623 define globe as 'A round bowle, or the description of the world, made in such a forme', leaving out the second meaning – the earth.[12] Thomas Blount's *Glossographia* of 1656 does not define globe, but includes it in defining a number of other words, including 'navigator'.

We use to say, Sir Francis Drake was the first that sailed round about the world, which may be true in a mitigated sence; viz. that he was the first Captain or person of note that atchieved this enterprize (Magellanus perishing in the midst of it) and therefore is reported to have given for his Devise, Globe with this Motto. 'Tu primus circumdedisti me.'[13]

Here, influenced perhaps by the cosmopolitan and egalitarian side rather than the narrowly territorial, colonialist or early capitalist associations of the idea of circumnavigating the globe, Blount takes what we might now term a generously global perspective, casting doubt on an English myth and appropriately crediting the Portuguese–Castilian voyage with priority.

In early modern English usage, then, some meanings of 'globe' are more prominent than in Latin and Middle English – the globe is more apt to mean the earth or the geographical or cosmological models of earth or the heavens, and the examples chosen for use in a number of dictionaries, from the sixteenth century to the *OED* suggest that the shift had to do with the common *use* of geographic globes and the actual crossings of the surface of the earthly globe by Magellan, Drake and other explorers. Blount's example also suggests a kind of circuit from the terrestrial globe to its models and representations that is relevant to Shakespeare: the word 'globe' in Blount refers to the representation of a globe in Drake's device. Was the representation that of the earth, or an image of a navigational globe, being, in the latter case, a model of a model? Did it have longitudinal and latitudinal lines, names of continents and oceans? The medal struck to commemorate

Drake's voyage of 1577–80 in the British Museum is a two-sided map of the world, cast in silver, with Drake's route, including the spur of the voyage to Northern California before Drake sailed across the Pacific, traced in dotted lines. The dates of English claims are inscribed as are longitudes, latitudes and place names.[14] Drake's coat of arms, on the other hand, includes a globe with no markings, surmounted by the Golden Hind. A celestial hand holds a banner on which the words *auxilio divino* are inscribed, and at the bottom of the device the legend *sic parvis magna*.[15]

No geographic model of the earth in the form of a sphere was produced in Europe between late antiquity and the late fifteenth century, when the famous Martin Behaim *erdglob* commissioned by the Nuremberg council was completed in 1492 (fig. 1). Recent studies, including Jerry Brotton's *Trading Territories*, John Gillies, *Shakespeare and the Geography of Difference*, and Gillies and Virginia Vaughan, *Playing the Globe* trace in detail the

---

11 John Florio, *A World of Wordes, or Most Copious, and Exact Dictionarie in Italian and English* (London, 1598).

12 J. B. [John Bullokar]; *An English Expositor* (London, 1616; facsimile repr. Menston (Yorks), 1967); Henry Cockeram, *The English Dictionarie* (London, 1623; repr. New York, 1930).

13 'You were the first person to go all the way around me' (my translation); Thomas Blount, *Glossographia* (London, 1656), s.v. 'navigator'. I am grateful to Ian Lancashire both for his on-line Early Modern English Dictionaries Database at *http://www.chass.utoronto.ca/english/emed/emedd.html* and for his performing searches of material not yet available on the public site.

14 BM CD 1852.5.7.1. See also Miller Christy, *Silver Map of the World: A Commemoration of Drake's Great Voyage* (London, 1900). An image of the medal appears in Peter Whitfield, *The Image of the World: Twenty Centuries of World Maps* (San Francisco, 1994), p. 75. I am grateful to Luke Syson, Curator of Coins and Medals. Syson believes the medal was struck *circa* 1590.

15 'With divine assistance'; 'thus great things from small'. I am grateful to Oliver Seeler for sending me a digital image of Drake's drum at Buckland Abbey, on which Drake's heraldic device is painted. See also Seeler's website on Drake at *http://www.mcn.org./2/oseeler/drake.htm*

role such globes and the associated maps of the 'new geography' played not only in the Renaissance voyages, but in the culture and discourse associated with discovery.[16] In the sixteenth century, globes and illustrated circular maps of the earth were often luxury items, of central symbolic importance in advancing the claims to possession of new territories by Castile, Portugal or England, but of less practical aid to navigation than portolan charts, logs and navigators' accounts. On Magellan's visit to Spain to seek sponsorship

he brought with him a well-painted globe showing the entire world, and thereon traced the course he proposed to take, save that the strait was purposely left so that no one could anticipate him.[17]

Las Casas also notes that Magellan actually knew where the strait was, having seen it on a chart made by one Martin Behaim in the treasury of the King of Portugal.[18] In Magellan's use, the globe was the sixteenth century equivalent of a computer demonstration in that it seemed to show that the thing could be done rather easily but that further research was required to find out exactly how. Magellan also brought globes on the voyage itself, tangible symbols of the whole journey, useful, perhaps, in motivating a crew greatly in need of encouragement, as most perished on the journey.

Thus, while any sphere could be a 'globe', in the sixteenth century globe was a particularly dynamic word for earth used preferentially when either its mapping or its traversal was in question, and it was also used when the earth was thought of in contrast to or in comparison with celestial spheres. What is unique about this word – and quite unlike the words sphere, earth, orb, or even theatre – is that both reality and representation not only *can* be meant by it, but are such equally possible meanings that in many contexts – and not only in Prospero's famous speech – one simply cannot tell whether 'the globe' means a tiny model or the earth itself; or, indeed, whether it means a tiny

model of the heavens or the heavens themselves. All this makes it a very rich name for a theatre, not requiring, but making possible a range of meanings depending on how the word was used in the fluid space of secular performance. Note also, in these examples, a reversal of the Latin idea of compression into a ball – sixteenth-century globes move, more often, from small to great. The sixteenth-century globe, whether theatrical or geographic, has often been regarded as microcosm. Of course it is that, but it is a dynamic, performative symbol, implying motion out into and around greater spaces; it is microcosm, map and talisman.

Shakespeare uses 'globe' in a dozen passages, written both before and after the construction of the playhouse, while 'earth' is used in hundreds.[19] 'Earth' is often though by no means always the more neutral term, while all Shakespeare's uses of the word 'globe' have the dynamic quality I have suggested – they refer either to circumnavigation, eclipse, or comparison of lesser spheres to great, either explicitly or metaphorically. 'And make a sop of all this solid globe' in *Troilus* (1.3.113) suggests transformation though not travel, and draws on the Latin meaning of compression. The kitchen

---

[16] Jerry Brotton, *Trading Territories: Mapping the Early Modern World* (Ithaca, NY, 1998); John Gillies, *Shakespeare and the Geography of Difference* (Cambridge, 1994). See esp. pp. 75–98 on the relation between the Globe theatre and the new maps and globes of the world; John Gillies and Virginia Vaughan (eds.), *Playing the Globe* (Pittsburgh, 1998). Work in progress by my colleagues Shankar Raman and Nicolas Wey Gomez will also contribute to this subject.

[17] Brotton, *Territories*, p. 123, quoting Bartolomé de Las Casas' account as translated in Samuel Eliot Morison, *The European Discovery of America* (Oxford, 1974), p. 324.

[18] Brotton, *Territories*, pp. 124, 194n, and Antonio Pigafetta, *Magellan's Voyage* (New Haven, 1974), I, 51.

[19] Marvin Spevack, *Complete and Systematic Concordance to the Works of Shakespeare* (Hildesheim, 1968–80), 9 vols. lists 330 references to earth and 670 to world; 'orb' and 'sphere' have ten each.

maid in *Errors* is 'spherical, like a globe' (3.2.116). Though she is difficult to circumnavigate, Dromio could, like Drake, 'find out countries in her' (117). In *Titus*, Tamora is imagined as the allegorical figure of revenge, traversing 'the globe' in her chariot like Hyperion (5.2.49). In *Contention* the Queen tells the exiled Suffolk 'wheresoe'er thou art in this world's Globe / I'll have an Iris that shall find thee out' (3.2.410–11). Other passages contrast one astronomical body with another – the sun and moon eclipse 'the affrighted globe' in *Othello* (5.2.109); Kent waits for the light of the moon, the 'beacon to this under globe' (*History*, Sc. 7.157; *Tragedy*, 2.2.154) in order to read a letter , and in *Richard II* the moon itself is, uniquely, referred to as the globe that lights the lower world (3.2.34). Falstaff, who is a 'globe of sinful continents', is a relatively small body compared to a much larger sphere (*2 Henry IV*, 2.4.288). Hamlet's 'distracted globe' (1.5.97) is one, perhaps, whose orbit has been wrenched from a regular path, but it is equipped with at least one seat (for 'memory', personified) and so alludes to the playhouse, as a number of the other instances might do if spoken in performance at the Globe.

'ALL WHICH IT INHERIT SHALL DISSOLVE'

Prospero's exquisitely complex lines on the fading or dissolving of the globe combine several levels of transformation and comparison. The passage draws on the conflation of representation and referent which the word globe had acquired in the period, praising, as is well known, the quasi-magical powers of theatrical representation at the moment of their interruption and renunciation. Whether *The Tempest* was written for or ever performed at the Globe, the passage would be diminished if we could not hear a reference to the playhouse in this passage. If the baseless fabric of the 'vision' Prospero refers to is the masque, then the 'great Globe' could mean the playhouse, even if the line were spoken elsewhere. If 'the baseless fabric of this vision' encompasses masque and stage, the 'great globe' can be the earth. If 'this vision' extends, as it may, to all of life on earth (the lower globe), then the 'great globe' is that of the celestial heavens. And this, too dissolves – as indeed it ought to do according to Revelations,[20] in which earth and heaven both vanish completely. And perhaps the passage implies an even greater apocalypse, a more complete extinction of life than any predicted by St. John, for in Shakespeare even the blessed, those who will inherit the earth at the end of time, 'yea, *all* which it inherit shall dissolve' in *The Tempest* whereas in *Revelations* the saved are spared the second death and live forever. At every point, lesser globes merge, lexically, with greater ones; relationships between performers and spectators shift, and representations change

---

[20] Vanish completely: Revelations 20:6; 20:11; 21:1; 22:5; 'dissolve': 2 Peter 3:12. 'Looking for and hasting unto the coming of the day of God, wherein the heavens being on fire shall be dissolved, and the elements shall melt with fervent heat.' The second death: Revelations 20:6; 20:14–15. 'All that it inherit' Matt. 5:5 and see the Arden *Tempest* (Arden 2), ed. Frank Kermode (Cambridge Mass., 1954). Kermode notes the relevance of Matthew 5 in his note to 4.1.154, but does not cite Revelations. The meaning of the biblical parallel becomes clear when both the 'blessed' of the Sermon on the Mount, who inherit the earth, and those who rule on earth and survive the second death after the vanishing of the earth in Revelations are thought of together. In addition, the Revelations and 2 Peter passages echo Isaiah 34:4: 'and all the host of heaven shall be dissolved, and the heavens shall be rolled together as a scroll: and all their host shall fall down, as the leaf falleth off from the vine, and as a falling fig from the fig tree'. The image is echoed in Revelations 6:4. In the Vulgate, the scroll is a book (*liber*) and the leaf at least potentially a page (*folium*). See John Ahern, 'Dante's Last Word: The "Comedy" as a *liber coelestis*', *Dante Studies*, 102 (1984), 1–14 and Peter S. Donaldson, 'Digital Archives and Sibylline Fragments: "The Tempest" and the End of Books', *Postmodern Culture* [online-only journal at *http://muse.jhu.edu/journals/postmodern_culture*] 8.2 (January 1998). See page 5 of the hypertext.

places with the realities to which they point. If those realities themselves are considered in their aspect of impermanence, illusion, or mutability, the passage becomes almost painfully complex – 'strangely disturbing' is Anne Barton's expression.[21]

To complicate matters slightly further, John Demaray has recently argued that the globe that dissolves in *The Tempest* would call to mind, for the play's first documented performances at Whitehall, the huge rotating globe in Jonson's *Hymenaei*, which held eight of the principal masquers during performance in 1606 and was re-used in the *Haddington Masque* in 1608 and possibly again in *Oberon* in 1610. Demaray speculates that this globe, suitably repainted, may actually have appeared on stage in the Whitehall stagings of *The Tempest* in 1611 and 1613.[22] Whether or not this was the case, the King's Men did perform in the Globe, at Blackfriars and at Whitehall, and because 'the globe' could have been and meant different things in each of these performance spaces, the argument that Prospero's speech can refer to the mutability of the forms of art – what we now call 'media in transition' – is strong. Jonson's wonderful globe of silver, 'filled with golden countrys' and apparently turning in midair, also seemed to him a kind of icon of the temporality of media and the passing of time: 'the envie onely was, that it lasted not still, or (now it is past) cannot by imagination, muche less description, be recovered to a part of that *spirit* it had in the gliding by'. Jonson's lovely passage is framed in terms that might apply to many of the evanescent pleasures and splendours of life, and, since the globe in *Hymenaei* is specifically 'a Microcosme, or Globe, (*figuring Man*)' this elegy for the passing moment of performance, like Prospero's lines on the fading of his masque, also proleptically laments the end of human life as a whole, and the dissolving (for that was the technical term for the disappearance of objects and persons in a masque) of the earth 'itself'.[23]

FROM 'GLOBE' TO 'GLOBAL'

To move from 'globe' to 'global', one must note that the latter word was not used in Shakespeare's time at all. Unlike 'globe', Latin provides no basis for it, as *globosus* is the adjectival form of 'globe'. The first edition of the OED lists the word 'global' as rare and offers only two instances, one in 1676 and 1849, where the earth is referred to as 'spherical, that is global'.[24] Despite the circumnavigation of the earth in 1522 and Marx's predictions of world economies in the *Communist Manifesto*, and the fact of instant intercontinental electronic communication in the 1870s, when telegraph cables connected Asia, Europe and the Americas,[25] these were not then called global phenomena, but world-wide, international, universal. In the second edition of the OED, we find 'global' in the sense of world-wide dating from 1892 – but until 1928, only in quotations, suggesting a new usage. *Harper's Magazine* (1892) has this passage:[26] 'M. de Vogüé loves travel; he goes to the East and to the West for colors and ideas; his interests are as wide as the universe; his ambition, to use a word of his own, is to be "global."' And in 1927, the *Contemporary Review* for 24 August has: 'The essence of the American proposal therefore was its "global"

---

21 Anne (Righter) Barton, *Shakespeare and the Idea of the Play* (London, 1962; repr. Westport, Conn., 1977), p. 203.

22 John Demaray, *Shakespeare and the Spectacles of Strangeness: 'The Tempest' and the Transformation of Renaissance Theatrical Forms* (Pittsburgh, 1998), pp. 91–2.

23 C. H. Herford, Percy and Evelyn Simpson, ed., *Ben Jonson* [works], Vol. 7 (Oxford, 1970), pp. 229, 213.

24 A Search on Chadwyck Healey's LION database yields earlier instances in Alexander Hart, *The History of Alexto and Angelica* (1640): 'glittering Phoebus doth begin his course, who lifting up his Globall front, from Cinthiaes glittering palme doth wash his face ...' and 'raise my Genius within the circle of this Globall head of mine, to limbe Angelica with poesie'.

25 John B. Thompson, *The Media and Modernity* (Stanford, 1995), p. 153.

26 *OED*, 2nd edn.

criterion.' In both cases, the new usage is doubly designated as foreign, placed in inverted commas and considered as a French or American innovation (the emphasis perhaps marks an anxiety lest the neologism triumph in fact as well as in speech – these places would, of course, no longer *be* quite so foreign if all the implications of M. De Vogué's word 'global' were ever realized.)

The 1920s bring accounting and commercial examples – 'global tonnage', 'global receipts', then 'global warfare' in the forties, and in 1946, in Julian Huxley's remarks on UNESCO, he speaks of 'A scientific world humanism, global in extent and evolutionary in background.'

The *OED* second edition has a separate entry on 'global village', Marshall McLuhan's phrase, first used in 1959:

9 'Whole Earth' from Space, Apollo 11 (NASA).

electronic media contract the world to a village or tribe where everything happens to everyone at the same time: everyone knows about, and therefore participates in, everything that is happening the minute it happens. Television gives this quality of simultaneity to events in the global village.

McLuhan's views have been rightly characterized as technologically utopian, locating collective authority in the as-yet-to be-realized cultural and political forms communications would supposedly foster – and they certainly did their part in distracting attention from the advance of the actual effects of global economics under late capitalism. (The expression 'global village, global pillage' might be taken as shorthand for this less optimistic view of the matter.) McLuhan made the word 'global' a global expression, but its use in the 1960s pales in comparison with its ubiquity, in a slightly altered sense, today. A search on the web in July 1998 turned up 11 million hits, while the poor distracted globe, in all its senses, not all of them Shakespearian, appeared 1,000,000 times.[27] Our use of the word is, as I have said, slightly different from McLuhan's. 'Global' is so often used in relation to digital communications

that it is easy to forget that he was not writing about computer networks at all – television was the electronic medium par excellence in the global village, and though the two are related, I would like to distinguish McLuhan's idea of televisual immediacy from the somewhat different implications of the digital variant of electronic culture (at least in the present, early phase of that culture).

As an illustration of the iconography of the global village, one might use the photographs of the whole earth as seen from space by the astronauts of the Apollo Saturn 11 mission. Illustration 9 is one of several such images that were published in the wake of the mission. It is one of the best known photographs of all time. In the context of the late 1960s, it seemed an object of stunning beauty, summing up, even

---

[27] Shakespeare himself appears in 500,000 web pages, and 'theatre' in two million. 'Electronic' yielded 22 million, and the great Web itself 66 million. Surely we have entered again the age of self-referential media. It is true that in the Middle Ages a book might begin 'heere begynneth the boke...' but it is not true that 'book' was the most frequently found word in books.

for many sceptics concerned with the expense of the space programs and its role in distracting attention from the global politics behind the United States' involvement in Vietnam, to combine human and technological adventure with the sense that there was a world that could be seen as a whole, and therefore as a mutually responsible community. Out of this cultural moment came such durable concerns as the ecological movement, along with a host of pseudoscientific and utopian ideas about the whole earth, and even the neopagan idea of the earth – Gaia – as a kind of organism. It is amazing how brief that moment was ('the envy only was, it lasted not still') – and in retrospect how enmeshed it was with a certain kind of modernist aesthetic now past peak. As in Clement Greenberg's notorious comparison of appreciating painting to hitting a baseball[28] – where the moving sphere is grasped, assessed, and responded to in a split second – the earth was seen by the camera in a small fraction of a second from a fixed point, in a single medium, and its image reproduced in the stunning detail made possible by Hasselblad engineering and Zeiss optics.

The earth image is photographic, while McLuhan's global village was televisual – yet this image belongs to the era and the aesthetic of televisual immediacy nevertheless and is one of its enduring symbols. Its publication history and its meaning were framed by and understood in the context of the great media event of the lunar mission, and of wide and immediate electronic access to that event through lower-definition video, a scratchy audio link to President Nixon, and that very odd message from the moon, with its awkward attempt to distinguish between 'Man' and 'mankind'. So universalizing was the discourse surrounding this event that Neil Armstrong, not heeding Rabelais' wise advice that 'man in general' has never been seen, forgot that he himself was only 'one man' or 'a man', and so flubbed his line and uttered the first lunar tautology. Whatever the reason, the broadcast was an erratic 'first step' in the transmission of

human presence from the moon. The published photographs, produced by the more mature technology of still colour photography, and not subject to the human errors of dramatic performance, made whole the fragmentary quality of the broadcast, and implied that first steps would be followed by others (though this did not happen).[29]

Olivier's *Henry V* presents the other Globe, the playhouse, but I will suggest that it, too, has televisual ambitions, and uses film like television. The film begins with the theatre – or rather with an aerial approach to the theatre, pausing at the Bear Garden and then, as if correcting the mistake made in Hollar's seventeenth century map, coming in for a close view of the Globe. We see tiring house activities, actors getting into costume, swigging ale, the boy actresses shaving and putting on wigs, stuffing oranges in their bodices and then deciding against the full-bosomed approach to female impersonation. We see the king (or the 'actor' who plays the king at the Globe), hesitate and cough nervously before entering the stage, and accompany him in his triumphal entrance and then on his heroic exploits and inward meditations as the film slowly moves outward from the Globe, in carefully planned steps, to the vast fields of France, as seemlessly as possible blending stage reality and cinematic location work. These hesitations – the shift

---

28 Rosalind Krauss, *The Optical Unconscious* (Cambridge, Mass., 1993), p. 7.

29 As I write, the integration of space voyage, photograph and broadcast enters another round as the Discovery mission is being shown to a limited audience at the Boston Science Museum as the first ever high definition broadcast in the Boston area. Portions of the broadcast are rebroadcast on the evening network news in conventional television resolutions, and, as the astronaut John Glenn flies over Perth, Australia, as he did in 1962, still photographs of Perth from space are promised as a gift to the city. (The Perth overflight was reported with images on 'The Ten O'Clock News' Channel 5, 30 October 1998, and see Don Avoin and Bruce Mohr, 'HDTV Blasts Off with Shuttle,' *Boston Globe*, 31 October 1998, pp. D1, D9.

from Bear Garden to Globe, the lead boy's rejection of his improvised bosom, the backstage drinking of the clergy, the king's cough – all suggest human imperfection, and perhaps also a contrast with the precise aerial descent into Nuremberg of Adolf Hitler's plane in *Triumph of the Will;* a contrast between the godman ruler Adolf Hitler and the imperfect, human, and improvisational nature both of Shakespeare's theatre and the culture that takes that theatre as its centre.[30]

Such acknowledgement of the poverty of the stage links the opening of the Olivier film to Shakespeare's chorus, but is not matched by comparable humility in its cinematic ambitions. Indeed, Olivier wrote quite immodestly of his work and of its medium, claiming that Shakespeare needed the representational resources of colour film and would have used them if he had lived today, and, further, that in enhancing the play in this way, he, the director, felt the spirit of Shakespeare within him, guiding his work.[31] While maintaining contact with its origins on the London stage, the film makes good the defects Chorus speaks of, filling the screen with the 'real' horses and battles, jumping o'er times and places – and its ability to do so is presented, I think, as a warrant of national character and determination in a perilous struggle. In *Film in the Aura of Art*, Dudley Andrew charts the complex chiasmic structure by which the film carefully grades its levels of realism – from the stage reality of the Globe to the intermediate world of the French court, with its artificial sets to the two scenes which are the centre of the film – the portrayal of a realistic battle and the companion scene, the presentation of the king's private thoughts in close-up voice-over.[32] We proceed from the theatrical to cinematic epic and cinematic intimacy – and then, by equally fine degrees, return to the stage of the Globe for the conclusion, for this is not a film about leaving the past or the theatre behind, but being inspired by it, fulfilling it. This *Henry V*, then, emphasizes precisely the dynamic, outward movement from the globe as model of a world

to the globe as an aid in traversing and possessing that world implicit in sixteenth-century cartographic as well as theatrical usage. Henry's return – not only to London, as in the text, but to the stage of the globe, with his victory achieved, and his princess beside him – is a triumph not only over the French and allegorically over fascism, but of the combined arts of the theatre and film over the reality they capture.

Olivier's *Henry V* has a place in television history as well. As John Cottrell and others have noted, the film is the successor to a planned television broadcast of the play. BBC Television service began in 1936, and its early production included televised Shakespeare. Dallas Bower, who had been producer-director on the BBC's *Kate and Petruchio, Julius Caesar* and *The Tempest*, wrote a script for *Henry V* in 1938.[33] BBC television broadcasts were suspended when war broke out. Bower himself was exempted from active duty to become supervisor of film for the Ministry of Information, and in that job continued to work on the idea of a *Henry V* film, rewriting the 1938 script. In 1942, the Ministry produced a fifteen-minute radio broadcast, 'Into Battle', in which Olivier performed the Harfleur and Crispin speeches. Filippo Del Giudice was drawn into

---

30 I owe this suggestion to Herbert Coursen.
31 Laurence Olivier, *On Acting* (New York, 1986), pp. 269, 275.
32 Dudley Andrew, *Film in the Aura of Art* (Princeton, 1984), ch. 8; see also Russell Jackson, 'Two Films of *Henry V*: Frames and Stories', in *Collection Astraea* No. 4: *The Show Within: Dramatic and Other Insets. English Renaissance Drama (1550–1642)* (Proceedings of the International Conference held in Montpellier, 22–5, November 1990, vol. I, 182–98 and Peter S. Donaldson, *Shakespearean Films/Shakespearean Directors* (Boston, 1990), ch. 1.
33 John Cottrell, *Laurence Olivier* (Englewood Cliffs, N.J., 1975), pp. 188–91; Brian McFarlane, *An Autobiography of British Cinema as Told by the Filmmakers and Actors who Made It* (London, 1997), pp. 80–4, (interview with Dallas Bower); Peter S. Donaldson, conversation with Dallas Bower, 31 August 1998.

the project of creating a film with Olivier by Bower, and Bower became associate producer on the film; his script was used as basis of the script for Olivier's film, and a number of his ideas, including the use of voice-over in soliloquies, were used in the film as produced. This 'background' to the 1944 film leaves its mark, I believe, on the formal structure of the film, and on particular devices that suggest broadcast. With the radio and televisual prehistory in mind, the film's interest in the *air* can be understood as drawing on the complex resonances of aerial attack, aerial photography, and the transmission of culture and history through the airwaves. The clear and peaceful skies over Shakespeare's London contrast with present air attacks, yet offer a confident promise of return to peace. As the flag is raised over the theatre, a piece of paper is seen tumbling through the air. It becomes visible as a playbill for *Henry V*, and begins to scroll, as playbill and cinematic credits become one. How is the audience placed or constructed by this device? Let me suggest that what is implied is a live broadcast model, bringing the spectator news of what is happening today at the Globe theatre, and doing so *through the air*. Shakespeare's work, and the heroism and humanity of his era, reach us individually and with immediacy.

Broadcast is also suggested by the amplification of the king's voice during track-back shots in the film. Olivier considered this technique an innovation – pulling back, past the king's immediate audience, on-stage members of the audience, groundlings, galleries – finally locating our own point of view as spectators just behind the last row in the second tier. At the same time, the king's voice actually becomes stronger at a distance, commanding the intervening space, integrating past and present, fiction and history. The same device is used in the Crispin speech, where the whole English forces are gradually encompassed in the shot, and the king's voice reaches the farthest reaches of the army. This device is also a wonderful blending or 'suturing' of theatrical,

broadcast and cinematic acoustics, extending what, in Renaissance treatises on the building of theatres had been called 'the orb of the voice'[34] through time and space to encompass, at least symbolically, the diachronic and geographically extensive community known as the 'nation', imperilled during the Second World War yet energized (once again) by the excitement of a just war and, by the time of the film's release, an heroic invasion of France.

Such techniques enable the film to retain the qualities of direct address, the 'broadcast to the nation' feel of 'Into Battle', and construct the cinema audience as heirs to the mostly anonymous yet fully participant 'brothers' of the king at Agincourt. This way of imagining film-as-television contrasts with the deployment of early television under the Nazis, which has been studied by William Uricchio.[35] The English model involved individual receivers in people's homes, much like radio, while the Nazis planned for reception in mid-sized public halls. If the Nazis saw such centres as extending the declamatory possibilities of radio speeches, the English model, as we glimpse it in the Olivier film, while not ignoring the declamatory, must link it to the intimacy and modesty of ordinary life – indeed, it is tempting to try and trace what specific connections there may have been between the radio 'fireside chat' as practised by allied leaders and the campfire scene before Agincourt.

I am suggesting that this film, McLuhan's theories and the media event of the lunar voyage all belong to what I have called the aesthetic of televisual immediacy – drawing, in more eclectic ways than are acknowledged, on older or not-yet-invented technologies to portray instantaneous video broadcast over great

---

[34] See Frances Yates, *The Theatre of the World* (Chicago, 1969), p. 204 on 'the swelling orbs of the voice' citing Leone Battista Alberti, *De re aedificatoria*, Eng. trans. James Leoni, *Ten Books on Architecture* (London, 1725; repr. edn. Joseph Ryckwert, London, 1955).
[35] William Uricchio, 'Rituals of Reception, Patterns of Neglect: Nazi Television and its Postwar Representation', *Wide Angle* (1993), 48–66.

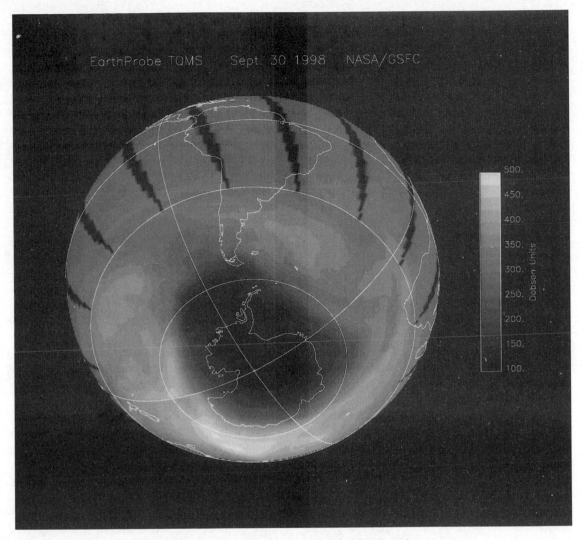

10 Ozone Concentrations, South Polar view (NASA).

distance, each with its own vaguely democratic ethos, and sense of the triumph of new media, and each with a certain degree of legerdemain and *bricolage* in the creation of their images of wholeness.

DISAPPEARING GLOBES AND DIGITAL AESTHETICS

The counterparts to Olivier's Globe and NASA's 'greater globe' in the digital age are somewhat different. In the current extensive 'Looking at Earth' exhibit at the National Air and Space Museum in Washington no example of the Apollo 'whole earth' photographs from the late 1960s is included among the many partial views and non-photographic imaging systems displayed.[36] The one picture of the

---

[36] Patricia Sprain and Fredricke Engle, *Looking at Earth* (Atlanta, 1992) is not a catalogue of the exhibition, but was based in part on the research conducted for the

whole disc of the earth in the exhibition is not a conventional photograph, but a digital composite image, showing the depleting concentrations of ozone from a South Polar view. More chart or circle diagram than portrait, it too is a beautiful image, in primary colours representing percentage concentrations against the black background where the ozone has fallen away to nothing. This is what is called a TOMS image, for Total Ozone Mapping Spectrography. These are now widely available for educational use and on the web (Illustration 10),[37] where animated versions show daily variations and long-term trends on a turning model of the earth. The TOMS images tell a double story characteristic of our time, a story of the thinning of the protective shield of the planet by its most intelligent inhabitants and the story of a technology so capable that it can record the progress of such a threat in daily increments. They are rendered in a medium in which, unlike still photography, there is no implication of a single, objective, and passively recorded visual truth. These images are 'false colour composites': because they synthesize data gathered from many points of view and from visible and non-visible portions of the spectrum, there can be little question of a single, untampered-with view.[38] Choice intervenes in every stage of the presentation and the information is narrativized by these choices which mingle objective data and storytelling. I find this digital emblem of the earth as rich as the others, and resonant with the 'globes' of Prospero and Jonson's masques in unexpected ways – digital images are contingent and fragile, they mingle what we can see and what we cannot see, and here they present a world that shares their contingency.

The TOMS images convey a narrative very different from the earlier images of the earth from space, one that has begun to affect how certain Shakespeare plays are understood and reproduced for audiences in the early digital age. It is a narrative of fascination rather than conquest.

Many features of our altered image environment, in which digital composites like the ozone maps of earth are replacing photographs as standard or canonical representations can be traced to aspects of an underlying reconception of the world as information rather than as place or picture, a reconception that conceives of the digital computer as a universal machine, able to model and replicate any aspect of reality that can be represented in numbers. The fascination of digital media, or of media enhanced or directed by computers, lies often in the blurring of the received boundaries between models and what they model, descriptions and commands, 'realities' and their representations.

Further, since it is the process by which information is generated, reproduced, or migrates from one form to another that compels attention, failures, lapses, and self-destructions often have an interest that they did not have in an earlier time. In part, this is because of the state of rapid transition in which the technologies of representation and communication find themselves – so much that is new can be done that it is often presented before it is perfected. No software is free of imperfection, and if it were it would be time to upgrade. Systems which function exceptionally well at one moment are subject to obsolescence, even unreadability as the larger digital environment of which they are a part changes. Uncertainties, failures of connection, and sudden disappearance or rendering into nonsense of text, speech or image are tolerated as annoyances in any period of media transition, as were the static, 'snow' or noise of early radio and television.

---

exhibit, and includes images of many of the artifacts on display.

[37] See TOMS home page at *http://jwocky.gsfc.nasa.gov* and follow links to ADEOS Northern Hemisphere Animation for 1997.

[38] The same is true for photographs, which of course are often highly manipulated, and do indeed tell stories. But in the digital realm, the mingling of automatic recording and design is often more self-evident. See William J. Mitchell, *The Reconfigured Eye: Visual Truth in the Post-photographic Era* (Cambridge, Mass., 1992).

But digital media are themselves constantly changing, and digital models tend to balance the wonder of their marvellous construction with an insistently foregrounded sense of its fragility and their fearful dependence on the complex systems and networks of which they are a part.

The present moment is one in which stable icons of the earth and of the journey around it – the contemporary successors of Drake's medal and his drum – have given way to representations of the earth's vulnerability, inscribed in media which, for all their magic, may be as ephemeral as the Stuart masque.

Peter Greenaway's *Prospero's Books* is the most obvious example of Shakespearian adaptation which takes aspects of the digital world – especially its ambivalent investment in both creation (quasi-magical) and destruction or dissolution as theme. As Greenaway makes clear in the book published to accompany the release of the film, Prospero's magic books, through which he creates the spectacle of *The Tempest* and even the animals and spirits who inhabit the island, are emblems of Greenaway's own medium of digitally enhanced cinema. Prospero renounces these arts, destroying his books by fire and water, in one of the film's longest and most technically demanding sequences. We watch with horror, but also with fascination, as what appear to be rare and precious early books and manuscripts are cast into the water, where they are mysteriously consumed by flame. Greenaway reads *The Tempest* – and its dissolution of media, first of the masque and then of the stage – in terms of the preservation and destruction of books, and the deployment and withdrawal of the technological wonders of special effects and digital editing.[39]

Prospero's Books is also part of global culture in a way in which Olivier's film was not. *Henry V* was notably international in several important senses: battle scenes were filmed on location in Ireland, several nationalities besides English – French, Irish, Welsh and Scots – were portrayed (though in now offensive stereo-

types), and it made the French war of the early fifteenth century relevant to a world war. But it was 'global' only in a mitigated sense, for its perspective on the world is designedly national, even local: the London Globe is the centre to which all virtual and actual voyages return. *Prospero's Books* was a joint French, English and Dutch production, digitally edited in Japan; its allegories celebrate a contemporary international avant-garde digital culture, and its settings – 'Milan', Prospero's books and study on the island – replicate the cosmopolitan world of Renaissance scientific, artistic and hermetic humanism. Though it is global, however, there are no allusions to Shakespeare's Globe at all. The Globe does not merely *not appear* in the film, but it might be accurate to say that the film leaves no room for public theatre in its otherwise comprehensive media allegory, since Prospero himself creates and controls the world of the play through incantatory recitation of words he has written with a quill pen, guided by lavishly presented early folios whose pages unfold into animated designs in three dimensions. The First Folio makes a brief appearance, there is a masque, and there are televisual references (Prospero's epilogue is delivered from a tiny screen). But, in so thoroughly imagining a bookish and literary origin for not only the text but the performance of the play (Prospero reads all the lines of the play as the characters move), Greenaway's Shakespearian media elide the theatre.

With *Prospero's Books*, Baz Luhrmann's *Romeo + Juliet* initiates a new genre of digitally enhanced film versions of Shakespeare that take digital technologies, digital images and the

---

[39] I have discussed *Prospero's Books* at greater length in 'Shakespeare in the Age of Post-Mechanical Reproduction: Sexual and Electronic Magic in 'Prospero's Books', in *Shakespeare the Movie*, eds. Lynda E. Boose and Richard Burt (New York, 1997), pp. 148–68 and in 'Digital Archives and Sibylline Fragments: *The Tempest* and the End of Books,' *Postmodern Culture* 8.2 (January, 1998). Special Issue on Film (Online Journal at *http://muse.jhu.edu/journals/postmodern_culture*).

cultural and human implications of global, electronic media as theme. They are meta-electronic or meta-digital, reflecting on their own relation to emerging technologies much as Shakespeare plays reflect on theatre and theatricality. Like *Prospero's Books*, *Romeo + Juliet* is a global work in a number of other ways as well: it was financed by one of the great global media companies, Rupert Murdoch's News Corporation, embodies a distinctively Australian pop-culture aesthetic, and moved, from its conception to completion, from Australia to Mexico City, Vera Cruz, San Francisco, and back to Australia. The setting of the film evokes Los Angeles, but it is generalized and de-localized, and, one might say placed under erasure by being unabashedly named 'Verona'. Through its various locations – Verona Beach, downtown Verona, the Mantua Outback and the most incongruously named Sycamore Grove (where there is ne'er a bush or tree) are all vividly evoked, the film works (as do other expressions of global culture such as the World Wide Web) consistently to weaken the sense of actual, historic or geographic place, because every place is equally a construction of a pervasive media culture.

Like *Prospero's Books*, Luhrmann's film belongs to a pointedly *post-theatrical* approach to Shakespearian film adaptation. But 'the Globe' is acknowledged, and its passing lamented, for the playhouse puts in at least a cameo appearance, its name being used for a disreputable pool hall. And unlike *Prospero's Books*, in which there is simply no theatre, the *lack* of a theatre is specifically called attention to in the film by the use of a large ruined proscenium arch, the remains of a theatre or cinema palace, as a crucial location. Though this theatre is not Shakespeare's Globe, any more than the renamed Vera Cruz pool hall that bears that name, together these locations pose the question of the relation of contemporary media culture to history; of 'Shakespeare' as Luhrmann has refashioned him for a new generation and the Shakespeare whose artistic practices

were other than, and perhaps alien to, such a refashioning.

Luhrmann's *Romeo + Juliet* places contemporary *media* – the integration and ubiquity of media images, their contribution to what Baudrillard has called the 'precession [*sic*] of the simulacra',[40] at the centre of the tragedy of Romeo and Juliet. The opening traverses media in a way that alludes to and confounds Olivier's careful move from the theatre to the real. The banner headlines contest the real, seek to supplant it, as Caesar's Palace (one of Baudrillard's examples) in Las Vegas seeks not to reconstruct any actual palace but to contest the hold of the past by appropriating its names and tokens. We begin not in a recreation of the Globe, but with a decontextualized television set, whose channels are changed by an unseen hand or remote control. We move from news coverage to the city 'covered' but the city we see is, at first, itself a low-resolution, televisual artifact. Though the world of Luhrmann's Verona is closer to us than that of Olivier's London, the stylized cartoon quality of the costumes, the disorienting changes of resolution and the temporal dislocations of the fitsec camera, which creates slow and fast motion on the fly as film is shot, work to undermine the sense of realistic location so that we are not sure we are in a real city, or within a world internal to the circular processes of media stardom, coverage of media events, broadcast and reception. Media forms abound – newspapers, newsmagazines, cinematic title cards, poster, and as we soon learn, there are televisions on the beach, balanced on the edge of billiard tables, in the passenger compartment of the Montague limousine, in bedrooms, multiple surveillance cameras in the swimming pool, television cameras in police helicopters, and all these media instantaneously transmit to the Montagues and Capulets in instant replay and feedback loops the giddy insouciance, fast pace, death-

---

[40] Jean Baudrillard, *Simulacra and Simulations*, trans. Sheila Faria Glaser (Ann Arbor, 1994).

dealing violence, pop art high style, and kitsch Catholicism of their own way of life.

The church has a central role in the proliferation of images. The city is dominated by a high-rise cathedral surmounted by a large statue of Jesus. Actually the church of the Sagrada Corazon in Mexico City, this structure works, in the film, not to oppose, but to extend the rule of media images into every recess of the imagined world of 'Verona'. Crosses and crucifixes appear in the back seats of cars, under shirts, as tattoos on the body, as posters, billboards, and in grotesque neon profusion, by the hundreds in the Capulet tomb in the central church. In the making of the film, so many Christian images were brought into the church by the production team that the authorities became suspicious and had to be assured that they were necessary to portray the devout culture of another place and another time.[41] The crosses, crucifixes and images of the sacred heart in the film work in tandem with what we more commonly think of as 'the media' to suggest the saturation of life by image.

Such an image-system is closely convergent with the situationist critique of late capitalism in the 1960s, as expressed in Guy Debord's *Society of the Spectacle*[42] – Debord believed that the fetishism of commodities was being replaced by an even more powerful fetishism of images, organized in a nearly unopposable system. While this culture is extremely attractive, the film offers tentative resistance to it, a resistance associated with the ruined theatre on the beach, where Romeo withdraws and is first seen looking at the sea and writing lines of verse in a small notebook with a pen. This location provides a hint of history at odds with the counter-myth of autochthonous television, and it was in fact the origin of the film in a different sense, for it was the originating image of the visual design, imagined and built as a model two full years before shooting began in Mexico City.[43]

Though the theatre is in ruins, it provides a setting for Romeo's withdrawal and his attempt to separate himself from the violence of the feud, and a location for the wild improvisations of Mercutio and the Montague boys, who watch his performances from the few seats that remain on the city-side of the structure. The 'place of the stage', to use Steven Mullaney's term,[44] is indeed marginal or liminal in Verona, and allows a free space for satire and poetry, and drag performance. However, we quickly come to see how dominated this marginal space is by the values of the centre – the fireworks that mark it as a place of festival actually originate in the Capulet festivities; the brash transgressions of Mercutio are welcomed as part of the masked ball – his drag replay of Lady Capulet's entrance is the high point of the ball itself.

The fight scene takes place at the ruined theatre, and Mercutio's final speech is played as a performance on the stage. In this sequence, such a stage's inability to structure levels of reality is evident; both Capulets and Montagues watch from the audience side of the arch, which faces the city, while for Mercutio's revelation to the screen audience of the extent of his wound, and his recognition that 'they have made worm's meat of me', he faces the beach side – yet it is precisely in handling action scenes with camera placements at 180 degrees from one another that film is least comfortable – in fact, the early rule against even crossing the axis of action, known as the 180 degree rule, still is basic cinematic wisdom – intentional violations of it, as in this sequence, can destroy the sense of a coherent space in which action takes place.

This moment is not only a turning point in the action, but in the film's visual design; what it suggests is that there is no liminal place from

---

41 *William Shakespeare's Romeo + Juliet* (Beverly Hills, 1997 (video laserdisc)), Audio Commentary track by Catherine Martin, side 1, time code 48:40–49:12.

42 Guy Debord, *The Society of the Spectacle*, trans. Donald Nicholson-Smith (New York, 1995; first published as *La société de la spectacle* (Paris, 1967).

43 Audio commentary track, 11:44–12:02.

44 Steven Mullaney, *The Place of the Stage: License, Play, and Power in Renaissance England* (Chicago, 1988).

which the action can be commented upon in this world in which illusion and reality are so intermeshed. This idea is extended by the portrayal of the 'Mantua Outback' to which Romeo is banished after the death of Tybalt. In the film it is a dismal trailer park in the desert, beyond the reach of the Verona media, but consigned by that removal to a drastically diminished existence. Shakespeare's plot device – the undelivered letter from Juliet – is worked into the film's portrayal of technologically mediated communication as ubiquitous, invasive and yet tragically necessary, for this conventional message, even when handled by a global overnight delivery service and marked 'extremely urgent', cannot be delivered expeditiously beyond the circle of the urban centre; there is no mailbox, the attempted delivery message falls from the trailer door with fatal results for the lovers.

The culminating aspect of the spatial allegory of which the portrayal of the ruined theatre is a part is the surprise that the Capulet tomb is located not at the margin of the town, or in a distant churchyard – but at the centre of the cathedral itself, and so Romeo must return to this centre at the end. The hundreds of neon crosses, with their techno-baroque religiosity, convey the triumph of the spectacle over the lovers. The final moments are unbearably bleak. Luhrmann revives the 'sentimental' ending of Garrick's adaptation, in which Juliet wakes before Romeo has died, but he does so in a way that withholds the possibility of even momentary reunion.

Barbara Hodgdon has made a compelling case for a different view of the ending of the film[45] – one in which Luhrmann's immersion in the current youth idiom is fully popular and learned at once, in which the religious imagery is repurposed for a transcendent conclusion on the level of romance while leaving room for a bleak but appropriate irresolution on the level of social realism, in which trenchant critique of what I have called the 'spectacle' is matched by joyous acceptance of its pleasures. But in her reading, as well, Luhrmann's 'global' *Romeo + Juliet* is a deeply ambivalent work in which participation in the contemporary fascination with media is countered by critique.

Luhrmann leaves the question of the theatre, the 'place of the stage', unresolved – although the ruined theatre was a generating image for his conception of *William Shakespeare's Romeo + Juliet* he does not portray its reconstruction, though such a project might be a fitting alternative to the golden monument Capulet proposes to erect to Romeo and Juliet. Luhrmann does not, that is, pursue the solution to the problem of how a global culture can continue the traditions of the Globe that have been explored by the International Globe Centre, embodied now in the successfully reconstructed theatre. The scenes of Romeo's withdrawal to the ruined theatre, where he finds momentary sanctuary and sustenance are not directly built upon in the film's conclusion – yet they remain in memory at the end, posing the question of how the past might have nourished the present. Indeed, in the world of contemporary London theatre and global tourism, the question of how the memory of the Globe can be a creative one has not been answered, as yet, even by the resumption of performances at 'Shakespeare's Globe'.

There, as in Luhrmann's film, the juxtaposition of Shakespeare and the contemporary 'global' culture of the present is tentative, dialogic, and sometimes patently awkward. Yet – in contrast to the myth of a seamless appropriation of the past in Olivier's treatment of the Globe – it may be precisely the incongruities that make the conjunction of Shakespeare 'as originally performed' at the Globe and Shakespeare as an artifact of, and presence in, the global contexts of the present an exciting and creative one.

---

[45] See her article in this issue, pp. 88–98.

'DELICIOUS TRAFFICK': ALTERITY AND EXCHANGE ON EARLY MODERN STAGES

ANIA LOOMBA

> ... we'll want no mistresses;
> Good swords, and good strong armours! [...]
> And fight till queens be in love with us, and run after us.
>
> *(The Knight of Malta, 2.5)*

For at least the last two hundred years, 'race' has functioned as one of the most powerful and yet most fragile markers of social difference. It is one of the great ironies of imperial history that ideologies of racial differences have hardened as a direct response to racial and cultural crossovers; conversely, colonial enterprises have facilitated contact and exchange between people of different ethnicities, religions and cultures. Notions of alterity or exchange thus derive their meaning from one another. Here I want to explore some aspects of this mirror-dance on the stages of Shakespeare's time – a time which can be characterized as either the last period in history where ethnic identities could be understood as fluid, or as the first moment of the emergence of modern notions of 'race'.

We are beginning to interrogate the crucial differences between twentieth-century and early modern ideologies of racial and cultural difference. Between the two stand four centuries of colonial relations which profoundly reshaped global relations. If, to use Stephen Greenblatt's words, Shakespeare's plays are letters we receive from the past, are we able to read and enjoy them only because there are powerful continuities and linkages between their vocabularies and our own? Or is it the case that these letters intimate alternate ways of being which denaturalize the dominant ideologies of our own age? The early modern period affords glimpses of other ways of being, some more flexible and generous, others more restrictive, than our own. Of course, precisely those aspects of the past which spell out a promise to some may signal danger to others. Our investment in interpreting these letters from the past, therefore, hinges upon our hopes and anxieties about the future.

Over the last two centuries, skin colour has dominated racist ideologies: races are commonsensically conceived of as

either 'black' or 'white' but never 'big-eared' and 'small-eared'. The fact that only certain physical characteristics are signified to define 'races' in specific circumstances indicates that we are investigating not a given, natural division of the world's population, but the application of historically and culturally specific meanings to the totality of human physiological variation.[1]

It follows that, in order to de-naturalize modern concepts of race, it is important to historicize the growth of colour-consciousness. However, I am struck by how many critics have recently claimed that colour was *unimportant* in the racial imaginary of early modern

---

[1] Robert Miles, *Racism* (London, 1989), p. 71.

England. Such claims suppose that colour consciousness was generated through colonial domination: since Africa was not colonized at the time that Shakespeare wrote *Othello*, one critic argues, the hero's colour did not necessarily connote bestiality or inferiority for its English audiences.[2] Another suggestion is that notions of Englishness were honed in opposition to the Islamic world of Asia and North Africa and therefore blackness carried little negative charge in England. I believe that we cannot historicize colour consciousness, or examine a time when it had not acquired the virulent connotations of imperial times by a downplaying of the vocabulary of colour. It is more fruitful to see how such a vocabulary is transformed during this period as it articulates itself through other markers of difference such as religion and gender.

It is certainly true that dark skin was not a prerequisite for either economic exploitation or cultural prejudice, as is evident from histories of Irish, Jewish or Islamic peoples. It is also true that because early modern scholarship has concentrated on the colonization of America, these other histories have not been adequately considered. Because imperialism was eventually to place natives of Asia, Africa and the Americas in similar positions of inferiority *vis-à-vis* Europe, we tend to assume that this was also the case during the sixteenth and early seventeenth centuries.[3] As Daniel Vitkus has remarked:

What has often been forgotten is that while Spanish, Portuguese, English, and Dutch ships sailed to the New World and beyond, beginning the exploration and conquest of foreign lands, the Ottoman Turks were rapidly colonizing European territory. Thus, in the sixteenth and seventeenth centuries, the Europeans were both colonizers and colonized, and even the English felt the power of the Turkish threat to Christendom.[4]

How does this doubleness affect the English sense of global relations, and more specifically, its representation on the English stages of the time? Elsewhere, I have suggested that Othello's difference from Caliban reminds us of the differ-

ence in perceptions of the Islamic East and the American West. Othello's mastery over language wins him Desdemona and charms the Venetian Senate; Caliban has to struggle to acquire and use Prospero's language. Othello serves the Venetian state as the captain of its army, Caliban's servitude is marked by punitive bondage. The differences between Othello and Caliban can be productively read against Hayden White's distinction between the Wild Man and the Barbarian in classical thought – the former (like Caliban) is imagined as outside civil society whereas the latter (like Othello) is regarded as living under an alien law.[5] Julia Reinhard Lupton uses a similar distinction to highlight the famous schism within Othello himself: a black Othello (whom Lupton reads as analogous to the uncivilized American or Caliban) is a barbaric figure outside all religion and therefore more easily convertible to Christianity, whereas a Muslim or Turkish

[2] Emily Bartels, '*Othello* and Africa: Postcolonialism Reconsidered', *The William and Mary Quarterly*, 3rd series, vol. 54, no. 1 (January 1997), 45–64. See also Lynda E. Boose, '"The Getting of a Lawful Race": Racial discourse in early modern England and the unrepresentable black woman', in Margo Hendricks and Patricia Parker, *Women, 'Race', and Writing in the Early Modern Period* (London and New York, 1994), 35–54.

[3] Ania Loomba, 'Shakespeare and Cultural Difference', in Terence Hawkes, ed., *Alternative Shakespeares 2* (London and New York, 1996), pp. 164–91.

[4] Daniel J. Vitkus, 'Turning Turk in *Othello*: The Conversion and Damnation of the Moor', *Shakespeare Quarterly* 48 (1997), 145–76; p. 146. For other revisionist views of the Renaissance world picture see Shankar Raman, *Looking East: 'India' and the Renaissance*, PhD thesis, Stanford University (1994); Julia Reinhard Lupton, '*Othello* Circumcised: Shakespeare and the Pauline Discourse of Nations', *Representations*, 57 (1997), 73–89; Jerry Brotton, *Trading Territories, Mapping the Early Modern World* (London, 1997) and '"This Tunis, sir, was Carthage": Contesting colonialism in *The Tempest*' in Ania Loomba and Martin Orkin, eds., *Postcolonial Shakespeares* (London and New York, 1998), 23–42 and Jonathan Burton, '"A most wily bird": Leo Africanus, *Othello* and the trafficking in difference' in the same volume, pp. 43–63.

[5] 'Shakespeare and Cultural Difference', pp. 176–7.

Othello is less convertible because he already owes allegiance to a rival religion of the book.[6] Lupton argues that a scandal of 'monstrous miscegenation' inherited from the nineteenth-century racial imagery has (wrongly) come to govern Othello's 'economy of differences'. In the Renaissance, a black Gentile could be legitimately placed within the narrative of an international romance, in a way that the Infidel Turk could not: 'whereas for the modern reader or viewer a black Othello is more subversive, "other", or dangerous, in the Renaissance scene a paler Othello more closely resembling the Turks whom he fights might actually challenge more deeply the integrity of the Christian paradigms set up in the play as a measure of humanity' (74).

In this argument, Islam, and not blackness, was the spectre haunting early modern Europe.[7] Of course the Muslim, as Lupton rightly points out, is connected to the Jew mythically via the figure of Ishmael, and bodily through the mark of circumcision.[8] Judaism and Islam both provide Christianity with a frightening image of alterity. Lupton compares this early modern proto-racism to what Etienne Balibar calls the neo-racism of our own times, which also does not hinge on the question of colour, indeed 'does not have the pseudo-biological concept of race as its driving force'.[9] In this important reading, to de-link racism from colour consciousness is to trace connections, rather than disjunctures, between our own times and Shakespeare's. Connections between sixteenth-century and twentieth-century anti-Semitic and anti-Islamic discourses become clear, and religious as well as cultural factors in the construction of racism are highlighted. However, Lupton highlights religious difference by explicitly downgrading the significance of colour: 'in Othello', she remarks, 'religious difference is more powerfully felt than racial difference, which was only then beginning to surface in its virulent modern form'. In conclusion she quotes Lynda Boose's assessment that 'circumcision rather than skin color is the trait

that Othello "invokes" as the final, inclusive sign of his radical Otherness' (81; emphasis added).

'Valiant Othello' with his 'bombast circumstance / Horribly stuffed with the epithets of war' (1.1.13–14), his 'sword of Spain' (5.2.260) and his violent jealousy certainly evokes a Renaissance stereotype of the 'malignant and turbaned Turk' (5.2.362) or Muslim. But I am unable to dismiss the forceful colour-coding of the play or the passionate repetition of explicitly colour-based image of monstrosity, too well known to require repetition here. How do we understand the images of monstrous coupling and animal imagery that kick-start the play's relentless exploration of love across the boundaries, or the repetitive harping on a black–white dichotomy, both by those opposed to the Othello–Desdemona marriage and by those sympathetic to it? Surely, these *images* have not been imported from the nineteenth century, reverberating as they do with hundreds of others evoked on Renaissance stages? Othello does not move from a glamorous black to a hated Turk: rather, we need to notice how both blacks and Turks can be glamorized as well as hated in contemporary representations, and how the two were inter-connected, both in Othello and in the culture at large, via the Spanish discourse on Moorishness, via medieval

---

6 Julia Reinhard Lupton, 'Othello Circumcised: Shakespeare and the Pauline Discourse of Nations', *Representations*, 57 (1997), 73–89.

7 Beerbohm Tree's assertion that 'Othello was an Oriental, not a Negro: a stately Arab of the best caste' makes it clear that some three centuries later it was the other way around. Quoted by Julie Hankey, ed., *Othello*, Plays in Performance Series (Bristol, 1987), p. 67.

8 Contemporary writers express this connection in a variety of ways: George Sandys claims that the Prophet Mohammed's 'father was a pagan, his mother a Jew both by birth and religion' (*A Relation of a Journey begun Anno Domini 1610*, third edition, London, 1627), p. 52.

9 Etienne Balibar, 'Is There a Neo-racism?' in Etienne Balibar and Emmanual Wallerstein, *Race, Nation, Class: Ambiguous Identities* (London and New York, 1991), pp. 17–28, esp. p. 23.

stereotypes of black Turks, or Egyptians, and also by more recent developments in global relations.

Ranking somatic, religious or national differences *vis-à-vis* each other is to continue to think of them as discrete categories. If we assume that racial thinking had not developed in early modern Europe because colour was not the primary marker of difference, we are still working with a conceptual equation of race and colour. It is more useful to trace the complex articulation between skin colour, religion, ethnicity and nationality during this period and to see whether *each of them* was viewed as a feature that could be acquired, or as derived from a more unchanging quasi-biological essence. I use the word 'articulation' to describe not a simple co-existence but a relationship between different categories which transforms all of them.[10]

Consider the argument that colour prejudice was produced by colonial relations. It is indeed true that it is 'premature to characterize, as some critics have done, the early seventeenth century as a society "exhibiting" cultural hegemony' and driven by 'the economic imperatives of imperial trade'.[11] But racial ideologies do not automatically and crudely *reflect* economic relations, although the two are always interconnected. Well before the actual enslavement and colonial plunder of Africans began, an obsession with colour and nakedness was firmly in place. As has been fairly well documented by now, contemporary writers drew plentifully upon biblical, classical and medieval images of black monstrosity which were often located in Africa.[12] Medieval morality plays routinely linked devilry and blackness, a link that Emilia reiterates in her outburst against Othello: 'O, the more angel she, and you the blacker devil' (5.2.140). Blackness was a staple (although not static) ingredient in images of wildness, of evil, of class difference, and of female disorderliness.[13] In fact in several colonial situations these earlier stereotypes provided an ideological *justification* for different kinds of exploitation.[14]

I am not suggesting that blackness has the

same negative charge over centuries, only that it becomes a highly mobile metaphor that can be reworked to establish a wide spectrum of differences. But what we also have to remember is that, despite England's tardiness, a larger European proto-colonialist discourse had been circulating awhile. African royalty provided occasional images of glamour: the fourteenth-century ruler of Mali, the King Mansa, captured the European imagination as equal in power and sophistication to any Christian Prince. By the mid fifteenth century, after the Portuguese penetration of Gambia, Mansa's heirs were depicted in terms of crude racial stereotypes 'with dangling simian sexual organs'.[15] Of

---

10 My usage derives from but is not identical to Stuart Hall's deployment of the term 'articulation' to describe the co-existence of pre-capitalist and capitalist modes of production. Hall emphasizes the dominance of the capitalist mode in that inter-relation whereas I want to emphasize greater equivalence between the concepts under discussion. However, like Hall, I want to draw attention to their mutually transformative power. Stuart Hall, 'Race, articulation and societies structured in dominance', in *Sociological Theories, Race and Colonialism* (Paris, 1980), pp. 305–45.

11 Daniel J. Vitkus, 'Turning Turk in *Othello*', p. 146, n. 4.

12 See for example, Eldred Jones, *Othello's Countrymen* (London, 1965) and *The Elizabethan Image of Africa* (Virginia, 1971); George K. Hunter, *Dramatic Identities and Cultural Tradition: Studies in Shakespeare and his Contemporaries* (Liverpool, 1978); Anthony Barthelemy, *Black Face, Maligned Race: The Representation of Blacks in English Drama from Shakespeare to Southerne* (Baton Rouge, 1987); Jack D'Amico, *The Moor in English Renaissance Drama* (Tampa, 1991); John Gillies, *Shakespeare and the Geography of Difference* (Cambridge, 1994) and Kim Hall, *Things of Darkness: Economies of Race and Gender in Early Modern England* (Ithaca, 1995).

13 Roger Bartra, *Wild Men in the Looking Glass, The Mythic Origins of European Otherness* (Ann Arbor, 1994); Richard Bernheimer, *Wild Men in the Middle Ages* (Cambridge, Mass., 1952); Louise Olga Fradenburg, *City, Marriage, Tournament, Arts of Rule in Medieval Scotland* (Madison, 1991).

14 Peter Fryer, *Staying Power* (London, 1984), 7; Miles, *Racism*, pp. 25, 27.

15 Felipe Fernández-Armesto, *Before Columbus, Exploration and Colonization from the Mediterranean to the Atlantic 1229–1492* (Basingstoke and London, 1987), pp. 146–7.

course, these negative images cannot be equated with the full-blown ideology of species difference, which had to a certain extent been retarded by the Christian belief in monogenism. As Robert Bartlett points out, 'while the language of race – *gens*, *natio*, "blood", "stock" etc. – is biological, its medieval reality was almost entirely cultural'. In practice, races were defined more in social terms of customs, language and law. Since customs and language, and even religion, could be acquired, pre-modern forms of ethnic differentiation were more fluid than their modern counterparts: 'When we study race relations in medieval Europe we are analyzing the contact between various linguistic and cultural groups, not between breeding stocks.'[16]

However, the seeds for a biological understanding of race were sown when, following the expulsion of Jews and Moors in 1492 and 1502, the Hebrew concept of purity of blood (*limpieza de sangre*) not only took ideological root in Spain but became the basis for discrimination in social and political and economic life. If racism is not just the belief that human beings are biologically different, but the translation of that belief into social inequalities, then sixteenth-century Spain certainly engendered modern racism.[17] Differences of faith now became signs of different interior essences:

Who can deny that in the descendants of the Jews there persists and endures the evil inclination of their ancient ingratitude and lack of understanding, just as in Negroes [there persists] the inseparability of their blackness? For if the latter should unite themselves a thousand times with white women, the children are born with the dark color of the father. Similarly, it is not enough for a Jew to be three parts aristocratic or Old Christian for one family-line [...] alone defiles and corrupts him.[18]

The important point about this passage is that a conflation of faith and genetic essence occurs *both* in the descriptions of Jews, where lack of colour differentiation becomes a source of anxiety, and in discussions about Moors, where colour is more obviously at stake. In fact, these overlaps are the basis for a comparison between Jews and Moors.

Balibar admits that 'bodily stigmata play a great role' in antisemitism, but suggests that 'they do so more as signs of a deep psychology, as signs of a spiritual inheritance rather than a biological heredity' (24). I would argue, instead, that 'spiritual inheritance' and 'biological heredity' are intricately connected. Therefore, the signs of visible difference are always translated into moral, and even religious alterity in the case of blacks. Thus Leo Africanus finds tawny or white Africans or 'Moors' who are Christians, but claims that in 'all the Negros Land' there are no Christians.[19]

16 Robert Bartlett, *The Making of Europe, Conquest, Colonization and Cultural Change 950–1350* (Princeton, New Jersey, 1993), pp. 197–9.

17 In England John Foxe's *Actes and Monuments* (published in 1570) used the word 'race' in the context of royal lineage but, according to Ivan Hannaford, such usage was not a starting point for a biological understanding of the term because kings could enter and depart from Foxe's 'course' or 'race' depending on the nobility of their actions, and ordinary people could not enter it under any circumstances. It is Jean Bodin's influential treatise *Method for Easy Comprehension of History* (1565) which marked one of the early transitions from a culturalist to a biologist meaning of race by arguing that human characteristics are drawn from nature rather than from variable (and therefore unreliable) social institutions such as religion. Form of the body and colour are two criteria Bodin uses to distinguish between his major groups of human beings – Scythian, German, African and 'Middler' (Ivan Hannaford, *Race, The History of an Idea in the West* (Baltimore and London, 1996), pp. 155–7.

18 Fray Prudencio de Sandoval, *Historia de la vida y hechos del emperador Carlos V* (1604) quoted in Jerome Friedman, 'Jewish Conversion, the Spanish Pure Blood Laws and Reformation: A Revisionist View of Racial and Religious Anti-semiticism', *Sixteenth Century Journal*, 18 (1987), 3–29; pp. 16–17. The same passage is also quoted by Mary Janell Metzger, 'Jessica, *The Merchant of Venice* and Early Modern English Identity', *PMLA* 113: 1 (1998), 52–63; p. 55.

19 Leo Africanus, *Navigations, Voyages, and Land-Discoveries, with other Historicall Relations of Afrike*, translated by John Pory in Samuel Purchas (ed.), *Hakluytus Posthumus or Purchas his Pilgrimes*, vol. 5 (Glasgow, 1905), p. 340.

Colour here operates as a sharp dividing line between Christians and non-Christians. In the case of Jews and Muslims religious difference is expressed in moral and often in physical terms. While circumcision certainly is a crucial and recurrent sign, these discourses also construct more indelible marks of difference. Thus Jewish men are said to menstruate, smell, be capable of breast-feeding or have hooked noses; blackness, mis-shapenness and grotesque features including swollen heads and hooked noses, are routinely attributed to many Muslims.[20] This is not to minimize the enormous anxiety produced by the physical similarities between Jews, Christians and Muslims, but to show that such anxiety results in a strenuous production of a discourse of difference.

The crucial question is: was England immune from colour prejudice, and especially prejudice against Moors? According to Eric Griffin, the strong anti-black discourse in *Othello* comments on Spanish, not English, attitudes to race and Moorishness, and Iago and Roderigo are portrayed as stereotypes of Spanish racists.[21] The play thus suggests an affinity between Othello the Moor and the English, an affinity that was evoked by several writers as Elizabethan England tried to establish trade with Barbary. Elizabeth herself claimed that both she and the Great Turk were enemies to idolaters.[22] Thus Griffin argues that Othello is a proto-Protestant Muslim who is attacked by Catholic racists, and whose own conversion to Catholicism pollutes him with the sin of idolatry.

Notice that Griffin and Lupton suggest absolutely divergent valencies for Islam in early modern England. For Griffin, Islam was viewed as an ally of Protestant England, Hispanic Roman Catholicism was the Other against whom an English identity was forged, and Othello's tragedy results from his conversion to Catholicism. Lupton argues that Islam and the Turks are the real adversary, and the tragedy is that Othello cannot fully convert from Islam. Griffin's argument, moreover, depends on an astute insistence on the double meaning of

Moor – as black *and* as Muslim – whereas Lupton's derives from a divorce between the meaning of Moorishness and blackness. What interests me is that despite their completely different assessments of Islam and blackness, both Griffin and Lupton suggest that somehow anti-black prejudice did not animate the *English* during this period.[23] The English are seen as romancing either Islam or blackness, and *Othello* is therefore a play about a racism elsewhere.[24]

'Spain's national obsession with purity of blood', says Griffin, 'had met its ideological reverse in an English Protestant obsession with purity of faith' (82). I want to suggest that, both in Spain and in England, purity of faith and purity of blood were necessarily yoked together, a yoking that is most clearly visible in contemporary discourses about conversion.

---

[20] James Shapiro, *Shakespeare and the Jews* (New York, 1996); Samuel Chew, *The Crescent and the Rose* (New York, 1937).

[21] Eric Griffin, 'Un-sainting James: Or, *Othello* and the "Spanish Spirits" of Shakespeare's Globe', *Representations*, 62 (1998), 52–99.

[22] Samuel Chew, *The Crescent and the Rose*, p. 103.

[23] Interestingly, Griffin's understanding of a larger international history of ideas where notions of race and religion travel across national borders directly contradicts Bartels's view where it would seem that the English had no access to the anti-black discourses of Iberia, but again the two arguments converge on the question of English prejudice against blacks.

[24] It is true that if on the one hand, the alterity between Christians and Jews/Muslims increasingly animated the ideologies of difference in this period, then on the other the Church itself had, from medieval times, become 'an arena of ethnic competition' (Robert Bartlett, *The Making of Europe*, p. 221). Later, the differences between Catholic and Protestant would be complexly mapped onto notions of ethnic, national and religious difference – thus Turks and Roman Catholics are viewed as equivalent by early modern writers such as Richard Knolles. But at the same time, the spectre of the Turk also serves, in a play such as Massinger's *The Renegado* (1621), to allow the differences between English and Italians, Protestant and Catholic to be bridged and the notion of a composite European, Christian identity to be posited.

Religious conversion, by signalling the possibility of crossovers, necessarily engenders several kinds of anxieties about authenticity.[25] If the faithful constitute a permeable and changeable body, then the purity of both the original body and those who are allowed to join it is always suspect. Worse, a permeable boundary can allow the faithful to both enter and leave: 'The institutionalized violence represented by the Inquisition was a product of the anxiety that this boundary of conversion might be transgressed in the wrong direction.'[26] Moreover, conversion was viewed as a perpetually unstable condition: converts to Christianity were suspected of covertly practising Judaism or Islam, or of interpreting Christianity in the light of their previous faiths.[27] The assimilation of Moriscoes (converted Moors) and Marranos (converted Jews) within the Christian community was an affair strenuously policed by civic and ecclesiastic authorities. Moriscos, for example, were even forbidden from dancing and singing in their traditional way, for they were suspected of using words and gestures with double meanings which mocked Christianity.[28] Such anxieties were not confined to Spain: James Shapiro points out that in an England where even the official religion had changed so often, the question of genuine versus assumed faith had a specially sharp resonance: 'Faith was disguisable, religious identity a role one could assume or discard if one had sufficient improvisational skill' (17).

But it is precisely when faith could be improvised that the question of authenticity became especially urgent. Fears that the exterior show did not match the inner faith were underlined by the fact that Jews, Moors and Christians were never simply religious categories, but variably articulated with nationality and ethnicity, and often colour. Categories such as 'A Christian Jew'[29] or 'a Turke, but a Cornish man borne'[30] attested to the fact that religion and nationality were affiliations which conversions could not entirely erase. The articulation of a religion which can be chosen and

an ethnicity which cannot is particularly complex in the case of the category called 'Moors'. The Spanish derived the word 'moro' from the Latin word 'maurus' which in turn came from the Greek 'mavros' meaning black.[31] But they used it to designate their conquerors who were not black at all but a mixture of Arab and Berber Muslims.[32] Earlier I suggested ways in which religious difference provides a vocabulary for the expression of racial difference. Here we see an instance of how religion and ethnicity were expressed through a vocabulary of colour.

Travel writings and plays of the period, including English ones, regularly play with and between these two senses of the word 'Moor':

[25] For early modern conversions see Samuel Chew, *The Crescent and the Rose*; N. I. Matar, 'The Renegade in English Seventeenth-Century Imagination', *SEL*, 33 (1993), 489–505. For thought-provoking discussions about conversion and Judaism in England, see James Shapiro, *Shakespeare and the Jews* and Peter Berek, 'The Jew as Renaissance Man', *Renaissance Quarterly*, 51:1 (1998), 128–62.

[26] David Nirenberg, *Communities of Violence, Persecution of Minorities in the Middle Ages* (Princeton, NJ, 1996), p. 128.

[27] See Andre Hess, *The Forgotten Frontier, A History of the Sixteenth century Ibero-African Frontier* (Chicago and London, 1978), pp. 151–2.

[28] Hess, *The Forgotten Frontier*, p. 151. In 1609, anxieties about converted Moors came to a head and Moriscoes were expelled from Spain.

[29] John Foxe's *Actes and Monuments* speaks of how Turks killed a converted Jew: 'A Christian Jew'. This is discussed by Shapiro, *Shakespeare and the Jews*, p. 146.

[30] Thomas Dallam, *The Diary of Master Thomas Dallam* (1599–1600), reprinted in *Early Voyages and Travels in the Levant*, ed. J. Theodore Bent (London, 1983), p. 79. Also cited by Vitkus, 'Turning Turk', p. 161, n. 62.

[31] The word may in turn be connected to the Hindi word 'Amavas' meaning moonless night or dark. According to Martin Bernal, 40–50 per cent of Greek vocabulary comes from the Indo-European group of languages, and 20–5 per cent from Egyptian (*Black Athena, The Afroasiatic Roots of Classical Civilization*, vol. 1 (New Brunswick, 1987), p. xiv). See also Barthelemy's discussion of the term, *Black Face*, 7–17.

[32] Albert Hourani, *A History of the Arab Peoples* (Cambridge, Mass., 1991), p. 41.

Caesar Fredericke's *Voyage ... into East India* clarifies that 'wheras I speak of Moores I mean Mahomets sect'.[33] But John Lok who brought five black men from Barbary to England in 1554 calls people of Ethiopia 'Moores, Morens, or Negroes, a people of beastly living, *without a God, lawe, religion, or common wealth ...*' (emphasis added).[34] Here Moors are not Muslims who obey an alien God, but people outside of civil society and organized religion. According to Leo Africanus, Moors come in various colours, and a variety of religious affiliations: some Moors 'are Gentiles which worship Idols; others of the sect of Mahumet; some others Christians; and some Iewish in religion'. But, as mentioned earlier, he also claims that there are no Christian Negroes, so that Moorishness, but not blackness, is compatible with Christianity.[35] *The Merchant of Venice* refers to the woman made pregnant by Launcelot as both a 'Moor' and a 'Negro' (3.5.37). In this sense Moorishness is something that cannot be either acquired or shed. Although Timon of Athens complains that gold can make 'Black white, foul fair, wrong right' (4.3.29), the black maid Zanche in Webster's *The White Devil* fails in her attempts to wash her colour by acquiring a large dowry.[36]

The word 'blackamoor' thus collapses religious and somatic vocabularies, which, despite knowledge about white Moors and non-Muslim blacks, could not be unknotted. In fact the same writer can make distinctions between the two and collapse them. Sexuality becomes a recurrent point of knotting Muslims and blacks: both are seen as promiscuous and desirous of white women, and this contributes to their being enmeshed in the 'common-sense' of the period.[37] Evidence can of course be amassed to bolster up two completely divergent assessments about Renaissance ideologies of colour: one, that black skin was thought of as a 'natural infection'[38] and was therefore indelible, like the proverbial leopard's spots and that the 'blackness of the Parent's sperm or seede' would overpower whiteness if the two were coupled, and two, that blackness was seen as derived from geographical location, and as mutable. But crucially, proponents of both views concurred that *blackness* was dominant and could contaminate whiteness, rather than the other way around. For example, a 1562 Act of Elizabeth expressed the fear that earlier laws against foreigners would be unable to deal with a new problem regarding gypsies or 'that false and subtil company of vagabonds calling themselves Egyptians'. Now, it says, 'persons as being born within this realm of England' are joining 'the fellowship or company of the said vagabonds, by transforming or disguising themselves in their apparel, or in a certain counterfeit speech or behaviour'.[39] This fear of 'turning gypsy' was most often expressed in relation to English rogues and vagabonds: thus the boundaries of culture are also imagined in class terms.[40] The

---

[33] 'The voyage and travell of M. Caesar Fredericke, Marchant of Venice into the East Indies' in Richard Hakluyt, *The Principal Navigations ... of The English Nation*, vol. 5 (Glasgow, 1904), p. 411.

[34] Hakluyt, *Principal Navigations*, vol. 6 (Glasgow, 1904), p. 167.

[35] John Leo, 'Navigations, Voyages, and Land Discoveries, with other Historicall Relations of Afrike', in Samuel Purchas, *Hakluytus Posthumus*, vol. 5 (Glasgow, 1905), p. 340.

[36] Colour, then, is a marker of moral difference: in *A Midsummer Night's Dream*, Lysander spurns Hermia by calling her both an 'Ethiop' and a 'tawny Tartar' (3.2.257, 263). Tartars of course were not tawny at all, but, like the Turks, they acquired connotations of moral and sometimes literal darkness.

[37] I am using 'common-sense' in the Gramscian sense of combining both everyday life but also earlier ideologies which have sedimented into it. See Errol Lawrence, 'Just plain common sense, the "roots" of racism', in Centre for Contemporary Cultural Studies, *The Empire Strikes Back, Race and Racism in 70s Britain* (London, 1982), 47–94.

[38] George Best described it thus in his *Discourse* (1578) reproduced in Hakluyt, *Principal Navigations*, vol. 7, p. 262.

[39] 5 Eliz. c. 20, 'An act for the further punishment of vagabonds, calling themselves Egyptians', Danby Pickering, *The Statutes at Large*, vol. 6 (Cambridge, 1763), pp. 211–12.

[40] See A. L. Beir, *Masterless Men* (New York and London, 1985), p. 62.

blurring of boundaries between English people and gypsies is conjured up via images of brown Englishmen rather than white gypsies. Thus blackness (both as a moral quality and as skin colour) can more readily contaminate whiteness rather than itself be washed into whiteness.

The tension between black skin and a Christian interiority, therefore, needs to be constantly negotiated, explained, addressed. The romance of a black Christian, perhaps like all romances, always contains within it the idea of its own impossibility. As a matter of fact, not only blacks but Moors and Turks were romantically treated in European literature. In Spain, 'the gap between the idealized picture of the noble Moor and the miserable circumstances of the Moriscos tended to confirm the belief of Old Christians that the maximum social distance, including expulsion, ought to be placed between the truly Spanish and ... recent converts.'[41] Thus a literary tradition of the Noble Moor indicates cultural stress rather than cross-cultural indulgence or harmony.[42] In English theatre, the figure of the noble Moor, such as Joffer in Heywood's *Fair Maid of the West*, was usually the exception that proved the rule of Moorish incivility, or devolved into a tragic figure like Othello who illustrated the impossibility of sustaining a perpetual contradiction.

But the Moorish convert to Christianity also represented something far closer to home – the possibility of self-fashioning. Peter Berek astutely suggests that English theatrical obsession with self-fashioning is expressed most powerfully through the figure of the converted Jew who represents 'the idea that identity is not stable and can be represented by individuals themselves'. Figures such as Othello (or indeed even Aaron or Morocco) can be credibly located within such a framework. However, whereas Berek suggests that the cultural anxiety represented by the Marrano 'isn't about Marranism, or Jewishness, or even [...] about emerging ideas of race and nation, but about cultural change and a fluid sense of self that one

could call "modern" (pp. 130, 158), I think the figure of the convert demonstrates precisely that emergent modernity or cultural change are inextricable from ideas of race and nation. All self-fashioning represents a transgression of boundaries that is both romantic and terrible, heroic and tragic. In the case of alien figures such crossings necessarily evoke anxieties about English, Christian or Protestant identity: the fluidity of the self is marked also by the changing boundaries of the faith or the nation. The romance and terror of self-fashioning becomes especially acute in the case of such figures: thus a Marrano or a Morisco cannot be a quintessential Renaissance man even though he may represent the essence of Renaissance self-fashioning.

II

More often than not, however, the converted Moor on the Renaissance stage is a woman. We have the recurrent spectacle of a fair maid of an alien faith and ethnicity romanced by a European, married to him, and converted to Christianity. Her story, unlike those of converted men, does not usually end in tragedy, nor does it focus on the tensions of cultural crossings. Whereas converted men must remain single or be destroyed, her religious turning is also a romantic turning to a Christian husband. Instead of a self-fashioning, hers is a re-fashioning by her Christian husband. Unlike

---

[41] Hess, *The Forgotten Frontier*, p. 195.

[42] As for the suggestion that the repeated English attempts to trade with Barbary resulted in a romancing of the Moor in England at the time when Shakespeare was writing *Othello*, we must remember that, despite official attempts to suggest commonality of interests between Muslims and Protestants, there was a far more widespread association of Muslims with Roman Catholics:

> If Mahomet, that prophet false,
> Eternetie doe gaine,
> Then shall the pope, and you his sainctes,
> In heaven be sure to raigne.

John Phillips, *A Friendly Larum, Select Poetry Chiefly Devotional of the Reign of Queen Elizabeth*, ed. Edward Farr (Cambridge, 1845), part 2, p. 528.

the Moorish man, she does not represent a fearful alterity to Christendom but the possibility of a controlled exchange. Nevertheless, her fair skin confirms that colour is in fact crucial to narratives of conversion and assimilation. Such a figure thus profoundly shapes ideas of both alterity and exchange in early modern England.

In an important essay, Daniel Virkus has drawn our attention to the sexual connotations of the drama of religious conversion. Conversion and perversion were both implied in the verb 'to turn'; the phrase 'to turn Turk' carried erotic connotations which drew upon ideas of Muslim hyper-sexuality as well as female immorality. Protestants viewed the conversion of Christians to Islam or Roman Catholicism as a sexual transgression or spiritual whoredom.[43] Turnings towards Christianity, I want to suggest, are also expressed through a sexualized vocabulary, but, when inscribed on the body of a 'fair' but 'alien' woman, this is a vocabulary of romance and marriage instead of whoredom.

Sexual intercourse between members of different groups was the kind of crossover that generated the greatest anxiety.[44] Since sperm was widely understood as man's purest blood, sexual activity was an exchange of blood, and a crossing of boundaries more profound than conversion. In the Christian, Muslim as well as Jewish communities, a double standard operated and punishments for female transgression were much harsher than those accorded to men: 'According to classic Islamic jurisprudence, Muslim men could marry Christian or Jewish women ... but Muslim women could not marry non-Muslim men' without risking a death penalty.[45] European travellers and commentators claimed Turkish harems were filled with abducted Christian girls, and Turkish strongmen or Janizzaries were captured Christian men who were converted to Islam and sometimes castrated. Othello's alliance with Desdemona evokes the popular and oft-told tale of Irene the Greek maiden who was abducted, loved and murdered by a Turkish emperor.[46] In Philip Massinger's play The

Renegado (1621), the fair Paulina has been sold to Asambeg, the Viceroy of Tunis and is, her brother Vitelli says, 'Mewde up in his Serraglio, and in danger / Not alone to loose her honour, but her soule' (1.1.129–30).[47]

The Turkish damsel Donusia, who falls in love with Paulina's brother Vitelli, rants against the double standard within Islam:

> Indulgent *Mahomet*, doe thy bloudy lawes
> Call my embraces with a Christian, death?
> [...] and yet want power to punish
> These that with scorne creak throgh thy Cobweb
>   edicts
> [...] to tame their lusts,
> There's no religious bit; let her be fayre
> And pleasing to the eye, though Persian, Moore,
> Idolatresse, Turke, or Christian ...   (4.2.128–36).

Donusia also draws attention to the difference between her fetters and the liberty enjoyed by Christian women:

> I have heard
> That *Christian* Ladies live with much more
>   freedome
> Then such as are borne heere. Our jealous Turkes
> Never permit their faire wives to be seene
> But at the publique *Bannias*, or the Mosques
> And even then vaylde, and guarded   (1.2.16–21).

Her English-born eunuch Carazie responds by picturing Englishwomen as leading a carnivalesque existence – hunting, hawking, feasting, entertaining, wearing breeches, commanding their husbands and apprentices, and cuckolding men freely: 'women in England / For the most part live like Queenes' (1.2.27–8). Paulina is eventually rescued from Asambeg and Donusia

---

43 Daniel J. Vitkus, 'Turning Turk'.
44 I am indebted to David Nirenberg, *Communities of Violence*, for rich connections between sexuality and conversion in the middle ages.
45 Nirenberg, *Communities of Violence*, p. 136.
46 Mahomet the Great, according to Richard Knolles's *The Generall Historie of the Turkes* (second edition, London, 1610, p. 353) and William Painter's *The Palace of Pleasure*, ed. Joseph Jacob (London, 1980), pp. 190–7.
47 Philip Edwards and Colin Gibson (eds.), *The Plays and Poems of Philip Massinger*, vol. 2 (Oxford, 1976).

also escapes the Turkish patriarchy by marrying Paulina's brother Vitelli and converting to Christianity.

In medieval Europe, the most common form of sexual transgression had in fact involved Christian men and Muslim women. In stories of Christians turning Turk that circulated in early modern times, Muslim women are temptresses who ensnare Christian men into a licentious faith. This spectre is repeatedly evoked in plays such as *The Renegado*, Robert Daborne's *A Christian Turn'd Turke* (1612) or Fletcher's *The Island Princess* (1620–1), in which Muslim women initiate sexual contact and ask the Christian hero to convert to Islam. But such fears are theatrically allayed by either the destruction of such women or their own conversions to Christianity and marriages to Christian men.

Fine race and colour distinctions always operated in the case of sanctioned inter-racial sex. Albuquerque 'invited his men to marry "the white and beautiful" widows and daughters of the defenders of Goa, making a distinction between them and the darker South Indian women whom he called "Negresses"'.[48] In English theatre, the desire of black people for those with fairer skins is usually lampooned, as in the case of the King and Queen of Fez in Heywood's *The Fair Maid of the West*. Such desire is either not reciprocated or clearly marked as foul lust, unredeemable by marriage or conversion. Black men, like Joffer in the same play, can be converted to Christianity and eulogized for their inherent nobility but only if they show no signs of a desire for white women.[49] The marginality of black women, on the other hand, is routinely expressed through the folly of their desire for white men. In play after play, black women, usually servants, are sexually but never romantically linked to white men. However, just as often we have an inter-racial romance featuring Muslim women, and such a romance is always also a story of religious conversion and marriage.

In a perceptive essay on Shakespeare's *The Merchant of Venice*, Mary Jane Metzger shows that Jessica's 'whiteness and femaleness make possible her reproduction as a Christian in the eyes of the "commonwealth"' and that her 'incorporation into Christian society is essential to defining her father's alien status' (57, 59). If circumcision was the major physical barrier to the idea of the converted Muslim (or Jew), then women, whose bodies did not bear this mark, could be more easily imagined as crossing the religious and racial divide. I have earlier remarked on the translation of circumcision into more indelible marks of difference. The uncircumcized body is imagined as literally fairer: thus, when Shylock claims a shared racial identity with Jessica, 'I say my daughter is my flesh and blood', he declares (3.1.34), Solanio tells him, 'There is more difference between thy flesh and hers than between jet and ivory, more between your bloods than there is between red wine and Rhenish' (3.1.35–37). Here gender difference produces a crucial difference *within* races.

A similar difference was suggested and amplified by an influential history of the Moluccan islands by Bartolemé Leonardo de Argensola, *Conquista de las islas Malucas* (1609), on which Fletcher's play *The Island Princess* was based.[50]

---

[48] The Jesuit priest Francis Xavier drew the finest of colour lines while urging the *casados* to marry their local concubines, encouraging the men to abandon the dark ones and even offering to find fair substitutes for them. M. N. Pearson, *The New Cambridge History of India, The Portuguese in India* (Cambridge, 1987), p. 101.

[49] The same logic governs, in my opinion, the casting of Denzel Washington as the Duke (Don Pedro) in Kenneth Branagh's film *Much Ado About Nothing*. Despite his high social status (or indeed because of it) the Duke is safe from romantic or sexual involvements; thus blackness is granted a nobility which does not threaten dominant sexual codes.

[50] It is a matter of some controversy how Fletcher amalgamated his story from the sources. Gordon McMullan, *The Politics of Unease in the Plays of John Fletcher* (Amherst, 1994) argues that he relied on a French novel by Le Sr de Bellan, *L'Historie du Ruis Dias*, published in 1615, which was based on Argensola's history. Edward Wilson, 'Did John Fletcher read Spanish?', *Philological Quarterly*, 27, 11 April 1948, suggests that Fletcher had enough knowledge of Spanish to use Argensola's text.

Argensola claims that the 'Natives Differ from one another, as it were through a Miraculous Bounty of Nature, for it has made the Women Fair and Beautiful, and the Men, of a darker Colour than Quince'.[51] Fletcher's play reserves this somatic difference for the Moluccan Princess Quisara. Unlike Shakespeare's Cleopatra, who is 'with Phoebus's amorous pinches black', 'the very sun', the Portuguese soldier Christophero tells us, dares not dye Quisara 'Into his tawny livery' (1.2).[52] But his companion Piniero contends that this is less a matter of nature than one of nurture: the princess 'dares not see' the sun,

> But keeps herself at a distance from his kisses,
> And wears her complexion in a case: Let him but like it
> A week, or two, or three, she would look like a lion.   (1.2).

He also suggests, taking a dig at the whole literary tradition of lovely princesses, that beauty is a matter of class power:

> She is a princess, and she must be fair,
> That's the prerogative of being royal;
> Let her want eyes and nose, she must be beauteous,
> And she must know it too, and the use of it,
> And people must believe it, they are damn'd else.
> . . .   (1.2).

Nevertheless, like Jessica and the 'too fayre' Donusia in *The Renegado*, Quisara is converted and married to a Christian man. Thus perceptions of colour, class and female tractability shape one another.

In play after play, conversion and penetration are often literally the same process. Quisara's maid is told by Piniero: 'I'll get thee with Christian, / The best way to convert thee' (5.4). In Beaumont and Fletcher's the *Knight of Malta* the soldiers want sexual access to the Turkish prisoner Lucinda '. . . to make her a good Christian' (2.1).[53] The children of such liaisons might be 'ill Christians' in genetic terms, but, says her master Miranda, 'We'll mend them in the breeding.' Like Jessica's

offspring, and unlike the offspring of the Moor impregnated by Launcelot, the children of Muslim women can be blanched of their inner stain. Thus the successful assimilation of Jessica and her ilk highlights the marginality, not only of men of their race, but also of darker women.

Lucinda's conversion is offset by the expulsion of the black maid, Zanthia, whose white lover is the evil Mountferrat. Zanthia is his 'black gib there, his Succuba, his devil's seed' and Mountferrat's villainous disposition is measured by his lust for her which, he confesses,

> . . . is not love, but strong libidinous will,
> That triumphs o'er me; and to satiate that,
> What difference 'twixt this Moor, and her fair dame?
> Night makes their hues so alike, their use is so;
> Whose hand's so subtle he can colours name,
> If he do wink and touch 'em? Lust being blind,
> Never in women did distinction find.   (1.2).

If 'lust' makes no racial distinctions, 'love' rests on a finely calibrated sense of difference.[54]

There were significant differences in Christian attitudes towards sex with Muslims and Jews in medieval times. Muslim women were generally poorer, and risked enslavement by consorting with Christian men. Jews, on the other hand, 'were closely tied to the Crown

---

51 English translation of Argensola, *The Discovery and Conquest of the Molucco and Philippine Islands* (London, 1708), 4.

52 All references to *The Island Princess* are from *The Works of Beaumont and Fletcher*, vol. 2, ed. George Darley (London, 1866). This edition has no line numbers.

53 All references to *The Knight of Malta* are from *The Works of Beaumont and Fletcher*, vol. 2, ed. George Darley (London, 1866). This edition has no line numbers.

54 Since the play rests upon distinctions of women's colour and virtue, at the end of the play Mountferrat is expelled from 'our society, . . . as a rotten, / Corrupted and contagious member'. He is told that since he has 'a Barbary mare of your own; go leap her, and engender young devilings' (5.2). Thus the romance of conversion works more easily with Muslim rather than black women.

and had a good deal of financial and political power that they could use to reinforce the sexual boundary around their community. A Jewish woman accused of miscegenation might be fined, tortured, mutilated, or even executed, but she could not become chattel.'[55] But on early modern English stages, the desirable Muslim and Jewish woman both promise wealth: as she elopes, Jessica pauses to 'gild myself / With some moe ducats' (2.6.49–50). Shylock's 'stones, his daughter and his ducats' are a package deal (2.7.22). In *The Island Princess* the fabled wealth of the Moluccas, 'The wealthy magazine of Nature' (1.2) is promised to Quisara's mate. In Massinger's *The Renegado*, Donusia woos her Christian lover Vitelli with 'bags stuft full of our imperiall coyne ... These Iems for which the slavish Indian dives / To the bottom of the Maine' (2.4.83–114). The motif of the converted wealthy Queen obviously harks back to the story of the black Queen of Sheba and to the black but comely bride in the Song of Songs. The blackness of these earlier figures is, whitewashed in theatrical representations, with the exception of those of Cleopatra, although it finds readier expression in the royal masque, in mayoral pageants, in poetry and in paintings of the period.[56]

Daniel Vitkus has remarked that Othello's turn towards Christianity and assimilation into Venice is jeopardized by Desdemona's potential waywardness: she 'can turn and turn, and yet go on / And turn again' (4.1.254–5). But if the changeability of women, a theme pervasive in the drama of the period, provokes anxieties and threatens to disrupt social stability, it is also necessary for the cementing and remodelling of social structures. Quisara in Fletcher's *The Island Princess* also 'turns, for millions ... For a ton of crowns she turns' but in the direction of Christianity, and her to be husband Armusia, and away from other men, including a Moorish priest who incites her to rebel against the Portuguese. Desdemona's fairness depends upon her fidelity: when suspected of being a whore, she is as 'begrimed' as Othello's face.

Quisara's beauty depends upon her religious faith: when she asks Armusia to convert to her religion, she spirals down from goddess to whore – her perfect beauty 'looks ugly now methinks'. Of course, once she declares her intention to convert to Christianity, she recovers her status as a 'blessed lady'.[57]

The changeability of women is thus both a threat and a promise. Their ability to adopt alien cultures is crucial to their value as currency that secures patriarchal alliances, just as it threatens the security of cultural borders. Foreign queens were an integral part of European feudal courts and their trans-national alliances. They brought along a different culture and would, if not properly assimilated, breed 'alien heirs'. Hence they spelt 'the danger of cultural alienation'.[58] But at the same time, as Louise Fradenburg astutely points out,

being liminal figures – such as the wild people also were – queens could be identified with 'land', 'people', 'nation', their liminality serving the very

---

[55] Muslim women were generally poorer, and risked enslavement by consorting with Christian men. Jews, on the other hand, were close to the Crown and had financial and political power that could be used to protect the sexual boundaries of their community. A Jewish woman accused of miscegenation might be fined, tortured, mutilated, or even executed, but she could not become chattel (Nirenberg, *Communities of Violence*, p. 140).

[56] For discussions of the poetry, artifacts and masques, see Kim Hall; *Things of Darkness*; for mayoral pageants, see Barthelemey, *Black face, Maligned Race* and my Introduction to Middleton's 'The Triumphs of Honour and Virtue' in *The Collected Works of Thomas Middleton*, general editor Gary Taylor (Oxford, forthcoming).

[57] Fairness, blessedness and virtue are knotted in these scenarios of exchange. Unsanctioned sex blackens women, as in the Thornton manuscript of *Thomas of Erceldoune*, for example, when Thomas meets a 'lady bryghte' who turns black after he lies with her seven times (quoted in Fradenburg, *City, Marriage, Tournament*, p. 251). In *The Renegado*, Vitelli comments that Donusia has lost her blinding fairness after her sexual contact with him, and Oriana in *The Knight of Malta* claims that she is 'A fragrant flower cropt by another's hand, / My colour sullied, and my odour changed' (5.1).

[58] Bartlett, *The Making of Europe*, pp. 230–1.

principle of identity – of the invulnerability rather than the vulnerability of the body of the realm. Queens themselves, then, are talismanic; they are a potential threat – a foreign body let in through open and even decorated gates, capable of causing internal torment – turned into an aegis of protection, a banner under which to ride against the enemy . . .[59]

The changeability, 'turnability' of the queen is thus central to her symbolic role. The ability to transform the queen from a foreign to a talismanic figure testifies to the power of the king, and assures 'the well-being of the whole body of the realm'. Fradenburg recalls the powerful connections between queen, wife and land encoded in James I's famous marriage metaphor ('I am the Husband, and all the whole Isle is my lawful Wife') and suggests that James's tournaments in Scotland featuring the black lady can thus be seen as representing the power of the sovereign to transform the land and his subjects.

However, rather than testify only to the power of the singular monarch, the romance of the foreign queen in English theatre also negotiates some of the wider national, religious, cultural and economic anxieties of the period. I have discussed how such gendered play underlines the power of colour differentiation while attempting to contain, and even invert, the meaning of Islamic or Jewish alterity. But the significance of female, especially queenly conversion or assimilation is not limited to religious otherness. The exchange of women has always signalled the vulnerability of cultural borders. This exchange took on new urgent meanings in an early modern England which was simultaneously looking outward and consolidating its national culture in linguistic, religious, and ethnic terms.

The disorderliness of figures such as Hippolyta, Tamora, Cleopatra and even Titania, and the necessity of their assimilation into the culture of their husbands can be set against this pattern. In *The Two Noble Kinsmen*, Hippolyta's transformation from a fighting to a domesticated Amazon is described thus:

> Most dreaded Amazonian, that hast slain
> The scythe-tusked boar, that with thy arm, as strong
> As it is white, wast near to make the male
> To thy sex captive, but that this, thy lord –
> [. . .] shrunk thee into
> The bound thou wast o'erflowing, at once subduing
> Thy force and thy affection   (1.1.78–85).

Unlike Hippolyta, Tamora, the Queen of the Goths in *Titus Andronicus*, and Cleopatra the Queen of Egypt resist such shrinking with varying degrees of success. Cleopatra's tawny skin as well as her political ambitions highlight a tension between her 'force' and her 'affection', whereas Tamora's liaison with the black Aaron problematizes her 'incorporation' in Rome. The convertible body of women is thus the 'delicious traffick' between cultures, religions and races.[60] On the stage, it provides a recurrent fantasy of exchange and mastery, while underlining the religious as well as somatic notions of alterity in the early modern period.

---

[59] Louise Olga Fradenburg, *City, Marriage, Tournament*, p. 252.

[60] I am appropriating the phrase 'delicious traffick' from the records of the Grocers' Company where it is used to refer to the sweetmeats which were strewn on London streets during the Mayoral pageants sponsored by the Company. See Baron Heath, *Some Account of the Worshipful Company of Grocers of the City of London* (London, 1869).

THE 1998 GLOBE SEASON

RICHARD PROUDFOOT

The 1998 repertoire at Shakespeare's Globe included two comedies, *As You Like It*, probably written for the original Globe in 1599, and *The Merchant of Venice*, revived there before Court performances in 1605. As in 1997, two further plays were added in August: Thomas Middleton's *A Mad World, My Masters*, written for the Children of St Paul's, at their small indoor theatre in the cathedral precinct; and *The Honest Whore* (part 1 by Thomas Dekker and Middleton; part 2 by Dekker alone), written for Prince Henry's Men at the Fortune (whose stage used the Globe's as its model). One play, then, was both Shakespeare's and a Globe play. Other performances at the Globe included a single performance of *King John* by the 'Original Shakespeare Company', and several concert performances of John Blow's opera *Venus and Adonis* (whose libretto bears no relation to Shakespeare's poem).

As the novelty of the Globe eases into familiarity, its attractions and its discomforts and discontents become clearer. Simply to enter the yard and stand in the building remains among its most reliable satisfactions. The enclosed space of the yard and timber galleries excludes the modern city around it. Even the nuisance of aircraft noise, especially hovering traffic helicopters, is taken in their stride by actors and audience alike, if anything creating a bond of sympathy. Less easily ignored are the hardness of the narrow backless benches in the three galleries (though cushions at £1 a show do much to alleviate it), the number of seats whose view is impeded by the structural uprights of the galleries or the two pillars which support the stage canopy, and the building's variable acoustics. I attended nine performances between July and September. The best position for hearing well was the central section of the second gallery. Least satisfactory was the Gentlemen's Room, next to the stage, which compensated for reduced audibility and skewed sight-lines by providing a moveable chair with a back.

The four directors showed no uniform awareness of these difficulties. Two plays, *As You Like It* and *The Honest Whore*, were staged with a main eye to the audience in the north-eastern areas of the building, from which the *frons scenae* and discovery space are clearly visible. This may, in part, have resulted from rehearsing in a rehearsal studio, leaving the Globe and its physical conditions to be explored in the dress rehearsal and previews, by when decisions about blocking were fixed. Use of the yard and the 'discovery space' in the middle of the tiring-house wall as acting areas further reduced visibility. For those who are seated in the side galleries on all three levels and in the Lords' Room above the stage, the discovery space might more aptly be named 'concealment space', as they can see nothing that happens or is placed behind the line of the tiring-house wall. Equally, action in the yard automatically becomes invisible to most of the seven hundred 'under-standers', who block each others' view of it, whatever heightened excitement it may offer to those close to it.

Performance time averaged three hours, with *A Mad World* clocking in at two hours and forty minutes. All the performances I saw had a fifteen-minute interval in addition to two-minute act pauses. In the Shakespeare plays, these pauses were announced by the Clown, who sometimes used them for improvised byplay with the spectators in the yard. Incidental music from the stage gallery served the same purpose in the other productions. However necessary for the comfort of spectators, the pauses reduced pace and continuity and left the actors to recover the attention of the audience as it straggled back after them. Pace seems hard to judge at the Globe: it was most satisfactory in *The Merchant of Venice*, especially in its second half, slackest in *The Honest Whore* and in the later acts of *As You Like It*.

It is no concern of the commercial Globe Theatre Company to engage in historical research into the use of its theatre but after the excitements of the opening season it was disappointing to sense that lessons learned from the experience of productions in 1996 and 1997 are not being passed on, or at least not being taken seriously, and that uses of the stage that many spectators must find unhelpful persist. Three examples may serve. Scene after scene of *As You Like It* was blocked with actors facing each other squarely across the width of the stage – especially the area of it in front of the pillars – rather than on diagonals, with inevitable and repeated masking of lengthy stretches of action for spectators seated in the lower side galleries. In *The Merchant*, the trial scene was undercut for many spectators by overuse of the area between the two pillars, where masking is at its maximum. In *The Honest Whore*, twentieth-century tables and chairs, even a bulky sofa, were overused, robbing scenes of their physical energy by making characters sit down, and reducing the mobility needed if an in-the-round audience is to be fully engaged with the action. Globe productions can be staged as for a proscenium theatre, but this robs the actors of

many chances of rapport with their audience, while leaving a minority of that audience out in the cold. Lucy Bailey's decision to open *As You Like It* with a ballad sung in the yard and a dumbshow played in front of a curtain strung between the stage pillars meant that spectators behind the line of the pillars, especially those in the first gallery, missed several minutes of the show. The time taken by the inserted ballad prologue also imposed a need to cut a short play in order to remain within the three-hour limit.

This invented prologue was symptomatic of general directorial unease about how to get the play started. Lengthy horseplay and music preceded the first scene of *The Merchant*; the opening funeral in *The Honest Whore* made up for its lack of ceremony by proceeding under the gaze of characters who are not on in the first scene – Bellafront drinking coffee at a café table; Candido, his wife and his prentices observing the meagre procession from the entrance of his shop (in the discovery space). In *A Mad World*, general turmoil by most of the cast turned into a mimed fight which culminated in Follywit being knocked down by the large actor who would return as the Constable in the final scene. Except in the Dekker play, these inventions took up time that might have been better spent in launching straight into the opening scenes. It was apparently assumed that audiences would take five or ten minutes to stop moving and talking, or to get used to looking at the stage, and that only then could the real show begin.

At the Globe, the disposition of the audience around the stage in a fully lit auditorium means that the actors have constantly to compel its attention. They risk losing it to the competing visual interest of the surrounding scene, or failing to sustain it when spectators have difficulty in hearing or seeing what is going on. In practice, audience attention was at its greatest when what was to be seen and heard was most significant, so that these opening gambits, which tried to engage their participation in insignificant activity, were counterproductive.

After this jeremiad about some aspects of current use of the Globe, it is time to redress the balance. All four productions included compelling and successful individual performances and all exerted a grip on audiences (some more intermittently than others). Once past the prologue, the opening acts of *As You Like It* had great clarity, directness and pace; *The Merchant of Venice* rose to a powerful climax in Act 4, and the power was sustained into the final scenes; *The Honest Whore* (especially in the scenes least mauled by heavy cutting) engaged spectators with its exploration of sexual double standards; and the two halves of *A Mad World* both built to hilarious climaxes. The claim that at the Globe the audience plays an essential role in the performance was ratified in these and other places, while the self-conscious over-reaction from the yard, and even the galleries, which was a marked feature of the 1997 season was happily absent.

In 1997, *Henry V* was designated 'period' production of the season. This status was marked by all-male casting, historically appropriate and lavish costuming and period music. Less whole-hoggingly, Richard Olivier's production of *The Merchant of Venice* was this year's equivalent, with women in the female roles and the model for costumes, music, carnival masks and comic style Venetian rather than English (barring the apparent anachronism of Bugs Bunny masking suits for Lorenzo and his friends). The discovery space was curtained with the lion of St Mark, flanked, on the adjacent panels, by hangings representing female figures in the manner of Veronese. The Venetian setting lent credence to the range and variety of an international company.

Before the play actors mingled with the audience. One of them, a masked man in orange (who would turn out to be Lancelot Gobbo, played by Marcello Magni) worked up the groundlings, clowning with a string of sausages. The Musicians of the Globe played on period instruments in the gallery, where Portia

and Nerissa, also masked, were briefly glimpsed. Gradually, the actors clambered onto the stage and a game of football ensued between the gentry and the lower orders. The competition then turned musical, the gentlemen trying in vain to sustain a madrigal in face of the increasingly noisy and percussive assault of a dance song sung by the plebs and accompanied on a drum. Music, arranged by Claire van Kampen, was a strong feature of the production. After Act 1, Jessica made a first appearance singing to lute accompaniment in the candle-lit discovery space, to the satisfaction of her approving father. After Act 4, Nicholas Monu, who had doubled as Morocco and the Duke of Venice, sang an unaccompanied counter-tenor song from the turret above the stage canopy.

To start each act, Gobbo rang a large hand-bell. Act 1, scene 1, hung fire, largely because Antonio (Jack Shepherd) seemed to belong in a different production from the rest of the cast. His inward, underplayed and vocally strained performance turned the enigma of Antonio's sadness from the focal point of the scene into a gap at its centre. Antonio attracted little interest or sympathy, either here or in later scenes, thus skewing the play heavily in the direction of Portia and Shylock. Mark Rylance was a callow and feckless Bassanio, still kicking the football on his first entry and presenting his request for Antonio's backing with conscious and disingenuous self-deprecation. The scene ended – bewilderingly for Antonio – as Bassanio parted from his friend and backer with a long kiss on the lips.

Belmont was introduced by drawing back the central curtain. Kathryn Pogson's tall, slender, bored Portia chatted languidly with Nerissa to the accompaniment of a lutenist in the gallery (who tactfully withdrew when the conversation reached Portia's suitors). Sonia Ritter's Nerissa was the perfect foil; short and energetic, speaking, in the earlier scenes, with a heavy Italian accent that later vanished. During her mockery of the suitors, Portia established easy and sympathetic contact with the audience.

11 *The Merchant of Venice*, Shakespeare's Globe. Kathryn Pogson as Portia, Nicholas Monu as the Duke of Venice.

The approach of the new suitors was announced from the gallery, still the area which poses most problems, as it is seldom required for action but has to be kept available for such scenes as Jessica's elopement and so cannot be entirely given over to audience – though a few spectators were seated in its outer bays for this and other productions. Perhaps, as early evidence suggests, it should be subdivided into bays or boxes with separate functions?

With 1.3 the production acquired its full momentum. The emergence of Portia into command of the stage is gradual; Shylock takes the initiative from his first moment. Casting the German actor Norbert Kentrup (suggested originally by the new Globe's only begetter, Sam Wanamaker) was daring. It is reported that he learned English specially to play the role, and his heavy German accent and intonation were an obstacle to understanding for many of the audience, despite his subtle grasp on the tone and nuance of his lines and his command of the acoustic of the theatre. The daring paid off in other respects. Shylock was physically dominant, tall and powerfully built. He was also the most intelligent and cultured man on stage, an effect fostered by costume. His sobriety, conveyed by a Rembrandtesque dark gown and skullcap, contrasted strongly with the fancy silks and velvets of the Venetians. The long aside in which he reveals his hatred of Antonio was given straight out to the audience from centre stage, with calm and thoughtful deliberation. Though given to hand gestures, notably a circling index finger, he was, in the early scenes, a centre of physical calm and stability, standing well above Antonio in height and remonstrating with him from a position of unshaken inner security. Similar security, and a proud, distant, affection, showed in his relations with Jessica (Lilo Baur) and in the amused detachment of his attitude to Lancelot. The intelligence and self-command of this Shylock would make him a formidable adversary, while his relaxed self-confidence spoke of financial and social ease. His misgivings on leaving

12 *The Merchant of Venice*, Shakespeare's Globe. Norbert Kentrup as Shylock.

Jessica were expressed with moderation: he passed her his keys slowly, with one discernible moment of hesitation, then removed his prayer-shawl and gave her that too.

Portia and Shylock can (and should) dominate *The Merchant of Venice*: Lancelot Gobbo can seem to embody the irrecoverable deadness of Shakespeare's verbal humour. The skills and personality of Marcello Magni, and his function, masked as Harlequin, of chief mediator between stage and auditorium, turned his Gobbo into a show-stealing success, and one which displayed the theatrical dynamic that so easily made the clown the dominant figure in Elizabethan acting companies. Without speaking more than was set down for him (unless during the intervals), Magni filled the theatre with his presence, from the violent physical tussle of his initial choice between conscience and fiend to a cadenza of acrobatic clowning which transformed the often dull (or cut) scene with his blind father into a comic high point. Using every corner of the stage, including the plinths of the pillars, he transformed himself into a dog, a cat and a horse before bringing the house down with a rapid mime of the many modes of his own alleged death. He had the audience eating out of his hand, alternately wooing and bullying it into total support.

An expected bonus was that the scenes of *The Merchant* were played in their proper order, without the cutting and rearrangement resorted to when Belmont requires a scene-change, while use of the sides of the stage for street-scenes helped to speed transitions. Morocco was young and sympathetic, Aragon (Morris Perry) old and infirm, and both were allowed the full arguments of their speeches. The location of the three caskets in the discovery space, while impeding sightlines for some spectators, placed the suitors in strong upstage positions, while leaving the front area of the stage for Portia to signal her reactions without impediment. She was passingly flattered by Morocco's compliment to her virginity, perhaps even fleetingly attracted; flattened to wide-eyed boredom by the tedious deliberateness of Aragon – though she robbed the audience of its final moment of uncertainty about the silver casket by registering her relief as soon as Aragon chose it, not waiting for him to open it.

Bassanio's choice was, once more, Portia's scene rather than his: her reactions were more immediate than his solemn meditation on the deceptiveness of appearances, delivered with little variety of pace or pitch. In the latter part of this scene the director's skill in use of the stage became fully apparent, with the seven characters grouped and moved so as to let the successive actions of the wooing of Gratiano and Nerissa, the arrival of Lorenzo and Jessica,

and the news of Antonio's jeopardy unfold with fluent clarity and an easy shifting of mood and pace, up to the climax of Bassanio's reading of Antonio's letter.

Shylock's rage after the elopement of Jessica was reflected in a new, aggressive mobility. Resisting the pleas of Antonio in 3.3, he suddenly, and to sinister effect, circled the stage-right pillar, leading the prisoner and his gaoler behind him. In the trial scene his composure was ostensibly restored, his manner once more quiet and confident. It was here that his superiority to the Christians in perceptiveness and in intelligence was most strongly projected. His reliance on that superiority robbed him of full sympathy in his defeat. Portia's questions did not, initially, take him by surprise. His dismissal of her request 'Have by some surgeon Shylock on your charge, To stop his wounds' – 'Is it so nominated in the bond?' – was off-hand – couldn't so clever a lawyer see for himself its obvious irrelevance? His final move to exact the penalty was so swift and unhesitating as visibly to shock Portia and prepare the ground for her own answering implacability.

On Portia's first entry as Balthazar 'his' youthfulness drew from Bassanio a gesture of incredulous indignation. Later in the scene his insistence on his readiness to pay for Antonio's release mounted to a pitch that forced her to shout him down (the only time she had to raise her voice and a useful preparation for the dynamic of Act 5). It was in Act 4 that Kathryn Pogson came fully into her own. The male disguise was uncommonly persuasive and there was no hint of sentimentality in her appeal for mercy – indeed its simplicity was so forceful that it troubled Shylock, who registered its force before brushing it too aside as irrelevant. The intelligent alertness of both players imparted to this scene the seemingly incompatible excitements of a fencing match and a game of chess. Shylock's collapse, when it came – on the mention of his conversion to Christianity – was complete, but muted: his pain, though inward, was real. His intelligence made the full extent of his disaster clear to him in a flash. As he left the stage he covered his head with his shawl, abandoning the bond, the knife and the scales which were the instruments of his intended revenge.

The opening of Act 5 was uncomplicated by any subtext of tension between the lovers. The banter of Lorenzo and Jessica, playing hide and seek round the left pillar, lacked foreboding undertones, and her melancholy at the music in no way reflected on her love of her husband (an attractive, if less than lyrical, performance by Clarence Smith). Centre stage provided the obvious position for the lovers to lie in after Lorenzo's description of the inaudible music of the spheres, and the painted undersurface of the stage canopy duly afforded a visual referent for his 'floor of heaven ... thick inlaid with patens of bright gold'. The authority gained by Portia in the trial scene carried through to the end of the play. Smugly delighted by Bassanio's initial refusal to part with the ring, she was correspondingly dismayed to receive it from Gratiano, and the business of punishing Bassanio was given a strong motive. In the final scene, when confronted by Portia's accusation, Bassanio, by the sincerity of his confusion and the openness of his confession, earned a sympathy that had previously eluded him (suggesting that the trickery with the rings may function precisely to win for him a regard he has not previously seemed to merit). Though weak, this Bassanio was neither a liar nor a prevaricator. Portia's final position was secure, and her welcome of the chastened Antonio showed no tinge of jealousy or mistrust of him as a potential rival for the affections of her docile and manageable husband.

In a period when *The Merchant of Venice* is regarded as a painfully problematic play, we are used to seeing productions which work hard to direct the sympathies of audiences, by selective emphasis, by cutting, or by tendentious casting. The casting of a German actor in the role of the Jew Shylock was unquestionably tendentious, as it would not have been in a German produc-

tion. The effect was to set up an unexpected, and complicating, potential anti-German prejudice against Shylock. This potential was exploited with some skill. To Globe audiences Shylock was audibly alien, while in terms of the play's dynamic he was also the superior of every other character, until he met his match in Portia. No prejudice against him could extend to Jessica or to his co-religionist Tubal. Otherwise the production did little to massage audience sympathies. Laying its emphasis on clear and detailed story-telling, it allowed those sympathies to grow and change as the play progressed. This production must have been very satisfactory as a first encounter with the play; elegant to look at, lucid and audible. More seasoned playgoers might have found it bland (and there were indeed scenes that made less than their full impact) but they must also have allowed that they had witnessed an uncommonly gripping and powerful rendering of the trial scene, a brilliant clown and a performance which gave the actors room to find their own ways of relating to the audience at their feet and all around them in the still unfamiliar space of the Globe. At two afternoon performances, early and late in the season, I saw capacity audiences respond to it with engaged and appreciative enthusiasm.

Impressions of a Globe performance are affected by one's place in the auditorium. Broiling in the afternoon sun in the front row of the second gallery, I could hear and see *The Merchant of Venice* and *As You Like It* with minimum impediment; seeing *As You Like It* again from a side first gallery seat level with the front of the stage was less satisfying – though I was less frustrated than the bored school party to my right, in the last bay, adjacent to the tiring-house. When one of them left his seat in eagerness to see better, he was promptly reproved by an usher for sitting in the aisle and required to return to his 'restricted view' seat. The steady stream of late-comers throughout the first half-hour was a further annoyance.

In Lucy Bailey's production of *As You Like It*

narrative was once more the top priority. In the opening dumbshow Sir Rowland de Bois took leave of his three sons before slumping dead in his chair, while a ballad of his story was sung in the yard. This opening introduced 'the second son of old Sir Rowland' prematurely, undercutting the arbitrariness of the role of Jaques de Bois (Wil Johnson) as *deus ex machina*. It also set up an inappropriate expectation of balladlike simplicity, to which the designer, Bunny Christie, responded by carpeting the stage with sheepskin, hanging the back wall and the central bays of the gallery with drab, dirty linen curtains, fitting the discovery space with heavy barn doors and supplying appropriate props to suggest the successive localities of Oliver's (apple) orchard, well-stocked with windfalls, and a wintery forest with bare skeletons of saplings tied to the pillars of stage, yard and gallery. Among these props was an alarmingly smoky late-Elizabethan barbecue for the exiled Duke's picnic party, which conjured fears of a second Globe fire in the minds of those spectators who could see the smoke coming from it, but not its source! Less was made of the play's self-critical artifice, its preoccupation with poetic language, or the fact that characters create their own mental visions of Arden. The staging evidently aimed to break down an imagined gulf between stage and auditorium. Steps that ran along the front edge of the stage gave easy access from stage to yard: many entries and exits were made through the audience and the outer doors of the yard. The gallery was unused, except for occasional visits by the musicians (when they were not scattered through the yard and galleries for antiphonal effects of birdsong and the like). A ladder propped against the gallery after the interval was climbed by several characters, but none got to the top. The music for this production, by Roderick Skeaping, was demotic, in the ballad tradition, and featured a dulcimer, bagpipes, recorders and cowhorns. The songs were built up into company numbers, insecurely led by Wil Johnson's Amiens, or into elaborate business – a bloody hunting mime in 4.2, with Amiens as the deer; a farcical striptease for Touchstone and Audrey in 5.3, to the accompaniment of 'It was a lover and his lass'.

The demotic touch extended to a tinge of Midlands in the voice of Orlando (Paul Hilton), which was doubtless designed to reflect his neglected education and which faded in Arden once he was in the company of Ganymede. He certainly hadn't picked it up from Leader Hawkins's well-spoken and gentle Adam (who doubled Sir Rowland in the dumbshow and Hymen, a startling apparition, horned like a stag and clad in a crown and jockstrap of straw and thorny twigs). Casting throughout was strongly to type and the success of the performance derived very largely from convinced and plausible characterization. Further effective doubling saw David Rintoul as a quick-changing pair of vocally forceful and energetic twin Dukes; Martin Herman as a professional Charles and a massive but docile William. Jonathan Cecil shifted from an affected Le Beau, with a strong taste for 'wrastling', first to a phlegmatic, bearded Corin, who patiently bore logs from the back of the yard onto the stage while maintaining the virtues of country life against Touchstone, and finally to a manic Sir Oliver Martext, surpliced and capped, and with a portable fit-up altar and cross in his capacious holdall. As usual, the creation of a woodland milieu for Arden left Silvius and Phebe, whose occupations are love and poetry and whose idiom is not that of the countryside, unlocalized. Guy Moore's mummerset accent made all but the simplest of Silvius' utterances unintelligible, while Belinda Davison's strapping Phebe was more akin to Touchstone's lost love, Jane Smile, than to the conventional Dresden figurine – capable of inflicting grievous bodily harm and relentlessly energetic in her pursuit of Ganymede, round pillars, up the ladder, almost off the edge of the stage. The ill grace of her final acceptance of Silvius was the production's one moment of real unease, ruffling the harmony of Hymen's atonement.

13 *As You Like It*, Shakespeare's Globe. Tonia Chauvet as Celia, Anastasia Hille as Rosalind, Paul Hilton as Orlando, Jonathan Cecil as Le Beau.

As Touchstone, David Fielder was primarily court fool, bauble, slapstick and bells to the fore in his first scene, but his glum manner and acidulous tone laid a stress on the satirical which, while accounting for Jaques's delight in him, blurred the distinction between his appetite for life and Jaques's rejection of it. Sonia Ritter's Audrey relied on stocky solidity, physical clowning and irrepressible good nature to qualify the sour note of Touchstone. John McEnery's Jaques was in relaxed control of theatre, audience and role. In scholarly garb and cap, he followed his quiet orbit among the Duke's foresters, puncturing pretension and revealing his own blindsides in crisp, rasping tones which lent themselves to parody by the courtiers. Throwing the apple from which he had just taken a first bite out among the groundlings, he disguised the undue familiarity

of the line as he launched into 'All the world's a stage'. In this play of many voices his carried full conviction.

Central to the production, as Rosalind, was Anastasia Hille. Her first entry with Celia (Tonia Chauvet), one fair, the other dark, but both tall, and dressed in gowns of the same light brocade, was striking. The balance of rank and power between the two cousins was level. Celia, indeed, retained the initiative until after their arrival in Arden, leaving room – and a need – for Rosalind to discover her ascendency as Ganymede. She was a thoroughly feminine Ganymede, whose sheepskin cap (more suggestive, together with her dirty face and unkempt appearance, of hired man than of master) had a habit of falling off, to reveal shoulder-length fair hair of indeterminate gender. Orlando seemed hardly to notice – his hair too was long –

because his time and attention were occupied with filling the forest with his verses, or carving 'Rosalind' on sticks from Corin's woodpile. By Act 4, all pretence of disguise was abandoned, bar the doublet and hose which 'Ganymede' retained, despite Rosalind's buttock-flashing panic attempt to shed them on first hearing of Orlando's presence in Arden: 'Alas the day, what shall I do with my doublet and hose?' The mock-wedding ended with a prolonged kiss that left Orlando gasping for breath while grasping nothing of the true situation. This Rosalind, indeed, consigned Orlando to a subordinate role and left Celia in a state of mounting frustration that snapped in sudden hysterical fury on 'And I'll sleep'. The frustration vanished in her instant passion for Oliver (Jonathan Bond), whom she seized and kissed intently over the body of the fainting Ganymede in 4.3. This said, Rosalind earned her prominence. It was a mercurial, relaxed and versatile performance, full of self-mockery and innocent of vanity. It found its natural climax in the yearning love-litany of 5.2, and in Rosalind's sudden deflation of it as 'the howling of Irish wolves'. She was both deep in love – prone to yell 'Orlando' to the sky – and a wary match for all the characters she encounters in Arden. Their reception of her epilogue demonstrated the audience's delight – but the sentence beginning 'if I were a woman' was rightly cut: this Rosalind was *all* woman.

The production had much in it to please, but the pace of the second half became self-indulgently slow, and by 4.30 on a cooling September afternoon (when an uncut text, played with brisker pace, might have been over), a full half-hour's playing was still to come, despite much cutting of the later scenes. The length of performances in Elizabethan and Jacobean theatres is much debated. Practical experience suggests to me that many, if not most, of Shakespeare's plays can be performed within two and a half hours, with only light trimming of impenetrable obscurities – and that furthermore the pace required to achieve this

timing is compatible with intelligible speaking, and can even allow the verse and rhetoric of the plays to make a stronger appeal than the slow and over-emphatic delivery which is fashionable today. The Globe would surely be the right theatre in which to restore reliance on the spoken word in the plays of Shakespeare and his contemporaries. Certainly the performances I saw this summer demonstrated that forceful and intelligent speaking of lines, without over-inflection or an imposed pattern of 'significant' disruption of rhythm, commanded the instant attention of the listeners. This was as true of the penitent speeches of Master Penitent Brothel in *A Mad World* or the unmasking of Hippolyto's double standards of sexual morality in *The Honest Whore* as of better-known passages in the Shakespearian comedies. Cutting may seem an inevitable expedient to achieve tolerable length of performance, but the paradox enunciated by George Bernard Shaw in a review of *As You Like It* in 1890 remains of force – 'somehow, the shorter you make your play in this fashion, the more tedious it becomes'.[1] Too often, cutting reduces the significance of the speeches on which it is practised by damaging their rhythm and structure. At times, it can pare them down to little more than the bare bones of plot necessity.

These thoughts were prompted by the decision to stage a text of *The Honest Whore* which reduced each of the two plays to the short span of some hour and twenty minutes, so that they could be performed together. A viable alternative would be hard to find: the first play is the less interesting, but without it the second lacks the context of its leading characters' earlier actions. Though the cutting permitted us to see two rarely read and never performed plays of great interest, its outcome was not wholly satisfactory, as it entailed the bleeding of vitality from some minor figures and wholesale removal of others (notably, in part 2, Brian, the

---

[1] *Shaw on Shakespeare*, ed. Edwin Wilson (Harmondsworth, 1969), p. 51.

Irish footman and Candido's second wife). A further obstacle in the way of full engagement, by cast and audience alike, was the location of the action in the Milan of the decades after World War II. Jack Shepherd had used the same period and place for his production of *The Two Gentlemen of Verona* in 1996, of which this *Honest Whore* conjured up frequent memories. Budgetary constraints may have affected the decision, but, in the words of the director himself, printed in the programme, 'though nominally Italy, much of it evidently depicted the low life and demimonde of London of the time'. The shift robbed the play, in which costume and appearance play an important role in defining character, rank and relationships, of one of its systems of signification.

The production offered a fair account of the plot, if not of all the characters. Candido (Marcello Magni) and his wife, Viola, played with Lancashire pugnacity by Kathryn Pogson, made their scenes the most entertaining in part 1, his unflappable, elegant equanimity and ironic detachment suggesting exactly how she might be provoked to the level of frustrated anger to have him locked up as a madman. Candido's comic business of cutting a penny-worth from the centre of a sheet of fine lawn was progressively polished during the run of the play into a contemptuous enactment of the principle that the customer is always right (even when the aim of that customer is simply to infuriate the shopkeeper by making unreasonable demands on him). The exiguous scrap of material was first cut out with meticulous accuracy, then carefully wrapped and finally deposited, with a flourish, in a very large, monogrammed carrier-bag and handed over with extreme courtesy. This routine provoked the audience to its first spontaneous applause, matched only by Candido's later departure for the Guildhall, gowned in a carpet, with holes cut in it for his head and arms, to avoid the heavy fine for appearing there improperly dressed to which his wife's confiscation of his gown would otherwise render him liable.

The main plot too was strongly centred, on Lilo Baur's small, tough but vulnerable Bellafront, played in Italian neo-realist idiom and capturing the essential pathos and helplessness of a woman oppressed by the indelible label 'whore' and by her role as scapegoat for the resentments and obsessions of the inadequate men who surround her. In part 1, Mark Rylance's Hippolyto recalled his Proteus of two years before, even to the raincoat and umbrella used for one furtive entrance. In part 2 the analogy was with Angelo in *Measure for Measure*, reinforced by his judicial robes, which the plot does little to justify. The double disclosure of his sexual hypocrisy, first by his wife Infelice (Sonia Ritter), then by Bellafront, gave genuine pleasure. As Bellafront's gambler husband, Matheo, Clarence Smith aimed at a level of inwardness and existential angst more in keeping with the novels of Dostoievsky or the subtextual theatre of Chekhov than the cheerily explicit social satire of Dekker. Ralph Watson, as Bellafront's sentimental father Orlando Friscobaldo, was also muted by the realist mode of the production (and heavy trimming of his role). It was hard to see how any middle-aged man in a shabby green macintosh and check tweed hat offering himself as a manservant to the impoverished Matheo in the kitchen of his council flat (defined by the sink and dresser in the discovery space) could have avoided either instant and forcible eviction, or referral to the police as a suspicious character. A further awkwardness arose from too literal a rendering of his stated intention to trim or tie his beard as a disguise: having shaved off his whiskers, he had twice to resume them at very short notice when he returned, briefly, to his true identity.

The late twentieth-century costumes, furniture and properties (even Hippolyto's *memento mori* skull was a modern cardboard cut-out model) need not have been obtrusive, but their effect, especially that of the ubiquitous table and chairs, and of Bellafront's zebra-striped brothel sofa, was to restrict gesture and to anchor the actors by seating them for scenes of confrontation, draining those scenes of much-needed physical and vocal energy. The only main-plot scene to provoke instant applause was part 2, 3.1, where Infelice's mock-confession of adultery, designed to trap her inconstant husband and expose his pursuit of Bellafront, was energised by Hippolyto's vigorous assault upon the duvet, linen and pillows of the marriage bed (or futon). Elsewhere, shouting too often served in place of significant speech, and rapport with the audience was perceptibly less than in the Shakespeare productions. Though in some respects the most ambitious production of the season, *The Honest Whore* was also the least persuasive, and the least resourceful in its use of the Globe stage. It could be relished mainly for a handful of enjoyable individual performances and for providing a rare chance of seeing at least the skeleton of two plays which richly merited revival.

The attractions of *A Mad World, My Masters* are much more obvious, and in general Sue Lefton's production had the good sense to let the play speak for itself. Unfortunately, though, the director somewhat muffled its voice by two decisions which detracted from clarity and ease of understanding. The first was to dress the cast in costumes which ranged in their suggestion of period from the 1890s to the 1970s without evoking any recognizable social world. The second was to play Middleton's astringent comedy as something between a farce (but without the deadly seriousness of true farce) and a pantomime (though without the support of pantomime songs and with only one general dance), which left the performance suspended in a void of improbable fiction, where its author anchored it securely and precisely in the manners, morals and topicalities of early Jacobean London.

Any sense of plausibility was further undermined by the choreographer-director's emphasis on movement rather than speech. Despite its committed energy, Wil Johnson's Follywit remained mannered and unfluent, rarely hinting at the improvisatory imagination

of an impoverished gentleman reduced to 'living on his wits'. As Sir Bounteous Progress, Jonathan Cecil, in a succession of voluminous gowns and nighties, was all gentle and vacuous affability, but suggested none of the character's self-promoting energy or self-congratulatory vanity, so that his grandson's successive depredations passed without provoking much sense that he had deserved them. Only the final scene, with its improvised play-within-the-play, came close to full realization of its comic ironies. Follywit's 'Have I scaped the constable to be brought in by the watch', when the watch he has stolen from his grandfather strikes in his pocket, was greeted with a spontaneous outburst of applause unmatched earlier in the evening. No doubt the source of many of the director's difficulties lay in the play itself. Written for an intimate indoor theatre, it relies more on talk than action and few of its scenes involve more than two or three characters at once. The bright costumes, stylized movement, acrylic-wigged jazz musicians and cheerful yellow hangings and stagecloth were all attempts to fill the empty space. Only in the final scene, which uses the full cast, did the stage seem full, with the onstage audience on stools along the front edge of it watching Follywit and his gang improvise their play, 'The Slip', at centre stage.

The sub-plot of Mr Penitent Brothel (David Rintoul) and his seduction of Mrs Harebrain (Tonia Chauvet) balances and reinforces the sexual hypocrisy of the Courtesan (Belinda Davison in silent cinema vamp mode) and her Mother – and bawd (Anastasia Hille). In this production it was the more successful of the two plots. The assignation of Brothel with Mrs Harebrain at the Courtesan's house is elaborately prepared by Middleton. Once they meet, they leave the stage: what they do – or don't – while off it is left to the imagination of the audience (and the ambiguity is crucial to the later scene in which Brothel, now penitent, is welcomed by her husband as his dearest and most trusted friend). Their absence is covered by a speech for the Courtesan in which she improvises a dialogue between herself and Mrs Harebrain designed for the ears of the prying husband, who is listening outside the bedroom in which she is pretending to be sick in bed. The scene invites virtuoso performance by the Courtesan, who is soon gravelled for want of matter, and signals desperately to the concealed (maybe) lovers that it is time for them to re-emerge. This effect was jettisoned in favour of a surefire farcical alternative. On the arrival of Mrs Harebrain, Brothel briskly withdrew with her, not offstage, but into the Courtesan's bed – which was instantly swathed from above by a celestially provided 'mosquito-net' that heaved and billowed throughout the rest of the scene to a crescendo of orgasmic groans. The Courtesan's covering speech was drowned by frantic spasms and cries from the bed, on whose downstage end she was precariously perched, and by raucous laughter from the audience.

No other moment so exactly defined to what extent this production sought easy alternatives to Middleton's ironies and cynicism. It did pay off, however, as preparation for the scene of Brothel's penitence, in which Mrs Harebrain – now embodied by a seductive *succuba* – emerged to embrace him from concealment as a bolster under the sheets of the same bed. David Rintoul as Brothel resisted the prevailing stylization to give a vigorous and attractive performance. Glimpses of the ironic humour latent, though too often untapped, in this witty and irreverent play emerged in flashes elsewhere; in John McEnery's catatonic Harebrain, Leader Hawkins's bothered and bewildered Gunwater and Anastasia Hille's surprisingly young Mother. The musicians, smocked in garish colours and with startling acrylic wigs, contributed to the prevailing bizarrerie, not least in their processional entries before and after the interval, scored for trumpet, four trombones, saxophone and drum.

In the end, the director's refusal to present the characters and their social world in consistent terms of any identifiable time or place prevented *A Mad World* from becoming more than a mildly amusing romp. It was hard not to contrast it with last year's ebullient production of Middleton's comic masterpiece, *A Chaste Maid in Cheapside*, which, despite the understandable reservations of purists, was, in my experience, the most simply enjoyable play yet staged at the Globe. This was largely because of the energy, inventiveness and unpretentious desire to amuse which pervaded it and invited its audience to recognize and respond to the life in it. It was, of course, written for an outdoor playhouse, the Swan, it is full of action and it has one of the largest casts, especially in female roles, of any surviving play of the period.

My last evening at the Globe, shortly before the end of the season, provided a strikingly different experience. Patrick Tucker's 'Original Shakespeare Company' presented an unrehearsed, costumed performance of the Folio text of *King John* – errors and all, so that, for instance, it wasn't until well on in their first scene that the audience was allowed to conclude that Philip was the name of the King of France and Lewis that of his son, rather than *vice versa*. Tucker's contention, that Elizabethan actors played on the basis of memorization of their lines and cues alone, with only the briefest of rehearsal of entries, exits and essential business, was tested to death in front of a paying audience, many of whom stayed the course, despite heavy defections at the interval. Perhaps the theory has a pinch of historical truth in it – certainly nothing resembling the rehearsal process of a modern company can be assumed as likely in the Elizabethan repertory system – and perhaps an established company of the best actors in England, who had worked together for years and who performed six days a week at the Globe, did manage to achieve something like unrehearsed performance of a standard fit for commercial presentation.

Tucker's *King John*, however, left even this proposition looking insecure. For actors not equipped with the full text of their play, lack of rehearsal dug a number of predictable pitfalls:

time and again moves were motivated by sudden awareness that a character was in the wrong company; time and again lines slowed in the desperate hope that someone else's business would be performed before it had to be described. Elaborate scenes involving many characters, such as the lengthy debates before Angers, lacked the visual focus that even minimal blocking would have supplied. Fortunately, Arthur, in his death scene, was not put in jeopardy by an unrehearsed fall from the gallery: a controlled, supported fall from the shoulders of a fellow actor was substituted (incidentally suggesting, however, that the gallery in the reconstructed Globe may be a bit too high). Mishaps less intrinsic to the process were missed cues – especially entry cues, no doubt because they were hard to hear from behind the tiring-house doors. The prompter, brisk, visible on stage and clearly audible to all, richly deserved her round of applause. Some of the valiant cast yielded, particularly in the first half, to an understandable temptation to enlist the complicity of the audience in sympathetic laughter at their predicament. The undisciplined movement, vigorous, improvisatory delivery and eager commitment of the unnamed actors did serve to communicate some of the play's energy, but feelings were too often generalized and the complex narrative remained hard to follow. Many of the audience must have found themselves increasingly reliant on the 'plot' supplied in the programme to retain any sense of who was who, or what was going on.

That the performance kept going at all was largely due to the presence of a nucleus of confident performers in key roles, among them the two Kings, the Papal legate, the Bastard, Queen Eleanor, and Constance. In the second half, where scenic structures are simpler and fewer actors are on at once, individual scenes began to develop their own dynamic. Undisciplined playing of minor roles remained, however, a recurrent hazard. The death scene of John was unfortunately upstaged by the misplaced ambition of the player of Prince Henry to make her mark by guying him as a mustachioed young fop with his crown awry. Once more reflection was prompted. Such indiscipline in a boy player would hardly have scaped censure: the freedom of the Elizabethan stage must have been the technically disciplined freedom of professional performers, expert in their art, finely tuned to each other and working within the understood constraints and conventions of a shared artistic and commercial enterprise.

Visible from all sides and with nowhere to hide, actors at the Globe are totally exposed: any lapse from engaged performance, any loss of focus or direction, translates itself immediately into loss of the interest and attention of the audience. If sustained, that loss can prove catastrophic; at the Globe, spectators readily vote with their feet. It must be counted a great achievement that the two main companies in 1998 played to 90 per cent capacity houses. The challenge now is to avoid complacency or contentment with the prevailing level of achievement. *The Merchant of Venice* and *As You Like It* are popular plays and reliable box-office. Next year's repertoire is rumoured to include *Julius Caesar*, perhaps Shakespeare's first Globe play, certainly his first tragedy for the new playhouse – as it will also be, in its quatercentenary year, at Sam Wanamaker's Globe. It will present a new challenge: how that challenge is met may determine what sort of theatre the Globe will become in the next millennium.

SHAKESPEARE PERFORMANCES IN ENGLAND, 1998

ROBERT SMALLWOOD

Of the eighteen productions covered in this year's review, eleven, including the whole of the RSC's main stage summer repertoire in Stratford, are of what the first Folio labels 'Comedies'. Whether this reflects financial managers' judgement of what will work best at the box office, or the current mood of directors, or whether there is felt to be a problem in matching available actors and the tragic protagonists' roles, are questions that might all be speculated upon; but not here. It is with this bumper crop of comedies that I begin.

Stephen Unwin made a spirited and energetic attempt to give a sense of newness to the distasteful story of the taming of Katharina Minola in his production of *The Taming of the Shrew* for English Touring Theatre, which made a national tour in the autumn. He set the play in a TV sit-com, lower middle-class world of Dagenham accents and rock music between the scenes. Kacey Ainsworth's Kate was a rebellious teenager in scruffy jeans and thick-soled trainers, sullen and surly, rather than angry, at her father's unfairness, making a journey through the play that was from androgyny to femininity rather than from shrewishness to tameness. David Cardy's cheeky Cockney Petruccio, ebullient and chirpy in a Max Miller sort of way and certainly not the kind of person to buy a second-hand car from, was oddly likeable in his apparently unquestioning self-confidence and bustling energy, his asides and soliloquies making the audience his allies in the taming process in a somewhat

disturbing way. It was, on the whole, a 'treat 'em rough' reading of the part, with little sense of tenderness even in the jay and lark speech and with spitefulness outweighing fun in the sun and moon scene and the encounter with Vincentio. The ending was clearly a set-up between Kate and Petruccio, she winking at Grumio as she began and at her husband as she called him her 'head', but even so there was a sense beneath the superficial irony of her delivery that a *modus vivendi* had been achieved that wasn't without understanding and might even arrive at a kind of rough affection.

The sub-plot of *The Taming of the Shrew* is not the most distinguished writing in Shakespeare but was given a little extra interest here by Daniel Goode's giving an Oxbridge Sloane flavour to Lucentio, who was certainly slumming it in the very suburban surroundings of the Minola household, and by Michael Cronin's presentation of Gremio as the opulent, vulgar, cigar-smoking owner of that second-hand car dealership that never seemed far away in this production. He was momentarily just a little pathetic in his crestfallen withdrawal from the auction for marriage with Bianca but cheered up remarkably at the prospect of free nourishment. The role had a rounded, identifiable modernity about it, part of the very good job the director had done in creating a believable world in which the characters could interact; whether, in the end, one thinks he was right to confront the play's awkwardness, and perhaps crudeness, by giving a degree of awkwardness and crudeness to its central pair of characters (and a patronizing shrug at the social world they inhabit) depends on one's assessment of the play. Of the fact that he created a clear, crisp, and entertaining piece of theatre there is no doubt.

Awkwardness, even ineptness, has been perceived also in *The Two Gentlemen of Verona* and this has led to its being regarded as Shakespeare's earliest comedy; it was certainly Edward Hall's directorial début at Stratford when his production opened in February and 'double first' turned out not to be too unapt for a searching, challenging production, with the alleged ineptnesses, especially in the final moments, an important part of the challenge. The journey of the play was marked by two single-gender, non-sexual embraces: at the end of the first scene by a valedictory hug of separation, expected all through the scene, between the leading men, Proteus and Valentine; at the end of the last scene, by an embrace of welcome and union, expected all through the scene, between the leading women, Julia and Sylvia. The embraces framed the intervening account of the awkwardnesses and inadequacies of the play's heterosexual relationships.

Hall's modern-dress production presented us with a rich and trivial society, Julia's and Lucetta's rather callous assessment of the former's suitors leading into a party with music and fireworks and all of them parading in with expensive presents for her: courtship had been turned into conspicuous consumption and Julia made the object of universal male desire. That idea of the objectification of woman was reinforced when we moved to Milan and the letter scene was played in a museum with a Damien Hirst-ish exhibit of a woman's head in a glass case, labelled 'Venus': woman as symbol of beauty and object of male desire set against Poppy Miller's gracious and astute Sylvia running rings round Tom Goodman-Hill's hopelessly uncomprehending Valentine. And at the end of the scene, 'Venus' turned out to be

alive, the model withdrawing her head from its glass case, her body from under its plinth, and lighting a cigarette – her shift as exhibit in the world of male fantasy over. When we next met Sylvia, *she* was being turned into the work of art, and with grim appropriateness into a miniature. Her father was the painter, the object of his admiration also his possession, for the painter was also the keeper of the key to her prison in the tower-bedroom. No wonder Sylvia was ready to give the miniature away to the unwelcome lover whose musical attentions beneath her window had disturbed her repose.

The production was at its most interesting in a complicated reading of this serenade scene that deliberately drained it of romance. 'If you send up "Who is Sylvia" it simply loses its point', wrote John Peter in *The Sunday Times*, rather missing the point himself. By handing over a fat roll of bank notes, Dominic Rowan's Proteus had secured the services of a professional singer, with a vulgar style and Pavarotti handkerchief, to sideline, with a flashy aria in pastiche Puccini manner, poor little Thurio's exquisite lyric 'Who is Sylvia'. Usurping the role of Julia's confidant the Host, and dressed up in clerical collar to pretend to the epithet 'Father' which she bestows on him, was Mark Hadfield's sad and knowing Launce, clearly determined to make her see the truth about the man she is foolish enough to love (a little like Rosalind forcing Silvius to hear Phoebe's letter): 'I am but a fool, look you, and yet I have the wit to know my master is a kind of knave.' The scene thus brought together the play's most generous, long-suffering, and put-upon lovers, Julia (in a touchingly yearning, vulnerable portrayal by Lesley Vickerage) of the ungrateful and worthless Proteus, and Launce, of the equally ungrateful and, in a most economically paced performance by the imperturbable Cassie, of the determinedly lugubrious and unresponsive Crab. It was a most perceptive examination of the undercurrents of the scene and a careful preparation for the play's ending.

All the superficial sophistication was stripped away for the final scene. The pretty pale blue shutters that had dominated the back wall were blasted open and the stage carpet was sucked down through a trap-door. The outlaws' hiding-place was through a grille in the floor (Harry Lime style); this was more a scene of urban dereliction than a forest, and to this place came Proteus, not just threatening but attempting and meaning rape to Sylvia, his hands bloody – from fighting an outlaw, we needed to remind ourselves, for the image was much more disturbing as he ran on stage with Sylvia, manhandling her obscenely and apparently about to expose himself as she struggled and cringed, coat ripped and stockings torn. Valentine's arrival was only just in the nick of time and Poppy Miller's face as she watched the last movement of the play through Sylvia's notorious silence was a remarkable tribute to what skilled performance can do when the author writes nothing for you. Terror, relief, approval, contemptuous disbelief, and the anguish of rejection passed in turn across her face as she held centre stage: the most important person in the scene was not invited to speak, and that told us everything about the society in which these things were happening. Then in came that society's dominant male, the boorish, cock-sure figure of Colin McCormack's Duke of Milan, handing over his daughter, taking the outlaws into his service (where, from what we'd seen of his other servants, they would be altogether at home), and presiding over the conventional embraces of the precarious pair of couples who seem to represent the future. Then off he strode, followed by the play's assembled males, leaving Julia and Sylvia to cling to each other in solace for what they had been through and, one could not help thinking, for what they would have to face in the future. There was nothing inept about this ending of *The Two Gentlemen of Verona*.

Sadly, Edward Hall was on nothing like this form when his earlier production of *The Comedy of Errors* from the Watermill Theatre did a few performances at Stratford's Other Place in the autumn. Its twelve actors, all men, brought huge commitment and exuberance to the play, with masked singing and dancing outside the theatre before the performance and during the interval, remorselessly noisy and energetic, invading the audience's space and trying the patience of several of its members. The performance itself, many of the actors retaining their *commedia* masks though others not (there seemed no rationale to the distinction), was equally energetic and equally short of tact and delicacy. I mention the production here only for the major negative example it provided: as Cheek by Jowl, and other companies, have repeatedly shown, there is not the least need for a Shakespeare performance in which men play the women's roles to take on the qualities of a drag show. Here, however, the simpering, mincing, high-camp demolition of Adriana's emotional pain and Luciana's sisterly sympathy took the heart out of the play. *The Comedy of Errors* is what it says, a comedy, not a farce. It is unforgivable to send it up as if it were 'Pyramus and Thisbe'.

'Pyramus and Thisbe' fared well in John Retallack's version of *A Midsummer Night's Dream* for the Oxford Stage Company, which opened at Cheltenham in October. The most interesting things in the production came in its closing moments. A crisp and witty performance of the interlude (with one funny piece of business new to me when Thisbe's blood-bags, that had been doubling as her bust, popped audibly at the moment of her self-slaughter) ended with a bergomasque that turned out to be a group rendering (beautifully performed) of 'The ouzel cock so black of hue' and then merged into a dance that involved the whole company. 'Lovers to bed', said Theseus, as the musicians departed and the lights dimmed – and the obedience of the lovers was immediate. 'A fortnight hold we this solemnity', he continued, in his usual tone of condescending explanation to the underlings, and Hippolyta (the only one of them left) decided that this was where she was going to begin the process of stopping him going on so. Since they were now alone and he had just mentioned bed, she started to undress him, first the rather masonic-looking ducal shawl, then the jacket, then the tie; he responded by removing her wrap and her stole: lovers preparing for bed. As Puck appeared, Theseus (Simon Coury) and Hippolyta (Victoria Woodward) were down to their Oberon and Titania costumes (the roles were doubled) and the blessing sequence was ready to begin, the fairies' 'field-dew' taking the form of tiny points of light at the tips of the wands they all carried. As the blessing was sung the stage-lights faded further and finally went out and we heard Puck's epilogue spoken from a stage that was, but for the pinpoints of 'field-dew', as dark as the auditorium. It had been throughout a production that was intelligent, clear, and well spoken, though for the most part it had not achieved in its earlier stages anything so memorable as this ending.

It was offered in modern dress by a company of only a dozen actors, lovers and mechanicals doubling as fairies and Philostrate as Puck, besides the central doubling of the ruling couples. Actors not involved in a scene watched from the stage-side, frequently providing music from a range of string and percussion instruments. Apart from a splendid purple carpet rolled out by Philostrate for the final scene, the 'set' was two wooden armchairs centre stage, Theseus's and Hippolyta's thrones, one of which, flown a few feet above the stage, became Titania's bower. The pace and energy of the performance, for the most part admirable, became excessive in the lovers' quarrel scene, in which words were lost in a frenzy of physical display, Anna Francolini's Helena seeming at times as if she would be more at home in a strip-show. Reason and the lovers' scene seem to keep little company together nowadays; the more the pity that some honest director will not make them friends. There were some good performances elsewhere: a fine, athletic Puck

14 *As You Like It*, directed by Michael Bogdanov for the English Shakespeare Company. Ivy Omere as Rosalind, David Shelley as Orlando. Act 4, scene 1.

from Christopher Beck, crisp and sharp with the language, relishing its rhymes; a wonderful gentle giant of a Bottom, dim but terribly well meaning, from Nicholas Beveney, a young actor of Curtly Ambrose proportions, towering above David Brett's tiny Peter Quince and carrying Titania off stage as if she were a china doll. And in Victoria Woodward, in her first professional role as Titania/Hippolyta, one saw a young performer with, surely (especially when she realizes that she doesn't need to *keep* smiling at the audience), a most promising future: striking physical presence, vocal clarity and range, and an intelligent responsiveness to verse that made 'These are the forgeries of jealousy', crackling with anger at one moment, full of wistful regret the next, a pleasure to listen to.

Another immensely promising professional début was that of Ivy Omere as Rosalind in Michael Bogdanov's English Shakespeare Company production of *As You Like It* for the Bath Shakespeare Festival in August, later seen at Salisbury and at the Hackney Empire. The director did not seem to have much that he wanted to tell us about *As You Like It*, but he had cast the central role splendidly, and the commitment, directness, and clarity of Ivy Omere's performance went a long way to making a success of the evening. The simple set of three wheeled frames, with Venetian blinds incorporated, could be moved about to suggest, vaguely, indoors or out; costumes, as ever with Bogdanov, were modern, which, as ever with *As You Like It*, turned Touchstone (Robert Barton) into a cockney spiv and created a problem with Rosalind's male disguise, for Ganymede's elegant buff trousers, tweed jacket, and jaunty cap might easily have been found in the pages of *Vogue* and did nothing to create a gender/identity change. The problem was solved by Ivy Omere adopting her native Nigerian accent as Ganymede, which added a dimension of fun and mischievousness to the persona that worked splendidly in such moments as the description of the 'divers paces' at which time travels and in the reprimand to Phoebe. The accent came and went very tellingly in the main wooing scene with David Shelley's refreshingly straightforward, gracious, and intelligent Orlando – what a pleasant change not to feel that Rosalind is throwing herself away – its presence or absence a barometer of her level of personal commitment. Her 'Rosalind voice' was absolutely dominant as she announced that she was taking Orlando for her husband and the kiss that followed was natural, inevitable, and altogether 'straight'. It was the immediacy and honesty of the sense of emotional commitment that made the performance so successful, a commitment not just to Orlando but also to Susannah Elliot-Knight's generous and affectionate Celia. The production overall was brisk, energetic, and unfussy,

though with those self-indulgent oddities here and there that seem to be an inescapable part of the Bogdanov experience: a gentlemen's club version of the wrestling scene, bets being taken in the haze of cigar smoke and the fight spreading all round the stalls (amusing at first, but long-winded); 'It was a lover and his lass' as a big rock number, brilliantly done, with aerobic dancing (funny, but forming its own show quite independent of the main enterprise); and the deer-killing staged as Orlando's nightmare of Rosalind killing him (irrelevant, except to the author of the article that must somewhere be in progress on recent directorial determination to treat this scene of less than twenty lines as one of the major events of *As You Like It*); and Tim Woodward's detached, observant, pipe-smoking, Irish Jaques, suitcase always to hand as though departure were imminent, conducting (with his pipe) the full-company chorus version of Hymen's (that is Corin's) song of wedding blessing, accompanied by old Adam on cello – all entirely out of character with anything we had seen of Jaques earlier or were about to witness. For the most part, though, it was the energy, pace, and directness of the production that impressed, and it was excellent to see Ivy Omere, like Victoria Woodward, moving so successfully direct from drama school to a major Shakespeare role.

From a beginning to an end: Cheek by Jowl's *Much Ado about Nothing*, directed by Declan Donnellan, which opened at Cheltenham in February and closed, after a British and international tour, in London in July, was the last production before this remarkable company disbanded. It brought to the play all the zest, élan, and invention that one has come to expect of them. Set in the Edwardian period, in a world of champagne parties, silver tea services, and parasols, it had a touch of operetta about it. With the men in dark green regimental dress-uniform (a far cry from the battle-dress they must just have left behind), hair groomed down and moustaches twirled up, and the women in narrow-waisted, high-

15 *Much Ado About Nothing*, directed by Declan Donnellan
for Cheek by Jowl. Ann Firbank as Ursula-Antonio,
Sarita Choudhury as Hero, Saskia Reeves as Beatrice,
Zoë Aldrich as Margaret. Act 4, scene 1.

there waiting for him to embrace her, the young man rushed instead into the arms of his general in celebration of his success in landing the dowry. The sight of Hero being laced into her corset for the wedding, lying akimbo on the floor as it was heaved to its maximum tightness, was a brilliant image of gender relations: the female body being prepared to come to the altar and to her man – like trussing up a chicken for consumption. 'Sigh no more ladies' opened the play and became virtually a leitmotif through the evening, the production seeming to exist largely as a lament for the women's failure to heed its warning. Antonio's lines were amalgamated with Ursula's and the role played by Ann Firbank, so that it was a redoubtable old aunt, thwacking Claudio with her glove, who first called the bluff of the swanking young man who had destroyed her niece. The production's feminist credentials were not in doubt.

And yet, on the whole, and ultimately, it did seem to ask us to approve that Beatrice should marry Benedick. The trick that deluded Matthew Macfadyen's gangling, awkward Benedick, with his absurdly braying laugh, drawlingly posh voice, and very modest intellectual gifts, into loving Saskia Reeves's spiky, sarcastic Beatrice, here seemed just another bit of masculine horse-play, hardly a promising source for a lasting commitment. Yet it allowed a glimpse of instincts perhaps fundamentally decent, and certainly insecure, beneath his goofy, inappropriately self-confident exterior, just as Saskia Reeves's coolly sarcastic Beatrice revealed a pathetic vulnerability below the surface, where emotional wounds were still unhealed, glimpsed momentarily at the party when she drank too much champagne, and plain to see in 'What fire is in mine ears'. She was fierce in her contempt for Claudio in the church scene, lashing out 'kill Claudio' after a pause in which fury was barely contained and which left not the faintest possibility of laughter in the house. Even at the end she refused Claudio's proffered hand, so that Benedick's 'Come, we *are* friends' became a

necked, ankle-length dresses in creams and whites, the production offered a searching examination of the play's gender relations. The men could dance with the women elegantly enough, but beyond that communication was much limited by their boarding-school, locker-room mentality, chortling and guffawing together and constantly exhibiting an urge to male bonding that bordered on the homo-erotic – and in Don Pedro's case clearly went beyond it: his perfunctory and inept little flirtations with Beatrice had far less commitment about them than the longing with which he looked at Claudio, and when Claudio's engagement to Hero was announced, and she stood very anxious attempt to keep the peace – and after the emotionless perfunctoriness of Claudio's penance at Hero's supposed tomb, perhaps Beatrice's hesitation was right. Both Beatrice and Benedick, one felt, had moved a little in the direction of self-awareness during the play and he, perhaps, had even grown up a little, but in spite of that long-awaited, and long, kiss in the final scene, it was still a very tentative conclusion. The evening was marred a little by the casting as Hero of the rising film-starlet Sarita Choudhury, whose precarious handling of the language made the role seem a lot longer than it is, but for the rest it was an elegant and consistently intelligent production, inviting us to see the play in new and illuminating ways, a highly appropriate valediction for this most innovative of companies.

Whether the mantle of Shakespearian theatrical innovator will pass to Tim Supple and his Young Vic company remains to discover. I very much admired Supple's production of *The Comedy of Errors* in 1996 (*Shakespeare Survey 50* (1997), 215–19) and went to his production of *Twelfth Night* at the Young Vic in July with high hopes: here was largely the same cast and the same style of eerie musical accompaniment on Middle Eastern string and woodwind instruments that had worked so well for *The Comedy of Errors*. Now, however, the effect seemed far less satisfactory – and not, I'm sure, through any sense of *déjà vu* (or *entendu*). Now the music got in the way of the language, possibly through less skilful arrangement than for the earlier production but more probably, I suspect, because the greater complexity, depth, and variation of the verbal texture of *Twelfth Night* is inimical to being generalized in this way. The haunting ritual beauty of the language in the final recognition scene, for example, was ruined by the unrelenting musical accompaniment. And a cast that had risen splendidly to the challenge of the roles in the earlier play here seemed suddenly underpowered, vocally and emotionally.

The production used a simple square playing area with a raised level up four steps at the back and the musicians seated below the front edge of the stage. Costumes were eclectic, Malvolio looking Jeevesish in a 1930s morning suit, Sir Andrew in a kilt, Sir Toby in grubby corduroys, Olivia taking the veilèd cloistress literally and dressed as a nun, and Sebastian and Cesario in black turbans, turquoise satin suits of eastern design, and silver scimitars, looking like an illustration from *The Arabian Nights*. (The inability of Robert Bowman's coolly rational Malvolio to describe to Olivia what the stubborn visitor at the door looks like became, in the circumstances, hilariously incredible.) The point of such costuming was, presumably, to render in visual terms the emotional isolation of the characters, theoretically not a bad idea, but the effect was to make the play's story disjunctive and to alienate the audience's belief.

The mood, too, was monotonously gloomy. There is, of course, a certain melancholy wistfulness about *Twelfth Night*, but there is hope too, even joy, and these were lost in the general dourness. One felt this particularly about Thusitha Jayasundera's Viola. That quiet, thoughtful gentleness that had worked so well for Luciana wasn't enough for Viola; she found a genuine boyishness for Cesario, and a certain detached intelligence and charm, but the role needs much more energy, a greater sense of fun, more emotional commitment, more vulnerability, than she was able to bring to it. As her brother Sebastian, Nitin Chandra Ganatra managed to be both charmless and inaudible, the latter a difficult feat in the Young Vic, while the snidely aggressive Feste of Dan Milne made one wonder about the perverse taste in household entertainment that Olivia's father must have had to find 'much delight' in such a fellow. (The current fashion for 'sad-clown', introverted knowingness in Festes does need to be tempered, I think, by attention to Viola's excellent advice about observing 'their mood on whom he jests'; instant dismissal for failure to fulfil the basic requirement of the job description – amuse the boss – would surely be

16 *Twelfth Night*, directed by Adrian Noble for the Royal Shakespeare Company. Scott Handy as Orsino, Helen Schlesinger as Viola. Act 2, scene 4.

the fate of many Festes one sees.) Christopher Saul's scruffy Sir Toby was interesting: a retired academic, perhaps, clever and lazy, with a malicious taste in practical jokes, though the 'two thousand strong or so' that he'd had of Andy Williams's noisy, hearty blockhead of an Aguecheek had clearly been well earned, for the painful tediousness of putting up with his company was felt also in the auditorium. By far the best performance was Robert Bowman's of Malvolio, an unctuous, quietly spoken, simpering smoothie with, seething beneath the surface and seen clearly in the letter scene, a maniacal ambition for power. His little twirl of glee as he thought he had it in his grasp was splendid – funny, but disturbing. Also ringing true was Sebastian's little moment of terror at first recognizing his sister, whom he took for a

ghost. But overall the production failed to fulfil one's hopes: *Twelfth Night* is certainly a play of shadows, but of sunlight too; a play not short of hate, but much concerned with love. This rather cheerless version seemed a long way from the heart of its mystery.

So too did Adrian Noble's production, which opened at the Royal Shakespeare Theatre late in 1997 and played through the 1998 Stratford season. Where Supple's version was dour and gloomy, Noble's was trivial and flash, failing to give the actors any sense of a 'world' for their characters to inhabit. The primary, poster-art colours of set and costume gave a cartoon or toybox feel to the production, and the placing of much of the action well down stage – in front of a lurid green plastic hedge for the garden scenes, or an enormous puce couch for the scenes between Viola and Olivia, or a ten-foot high refrigerator for the cakes and ale scene – gave a two-dimensional quality to it all. The costumes had a cut-out-book look that confirmed one's sense that, at the end of the play, there was nothing that would happen to the characters beyond their all being put back in the toybox. Viola's disguise as Cesario was a sailor-doll costume; Sir Toby wore a Mr Toad check suit; little Noddy policemen gave chase to a bicycling Antonio; Olivia wore a Barbie-doll pink wedding dress; and the giant fridge took us to *Alice in Wonderland*. The actors were given an impossible task in asking us to care about the emotions of people who lived in this ever-so-jolly Toytown world.

The wonder was that they got some way with it. Helen Schlesinger, in her first season at Stratford, presented a Viola who responded with a touchingly vulnerable delight to Orsino's attention to the beauty of her lip, was wonderfully open to the bewilderments of the story in which she finds herself in 'Time thou must untangle this', and spoke the willow cabin speech with a passionate earnestness that pulled us into Viola's emotions as firmly as she did when contemplating, through her tears, the hopelessness of her imaginary sister's love. There was a delightful Sir Andrew from John Quayle, a floppy-haired ninny in blazer and Garrick Club bow-tie, and David Calder, as Sir Toby, showed flashes of the dangerously melancholic, self-destructive alcoholic he might have given us in another production. Philip Voss's Malvolio might actually have wandered in from that other production, his immaculate morning suit looking as though it belonged to a world of pompous officialdom that one could recognize as real. Two moments gave the character a pathetic vulnerability: his joy at discovering his mistress's supposed love issued into sobs, and his previously impeccable diction turned into a stammer on the word 'notorious' in his exit speech, as though everything else might be lived down, but to have become

17 *The Tempest*, directed by Adrian Noble for the Royal Shakespeare Company. David Calder as Prospero, Scott Handy as Ariel. Act 5, scene 1.

'notorious' was career-terminating. The performance that seemed to sit most easily in the production was Stephen Boxer's Feste, the wry observer seeing through pretensions (and disguises), the professional joke-teller in a production that was so anxious to tell jokes. His final song, ending with an imploring gaze into the auditorium that distilled the yearning to please, was very fine. But for the most part this was a *Twelfth Night* to draw a veil over.

The RSC's Artistic Director was on rather more artistic form with his production of *The Tempest*, also on Stratford's main stage later in the season. The stage, empty except for a great conch-shell from which Caliban emerged, was a simple circle round which a gauze curtain could be drawn, to wipe it clean, as it were, between scenes, or behind which the shipwreck, or the masque of the goddesses, could be presented. There was a ramp down the left-hand aisle into the stalls, from which Ferdinand and Miranda watched the masque, or Prospero watched Ferdinand and Miranda, and down which Scott Handy's impressively athletic Ariel, his body painted white and naked except for a loin cloth, made many a speedy exit.

The production began well, with a silk floor-cloth billowing into benevolent little waves and, to calm-sea-and-prosperous-voyage music, and the gentle creaking of timbers, a model galleon sailing in the distance. The arrival of storm and lightning, the ship's deck now in the foreground, the boatswain clinging to a slender bowsprit that would soon turn out to be Prospero's staff (no wonder they were lured off course) was well done, with good refereeing of the usual competition between the dialogue and the sound effects. And then we were with David Calder's impressive Prospero, staff in hand, his magic cloak swirling away behind him and becoming part of the backcloth and so directly linking him to the sky – now there's magic for you – and a great circle of fire in front of him and Penny Layden's Miranda sprinting down the aisle walkway, from among us, desperately demanding what's going on: it was a fine, bold picture. Calder's was a troubled, unpredictable Prospero, constantly struggling with the hurt and resentment of past memories. One often wished it were just a little bigger, but of the interest of its progress from vengeance to virtue there was never any doubt, particularly in the precariousness of that pro-gress, the fear that the vengefulness of the man might triumph after all and he would destroy them all – no doubt by electrocution, moving beyond the stage of reduction to a blue quivering heap that he had imposed on Ariel for grumbling, to complete incineration. The decision finally to forgive was clearly marked. Prospero could not see his Ariel and seemed merely to take him for granted as a sort of high-powered personal computer. Then, suddenly, provoked by his puzzled observation of

Ferdinand and Miranda together, Ariel asked 'Do *you* love *me*, master', and touched him on the breast, sending a huge shock wave through him. The action was repeated on 'Mine would, sir, were I human', and the path to the conclu-sion was immediately clear. 'And mine shall', he managed to say, with a sense of relief at the chance at last to let go. 'I do forgive thy rankest fault', he said to his brother, simply and yet profoundly, and his kiss of peace expected (and of course got) no response.

The production's best sequence came just before the Epilogue. 'Then to the elements thyself be free', said Prospero, and touched Ariel on the forehead, again with that little shock of communion passing between them. Ariel tried to run away along the parados, as he had done so often, but now he could only struggle and limp, either because the bond between them was hard to break or because the first steps to freedom are inevitably uncertain. As he heaved himself along, his song of 'Where the bee sucks' was heard on the air and Prospero caught and hummed it to himself, several registers lower, standing looking into the distance, his staff across his back. Then, all of a sudden, when we weren't ready and, more important, when he wasn't ready either (for he'd liked being magic, this Prospero), he snapped the staff with a crack across his shoulders and we were into the very simple, direct speaking of the Epilogue.

There was good work around Calder. Scott Handy's Ariel spoke the lines with an intelli-gence that was as much musical as intellectual and charted the relationship with his master with an attentiveness that refused to be senti-mentalized. Robert Glenister, semi-recumbent and earth-caked, his eyes flashing red with anger from his muddy face, was a powerful and moving Caliban, putting up his hand to take Prospero's as their past was recalled at the beginning, or Stephano's, as he sought alterna-tive domination, only to be flung to the ground by both of them. At the end, as he determined to be wise and seek for grace, that hand again

18 *The Merchant of Venice*, directed by Gregory Doran for the Royal Shakespeare Company. Philip Voss as Shylock. Act 4, scene 1.

sought Prospero's, and was met and held and not flung away, as though Prospero, too, had learned something about relationship: 'This thing of darkness I acknowledge mine'.

The courtiers' scenes were no more interesting than they usually are, but the comic scenes had enormous vitality, with a wispy, sad Trinculo from Adrian Schiller and a Stephano from Barry Stanton who seemed, quite rightly, to have a real streak of nastiness and violence in him that presented a genuine threat to Prospero. It was good, too, that he was of exactly the same dominant physique as the play's other would-be usurper, Antonio. Penny Layden offered a convincingly wide-eyed version of youthful commitment as Miranda, but Evroy Deer's Ferdinand overdid the vehemence and energy, his constant vocal top gear

becoming a little wearying. Nor, in a theatre rightly committed to blind casting, and in a production not (for a change) offering the modern cliché colonialist reading, did there seem much relevance in the sudden appearance of a log-bearing Ferdinand in chains that invited us to equate Prospero with a Confederate slave-master. There were little moments of thoughtfulness though, too: the masquers who wouldn't go away immediately when Prospero changed his mind, spirits who'd learned their lines and put on the play he'd asked for and who didn't see why they should give it all up at his whim; and an Antonio who lingered at the final exit to have another look at his brother, perhaps out of mere curiosity, perhaps because thoughts of a second usurpation were beginning to form; and a bold theatrical effect for Ariel's appearance as harpy, lowered from the flies on huge red wings. It was, all in all, by no means a bad shot at this most difficult of plays.

From a director working on the daunting space of Stratford's main stage for the umpteenth time to one making his début there – and one could tell: Gregory Doran's *The Merchant of Venice* started as it meant to go on, with a determination to *fill* the space, its opening dumb-show of merchants, Jewish and Gentile, congregating on the Venetian dockside in the half light of a February day, lasting several minutes before the play's first line. With a dark mist rising and black stone walls oozing damp, cargo was examined and valued while prostitutes stood around hopefully waiting for customers: everything was for sale here, including sexual companionship; and from this we moved to the scene in which Bassanio seeks another loan from Antonio.

Doran's production had nothing particularly startling to tell us about the play, no new directorial reading to offer. In some ways it was rather safe; but what it did well was to provide actors with the chance to explore their roles in organic interaction. One saw this at once in the first scene, with Julian Curry's pale, austere, emaciated Antonio, terribly unbending but with a kind of wasted elegance, confronting Scott Handy's noisy, boisterous Bassanio. In Bassanio slid, flat on his stomach, from some bit of off-stage larking about with others of the laddish crew with whom he drinks too much and makes lots of noise in the streets. He had arrived late, and half-drunk, for an important meeting with a man who – and this we learned as soon as their eyes met – loved him deeply. Bassanio tried to touch him on the cheek; Antonio flinched, not wanting to be patronized, or teased, in this way. There was impatience from Antonio at Bassanio's slowness in coming to the point, a touch of tetchiness at his indirectness in asking for money, and a foreboding appropriateness in his giving Bassanio his ring to help in the attempt to raise it. The

understatedness of Curry's performance was absolutely right in establishing the tensions of the relationship.

Philip Voss had *not* chosen to understate his Shylock, and the result was equally appropriate to the overall balance of the production. His first scene established his loathing for Antonio, smarming round and pawing Antonio's young friend, insisting on lots of handshakes, using the story of Laban's sheep to mime the homosexual act, swiping at Antonio's genitals as he spoke of the pound of flesh. His farewell to Jessica was very precisely observed: he was obsessed with the handing over of the keys, while she, anxious not to seem anxious to get hold of them, wrapped his scarf a little more neatly round his neck, then dodged back to him for a last little kiss – of guilt and of tenderness too. The invention of Shylock's vision of Jessica being carried away on someone's shoulders in the swirl of music and torches and hideously pig-masked revellers was, perhaps, to hammer home the point a little strenuously, but it led to a rather nice little Irvingesque moment as Shylock returned to his empty house to find his world, and his entrance hall, spinning out of control. 'Let him look to his bond', he was saying when we next met him, and the second time he said it we saw, with startling clarity, the idea suddenly strike him – a brilliantly focused moment. The fierce anger (no self-pity at all) of 'Hath not a Jew eyes', the tenderness with which he wiped off the spit that Salerio and Solanio had deposited on Tubal's beard, the anguished immediacy of his recall of Leah's turquoise, led to the howl of pain that ended the first half of the production and that seemed to come from a very 'ancient grudge' indeed.

The production would have been offering us 'The Tragedy of Shylock' if Helen Schlesinger's Portia had not been so striking and intelligent a performance. Her restless energy when we first met her, pacing around the room taking the labels off her suitors' ostentatious gifts, her wry humour, her clear resentment of the restrictions of her father's will and loyal determination to obey them, her obvious fear that Morocco or Aragon might choose right (and the hamming up of those performances made that fear understandable), all this put enormous pressure on Bassanio's choosing scene. This was played with total commitment and seriousness, as though the feckless young man we had watched in Venice had suddenly, through the influence of Belmont, seen things clearly for the first time in his life. The wonderful sense of pent-up joy released when he chose right, then dashed again by the arrival of the messengers from Venice, was impressive. 'O *love* … dispatch', she said when Antonio's letter was read, and 'love' was not a vocative but the abstract noun, signalling her realization of the emotional complexities she would face in Venice.

In the trial scene Portia was, believably enough, uncomprehending at first that Shylock would not be bought off. She clearly expected the graciousness of her argument about mercy, the persuasive eagerness with which it was uttered, the self-evident need for a surgeon, to be convincing to her adversary. Only slowly did she begin to perceive the full depth of loathing with which she had to deal and the extent of her husband's commitment to Antonio as she was forced to watch the long, slow hug between them that provoked Shylock's sardonic 'These be the Christian husbands'. This Portia didn't have her clever little solution all sewn up before she came into court; the acting was on the moment, with the contest between the play's two impulses, to comedy or to tragedy, on the knife-edge. Moments later, as Shylock's own knife-edge lingered for a long time on Antonio's chest, trying different angles for slicing, there was a slight danger that a third genre, melodrama, might come into the equation. At the end of the scene there was another flirtation with the melodramatic as Shylock, who had collapsed in the heap of gold coins that Bassanio had thrown down in evidence that he had the repayment money 'here, in the court', struggled to rise to his feet. He skidded and slithered about, his

forlorn gestures for help ignored, providing an image that was undoubtedly impressive, iconic even, but perhaps just too self-consciously contrived. The coins remained there for the final scene's return to Belmont, so that Lorenzo sat with Jessica on a bank thick inlaid with ducats of bright gold, an image that insisted on the play's constant shuttling between love and money: 'Since you are dear bought I will love you dear'. Its final image was of four men clinging to the prizes that the story has given them, three of them to women who have brought them wealth, the fourth to a letter, a sort of 'bond', that promises him wealth too. A fifth man, who signed a bond to 'buy your love' and ended with neither love nor money, was not there.

Last play onto Stratford's main stage in 1998 was Michael Boyd's production of *Measure for Measure*. It divided the critics in the national press, the left largely in favour, the right very hostile. It started as it meant to go on, in bold defiance of tradition, with Robert Glenister's Duke alone and in a state of apparent collapse. He was clearly on the edge of the abyss, and his dukedom (somewhere in the Balkans in the early twentieth century, it seemed) was on the verge of the destruction visited upon that earlier corrupt city, Babylon, in the biblical quotations flickering in the beam of a slide-projector on the wall behind him. The empty bottle of vodka, the slumped figure, the little cell of a room, the noise beyond it, the sudden lurching flight down the walkway (still in position from *The Tempest*) through the auditorium, vividly presented a state, and its ruler, in terminal disintegration, ready for the *coup* that was soon made manifest by the smashing down of the door in Laertes-like rebellion. Through a message left on a phonograph (the play's first speech), the Duke just preserved the fiction of having voluntarily abdicated power before it was taken from him perforce by Stephen Boxer's smoothly confident Angelo, drifting apparently nonchalantly in through the broken door, smirking at the empty bottle, accepting

19 *Measure for Measure*, directed by Michael Boyd for the Royal Shakespeare Company. Jimmy Chisholm as Pompey, and prisoners. Act 4, scene 3.

the power he had clearly long been seeking – and no doubt felt it his religious and moral duty to seize. His moral crusade, alias his tyranny, could now begin, and very soon, in little sinister moments between scenes, one began to catch glimpses of his spies and bodyguards. Then he stopped pretending and filled the stage with soldiers, changing his own high-buttoned white suit of fake innocence for the grey officer's uniform of totalitarian despotism.

Boxer's was a fine performance, controlled and concentrated, an Angelo unquestioning of his own right to power. He easily dismissed Isabella's appeals for mercy in crisp half lines until she grabbed hold of him on 'O spare him', and his tongue flicked out, momentarily, to moisten his lips, the attempt to maintain articulate coolness in the face of a sudden surge of

feeling already a lost cause. Before the second interview he watched her with a terrible intensity as she came down the long curving upstage staircase, aware of every movement of her body in a way that was already a violation. The suave savagery with which he turned her armchair into a small prison as he leaned over her, and the horrifying coolness with which he lifted her skirts to inspect, with ruthless detachment, what he meant to take – just to prove that he could – provided spine-chilling moments.

The journey of Robert Glenister's Duke from disintegration to determined self-assertion was something of a *tour de force*. I was never wholly convinced of the idea of his pretending to be blind as part of the friar's disguise. Justice is blindfold, of course, and he is in pursuit of justice; as Duke, too, he has ruled with a kind of myopic failure to perceive the destruction to which his city is heading and now he returns, seeing clearly, and delving, mole-like, into the aftermath of his own misgovernment as he tries to clear it away; theatrically, too, it had its uses in allowing him often to drop the pretence and make direct eye-contact with the audience. In spite of all this, however, the disguise had, in a production full of trap-doors, the unfortunate effect of allowing worry for the actor's safety to impinge on one's commitment to the fiction.

It was a sense of containment only just achieved that was most interesting about Clare Holman's Isabella: the long white dress severely buttoned up from ankle to throat, the desire for more restraint upon the sisterhood, the anguished horror at the polluting touch of Angelo's hands, were all part of this. But the most impressive thing about the performance was that Isabella's ardour and youth and energy and capacity for love were never in doubt, so that the proposition that this young woman would, at the end, find the courage to leave the stage with her hand in the Duke's was also perfectly credible.

Around the central trio there was good work from Jimmy Chisholm, presenting an epicene Pompey in heavy make-up and a pin-striped suit, uttering the play's truisms about the inevitability of lechery in a cut-glass Morningside accent of exquisite phoneyness before being forced into prison through the hole that dominated the centre stage. Through this hole the great upstage staircase wound downwards and from it Pompey only escaped by becoming the lackey of the state tyranny, administering bread and water (from a watering can) to the up-turned bruised and bloody faces of the detainees of the moral crusade as they peeped through their trap-doors like larvae from their cells – a surreal and disturbing scene. Part of the team forcing him down the Hole, and giving him a savage kick in the face in doing so, was Adrian Schiller's Lucio, a strange, self-loathing roué with a sad hint of faded elegance, bitter at the

futility of his existence, but nasty, too, in his destructive cynicism.

In the remarkable final scene this dangerous Lucio pulled a pistol on the disguised Duke as Lucio struggled to unmask him, unleashing as surprising and exciting a piece of Shakespearian theatre as I have seen in a long time. The Duke's pompous return up the aisle down which he had fled at the start, with Angelo's fake applause from a stage which he had filled with soldiers, the braying of a military band only half-disguising the sham, had done what many a reader of this play must often have done – dared to question what seems to be its assumption that heads of state who hand over power can expect to be welcomed back with open arms whenever the whim to return comes over them. Now, as the Duke managed to grab Lucio's pistol and pointed it at his Deputy's head, and Friar Peter and the rest of his carefully planted followers (the production used a great many unpaid extras) disarmed the presidential bodyguard and placed them under arrest, the production that had begun with a *coup d'état* ended with a counter-coup that was something of a *coup de théâtre*. With a huge effort of self-control, and by only a whisker, the Duke managed to avoid pulling the trigger on Angelo, and the sequence of revelations that is the last phase of the last scene began, with directorial choices that had a touch of inspiration about them. From the Hole, in a long shambling line, blinking in the light, came the prisoners of Angelo's régime. Up they climbed, battered, filthy, and bewildered, Master Froth, Mistress Overdone, Juliet with her baby, Claudio, and the rest – a remarkably moving moment. And among them was a prisoner of the old régime, kept nine years on Death Row, whom the Duke had thought a convenient source of the spare head that his little scheme required: to kneel to Barnadine was the least the Duke could do, though I've never before seen a Duke with the guts to do it. The production had begun with a duke fleeing from authority; it ended with one kneeling in humble acceptance of its awful responsibilities.

And yet not quite ended. The audience had been allowed its little laugh on 'but fitter time for that' after the Duke's first mistimed proposal to Isabella. By moving the play's final couplet a little earlier, the stage had been cleared before his second attempt. After it, half-yielding, half-resisting, she accepted a kiss, then turned away and wiped it from her mouth as the Duke moved slowly to the upstage exit, accepting rejection. Her hands moved from her face to her throat, passed near but did not touch the cross at her breast, and then, not without a certain sensuousness, slid down her body. She then walked, hesitantly, to join the Duke (who had paused in his exit and looked back) and their hands joined. And we realized that the set that had hitherto presented an unbroken curve at the back was now open on one side, the bare bones of the theatre, the wall of the back dock, plainly visible through it; and we were watching two actors now heading for their dressing-rooms at the end of the theatrical fiction. But the stage had yet one more moment of its own. As Friar Peter was disappearing at the top of the long curving back-wall staircase, we got the last of the production's wonderful lighting effects as dozens of slats opened for the first time in the plain wall beside the staircase and a bright, warm light flooded the stage. The trap-doors to hell of the prison scene had been replaced by these portals of light that might just possibly have been from heaven – hard to ask a director to provide better illumination.

The two productions of history plays that came my way in 1998 could not have been more contrasted. Edward Hall's 1997 Watermill production of *Henry V*, in modern dress and using just a dozen actors, came to Stratford's Other Place in the autumn; Elijah Moshinsky's RSC production of *Richard III*, on a national tour through the autumn, had a large cast, a massive set, and elaborate period costumes.

Henry V began beautifully with a group of soldiers, all alike in battle fatigues, marching in and collapsing exhausted on the ground. Slowly they began a game of passing a baton among them and then, after a few seconds, as each man took it, he spoke a line of the opening chorus: this was to be their story. They acted it out very simply before us, bits of extra costume – a general's jacket for the King, a little white cotter for the Archbishop, a scruffy dress for Katherine – going on over the camouflage trousers. For some of the scenes, the siege of Harfleur for example, we were led outside and became part of the army being harangued to attack the breach. It was all energetic, brisk (the textual cutting was ruthless), and very honest, the brutality of war being clear at every moment – though, oddly, this did not undermine our basic sense of trust in Alexis Daniel's Henry. What struck me as most interesting about this production was its development of the effect that Ron Daniels's modern-dress *Henry V* had produced last year (*Shakespeare Survey 51* (1998), 236–9). The sense then of the invading English army as brutal and threatening was here taken further, so that we saw them at times as a gang of English football hooligans, complete with lager cans, shouting their jingoistic chants in sickening imitation of scenes in Marseille and other French cities during the recent football World Cup. It is instructive that two modern-dress versions of the play should expose such uneasy responses to its nationalism when the 1997 Globe production, in Elizabethan costume (down to the underwear, we were assured) actually extended its jingoism from stage to auditorium, encouraging spectators in mindless booing of the French every time they appeared. For reminding us of the loathsomeness of such behaviour, and, in its small-scale intensity, for keeping the complex and conflicting emotional currents of the play in theatrical tension, there was much to admire in Hall's production.

Elijah Moshinsky's *Richard III* (like any other director's, no doubt) was to a large extent a vehicle for the player of its title role. There

20 *Richard III*, directed by Elijah Moshinsky for the Royal Shakespeare Company. Robert Lindsay as Richard III.
Act I, scene I.

were some good performances around Robert Lindsay's Richard: a suavely intelligent Buckingham from David Yelland, 'all ice' indeed when the suggestion of killing the princes was put to him and foreseeing his own doom with grim clarity as he headed off for Brecknock; and a fierce and inexorable Queen Margaret from Anna Carteret, taking out a little talismanic dagger for the succession of curses in her first scene and presiding over the final battle, hunched and motionless downstage, looking, in her tatty dark green dress, like some mossed-over tree-trunk, but spreading her arms in triumph to take over the stage after Richmond's final speech.

Overall there was a rather old-fashioned feel to the production. The set presented massive gothic walls on the two upstage sides of a square playing-area set on the diagonal, its leading corner thrust into the stalls to give a theatre-commanding position – mostly for Richard (above all in the soliloquies), but also occasionally for others, including Margaret in the final battle. For the first of the court scenes massive chains came down from the flies, suggesting a rather macabre Yorkist taste in wall-hangings; they remained, swaying and clanking, until the final battle, when they crashed to the stage floor to lie in messy heaps that had to be struggled over by the combatants. A triangle of high-backed gothic benches occupied centre stage for the council scene, the seat at its apex conspicuously empty; it was here that Richard seated himself, with a huge zest and enthusiasm that one would have liked to see more of in the performance, at the end of the scene with the mayor and citizens. The old-fashionedness of the production was at its best in this scene, Richard working hard (though engagingly transparently for the audience) to produce an impression of sanctity that was perfectly plausible: too many recent productions have here offered a Richard so absurdly histrionic as to make the acquiescence of the citizens simply unbelievable. Elsewhere the old-fashionedness seemed a little more irksome. Black was the production's dominant costume colour; there were sheens of green, or purple, in the women's dresses, and Richard shifted to crimson velvet as he seized power, but black and grey are what one remembers. The major characters carried massive staffs topped by their heraldic devices, their clonk-clonk on the stage punctuating the action. For the pre-battle scenes we had the time-honoured image of the two tents pitched side by side, Richmond's white, Richard's red. For the execution of Grey and Rivers the gaolers carried massive axes. King Edward was propped up in his death-bed wearing a very large crown. (His death occurred on stage, so that one was treated to the remarkable spectacle of Rivers, Buckingham and the rest cheering up the lamenting widow actually beside the corpse.) A red glow loomed behind the gothic wall as Clarence was dragged off to be drowned in the wine butt – wouldn't amber have been more appropriate for malmsey? 'As we have ta'en the sacrament' said Richmond in his final speech, and in a trice there was a priest to administer the bread and wine. And so on.

Robert Lindsay's performance grew quite naturally from this context. With massive hump and lurching gait, and a black finger-nailed pottery hand (which he removed in the council scene to demonstrate that his arm was indeed 'withered up'), this was a Richard in the *grand guignol* tradition. There was a certain childishness about him, a desire for dominance that had a brutal simplicity about it. He spoke with a Yorkshire accent – well a Yorkist would, wouldn't he? His brother Edward did too, but

not his brother Clarence, no doubt on account of his marriage into the posh family from down south at Warwick. The virtually inescapable signal given by regional accents in productions where the rest of the cast speaks 'standard' English is of intellectual inferiority – or pretended intellectual inferiority, but as Richard's accent remained unchanged in his soliloquies the latter was not an option. The device produced some interesting moments, particularly in the scene of Prince Edward's arrival in London, when Richard hadn't the faintest idea of the answers to the pompous little swot's questions about Julius Caesar's connexions with the building of the Tower. He diverted them all to Buckingham and turned to the audience with a toothy grin to remark in that Wilfred Pickles voice: 'So wise so young, they say, do ne'er live long'. But the price paid for such moments was a heavy one, it seemed to me: not to have a sense of Richard's dazzling intelligence, and a share in its brilliant destructiveness, was a sad loss.

The text was heavily cut to give a playing time well inside three hours, and there were several textual tinkerings: the decision to keep Lady Anne on stage after the wooing over the corpse of Henry VI (literally across the bier), she kissing Richard erotically through the soliloquy that follows; and the postponement of the appearance of the ghosts from Richard's dream (thus removing the reason for his awakening in terror) to the battle itself. This took the form of a long-drawn-out single combat between Richard and Jo Stone-Fewings's smug Welsh Richmond, slugging it out in this medieval version of the Yorkshire-Glamorgan match, Richard persistently getting on top until one of the ghosts came forward and told him to 'despair and die'. Each time he managed to recover, until his wife Anne came to demand that he 'let fall' his 'edgeless sword', which proved irresistible. Richmond skewered him and he writhed and twitched, screaming in agony, before we were invited to look forward to the future with the young Welsh commu-

21 *Romeo and Juliet*, directed by Michael Attenborough for the Royal Shakespeare Company. Ray Fearon as Romeo, Zoë Waites as Juliet. Act 2, scene 5.

nicant, after which Queen Margaret took over the stage in glee. It was somehow appropriate that this production should be played against a gothic set, for there was something distinctly gothic in its directing and acting styles.

Among the year's productions of the tragedies, Michael Attenborough's of *Romeo and Juliet*, which played at the Barbican and then at Stratford's Swan Theatre through the 1997–8 winter before a national and international tour, was a welcome change from a recent run of rather disappointing versions of this play. Coleridge used the word 'precipitate' of *Romeo and Juliet*, and it was this quality that gave energy, excitement, and danger to Attenborough's production. With a wall of crumbling, sun-baked brick as background (which, with the addition of candles in niches, became the inside of a church, or from which Juliet's little iron-railed, green-shuttered balcony, with its potted geranium, was hung), the set had a central raised area which served at the beginning as the lounging place for the town's youth to eye the girls doing the washing at the fountain alongside, in the middle as the bed for the lovers, and at the end as their bier. It was here too, in the dumbshow with which the production began – a procession in near darkness, with umbrellas, led by Friar Lawrence to gloomy clarinet music, the dull thud of a drum, and the smell of incense – that the corpses of the lovers were laid. The same images, the same darkness, the same music ended the play, the two ends of an arc that had at its zenith the production's mid-point, the moment before the interval, the two lovers kneeling in brilliant light in front of Friar

Lawrence: 'Till holy church incorporate two in one'.

It was a strength of the production that it created a genuine sense of a small-town community where everyone knew each other and where old hatreds ran deep. The play was taken several steps down the social scale to achieve this: the 'grove of sycamore' here rooted westward (with some disservice to the scansion), from 'this *town*'s side'; Capulets and Montagues fought in the first scene with bill-hooks and other agricultural implements; Peter became the Nurse's 'friend', not her 'servant' and Romeo's 'man' became *his* friend 'Abraham'; Juliet was busy helping with the baking when the idea of her marriage was first broached; Capulet drank wine from a bottle as he discussed marriage with a Paris noticeably smarter than the other young men because he wore a shirt rather than a dirty vest; and the head of this little community, with its square and its fountain baking in the sun somewhere in southern Italy sometime between the wars, was a very ordinary little mayor, far from ducal. The sense of violence simmering beneath the sweat and the sexual swagger of the young men was never in doubt. This was a world in which the energy, the recklessness, the precipitateness were believable, in which the plunge to catastrophe in the second half was headlong – and assisted, it has to be said, by some hefty textual cutting in the later stages.

Speed was the essence of the evening. The cut from that opening funeral procession, all umbrellas and darkness, to the sunlit square and the boys watching the girls, joking, fighting, bleeding, set the pace. Juliet danced a tango, very sensually, with Paris; for a moment we went into slow motion as she and Romeo caught each other's eyes; then off it all went again, helter-skelter, the eager urgency of their meeting, her passionately kissing him, the wild energy of Chook Sibtain's Mercutio 'conjuring' Romeo with every sexual innuendo semaphored. The drive forward was never allowed to relax. The fight among the young men flared up with a ferocity that was terrifying, Ray Fearon's headstrong, passionate Romeo stabbing Tybalt repeatedly in a sort of wild frenzy. Zoë Waites's Juliet had the same vulnerable, dangerous commitment and spontaneity, particularly evident in the open-hearted frankness and sensuality with which she spoke the 'Gallop apace' soliloquy. Her relationship with Romeo was wholly believable (how often can one say that?), both in its freshness and vitality and in its unstoppable plunge to destruction. Trying to stop it was the warm humanity, reliability, and obvious goodness of Richard Cordery's Friar Lawrence, a massive figure, very moving in his farewell embrace of Romeo after calming him down and sending him off to Mantua. But in spite of the friar's love, and the energy, and joy, and precipitateness which we felt so vividly, the outcome was never in doubt: we ended in the dark, the candles flickering in the niches of the wall, and the lovers' corpses on that central platform, their brief, brilliant flame extinguished.

Italy between the wars was also the setting for Anthony Clark's production of *Julius Caesar* at Birmingham Repertory Theatre late in 1997. It was played in a curved amphitheatre of a set, a mixture of debating chamber and stadium, in 1930s costumes – the conspirators furtively arriving at Brutus's orchard, as if from a gangster film, in overcoats with big, turned-up collars and trilby hats, Caesar and Calphurnia sitting at their art deco breakfast table, she in her cardigan he in his silk dressing gown, Antony in a very sharply cut pin-striped suit for the Forum scene. The period was interrupted at times, however, by suggestions of ancient Rome – Caesar in purple robe and golden laurel wreath for the Senate scene, the assassins putting on togas over their three-piece suits; or by allusions to the present day – the Soothsayer in a modern anorak, foretelling the future with the benefit of hindsight, refugees pushing prams across the battlefield at Philippi, or all of us, all the time, seeing ourselves in the mirrors that surrounded the set.

These were interesting attempts to sustain the relevance of the play to more than one historical period, but perhaps there were rather too many of them to allow the production to develop real drive and focus. The most exciting part about it was the sequence before the interval, the trapping of Cinna the poet by the hooligan mob, his taunting and murder and the throwing of his corpse into a fine imitation of a fire, along with heaps of books and great armfuls of the set: 'Pull down forms, windows, anything'. Here was a superb sense of a mob on the rampage – and it was in curious contrast to the terribly stodgy way they'd received the speeches (crudely amplified) of the politicians from the pulpit. David Bark-Jones's Mark Antony, wafting a totally blank piece of paper at the audience at the end of his speech about Caesar's will, had a disturbing Michael Portillo streak in him, and his régime, with the names for liquidation chalked up on a blackboard, was clearly going to be even more ruthless than that of Michael Cashman's Caesar, jack-booted of course and posing on a plinth as the play began, as if already a figure from the past. All the conspirators were cast young, which made the assassination seem, not uninterestingly, like a junior officers' coup, and Timothy Walker had the courage to make Brutus (in another very sharp suit) both mentally dim and seriously pleased with himself, that most dangerous political combination. The most interesting performance was that of James Dreyfus as Cassius, fiercely intellectual and emotionally prickly in his little rimless spectacles, just managing to hold in the passions that burned within him, knowing he lacked the popular charisma of Brutus and bitter at having to give in to the latter's consistently mistaken political choices. His long stare into the void as he conceded to Brutus's desire to give battle immediately at Philippi, his fellow officers staring at him in horrified disbelief, was very memorable.

Also at Birmingham Repertory Theatre, in October, was Bill Alexander's production of *Hamlet*. Like Matthew Warchus's recent version for the RSC (*Shakespeare Survey 51*, (1998) 242–44), it cut Fortinbras and all the play's politicking with Norway (and with it, of course, 'How all occasions do inform against me') and turned the play into a family tragedy. There was also a certain amount of tiresome importation of footnote glosses into the dialogue – 'probe' for *tent*, 'burdens' for *fardels*, and so on – that was unworthy of a production otherwise thoughtful and intelligent. Played on a largely bare stage, with one upstage door that occasionally appeared downstage to suggest the claustrophobia of the room where Claudius prays, or plots with Laertes, it was remarkable for some splendid lighting effects by Tim Mitchell. The use of narrow beams of light, vertical and horizontal, to suggest the grid of a portcullis, was particularly effective: everyone walked carefully through the gap in it until the ghost, with no other 'ghostly' effects about his very human-looking person, walked straight through the bars to bring his news from Purgatory. Costumes were difficult to date, perhaps nineteenth-century, but their effect was to create the sense of a stifling, shadowy world, intent upon itself, without reference to where or when.

At the centre of that world was the fierce struggle for supremacy between Richard McCabe's engaging, disturbing Hamlet and Gerard Murphy's powerful, brutal Claudius. We saw Hamlet first alone on stage before the court scene, seated on the royal chair from which Claudius would shortly make his speech of self-justification, Anna Nicholas's Gertrude, in white bridal gown with red underskirts, making a grand entry through the upstage door in the middle of it, as he mentioned their marriage. Hamlet sat again in that royal chair after Claudius's terrified rush from the play scene, his screams for 'lights' answered by men rushing after him with blazing torches. The conflict for supremacy was played out to the last, Claudius fleeing upstage as he realized the game was up after the final duel, chased and caught by Hamlet, with great clashing of bodies by that upstage door, and dragged back to be stabbed clumsily, brutally, with the sword which, just moments before, had been so elegantly used in the foil play with Laertes.

If Hamlet's relationship with his uncle centred on a chair, his relationship with his father had to do with a stool, or rather two. We had earlier seen a downstage high and low stool used by Polonius and Ophelia, the easy-going-ness of their relationship reflected in the fact that she sat on the higher. It was not so when the Ghost passed for a second time through those bars of light and took the higher stool. Hamlet obediently sat below him listening intently, McCabe's podgy face looking up, open-mouthed, those remarkable bugle eyes taking it all in, pathetically trying to touch his father comfortingly as the 'horribles' were repeated. And as one watched those two figures sitting on stools, spotlit on a bare stage, the image of a little boy listening to daddy was strangely displaced by the image of a ventrilo-quist and his dummy – a curious and disturbing gloss on the scene.

A white sofa, downstage, back to the audience, dominated Hamlet's scene with his mother, he repeatedly forcing her head back in his violent attempts to make her understand, so that we constantly saw her face upside down against the white back of the sofa. And for his big scene with Rakie Ayola's Ophelia, it was again what he sat on that set the tone. For 'To be or not to be' he was on the top of an enormous library step-ladder, reading a book from a huge square pillar of a four-sided book-case, twenty feet high. She stood at the bottom as he addressed us, perforce loftily, and very emphatically over her head, and then met him, half way up the ladder, to give him back his 'remembrances', which took the form of a little teddy-bear. Again it made a remarkable, though here I found an over-self-conscious, image.

McCabe's earlier Shakespeare roles have largely been comic (or comic-cynical, as his recent Thersites at Stratford). One wondered

whether he quite had a Hamlet in him – and one was wrong. This was a remarkably inter-esting performance, touching and sad, bitter and mocking, anti-heroic and immensely like-able, a man on the edge of disintegration but still agonizingly sane. He found a dangerous kind of solace in shamming madness, prancing and dancing anarchically about in his long white cassock, goading and undermining Clau-dius with those insolent eyes, until one feared that that bull-necked, bullet-headed, blotch-faced tyrant (who could yet crack up in tears as he failed to pray) would pash him to pulp, so threatening and subversive an opponent was he. And yet he could be tender and emotional elsewhere, his sudden mood-switches dis-turbing and believable, howling in distress at the sight of the corpse of Polonius, weeping helplessly as he berated himself that 'this thing's to do', in utter despair to have lost 'all my mirth', sobbing after the graveyard scene but finding a kind of weary peace in the futility of it all at the end. As he died he toppled from the little stool on which he had taken such careful note of his father's instructions, his head falling against his dead mother's breast. There has always been a sense of danger about McCabe's acting and it was put to fine effect in this moving, urgent performance.

It was a far cry from this highly emotional version of *Hamlet* to the crisp intellectual challenge of Michael Bogdanov's English Shakespeare Company production of *Antony and Cleopatra* at the Bath Shakespeare Festival in August (and later at the Hackney Empire). It was in modern dress (of course), Antony's soldiers in khaki drill, Antony in a general's uniform, the Roman leaders as naval officers, and it had a simple set of a dividing screen with airport-style clocks on one side of it showing the time in Rome, Athens, and Alexandria. The screen opened from time to time so that, for council and parley scenes, a long table could be thrust between its halves (in a way that was, I fear, intended as a sexual allusion). The remarkable thing about the production was that it handed over the play, in a most determined way, to David Shelley's Octavius Caesar. Shelley had played Orlando in the companion production of *As You Like It* (see above, p. 233), and here again he gave a refreshingly straightforward reading of the part, presenting Octavius as loving brother, courteous and conscientious ruler, and honest, likeable man. There was no doubt that the Roman Empire would be decently and humanely governed with him in charge. His opponents' first appearance – after quick-talking journalists in the sunglasses–notebooks–battered-hats tradition had given a newspaperese version of 'the story so far' – turned us against them immediately and in a manner, surely deliberate, from which there was no way back: Antony, drunk, slobbering with a masseuse who was oiling his body; Cleopatra, in top hat and white tie, riding a bicycle and laughing inanely. 'Nay, but this dotage of our general's ... '.

Tim Woodward's Antony had clearly been watching too many Trevor Howard war films: the clipped, studiedly throwaway speech, the gruff voice, the constant lighting of cigarettes, the little past-regretting shrug, were all part of the hard-bitten old soldier act, sexually experienced but with a heart of gold, a fine version of the cliché. Cathy Tyson's Cleopatra was everything the Romans say about her: shallow and selfish, always putting on a performance – not even genuine, one felt, at Antony's death – dressed, again with obvious cinema reference, as the stereotype tart, high heels and short nighties, long boots and skin-tight trousers, hair scraped up in a way that was presumably intended to allure Antony but was most unlikely to allure anyone else, and finding a way of saying the lines that made them seem banal, she came over as fundamentally cold and heartless, for all the superficial pretence at sensuality.

I thought this a bold and challenging reading, absolutely clear in its telling of the story in its own way and consistent in its invitation to us to clear our minds of what the director clearly saw as the fustian romantic nonsense that has surrounded the performance history of this play. It was certainly a more sharply focused version than the much grander affair directed by Sean Mathias for the Royal National Theatre. This had promised to be the Shakespeare production of the year, its director, with a fine record and a high reputation, embarking on his first major Shakespeare production and, in the title roles, two actors with star names who had been too long absent from the stage. It sold out before it opened and then received one of the worst sets of notices ever experienced by the National Theatre. In so far as it is the purpose of this annual essay to record what was illuminating and perhaps innovative in Shakespeare productions during the year, it might best be passed over in silence, but some assessment of the failure of so high-profile a theatrical event may perhaps be appropriate.

Although much of the blame was laid by reviewers on Alan Rickman's performance as Antony (and there was indeed much about which one could be disappointed), the problem went deeper. The evening was bland, and fundamentally empty, because the director seemed to have nothing he needed to say about the play, no great reason for wanting to direct it other than the availability of Helen Mirren and Alan Rickman for the star roles and a big budget for a very large cast and lavish period costumes. The set (by Tim Hatley) featured a wide arch (of the ranged empire, presumably) through which the revolve alternately delivered a horizontal, cushioned Egypt or a vertical, glass-paned Rome, saving its most impressive effect for the monument scene in which Cleopatra appeared in front of hundreds of lighted candles racked in multi-levelled semi-circles behind and around her. Helen Mirren's Cleopatra achieved an impressive stillness and concentration in these final scenes, the speaking of the language and the disposition of the actors on the set in the death scene releasing at last some of the play's latent power. Earlier she was at her most interesting in moments of sarcasm or wry humour – referring to her 'salad days'

22 *Antony and Cleopatra*, directed by Sean Mathias for the Royal National Theatre. Helen Mirren as Cleopatra, Alan Rickman as Antony. Act I, scene I.

with a challenging little look at the audience, shrugging off the news that Octavia is thirty, demanding at the beginning, with searching irony, 'if it be love indeed'.

As every reviewer (and no doubt every playgoer) remarked, there wasn't the faintest whiff of sexual chemistry between her and Alan Rickman's Antony – which shouldn't have been as surprising as people seemed to find it, given Rickman's extraordinary ability to play the detached, the languorous, the sardonic. He was quite unable to suggest the struggle between sexual thraldom and the resultant shame that his Roman past imposes upon him, the little joke of collapsing back horizontally onto the cushions on 'we stand up peerless' seeming to sum up the reading of the part. It was deeply sad to see a fine actor so miscast, wandering apparently dazed and woebegone about the stage in the attempt to depict the struggle with himself, the half-closed eyes instead suggesting boredom, and the often-repeated gesture of wafting his hands wearily down – in a vague, ineffectual gesture of futility – in danger of being applied by the audience to the evening they were passing rather than to the situation in which Marcus Antonius found himself. He had, however, one glorious moment, the last before the interval. 'In the east my pleasure lies', he had said with a kind of grim sense of the inescapable (and certainly no vestige of pleasure), and as he dismissed Octavia back to her brother, he watched her walk away before turning to the audience with a long, doleful glance of guilt, and pain, and despair.

There was some excellent verse speaking from Finbar Lynch's interesting Enobarbus, his earlier ironies about his general hard-edged and with a certain slyness in their detachment, so that his defection was less surprising than it sometimes is – a fact that made the director's decision to have stardust fall at his death alarmingly sentimental and banal. Sam West was an Octavius of the old school (quite unlike David Shelley's for the English Shakespeare Company), his diction clipped, monotonous, mean, his manner crisp and prissy, his possessiveness towards his sister disturbing. But at least he was vocally clear: around the principals there was far too little attention to scansion, to clarity, and at times even to audibility. A production that had promised much delivered little – not for the first time with this theatrically elusive play. A star cast and a big budget are not sufficient answer to the question that needs to be asked about every Shakespeare production: why did *this* director want to do *this* play *this* year? If for nothing else, the production was instructive in reinforcing that simple truth.

PROFESSIONAL SHAKESPEARE PRODUCTIONS IN THE BRITISH ISLES JANUARY–DECEMBER 1997

compiled by

NIKY RATHBONE

Most of the productions listed are by professional or semi-professional (pro/am) companies. Productions originating in 1996 or earlier have only been included if there is new information. Details are mainly taken from newspaper reviews held in the Birmingham Shakespeare Library.

ALL'S WELL THAT ENDS WELL

The New Shakespeare Company, the Open Air Theatre, Regent's Park: June 1997–
Director: Helena Kaut-Howson
Designer: Claire Lyth
Set against the background of the Bosnia war.

The Oxford Stage Company, tour: August 1997
Director: Irina Brook
Set in a North African country and played as though by strolling players.

ANTONY AND CLEOPATRA

The Bridewell Theatre Company, London: April 1997–
Director: Carol Metcalfe
Designer: Bridget Kimak
The set consisted of white hangings, lit red for the Egypt scenes.

The Lincoln Shakespeare Company: November 1997
Director: Rob Smith
A pro/am production

AS YOU LIKE IT

Bristol Old Vic and West Yorkshire Playhouse February 1997–
Director: Polly Irvin
Designer: Atlanta Duffy
Music: John O'Hara
Set in the 1990s, played as though by strolling players. The set consisted of a latticed steel tower on a black stage.

The Mercury Theatre, Colchester: February 1997
Director: Pat Trueman
Designer: Christopher Oram

Nottingham Playhouse: February 1997
Director: David Pountney
Designer: Marie-Jeanne Lecca
Music: Thomas Gray
Set in the 1990s

Inside Intelligence at the Jermyn Street Theatre and Greenwich Festival, London: May 1997
Director/music: Robert Shaw
Set in the Twenties with period songs and dances.

The Festival Players Theatre Company, tour of historic open-air sites: June 1997–
Director: Trish Knight-Webb
Music: Johnny Coppin

The Lincoln Shakespeare Company, open-air production at historic sites around Lincoln: July 1997

Director: Karen Crow
A strongly comic pro/am production.

Albion Shakespeare Company, tour of open-air sites with *The Tempest:* July 1997–

OpenHand Productions, the Cambridge Shakespeare Festival: August 1997.
Played in college gardens.

Wooden O Productions at the Bridewell Theatre, London: September 1997–
Director: David Terence
Designer: Bridget Kimak

The Perth Theatre: November 1997
Director: Michael Winter
Designer: Monique Jones
An all male cast. The players opened in rehearsal clothes and slowly assumed period costume.

Adaptation

Call me Ganymede
The James Arnott Theatre, University of Glasgow: November 1997
Director: Giles Havergal
A student production, exploring androgyny in *As You Like It.*

THE COMEDY OF ERRORS

The Nuffield Theatre, Southampton: February 1997
Director: Patrick Sandford
Designer: Paul Farnsworth
Set in present-day Southampton, but given a comically surreal atmosphere.

CORIOLANUS

Steven Berkoff Company, tour to the Edinburgh Festival, Japan and Israel. See *Shakespeare Survey 50.*

CYMBELINE

Galleon Theatre Company at the Prince Theatre, London Fringe: February 1997

The RSC at the Royal Shakespeare Theatre, Stratford: February 1997–
Director: Adrian Noble
Designer: Anthony Ward

HAMLET

The New Shakespeare Company, Regent's Park Open Air Theatre, London: July 1997–
Director: Tim Pigott-Smith
Hamlet: Damian Lewis

Wales Actors' Company, tour of open-air sites in Wales: July 1997–
Director/Hamlet: Paul Garnault
Cut as a Jacobean touring production might have been.

The RSC at the Royal Shakespeare Theatre, Stratford: May 1997–
Director: Matthew Warchus
Designer: Mark Thompson
Hamlet: Alex Jennings
Music: Gary Yershon
The production made interesting use of film sequences for flashback.

Adaptations

Elsinore
Written and performed by Robert Lepage.
The Royal National Theatre at the Lyttleton Theatre: January 1997
See *Shakespeare Survey 51.*

Hamlet

Two-Way Mirror Theatre Company at the Springfield Park Tavern, London: February 1997–
Director/Hamlet: Ricardo Pinto
The text stripped to the essentials, and played very fast.

Hamlet
The Soho Group at the Thorndike Exchange, Leatherhead: March 1997

An adaptation for an all-female group. Oriental shadow puppets were used for the play within the play.

Amiod's Journey, directed and devised by Runar Gudbrandsson
RSC Fringe Festival: August 1997
An exploration of the Hamlet myth, following Amiodi Heinski (Hamlet the Fool) and Ophelia on a journey through time, space and literary iconography.

The Prince of West End Avenue, adapted from the novel by Alan Isler.
Adapted and performed by Kerry Shale
The Hampstead Theatre, London Fringe: September 1997.
Directed by Sonia Fraser.

HENRY V

Mappa Mundi, the Sherman Theatre, Cardiff and tour with *Julius Caesar*: January 1997–
Director: Lloyd Llewellyn-Jones
Music: Christopher Knight
Performed by a cast of six.

Shakespeare's Globe, London: May 1997–
Director: Richard Olivier
Designer: Jenny Tiramani
Henry: Mark Rylance
An all-male cast, playing in traditional Elizabethan costume, including period underwear.

The Watermill Theatre, Newbury: May 1997–
Director: Edward Hall
Henry: Jamie Glover
An all-male cast. The production took place partly out of doors.

Fast and Loose Theatre Company at Bramber Castle: June 1997
Hamlet: Keith Charles
A pro/am production played in traditional period costume.

The Berenger Theatre Ltd. Shakespeare at Barnwell; Barnwell Manor: July 1997
Director: Godfrey Davies

Designer: David Neal
Henry: Nigel Wrightson
Chorus: Robert Hardy
Duke of Burgundy: Richard Todd
An open-air pro/am production.

The Cherry Tree Theatre Company at the Bellairs Playhouse, Guildford: August 1997

The RSC at the Swan Theatre, Stratford and tour: September 1997–
Director: Ron Daniels
Designer: Ashley Martin-Davis
Music: Colin Towns
Henry: Michael Sheen

JULIUS CAESAR

Birmingham Repertory Theatre: October 1997
Director: Anthony Clark
Designer: Patrick Connellan
Music: Mark Vibrans
Set in the Thirties, with echoes of ancient Rome given by token togas draped over business suits. A semi-circular Forum faced the audience, which became the crowd for the actors' orations. At the interval, following the death of Caesar, the Forum was torn apart to symbolize civil war.

Adaptation

Julius Caesar
Seigy Tamura, Teatre du Sygne and Haiyu-za, Tokyo at the Riverside Studios, Hammersmith and tour to Greece: August 1997
A ninety-minute adaptation based on *Julius Caesar*, *Antony and Cleopatra* and Plutarch's *Lives*. The production combined elements of classic European drama and traditional Japanese kabuki.

KING LEAR

Leicester Haymarket and the Young Vic, London: February 1997–
Director: Helena Kaut-Howson

Designer: Pawel Dobrzycki
Lear: Kathryn Hunter
The production opened and closed in an old-people's nursing home, and the play became the dream of a dying woman.

The Cottesloe Theatre, Royal National Theatre
London: March 1997–
Director: Richard Eyre
Designer: Bob Crowley
Music: Dominic Muldowney
Lear: Ian Holm
The production was also televised.

The Peter Hall Company at the Old Vic, London: August 1997–
Director: Peter Hall
Designer: John Gunter
Lear: Alan Howard

The Crucible Theatre, Sheffield: October 1997
Director: Deborah Paige
Designer: Simon Vincenzi
Lear: Tim Barlow
The Folio text was used. The set gave the feel of a fortress or bunker with Tim Barlow's Lear very much the old soldier.

Adaptations

The Dying of the Light, an adaptation by Pete Barrett
The Wolsey Studio Theatre, Ipswich: May 1997
Director: Caroline Smith
A small cast played multiple roles. The action was set by the seashore, the seascape evoking the essential loneliness of the individual.

Film adaptation

A Thousand Acres
Based on the book of the same title by Jane Smiley
Director: Jocelyn Moorhouse
With Michelle Pfeiffer as Rose (Regan) and Jessica Lange as Ginney (Goneril)

LOVE'S LABOUR'S LOST

The Cliveden Festival, Cannizaro Park, Wimbledon: July 1997
Director: Richard Frost

MACBETH

Drayton Court Theatre, Ealing, London: February 1997–
Director: Philip d' Orleans

Jactito Theatre of Visual Arts, schools tour: April 1997–

Black Box Theatre, Liverpool Playhouse Studio: July 1997
Director: Ian Karl Moore

OpenHand Productions, Cambridge Shakespeare Festival: July 1997–
Played in Cambridge college gardens.

Shakespeare in the Park, Regent's Park Open Air Theatre: August 1997–
Director: Philip Ayckbourne

Theatre Babel at the Tron, Glasgow and tour: September 1997–
Director: Graham McLaren
Played in modern dress with no stage set, the cast sitting on chairs at the side of the stage when not involved in the action.

The Tatar National Theatre at the Assembly Rooms, Edinburgh Festival: October 1997. Played in the Tatar language.

Rebbeck Penny Limited, Bristol Old Vic and tour: October 1997–
Director: George Costigan
Designer: Ashley Martin-Davis
Macbeth: Pete Postlethwaite
Mainly modern dress, with one of the witches dressed as a Red Cross nurse, radio interviews and ending with Macbeth hanging from a butcher's hook.

Adaptations

Macbeth
The Custard Factory, Birmingham, tour: February 1997–
Director: Theresa Haskins
Designer: Juliet Forster

Macbeth
Classworks Theatre, schools tour: March 1997–
Director: Jenny Culank

From a Jack to a King, a rock musical by Bob Carlton
Pola Jones in association with the Theatre Royal Plymouth, tour: September 1997–
Director: Bob Carlton
Designer: Rodney Ford
Eric Glamis, back-stabbing member of a rock and roll band, disposes of Elvis look-alike lead singer. A witty musical set to fifties rock and roll classics. Originally written for Bubble Theatre Company.

Macbeth
A solo adaptation by Simon Floyd of Loosewig Theatre Company, performed at the Norwich Festival of Theatre: June 1997

Scenes from Leviathan, a modern Macbeth by Rod Wooden, playwright in residence at the University of Swansea
The Mercury Theatre, Swansea: June 1997
Director: Adrian Stokes
Presented as a work in progress meditating on colonial experience through examination of conflict in South Africa and Ireland under Cromwell. The cast included professional actors and students.

Umabatha, the Zulu Macbeth
Adapted and directed by Welcome Msomi
Shakespeare's Globe Theatre, London: August 1997
A spectacular adaptation of *Macbeth* to a tribal African setting.
First UK performance 1972, in Peter Daubeny's World Theatre season. The production has been performed in many parts of the world.

Macbeth from Manipur: Stage of Blood
Writer/translator: Somorendra Arambam
International Arts Production in association with the Forum for Laboratory Theatre of Manipur, India at the Waterman's Arts Centre: August 1997
Director: Lokendra Arambam
An all-male cast played on a floating stage on the river Thames, making use of the river for dramatic entrances by canoe, lit by flaming torches. The production has developed over several years from a 1995 pilot project on Loktak lake, Manipur. The action was difficult to follow, as it was played in reverse, taking Macbeth's eventual fate as its starting point and re-interpreting the story. One reviewer described the magical experience of seeing the production on the lake in Manipur played to an audience of 2,000 local people.

Akogun by Rufus Orisayomi
A Nigerian adaptation of *Macbeth*
African Popular Theatre at Hackney Empire, London: September 1997

Macbeth the Panto
Oddsocks Theatre Company, tour: November 1997–
A comedy illustrating the folly of ambition.

Macbeth: Information is Power
GRIP Theatre, the Rose and Crown, Wimbledon: November 1997
Director: Martin Richards
Cut to two hours, with a cast of eight making extensive use of computer graphics and visual projections.

Macbeth
TILT Theatre Company at the Everyman Theatre, Cheltenham; November 1997
An adaptation for five actors.

Film versions

Macbeth
Grampian TV and Cromwell Productions: May 1997

Director: Brian Blessed
Producer: Bob Carruthers
Macbeth: Jason Connery
Lady Macbeth: Helen Baxendale
A traditional production intended for schools. The murder of Lady Macduff and her children was cut.

Macbeth
Wolf and Water, Beaford Arts Centre, North Devon: January 1997
Directors: Peter Harris and John Morrison
Designer: Steve Newton
A video project involving adults with learning difficulties as artists and technicians, using an improvised script.

MEASURE FOR MEASURE

Lincoln Shakespeare Company: March 1997

Electric Theatre Company at the North Pole public house, Greenwich: April 1997–
Director: Toby Summers

Word of Mouth at the Cockpit, London and tour: April 1997–
Director: David Salter

North Devon Renaissance Theatre, tour of Devon: June 1997
Directors: Leo and Paul Donner

Nottingham Playhouse and the Barbican Centre, London at the Edinburgh Festival, British and foreign tour: August 1997–
Director/set designer: Stéphane Braunschweig
Music: Gualtiero Dazzi
The Duke: Jim Hooper
Angelo: Paul Brennen
Isabella: Lise Stevenson
In this production the Duke was clearly not in control of events, but frequently confounded by them. Solutions to unexpected dilemmas such as Angelo demanding Claudio's head were thrown together, making the Duke's behaviour more plausible than sometimes appears.

A and BC Theatre Company at the North Lawn, Lincoln's Inn, London: August 1997
Director: Gregory Thompson

The Court Theatre Company at the Courtyard Theatre, King's Cross, London: August 1997–
Director: Graham Watts
Designer: Rachel Oliver

The English Touring Theatre, UK tour: October 1997–
Director: Michael Gordon
Designer: Conor Murphy
Isabella: Catherine Cusack
A stark set of white bars on a black backdrop.

Adaptation

Measure for Measure
Diverse Attractions at the Edinburgh Fringe Festival: 1997
Director: Andrew Sawford
A Duchess replaced the Duke, and at the end of the play Angelo was punished for his crimes.

THE MERCHANT OF VENICE

Birmingham Repertory Theatre with Thelma Holt Productions, Birmingham and tour: February 1997–
Director: Bill Alexander
Designer: Ruari Murchison
Portia: Cathy Tyson
Shylock: David Schofield

Compass Theatre Company (Sheffield) the Gulbenkian Theatre, Canterbury and tour: February 1997–
Director: Neil Sissons
Designer: Liam Doona

Second Age Theatre Company at the Everyman Palace Theatre, Cork and tour of Ireland: April 1997–

Prime Productions at the Edinburgh Fringe Festival: August 1997
Director: Lewis Hancock
Playing the First Folio text, unrehearsed to

simulate the supposed acting conditions of the Elizabethan stage.

The RSC at the Royal Shakespeare Theatre, Stratford: December 1997–
Director: Gregory Doran
Designer: Robert Jones
Portia: Helen Schlesinger
Shylock: Philip Voss

THE MERRY WIVES OF WINDSOR

The RSC at the Royal Shakespeare Theatre, Stratford: December 1996–
The Barbican Theatre, London: December 1997–
Director: Ian Judge
Designer: Tim Goodchild
Music: John White
Falstaff: Leslie Phillips

Crew of Patches, tour: August 1997–
Director: Jo Greenhalgh
A pro/am production.

A MIDSUMMER NIGHT'S DREAM

Tara Arts at the Lyric, Hammersmith and tour: January 1997–
Director: Jatinder Verma
An international cast in a production which contrasted urban and rural worlds.

The Lyric Theatre, Belfast: March 1997
Director: Robin Midgley
The play was seen as Bottom's dream and played in a modern urban setting.

Third Party Productions, tour: March 1997–
Director: Ben Bennison
The production designs were inspired by Klimt.

Blue Raincoat at the Factory, Sligo, tour of Ireland and Riverside Studios, Hammersmith: April 1997–
Director: Niall Henry
Costumes: Mudita Procter

Played with minimal props and scenery in a flowing, choreographed style apparently influenced by Peter Brook.

The New Shakespeare Company at the Open Air Theatre, Regent's Park: May 1997–
Director: Rachel Kavanaugh
Designer: David Knapman
Bottom: Ian Talbot
Set in the Edwardian period.

The English Shakespeare Company (Newcastle-on-Tyne) tour: June 1997–
Producer: Michael Bogdanov
Directed and designed by Phelim McDermott and Julian Crouch
Male fairies and a set design which used many reels of Sellotape to create the sticky coils of magic in which the mortals are entrapped.
Barclays Theatre Award: Best Touring Production

Heartbreak Productions, tour of open-air venues: June 1997–
Director: Louise Jameson

A Midsommer Night's Dreame
Midsommer Actors (Manchester) tour of open-air venues in the north of England: June 1997–
Director: Simon Corble
A promenade production.

OpenHand Productions playing in Oxford college gardens at the Oxford Shakespeare Festival: July 1997–

OpenHand Productions playing in Cambridge college gardens at the Cambridge Shakespeare Festival: July 1997

Off the Ground Productions, tour of open-air venues in the North West of England and North Wales: July 1997
Director: Elinor Morgan Jones
Played in Elizabethan costume. The company aims to make Shakespeare accessible for modern audiences.

Contact Theatre Company (Manchester) at the Forum, Wythenshaw: October 1997

Director: Benjamin Twist
Designer: Andrew Wood
Played by a cast of eight, doubling roles.

The Popular Mechanicals, Sydney, Australia, at the Arts Theatre, London: November 1997
Director: Geoffrey Rush
Designer: Stephen Curtis

Adaptations

A Midsummer Night's Dream
Cwmni Ballet, Gwent, tour: May 1997
Choreography: Darius James
Music: Mendelssohn
A new ballet for a cast of seven.

A Midsummer Night's Dream
The Orange Tree Theatre, Richmond: June 1997
Director Tim Sheader
Four actors in a version for children using audience participation.

A Midsummer Night's Dream
Shakespeare 4 Kidz, tour of Worthing and district: June 1997
Adaptation by Julian Chenery and Matt Gimblett
A musical adaptation for adults and primary school children, involving audience participation.

Dream Nights
The Key Theatre, Peterborough: August 1997–
Adapted and directed by Derek Killeen and Michael Cross
Music: Simon Pearce
Set to Sixties pop music. Another successful Shakespeare musical by this amateur group.

A Midsummer Night's Dream
The Salberg Studio, Salisbury Playhouse: November 1997
A cast of five playing a severely cut text in modern dress.

Film version

A Midsummer Night's Dream
The RSC in association with Channel 4 TV. UK release January 1997
Director: Adrian Noble
Oberon: Alex Jennings
Titania: Lindsay Duncan
Bottom: Desmond Barrit
Based on the 1994 RSC production, and mainly using the original cast The film version opens in the moonlit bedroom of a small boy, who becomes the 'little Indian boy' of the play and observes throughout, the play becoming his dream.

MUCH ADO ABOUT NOTHING

Ludlow Castle Shakespeare Festival: June 1997
Director: Glen Walford
Designer: Rodney Ford
Music: John Oakley-Smith
Beatrice: Toyah Wilcox
Benedick: Martin McKellan

OpenHand Productions playing in Cambridge college gardens for the Cambridge Shakespeare Festival: July 1997

A and BC Theatre Company, the North Lawn, Lincoln's Inn, London: August 1997
Open-air production.

Manchester Royal Exchange Theatre: September 1997
Director: Helena Kaut-Howson
Designer: Johanna Bryant
Beatrice: Josie Lawrence
Benedick: Michael Mueller
Music: Akintayo Akinbode
Set in Garibaldi's Italy.

The Royal Lyceum Theatre, Edinburgh: November 1997
Director: Kenny Ireland
Music: Ricky Ross
Beatrice: Elaine C. Smith
Benedick: Forbes Masson

Set in Scotland using Scots accents as a feature of the production.

OTHELLO

OpenHand Productions playing in Cambridge college gardens for the Cambridge Shakespeare Festival: July 1997

Garage Theatre at the Edinburgh Fringe Festival: August 1997
Director: Nigel Roper

Asylum Theatre Company at the Edinburgh Fringe Festival: August 1997

The Cottesloe Theatre, Royal National Theatre: September 1997
Director: Sam Mendes
Designer: Anthony Ward
Music: Paddy Cunneen
Othello: David Harewood
Iago: Simon Russell Beale
Desdemona: Claire Skinner
The production opened at the Salzburg Festival in August 1997, embarked on a world tour in 1998 then returned to the Lyttleton Theatre.

Talawa Theatre Company at the Drill Hall, London and tour: October 1997–
Director: Yvonne Brewster
Designer: Ellen Cairns
Othello: Ben Thomas
Ben Thomas was not the only black actor in the cast, consequently the sense of Othello's racial difference and isolation was weakened.

Second Age Theatre company, the Tivoli Theatre, Dublin and tour of the Irish Republic: November 1997–
Director: Ozzie Jones
Othello: Michael Grennell
Iago: Johnny Lee Davenport
A black actor played Iago, and a white actor, blacked up, played Othello in a production intended to make a statement about race.

PERICLES

Dolphin Arts at the Wolsey Studio, Ipswich: September 1997
Director: John Southworth
A pro/am production.

RICHARD II

The Barbican Theatre Company at the Pleasance Theatre, London Fringe: October 1997
Director: Phillip Joseph
Designer: Andy Dixon

Film version

Richard II
The Royal National Theatre with BBC 2
Director: Deborah Warner
Richard: Fiona Shaw
A version for TV and film of the 1995 National Theatre production. See *Shakespeare Survey 50*.

RICHARD III

Illyria Theatre Company, tour of National Trust sites with *The Tempest*: August 1997
Director: Oliver Grey
Richard was played by a woman, Liz Brimilcombe.

Adaptations

Richard III
Oddbodies London International Mime Festival, Edinburgh Festival and tour: August 1997
Director: John Mowat
An adaptation for two people blending music, text and mime. The production also toured Europe and, in 1998, the USA.

Richard III
Shirtsleeves Theatre Company, Redbridge at the Camden Palace Theatre, London: October 1997. Text cut to ninety minutes.

ROMEO AND JULIET

Harrogate Theatre: January 1997–
Director: Andrew Manley
The actors opened in Elizabethan costume, and gradually changed to modern dress, teasing out the contemporary relevance of the play.

ACTER at the Bridge Lane Theatre, Battersea: April 1997
ACTER is an American company and also toured the USA.

Box Hedge Theatre Company, tour of open-air venues around London: July 1997.

The King's Head Theatre, Islington, London: July 1997–
Director: Dan Crawford
Designer: Nigel Hook
Romeo: Sean Maguire

OpenHand Productions playing in Cambridge college gardens for the Cambridge Shakespeare Festival: July 1997

The Stafford Shakespeare Festival, Stafford Castle: July 1997
Director: Julia Stafford Northcote
Designer: James Pointon
Romeo: John Pickard
Juliet: Kellie Bright

Lemmings, Northampton, Edinburgh Festival and tour: August 1997
The company has been founded by Hazel Barney and Hannah Jack to provide struggling actors with a platform for their work.

R. J. Williamson Productions, Nottingham and Leeds Shakespeare festivals: August 1997
An open-air production with *The Taming of the Shrew* for the first Nottingham Shakespeare festival. R. J. Williamson is the originator of the Leeds Shakespeare festival.

The Bloomsbury Theatre, London: September 1997
Director: Gwenda Hughes

Imaginary Forces Theatre Company, the Key Theatre Peterborough and tour: September 1997–

The Chester Gateway Theatre: September 1997
Director: Deborah Bruce

The RSC at the Barbican Theatre, London, the Swan Theatre, Stratford and tour: October 1997–
Director: Michael Attenborough
Designer: Robert Jones
Music: Stephen Warbeck
Romeo: Ray Fearon
Juliet: Zoë Waites

The Belgrade Theatre, Coventry: October 1997
Director: Chris Monks
Set in Central America and played by a multi-cultural cast.

Adaptations

Romeo and Juliet
Théâtre le Ranelagh at the London International Mime Festival: January 1997
Adapted for mime and music.

Romeo and Juliet
Virtual Stages, schools tour: February 1997
Directed and adapted by Michael Woodwood and Keith Homer.

Rock'n' Rolling Romeo
Shakespeare 4 Kidz, tour of primary schools around Worthing with an adaptation of *A Midsummer Night's Dream:* June 1997
Devised by Julian Chenery and Matt Gimblett.

Ballet version

Romeo and Juliet
Northern Ballet Theatre, tour: May 1997–
Choreography: Massimo Moricone
Director: Christopher Gable
Music: Prokofiev

Film version

Romeo + Juliet
20th Century Fox: March 1997
Director: Baz Luhrmann
Romeo: Leonardo Di Caprio
Juliet: Claire Danes
An extremely popular film by the director of *Strictly Ballroom*, set in modern Miami Beach America but retaining much of the original text.

THE TAMING OF THE SHREW

R. J. Williamson Productions, Nottingham and Leeds Shakespeare festivals: August 1997
Director/Petruchio: Robert J. Williamson
An open-air production for the first Nottingham Shakespeare festival. The company also staged *Romeo and Juliet* for the festival.

Traffic of the Stage, tour: October 1997–
Director: James Reynard

Adaptation

The Taming of the Shrew
West 28th Street Theatre Company at the Ashcroft Theatre, Croydon: February 1997
Director: Mark Helyer
Played by five actors doubling roles, with theatrical workshops staged by Kicking Bardom. Included the Christopher Sly scenes.

THE TEMPEST

Shared Experience, tour continues, see *Shakespeare Survey 51*.
The production also toured Japan, Israel and Korea.

The Grace Theatre, the Latchmere pub, Battersea, London Fringe: April 1997–
Director: Richard Hurst
Music: Christopher Slaski
Each actor played two widely differing characters, Caliban and Ferdinand; Prospero and Alonso being played by the same actors.

Illyria, tour of open-air venues with *Richard III*: summer 1997
Performed by a cast of five. Caliban doubled with Ferdinand.

Albion Shakespeare Company, tour of open-air venues with *As You Like It*: summer 1997
Director: David Terence
Designer: Bridget Kimak

Bold and Saucy Theatre Company, tour of open-air venues: July 1997

OpenHand Productions playing in Cambridge college gardens for the Cambridge Shakespeare Festival: July 1997

Adaptations

Caliban's Island
Touched Theatre Productions, Shrewsbury Music Hall: June 1997
The play explores the plight of Caliban, who feels his island has been invaded. Set in the present.

The Tempest
Little Eyases Theatre Company, Telford in the Town Park Amphitheatre and Edinburgh Fringe Festival: July 1997–
An adaptation for children played as though by one of the Elizabethan child acting companies. A cast of five.

Strangest of Islands
Tempest Productions at the Gardner Arts Centre, Brighton: July 1997
Director: Marie Pattinson
Designer: Garry McCann
Music: Guy Richardson
A pro/am musical adaptation, the lead parts played by professionals.

Play for England by Rex Obano
The RSC Fringe Festival, Stratford: August 1997

Director: Josette Bushell-Mingo
'The tempest on Prospero's island marked the dawning of time. The spirits of that time inhabit the people of England in 1988.'

Caliban
Written and performed by Marcos Azevedo from Brazil.
The Riverside Studios, Hammersmith: September 1997
Director: Eduardo Bonito

TV film

The Tempest
Filmed for BBC Wales: March 1997
Director: Michael Bogdanov
A neighbourhood production filmed around Tiger Bay, Cardiff, set in the Sixties.
Prospero, Caliban and Ariel were all played by four or five different actors.

TIMON OF ATHENS

Andrew Jarvis Theatre Company in association with the ESC at The Brix, St Matthews Church, Brixton, London: September 1997

TITUS ANDRONICUS

The National Theatre of Craiova, Romania, Nottingham Playhouse and tour: May 1997–
Director/music: Silviu Purcarete
Designer: Stefania Cenean
A simple set of white sheeting, descending or moving forward, capturing Lavinia by enfolding her. Modern life and the primeval were cleverly juxtaposed in a production played as black comedy. First performed Bucharest 1992.

TWELFTH NIGHT

The British Actors Theatre Company at the Haymarket Theatre, Basingstoke: February 1997
Director/Olivia: Kate O'Mara

Northern Stages at the Playhouse, Newcastle-on-Tyne: June 1997
Director: Alan Lyddiard
Designer: Neil Murray
The action began and ended with the actors as a group of travelling players.

Theatre Set Up, Sarajevo Festival of Peace, British and international tour: June 1997–
Director: Wendy McPhee
Designer: Michael Palmer
Set in the Balkan States, since Illyria was once a Balkan province of the Roman Empire. Sir Toby Belch was played as a Serbian grandee run to seed.

The Northcott Theatre, Exeter, annual open-air production in Rougemont Gardens: July 1997
Director: John Durnin
Designer: Emma Donovan

Border Crossings and Forum for Laboratory Theatre of Manipur at the Studio Theatre, the Haymarket, Leicester and short tour: September 1997–

The RSC at the Royal Shakespeare Theatre, Stratford: November 1997–
Director: Adrian Noble
Designer: Anthony Ward
Music: Jason Carr
Viola: Helen Schlesinger
Olivia: Clare Holman
Malvolio: Philip Voss

Night Witches, open-air production in Ravenscourt Park, London: August 1997
Director: Chalkie Horsefall

Adaptation

Twelfth Night: Shakespeare Unplugged
The Royal National Theatre in Education, Spitalfields Market Opera House and tour: February 1997–
Director: Brigid Larmour
Designer: Nettie Edwards

A promenade production playing both schools and public venues.

THE WINTER'S TALE

Method and Madness, tour: January 1997–
Director: Mike Alfreds
A cast of eight playing on a bare stage. The company was previously Cambridge Theatre Company.

Shakespeare's Globe Theatre, London: June 1997–
Director: David Freeman
Designer: Tom Phillips
Music: Claire van Kampen

The Maly Drama Theatre of St. Petersburg, Russia: November 1997
Director: Declan Donnellan
Designer: Nick Ormeod
Included for interest. Cheek by Jowl and the Maly Theatre have long expressed mutual appreciation. Declan Donnellan and Nick Ormerod intend returning to Russia to direct in Moscow.

ATTRIBUTED PLAYS

Edmund Ironside
The RSC Fringe Festival, Stratford: August 1997
Director: Matthew Telfer
Music: Alex Patterson
Performed as a collaboration between members of the RSC and the local community.

POEMS AND SONNETS

Sonnets in the Garden
The Rosemont Players at Tan-y-Llyn, Wales: September 1997

MISCELLANEOUS

Falstaff or The True and Valient Death of Sir John Falsof by David Buck

The Grace Theatre, Battersea: February 1997
David Weston played Falstaff in this adaptation which drew on *Henry IV* and *The Merry Wives of Windsor*.
Director: David Delve
Designer: Andrew Hunt
Adapted from the novel by Robert Nye.

Came Each Actor on his Ass
The RSC Fringe Festival: August 1997
John Kane one-man show covering four centuries of Shakespearian acting styles.

The Quiney Affair by Reg Mitchell
RSC Fringe Festival: August 1997
Staged reading of a new play reconstructing the story of the lust and deceit of Shakespeare's son-in-law.

Shakespeare: The truth
RSC Fringe Festival, August 1997
Patrick Barlow playing Oliver Dingle, Artistic Director of the National Theatre of Brent on How to Do Shakespeare.

Operation Shakespeare
WellMade Theatre, schools tour of South Wales valleys: September 1997
Three actors presenting the essentials of *Macbeth, The Merchant of Venice* and *The Tempest*, with workshops. For the campaign for increased literacy among ten to eleven-year-olds.

Vortigern by William Henry Ireland
Tour de Force Company at The Bridewell, London: October 1997
Director: Joe Harmston
A rare staging of the best known of the Ireland forgeries. 'Shakespeare must have been very young when he wrote it' (Sheridan.)

Mutabilitie by Frank McGuinness
The Royal National Theatre, London: November 1997
Director: Trevor Nunn
Designer: Monica Frawley
Music: Shaun Davey

Edmund: Patrick Malahide
William: Anton Lesser.
In 1598 Edmund Spenser and his family were living at Kilcolman Castle, Ireland.

The play weaves an account of the Irish rebellion around mythic Irish figures, Spenser's account of the decimation of Munster and a small band of English actors, William, Ben and Richard.

THE YEAR'S CONTRIBUTIONS TO
SHAKESPEARE STUDIES

1. CRITICAL STUDIES
reviewed by JANETTE DILLON

Probably the most important contribution to Shakespeare studies to appear within the last year is Helen Vendler's *The Art of Shakespeare's Sonnets*, which includes two full texts (a facsimile of the 1609 edition and a modernized version). Commentaries are printed following individual poems, and the book comes with a CD-ROM of Vendler's own readings of just under half of them. Vendler's rationale for offering yet another account of the Sonnets is that previous editors have not paid enough attention to them as poems, 'that is, as a writer's projects invented to amuse and challenge his own capacity for inventing artworks'. Citing W. H. Auden's insistence that a poem is primarily a 'verbal contraption', she argues that lyric poems have 'almost no significant freight of "meaning" at all, in our ordinary sense of the word' and aims to direct attention forcefully back towards poetic form. For Vendler the poet's duty is the creation of 'aesthetically convincing representations of feelings felt and thoughts thought', and it is not the nature of those thoughts and feelings but the ways in which they are expressed that are the appropriate area of interest for the literary critic. This is straightforward and persuasive. More problematic, however, is her next step, which is to claim that 'the ethics of lyric writing lies in the accuracy of its representation of inner life, and

in that alone. Shakespeare's duty [is] ... to be accurate in the representation of the feelings of his speaker'. Ethics and accuracy seem an unlikely set of criteria with which to follow on from a concentration on form, and accuracy seems to claim more objective value as a category than 'aesthetically convincing representation'. But the real criterion for judging this book must be the success of Vendler's method in practice, and here she is superb. While her approach might broadly be categorized as 'close reading', she demonstrates that different kinds of attention need to be paid to different sonnets. Take her attention to sound-patterns, for example. They emerge as closely allied to features particular to the sonnet in question: to a kind of thematic plotting in Sonnet 25; to the changing grammar of the phoneme *-ing* in Sonnet 87; and to the visual patterns of the written word in Sonnet 9, which Vendler renames 'Fantasy on the Letter W'. On the other hand, there are certain strategies that are part of her regular apparatus for anatomizing each sonnet: the identification of key-words (those occurring in each of a sonnet's four parts – the three quatrains and the couplet) and hence also of 'defective' key-words (where the word is expected and absent in one of the four sections), and the highlighting of other words that function specifically to tie the couplet to the main body of the sonnet. Each of these strategies is deployed in a way that reveals much about the architecture of the Shakespearian sonnet. And Vendler's attention to the detail of vocabulary and grammar sometimes yields unexpected results, as in her reading of Sonnet 116, in which the predominance of negative forms leads her to the view that this is a poem of rebuttal, thus incorporating by definition the less than ideal view of love it seeks to refute. Vendler's prose is packed, precise and consistently up to the challenge of explicating the dense patterning of the Sonnets, though she also presents some of her insights with particular clarity by tabulating them. Her strategy of presentation, as of exploration, is developed in response to the given sonnet. The achievement of this book is that it allows comprehensive insights to emerge by way of privileging the individuality of each poem.

Jonathan Bate's analysis of *The Genius of Shakespeare* has aims that to some extent parallel those of Michael Bristol's *Big-Time Shakespeare* last year. Though the ground each covers is very different, both seek to rescue Shakespeare's 'genius' from the politics of theoretical infighting. Bate's book, like Bristol's, is wide-ranging, well-informed, suggestive and stimulating. He writes with a light touch underpinned by unobtrusive scholarship, though occasionally the attempt to engage the general reader can be a little condescending (as in the use of italics to signpost the lines of argument). The book is divided into two parts, which respectively examine the origins and the after-life of Shakespeare's genius; and one thing this structure makes very clear is that it is impossible to approach the question of origins without coming via afterlife. At every point, from the anecdotes to the more formal biographies, the documentary records, the authorship controversy and the printed texts, the 'origins' are steeped in the dye of later mediations. Bate's strengths are his range and enthusiasm. He writes about old chestnuts like the identity of the young man of the Sonnets and whether the

plays were written by the man from Stratford in a way that emphasizes the endless fascination of these subjects even where the ground covered is well trodden. But Bate also has new suggestions to offer regarding the young man and the dark lady of the Sonnets, though these seem to me the areas of the book least likely to convince academic readers. Bravely, the book seeks to tackle the question of genius head-on, but the argument that the sheer variety and pervasiveness of Shakespeare's survival is evidence of his genius doesn't take us very far. In arriving, via Empson and Wittgenstein in the last chapter, at 'aspectuality' and 'performativity' as the laws of the Shakespearian universe, Bate seems to say that it is ambiguity that defines genius, and survival that proves its presence. It would, however, be equally logical to argue that ambiguity creates the conditions for survival, but that neither ambiguity nor survival has any necessary connection with genius, whatever that is. But this is not a book that stands or falls by the extent to which its arguments about genius persuade. Its force lies in the range and richness of individual chapters rather than in its overall shape. Bate is excellent at describing and comparing how and why specific appropriations of Shakespeare have emerged out of particular times and places and at making us pay attention to cultural specificity. Above all, it makes that paying attention a pleasurable experience.

Shakespeare's Storytellers is a fertile study of an area that Barbara Hardy identifies as characterized by a general lack of critical interest. Her interest is in the variety of narrative forms Shakespeare uses in his plays and the different ways they function. Her observations are sharp and to the point, densely packed and concisely expressed. Building on apparently simple points, she explores the wider implications of narrative within dramatic structures. Beginning, for example, from the recognition that a 'narrative injunction' (that is, the command to tell a story) appears at the end of a majority of the plays, she notes its different effects in tragedy and comedy: its intensification of the tragic in the first and its creation of a sense of the play continuing offstage in comedy. Close attention to narrative yields insights not only about genre but about individual plays: where *King Lear*, for example, is singled out by its inclusion of a rare kind of story projecting into the future ('We two alone will sing like birds i'th' cage . . .'), the significant factor about narrative in *Macbeth* is that the play lacks the 'characteristically Shakespearian closing invocation of narrative order'.

In his book, *Poetic Will*, David Willbern seeks to 'rescue' Shakespeare from the 'limitations and distortions of dramatic performance', in order to reclaim the fullest possible implications of his poetic language. His approach illustrates a psychoanalytic methodology at its most sophisticated and persuasive. The sketch of his thesis summarized in his prologue as 'will = unconscious = (female) sexuality' is initially off-putting, but its working out in practice is playful, richly suggestive and much less schematic than this suggests. And though psychoanalysis is much more dominant in Willbern's approach than in the work of Patricia Parker or Harry Berger, his strategies for close reading are not dissimilar. He offers, in his own terms, 'an erotics of reading Shakespeare' and sees his analysis as one that consciously tests the limits not only of language and sexuality but also of criticism. This attention to limits means that Willbern is always anticipating potential rebuttals and playing with the back-and-forth of argument in exploratory and illuminating ways. Despite his explicit rejection of performance as limiting, some of his readings are more closely tied to performance than to the written text. The opening pun on 'Know/No' in *King Lear*, for example, is unlikely to be noticed in a silent reading of the text, and Willbern admits that it was first brought to his attention by Scofield's delivery of the line with a pause after 'Know' in Brook's film of the play. Furthermore, in its preoccupation with circles, zeros and sounded 'o's, this chapter almost

inevitably encounters the replication of the circle in the material shape of Elizabethan amphitheatres. The return of the repressed, perhaps?

Much less persuasive in its attempt to banish performance is David Lowenthal's *Shakespeare and the Good Life*, which aims to get rid of most critics too. Here the basic premise is that 'reason, not imagination, is the deepest source of [Shakespeare's] work', though Lowenthal suggests that it is not surprising if we fail to penetrate these rational depths, since Shakespeare 'generally sought to conceal, rather than reveal, his own systematic thought or philosophy'. And as if the difficulty of deducing Shakespeare's rational thought-system were not enough in itself, Lowenthal goes on to argue, we must face the 'new and more formidable barriers' put in our path by recent critics. Four critical barriers are then listed, climaxing in the supposedly misguided view 'that Shakespeare wrote primarily for the stage rather than the study, from which it would follow that he wrote his plays for instant appreciation on the stage and avoided placing anything deep or complicated in them'. Lowenthal, however, rejects the need to cite the work of other critics, since he sees himself as 'striking out on new paths', taking as his models the work of A. C. Bradley and Harold C. Goddard. It may be this cavalier approach to other scholars' work which leads him to suppose that *King Lear* predates the history plays and that *Othello* predates *The Merchant of Venice*, assumptions so far from the mainstream that one would expect them to merit some defence, though none is offered. Nor does Lowenthal offer any explanation for the sequence of his chapters, which discuss the plays in apparently random order, beginning with *The Tempest* and ending with *A Midsummer Night's Dream*. There is no need, of course, to discuss plays in chronological order, but one looks for some rationale to emerge if it is not made explicit. The book is of a kind Shakespeare's plays seem to stimulate with some regularity, adopting an approach that masquerades as mere good sense, while dismissing all that goes before it with lofty assurance.

The title of Heather James's book, *Shakespeare's Troy*, suggests a somewhat narrower scope than the book really covers. Its subtitle, *Drama, Politics, and the Translation of Empire*, gives a clearer sense of its concern with appropriating and remaking the authority of classical texts. James is interested in Virgil, Augustan ideology and Ovidian refusals of their terms, and her focus is not on the traditionally grouped 'Roman' plays, but on a development running from *Titus Andronicus*, through *Troilus and Cressida* and *Antony and Cleopatra*, to *Cymbeline* and *The Tempest*. In them she sees Shakespeare 'undoing and regluing the idea of England in terms of authoritative books on England's cultural market', as well as exploring the legitimacy of a developing national theatre within that wider context. It is the contaminations of myth to which the book keeps returning: Tamora's appearance as Astraea, Troilus' failure to die, Cloten's headless body (with its implicit echo of the fallen, headless Priam); and these contaminations, James argues, demonstrate a deliberate intervention to contest the ideological authority the myths carry, an intervention begun under Augustus Caesar himself by Ovid. James knows her chosen area well and her study repeatedly illuminates broader questions, such as the function of women in the plays, or points up surprising general observations, such as the prominence of books at moments of crisis. The chapter on *Titus* offers a new perspective on the play which, if not totally persuasive, certainly demands further consideration, and the chapter on *Cymbeline* shows how far James's particular avenue of approach can go in illuminating difficult areas of the play. The chapter on *The Tempest* seems to me most resistant to the general shape of the argument. Its closing sentence, arguing from the evidence of the play's epilogue that the play 'aligns the theater with constitutional theory that derives the royal

authority from the people, who technically have the right to withdraw their consent and leave the prince stranded on a desert island' demonstrates the strain. But, the disappointment of this closure aside, this is a revealing and stimulating book with an important case to argue.

David Hillman takes up the same question as James in his essay on *Troilus and Cressida*, 'The Gastric Epic', pondering why Shakespeare chose to write on such overdetermined subject matter as the Troy story. The very multiplicity of its reworkings, he argues, makes its heroes 'deeply textual', inextricable from earlier literary versions. Hillman looks again at the play's disgust with the body and argues that its primary interest is in relations between language and the body. Its thrust, he suggests, is not so much against the body as leading back into it, and that return, he proposes, implies a corresponding distrust of language.

Jodi Mikalachki's project in *The Legacy of Boadicea* further complements Heather James's unravelling of the Roman contribution to the making of English nationhood. Her aim is to uncover the basis of the English preference for Roman over pre-Roman Britain in sixteenth-century attempts to recover native origins. The problem, she argues, is that pre-Roman British history emerges as barbaric, not least in the prominence of powerful and rebellious women amongst its figures of authority. Early modern historiographers thus commonly construct British history in terms of a gendered struggle between savage female excess and a masculinist Roman hierarchy. Mikalachki's opening chapter looks at the development from early chorographic texts that conceived of the land through a feminine iconography to the strongly masculinist rhetoric of the state as figured in Hobbes's *Leviathan* in the mid-seventeenth century. The chapter concludes with a study of the counter-example offered by Margaret Cavendish's *Blazing World*. The next two chapters look at *King Lear* and *Cymbeline* respectively. The argument, as reduced to its simplest terms by Mikalachki herself, is that 'Cymbeline is a "romance" because it incorporates "Romans"', while 'Lear . . . is a tragedy because it is inescapably locked in the *huis clos* of pre-Roman Britain'. The chapter on *Lear* is full of fascinating material, exploring the play via contemporary cartography and cosmography, comparison with Rastell's *Four Elements* and an extended meditation on the place of Dover at the intersection of history and topography. The conclusions are perhaps overstated but the journey towards them is instructive. The final chapter returns to consider representations of Boadicea within the fuller context of the gender anxiety outlined in preceding chapters, and followed up here with particular reference to questions of gender reversal and female rule.

The central argument of Cynthia Lewis's *Particular Saints*, that characters called Antonio and Sebastian, specifically in Shakespeare's *Merchant of Venice*, *Twelfth Night*, *Antony and Cleopatra* and *The Tempest*, consistently look back to St Antony and St Sebastian, is difficult to accept, particularly since Mark Antony's name, as Lewis recognizes, is determined by history rather than by Shakespeare. Antonios, Lewis argues, are characteristically fools for love; but this aspect of her thesis also presents problems, since the Antonio of *The Tempest* is consumed by hate. To be fair, Lewis openly acknowledges and tries to confront these difficulties, but it is hard to avoid the sense that the result is special pleading. The book also tends generally to overstate Christian parallels in the plays. Where psychoanalytical criticism has a tendency to overplay sexuality, this study pulls in the opposite direction, underplaying the sexual element in relationships on account of its determination to see love, particularly on the part of characters named Antonio, as manifestations of Christian charity. (Both Lewis and Yu Jin Ko, in 'The Comic Close of *Twelfth Night* and Viola's *Noli me tangere*', see the moment at which Viola defers Orsino's embrace as an echo of Christ's warning to Mary Magdalene in the

Garden of Gethsemane.) Yet there is much that is useful and perceptive in Lewis's book. She is particularly acute, for example, on uncertainties of tone in *Antony and Cleopatra*; but her sharpest observations, it seems to me, are often those least directly associated with the overall argument.

In reviewing Lisa Hopkins's *The Shakespearian Marriage*, I should admit straight away to an instinctive hostility towards books that work through all or most of the canon play by play. The relevance of the book's subtitle, *Merry Wives and Heavy Husbands*, moreover, did not seem to me to be demonstrated. Having said that, the sense of argument, though not an argument concerning merry wives and heavy husbands, is strongest in the later chapters of the book. The way in which the tragedies problematize marriage, for example, or the history plays focus on its political importance, emerges clearly. In the chapters on the comedies, however, the observations on individual plays seem curiously cut off from one another. Thus, in the chapter entitled 'What Makes a Marriage', for example, Hopkins concentrates on unseasonality in *Love's Labour's Lost*, food imagery in *Much Ado* and rampant fertility in *Measure for Measure*, and it is hard to see what holds the chapter together. She often illuminates the focus of a play by calling attention to a single striking feature, such as the consuming interest in marrying above or below one's station in *Twelfth Night* or the 'continuity of motherhood' in *All's Well*, but the observation is left undeveloped. The survey approach, nevertheless, does demonstrate the validity of Hopkins's conclusion that: 'Where the ultimate insult is "bastard", marriage must always be the transcendental authenticator.'

Nicholas Marsh's study of the tragedies in the Macmillan series, *Analysing Texts*, provides an excellent student introduction to the four 'great' tragedies. Though the book appears to be aimed in the first instance at sixth-form students, with the introduction and suggestions for further reading targeting absolute beginners, everything in between is entirely suitable for an undergraduate audience. Indeed, university students coming from schools where the teaching is less well informed and thorough than Marsh's would do well to read this short book as a way of both disabusing themselves of unhelpful approaches (Marsh incorporates useful and constructive caveats about the dangers of giving static accounts of characters, thinking of characters as real people, dismissing humour in the tragedies as 'comic relief', approaching the tragic hero via half-baked Aristotelian theory) and familiarizing themselves with a range of good practice. The book is divided into two parts, of which the first and more substantial is devoted to close reading and analysis and the second to context and criticism. Each chapter in part I follows the same model, beginning with analyses of brief extracts from each of the four tragedies, summarizing conclusions, explicitly reviewing methods of analysis and offering suggestions for further work. This may sound reductive, but it is not. Into this framework Marsh packs clearly and concisely formulated arguments, shows how he derives them from the texts and leads student-readers to build on knowledge accumulated chapter by chapter. Part II uses a mere fifty pages to introduce readers to the canonical and historical contexts of the plays and to a few selected critical approaches. I know of no other short introductory book which hands students the critical tools more helpfully without becoming banal or reductive.

Several useful anthologies have appeared this year. The most general and wide-ranging of these is the collection of twenty-six essays in honour of E. A. J. Honigmann gathered together under the title *Shakespearian Continuities*. The essays are grouped into four sections: Shakespeare and his Predecessors; Shakespeare and his Contemporaries; Shakespeare in Performance; and Shakespeare and Later Writers. Oddly, given the span of Honigmann's work, there is no section on editing or textual matters, though R. A. Foakes does contribute his

thoughts 'On Finishing a Commentary on *King Lear*', placed in the third section because of the visible shift in recent editing practice generally towards taking more account of staging. The subject matter ranges widely, and the essays are generally thoughtful, lively and concise. Essays in the first section consider Shakespeare's sources, with Brian Vickers offering particularly interesting parallels between *The Mirror for Magistrates* and the chorus in *Henry V*. Philip Edwards's rich study of the topos of underwater transformation and its associations with restoration, persons and personality stands out in the second section, while in the third R. S. White usefully extends Margot Heinemann's exploration of shared concerns between Brecht and Shakespeare, and G. K. Hunter offers some sharp observations on common ground between Hollywood and the Elizabethan theatre. Contributions to part IV range from N. E. Osselton's comparative study of the glossing of Shakespeare and Judith Hawley's analysis of the different ways eighteenth-century women read Shakespeare to considerations of Shelley, Ruskin, Strindberg, Angela Carter and the many remakings of Falstaff. The section closes with the late Kenneth Muir's observations on 'base uses', or misappropriations, of Shakespeare. The book itself has a poetic coda: a set of poems by Desmond Graham, imagining versions of Shakespearian characters in modern-day Newcastle, and Honigmann's own poem, 'A Book-Binder's Grumble'. Honigmann's poem rounds off the volume with a nice irony, ruminating on Shakespeare as a 'wordy man'

> Who missed his market, who might have been
> A Silver-Tongued Smith, a Dean of St Paul's,
> If only he'd known how the round world rolls
> And had studied good books, and had loved
>   men's souls.

Michele Marrapodi's collection, *The Italian World of English Renaissance Drama*, groups its contributions into the two areas indicated by the subtitle: cultural exchange and intertextuality. Both parts are full of interesting material, exploring a range of influence from the late classical period, through the Middle Ages, to the Renaissance. In part I I found Viviana Comensoli's study of the significance of music in *Othello* within the context of *The Book of the Courtier*, A. J. Hoenselaars's unfamiliar slant on Machiavelli by way of English appropriations of his 'Novella di Belfagor Arcidiavolo' and J. R. Mulryne's argument that the London of *Women Beware Women* is shaped by Middleton's understanding of the 'myth of Florence' especially rewarding. Comensoli's essay is the only one to focus on Shakespeare in part I, but part II contains two good pieces on *Much Ado* by Leo Salingar and Juliet Dusinberre. Salingar argues that Shakespeare turns a source-story which in all versions centres upon slander and masquerade into an exploration of the larger issue of social communication itself, while Dusinberre examines parallels between the character of Benedick and the expressed attitudes of Sir John Harington, translator of Ariosto's version of the Hero/Claudio story in *Orlando Furioso*. Both, she suggests, may be seen as figures who paradoxically prove their underlying honesty by their capacity to turn and turn again. Other essays widen the focus: Robert Henke and Keir Elam both build on work reviewed here last year and the year before (Henke on his book, *Pastoral Transformations*, and Elam on his study of 'The Fertile Eunuch'); Robert Miola looks at the Italian setting of the Quarto text of *Every Man in His Humour*; Michele Marrapodi pursues the popularity in English Renaissance drama of the Italianate motif of revenge; and Zara Bruzzi argues a more specific and to my mind less persuasive case than Mulryne with regard to parallels between *Women Beware Women* and contemporary Florence.

Ronald Knowles's collection, *Shakespeare and Carnival*, is, the blurb points out, 'the first collection to assess a range of Shakespeare's plays in relation to the theory of carnivalesque'. This comes as something of a surprise, given the dominance of Bakhtin in the western critical tradition over the last fifteen years or so. This collection, however, manages both to address the beginner, by including, for example, an excellent brief introduction to Bakhtin's life and work, and to represent the sophistication and variety of work done following Bakhtin. Several essays particularly emphasize the point that Bakhtin was not the first or only person to think about carnival, and pointedly acknowledge Bakhtin's important forebears: the first part of David Wiles's essay on 'The Carnivalesque in *A Midsummer Night's Dream*' offers a wonderfully brief and clear outline of approaches from Plato onwards, and Anthony Gash emphasizes the central importance of Erasmus for subsequent understandings of folly. There is also widespread attention to the crucial distinction between conceiving of carnival as a safety valve or, as Bakhtin does, in Utopian terms. Falstaff is the focus of three very different approaches by François Laroque, Kristen Poole and Jonathan Hall, and the history plays constitute the dominant genre under consideration. The last two essays offer particularly illuminating ways of thinking about Shakespeare in relation to carnival: Anthony Gash argues that carnival borders on the sacred, illustrating his thesis via *The Winter's Tale* and *Measure for Measure*, while Gordon McMullan demonstrates the centrality of a process of 'dialogic degradation' to the meanings made by *Henry VIII*. As these and other essays demonstrate, Bakhtinian analysis need not and should not concentrate only on fools and clowns.

It is worth mentioning Harry Berger's essay, 'The Prince's Dog: Falstaff and the Perils of Speech-Prefixity', alongside Knowles's collection. Published in *Shakespeare Quarterly*, it engages with questions of carnival from yet another angle, opening up significant methodological issues along the way. The thesis in relation to Falstaff is basically that Falstaff actively seeks out and co-operates in his own rejection, and in pursuing this thesis in dialogue with other critics Berger gives detailed consideration to an earlier published version of

Kristen Poole's essay (in the Knowles collection); but underpinning the localized exploration of how Falstaff functions within the Henriad is a complex and densely argued meditation on what a dramatic speaker is. Berger's arguments are always reduced by the attempt to condense them, but the theoretical interest of this piece lies in its careful teasing out of the dramatic speaker's object status from his/her subject status. 'When critics . . . transform the speech prefix into a speaker and a subject, the subject is dissociated from the speaker; the real subject is not the character but the playwright, the actor, the audience, or the culture – whatever is presumed to speak through the character.' There is, then, 'no presence on the other side of the representational meaning of speech, only a speech prefix'.

The focus of *Shakespeare Survey 50* is on language. John Kerrigan's richly contextualized piece on the importance of secrecy and gossip in *Twelfth Night* makes one wonder why these topics have not been central to discussion of the play before now, and Meredith Skura contributes an interesting essay on how Shakespeare responds to Marlowe's *Edward II*, sublimating its sex and violence into language and imagery, while keeping them out of the plot. Her discussion centres mainly on *Richard II*, but she also glances at echoes of *Edward II* in *Hamlet* and *The Comedy of Errors*. John Astington insists on some very important caveats with regard to interpreting early illustrations that may seem to bear on staging practice and makes a plea for further research on the range of material factors relevant to these pictures necessary to prevent us making false assumptions about their relevance to dramatic texts.

Critical anthologies on *As You Like It* and *Richard II* have appeared this year in the Garland Shakespeare Criticism series and Athlone Press's Shakespeare: The Critical Tradition series respectively. Though Tomarken's collection on *As You Like It* claims to cover the period from 1600 to the present, while Forker's on *Richard II* includes only material written

1780–1920, the difference in range between the two collections is less pronounced than these avowed parameters would seem to indicate. Tomarken notes the absence of any recorded productions of *As You Like It* before 1740 and includes only four pieces dating to before 1780. A peculiarity of his selection is that he includes no critical work published between 1944 and 1996, and the single, previously unpublished, 1996 piece, by Margaret Maurer, looks at the eighteenth century, examining Pope's edition and Johnson's *Love in a Forest*. Some more recent material is included in the Reviews section, but this gives the reader little sense of the directions of critical thinking on the play over the last half-century. Tomarken includes a brief survey of recent criticism in his introduction, but this hardly substitutes for the opportunity to sample the important work by Empson, Barber, Frye, Montrose and others that he mentions in passing. Forker's introduction covers the same period in almost as much detail, despite the fact that his selection excludes it. Two of the pre-1780 texts Tomarken includes, however, are particularly useful: the complete text of Charles Johnson's adaptation of *As You Like It*, *Love in a Forest*, published in 1723, and Samuel Johnson's text and notes, published in 1765. This fullness is in line with the expressed aim of the series to reprint material in its entirety as far as possible. Forker, by contrast, chops and edits many extracts, but offers a more user-friendly format, including dates throughout the contents, critical headnotes on the authors of his selections and three separate indexes. Whatever the omissions, and those are inevitable in any anthology, both books are rich resources, well produced.

Robert Miola's collection of critical essays on *The Comedy of Errors* demonstrates the seeming capacity of this play to entertain all manner of critical approaches without necessarily revealing contradiction, and contributors almost all comment on this multifaceted quality of the play. The two earliest essays reprinted here highlight it (Coleridge calls it 'poetical farce', while G. R. Elliott calls it 'weirdness'), and later pieces generally exemplify the shift from a critical mode that sees this as incoherence to one that is more prone to see it as the pointed bringing together of differences (farce with romance, classicism with medievalism, paganism with Christianity, and so on). The volume displays a recurrent emphasis on sources, often looking to the disparity of the sources as a route into assessing the play's own heterogeneity. The essays seem to mesh together, expanding on aspects of the detail of one large enterprise. Louise Clubb argues that mixedness is a characteristic already visible in Italian *commedia grave*, a likely influence; Candido argues that it is already inherent in Plautus. Alexander Leggatt's study of the mix of styles is usefully extended by Arthur Kinney. Barbara Freedman recasts the collision in psychological terms, using Freud's terminology to name what she finds resistant to a unified reading as 'the uncanny', and Brennan O'Donnell links even the plurality of metrical styles to loss of identity. The cumulative sense of the volume is not one of tired repetition, but rather of the gradual mounting of a shared argument demonstrating the play's tense relations with its source materials, its concern with identity and its insistent doubleness. About a third of the collection is devoted to reviews of performance. This is a useful feature of the book; but it is a pity that the last review printed sums up the play as 'not particularly deep but very clever', after so many contributors have argued for a depth beyond mere cleverness.

Three volumes on Shakespeare have so far been published in the Writers and their Work series published by Northcote House in association with the British Council. The format of these is short and unpretentious, clearly targeting a student audience and supplying commented bibliography as well as an introduction to the play. Terence Hawkes's volume on *King Lear*, published in 1995, makes an excellent beginning. He offers his chapters as a group of linked seminar discussions, in which

he ranges across an impressively wide terrain with a surprising amount of detail and quotation for such a short book. Hawkes is engaging and accessible without being reductive or patronizing, and constantly encourages students to become aware of the critical methodologies that operate in any given analysis of the play, with the result that his book is as helpful on recognizing and describing particular theoretical approaches as it is on the play. Ann Thompson and Neil Taylor's study of *Hamlet* covers the play from many of the same angles as Hawkes's study of *Lear*, taking into account textual matters, canonicity, the uses of history, gender issues and the play's 'afterlife' both on the stage and in critical discourse. Though useful, this volume is less fun to read than Hawkes's strongly personalized approach, and the introduction of other critics into the discussion is sometimes awkward. Helen Hackett's book on *A Midsummer Night's Dream* differs from these two in being more selective. Taking the changeling as its starting point, it focuses first on exchange and transformation and moves through consideration of love, female power, nature and supernature. As this outline suggests, the approach is oriented towards themes and images, though a separate chapter also looks at the play on stage and film.

Another book devoted to one play and presumably aimed at a student audience is H. F. Coursen's *Macbeth: A Guide to the Play*, but one of the problems with this publication is precisely that of target audience. The opening chapter surveying editions is evidently not aimed at scholars: one sentence covers the Arden and New Variorum editions, while a page is devoted to the Everyman Shakespeare. Yet the chapter on themes (which is almost entirely given over to religious issues) assumes a basic understanding of Calvinism, election and Arminianism. More serious than the problem of audience, however, is a basic contradiction at the heart of the enterprise. Intended, according to the preface, as 'a systematic and objective reference work', the book organizes its chapters by topic headings which are predominantly by definition interpretive: dramatic structure, themes and critical approaches, for example. Coursen acknowledges in the preface that 'no discussion of responses to this or any Shakespeare play can be neutral', but the disclaimer greatly understates the degree to which the book is not only interpretive but directive. Though some of its features, such as the list-like structure of chapters and the often flat tone, are suggestive of reference mode, opinion is also stated as if it had the status of fact. Surveying the history of performance, for example, Coursen pronounces: 'it is usually a mistake for a director to place a production precisely in a modern context'. Belatedly, towards the end of his chapter on critical approaches, he admits to pursuing an 'essentialist thesis' in this book. Though one might admire the openness of this stance, it is hardly compatible with the claim to offer an objective reference work.

Much more work is devoted to *King Lear* and *Othello* than to *Macbeth*, as has been characteristic over recent years, but more surprising is the relative sparsity of *Hamlet* criticism this year. Work on *Lear* is most notable. Judy Kronenfeld's *King Lear and the Naked Truth* returns to the much-studied theme of clothing and nakedness in the play. Underpinned by a theoretical framework that Kronenfeld describes as 'extensionist semantics', the book centres on the close study of a few crucially important quotations, used by other critics to argue for or against particular politics or value-systems inherent in the play. Kronenfeld takes a hard look at the precise vocabulary of these verbal cruces within the context of their wider contemporary semantic field, drawing from a range of texts, but especially those of religious controversy, and forcefully demonstrating the need to look beyond anachronistic assumptions about meaning at the detail of cultural struggle. Anglicans and Puritans, she shows, can often wrest their words and images into uncharacteristic shapes in mounting the argument against their opponents, and the easy assumption that, for example, the naked is morally superior to the clothed, has to be situated within the richer environment of texts and emblems that reveal a far more conflicted set of ideas. Kronenfeld argues strongly against critics who wish to enlist *King Lear* for radical religious or political agendas. While terms like 'plainness' and 'truth', she argues, 'have the potential to become politically charged in specific contexts, they also participate in broadly shared frameworks that permit non-partisan readings'. This is a sensible caveat, and one that no doubt needs emphasizing in the present critical climate. On the other hand, such 'good sense' carried too far can have the effect of erasing the possibility of radical texts. Too much emphasis on the broad framework can blind us to what is going on at the edges, as all the old arguments against Tillyard's Elizabethan world-picture insist. The broad sense in which words are used and understood within a culture is never the only sense, and there has to be a space in which new and radical meanings, pushing new and radical political agendas, can emerge. Though Kronenfeld, quoted above, recognizes that specific contexts can produce a political charge, it is the shared framework rather than the specific context in which she is primarily interested. The most obvious specific context in which the words of a play may take on sharp and particular meanings is of course performance, which is not an area within this book's scope. But the point is one that should not be ignored. To try to resolve, as Kronenfeld does through the study of language use, whether a text is or is not to be understood as radical, is to essentialize that text and ultimately to deny the processes by which language and culture change.

Michael Holahan, in '"Look, her lips": Softness of Voice, Construction of Character in *King Lear*', argues for subjectivity as emerging most clearly in the play not via the apparent interior of any one character, but 'in the intervals disclosed by the verbal response of one character to another's silence'. Oddly, however, Holahan wants to attack 'theory' for its insistence on dramatic character as constructed while at the same time mounting a powerful demonstration of one of its specific modes of construction here. In a brief piece on 'Anglo-Saxon Elements of the Gloucester Sub-Plot in *King Lear*', Tony Perrello examines some suggestive parallels between *King Lear* and the chaos in Anglo-Saxon Wessex following the quarrel over the succession between the legitimate and illegitimate sons of Edgar, who died in 975. Amy Wolf returns to the question of the play's engagement with Samuel Harsnett's writing in order to argue that *Lear* offers a critique of Harsnett by resituating his cynical exposures of fraudulent demoniacs within a context of real suffering and madness. The essay comes perilously close to arguing that *Lear* is centrally about Harsnett.

Criticism of *Othello* remains primarily focused on race. Julia Lupton, in 'Othello Circumcised: Shakespeare and the Pauline Discourse of Nations', argues for circumcision rather than skin colour as the ultimate sign of Othello's otherness, since circumcision simultaneously allies Muslims with Jews and differentiates them from both pagans and Christians. For Ian Smith, in 'Barbarian Errors', eloquence is central to racial definition, and Othello's linguistic performance initially enacts a claim to cultural whiteness; but that performance of eloquence is vulnerable to a collapse engineered by Iago in a racial reversal that questions, Smith argues, 'the supposed discreteness of racial categories'. In 'The Arabization of *Othello*' Ferial Ghazoul reviews a century of the play's history in the Arab world, looking at translations, criticism, adaptations and the play as intertext and showing how the play has repeatedly been used to confront issues of self and other. Camille Wells Slights's 'Slaves and Subjects in *Othello*' provides a variation on the dominant racial focus, looking at the simultaneous emergence of English awareness of slavery and new ways of thinking about the self, and arguing that the two preoccupations, with slaves and subjects, are interdependent.

Moving away from race altogether, Andrew Sofer turns to props, and in particular to the handkerchief. Sofer's phenomenological reading of the way the prop functions, its 'oscillation between sign and thing', is productive, but his conclusion that the play may be read as 'a witty and disturbing meditation on the magical properties of props' seems to me to reduce the possibility of responding to the play as tragedy. It is surely not ultimately or most centrally *about* either the handkerchief or the status of props. Sofer pursues his interest in props more widely in a piece entitled 'The Skull on the Renaissance Stage'. Here he formulates the doubleness of props slightly differently, seeing their capacity to function as both live attributes and dead objects as having the potential to set the spectator, quite literally, 'on edge'. Critics intent on the emblematic quality of Yorick's skull, for example, he argues, miss a special quality of irony in the scene.

Apart from Hackett's study of *A Midsummer Night's Dream*, the only book-length study of a comedy I was sent for review this year was Lawrence Ross's extended essay on *Measure for Measure*. Unlike *The Comedy of Errors*, which seems to accommodate so many critical approaches without them cancelling each other out, this play, Ross suggests, may function as a touchstone for critical methodology itself. Ross, like Lowenthal, is dismissive of other critics, but unlike him, places great emphasis on performance, ranking attention to dramaturgy and scenic structure high in his critical priorities. He insists (rightly, I think) on the non-existence of Act 3, scene 2, arguing that the Duke and the Provost remain hidden on stage throughout. Ross's emphasis on performance includes a special interest in costume which overlaps with Andrew Gurr's exploration of '*Measure for Measure*'s Hoods and Masks'. While Ross visualizes Isabella dressed as a nun, however, Gurr argues a strong case for Isabella wearing secular dress throughout the play, including quite probably the black velvet mask of a gentlewoman, and proposes a symmetrical progress towards unmasking on the part of both Isabella and the Duke. Surprisingly, perhaps, he does not consider at precisely what point Isabella unmasks. If he is right about Isabella's costume, however, then her acceptance of the Duke might be represented, via the same emblematic symmetry, by her unmasking to look directly in the Duke's own, now unmasked, face. Alternatively, of course, rejection might be enacted by a refusal to unmask at all. This is the point of view adopted by Jessica Slights and Michael Holmes, whose essay, 'Isabella's Order', argues that Isabella's spiritual desires empower her to resist the Duke's offer of marriage.

Some of the general issues raised by books reviewed above are taken up more widely. Marriage, for instance, is the subject of several essays. Sid Ray proposes that questions of marriage, in particular the focus on marital consent, in *Titus Andronicus* are in fact a way of exploring nonconsensual government. Laurie Shannon, in 'Emilia's Argument: Friendship and "Human Title" in *The Two Noble Kinsmen*', argues that the play uses marriage as a figure for unreasonable rule and questions the characteristically male friendship usually offered in other literature of the period as a paradigm of resistance to such oppression by substituting for it ideal relations between women, as expressed through a common bond of chastity. Emily Detner, in 'Civilizing Subordination: Domestic Violence and *The Taming of the Shrew*', argues that the *Shrew* constitutes a shift towards a more 'modern' way of managing the subordination of wives by legitimizing non-physical domination. Detner's reading of the play through the 'Stockholm syndrome' (whereby hostages bond with their captors) seems to require us to erase the differences between the structured fiction of the play and actual social situations and turns into a somewhat awkward exercise in political correctness, whereby Detner as teacher sees her role as giving students 'the tools to resist reading as an abuser'.

More nuanced feminist readings appear in essays by Cynthia Marshall, Jyotsna Singh and Laura Levine in the collection *Feminist Readings of Early Modern Culture*, edited by Valerie Traub and others. Marshall's 'Wound-man: *Coriolanus*, Gender, and the Theatrical Construction of Interiority' works in the same territory as Coppélia Kahn's *Roman Shakespeare*, reviewed here last year; Singh examines race and gender conflicts in *The Tempest* through Caliban and Miranda; while Levine's, the most original piece, looks at the conjunction of theatrical transformation and sexual violence in *A Midsummer Night's Dream*. Kathryn Schwartz's 'Fearful Simile' also takes up the concerns of another feminist study reviewed here last year, Jean Howard and Phyllis Rackin's *Engendering a Nation*. She argues that the spectacles of female agency visible in the first tetralogy are less the symptoms than the cause of the dissolution of male bonds in these plays. Two companion pieces in *New Theatre Quarterly* study contemporary feminist theatre playing, or playing with, Shakespeare. Jane de Gay, building on a suggestion by Lorraine Helms for recuperating the women's parts in Shakespeare, looks at Bryony Lavery's *Ophelia* and Jane Prendergast's *I, Hamlet*, while Teresa Dobson looks at Beau Coleman's *Queen Lear*.

New Comedy, which receives a good deal of attention in both Marrapodi's *The Italian World of English Renaissance Drama* and Miola's collection on *The Comedy of Errors*, is also the subject of 'The Many Masks of Parolles' by R. J. Schork, which argues for adding the clever slave and the pimp to the range of types contributing to the characterization of Parolles. *Much Ado About Nothing*, also prominent in Marrapodi's collection, is the subject of two further essays. Courtney Lehmann, in a piece entitled '*Much Ado About Nothing*: Shakespeare, Branagh and the "National-Popular" in the age of Multinational Capital' exploring Branagh's characteristically postmodern 'quilting' between high and low cultures, argues that the casting of Denzel Washington as Don Pedro represents the faultline in the film's determination to universalize and deterritorialize the play, 'the point at which Branagh's "collective project" slides into hey nonny nonsense'; and Stephen Dobranski, in 'Children of the Mind: Miscarried Narratives in *Much Ado About Nothing*', explores hints of a fragmentary relationship between Beatrice and Benedick before the play opens.

Other work on the comedies usefully extends existing scholarship. Shakespeare's debt to Golding's Ovid is reassessed by Madeleine Forey, who argues that Golding is a more conspicuous presence in *A Midsummer Night's Dream* than has hitherto been acknowledged, and that Shakespeare's tone of parodic irreverence is in part a response to Golding's serious-minded anxiety about his material, as expressed in his preface. Mary Crane's 'Linguistic change, Theatrical Practice, and the Ideologies of Status in *As You Like It*' takes up some of the concerns of David Wiles's recent work on Shakespeare's clowns. The play, she argues, repeatedly gestures towards the absence of Kemp and his jigs in a way that exposes a deep-rooted ambivalence around issues of social status and upward mobility. Mary Janell Metzger's essay on *The Merchant of Venice*, picking up from James Shapiro's explorations of the Jew in English Renaissance culture, argues that more attention needs to be paid to the difference between Jessica and Shylock as alternative constructions of Jewishness within the play. Nora Johnson's 'Body and Spirit, Stage and Sexuality in *The Tempest*' uses the body more thoughtfully than much existing published work to think through contemporary objections to the performing body (as opposed to the dramatic text) and to argue for Prospero's failure to rescue theatre from its associations with illicit desire and the undoing of identity.

Anxieties about theatre and issues of identity are also central to several essays on the tragedies. Dennis Kezar's essay, '*Julius Caesar* and the Properties of Shakespeare's Globe', argues for the dismemberment of Cinna the poet as a metatheatrical emblem of anxieties about theatre's appropriation of its subjects as spectacles and the potential dangers of an audience's response to such appropriations. The essay further seeks to locate this anxiety in the historical moment of the Globe's opening. Burton Hatlen, in 'The "Noble Thing" and the "Boy of Tears": *Coriolanus* and the Embarrassments of Identity', seeks to make links between the political, psychoanalytical and linguistic approaches that have identified and segregated recent critical work on the play. Centring on the topics of identity and shame, the essay uses all three methodologies to argue that the play demonstrates the impossibility of creating an autonomous subjectivity. Robert Appelbaum examines the issue of masculinity in *Romeo and Juliet* in a piece that is as much a meditation on the possibility of defining or even discussing such a thing as 'healthy masculinity' in the present academy as a study of *Romeo and Juliet*. Appelbaum uses the play as a test-case for the argument that Shakespearian tragedy is virtually by definition a tragedy of failed masculinity which nevertheless idealizes a notionally full masculinity as its principle of order.

The best piece on the histories this year is Harry Berger's essay on *Henry IV*, discussed above in relation to the subject of carnival, but two other pieces concentrating on plays in the second tetralogy offer new ways of thinking about them. In 'Speaking Freely about *Richard II*' Paula Blank makes the case for the play as practising self-censorship (whether or not Shakespeare self-censored the notorious deposition scene). She argues that the play is 'preoccupied with the way stories are written and rewritten' and that its real threat to Queen Elizabeth was not the representation of a monarch deposed but rather the other kinds of 'depositions', the testimonials against the king, inserted throughout the play. Cyndia Clegg, on the other hand, argues that the deposition scene was subject to press censorship, but not for any of the reasons usually put forward. In her view it is the play's representation of parliamentary authority in the deposition scene that made it unacceptable in the political climate following the publication of Robert Parsons's *A Conference about the Next Succession* in 1595. Richard Dutton's survey of 'Shakespeare and Lancaster' provides a careful study of the resonance of 'Lancaster' for a late sixteenth-century audience, highlighting the degree to which the Duchy of Lancaster functioned as a reminder that the monarchy was compromised after the reign of Richard II (and proposing that the second tetralogy should be read as succession plays.)

Nothing on the poems compares with Helen Vendler's work on the Sonnets, but Heather Dubrow notes the particular frequency of tropes of thieving in the Sonnets and examines them in the context of the flood of legislation on rogues and vagabonds in the period. She looks especially at Sonnets 35, 40, 48 and 92, and follows her analysis with a review of the state of critical studies on the early modern period. Stephen Booth argues for the unique-ness and inherent superiority of Shakespeare's language, using the Sonnets to demonstrate his case most fully; Emily Stockard looks at the sequence from 1–126 within the tradition of consolation literature and sceptical thought; and David Willbern writes especially perceptively on *The Rape of Lucrece* in *Poetic Will*.

WORKS REVIEWED

Appelbaum, Robert, '"Standing to the Wall": The Pressures of Masculinity in *Romeo and Juliet*', *Shakespeare Quarterly*, 48 (1997), 251–72.

Astington, John, 'Rereading Illustrations of the English Stage', *Shakespeare Survey 50* (1997), 151–70.

Batchelor, John, Tom Cain and Claire Lamont, eds., *Shakespearean Continuities: Essays in Honour of E. A. J. Honigmann* (Basingstoke, 1997).

Bate, Jonathan, *The Genius of Shakespeare* (London, 1997).

Berger Jr., Harry, 'The Prince's Dog: Falstaff and the Perils of Speech-Prefixity', *Shakespeare Quarterly*, 49 (1998), 40–73.

Blank, Paula, 'Speaking Freely about *Richard II*', *Journal of English and Germanic Philology*, 96, (1997), 327–48.

Booth, Stephen, 'Shakespeare's Language and the Language of Shakespeare's Time', *Shakespeare Survey 50* (1997), 1–18.

Clegg, Cyndia Susan, '"By the choise and inuitation of al the realme": *Richard II* and Elizabethan Press Censorship', *Shakespeare Quarterly*, 48 (1997), 432–48.

Coursen, H. R., *Macbeth: A Guide to the Play* (London, 1997).

Crane, Mary Thomas, 'Linguistic Change, Theatrical Practice, and the Ideologies of Status in *As You Like It*', *English Literary Renaissance*, 27 (1997), 361–92.

de Gay, Jane, 'Playing (with) Shakespeare: Bryony Lavery's "Ophelia" and Jane Prendergast's "I, Hamlet"', *New Theatre Quarterly*, 54 (1998), 125–38.

Detner, Emily, 'Civilizing Subordination: Domestic Violence and *The Taming of the Shrew*', *Shakespeare Quarterly*, 48 (1997), 273–94.

Dobranski, Stephen B., 'Children of the Mind: Miscarried Narratives in *Much Ado About Nothing*', *Studies in English Literature*, 38 (1998), 233–50.

Dobson, Teresa, '"High-Engender'd Battles": Gender and Power in "Queen Lear"', *New Theatre Quarterly*, 54 (1998), 139–45.

Dubrow, Heather, '"In thievish ways": Tropes and Robbers in Shakespeare's Sonnets and Early Modern England', *Journal of English and Germanic Philology*, 96 (1997), 514–44.

Dutton, Richard, 'Shakespeare and Lancaster', *Shakespeare Quarterly*, 49 (1998), 1–21.

Forey, Madeleine, '"Bless Thee, Bottom, Bless Thee! Thou Art Translated!": Ovid, Golding, and *A Midsummer Night's Dream*', *Modern Language Review*, 93 (1998), 321–9.

Forker, Charles R. ed., *Richard II* (London, 1998).

Ghazoul, Ferial J., 'The Arabization of *Othello*', *Comparative Literature*, 50 (1998), 1–31.

Gurr, Andrew, '*Measure for Measure*'s Hoods and Masks: the Duke, Isabella, and Liberty', *English Literary Renaissance*, 27 (1997), 89–105.

Hackett, Helen, *A Midsummer Night's Dream* (Plymouth, 1997).

Hardy, Barbara, *Shakespeare's Storytellers: Dramatic Narration* (London, 1997).

Hatlen, Burton, 'The "Noble Thing" and the "Boy of Tears": *Coriolanus* and the Embarrassments of Identity', *English Literary Renaissance*, 27 (1997), 393–420.

Hawkes, Terence, *King Lear* (Plymouth, 1995).

Hillman, David, 'The Gastric Epic: *Troilus and Cressida*', *Shakespeare Quarterly*, 48 (1997), 295–313.

Holahan, Michael, '"Look, her lips": Softness of Voice, Construction of Character in *King Lear*', *Shakespeare Quarterly*, 48 (1997), 406–31.

Hopkins, Lisa, *The Shakespearian Marriage: Merry Wives and Heavy Husbands* (Basingstoke, 1998).

James, Heather, *Shakespeare's Troy: Drama, Politics, and the Translation of Empire*. Cambridge Studies in Renaissance Literature and Culture, 22 (Cambridge, 1997).

Johnson, Nora, 'Body and Spirit, Stage and Sexuality in *The Tempest*', *English Literary History*, 64 (1997), 683–701.

Kerrigan, John, 'Secrecy and Gossip in *Twelfth Night*', *Shakespeare Survey 50* (1997), 65–80.

Kezar, Dennis, '*Julius Caesar* and the Properties of Shakespeare's Globe', *English Literary Renaissance*, 28 (1998), 18–46.

Knowles, Ronald, ed., *Shakespeare and Carnival: After Bakhtin*. Early Modern Literature in History (London, 1998).

Ko, Yu Jin, 'The Comic Close of *Twelfth Night* and Viola's *Noli me tangere*', *Shakespeare Quarterly*, 48 (1997), 391–405.

Kronenfeld, Judy, *King Lear and the Naked Truth: Rethinking the Language of Religion and Resistance* (London, 1998).

Lehmann, Courtney, '*Much Ado About Nothing*: Shakespeare, Branagh and the "National-Popular" in the age of Multinational Capital', *Textual Practice*, 12 (1998), 1–22.

Lewis, Cynthia, *Particular Saints: Shakespeare's Four Antonios, Their Contexts, and Their Plays* (London, 1997).

Lowenthal, David, *Shakespeare and the Good Life: Ethics and Politics in Dramatic Form* (Oxford, 1997).

Lupton, Julia Reinhard, 'Othello Circumcised: Shakespeare and the Pauline Discourse of Nations', *Representations*, 57 (1997), 73–89.

Marrapodi, Michele, ed., *The Italian World of English Renaissance Drama: Cultural Exchange and Intertextuality* (London, 1998).

Marsh, Nicholas, *Shakespeare: The Tragedies*, Analysing Texts (London, 1998).

Metzger, Mary Janell, '"Now by My Hood, a Gentile and No Jew": Jessica, *The Merchant of Venice*, and the Discourse of Early Modern English Identity', *PMLA*, 113 (1998), 52–63.

Mikalachki, Jodi, *The Legacy of Boadicea: Gender and Nation in Early Modern England* (London, 1998).

Miola, Robert, ed., *The Comedy of Errors: Critical Essays* (London, 1997).

Perrello, Tony, 'Anglo-Saxon Elements of the Gloucester Sub-Plot in *King Lear*', *English Language Notes*, 35 (1997), 10–16.

Ray, Sid, '"Rape, I fear, was root of thy annoy": The Politics of Consent in *Titus Andronicus*', *Shakespeare Quarterly*, 49 (1998), 22–39.

Ross, Lawrence J., *On Measure for Measure: An Essay in Criticism of Shakespeare's Drama* (London, 1997).

Schork, R. J., 'The Many Masks of Parolles', *Philological Quarterly*, 76 (1997), 263–9.

Schwartz, Kathryn, 'Fearful Simile: Stealing the Breech in Shakespeare's Chronicle Plays', *Shakespeare Quarterly*, 49 (1998), 140–67.

Shannon, Laurie J., 'Emilia's Argument: Friendship and "Human Title" in *The Two Noble Kinsmen*', *English Literary History*, 64 (1997), 657–82.

Skura, Meredith, 'Marlowe's *Edward II*: Penetrating Language in Shakespeare's *Richard II*', *Shakespeare Survey 50* (1997), 41–56.

Slights, Camille Wells, 'Slaves and Subjects in *Othello*', *Shakespeare Quarterly*, 48 (1997), 377–90.

Slights, Jessica and Michael Morgan Holmes, 'Isabella's Order: Religious Acts and Personal Desires in *Measure for Measure*', *Studies in Philology*, 95 (1998), 263–92.

Smith, Ian, 'Barbarian Errors: Performing Race in Early Modern England', *Shakespeare Quarterly*, 49 (1998), 168–86.

Sofer, Andrew, 'Felt Absences: The Stage Properties of *Othello*'s Handkerchief', *Comparative Drama*, 31 (1997), 367–93.

'The Skull on the Renaissance Stage: Imagination and the Erotic Life of Props', *English Literary Renaissance*, 28 (1998), 47–74.

Stockard, Emily E., 'Patterns of Consolation in Shakespeare's Sonnets 1–126', *Studies in Philology*, 94 (1997), 465–93.

Thompson, Ann and Neil Taylor, *Hamlet* (Plymouth, 1996).

Tomarken, Edward, ed., *As You Like It from 1600 to the Present: Critical Essays* (London, 1997).

Traub, Valerie, M. Lindsay Kaplan and Dympna Callaghan, eds., *Feminist Readings of Early Modern Culture: Emerging Subjects* (Cambridge, 1996).

Vendler, Helen, *The Art of Shakespeare's Sonnets* (London, 1997).

Willbern, David, *Poetic Will: Shakespeare and the Play of Language* (Philadelphia, 1997).

Wolf, Amy, 'Shakespeare and Harsnett: "Pregnant to Good Pity?"', *Studies in English Literature*, 38 (1998), 251–64.

2. SHAKESPEARE'S LIFE, TIMES, AND STAGE

reviewed by ALISON FINDLAY

You go not till I set you up a glass
Where you may see the inmost part of you   (*Hamlet* 3.4.19–20)

Peter Holland concludes his book *English Shakespeares* by praising foreign productions for 'rightly showing us that not everybody's Shakespeare is the one we possessively think we know' (p. 269). Several recent publications show the effects of Shakespeare's transposition within German, French, Russian and Irish cultures, past and present. In *Redefining Shakespeare: Literary Theory and Theatre Practice in the German Democratic Republic*, J. Lawrence Gunter and Andrew M. McLean have brought together an illuminating range of essays and interviews with theatre practitioners which chart the changing production styles in the former East Germany in relation to their political contexts. For me at least, much of this was undiscovered country. A useful chronology of key productions and events from 1945 to 1990 sets a historical framework for the development of a tradition in which the German Shakespeare Society, and the work of Brecht and Robert Weimann are shown to be important influences. Weimann's own lucid essay gives 'a personal retrospect' of how 'Shakespeare' has been redefined over the period, assessing the 'uncanny threshold between unorthodoxy and complicity' (p. 137) unique to theatre practice in the GDR.

Between the twenty contributions, the pressing need to record what Alexander Lang calls 'a page in the history of theater on which it will be remembered that a different kind of theater was developed' (p. 168) leads to some repetition of material but also shows a strong sense of dialogue between scholars and theatre practitioners. Anna Nauman's fine article on

'Dramatic Text and Body Language' reads critiques of the socialist regime in performances of Ophelia and Titania as oppressed women. Details of the harsh realities of working under authoritarian surveillance reveal the daring of subversive productions like Christoph Schroth's 1986–7 *Romeo and Juliet* and *The Winter's Tale*, 'a reaction to the encrustation and disorientation of our own socialist society' (p. 142). Working in the GDR also gave a special understanding of the postmodern condition. Heiner Müller, author of *Hamletmaschine* (1977), argues '[w]e had parodies of Shakespearean characters' and many productions exposed East Germany itself as 'only a parody of the Soviet Union' (pp. 186–7). Katja Paryla's account of how she played Titania 'à la Marilyn Monroe' gives a specific example of this politicized use of pastiche (pp. 253–6). Such insights indicate what this exciting book has to teach us. Perhaps more than anything, the candid enthusiasm of the contributors reminds us of the importance of ideals, the need to speak 'what we feel, not what we ought to say' (*King Lear* 5.3.300).

A broader perspective on the huge popularity and reproduction of Shakespeare in Germany is provided by Wilhelm Hortmann's *Shakespeare on the German Stage: The Twentieth Century*. In spite of the author's regrets about its selectivity, this monumental book of nearly five hundred pages and over a hundred illustrations provides a wonderfully comprehensive picture of German traditions of staging. (The chapter on East Germany, with a contribution by Maik Hamburger, makes a useful companion piece to the book of essays just discussed.) Working through chronologically, the chapters introduce the political and artistic environments of each key period before considering a selection of major artists and distinctive productions (marked by sub-headings for easy reference). What emerges is an intricate picture of how different Shakespeare traditions and individual talents have interacted to produce a varied tapestry of interpretations even under apparently oppressive regimes. For example, Hort-

mann uncovers subversive elements in Jurgen Fehling's productions of histories and tragedies at the Staatstheater during the Third Reich, where his *Richard III* seems to have anticipated the Richard Eyre / Ian McKellen 1990 Royal National Theatre production with some daring. Not surprisingly, Hortmann singles out *The Merchant of Venice* for special attention in this and the subsequent chapters on the postwar stage, arguing that 'the Holocaust taboo on negative traits in the Jewish character was so strong that it took Jewish directors to break it' (p. 256).

Hortmann's sensitivity as a theatre historian and cultural critic allows him to give persuasive reassessments of the significance of 'traditionalists' like Reinhardt, or directors of the fifties like Sellner and Kortner. The attention the book pays to provincial as well as national theatre has the virtue of showing how, often, not even the strongest trends held total dominance, as directors experimented with alternative styles. Hortmann also gives incisive critiques of the excesses and shortcomings of productions. He assesses the situation since 1989 as one of radical, sometimes undisciplined experiment which 'had little to do with Shakespeare' but ironically proves his central position in German culture as a testing ground for new ideas (p. 453). *Shakespeare on the German Stage* makes a major contribution to theatre history and will be used and valued by scholars for many years to come.

Another part of the world is opened up in *Russian Essays on Shakespeare and his Contemporaries*, ed. Alexandr Parfenov and Joseph G. Price. This collection is designed to 'lift, though slightly, the curtain' that exists between studies of Shakespeare in Russia and in the rest of the world (p. 10). When the curtain is lifted, the volume provides ample evidence that Shakespeare holds a special place in Russian culture as well as German: *Pravda* proclaims 'he has always been our contemporary, a participant in the great struggle for the fair future of mankind to which the Soviet people are also committed'

(p. 15). What is revealed is, for the most part, not the shock of the new or the different.

Several essays, offering introductory or obvious comments, are of limited interest since it is difficult to see beyond the basic, sometimes dated, statements to identify particular Russian historical and cultural perspectives on the plays. More interestingly, Leonid Pinsky's article argues that Russian interest in tragedy played out a crisis in the humanism of the past brought by the emergent bourgeois absolutism of the present. His view that 'implanting the personal history of a hero in a tragedy is inappropriate and groundless and is a modernization of Shakespeare in the spirit of the new age' (p. 47) strikingly prefigures Francis Barker's proclamation 'at the centre of Hamlet, in the interior of his mystery, there is, in short, nothing'.[1] Yuri D. Levin and Nina Diakonova both draw attention to a process of creative appropriation which 'was started in Russia more than half a century earlier than in England' (p. 101). Some fascinating nineteenth-century rewritings, including Leskov's short story 'Lady Macbeth of the Mcenskij District' (1865), are examined with reference to their cultural contexts.

A highlight of the book is Ilya M. Gililov's piece 'For Whom the Bell Tolled: A New Dating for Shakespeare's "The Phoenix and the Turtle" and the Identification of Its Protagonists'. Gililov's painstaking research on the surviving copies of Chester's *Love's Martyr* in which the poem was first printed, lead to the claim that the 1601 publication date is 'a deliberate mystification' (p. 163) and that the volume was, in fact 'published during the 1612–1613 period (p. 165). Gililov makes a good case for considering Elizabeth, Countess of Rutland and her husband Roger as the protagonists, Elizabeth's identity as Philip Sidney's daughter leading him to propose a connection between Shakespeare and the Pembroke circle. Gililov's piece contributes usefully to the international scholarly debate rather than constituting a specifically Russian angle on the material. Although this collection

makes a useful start, one senses that there is much more to discover when the curtain is lifted further.

The French too have taken Shakespeare as their own, turning towards his work to speak 'de nos rêves, de nos doutes' and of the crises 'de cette fin de siècle' (p. 7) as Jean-Claude Lallias remarks in his introductory essay to *Shakespeare: La Scene et Ses Miroirs*, volume 6 of the French journal *Théâtre Aujourd' Hui*. The volume is devoted to a comparative study of *Hamlet* and *Twelfth Night*. François Laroque's astute introductory essay considers these plays as twins or mirrors concerned with absent paternal figures, vengeance, metatheatre and deception, and sketches parallels between Hamlet, Viola and Maria.

Shakespeare is seen, via these plays, as an infinite prism, 'un miroir déformant' for theatrical practitioners, reflecting the aesthetic and political stakes of a period (p. 4). The volume admirably displays the multi-dimensional qualities of interpretation with essays on translation, theatre spaces and design, songs, music and sound effects. Catherine Treilhou-Balaudé offers concise French stage histories of each play, followed by a selection of interviews. Peter Brook discusses his 1995 fragmentation of *Hamlet* as *Qui est Là* as a way of releasing the play from its stage history; Maurice Durozier gives an actor's perspective on working within Mnouchkine's kathakali style *Twelfth Night*; and Yannis Kokkos discusses his remarkable geometric design as a key factor in de-sentimentalizing Hamlet in Antoine Vitez's 1983 production. The high quality photographs, accompanying set of colour slides and compact disc, offer immediate evidence of the editors' commitment to representing the many facets of theatre production as equally significant interpretations of the texts. Although the recordings

---

[1] Francis Barker, 'Hamlet's Unfulfilled Interiority', in Richard Wilson and Richard Dutton, eds., *New Historicism and Renaissance Drama* (Harlow, 1992), 157–66, pp. 163–4.

of selected speeches do not have the clarity of radio broadcast quality, they suggest the choices made in performance. Particularly enjoyable are Jean-Jacques Lemêtre's musical cameos for Mnouchkine's *Twelfth Night*, in which Sir Toby is portrayed by a shambling bass clarinet and Maria, 'the youngest wren of nine' (3.2.63), by a vivacious piccolo.

As well as reflections on French theatre and culture, this book offers a mirror to English-speaking Shakespearians 'Où vous puissez voir la part la plus intérieure de vous-même' (p. 1). It explicitly addresses English academics and theatre practitioners in interviews with Terry Hands and Peter Holland, and a discussion with Trevor Nunn about his film version of *Twelfth Night*. Jean-Claude Lallias provocatively argues that in England it is barely admitted that a theatre practitioner could be a primary inter-preter of the text as in France (p. 6), regarding the status of the reconstructed Globe as a test case for Anglo-American interests. By ques-tioning whether the theatre will be a museo-logical celebration of Elizabethan theatre or an opportunity to create genuinely new forms of theatricality (p. 7), he fails to appreciate that the two might, in fact, be compatible. Nevertheless, the book's insistence on the importance of experimental, often eccentric production techniques constitutes a stimulating challenge to conventional ways of thinking about Shakespeare.

Shakespeare and Ireland: History, Politics, Culture, edited by Mark Thornton Burnett and Ramona Wray, explores yet another context for understanding alternative Shakespeares. The collection is divided into three sections, covering the early modern period, national and postcolonial cultures, and modes of transmission ('performance, pedagogy, language'). Particu-larly striking is Wray's own essay 'Shakespeare and the Sectarian Divide: Politics and Pedagogy in (post) Post-ceasefire Belfast' which bravely describes her teaching practice and the reactions of her highly politicized students to Shake-speare's texts, plays which offer 'metaphorical positions' (p. 251) from which to discuss the most controversial aspects of Irish society. Richard English's absorbing piece 'Shakespeare and the Definition of the Irish Nation' under-mines simplistic models of colonization and resistance with fascinating evidence of early twentieth-century Republican appropriations of Shakespeare – quite literally in the case of IRA member Peadar O'Donnell, who stole a copy of the Complete Works from the officers' lavatory on the day of his release from prison! (p. 136). Articles by Richard Brown, Jonathan Allison and Neil Rhodes illustrate the process of cross-cultural exchanges by concentrating on the influence of Shakespeare on important Irish literary figures; Rhodes's essay links Ireland to a feminized Catholic ideal in the work of both Laureate Ted Hughes and Irish-born Seamus Heaney. Beverly E. Schellner examines Sheri-dan's promotion of Shakespeare in eighteenth-century Smock-Alley theatre in Dublin, and his unique policy of advertising his productions to ladies of quality (p. 181). These different points of focus give a pleasing diversity to the collec-tion, in which the localized nature of any positioning of Shakespeare within Irish culture is clear.

Contributions to the early modern section of the book discuss Ireland's curious position as both English colony and kingdom. Essays by Willey Maley and David J. Baker consider Holinshed's Chronicle and *The Tempest* to give contrasting views of Ireland as a central element of English imperialism in a localized British context and further afield. The early modern context to Shakespeare's history plays is more fully explored by Christopher Highley in *Shakespeare, Spenser and the Crisis in Ireland*. The author rejects parallels between English activities in the New World and the case of Ireland as inadequate, choosing to concentrate on the ways in which Wales, Scotland and France figured alongside English preoccupa-tions with 'their oldest "colony"' (p. 2). This really in-depth study uses important political tracts such as Richard Beacon's *Solon His Folie*

(1594) and John Derricke's *The Image of Irelande* (1581) to set up interesting perspectives on Spenser and Shakespeare's work.

In Shakespeare's *Contention*, York's return from Ireland to challenge Henry's crown is read as symbolic of the 'nation's geographical margins' turning aggressively in on the core in a 'nightmare of collapsing boundaries' (p. 49). Convincing parallels are drawn between York and Sir John Perrot, although the argument that Jack Cade is another image of threatening Irish disorder is less persuasive. The use of Wales as 'a kind of living museum or memory theater' (p. 71) and Welshwomen as representative of dangerous forces in Ireland is examined with reference to Peele's *Edward I* and *1 Henry IV*. Highley contends that alongside the re-figuring of Tyrone's rebellion in the rebels of Shakespeare's play, Glendower is deliberately presented as a feminized figure who, with his daughter and the unseen Welshwomen, are gradually disempowered in a form of 'theatrical magic' which assuages English fears about Irish Celtic 'chieftains' (p. 97). Tyrone's heroic masculine appeal is also recontained, the book argues, in Hal's defeat of Hotspur at Shrewsbury. The final chapter on *Henry V* returns to masculine military heroism, bringing together the figures of Tyrone and Essex in a reading which goes beyond previous discussions to show how the play registers 'Shakespeare's disillusioned ambivalence' about English empire-building (p. 135). Even figures like the Archbishop of York display a non-censorious view of those unwilling to fight for the English cause (p. 152). Here, as in so much of the book, Highley's use of contemporary writings deftly verifies the varied opinions of early modern English subjects on ideas of nationhood.

II

A different kind of reflective mirror is set up in *Shakespeare and the Authority of Performance*, an important book which draws on recent theories of performativity and editorial practice to rigorously question the relationship between scholarship, performance and authority. In the excellent opening chapter, W. B. Worthen uses Barthes' terms 'work' and 'text' to define the 'ideal' category of a play like *Hamlet* (which is always absent), and the material manifestations we have of it in staged and printed forms. He deconstructs the parasitic dependence of performance on text as the product of nineteenth-century literary tradition, proposing an equality between production and edition, where performance is 'a separate iteration of the work' with an equal claim to authority (p. 16).

The book backs up this balance by devoting its three remaining chapters to an exploration of the different routes directors, actors and critics use to claim authority and access to 'Shakespeare'. The powerful 'auteurs' in a director-centred theatre can be aligned with authors, the book argues, as abstract figures 'for the attribution of intention or meaning' (p. 49). Familiar material from Charles Marowitz, Peter Brook and Jonathan Miller is quoted to illustrate how the director functions as a legitimator of performance, a negotiator between the transcendent values associated with the text as literary artefact and its use as theatre script. This is followed by a thoughtful close reading of Peter Sellars' 1994 production of *The Merchant of Venice*, in which Worthen compares Sellars' ambiguous undermining of unified subjectivity and the techniques used by Anna Deavere Smith's television series *Twilight*.

The third chapter moves on to examine how actors are instrumental in reproducing the hegemony of modern individualism in the theatre. It contends that while actors' work on body and voice may seem to liberate them from social and ideological constraints, in fact it tunes them in even more firmly to the recovery of authorial intention. In spite of their apparent affinities with the postmodern master-mistress of pastiche, most actors understand their self-fashioning not as authors of themselves but as 'a mode of fidelity to Shakespeare' (p. 128). Shakespeare becomes the big 'Other' which confirms their own identities. Worthen is not hostile to actors; his discussion properly appreciates their intelligent insights and the contribution performance can make to an understanding of a play. However, he presents a strong argument for the need for theatre to focus more critically on 'how "Shakespeare" is produced and implemented' (p. 141). The final, much shorter chapter, turns the spotlight onto performance critics, re-configuring many of the earlier arguments of the book. What makes *Shakespeare and the Authority of Performance* so pertinent is its eloquent insistence that we should all pinpoint the hidden assumptions on which our work is based and the implications this holds for how we view the relationship between page and stage.

Shakespeare and the Theatre: An Anthology of Criticism, compiled and edited by Stanley Wells, takes a completely different approach to the art of theatre criticism by presenting an extensive menu of eighty pieces, dating from the beginning of the eighteenth century to the present, for the reader's enjoyment and use. The book fulfils both these functions. The collection of so wide a range of articles in a single volume makes this an extremely useful resource as I can attest, having already used my review copy on several occasions in teaching. Familiar pieces such as Shaw's delightfully acerbic comments on Augustin Daly's productions, or Morley's enchanted view of Phelps's *A Midsummer Night's Dream*, are accompanied by critiques either previously unpublished or very difficult to get hold of. Theodor Fontane's account of Kean's *The Winter's Tale*, for example, provides a refreshingly objective German perspective on the elaborate spectacle where 'pretentiousness ... attaches itself to everything' (p. 96). James Murdoch's comments give a rare 'bird's eye view' (p. 65) of Charles Kean's emotionally charged performance of Posthumus, a role he played only once while on tour in Philadelphia.

Throughout the book, editorial intervention is restrained; the introduction outlines a broad historical perspective to theatre criticism

without explicitly interrogating the relationships between authority, page and stage as Worthen does. Instead, notes on each article provide basic factual information, and the reader is at liberty to tease out the implications which so rich a range of articles provide. These are many: Virginia Woolf's review of a production of *Twelfth Night* is a pretext for anatomizing the relationship between reading and seeing a play; Shaw's remarks on Ada Rehan's performance as Helena in *A Midsummer Night's Dream* give a glimpse of changing attitudes to the social functions of theatre for female spectators. Wells advises the reader that he has chosen criticisms for their power to 'stimulate the imagination' by means of their enthusiasm and skilful use of language (p. 1). Such criteria make the book genuinely entertaining and the historical significance of certain productions is effectively registered through emotionally charged responses. Hubert Griffith's reaction to Barry Jackson's *Hamlet*, seeing the play as a crowning achievement of drama which 'could make one huge bonfire of the lot and soar aloft in the combined radiance of them all' (p. 206) is passionate testimony to the revolutionary power of staging Shakespeare in modern dress in 1925. In the latter section of the book, the choice of productions covered does reflect recent interests in issues of gender, race and marginalization, and regionalism, but the reviews are not especially representative of postmodern sensibilities.

Peter Holland takes up the challenge of evaluating recent production trends in more detail in *English Shakespeares*, which concentrates on stagings in the 1990s. As a preface to his discussions, he outlines many practical elements which can be easily overlooked. For those not close to the business of theatre, or familiar with the working practices of so large an institution as the Royal Shakespeare Company, it is useful to be reminded that factors like the time of the last train home or the 'frequency cycle' (p. 9) governing choice of plays for the repertory all play significant parts in production choices. In spite of his proximity, Holland is not uncritical of the Royal Shakespeare Company's practices; he examines the predominant style of 'big set' productions for the main house as the result of a short-sighted view of audience expectations, which often has limiting consequences for actors and spectators alike.

The following chapters successfully retain an explicitly subjective account of individual performances within an overview of different styles of Shakespearian production in the 1990s. Indeed, one of the most valuable things about the book is the luxury it affords Holland to undertake lengthy discussions in the style of the reviewer. He sharply observes actors' achievements, and yet also elaborates his commentaries with immense detail, as in his appreciative remarks on Sally Dexter's performance of a single line by Regan 'How is't my lord' (3.7.92), directed at Gloucester as a substitute father in Nicholas Hytner's 1990 *King Lear* (p. 43). Such moments of focus will make this book a really useful reminder for those who saw the productions. For someone, like myself, whose theatre-going has recently been interrupted, it is also immensely valuable in filling in the gaps in a way that conventional theatre reviews cannot. I did find myself at odds with some of Holland's opinions: his view that Alex Jennings' beautifully coiffured, ostentatious Richard II contained 'no tinge of camp' (p. 76), or his damning account of Ian Judge's *Comedy of Errors*, though in fairness to that production, he acknowledges its immense popularity.

The book is primarily concerned with the work of large theatre companies, yet it achieves a broader perspective through a well-chosen selection of other unusual productions. Cheek by Jowl's all-male *As You Like It* (1991), the Medieval Players' excellent Q1 version of *Hamlet* (1992) are rightly appreciated as important recent stagings of Shakespeare. In addition, Holland considers the achievements of Northern Broadsides as a company which has 'reclaimed Shakespeare in a piece of cultural

annexation that reappropriated high culture and its geographical polarity' (p. 152). In order to give a balanced picture, Holland does not pull back from describing problematic and even disastrous productions like Phyllida Lloyd's 1994 *Pericles*, arguing rather pessimistically that all too often 'directors are only too willing to ignore the lessons of history' (p. 216). However, his discussions of Deborah Warner's *Richard II* (1995) and Karin Beier's *Romeo and Juliet* (1994) end the book on an enthusiastic note. Taking his view that 'in the end, our reactions measure ourselves' (p. 20), Peter Holland's own achievement in *English Shakespeares* is to be applauded.

Shakespeare, the Movie, edited by Lynda Boose and Richard Burt, sets out to explore the pleasures and problems of popularization for the critic reading Shakespeare on film. By offering sixteen short essays, the book manages to cover a good range of topics and recent film texts. The cross-fertilization of Hollywood cinema and Shakespearian script is addressed particularly well in essays by Donald Hedrick and James Loehlin. Hedrick engagingly reads Branagh's *Henry V* as 'an importation of the mud of Dirty Harry into the British text and film' (p. 54) while Loehlin discusses how Richard Loncraine's *Richard III* (starring Ian McKellen) rewrites Shakespeare in the light of Anglo-American film history, parodying the English 'heritage' film in its presentation of modern British fascism of the 1930s. The film's structure, with McKellen's paranoid Richard at its centre, is, he argues, deeply embedded in the American gangster movie tradition (especially James Cagney's performance in *White Heat*). This is a useful way of understanding the emphasis placed on Richard's relationship with his mother in the film.

Impressive essays by Peter Donaldson on *Prospero's Books* and Laurie Osborne on *The Animated Shakespeare* illustrate how technical aspects of film are also bound up in the cultural reproduction of Shakespeare. Donaldson gives thoughtful consideration of the anxieties of authorship and paternal control in Greenaway's film, as represented through the protagonist's (and director's) ostentatious use of digital image technology. Osborne demonstrates that the different animation techniques in *The Animated Shakespeare* films are instrumental in creating varied levels of distance between viewers and characters and narrative. The difficulties created by moving a Shakespeare play into television format are explored by Tony Howard, whose critical assessment of Orson Welles and Peter Brook's 1953 collaboration on *King Lear* is especially useful since this film has received little attention.

The politicization of race, gender and sexual orientation in recent Shakespearian films gets its fair share of analysis in essays by Valerie Wayne, Lynda Boose, Katherine Eggert and Diana Henderson. Barbara Hodgdon's re-reading of *Othello's* racist and misogynist discourses through the television films of productions by Janet Suzman and Trevor Nunn contains much sensitive observation of detail. Sue Wiseman and Richard Burt take different approaches to the ways Shakespeare has been used to unsettle heteronormality, the former focusing on crises of masculinity in *My Own Private Idaho* and the latter intriugingly arguing that Shakespeare becomes 'a mainstream signifier of queer sex *and* popular culture' (p. 244) in straight films like *Dead Poets Society*. Although one laments the brevity of some of the essays, the range of material covered by the book, and its reasonably priced paperback edition, make this an ideal introduction to Shakespeare on film for students and teachers.

Gary Jay Williams presents a well-crafted stage history of a single play in *Our Moonlight Revels: A Midsummer Night's Dream in the Theatre*. The book covers important English and American stagings such as Madame Vestris' 1840 restored text, the Victorian pictorialism of Charles Kean, the modern revolutionary approaches of Granville Barker, and Peter Brook, and there is also a section on Max Reinhardt's range of neoromantic *Dream*s.

Although details of many of these famous productions will already be familiar to theatre historians, Williams' aim, 'to understand each production in its cultural moment' (xi), produces some striking insights. For example, the nineteenth-century tradition of casting a woman as Oberon (begun by Vestris in 1840 and not broken until Benson's production of 1889), is seen as addressing 'Victorian patriarchal culture in complex, fascinating ways' since a woman occupied the English throne as in the 1590s (p. 93). Williams complains that Granville Barker's productions 'have been idealized and dehistoricized' (p.143) but, sadly, his own account of this ground-breaking *Dream* does little to set its choices of oriental fairies, modernist staging or English folk music against the changes and insecurities of England in 1914.

A particularly strong element of the book is its focus on the musical dimensions of productions. Williams gives an engrossing account of Purcell's 1692 opera *The Fairy Queen* as a tribute to William and Mary composed deliberately in the style of court entertainments. This, it is argued, is one example of how the play has been appropriated to celebrate royal marriages. Re-surveying the arguments that *A Midsummer Night's Dream* was originally written for an aristocratic nuptial, Williams firmly rejects the idea, arguing that 'never far from the wedding play myth and its court orientation is the celebration of Shakespeare as England's national poet' (p. 16). The book concludes on the wry note that *Dream*s as radical as Peter Brook's have all but disappeared, since the programme for Adrian Noble's 1994–5 production displayed a colour photograph of Prince Charles and a note that 'the play had been composed for a wedding in a noble household' (p. 257). Such self-conscious wit is typical of the book as a whole; the author never forgets that he is part of the process of reinterpretation and uses an engaging style to entertain as well as inform his readers. By virtue of its detail and perceptive readings, it will prove a very rich resource for those working on the play.

Like Williams' book, John Ripley's *Coriolanus on Stage in Britain and America 1609–1994* is remarkably comprehensive, although the main focus is on eighteenth and nineteenth-century British productions. In reading the book from cover to cover, the detail is sometimes overwhelming but as a source of information it is magnificent. A very full index, including entries on individual characters, scenes, and even Menenius' belly speech, allows the reader to make selective use of the material. The author's introductory remarks that *Coriolanus* is characterized by a 'user-unfriendly aesthetic' (p. 33) to which productions consistently respond by stabilizing its disparate elements is borne out in the following chapters. Adaptations by Tate and Dennis are revealed in their full political resonance as Tory and Whig propaganda pieces in response to the Popish Plot and the Old Pretender's invasion attempt. The eighteenth-century tradition of laundering and simplifying Martius as a great classical hero, dating from Thompson's 1749 adaptation, is explored with reference to productions by Sheridan, Garrick and Kemble. Useful reminders of England's constant military activities from 1752–1817 and the impact of the French Revolution, help to contextualize these celebrations of military prowess and bourgeois individualism. The persistence of the celebratory style in England and America is traced through to Olivier's famous performances. The strength of the book's attention to nineteenth-century prompt books and reviews is especially obvious in suggesting variety within the overall style.

Ripley identifies the first radical challenge to the Kemble tradition in Edmund Kean's little known production of 1820, a 'pivotal' production, rejecting interpolations and restoring 'something of the character's original roughness and inconsistency' (p. 158). Twentieth-century reinventions are dealt with more briefly than their theatrical predecessors, although Ripley is to be commended for redirecting attention to marginal productions like Monck's at the Maddermarket in 1928 or Roche's overtly political interpretation at Manchester Repertory Theatre in 1935. In the final chapter of the book, one senses the author's frustration that, even now, theatre practitioners continue to 'stabilize' the play rather than staging its radical 'overdeterminacy and indeterminacy' (p. 335). This is an unfair criticism and an impossible task. Directors and actors must make choices; it is impossible to play all the ambiguities and contradictions in the text. Happily, Ripley's search for an elusive definitive production never clouds his clear critical judgement or appreciation of what has been represented. The book makes an invaluable contribution to study of the play and the theatrical traditions of the eighteenth and nineteenth centuries.

Another little-known piece which invites an adjustment to our reading of the eighteenth century's appropriations of Shakespeare is Horace Walpole's *The Dear Witches* (1743), which is uncovered and analysed in an interesting article by Catherine Alexander. Alexander provides details about the piece and its context, to show that Walpole's parody of scenes from *Macbeth* 'makes sophisticated political points' (p. 142) by attacking the Patriots who were responsible for his father's political downfall in 1742. She convincingly argues that Walpole's use of Rowe's edition of Shakespeare as the basis of his 'duplicitous act of parody' ironically allowed him to 'achieve a veracity that evaded his opponents' (p. 142).

Sexual rather than national politics are the focus of John Cox's Shakespeare in Production volume on *Much Ado About Nothing*. Like others in the series, this book is divided into an extensive introduction charting the stage history of the play, and a copy of the New Cambridge text, annotated with details of different interpretations of settings, lines or pivotal moments. This theatrical variorum is the most valuable part of the study; as a tool for making comparisons between different approaches to specific lines it will be useful to researchers and actors. A handy chronology of the productions cited is included at the beginning of the volume and the bibliography provides further guidance for those wishing to follow up a specific production.

The critical introduction is less satisfying, mainly because it chooses to focus almost exclusively on the play's treatment of gender issues. It is interesting to learn that in the period of Garrick, Beatrice's unconventional behaviour was relished rather than criticized by reviewers (p. 14), and that only later did actors such as Maria Foote transform the character into a 'Beatrice of the drawing room of 1829' (p. 22). However, to be constantly reminded of how the character 'disrupts the conventional gender polarities' (p. 5) becomes tedious, even though Cox takes trouble to show how Victorian actors such as Ellen Terry negotiated ways of playing the role which still allowed for the display of spirit. Other important dimensions of the play are sidelined to short descriptions instead of being explored with the depth they merit. For example, the changing interpretations of Don John, Don Pedro, Claudio and Leonato are discussed in three short paragraphs (pp. 34–5, 56–7 and 68) in spite of the fact that annotations to the playtext offer evidence of variations on these roles. Scenery and design receive more attention but it is unfortunate that the issues of class, alienation and insecurity in *Much Ado About Nothing* are discussed only in the context of a battle of the sexes. Cox quotes Jonathan Miller's comment that the play 'has an afterlife different from the life conceived of by its author'. Or by this editor, one might add.

Changes in theatrical tradition are considered from a biographical perspective in Michael Morrison's study *John Barrymore: Shakespearean Actor*. Wisely avoiding the more colourful elements of his subject's private life, Morrison concentrates instead on Barrymore's revolutionary productions of *Richard III* (1920) and *Hamlet* (1922–5). These are examined in the central chapters of the book, where Morrison's extensive use of accounts by those who knew or worked with Barrymore creates a vivid picture of a collaborative production process with director Arthur Hopkins and designer Robert Edmonds. Scene by scene descriptions of the productions are followed by analyses of the critical response to each, drawing on reviews and eyewitness reports. Clearly headed sub-sections within each chapter generously allow readers to use this material selectively.

Morrison's well-written biography is a powerful tribute to 'a great actor of Shakespeare' who was able to reinterpret 'classic roles with an innovative artistry that redefined those characters for the postwar generation' (p. 302). The significance of Barrymore's contribution in the metamorphosis of a Victorian theatre tradition into modern conceptions of acting, design and direction is demonstrated by two flanking sections of the book. The preliminary chapters outline the legacy of figures like Booth, Irving, and Mansfield and the American Shakespeare star system on which Barrymore's own magnetic appeal drew, while chapter 5 considers Barrymore's attempts to bring Shakespeare to film, most of which were aborted or were not received with great critical acclaim. Given the lack of recordings of Barrymore's great stage performances, Morrison's achievement in reconstructing a record of those theatrical highlights in a lively, engaging account, is of especial importance.

In another form of recording, two new audio productions of *Romeo and Juliet* and *Hamlet* demonstrate the advantages of putting Shakespeare on compact disc. These performances, using the text of the New Cambridge Shakespeare, are divided into 'tracks', allowing the listener to select individual scenes or speeches. The productions are more than the sum of their parts, with their own integrity and sense of direction. The opening scene of *Romeo and Juliet*, directed by Michael Sheen, suggests an Irish context (possibly Belfast) for the play, an impression that is furthered by Fiona Shaw's excellent performance of the nurse, who brings a strong sense of material reality to the Capulet household. The hysteria of the Capulets in the wedding morning scene is pointed up to suggest a potentially ridiculous situation, a nice contrast to the more poignant emotion of the protagonists. Kate Beckinsale gives an impressive performance as an appropriately more mature and thoughtful Juliet. Michael Sheen's Romeo is also consistently good, often highlighting apparently 'ordinary' lines with particular poignancy. It is a tribute to his skills as director and actor that the speech I remember as the most touching from the whole production was his words to the apothecary, torn with desperate emotion.

In Neville Jason's production of *Hamlet*, the word that immediately comes to mind for Anton Lesser's protagonist is 'wormwood' (3.2.172). This is a very unsympathetic Hamlet whose general bad temper gives little sense of a noble mind o'erthrown and whose savagery in the nunnery scene is genuinely disturbing. The occasional glimpses of the former Hamlet, in his first greeting of Rosencrantz and Guildenstern, bring a genuine warmth, but the performance is dominated by Lesser's nasal voice and clipped accents. This does suggest Hamlet's extreme sense of frustration, even thwarted ambition, but given the length of the recording, his announcement 'the rest is silence' (5.2.310) comes as rather a relief, both for him and us. Claudius (played by Edward De Souza) uses much more rounded vowels which give a wonderful sense of false generosity. That this is only a thin mask is clear when he says 'And we beseech you, *bend* you to remain / Here in the cheer and comfort of our eye' (1.2.115). A threatening pause on the word 'bend' signals already the destructive power of Claudius, and his determination to crush Hamlet. Another notable feature of the production is the decision to play the ghost using an echo effect. The 'questionable shape' (1.4.24) of the spirit and its demands are well suggested by this audio equivalent of dry ice, which blurs the clarity of its lines. Many of the performances and scenes are effective, although enjoyable is not a word I would use of this production.

Two different approaches to theatrical production in Shakespeare's own times are taken in *Stages of Play* by Michael Shurgot and *The Queen's Men and Their Plays*, by Scott McMillin and Sally-Beth MacLean. Shurgot announces an exciting agenda by promising to explore how the physical shape of thrust stages 'and the crisscross patterns of sight lines and varied actor-audience relationships' they created (p. 21) could have contributed to the theatrical energies woven into texts and performances. His project seems especially valuable given the work being undertaken at the new Globe and the author writes with an undeniable energy and commitment of his own. Sadly, however, the book does not always live up to its promising beginning. In the chapter on *A Midsummer Night's Dream* and *Love's Labour's Lost*, the central point about on-stage audiences is elaborated with occasional insights into the potential discrepancies between the sympathies of different sections of the audience, depending on where the characters are placed, but little attention is given to the implications of meta-theatre, though there have been fine essays on this topic by other scholars.[2] Similarly, by taking an oppositional stance to historicist feminist work and insisting on the importance of the audience's sequential experience of *The Taming of the Shrew*, Shurgot misses the chance to follow up the ideas of theorists like Judith Butler, with a more trenchant examination of the performativity of gender.

The chapters on *The Merchant of Venice* and *Troilus and Cressida* offer richer analyses. Shurgot begins to tease out the complexities of the trial scene in *The Merchant of Venice* by suggesting that Antonio skilfully 'combines the downstage *platea* with the upstage *locus* of Venetian authority' to condone Jessica's

---

[2] See, for example, Laura Levine, 'Rape, repetition and the politics of closure in *A Midsummer Night's Dream*', in Valerie Traub, M. Lindsay Kaplan and Dympna Callaghan, eds., *Feminist Readings of Early Modern Culture: Emerging Subjects* (Cambridge, 1996), 210–28.

behaviour and force Shylock's conversion (p. 97). Proposing that the physical proximity of an actor encourages audience members to 'share more directly his experience' (p. 93) allows Shurgot to demonstrate, convincingly, that in the wooing scene of *Troilus and Cressida*, the audience's views of Cressida are deliberately set up as irreconcilable (p. 194). The book's exclusive concentration on the physical plane tends to obliterate the possibility of cultural differences between audience members, between fathers and daughters standing in the same place at a production of *Merchant*, for example. The particular experiential baggage carried by individual spectators may be impossible to identify but it surely played a significant part in their response to scenes or moments. Failure to take account of such variations inevitably limits the usefulness of the book's insights.

In *The Queen's Men and Their Plays* McMillin and MacLean argue for a reorientation in theatre history, to focus on acting companies and their repertories rather than the canons of writers. Their detailed study of the company presents a persuasive case for the new insights which can be revealed by such an approach. The first part of the book proposes that the founding of the Queen's Men in 1583 was 'a more sharply political venture than has been supposed before' (p. 17), motivated by Tilney and Walsingham's wish to tighten governmental control over theatrical activity and to promote Protestant propaganda on behalf of the royal patron (p. 27). An examination of the company's extensive touring schedule in the years 1583–1603, drawing on carefully researched evidence from the Records of Early English Drama, furthers the book's more general argument that theatre history should shift attention away from London venues to the provinces. The Queen's Men's continued vigorous activities on tour, counter to the popular opinion that they broke up or went into immediate decline once they lost prominence in the capital after 1594.

The second part of the book concentrates on the Queen's Men's plays as bodying forth a company style which would be superseded in the later 1590s by the work of the Admiral's and Lord Chamberlain's Men. The authors are deliberately conservative in their claims about the repertory, choosing to concentrate on the nine 'certain' plays (although evidence about a further thirteen 'apocryphal' plays is also usefully listed for the reader's information). With precise, exacting analysis, the book shows that plays dating from 1591 required a minimum of fifteen and seventeen actors, yet later plays from 1594 could have been performed with a cast of fourteen, later ten, reinforcing the theory that the Queen's Men branched into two sister touring troupes. The book's insights into the company offer many suggestive ideas, one of the most radical being a review of the status of so-called 'bad quartos'. Using the examples of *The Famous Victories of Henry V* and *The True Tragedy of Richard III*, the authors propose that mislineation of prose as verse in these is the result of mistakes introduced in the copy texts: prompt-books of the revisions of these plays which were dictated to a scribe in the rehearsal process '*after* the actors knew their revised parts' (p. 116). This is an ingenious theory which deserves to be treated seriously; its implications for reassessing so-called bad quartos in terms of their theatrical coherence are indeed far-reaching.

A final, short chapter reiterates the suggestion that Shakespeare could have possibly been a junior member of the Queen's Men in the early part of his career. 'His connection with the published texts of the Queen's Men seems close and deep' (p. 162), given the mirroring of incidents from four of the Queen's Men plays in his own, so the theory that he may have been one of several collaborative authors of *The Troublesome Raigne of King John* before rewriting this for the Lord Chamberlain's company is persuasive. A far less convincing biographical argument is put forward by Robert Fleissner, in an article published in the journal *Manuscripta*. Fleissner proposes, with negligible substantiating evidence, that Shakespeare may have been a visitor to Oxford and used the Bodleian library before writing *Julius Caesar*.

III

The difference between the personal styles of Queen Elizabeth and her successor has been the subject of some important work on the times in which Shakespeare wrote. Curtis Perry's book *The Making of Jacobean Culture* is an impressive re-examination which brings many new insights. A specific discussion of the nostalgia for Elizabeth and her reign is found in chapter 5, but the majority of the book takes a more oblique approach, using different genres to give subtle, nuanced readings of the changes from Elizabethan to Jacobean culture and their political meanings. In a fine chapter on pastoral, for example, Perry demonstrates how fragmentation is a characteristic feature of texts whose dramatists strove to negotiate their way between residual and emergent royal styles. Chapter 3 examines the crisis of counsel in the introverted world of the Jacobean court, in which, Perry argues, James's self-styling calls forth a reiterative response from his subjects which actually verges on parodic mimicry. The dangers of this specular environment are played out in texts like Marston's *The Fawne* and Daniel's *Philotas*. The book gains a pleasing breadth by devoting its final chapter to the city, a world elsewhere with its own audience and interests, which also moulded Jacobean culture through entertainments and pageants staged to celebrate successful citizens and the King.

The subject of kingship is addressed with reference to Shakespeare in chapter 4. Perry takes as his starting point the assimilation of maternal bounty into patriarchal rule under James. That the fantasy of quasi-maternal kingship is always shadowed by crisis and doomed is demonstrated through the tragedies of *King Lear* and *Macbeth*. Much of Perry's argument on *King Lear* relies on previous work by Kahn and Erickson, but he reaches the striking conclusion that the disempowerment and death of Cordelia represents the ideal of a feminized, nurturing king as a 'politically insufficient' failure (p. 137). *Macbeth* continues this critique of patriarchy's attempt to appropriate maternal functions, he goes on to argue, reading Lady Macbeth's monstrous parthenogenesis as an inversion of the self-created monarchs Duncan and Macbeth. This is intriguing, drawing attention to a sense of uneasiness at the end of the play, where the victorious Macduff 'not born of woman' (5.7.3) is a paternal failure who deserts his household.

Another dimension of the household community receives attention in Mark Thornton Burnett's *Masters and Servants in English Renaissance Drama and Culture*. Given the ubiquity of servant characters in Renaissance drama it is surprising that this is the first study devoted to this topic. The book provides a valuable survey of the territory, devoting chapters to apprentices, craftspersons, male and female domestic servants, and concluding with a discussion of the elaborate hierarchy of aristocratic great houses. In keeping with the aim of the series 'Early Modern Literature In History', each section outlines a historical context with which to approach the dramatic texts. Burnett is alert to the difficulties of recovering some of the histories, such as those of women in domestic service, and the general statements he makes about the positions of different servant types are backed up with a wealth of references to documents in record offices and research libraries. Since many of these are previously unpublished, their use opens a new angle on figures like De Flores or Bosola.

The arrangement of the chapters does not make the most of this opportunity. Cultural context and dramatic text are treated in parallel and Burnett makes his aims abundantly explicit in introductions and conclusions to each chapter. While such clarity is useful (particularly for the undergraduate reader), one feels, frustratedly, that the book's ideas could have been taken further by juxtaposing plays and documents in more pointed discussion, and at the expense of such elaborate signposting of the argument. Fascinating suggestions, like the comparison between the status of the acting companies as 'servants' and their possible identification with on-stage characters are left undeveloped (p. 96), for example. The focus on servant 'types' also prevents the book from giving fuller readings of the interactions within a household and play.

Nevertheless, Burnett makes a strong case for the servant's ability to function as 'symbolic property' or 'a barometer' of change in a times of economic and social fluctuation (p. 89), and provides illuminating analyses, such as his discussion of Kent, Oswald and Cornwall's servant in *King Lear* (pp. 83–6). In the final section of the book, the argument comes together strongly, using text and context to show how a decline of the noble household in the 1630s is dramatized in plays like Shirley's *The Lady of Pleasure* where the Steward's voice obliges the fashionable audiences to confront the price of 'abandoning pastoral pleasures for city leisure' (p. 180). One welcomes the attention Burnett pays to work by Shirley and Brome alongside more mainstream texts. The book includes discussion of plays like *Twelfth Night, The Changeling* and *The Shoemaker's Holiday*, though surprisingly Heywood's *A Woman Killed With Kindness*, in which the servant community plays such a vital role, is not considered. However, the observations about servant types provide good starting points for readers to construct interpretations of individual texts. This is the real strength of the book: while it does not offer transformative analyses of full plays, it does present a wealth of authoritative information on its subject.

This can also be said of Mario DiGangi's *The Homoerotics of Early Modern Drama* which begins by giving a clear outline of recent critical work in this field. The author correctly remarks that, on the vexed issues of sexual orientation in Shakespeare's period, we have 'lost the ability

to recognize the signs of orderly Renaissance homoerotic relations' within a modern ideology which 'posits heterosexuality as the norm' (p. 170). The book endeavours to correct this blinkered mode of perception by concentrating primarily on erotic relations between men in the drama. This project is pursued with energy using mainly non-canonical texts. The author makes a deliberate choice to decentre Shakespeare, although the opening chapter on Ovidian comedy contains a lucid analysis of the complex erotic energies circulating at the end of *Twelfth Night* around the maid / man figures of Sebastian and Viola. Sometimes DiGangi's enthusiasm for the topic leads to unconvincing statements such as the view that all the objects of erotic desire in the play are male, that 'Sebastian and Antonio desire each other' (p. 41). This focus threatens to reduce the wonderful ambivalence of 'what you will' just as exclusively as the heterosexual norm DiGangi complains about.

The book approaches satiric comedies by Jonson, Chapman and Middleton via a 'homoerotics of mastery', which allows for trenchant analysis of the power dynamic between masters and servants and inherent in the genre itself. The following chapter considers the figure of the court favourite, concentrating on sodomy as a cause of tragedy in *The Massacre at Paris*, *Edward II*, and on the relations between men in Chapman's tragedies of the French court. DiGangi's astute comments on *The Revenge of Bussy D'Ambois* give an example of the fruitful nature of his approach, when he aptly identifies the repressive nature of Clermont's stoicism as a refusal to recognize that 'the system of royal patronage that sustains him is *openly* and *normatively* homoerotic' (p. 131).

The popularization of less well-known plays which DiGangi promotes is assuredly helped by the availability of reasonably priced, well-annotated texts and Keith Sturgess's collection of plays by John Marston is a welcome addition to the Oxford World Classics series. Sturgess's introduction gives important points of access to each of the five plays: *Antonio and Mellida*, *Antonio's Revenge*, *The Malcontent*, *The Dutch Courtesan* and *Sophonisba*. More important than the issues of genre, however, is the focus on theatrical aspects of the plays. Sturgess stresses Marston's confident use of music, visual language, and reliance on metatheatre to 'break the frame of the fiction' (p. xiv), and carefully points out that we should not assume that the boys' companies for whom the scripts were written 'were incapable of playing "straight"' (p. xi). Like Jackson and Neill's 1986 edition, Sturgess uses the King's Men's QC text of *The Malcontent* but relegates the Webster additions to sections in the helpful explanatory notes.[3] This edition will make Marston's work easier to place for the modern reader or theatre practitioner.

Several recent publications open up European contexts to the early modern period. It is good to see a paperback edition of the 1996 collection *Witchcraft in Early Modern Europe: Studies in Culture and Belief* which successfully orientates ideas about English witchcraft within a European dimension. There are contributions by many prestigious scholars. Peter Elmer's useful piece on 'Saints and Sorcerers' draws attention to the charges of witchcraft levelled against Quakers in the mid seventeenth century (pp. 145–79), and Jim Sharpe thoughtfully reassesses the East Anglia trials of 1645–7, which, he suggests, provide evidence not of 'peculiarity' but of a more pervasive integration of so-called European witchcraft beliefs (pp. 237–54).

Several essays focus specifically on the relationship between witchcraft and gender. Gareth Roberts shows how the powerful figure of Circe, frequently associated with witchcraft in literary contexts, contributed to the construction of the witch as a symbol of overbearing female power in early modern English culture, and offers a brief, interesting reading of *The Comedy of Errors* in support of this thesis. In 'Witchcraft and fantasy in early Modern Germany' (pp. 207–36), Lyndal Roper brings a

new angle to bear on the model of witch as victim, regarding the lying-in maid as the scapegoat of women's own suppressed fears and desires surrounding maternity and childbirth. The conclusions of this stimulating essay perhaps suggest new ways of assessing women's involvement in English witchcraft prosecutions and the importance of paying attention to a European context. The book's publication in paperback is to be warmly welcomed since the editors have brought together essays which offer detailed case studies while raising important methodological questions.

Scholars working on early modern Europe will also be pleased by the publication of *Marriage in Italy 1300–1650*, a collection edited by Trevor Dean and K. J. P. Lowe. Some of these articles illuminate interesting contexts for work on Shakespeare's plays. Patricia Allerton's essay on wedding finery and entertainment in sixteenth-century Venice, centred around the bride (p. 32), makes Petruchio's monstrous parody and subsequent rejection of festivities in *The Taming of the Shrew* seem all the more outrageous. Similarly Kate Lowe's comparison of secular and convent brides involved in ceremonies with many clear parallels, casts an interesting light on Isabella's position at the end of *Measure for Measure*. In addition there is a fascinating essay by Piet van Boxel on Catholic attempts to convert Jews by providing Jewish women with dowries if they were willing to renounce their culture and faith. Although the context here is Counter-Reformation Rome, its relevance to *The Merchant of Venice* is apparent.

A less successful book is Kwang Soon Cho's *Emblems in Shakespeare's Last Plays* which attempts to place the romances within the context of English and European emblem collections and famous Renaissance paintings such as Botticelli's *Primavera*. The idea of using emblems to read the last plays is potentially

---

[3] MacD. P. Jackson and M. Neill, eds., *The Selected Plays of John Marston* (Cambridge, 1986).

interesting but the execution here is weak. The study of *Pericles*, for example, isolates a few elements of the text and discusses them in what reads like a series of footnotes rather than a coherent argument about the play. There is, remarkably, no discussion of the opening spectacle at Antiochus' court, nothing about the other knights' impresas at the Pentapolis joust. In considering Pericles' own impresa, the author takes no account of work on the probable source for this.[4] Discussions of the other plays demonstrate a similarly limited approach. In the final chapter on *Henry VIII* the author begins to construct an argument about the relationship between symbolic visual spectacle and royal power, but politicization of the emblem tradition is not fully developed, and is notable by its absence from the chapter on *The Tempest*. The book is also marred by numerous careless typographical errors, which come to a climax in the final chapter's indiscriminate use of 'Katherline' and 'Katherine' for the Queen. One is forced to conclude that this is a disappointing, unscholarly and under-researched piece of work.

Verbal as opposed to visual language is the subject of Janette Dillon's *Language and Stage in Medieval and Renaissance England*. It is pleasing to find a study which constructs the late medieval and early modern along a continuum rather than treating them as isolated, discrete, periods. Dillon stresses change, but traces a development of responses to alien languages in English drama and the wider culture. Foreign languages, associated with attitudes to the immigrant population of early modern London, are briefly examined in *The Merry Wives of Windsor* and *Henry V* alongside *The Weakest Goeth to the Wall* and Richard Wilson's *The Lords and Ladies of London*. However, the majority of the book concentrates on religious discourse and the biblical Word as a potent symbol of truth; Dillon skilfully explores the negotiations between a Latin liturgy, 'at once so remote from and so familiar to ordinary people' (p. 1), and the impulse to construct an independent national identity through English.

She uses the context of the Lollard movement to suggest the subtlety with which texts like the Wakefield *Second Shepherds' Play* and *Mankind* present the voice of God and the sacramental language of authority. As the book argues, the Protestant dilemma over 'learning' was played out in a variety of forms in Tudor morality plays in which the Latinity of traditional scholarship is curiously endorsed, and where the book becomes a prop of especial importance. The ambiguity of Latin is further explored in an effective reading of *The Spanish Tragedy*, where Hieronimo's book, representing both Seneca and the Bible, signals the breakdown of unitary truths, and his use of Latinate vocabulary creates a deliberately heightened artifice to intensify emotional engagement. The final chapter discusses Latin in *Doctor Faustus* and *Contention* as a language associated both (negatively) with Catholicism and conjurers and more positively with authority as the language of philosophical debate.

Although Dillon makes some passing references to Bakhtin, the dialogic nature of the speeches she discusses is often underplayed. The performed nature of the language – and its inherent instability as parasitic utterance – does not receive any detailed consideration. Nevertheless, one of the book's great strengths is its clarity. Its use of quotations and close reading means that its points are always well illustrated.

Another example of the value of close reading and the importance of language is Philip Edwards' *Sea Mark: The Metaphorical Voyage, Spenser to Milton*, which studies the voyage as a motif central not only to romance narratives but to tragedy and history. Edwards takes his title from Othello's lines 'Here is my journies end, heere is my butt / And verie Seamarke of my utmost Saile' (Folio 5.2.274), where the sea mark is the guiding point which

---

[4] Alan R. Young, 'A Note on the Tournament Impresas in *Pericles*', *Shakespeare Quarterly*, 36 (1985), 453–6.

gives direction to one's life. Navigational imagery provides a clear way into reading the tragedies of Othello and Macbeth, where Edwards' writing, based on years of close acquaintance with the texts, is characterized by confident eloquence. He makes a strong case for reading Othello's 'excuses' in the final scene sympathetically, as the bitter realization of personal responsibility for what has happened. In *Macbeth*, the weird sisters' spell on the Master of the Tiger (1.3.1–29) is read as the point which generates the tragic action in which the protagonist degenerates into a pilot who has 'wrecked his own ship' and 'denied "navigation" to others' in Scotland (p. 127). Less effective is Edwards' chapter on the comedies and romances, which simply traces the recurrence of the shipwreck and restoration pattern through from *The Comedy of Errors* to *The Tempest*.

A notable feature of Edwards' approach is his insistence on using Folio readings of the plays as 'infinitely superior' and 'necessary' (p. 102). Use of Folio capitalizations and spellings often has the virtue of estranging the reader and encouraging a new focus on the language in the technique of close reading which Edwards promotes. Bridget Cusack's edition of less familiar documents in *Everyday English 1500–1700: A Reader* is another very useful teaching tool, using original spelling and punctuation. The sixty-four texts from different areas of England, Scotland, America amply illustrate regional variations in language use. Their grouping under the headings of accounts, wills, journals, letters, memoirs, depositions, presentments and abuse, makes the book interesting from a socio-historical as well as a linguistic point of view and readers will be pleased to find many previously unnoticed texts, transcribed from manuscripts and brought to light here.

The language of abuse is the concern of M. Lindsay Kaplan's important new book *The Culture of Slander in Early Modern England*. Kaplan opens with a rather narrow critique of

recent studies of literary censorship, arguing that they fail to pay proper attention to the ways in which defamation is configured in early modern society. The book sets about to fill this gap and outlines a picture of slander as an ambiguous weapon used by both the state and its opponents. In a well-argued opening chapter, Kaplan examines defamation as a deeply paradoxical form, its unstable status as either a true exposure or a false claim undermining any notion of transcendent 'truth' and making accusations dangerous to both the antagonist and his or her 'victim', who may be the perpetrator of a crime. Even more disturbingly, slander is shown to be a central technique employed by those in authority to enforce order via the public humiliation of dissidents, yet its use could easily implicate the state rather than the criminal.

The book's subsequent chapters illustrate how writers negotiate a route through the slippery terrain of defamation in order to support their own positions and freedom of expression while still offering a critique of those in power. Kaplan shows that although Jonson and Spenser adopt a clever manipulation of the politics of defamation, this unravels as each is finally unable to escape the charge of slander he levels against others. The final chapter demonstrates how Shakespeare dramatizes the problem of slander more successfully in *Measure for Measure*. Kaplan picks up on the description of Lucio as 'a fantastique' (dramatis personae) to read him as a satiric poet whose elaborate slanders actually pinpoint the truth about Vienna's laws and government, drawing attention to 'significant inadequacies in the Duke's actions as a ruler' (p. 99). While this may seem self-evident, the analysis pushes further to reveal the way in which Lucio's creative power in the invention of slanders is mirrored by the 'fantastical Duke' (4.3.152) whose use of slander as a tool of subjugation actually 'subverts the authority of the state' (p. 107). In addition to such stimulating analyses, readers will find the general arguments which the book presents extremely useful starting points for thinking about the wider context of slander and defamation.

The power of language as a moulding force is taken up again in Howard Marchitello's *Narrative and Meaning in Early Modern England*. From the beginning, this book ingeniously teases the reader in the introduction of its thesis that meaning is produced discursively in a temporal paradox where the narrational voice (or writing) forgets its own beginning and unself-consciously imagines that it can construct pure meaning 'in what is in fact a thoroughly narrativized world' (p. 8). Hamlet's words 'I am dead, Horatio' (5.2.285) and Derrida's discussion of the ghost as a '*revenant*' illustrate the complex theoretical position Marchitello wishes to outline, and his playful comments on his own writing practice look forward to the book's interrogation of current critical and editorial narratives.

The subsequent chapters take up the idea of narration in maps, colonialist discourse on the New World, medical and scientific writing. Much of this material is familiar, yet the book often gives it an interesting new spin, as in the discussion of a modern Automobile Association route as a dominant narrative where 'orientation is utterly disregarded' and 'trajectory becomes the equivalent of plot, and the plot alone exists in the very midst of what is evidently a blank space' (p. 87). Shakespeare's *Othello* and *The Merchant of Venice* feature in Marchitello's discussions. The first chapter compares Othello's search for 'ocular proof' (3.3.365) of Desdemona's sexual identity and Vesalius' dissection of female bodies in the anatomy theatre, to show that the woman's hymen loses its corporeality in its role as a 'narrational signifier' within a 'politically motivated reading which offers justification for domination' (p. 19). While not altogether new, the argument is elegant, ending with a spotlight on Giovanni's futile attempt to possess Annabella's love by physically displaying her heart in the final scene of *'Tis Pity She's A Whore*.

Letters and writing provide the focus for the book's most absorbing discussion: of *The Merchant of Venice* and the practice of editing. Marchitello analyses the letters, will and bond in the play, including the final missive to Antonio which 'comes from nowhere and from no one's hand', as forms of writing that destabilize 'the epistemology of presence' they appear to construct (p. 51). This intelligent discussion, however, turns out to be a pre-text for the real argument of the chapter, for a move away from editorial practices which attempt to construct and explain all the disparate elements of a text in relation to agency and recognisable meaning. Using the example of the crux of the three characters Solanio, Salarnio and Salerio as a possible 'accident' in the play, Marchitello proposes that such 'accidents' need to be preserved in the printed text because 'they mark eruptions of phenomena for which we simply cannot account' (p. 61) and therefore return the text and us more fully to history. This challenging argument illustrates the most important quality of the book: its ability to cast a new light on current critical practice from an apparently familiar angle.

Accident, narrativity and authority are also the subjects of Jacques Lezra's book *Unspeakable Subjects: The Genealogy of the Event in Early Modern Europe*. Like Marchitello, Lezra aims to expose the gaps which exist between 'the formalization of matter and the materialization of form' (p. 32). The introduction attempts to explain 'eventful reading' as a 'practice of material poetics' in which 'etiologies or genealogies of the eventful emergence of power are always phenomenonalized according to regressive patterns' so that 'the event *as such* is also the name we give to the mystification of the origin of ideology' (p. 33). Lezra deliberately juxtaposes early modern texts and modern theoretical writing in the pursuit of his topic. Although this is an exciting methodology, and certainly shows the author's sparkling mental agility, the jumps he makes from Lucretius to Hegel, *Don Quixote* and Fray Luis de Léon to

Freud and Derrida, or Descartes and Shakespeare to Nietzsche and Foucault, are often baffling to all but the most informed reader. Indeed, one feels that the avalanche of ideas launched in the opening chapter is in danger, like Falstaff, of 'o'erwhelm[ing] all her litter but one' (*Henry IV Part 2* 1.2.11).

Happily, the discussions which emerge in the following chapters are not so overburdened. In *Measure for Measure*, Lezra takes the event of Barnadine's point blank refusal to be executed as a starting point for examining the insecure relationships between signs or figures and authority. Piracy, in the person of Ragozine, is read as a key trope which links together the figures of the Duke and Lucio and Angelo within the text, and King James and Shakespeare the dramatist outside it. Ragozine's identity as a 'substitute' is cleverly read as a symbol of the absence at the heart of monarchy, a symbol which 'risked showing the inadequacy of the "substitute" to the "absence" he or she supplied' (p. 259). Lezra argues that Vincentio's sinister side is imaged in the pirate, that the slippery signification which characterizes piracy always threatens to consume the discourse of state power. This reading unfortunately pays little attention to the Isabella plot, but it certainly establishes Lezra's own voice as a lively intervention into the critical debate. To return finally to Hamlet's wish to set 'up a glass / Where you may see the inward part of you' (3.4.19), these recent studies on Shakespeare's times and stage indicate a continuing interest in mirroring and reflection, a fascination with the other, be it from the past or the present, as a way of illuminating the self.

WORKS REVIEWED

Alexander, Catherine M. S., 'Horace Walpole's *Macbeth*', in *The Review of English Studies*, 49 (1988), 131–44.

Barry, Jonathan, Marianne Hester and Gareth Roberts, eds., *Witchcraft in Early Modern Europe: Studies in Culture and Belief*. Past and Present Publications (Cambridge, 1998).

Boose, Lynda E. and Richard Burt, *Shakespeare, The Movie: Popularizing the Plays on Film, TV and Radio* (London and New York, 1997).

Burnett, Mark Thornton, *Masters and Servants in English Renaissance Drama and Culture: Authority and Obedience*. Early Modern Literature in History (Basingstoke, 1997).

Burnett, Mark Thornton and Ramona Wray, eds., *Shakespeare and Ireland: History, Politics, Culture* (Basingstoke, 1997).

Cho, Kwang Soon, *Emblems in Shakespeare's Last Plays* (Lanham, New York, Oxford, 1998).

Cusack, Bridget, ed., *Everyday English 1500–1700: A Reader* (Edinburgh, 1998).

Dean, Trevor and K. J. P. Lowe, eds., *Marriage in Italy 1300–1650* (Cambridge, 1998).

DiGangi, Mario, *The Homoerotics of Early Modern Drama* (Cambridge, 1997).

Dillon, Janette, *Language and Stage in Medieval and Renaissance England* (Cambridge, 1998).

Edwards, Philip, *Sea Mark: The Metaphorical Voyage, Spenser to Milton* (Liverpool, 1997).

Fleissner, Robert F., '"Et Tu Brute" and "Recte Brutus ... improbe, qui interfecto Caesare ... ": or, did not Shakespeare ever utilize the Bodleian?', *Manuscripta*, 39 (1995), 51–5).

Gunter, J. Lawrence and Andrew M. McLean, *Redefining Shakespeare: Literary Theory and Theater Practice in the German Democratic Republic* (Newark, 1998).

'*Hamlet / La Nuit des Rois:* Shakespeare, La Scène et Ses Miroirs', *Théâtre Aujourd' hui*, 6. (Paris: Ministère de L' Education Nationale de la Recherche et de la Technologie, 1998).

Highley, Christopher, *Shakespeare, Spenser and the Crisis in Ireland* (Cambridge, 1997).

Holland, Peter, *English Shakespeares: Shakespeare on the English Stage in the 1990s* (Cambridge, 1997).

Hortmann, Wilhelm, *Shakespeare on the German Stage: the 20th Century* (Cambridge, 1998).

Lezra, Jacques, *Unspeakable Subjects: The Genealogy of the Event in Early Modern Europe* (Stanford, 1997).

Kaplan, Lindsay M., *The Culture of Slander in Early Modern England* (Cambridge, 1997).

Marchitello, Howard, *Narrative and Meaning in Early Modern England* (Cambridge, 1997).

Marston, John, *The Malcontent and Other Plays*, ed. by Keith Sturgess (Oxford, 1997).

McMillin, Scott and Sally-Beth MacLean, *The Queen's Men and their Plays* (Cambridge, 1998).

Morrison, Michael A., *John Barrymore: Shakesperian Actor* (Cambridge, 1998).

Parfenov, Alexandr and Joseph G. Price, eds., *Russian Essays on Shakespeare and his Contemporaries* (London, 1998).

Perry, Curtis, *The Making of Jacobean Culture: James I and the renegotiation of Elizabethan literary practice* (Cambridge, 1997).

Ripley, John, *Coriolanus on Stage in England and America, 1609–1994* (Madison, 1998).

Shakespeare, William, *Hamlet*, Dir. by Neville Jason (Naxos AudioBooks, 1997).

Shakespeare, William, *Much Ado About Nothing*, ed. by John F. Cox, Shakespeare in Production Series (Cambridge, 1998).

Shakespeare, William, *Romeo and Juliet*. Dir. by Michael Sheen (Naxos AudioBooks, 1997).

Shurgot, Michael W., *Stages of Play: Shakespeare's Theatrical Energies in Elizabethan Performance* (Newark and London, 1998).

Wells, Stanley, ed., *Shakespeare in the Theatre: An Anthology of Criticism* (Oxford, 1997).

Williams, Gary Jay, *Our Moonlight Revels: A Midsummer Night's Dream in the Theatre* (Iowa, 1997).

Worthen, W. B., *Shakespeare and the Authority of Performance* (Cambridge, 1997).

3. EDITIONS AND TEXTUAL STUDIES

reviewed by ERIC RASMUSSEN

EDITIONS: ARDEN 3

The new Arden edition of *Shakespeare's Sonnets* has been a long time coming. C. K. Pooler's edition in the original Arden series was issued in 1918; a revised second edition appeared in 1931. For many decades, students of the *Sonnets* awaited publication of a New Arden, long-announced as in preparation by Winifred Nowottny, which never came forth. Katherine Duncan-Jones begins her edition in the Arden 3 series with no mention of the lack of an Arden 2, although an explanation for the delay may be implicit in her observation that an edition prepared with due diligence necessarily takes time:

With reference to the text of individual sonnets, the minutest features of spelling, punctuation and format have momentous consequences for resonance and meaning. I have never felt more strongly than when

working on this text the force of Oscar Wilde's account of a writer's hard labours: spending the whole morning putting in a comma, and the whole afternoon taking it out. (p. xiv)

Regrettably, this careful attention to detail is not always evident in the edition itself. There is an error in the text ('ye' for 'you' in line 71 of *A Lover's Complaint*), and over two dozen errors in the line references and lemmas in the notes.[1] Moreover, in an announced 'divergence

---

[1] *Reviewer's note*: In all of the editions under review, textual collations and commentary notes begin with a line number followed by a lemma (the word or phrase from the text). The line number reference in the note should, of course, be the line number in which the word appears in the text; and the word in the lemma should replicate the word in the text exactly. For each edition, I have noted any instances in which a line reference or lemma is incorrect. Although it may seem that such details have nothing to do with content, a failure to pay

from normal Arden 3 practice' Duncan-Jones has not collated any of the eighteenth-century editions of the *Sonnets* except for Capell's manuscript notes for a proposed edition that never saw print and Malone's edition of 1780; nor has she collated any of the more than one hundred editions that appeared between Malone (1780) and Pooler (1918). An Arden edition is not intended to be a Variorum, but to ignore the editorial activities of several centuries has real consequences for anything resembling an accurate record of textual history.

Nearly every emendation that Duncan-Jones claims is unique to her edition was anticipated in earlier editions that she has not collated. The edition's thrice-trumpeted claim (made on pages xiv, 103, and 366) to be 'the first modernized text ever to reproduce the two pairs of empty italic parentheses' which conclude sonnet 126 is manifestly untrue: Samuel Butler's edition of the *Sonnets* (1899) and G. B. Harrison's in the Penguin Shakespeare series (1938) both reproduce the parentheses. The commas setting off 'all, tyrant', in 149.4 are flagged as an emendation 'adopted for the first time in this edition', but the same commas appear in George Sewell's edition of *Mr Sh.'s Miscellany Poems* that was issued as volume seven of Pope's Shakespeare (1725). The conjectural emendation of 'their' to 'your' in 85.3, which Duncan-Jones claims for '*this edn*', giving credit to series general editor Richard Proudfoot for suggesting it to her, was proposed long ago and is recorded in Wright's Cambridge Shakespeare (1893). Duncan-Jones notes that, on the advice of Helen Vendler, she has emended 'My sinfull earth' to 'Feeding' in 146.2 and claims the emendation as her own; but the conjecture should properly be credited to Sebastian Evans who made it well over a century ago.

The spirit of error haunts the introductory essay as well. Duncan-Jones's assertion that '*Venus and Adonis* went through at least sixteen editions in Shakespeare's lifetime' (p. 8) is challenged by the *Short-Title Catalogue of Books Printed in England* which lists only ten (STC

22354–22360b). Even when she playfully charges Emma Thompson with historical inaccuracies, Duncan-Jones is herself less than accurate:

In her screenplay of Jane Austen's *Sense and Sensibility* (1995) Emma Thompson shows Willoughby and Marianne as each equipped with a little volume of *Shakespeare's Sonnets*. Though this scene works well as a visual signal of the natural erotic and literary sympathy between the young people, it is wholly anachronistic, for in 1811 no such dainty edition existed. (p. 78)

In fact, Willoughby and Marianne might well have had Armstrong's *Sonnets from Shakespeare* (1791), or Cooke's edition of *The Poetical Works of Shakespeare* (1797), or the Oliver & Munroe edition of *The Poems of Shakespeare* (1807), the last two of which were printed in duodecimo — a dainty format in anybody's book.

At other points in the introduction, factual errors are intermingled with rather questionable

---

attention to details in superficial features is unfortunately often a signal of sloppiness in more substantive aspects. I am indebted to Arthur Evenchik, Bernice W. Kliman, and Stanley Wells for reading early drafts of this review essay and pointing out my own errors, both superficial and substantive.

Errors in Duncan-Jones's commentary notes include sonnet 13, line 1, for 'Yourself' read 'yourself'; sonnet 21, line 9, for 'True' read 'true'; sonnet 46, for '3, 13, 148' read '3, 8, 13, 14'; sonnet 59, for '1–2' read '1'; sonnet 77, the second 'memory' is listed under line 6 rather than line 9; sonnet 87, line 14, for 'in' read 'In'; sonnet 105, line 6, for 'still' read 'Still'; sonnet 118, line 5, for 'ne'er cloying' read 'ne'er-cloying'; sonnet 119, 'blessed' is listed under line 7 rather than line 6; sonnet 133, the commentary on line 8 is placed after that on line 9; sonnet 153, line 2, for 'a maid' read 'A maid'; sonnet 153, 'distempered' is listed under line 14 rather than line 12; *A Lover's Complaint*, 'anon' is listed under line 28 rather than line 26. Errors in the textual collations include sonnet 24 for 'good-turns' read 'good-turnes'; sonnet 30, 'foregone' is listed under line 7 rather than line 9; sonnet 33, line 4, for 'gilding' read 'Gilding'; sonnet 62, line 13, for 'Tis' read ' 'Tis'; sonnet 81, for '5' read '6'; sonnet 99, two stray semi-colons appear in the first two collations; sonnet 118, line 5, for 'ne'er cloying' read 'ne'er-cloying'; sonnet 138, line 7, for 'credite' read 'credit'; *A Lover's Complaint* line 182 for 'vow' read 'vovv'.

logic. Duncan-Jones argues, for instance, that the survival of thirteen copies of the 1609 *Sonnets* Quarto, whereas 'only four copies' of the 1609 *Troilus and Cressida* Quarto are extant, suggests that '*Troilus and Cressida* was three times as popular among readers as *Shakespeare's Sonnets*' (p. 8). She argues that *Troilus and Cressida* was read so voraciously that all but four copies crumbled, while multiple copies of the *Sonnets* remained unread and untouched. But couldn't the converse be argued with equal plausibility? That is, might not the higher survival rate suggest that the Quarto of the *Sonnets* was not treated as a disposable paperback by its early readers, but a text to be treasured and preserved? It may be a moot point since there are, in fact, *fifteen* extant copies of the *Troilus and Cressida* Quarto (and one of these, the uncut Martin Bodmer copy, has never been opened).

Duncan-Jones conjectures that in the severe plague year of 1609, an out-of-work Shakespeare sold the *Sonnets* manuscript to the quality publisher Thomas Thorpe ('price must have been an important consideration') before leaving London for Stratford. In order to maximize the return on his investment, Thorpe divided the copies between two booksellers: William Aspley, whose name appears on the title-pages of four of the extant copies, had a shop in St Paul's Churchyard; John Wright, whose name appears on seven extant copies, had a shop at the door of Christ Church nearest to Newgate. Duncan-Jones suggests that Wright may have been chosen 'precisely because his shop was in a conspicuous position . . . When the moneyed classes returned to the City after the plague-ridden summer of 1609 by way of the Strand or of Holborn, they would pass near one of the shops at which *Shakespeare's Sonnets* was on sale' (p. 37). The assumption here is that the bookseller identified on a title-page was the book's exclusive *retailer*. But, as Peter Blayney has recently explained in no uncertain terms, 'the primary purpose of an imprint was the same in early modern England as it is today: to inform *retailers* where a book could be purchased *wholesale* . . . The goal of whoever handled the wholesaling of a book (either its publisher or chosen agent) was to sell as many copies as possible, and that meant selling them to as many of England's hundreds of *bookshops* as possible. The idea that anyone could benefit from restricting retail sales to a single shop in a single city is nothing less than absurd.'[2] Blayney's important caveat renders Duncan-Jones's narrative about the distribution of *Shakespeare's Sonnets* untenable.

The occasional inaccuracies notwithstanding, there are things to admire and value in Duncan-Jones's edition: she offers some genuine food for thought on the overlooked January 1599/1600 entry in the Stationers' Register for 'certain *other sonnets* by W.S.'; her discussion of the textual implications of the 'mock-lapidary' form of the dedication is compelling; and the layout of the edition itself is particularly appealing. Each sonnet is printed on a separate recto page, with the commentary for that sonnet on the facing verso. When the commentary runs longer than a page, the sonnet is reprinted on the subsequent recto so that the commentary is never out of its text.

Duncan-Jones provides narrative summaries for each sonnet and concise commentary. For readers accustomed to the voluminous notes in Stephen Booth's edition, it may seem odd that the text of the sonnet frequently occupies more space than the text of Duncan-Jones's commentary notes. In general, Duncan-Jones suggests far fewer multiple meanings for individual words than does Booth. The apparent pun in the opening line of Sonnet 116 ('Let me not to the marriage of true minds admit impediments') is a case in point: whereas Booth gives a range of possibilities for *admit* including 'concede the existence of, acknowledge; permit consideration of . . . allow to

---

[2] 'The Publication of Playbooks', *A New History of Early English Drama*, ed. John D. Cox and David Scott Kastan (New York, 1997), p. 390.

enter',[3] Duncan-Jones suggests only 'acknowl-edge'. So too, the narrative summaries, which are no doubt intended to assist a reader en-countering *Shakespeare's Sonnets* for the first time, may have the net effect of appearing to close off certain interpretative possibilities. Although Duncan-Jones is usually attuned to nuances of sound, I would suspect that even advanced readers could have used a note on the 'taste'/'last' rhyme in *A Lover's Complaint* (lines 167–8). Booth admitted that many of the puns and allusions he described were probably farfetched; only a few of Duncan-Jones's notes deserve this label, but it might apply to her suggestion that in Sonnet 144 the poet is numerically punning by being really 'gross'.

The Arden 3 cover blurbs have a fondness for the definite article: 'The critical edition of Shakespeare', 'The established scholarly edition', 'The finest edition of Shakespeare you can find'. One might question whether all editions in the series are uniformly deserving of these claims of distinction, but David Beving-ton's new *Troilus and Cressida* stands out as the genuine article. Bevington's edition begins, co-incidentally, with a stimulating discussion of 'an enigmatic publicity blurb'. The first issue of the 1609 *Troilus and Cressida* Quarto (Qa) offers the play 'As it was acted by the Kings Maiesties seruants at the Globe'; a second issue (Qb) claims that the play was 'never staled with the stage, never clapper-clawed with the palms of the vulgar', and offers the text to a reading audience with a title-page highlighting its literary qualities: 'The Famous Historie of Troylus and Cresseid. Excellently expressing the beginning of their loues, with the conceited wooing of Pandarus Prince of Licia'. The ambivalence in the play's status as a theatrical text (Qa) and/or a literary text (Qb) extends to its genre: Qb presents the play as a comedy, 'passing full of the palm comical'; both Quarto title-pages offer the play as a 'Historie'; the Folio text calls it a 'Tragedie'. In the Folio, the first page of *Troilus and Cressida* was initially printed on the verso of the last page of *Romeo*

and Juliet, but it was then reset and re-placed to come first among that volume's tragedies – *or* last among the histories; the table of contents for the Folio omits the play and thus does not make it clear to which category it belongs.

This edition is fascinated by *Troilus and Cressida*'s many indeterminacies: its stop-and-go publication, its experimentalism, its three centuries of neglect, and its explosive revival in recent years both critically and theatrically. Bevington credibly claims to have read 'every-thing written on the play' and to have reviewed 'the entire history of production' (the biblio-graphy of works cited runs to well over six hundred entries).[4] Instead of presenting a tiresome précis of this enormous amount of critical material, Bevington offers an eloquent synthesis. His introductory essay moves deftly from the sacred to the profane – the Bible's Song of Solomon rubs shoulders with 'a bill-board poster reminiscent of Madonna' (presum-ably not the biblical one) – in a genuinely engaging narrative account of the play's histor-ical context, its theatrical representation, and its cultural implications, including an especially valuable discussion of commercial and subjec-tive valuation of identity and worth.

Rather than obfuscate the play's famous textual indeterminacies, Bevington initially proposed editing both the Quarto and the Folio on facing pages or sequentially, as he and I had done with *Doctor Faustus* in the Revels Plays series, but such version-based editing apparently goes against Arden 3 general policy (with the rule-proving exception of the forthcoming

---

[3] Stephen Booth, ed., *Shakespeare's Sonnets* (New Haven, 1977), pp. 384–90.

[4] Bevington's claim to have collated the uncorrected and the corrected states of the Quarto is not entirely credible: the press variants 'lone' (Qu) 'loue' (Qc) at 3.1.107, '*Deipholus, Helenes*' (Qu) '*Deiphobus, Henenus*' (Qc) at 3.1.129, 'thene then' (Qu) 'then' (Qc) 3.2.82, and 'shooing-horue' (Qu) 'shooing-horne' (Qc) at 5.1.54 are not listed in the textual notes. At 2.3.223, 'Yon' is given as the Q reading but should be properly be listed as Qu, since Qc has 'You'.

Hamlet). 'As a result', Bevington laments, 'the textual notes in this edition are burdensomely numerous, and the commentary notes necessarily take up issues of competing readings on a case-by-case basis'. In dozens of instances, a concise commentary note (that can hardly be called burdensome) alerts readers interested in 'textual choices' to consult the section of longer notes printed after the text where Bevington adjudicates between the rival claims of early texts in a model of humane textual criticism.

Bevington's text is flawless; the commentary full and helpful; the account of the complex textual situation should prove accessible to all readers. Bevington proposes a scenario in which *Troilus and Cressida*'s seeming comment on the Earl of Essex made the play 'too hot to handle' in the wake of the failed rebellion. 'The play was so politically controversial that Shakespeare's acting company prudently withheld it (after, perhaps, a very few performances) and dissociated themselves from it on the revised title-page of the 1609 Quarto' (p. 89). He also suggests that the duality of Qa and Qb may reflect 'diverse impulses in Shakespeare himself' in that he cared about his plays as theatrical texts for performance *and* as literary texts 'to be read and remembered' (pp. 400–1). Bevington might have observed that this duality is nicely, if serendipitously, preserved in the Daniel-Huth copy of the Quarto which includes both the original and the revised title-pages.

Bevington ascribes the legional Q/F differences to authorial revision, made when Shakespeare had occasion to write out a new script for his company or perhaps for an influential patron (p. 412). The three-line passage, in which Troilus dismisses Pandarus, that appears at the end of 5.3 in the Folio and then again, slightly altered, at 5.11.32–4, is central to any account of the *Troilus and Cressida* texts.[5] Whereas E. K. Chambers saw 5.3 as Shakespeare's first shot, Gary Taylor argued that the 5.3 version was added in revision for the purposes of ending Pandarus' relationship with Troilus at that point in order to allow the play

to end on Troilus' bitter note of revenge and inward woe for the death of Hector. In this putative revised version of the play, Pandarus' Epilogue was also cut, but the F compositor missed the deletion markings. The Oxford *Complete Works* did not include Pandarus's final soliloquy in the text of the play, but printed it as Additional Passage F. More recently, the Oxford editors have modified their position and now argue that the passage perhaps ought to be printed at the end of 5.3.[6]

Bevington's decision to retain Pandarus' Epilogue (while deleting the 5.3 version of the three lines) is rooted in the textual history of the Folio. When the Folio printers began setting *Troilus and Cressida* (beginning on the verso of the conclusion to *Romeo and Juliet*), they were apparently working from a copy of Q and simply reprinting the Quarto text. After three pages had been set in this way, a different sort of printer's copy seems to have become available, and the first page was reset with the new Prologue on the recto. From there on, it appears that the compositors were working from a copy of Q that had been annotated with reference to a manuscript. Bevington argues that if we credit Heminges and Condell with 'knowing what they were doing when they turned to an authoritative manuscript as a way of updating the Q printed text, we should also consider that the inclusion of the ending common to Q and F was their choice' (p. 421). The decision to retain the Epilogue seems reasonable enough, but Bevington might have given more attention to the Folio-only Prologue, the addition of which, Taylor argued, may be related to the altered ending. Indeed, Bevington's assertion that 'the longest passages

---

[5] Bevington's comment that the two versions of this passage are 'modified in one word only' (p. 352n) is not strictly correct. The Folio version at 5.3 reads 'Why, but heare you? / Hence brother' whereas at 5.11 the lines are 'But hear you, hear you / Hence, broker'.

[6] Stanley Wells and Gary Taylor, 'The Oxford Shakespeare Re-viewed by the General Editors', *Analytical and Enumerative Bibliography*, n.s. 4 (1990), 14–15.

occurring in F alone' are 'five lines each' inadvertently neglects the 31-line Prologue altogether (p. 412). The single sentence describing the Prologue's role in the revision ('A prologue came along at some point and became part of the copy for F' (p. 423)) might be said to lack precision.

But the vagueness in discussing the Prologue may be part of Bevington's avowed philosophical commitment to respect and represent 'the play's own indeterminate nature' while (the cover blurb notwithstanding) 'making no claim to be definitive' (p. 426). Rather than dogmatically insisting upon solutions, Bevington positively celebrates *Troilus and Cressida*'s many puzzles with infectious enthusiasm ('This is an amazing play'). Bevington's edition is so clearly the best now available that it will no doubt quickly become standard practice for all study of this remarkable play to begin with this remarkable edition.

David Daniell's monumental introductory essay to his Arden 3 edition of *Julius Caesar*, a monograph in itself, opens with a provocative discussion of the 'calendar conflicts' at the end of the sixteenth century. In 1582, the Papal states had adopted the new Gregorian calendar, which added ten days and made the summer solstice the 21st (not the 12th) of June, while Protestant countries clung tenaciously to the Julian calendar. Instituted by Julius Caesar in 46 BC (Daniell mistakenly dates it 44 BC, the year of the assassination), the Julian calendar was viewed by many Romans as tyrannical interference with the course of nature and was, according to Plutarch, one of the reasons that Caesar was hated. As Sigurd Burckhardt and others have pointed out, the situation in Europe in the 1580s and 1590s was thus analogous to Rome in 44 BC in that 'the most basic category by which men order their experience seemed to have become unstable and untrustworthy' (p. 19). Daniell's discussion of the cultural analogy (based in part on forthcoming work by Steven Sohmer) is interesting in and of itself, but Daniell then ingeniously brings it to

bear on a famous textual crux. At 2.1.40–2 in the Folio, Brutus asks Lucius 'Is not tomorrow, boy, the first of March?' Lucius doesn't know, so Brutus requests that he 'Look in the calendar and bring me word'. The calendar reveals that it is 15 March. Theobald's emendation of 'first' to 'Ides' in line 40 is almost universally followed, but Daniell makes a compelling case for retaining the Folio reading. Once one acknowledges the intensity of the conflict over Caesar's reform of the calendar and the parallel conflict between the rival Julian and Gregorian calendars in the 1590s, it becomes clear that the focal point of this exchange is 'the calendar' (line 42) since only when *the* calendar (i.e. the right one) has been consulted can the fifteen-day discrepancy be settled. Daniell observes that Shakespeare is here 'writing to the historical and contemporary moments at once' and may also be using the calendar shift to 'bring into prominence the concentration of time' in the first three acts of the play (p. 199).

With introductory sections on character, structure, sources, criticism, performance, and text (and all Shakespeare cross-references made to the Alexander edition), Daniell's edition has a decidedly old-fashioned feel to it. I do not necessarily mean this in a pejorative sense, since some readers may welcome a return to traditional scholarship in which character criticism is pre-eminent. Thirty pages of Daniell's introduction are devoted to analyses of Julius Caesar, Brutus, Cassius, Portia, Antony, Flavius, Murellus, and Lucius. The noticeably thin section on '*Julius Caesar* and the Critics', at only five pages, calls into question the dust-jacket's promise of 'an in-depth survey of critical approaches to the play'. Daniell greatly admires a 1957 essay by T. J. B. Spencer, but seemingly has little use for more recent criticism; he invokes Richard Wilson's influential study of Roman carnival only to dismiss it: 'like other New Historicist critics, Wilson offered historical evidence that was scattered, to put it no higher, and like them he was cavalier with mere facts' (p. 98).

In general, Daniell's tone is scholarly and his readings of individual characters are as solid as the marble busts in the accompanying illustrations. There are instances, however, such as the second paragraph in his discussion of Caesar (which I quote in full below), where Daniell presents a confusing pastiche of quotations and paraphrases of earlier critics, snippets of source material and analogues, and even newspaper reviews:

Caesar was freshly interpreted by Shakespeare (Rees, 'Caesar'). 'The most common fault attributed to the Roman leader in the Elizabethan period was pride' (Barroll, 340). In *The Mirror for Magistrates*, Caesar's whole 'pretence' was 'glorye vayne . . . Without remorce of many thousands slain' (Bullough, 5.173). He is a braggart in *Caesar's Revenge*, and his 'strut' was much noticed. 'At all times it is, as it should be, Caesar's play', wrote J. C. Trewin in the *Birmingham Post* (4 May 1972) about Trevor Nunn's 1972 production; he saw Caesar 'made of coagulated iron filings'; Michael Billington in the *Guardian* (13 May 1972) noted his 'testy Fascist omnipotence'. But in Shakespeare's play, even his dismissal of his antagonists just before his killing, 'Hence! Wilt thou lift up Olympus?' (3.1.74), has an elevation as well as arrogance. Shakespeare needed a defining language for this living and vulnerable man.   (p. 47)

I confess that I have difficulty finding the narrative thread in this paragraph; it seems to imply that Trevor Nunn staged the anonymous *Caesar's Revenge* in 1972, but surely the reviews refer to Nunn's landmark production of Shakespeare's play in Stratford in that year?

In discussing the 'thick crop of allusions' to *Julius Caesar* in the early seventeenth century, Daniell asserts with some confidence ('This is important') that since the play was not printed until the 1623 Folio, knowledge of it must have come from stage performances: 'It is extremely unlikely that there could have been access to a manuscript copy' (p. 14). In fact, when Humphrey Moseley published the Beaumont and Fletcher Folio in 1647, he assumed that there were so many manuscript copies of the plays in circulation, 'transcribed' by the actors

for their 'private friends', that he felt compelled to explain the potential differences between those manuscripts and the printed texts. If Moseley's assumptions were well-founded, the possibility that manuscript copies of *Julius Caesar* might have been available in the first decades of the 1600s may be more likely than Daniell suggests.

At nearly 400 pages, Daniell's edition is more than twice as long as T. S. Dorsch's in the Arden 2 series. In what may be a unique case of an Arden 3 being *more* scholarly than its Arden 2 predecessor, Daniell's commentary notes are everywhere fuller and more learned than their counterparts in Dorsch. Dorsch, for instance, does not provide a gloss on Pompey (1.1.38), where Daniell offers a richly detailed note on the historical Pompey the Great and the manifold appearances of the name (over ninety times) throughout Shakespeare's work. In a few scattered places, the verbal texture of Daniell's commentary derives from Dorsch and his notes seem derivative. In glossing the feast of Lupercal (1.1.68), Dorsch's note reads 'Caesar's triumph celebrating his victory over Pompey's sons had been held in the previous October, but for dramatic effect Shakespeare had combined it with the Lupercalia'; Daniell's comment is essentially the same: 'Caesar's triumph had been in October, five months before. Shakespeare gets dramatic value out of combining the two' (p. 161). Similarly, at 5.1.35, 'Cassius recalls the honeyed words with which Antony declared his friendship for the conspirators after the assassination' (Dorsch); 'Cassius sneers at Antony's words in the light of his declaration of friendship immediately after the assassination' (Daniell).

Daniell's edition is a hefty piece of serious scholarship that makes a genuine contribution. Something needs to be said, however, about the printing and proofreading of this edition: there are a dozen typographic errors in the notes,[7] the marginal line-numbers are printed

---

[7] Errors in the commentary notes include: for 2.1.109–10 read 109; 2.2.46 for 'We were' read 'We are';

on the wrong lines at 1.2.235, 3.2.35, 3.2.40, 5.1.115, 5.4.10, and 5.5.50, and there is a gap of nearly an inch between two words, 'Decius' and 'house', on the same line at 3.3.37 (seemingly caused by a need to right-justify the prose line?) that gives the passage the strange typography of shaped verse. Surely Daniell, the Arden editorial team, and Thomas Nelson and Sons could have exerted more care to ensure that this edition was not sent forth so misshapen into the world.

H. R. Woudhuysen sees the 'great feast of languages' in *Love's Labour's Lost* (5.1.35) as 'a wild and carnivalesque spread' (p. 41); similar terms might justly be used to describe Woudhuysen's Arden 3 edition of the play. Woudhuysen treats his readers to a multi-media celebration of the play's 'painterly' qualities (following directors in their search for an appropriate visual style in Velázquez, Monet, Manet, and especially Watteau), its musical qualities (Holofernes's snatch of a scale supplied Anthony Burgess with the theme for the finale of his third symphony), and even its operatic qualities (it has been used as the basis for a libretto adapted to Mozart's *Così fan tutte*). Throughout, Woudhuysen wears his learning so lightly that he can pause to note a connection between Auden and Kallman's 1969 libretto based on the play and E. K.'s gloss to January in Spenser's *The Shepheardes Calender* without any disruption in the flow of this introductory tour de force.

Love's Labour's Lost, Woudhuysen reminds us, was the only one of Shakespeare's plays that was not performed in the eighteenth century when its particular type of humour was far from popular. Instead of engaging in what John Jowett once characterized in this space as 'the dutiful long march from the Globe to the latest production at the RSC', Woudhuysen (who also once held forth in this space with aplomb) discusses the play's performance history in the context of an inquiry into the reasons that the play has traditionally proven so challenging for acting companies and audiences. He notes,

for instance, that the centre of dramatic power is by no means self-evident: there have been Berownes who dominate the stage (Ian Richardson), but Boyet (in the person of Brewster Mason), Armado (Paul Scofield),[8] and even Holofernes (Kenneth Tynan) have been known to steal the show. This discussion of the dramatic representation of individual characters might usefully have been extended to consider Irene Dash's study of the ways in which directors have traditionally toned down the 'sexually outspoken' Princess (Dash's term),[9] particularly since Woudhuysen represents the Princess as the only character who 'never herself contributes to the obscene and sexual exchanges' (p. 43).

Woudhuysen sees the self-conscious theatricality of the play as presenting one of the central problems, faced by actors and audiences alike, in judging its tone. He poses a series of provocative questions ('How seriously is an audience to take the play's opening vows? Are the King and his courtiers to be portrayed as ridiculous from the start? If so, should the Princess and her party be seen as the centre of sense and order? . . . If the play is Arcadian, does Marcadé's arrival destroy or fulfil the audience's expectations of the setting?') but ultimately leaves them all to be answered by future directors and their audiences. This open-endedness is characteristic of what may be the

---

3.1.114–16 for 'dust.' read 'dust?'; 3.2.7, 10 the lemma should be in bold face; 3.2.111 for 'Has he masters?' read 'Has he, masters?'; 4.3.42 for 'Fret' read 'fret'. Errors in the textual collations include the 1.2. collation that appears erroneously on page 161; 2.1.121 for 'women. Then' read 'women: then'; 2.3.14 for 'may'st' read 'mayst'; 3.1.115 for 'lyes' read 'lies'; 3.2.111 for 'H'as he' read 'Has he'; at 5.3.90.3 an editorially added stage direction is not collated.

[8] Stanley Wells has pointed out to me that the captions on pages 99 and 100 for the photos of Peter Brook's 'Royal Shakespeare Company' production starring Scofield in 1946 considerably anticipate the founding of the RSC in the early 1960s.

[9] *Wooing, Wedding, and Power: Women in Shakespeare's Plays* (New York, 1981), p. 14.

only unsatisfying aspect of Woudhuysen's introduction: his tendency to raise pointedly interesting issues (such as the observation, made in passing, that the play consists of nine scenes, 'the same number as in Shakespeare's other "source-less" plays, *A Midsummer Night's Dream* and *The Tempest*' (p. 54)) only to leave their provocative implications for the reader to puzzle out.

Woudhuysen's text is impeccable. This is especially impressive given the play's legendary textual difficulties but hardly surprising given Woudhuysen's sensitivity to the smallest textual nuance. His very first commentary note finely observes a potentially substantive difference in the running-title of both the Quarto and Folio texts ('*Loues Labor's lost*') in that 'if the apostrophe in *Labor's* is correct, then the title means "the labour of love is lost" rather than "the lost labours of love"' (p. 111). Woudhuysen's commentary revels in the play's carnivalesque language while revealing its fundamental connections; he trenchantly points out that the discussion of the pronunciation of *debt*, *calf*, and *half* in 5.1 looks forward to specific couplets in 5.2 where *debt* rhymes with *Boyet*, *debtor/letter*, and *calf/half*. Woudhuysen's notes are always worth consulting; it is unfortunate that in two places the notes are mistakenly printed on the previous page from the text that they gloss (5.2.631 and 5.2.651–2) where a reader moving from text to commentary may have difficulty finding them.

Woudhuysen's lively essay on 'The Text' splendidly transcends the boundaries of that generally lack-lustre genre (although it is here, as in other Arden 3 editions, relegated to an appendix). His word-by-word analysis of the Q1 title-page is rich in textual and contextual detail. The history of the 'pleasant Conceited Comedie' epithet reveals that it may have been a formula favoured by Cuthbert Burby; Woudhuysen observes that its use on the title-pages of Q1 *Love's Labour's Lost* and Q1 *Merry Wives of Windsor*, combined with its cousin '*humorous conceits*' (on the title-pages of the Falstaff plays)

may give evidence of Shakespeare's reputation as a humorist at the end of the century. The title-page's claim to present a text 'Newly corrected and augmented', by analogy with similar claims on Q2 *Romeo and Juliet* and Q2 *Hamlet*, may suggest an earlier quarto (Q0) now lost; but the false claim of Q2 *1 Henry IV* to be 'Newly corrected' and of Q3 *Richard III* to be 'Newly augmented' suggest that such title-page advertisements be treated with scepticism, and Woudhuysen points to evidence of short pages which gives some indication that the Q1 printers were setting from manuscript copy rather than producing a page-for-page reprint.[10] Woudhuysen's approach to the implications of the title-page's assertion that *Love's Labour's Lost* 'was presented before her Highnes this last Christmas' is also cautionary. The stated occasion of this performance offers little help in dating the play, since such claims often survived into later editions. *The Shoemaker's Holiday* (coincidentally another play-title whose apostrophe presents problems for modernizing editors) went on claiming it was acted before the Queen on New Year's Day at night in 1600, 1610, 1618, 1624, 1631, and 1657.

Whereas several of the editions under review tend to be somewhat dogmatic in repeating the New Bibliography's narratives of textual production and reproduction, Woudhuysen's analysis of the apparent features of authorial copy evident in the Q1 text (irregularity about the naming of characters, false starts in composition, unclear action, unsatisfactory, permissive and vague stage directions) is appropriately tempered by an awareness that (as Paul

---

[10] On page 300, Q2 of *1 Henry IV* is mistakenly included in a list of texts published in 1598, but is correctly dated 1599 on page 302; on page 298, *Edward III* is misdated 1595 (for 1596). Woudhuysen acknowledges that Cuthbert Burby published Q2 of *Romeo and Juliet* 'without entry in the Stationers' Register' (p. 298) but then suggests that the putative lost quarto of *Love's Labour's Lost* would be unique in its 'lack of entry as a "good" text of one of Shakespeare's plays in the Stationers' Register' (p. 306).

Werstine has been insisting for some time now), in the absence of an extant example of early modern dramatic 'foul papers', the traditional narrative often transcribes a circle in which foul-paper texts are identified by the presence of those features which are thought to be characteristic of foul-paper texts.

Woudhuysen's extended discussion of a single Q1 page, with the page reproduced in facsimile, provides a sample of the barely surmountable difficulties faced by an editor of *Love's Labour's Lost*; this section may also prove useful to teachers who want to impress upon their students the degree to which Shakespeare's texts as they appear in standard critical editions are constructed by editors. Holofernes (referred to by his generic name *Pedant* in this section of the Quarto) complains about affected pronunciation such 'as to speake dout fine, when he should say doubt'. This line, in the edited text, becomes 'as to speak "dout" *sine* "b", when he should say "doubt"' (5.1.19–20). With the textual notes rusticated to the bottom of the page by Arden 3 convention (much to the chagrin of textual critics everywhere), it would take an almost unimaginably careful reader to be fully aware of all of the places in which the text is editorially emended, so Woudhuysen is to be commended for foregrounding the process.

Woudhuysen has largely succeeded in cutting through the gordian knots of the *Love's Labour's Lost* text, but one tangle remains. Opting not to follow previous editors in changing the Princess's speech prefix to *Queen* at 5.2.721 after Marcadé has told her that the King, her father, is dead, Woudhuysen argues that 'her immediate social status is changed by the news . . . but not her absolute essence . . . suddenly to change from "Princess" to "Queen" at this point is unjustified and invites novelistic speculation as to the precise point in the play at which the King of France dies and how long it took Marcadé to get to Navarre' (p. 338). Woudhuysen's points are well taken, but his textual note may occasion confusion: '721 + SP

PRINCESS] *F2*; *Quee. (Queen., Qu.) QF'*. A reader might assume that both the Quarto and F1 texts here change the speech prefix from *Princess* to *Queen*, and this assumption would seemingly be confirmed by a glance at the Princess's preceding speeches (lines 711 and 715) where there is no indication in the textual notes that the 'PRINCESS' prefix differs in any way from QF. But this is not the case. The Princess's speech prefixes are, in fact, *Quee.*, *Queen.*, or *Qu.* throughout this scene in the early texts (the emendation to 'PRINCESS' is collated at lines 563 and 581, but not at 625, 662, 711, or 715). Readers who might initially want to take Woudhuysen to task for not following his control text in granting the Princess her majesty at this point, find instead that they have reason to complain (at least in this lone instance) that he has not provided them with sufficient information with which to evaluate his textual decisions.

In the spirit of complementarity that guides his edition, Woudhuysen attributes the play's current popularity to three critical studies 'which have influenced directors and themselves been influenced by productions' (p. 93): Harley Granville-Barker's rehabilitatory preface of 1930; Bobbyann Roesen's (Anne Barton's) 'brilliant article published in 1953 when she was still an undergraduate', and William Carroll's 1976 book *The Great Feast of Language*. Woudhuysen does not observe that these key studies appear at regular 23-year intervals, so a new landmark in *Love's Labour's Lost* scholarship is clearly due this year. I would suggest that, with the publication of Woudhuysen's Arden 3 edition, the magisterial study of the play that will energize a new generation of readers and directors has now arrived.

EDITIONS: NEW CAMBRIDGE

In a day and age in which it is not always clear that yet another edition of a Shakespeare play is really needed, Kathleen O. Irace's *The First Quarto of Hamlet* in the New Cambridge Early

Quartos series stands out as a genuine contribution to the field. Discussion of QI *Hamlet* has been hampered for some time by the lack of a good modern-spelling edition (Albert Weiner's 1962 edition being long out of print). Irace's meticulously edited modernized text with scene and line numbers as well as the Consecutive Line Numbers (CLN) devised by Paul Bertram and Bernice W. Kliman (which Irace mistakenly calls 'Complete Line Numbers'), bracketed QI leaf-signature numbers in the margins, and judicious textual notes combine to form what will no doubt become the standard critical edition that will now enable discussion of this text to flourish.

Irace's brief introductory essay provides a good overview of the theories of memorial reconstruction, theatrical adaptation, and the distinctive features of the QI textual version. Much of the introduction distils material from Irace's important study *Reforming the 'Bad' Quartos* (1994). (Indeed, in what may be a record for self-referentiality, Irace cites her previously published work eight times within the course of six pages.) In a sign of the extent to which QI *Hamlet* has been successfully rehabilitated, the ideologically charged 'bad quarto' designation does not appear anywhere in the text of Irace's introduction. She begins by averring that the 1603 title-page 'gives no hint that this version of *Hamlet* is in any way irregular or unusual' (p. 1). QI claims to present 'The Tragicall Historie of Hamlet . . . As it hath been diuerse times acted by his Highnesse seruants in the Cittie of London: as also in the two Vniuersities of Cambridge and Oxford, and else-where'. The title-page may not appear suspicious to us and we might agree with Irace that 'QI apparently preserves an authorized script of the play as performed by Shakespeare's company, the King's Men, in various locations in England' (p. 1). But the claim that the King's Men played at the universities might have suggested something highly irregular to an educated Jacobean reader, who would have known (as John R. Elliott's recent study of

Renaissance staging in Oxford has reminded us) that 'no professional companies ever performed within university precincts'.[11] Thus, the title-page may, in fact, hint at something unusual, but in a critical context in which the early Quartos are no longer viewed as 'stolne and surreptitious' but merely 'short' (Irace's preferred term) clues such as this may get overlooked.

The central difficulty faced by an editor working on QI *Hamlet* is deciding how to deal with its unique textual features; its differences from the Q2 and FI texts are, after all, what make it interesting, but its palpable errors may need to be emended by reference to Q2 and F. Irace rightly observes that the prejudice many readers have for the more familiar readings is so strong that QI's differences 'may at first seem to be errors, but in almost all cases, QI's readings make sense' (p. 29). Irace generally retains the QI reading when it can be defended and makes good arguments for preserving QI's puns 'my chief' (9.68), 'trapically' (9.117), and 'shroud' (11.2). Occasionally, however, QI's seemingly defensible (albeit quirky) verbal variants are emended to conform to the standard Q2/F readings: thus Old Norway is not 'impudent' (QI) but 'impotent' (Q2/F) and Horatio's description of 'The strauagant' (QI) spirit becomes 'Th'extravagant' (Q2/F). Moreover, many of the unique textual features of QI are obfuscated in the course of modernization: QI's distinctive 'Ceasen your admiration for awhile' (2.106), which Irace acknowledges could be heard as 'cease in', is modernized to 'Season' (2.106); 'Marshall' is modernized to 'martial' (1.56); 'happly' to 'happily' (1.93); 'One wholesome life' to 'On wholesome life' (9.145); 'viz' is expanded to '*Videlicet*' (6.25). In each of these instances the process of modernization produces the Q2/F reading. The requirements of a modern-spelling edition notwithstanding, should not these QI variants be preserved in an

---

[11] 'Early Staging in Oxford', *A New History of Early English Drama*, p. 69.

edition claiming to present 'the first printed text of Shakespeare's *Hamlet*'?

A number of critics have recently argued that one of the key differences between Q1 *Hamlet* and the longer texts is that 'several characters differ in significant ways from their counterparts in Q2 and F' (p. 12). In order to preserve these differences, Irace retains the Q1 spellings of character names. There is no question that the distinction between Polonius and Q1's Corambis ought to be maintained, but it is less clear that an insistence upon preserving minor spelling variants does not create differences where none exist. In her notes to the list of Q1 characters, Irace provides their counterparts in Q2 and F: 'GERTRED parallel to Gertrude in Q2/F'; 'ROSSENCRAFT parallel to Rosencrantz in Q2/F' (p. 33). In point of fact, neither *Gertrude* nor *Rosencrantz* appears in Q2, in which Hamlet's mother is spelled *Gertradt* or *Gertrard* and his boyhood friend is invariably *Rosencraus*. It took well over a century for the familiar *Rosencrantz* to evolve: it's *Rosincrane* or *Rosincrance* in F1; *Rosincrosse* in the later Folios; *Roseneraus* in Rowe; *Rosincrantz* first appears in Theobald's 1733 edition. Given the instability of these names in the early texts, it may be misleading to suggest that a variant Q1 spelling be taken as a sign of a difference in character.

In Irace's edition, the 'King of Denmark' receives a local habitation but no name: 'in Q1, the king is never called "Claudius" as he is in Q2 and F' (p. 95). Again, this distinction is problematic. Strictly speaking, he is never *called* 'Claudius' in either Q2 or F; others in the play refer to him as *my lord* or as *king*. Q2 names Claudius only twice, once in the entrance list for the second scene and once in his first speech prefix; in the F text he is named only in the entrance list. If Q1 represents a memorially reconstructed text, it should surprise no one that it fails to record 'Claudius', a name that is never spoken on-stage.

Irace makes nearly two hundred changes in Q1's lineation, in the course of which a few of Q1's seemingly adequate pentameters are unac-

countably bisected and rearranged. Horatio's 'My Lord we did, but answere made it none / Yet once me thought it was about to speake' (sig. C1r) becomes

HAMLET Did you not speak to it?
HORATIO   My lord, we did,
     But answer made it none. Yet once methought
     It was about to speak and lifted up ...(2.130–2)

Mislineation has long been thought to be a characteristic feature of memorially reconstructed texts (an assumption that has recently been challenged by Laurie Maguire).[12] Editors, of course, standardly re-align mislined verse in the course of preparing early dramatic texts for modern readers. But the fact that Irace rearranges lines 2.130–2 so that they now match the lineation of Q2/F raises an important issue about whether or not (mis)lineation perhaps ought to be treated as a substantive difference that should be preserved in an edition such as this.

Irace mentions in passing the 'heated exchanges' in the *TLS* occasioned by the publication of Q1 *Hamlet* in *The Shakespearean Originals* series under the general editorship of Graham Holderness and Bryan Loughrey, but she might have explored more extensively the merits and demerits of the continuing debate.[13] Although Irace is an effective champion of the Q1 text, surely there ought to have been space in her edition for opposing voices. Most Shakespearians would, I think, agree with Stanley Wells, who acknowledges that making early quarto texts more readily accessible than they have previously been 'is in itself good', but continues to believe that they have no place in

---

[12] *Shakespearean Suspect Texts: The 'Bad' Quartos and their Contexts* (Cambridge, 1996), pp. 221–2.

[13] There is rich irony, for instance, in the invoking of textual authority by Holderness and Loughrey in their recent 24-page apologia in which they argue that much of the adverse criticism of the series was responding to claims made in 'unauthorized advance publicity' and on 'unauthorized back-cover blurbs' ('Shakespeare Misconstrued: The True Chronicle Historie of *Shakespearean Originals*', p. 399).

Shakespeare's *Complete Works* since 'these texts are all inferior, many of them grossly inferior, as works of art to the corresponding texts in the accepted canon' ('Multiple Texts and the Oxford Shakespeare', p. 389).

Giorgio Melchiori opens his excellent New Cambridge edition of *King Edward III* with a brief history of the righteous indignation expressed by the play's early advocates, forcefully articulated in the title of Alexander Teetgen's 1875 pamphlet: *Shakespeare's 'King Edward the Third', absurdly called, and scandalously treated as, a 'DOUBTFUL PLAY'*. Now that the play has found its way fairly comfortably into the canon (by virtue of its inclusion in the New Cambridge Shakespeare, in the second edition of the *Riverside Shakespeare*, and in a forthcoming Arden 3 edition) its champions can afford to be more muted in their assertions. Even the cover blurb tempers its presentation of the play as 'a major new addition to the Shakespearean canon' with the acknowledgement that 'Melchiori does not claim that Shakespeare is the sole author'. Indeed, Melchiori is so careful in discussing the play's authorship that the issue of agency becomes somewhat muddled in his introductory essay: page 19 posits a single, anonymous, controlling intelligence behind *Edward III* ('the original deviser'); by page 24, the originator has multiplied ('the devisers of the play originally'); page 27 returns to a lone dramatist ('the author's mind') who maintains his singularity through page 33 ('the playwright'); page 36 then returns to the plural ('the devisers of a well-planned play'). At times, passive constructions allow the play to author itself: 'To ensure a firm dramatic structure, the third part of the play presents a more drastic manipulation of the sources . . . The central event is placed in an inner dramatic frame . . . Links are established between this double concentric structure and that of the first dramatic block' (pp. 34–5).

Melchiori treats the attribution of part of *Edward III* to Shakespeare as a *fait accompli*: at first proposed tentatively ('probably involves Shakespeare at least as collaborator' (p. 14)), the attribution becomes more specific ('Shakespeare contributed in some measure, in conjunction with other more or less experienced script-writers' (p. 16)), and ends in certainty ('his sole authorship of at least Act 2 is undeniable' (p. 17)). In refreshing contrast to previous critical studies, Melchiori's introduction does not cite a single parallel-passage linking *Edward III* to works in the established canon. The attribution here rests largely upon the 'support of serious investigators as arguably the work of Shakespeare' (p. 3, quoting Richard Proudfoot). It is notoriously difficult for literary scholars to evaluate stylometric computer-aided authorship studies; and it is perhaps too easy to dismiss what we do not fully understand, especially when the terminology employed in such analyses often seems to derive from science fiction. Using 'multilayer perceptrons' and 'radial basis functions', for instance, several recent studies undertaken by Thomas Merriam have suggested that Act 3 of *Edward III* may show traces of Marlowe's stylistic fingerprints. Although Melchiori summarily dismisses this conclusion ('there is no need to suspect Marlowe's hand in *Edward III*' (p. 35)), he would presumably approve of the fact that Merriam's study assigns Act 2 to Shakespeare. And yet, there is a circularity in Merriam's acknowledgement that 'the strongest confirmation of the method' he employs is that in identifying Act 2 as Shakespeare's it confirms, and is itself confirmed by, the 'virtually unanimous' scholarly ascription of Act 2 to Shakespeare ('Heterogeneous Authorship', p. 25).

This is not to say that Melchiori's edition finds its entire focus in the question of authorship (as might be said of Eric Sams's recent edition). By finessing the issue of authorship to a certain extent, Melchiori is able to concentrate on several overlooked aspects of the play, making this the most comprehensive edition available. Melchiori's richly contextual introduction detailing the interplay between

Edward III, its chronicle sources, and other history plays in the 1590s, is finely supplemented in the appendix by a scene-by-scene account of the play's use of Holinshed and Froissart.

Melchiori speculates that *Edward III* was the play referred to in a 1598 missive from George Nicolson to Lord Burghley as 'stayed', that is, withdrawn from public performance, because of its scornful attitude towards the King and people of Scotland. This would account for the title-page advertisement ('As it hath been Sundry times played about the Citie of London'), which is unusual in that it does not specify a particular company, since clearly no company would be eager to claim a suppressed play. Subsequently, *Edward III* was 'forgotten by the theatrical profession for more than three centuries' (p. 46). Although this makes for a pleasingly brief section on performance history, Melchiori might have attended to the evidence that a play about Edward III and the Countess of Salisbury was presented in Danzig *circa* 1591 by members of the Admiral's Men who were on a foreign tour.[14]

Melchiori posits a rather tenuous link between Shakespeare and Act 2 based upon the single appearance of the supposedly unique Shakespearian spelling 'emured' for 'immured' (2.1.178). As it happens, the Chadwyck-Healey literary databases of English drama (1250–1660), English prose fiction (1475–1700), and English poetry (1250–1660) confirm that the spelling 'emured' appears only in *Love's Labour's Lost* and *Edward III*.[15] But this single spelling, coupled with what Melchiori acknowledges is an even less cogent bit of evidence (the use of capital instead of lower-case 'c' for a mid-sentence 'Cannot' at 2.2.148), hardly provides sufficient grounds for the conclusion that 'the printer of the first quarto of *Edward III* was setting from copy in the same hand responsible for Addition II in Hand D to *Sir Thomas More*, a hand generally recognized as Shakespeare's' (p. 175).

Like *Sir Thomas More*, *Edward III* may represent the collaborative work of several playwrights, with multiple layers of addition, revision, playhouse annotation and censorship. From the *More* manuscript, Melchiori extrapolates a narrative account of what 'generally happened' in dramatic collaborations. However, given the uniqueness of the *More* text, some of Melchiori's inferences may prove of limited value in helping us to understand the text of *Edward III* (e.g., the assertion that it was 'a normal practice' (pp. 173–4) in preparing a fair copy of a collaborative manuscript to transcribe only the speeches on each page, leaving the speech headings to be added at a later time, is not particularly believable). And yet, there do seem to be genetic affinities between the two plays, especially regarding Shakespeare's role as collaborator. Melchiori argues cogently that, along with writing individual scenes of the original version of *Edward III*, Shakespeare contributed additional passages (the so-called 'Countess of Salisbury' scenes, which derive from a different source) after the play had been ostensibly finished, as he had done for *More*. Melchiori, who edited the full text of *More* for the Revels Plays series, has again chosen to present the Shakespearian passages in 'their natural contexts, rather than as mere excerpts' (p. ix). I cannot imagine that anyone would question the legitimacy of this editorial decision, or wish it undone, the issue of it being so proper.[16]

---

[14] See Emil Herz, *Englische Schauspieler und englisches Schauspeil zur Zeit Shakespeares in Deutschland* (Hamburg and Leipzig, 1903), pp. 5–6.

[15] Melchiori mistakenly claims that 'emures' appears 'both in the Quarto (1609) and in the Folio text of *Troilus and Cressida*, Prologue 9' (p. 174); in fact, the Prologue appears only in the Folio text of that play.

[16] There are only a few scattered errors in the edition: Wolfgang Iser is called 'Isar' on pages 41 and 217; the textual collation for 1.2.14 SD comes one page too early; the lemma at 1.2.34 for 'out: "Enough ... pity"' should read 'out: "Enough"'; in the lemma in the commentary at 5.1.78 for 'doth' read 'Doth'; the textual notes are set entirely in bold face on several pages (pp. 59, 75, 76, 134, 135, 140, 143, 155, 156).

The late Antony Hammond has left a lively legacy in the New Cambridge *Pericles*, co-edited with Doreen DelVecchio. Their unabashedly iconoclastic edition opens with a Government Health Warning ('THIS EDITION OF *PERICLES* MAY BE HARMFUL TO YOUR PREJUDICES') as the editors map out their mission to do 'what no other editor has done . . . to trust the text and to respect the integrity of the play' (p. vii). Gary Taylor once characterized the *Pericles* Quarto as 'bewilderingly corrupt'.[17] and Stanley Wells continues to refer to it as an 'obviously damaged text' ('Multiple Texts and the Oxford Shakespeare', p. 385). Even given the current shift in paradigm in which many formerly 'bad' quartos have now been re-classified as authorial first drafts, it is nevertheless stunning that DelVecchio and Hammond conclude that Q1 'seems to have been based on very primitive, and perhaps not homogeneous, foul papers' (p. 208). Such a revolutionary conclusion ought to be supported by a detailed consideration of the hundreds of textual anomalies in the Quarto text in which the editors demonstrate that these anomalies can be best explained by the hypothesis of rough authorial copy. One would want to know, for instance, what to make of the Latinate speech prefixes '*Omnes*' at 1.4.95 and 2.4.40 (the first of which the editors silently translate without collation). As Lee Bliss has recently observed, the use of '*Omnes*' as a speech prefix is exceedingly rare in Shakespearian printed texts, especially those thought to derive from authorial manuscripts ('Scribes, Compositors, and Annotators', p. 337). However, DelVecchio and Hammond's brief and unconvincing section of 'Textual Analysis' tends to argue by analogy ('the copy for Q1 *Pericles* probably resembled the copy for Q1 *Lear* . . . If the memorial theory can be abandoned for Q1 *King Lear*, there is no compelling reason to retain it for *Pericles*' (p. 208)) without addressing many of the specific details that make *Pericles* such a unique and challenging text.

Even those of us who remain unpersuaded by the foul-paper hypothesis can still appreciate some of the fruits of DelVecchio and Hammond's decision to trust the Quarto. A case in point is Lysimachus' long run-on sentence at 4.5.96–107 into which Hoeniger's Arden 2 edition inserted no less than seven full stops. DelVecchio and Hammond retain the Quarto's commas and reasonably argue that since Lysimachus 'is trying to make a graceful exit with his foot in his mouth . . . his discomfort is better conveyed by running on his phrases than by grammatical correctness' (p. 170). The editors' contention that the 'characteristic prose rhythms of Cockney speech' in the Miteline brothel scenes (4.2 and 4.5) are 'caught well by Q's punctuation, which we have consequently on the whole retained' and the stronger claim that 'it seemed absurd to regularise the bawds into conventional modern syntactical punctuation' (pp. 44, 80) might have been more compelling if they had indeed followed the Quarto more faithfully in these passages. In the event, the Q1 punctuation of the Bawd's speech at 4.2.95–7, 'where you haue most gaine, to weepe that you liue as yee doe, makes pittie in your Louers seldome, but that pittie begets you a good opinion' (sig. G1), is modernized and regularized: 'where you have most gain. To weep that you live as ye do makes pity in your lovers: seldom but that pity begets you a good opinion' (4.2.95–7).

Along with sweeping away the orthodox view that the Quarto is seriously corrupt, DelVecchio and Hammond declare that 'we do not regard the stylistic differences in the play (which have often been exaggerated) as in any way conclusive evidence of collaboration' (p. 11). As it happens, Thomas Merriam's recent 'multivariate' analysis provides new evidence corroborating the editors' belief that *Pericles* may not be a collaborative effort after all

---

17 Gary Taylor, 'The Transmission of *Pericles*', *Publications of the Bibliographical Society of America*, 80 (1986), 193–217.

('Invalidation Reappraised'). But was it really necessary that so many previous critics of the play be so clearly stamped with their one defect? G. Wilson Knight and Kenneth Muir's arguments 'can only be called grotesque' (p. 56); Gary Taylor and Macd. P. Jackson 'can only be called reckless' (p. 209); F. D. Hoeniger is 'misguided' (p. 9); Roger Warren's 'missionary view' of the Oxford *Pericles* 'distorts many of his statements and all of his opinions' (p. 20); Steven Urkowitz is 'aggressive and acerbic' (p. 200). Much of the editors' vitriol is directed at Taylor and Jackson's conjectural reconstruction of *Pericles* and *The Painfull Aduentures* in the Oxford edition with little acknowledgement that the Oxford editors also reprint the 1609 Quarto *literatim* in their original-spelling edition.

This take-no-prisoners attitude is part of an overall approach that, I assume, is intended to be engagingly trendy – Julian Barnes, John Fowles, Elton John, and *Star Wars* are all cited in the notes – but the editors sling so much mud that the cumulative effect can be rather cloying; and their tone is often less than gracious. DelVecchio and Hammond acknowledge that their enthusiasm for the play was originally fired by a 1986 production in Stratford, Ontario, but seem to believe that they have a right to reproduce photographs from the production and curse Canadian Equity for the 'absurd conditions' it imposed when they requested permission to do so. The RSC apparently furnished DelVecchio and Hammond with an archival videotape of David Thacker's 1989 Stratford-upon-Avon production, but the editors complain that 'it is a scandal that this tape is so poor that only a handful of brightly lit scenes can be made out' (p. 24). Unfortunate perhaps, but a *scandal*?

A few of the features of DelVecchio and Hammond's edition ought to be emulated by all editors of early modern drama, especially the enormously useful key to pronunciation of names and places provided as an extended gloss on the List of Characters. The editors' overview

of stage history, with its awareness of and caution against over-reliance on reviews (noting that theatre critic Michael Coveney characterized Rudolph Walker's Gower as 'haltingly half-comprehensible' whereas Michael Billington said the same actor in the same performance 'articulated beautifully'), is also commendable. But, on the whole, this is not a very accurate edition, and its occasional moments of sheer nastiness will not endear it to many readers.[18]

David Crane's New Cambridge edition of *The Merry Wives of Windsor* begins with a discussion of the cultural position of married women in early modern England. But readers expecting an ideologically driven narrative to follow may be surprised to find, instead, a sort of cheerful nihilism. Since wives 'in a certain contemporary social sense can by definition do nothing of significance' they are ideally suited to Crane's reading of the play in which a plot 'which does nothing' and language 'which does nothing' combine to form a play which 'is about nothing' (pp. 8–10). A reader fearing that nothing will come of this might ask Crane to speak again, but his introduction ends after a mere twenty pages of text. If there were ever anything written that was wished longer by its readers (to expand upon Dr Johnson's short-

---

[18] There is an apparent lineation error at 3.2.9–10. Errors in the commentary notes include Prologue 0, for 'Enter' read '*Enter*'; 1.1.65–71, for 'viper . . . breed . . . kindness . . . He's father . . . child . . . How they . . . in two' read '*viper . . . breed . . . kindness . . . He's father . . . child . . . How they . . . in two*'; 1.1.73, for 'sharp' read 'Sharp'; 1.1.168, for 'make sure' read 'make him sure'; 2.1.74–5, for 'fasting days' read 'fasting-days'; 3.2.85–6 for 'the rough' read 'The rough'; 5.0.8 for 'inkle' read 'inckle'. Errors in the textual notes include 1.1.3–5 for 'hazard' read 'hazard,'; 3.1.35 for 'womb:' read 'womb.'; 3.1.52–4 for 'over board' read 'overboard'; 3.2.73 for 'Besides' read '*Besides*'; 3.2.102 for '2 Gentleman' read '2 GENTLEMAN'; collation at 4.1.5 should read '5–6'; 4.4.32–3 for 'writ,' read 'writ'; 4.5.85–7 for '*Marina*' read 'MARINA'; 5.1.16 for '*Lysimachus*' read 'LYSIMACHUS', for '*Hellicanus*' read 'HELLICANUS', for 'This.' read 'This'.

list) Crane's introduction might be a candidate. Whereas a section of 'Literary Sources and Analogues' occupies half a dozen pages in Oliver's Arden 2 edition of the play, Crane devotes all of two brief paragraphs to 'sources' in which the analogous story in Fiorentino's *Il pecorone* (1558) is summarily dismissed as yet another nothing: 'Nothing, of course, can be done with such a piece of information as this about *Il pecorone* except to acknowledge it. Shakespeare, if he knew this story, plainly transmuted it beyond a point where it is any longer useful to think of it' (p. 6).

On a more positive note, Crane has a director's eye for the 'shapes and energies' in *The Merry Wives of Windsor* and a gift for describing its effervescent qualities: 'words are easily released in this play to glory in their independent moment' (p. 15). Crane's commentary frequently draws pointed distinctions between reading and performance (e.g., 'often, what seems redundant and over-obvious in the study is just what an actor wants on stage' (p. 49n)). In defending his decision not to emend Mistress Quickly's interrupted line in the Folio '*An – fooles head*' (1.4.106–7) to '*Anne – ass-head*' (as the Oxford editors do), Crane explains (in part):

In the study, the linguistic joke works clearly and precisely: the sound 'an' can be written '*An*' to signal a quibbling use of the proper noun, and Caius can exit in a flash to enable the sentence to run on past the point of fracture rapidly enough to take up the indefinite article smoothly. Not so on the stage. Here the player must say '*An*' as '*Anne*' (with no possibility of an indeterminate stressing that could be either indefinite article or proper noun) because he is cut off not by another speech sound but by Caius' exit, which takes longer than a speech interruption and must allow the sound of the word to emerge fully. On the stage, then, the word Mistress Quickly says is at this point not the indefinite article at all; it is wrenched suddenly, after a pause for the exit, into being the indefinite article by the common nouns that follow.

As is the case in many of Crane's 'page vs. stage'

notes, this one is both theatrically alert (notice that the imagined early modern player in the role of Mistress Quickly is male) and rather pleasantly pedantic.

Crane embraces Malone's suggestion that the play was commissioned by Lord Hunsdon for the yearly feast for the Order of the Garter knights at Westminster, in Whitehall Palace on St George's Day, 23 April 1597, but does not address Giorgio Melchiori's recently reiterated conviction that the play 'could not possibly be the entertainment offered on the night of 23 April 1597' ('What did Shakespeare Write?', p. 349; Melchiori argues the case at length in *Shakespeare's Garter Plays* (1994), pp. 82–112) except to say that Melchiori 'does not explain why Shakespeare includes in a play written for the public stage specific lines about the Garter ceremonies' (p. 5n).

The Quarto of *Merry Wives* is among the last of a vanishing breed: a text still widely viewed as a memorial reconstruction. Crane accepts the 'bad quarto' classification and points to additional evidence in the Quarto text of 'intimate and detailed response to theatrical circumstance', that is, places where the play may have been modified by the players during performance (rather than intentionally revised by the author), modifications which may then have been recorded in a memorially reconstructed version. These are useful contributions to the on-going discussion of memorial reconstruction, but Crane employs the unfortunately prejudicial terms associated with Pollard's now widely discredited narrative in which the text is 'the product of a corrupt memorial report' by a 'culprit' actor so that a printer could 'produce a pirated or "bad" quarto of the play for illicit profit' (pp. 151–3). In fact, there is no evidence that memorial reconstruction was ever used for the illegal acquisition of texts, and Crane does not offer an alternative scenario.

There is little to object to in this edition, although some readers might question the appropriateness of the stereotypes invoked in the list of the characters where Doctor Caius is glossed as 'Very French. Easily angered', and Sir Hugh Evans is defined as 'Very Welsh. Stupid but occasionally accurate'. Overall, Crane's text is remarkably accurate, but he occasionally does not record in the textual collations editorially added *Exit* directions at the ends of scenes (1.4.139, 2.2.245, 2.3.79).[19] Readers interested in an extensive discussion of sources and analogues or a cultural analysis of the ways in which the upper- and lower-class figures in the play function to underscore the assimilating power of the middle class should probably consult other available editions of *The Merry Wives of Windsor*. But then they would miss Crane's agreeable idiosyncrasies, and that would be a loss.

Herbert Weil and Judith Weil's New Cambridge *Henry IV Part 1* is a solid edition that seems geared to an audience of beginning students rather than seasoned scholars.[20] The gloss on the Carrier's lantern at the opening of Act 2, for instance, provides fairly rudimentary information: 'the play would originally have been performed at an arena playhouse in daylight. The lantern conventionally signifies that the action takes place at night or near daybreak' (p. 94). Weil and Weil acknowledge the relative absences of women and middle- and lower-class characters in the play and provocatively suggest (in their 'Acknowledgements', of all places) that these absences may figure as important presences; but the editors seem reticent about engaging critical discourses relating to gender or class. Although their introduction occasionally touches upon significant articles by recent critics, the only essays discussed in depth are those by Maurice Morgann (1777), W. H. Auden (1962), and William Empson (1953). The Falstaff/Oldcastle controversy, which has, of course, been at the forefront of *Henry IV* studies in recent years, receives barely three pages, in which Weil and Weil unaccountably assert that the Epilogue to *Part 2*, with its explicit denial of the link between Falstaff and Oldcastle, was 'omitted from the 1600 quarto' (p. 28). This is an unfortunate misstatement of

fact (the Epilogue is very much present in the Quarto text) that will no doubt seriously mislead all students who begin their study of this important textual and historical issue with this edition.

EDITIONS: OXFORD

Weil and Weil's *Part 1* may be usefully compared with René Weis's *Henry IV Part 2* in the Oxford Shakespeare series. Both editions include a photograph of Richard Burton playing Prince Hal in a 1951 production in Stratford-upon-Avon. Weil and Weil provide the caption 'A typical publicity photograph' and identify only Burton and Anthony Quayle, leaving the actors playing Poins and Bardolph unnamed (p. 49). Weis identifies all four actors in the picture, which he includes not in his account of performance history, but in a discussion of the possible historical basis for the comic characters' names. Weil and Weil seem to be going through the motions of a standard stage history with a certain ironic distance implied in 'A typical publicity photograph'; and their readers may feel that some pertinent information has been left out. Weis is using the photo-

---

19. In the commentary notes at 4.2.82 SD for 'Exit' read '*Exit*'; 4.2.92 SD.2 for 'Caius' read '*Caius*'.

20. In moving from Crane's edition to Weil and Weil's, I was struck by the lack of uniformity between these two volumes published in the same series in the same year. One would imagine that the abbreviated sigla used for early editions of Shakespeare would be a series convention that, by this late date in the life of the New Cambridge, would by now be etched in stone. And yet, the abbreviations used in these two editions are consistently inconsistent: in Crane, the 1773 Johnson and Steevens' variorum is cited throughout as 'Steevens' whereas Weil and Weil use 'Var. 1773'; similarly, the 1778 variorum is 'Steevens²' in Crane and 'Var. 1778' in Weil and Weil; Isaac Reed's 1785 variorum is 'Reed' in Crane but 'Steevens' in Weil and Weil. There are a few errors in Weil and Weil's edition: an editorially added stage direction at 2.2.42.1 is not collated; in the commentary note at 1.3.67, for 'come' read 'Come'; the textual collation at 2.4.102 should read '103' and be placed on the subsequent page.

graph as an appropriate illustration for a particular moment in his critical narrative; and his readers may feel more assured that they are indeed getting the full picture.

Weis's elegant introductory essay focuses squarely on Falstaff, who, with more lines in the play than Prince Hal and King Henry combined, is clearly the dominating presence in *Henry IV Part 2*. While demonstrating an appropriate awareness that for the overwhelming majority of audiences the Falstaff/Oldcastle debate is 'in the strictest sense a scholastic one', Weis presents an engaging overview of the controversy and further enriches the debate by proposing that it may have been the appearance of Oldcastle in *2 Henry IV* that precipitated intervention by Cobham in both plays, because *Part 2* was probably submitted for licensing in 1596 during Cobham's tenure in the office of Lord Chamberlain (pp. 7–15). He draws an interesting connection between the Epilogue's famous disclaimer that 'Falstaff shall die of a sweat . . . Oldcastle died a martyr, and this is not the man' and the intriguing use of 'sweat' earlier in *1 Henry IV* where, after robbing the robbers at Gad's Hill, Hal turns to Poins with 'Away, good Ned. Falstaff [Oldcastle] sweats to death'. Weis acknowledges that if the trisyllabic 'Oldcastle' were used instead of 'Falstaff', the line would be a perfect pentameter; 'and it might arguably confer a piquancy (perhaps even poignancy) on the comic idiom of sweating and lard that audiences of a Protestant nation reared on Foxe's *Acts and Monuments* could perhaps be trusted to recognise' (p. 37). Shakespeare's use of 'sweat' may be echoed in the Epilogue, Weis suggests, to signal that he has still not entirely let go of his character Oldcastle.

Weis's ultimate decision to retain 'Falstaff' in the text is based largely on reception history ('Falstaff has become powerfully real through being a fiction'), a sense that we should implicitly trust Heminges and Condell, and a feeling that a decision to restore Oldcastle 'is bound to focus any audience's attention on the change

itself and its legitimacy, at the expense of the imaginative part played by the character' (p. 40). Readers familiar with the arguments advanced in Bevington's Oxford edition of *1 Henry IV* will see manifest similarities here, which Weis proudly acknowledges. Like the two parts of the play, these two editions are connected in fundamental ways while maintaining a considerable degree of autonomy as well (Weis, for instance, follows the *Complete Works* in the spelling 'Glyndŵr' where Bevington prefers 'Glendower').

Weis observes that an essential difference between *Part 1* and *Part 2* is that 'in *Part 2* the wider politics of the realm are marginalized to a degree that is unthinkable in the earlier play-world' (p. 3). These apparent thematic differences are a critical element in the play's textual history. John Jowett and Gary Taylor have suggested a two-stage process of revision in which Shakespeare incorporated passages of a specifically political nature into the text of *Part 2*, emphasizing links with his earlier history plays, beginning with the addition of 3.1, a retrospective on the usurpation of Richard II that first appears in the second issue of the Quarto (Qb), and continuing in the addition of several short passages that are present only in the Folio text.[21] Where Jowett and Taylor saw expansion, Weis sees subtraction. He argues that 3.1 must have been part of the original composition, since without it the play's careful alternation of verse and prose scenes would have been thrown out of balance. 3.1 and the F-only passages were, in Weis's view, 'an integral part of the play from the beginning' (p. 89), but were all cut from Shakespeare's foul papers to satisfy the licensers of printed matter when the copy for Qa was presented to them in 1600; these authorities, however, 'unexpectedly gave the green light' to 3.1 during the course of the printing of Qa (p. 84); so signatures E3–4v were cancelled from Qa and replaced by a new

---

21 'The Three Texts of *2 Henry IV*', *Studies in Bibliography*, 40 (1987), 31–50.

four-leaved sheet containing the scene on signatures E3–6v, now designated Qb. A copy of Qa was, at some point, collated with the post-1606 playbook (one that had been purged of profanity but still retained the politically-sensitive material) for a private literary transcript which in due course served as printer's copy for the First Folio.

Whatever one thinks of the idea that 3.1 received an eleventh-hour reprieve from the Bishop of London, the editorial use that Weis makes of this narrative textual history is decidedly curious. Given Weis's argument that F recovers (rather than rewrites or revises) passages that were originally part of the play, no one would question his use of F for those passages, even in an edition for which Q is the stated control-text. But 3.1 exists in both Qb (apparently set from authorial papers) and F (where the text may derive from a transcript of a playbook). In editing 3.1, Weis follows the F entrance direction '*Enter the King, with a Page*', and a subsequent '*Exit*' for the Page, rather than Qb's '*Enter the King . . . alone*'; F's '*Enter Warwicke and Surrey*' then erases Qb's ghost character '*Enter Warwicke, Surrey, and sir Iohn Blunt*'. Weis also adopts several key F variants (3.1.18 'mast' for Qb 'masse'; 22 'billows' for Qb 'pillowes'; 26 'thy' for Qb 'them'; 27 'sea-boy' for Qb 'season'), all without comment, except in one remarkable instance where he defends the rejected reading of his control-text: 'Q's "season" (for, probably, "sea-son") is not implausible . . . particularly since "sea-boy" is not recorded elsewhere in the period and may be thought rather awkwardly to echo "ship-boy" [in line 19]' (p. 191n). One would have thought that, with Q as control-text, Weis would incline toward the Q reading in cases of indeterminate claims between the early editions. In practice, Weis's textual choices here are identical to those made by the editors of the Oxford *Complete Works* where the aim was 'to reproduce the substantive features of the stage version of the text underlying F' (*Textual Companion*, p. 353) – a fact that may challenge

Weis's assertion that his text 'differs significantly from theirs' (p. 101).

Aside from a typo on page 80 of the introduction (describing 3.1 as a 'long restrospective'), Weis's text and notes are generally accurate.[22] But his commentary is noticeably thin in places, often glossing fewer than half a dozen words per page. Several years ago, H. R. Woudhuysen, remarking in this space upon the paucity of commentary in some Oxford and Cambridge editions, proposed a prize for the first editor 'who manages to print a page of text without any annotation'. This dubious honour now belongs to Weis's edition, on page 240 of which 4.3.171–89 is presented without comment.

Roger Warren's new Oxford *Cymbeline*, the first critical edition of the play to appear in nearly four decades, presents a scrupulously edited text imbued throughout with the careful attention to theatricality that one would expect from the author of *Staging Shakespeare's Late Plays* (1990).[23] Warren, who served as dramaturg for Peter Hall's 1988 production of the play at the National Theatre, acknowledges that 'working on every line of the text with the company for several months was an invaluable preparation for this edition' (p. v). His introduction explores a genuinely reciprocal relationship between theatrical interpretation and editing. At an early rehearsal for the production at the National, the ghosts' speeches in Posthumus's dream 'were spoken slowly, steadily, marking the short-line layout as printed in this edition, with a simple dignity that evoked a world of heroic antiquity; but in performance, they were treated as fourteeners and spoken very rapidly, with the rhythms exaggerated. . .

---

22 The lemma in both the textual note and commentary note for 1.1.6 should read 1.1.6.1–2; the stage directions given in broken brackets at 2.2.89 and 3.2.93 are not collated.

23 There is a lone error in the textual collations at 3.3.78: for 'nor here, nor' read 'Nor here, nor'; in the commentary notes at 1.1.15 for 'glad' read 'Glad'; 4.2.72 for 'let' read 'Let'.

The experience of the National Theatre's versions suggested that the lines sound less threadbare, less like doggerel, when they are delivered simply, without calling too much attention to their origin in the fourteener; and this has influenced my decision to print them substantially as they appear in the Folio text' (p. 55).

Interpretive possibilities suggested by stage history find their way fruitfully into Warren's commentary as well. A note on Innogen's 'O no, no!' (1.6.199) observes that 'this simple phrase permits widely different interpretations, from Peggy Ashcroft's generous warmth to Judi Dench's icy politeness which did not conceal intense dislike of Giacomo and his methods'. Although Warren's comments on specific staging practices make for particularly satisfying notes, the repetition of some single-word glosses throughout the text can become redundant (*Haply* is glossed as 'perhaps' at 3.3.29, 3.4.148, 3.5.60, and 4.1.18).

Cymbeline presents few textual problems, but the name of its central character has become a matter of debate in recent years. Should an editor retain the Folio's invariable 'Imogen' or acknowledge that the spelling probably represents a minim error, made by Ralph Crane in preparing the Folio copy, for 'Innogen', the spelling (of Britain's first queen) in Holinshed and in Simon Forman's eyewitness account of the play? Warren follows the editors of the Oxford *Complete Works* in opting for 'Innogen'. He notes that with its overtones of innocence, Innogen gives the character's name a significant etymology corresponding to those of other late-play heroines: Marina (born at sea), Perdita (the lost one), Miranda (the top of admiration). A ghost character named Innogen, Leonato's wife, appears in the opening stage direction of *Much Ado About Nothing*. The fact that Shakespeare apparently intended to name that husband and wife pair Leonato and Innogen provides further evidence that Posthumus Leonatus's wife was called Innogen as well. Finally, and perhaps most importantly for

Warren, the emendation has been shown to be effective in the theatre. In Hall's 1988 production, 'Innogen' was used in rehearsal on an experimental basis, and it was 'Posthumus's constant anguished reiteration of the name in the last act . . . that clinched its appropriateness for Hall' who remarked that the name becomes 'a kind of talisman for Posthumus, a symbol of innocence and integrity, the qualities he has lacked himself' (p. 268).

Although the Oldcastle/Falstaff controversy does not present an entirely analogous situation to Innogen/Imogen (where there is no suggestion of censorship), it may be salutary to compare the two. René Weis's arguments for retaining Falstaff have to do with respecting the Folio text and four hundred years of tradition; Warren, on the other hand, trusts Simon Forman more than the Folio editors, and thinks the change is called for despite the 'powerful tradition supporting the Folio reading' (p. 268). Warren provides a useful new piece of archival evidence, an entry for the Forman manuscript in a 1697 catalogue of Ashmolean manuscripts, proving beyond any doubt that it is not a Collier forgery but an authentic document. Nevertheless, one wonders if Warren's faith in Forman may be misplaced. After all, Forman in his account of *Macbeth* made such homonymic errors as 'Mackbeth, king of Codon', 'Bancko', and 'Mackdoues wife & children'. The decision to emend to 'Innogen' implies that Forman's recollection of one performance is right, and that Heminges and Condell, who presumably acted in the play on a number of occasions, did not notice that the name was wrong.

Emending 'Imogen' to 'Innogen' in the text of the play is one thing, but incorporating 'Innogen' into the discussion of the play's stage history and its critical reception seems anachronistic. Keats, Tennyson, and Swinburne were not members of 'the cult of Innogen'; nor was Ellen Terry 'the most famous Innogen of the nineteenth century' (p. 6). When Swinburne referred to 'the woman above all Shakespeare's women' he was talking about Imogen; so too, when Terry corresponded with George Bernard Shaw about her speech beside the headless body of Cloten, they were analysing Imogen. Warren's emendation may now provide a text of the play as Shakespeare intended it, but it cannot or at least *should* not change what Warren himself calls 'the seductive theatrical and literary associations that have accumulated around "Imogen"' (p. 268).

The project to translate the text of the Oxford Shakespeare into French, under the general editorship of Michel Grivelet and Gilles Monsarrat, has produced a handsome boxed set of the *Histoires*, including the two tetralogies, *King John*, *Sir Thomas More*, and *Henry VIII* (the title of which the editors tellingly choose over Oxford's *All is True*) with facing-page translations. Grivelet introduces the series with a brief discussion of the art of translation, poking fun at Voltaire's first translation of *Hamlet* ('une belle infidèle') for emulating the elevated diction of classical French tragedies and departing too much from Shakespeare's text, and concluding that a good translation is one that is faithful to the thought of the text ('D'une bonne traduction on attend qu'elle soit fidèle, fidèle à la pensée du texte').

Despite this apparent uniformity of mission, the team of translators involved in this project have dramatically different styles: Victor Bourgy, who translated the *Henry VI* plays, often seems more willing to alter syntax and change idioms than Pierre Spriet whose translation of *Henry VIII* is quite literal. Bourgy's translations in particular often seem to miss the subtleties of the original. In the introduction to *3 Henry VI*, Bourgy translates the oft-cited passage from Greene's *Groatsworth of Wit* with no apparent awareness of the pun in 'Shake-scene in a country' which is rendered 'Branle-scène du pays' (p. 400). In the first scene of *3 Henry VI*, Henry enters to find York seated on the throne and deduces that York intends 'To aspire unto the crown and reign as king' (1.1.53), which Bourgy renders as 'Réclamer la couronne, avoir titre de roi'. *Réclamer* is used in

this case as claiming an actual right, which seems to miss the accusatory tone of 'aspiring'. Bourgy regularises the speech heading 'KING HENRY' to 'LE ROI' throughout the play, which would not cause any difficulty were it not that he regularises 'KING EDWARD' to 'LE ROI' as well. When a reader finds Henry's speech-heading at 4.7.68 is 'LE ROI', and Edward's speech-heading thirty lines later at 4.8.1 is also 'LE ROI', one suspects that, whoever is king, confusion will reign. (I am indebted to Jennifer Forsyth for several of these observations.)

ELECTRONIC EDITIONS

The potential use of the Internet as a research tool in Shakespeare studies is showcased by Bernice W. Kliman's *Enfolded Hamlet* on the World Wide Web. Kliman originally developed this innovative edition as a working text for the New Variorum *Hamlet*. (Full disclosure: I am one of the four co-editors at work on this project and am one of the dedicatees of the *Enfolded Hamlet*.) In its paper format, the enfolded text is a diplomatic reprint of the Second Quarto employing a system of curly and pointed brackets so that Q2 and F1 readings can be present, and distinguished, in the same line of text. In the electronic version, browsers that support font colours can display the different texts with colour coding. The enfolded text appears as dark blue with passages unique to Q2 in green and passages unique to F1 in purple. Readers can select a variety of display options: the enfolded version, the full Q2 version, the full F1 version, a Q2-Only version (displaying those lines or parts of lines that occur *only* in the Second Quarto), and a F1-Only version (displaying those lines or parts of lines that occur only in the First Folio).

Jeffery A. Triggs, director of the North American Reading Program for the *Oxford English Dictionary*, has developed a search engine for the *Enfolded Hamlet* which incorporates a sophisticated 'Variant Spellings' option that pre-processes a modern spelling into a number of likely early modern English variations and then searches the *Hamlet* texts for any of these. Although the hard-copy version of Kliman's edition has been available to Shakespearians for a number of years (*The Shakespeare Newsletter* devoted a special issue to the publication of *The Enfolded Hamlet* in 1996; in 1995 it was used as an acting text by the Shenandoah Shakespeare Express, under the direction of Ralph A. Cohen), scholarly usage has jumped exponentially now that the electronic version is available on the Internet (http://narp.oed.com/enfolded.html): the site currently receives between 5,000 and 6,000 'hits' per day; on an average day, the search engine is run over a thousand times.

A copy of John Benson's edition of *Poems: Written by Wil. Shake-speare. Gent* (London, 1640) recently sold at Sotheby's for $110,000. Octavo Digital Rare Books, a small start-up company in California, now offers a picture-perfect electronic edition of the Warnock Library copy on CD-ROM for a mere $25. The entire book has been digitally photographed in two-page spreads, including the original calf binding and the endpapers. Readers can choose a variety of resolutions, suitable for different purposes: one at 'screen' resolution for browsing and paging through the text, one at a higher resolution for zooming-in to a comfortable distance to read, and another resolution optimized for printing. For $50, Octavo offers an 'Archival' edition that provides very high resolution that enables users to zoom-in up to 800 per cent in order to study details of printer's ornaments, individual letters, or even the chain lines on the paper. Octavo's most interesting innovation is what it calls 'live text': digital text that can be scrolled through, copied, and searched. This is done essentially by hiding an Adobe PageMaker file behind the image on every page, with invisible PostScript type that corresponds to the printed type shown on the page. The result is an extraordinary edition and research tool: students can get a sense of a

Renaissance reader's experience of the 1640 octavo; teachers can cut, paste, and print a selection of sonnets for classroom use; critics can search for key words; and textual scholars can even undertake detailed study of the recurrence of identifiably damaged pieces of type.

TEXTUAL STUDY

Many textual critics and editors, exulting in what they perceive to be their recent move 'from a prestigious but somewhat marginal role within Shakespeare criticism to centre stage', firmly believe that 'few critics today are likely to discuss or quote, say, *Hamlet* or *King Lear* without indicating at least a consciousness of the differences between the respective Quarto and Folio texts' (Elam and Thompson, p. 335). Such assertions may be tested by a consideration of *'Lear' From Study to Stage*, a new collection of essays that foregrounds textual study but ultimately serves to reaffirm its continuing marginal role. James Ogden and the late Arthur Scouten set out to design an anthology that would prove useful to school teachers of *King Lear* 'who will certainly know that since Bradley there has been much work on the play, but will probably not be Shakespeare specialists themselves, and will possibly feel they cannot cope with it all' (p. 11). The collection, which reprints previously published articles that the general editors thought deserved more prominence (such as William A. Ringler's 1981 essay on 'Shakespeare and his Actors'), begins with several newly commissioned essays by leading textual critics intended to introduce students and teachers to the various sides of the revision debate.

T. H. Howard-Hill offers a history of 'The Two-Text Controversy', drawing an important distinction between 'preperformance' and 'postperformance' revision, and providing useful tables of Q-only and F-only passages. Howard-Hill writes with his characteristic authority and grace, but one wonders if his discussion of the 'plurisignative' nature of textual phenomena might be over the heads of the book's intended audience. Grace Ioppolo argues for revision in 'The Idea of Shakespeare and the Two *Lears*' while Richard Knowles presents the case against revision in 'Two *Lears*? By Shakespeare?' The contributors apparently did not have access to each other's work, so potentially lively internal debate between essays is not possible except in the few instances in which they coincidentally respond to each other. Ioppolo, for instance, argues for a pattern of revision in which Folio passages 'omit references to a French invasion and replace them with passages on civil war' (p. 52). Knowles effectively undercuts this thesis by quoting R. A. Foakes, himself a champion of revision, who observes that 'arguments that the Folio changes a French invasion into a civil war . . . [are] not borne out either by the text, which in F, in spite of omissions, still emphasizes that Cordelia leads a French army, or by the stage directions calling for the 'colours' of what must be a French army' (p. 70).

Impartial observers will be amused that both sides claim Nicholas Hytner's 1990 Royal Shakespeare Company production as a victory. Ioppolo points to the RSC production, based on the Folio text, as evidence of a *zeitgeist* at work in which scholars, theatre people, and 'even non-Shakespearians' acknowledge 'that the play was authorially revised' and Hytner himself 'spread the doctrine in the London *Times*' (p. 53). On the other side of the fence, Robert Clare in 'Quarto and Folio: A Case for Conflation', observes that Hytner, in fact, could not convince his actors that the major Folio cuts were theatrically viable, and, after testing the variants of 3.6 in rehearsal, even Hytner agreed that the mock trial had to be included, as was the whole of Edgar's fourteen-line soliloquy in rhymed couplets that closes the Quarto version of 3.6. 'Hytner's production was far from providing the revisionists with the vindication of their argument for which they may have hoped . . . His text was, after all, a conflation' (pp. 95–6).

The quiet irony of *'Lear' from Study to Stage*

comes in a footnote to Richard Levin's '*King Lear* Defamiliarized', a lucid review of thirty-six recent critical studies (including important essays by Adelman, Dollimore, Erickson, Goldberg, Greenblatt, Heinemann, Kahn, Patterson, and Tennenhouse), in which Levin notes that only *one* of these interpretations relies upon the two-text theory (Leah Marcus's occasionalist reading of the Quarto version which, she argues, contains material written especially for the court performance on St Stephen's Night 1606). Equally tellingly, Benedict Nightingale's twenty-page review of London productions of the play in the last two decades never once mentions the Quarto or the Folio and never raises the spectre of revision. No matter how boldly textual scholars proclaim themselves the acknowledged legislators of the Shakespearian world, those engaged in the business of critical interpretation and performance continue, it would seem, to have little interest in textual criticism or in the two versions of Shakespeare's *Lear*.

WORKS REVIEWED

Bliss, Lee, 'Scribes, Compositors, and Annotators: The Nature of the Copy for the First Folio Text of *Coriolanus*', *Studies in Bibliography*, 50 (1997), 224–61.

Elam, Keir and Ann Thompson, 'The One and the Many'. Introductory essay to a special issue of *Textus* devoted to 'Shakespeare's Text(s)', *Textus: English Studies in Italy*, 9 (1996), 335–8.

Holderness, Graham and Bryan Loughrey, 'Shakespeare Misconstrued: The True Chronicle Historie of *Shakespearean Originals*', *Textus: English Studies in Italy*, 9 (1996), 393–418.

Kliman, Bernice W., ed., *The Enfolded 'Hamlet'*, The World Wide Web (http://narp.oed.com /enfolded.html).

Melchiori, Giorgio, 'What did Shakespeare Write?', *Textus: English Studies in Italy*, 9 (1996), 339–56.

Merriam, Thomas, 'Heterogeneous Authorship in Early Shakespeare and the Problem of *Henry V*'. *Literary and Linguistic Computing*, 13 (1998), 1–28.

'Invalidation Reappraised', *Computers and the Humanities*, 30 (1997), 417–31.

'Marlowe's hand in *Edward III* revisited', *Literary and Linguistic Computing*, 11 (1996), 19–22.

Ogden, James and Arthur Scouten, eds., *'Lear' from Study to Stage* (Madison, Teaneck, and London, 1997).

Shakespeare, William, *Cymbeline*, ed. by Roger Warren, Oxford Shakespeare (Oxford, 1998).

King Edward III, ed. by Giorgio Melchiori, The New Cambridge Shakespeare (Cambridge, 1998).

The First Quarto of Hamlet, ed. by Kathleen O. Irace, The New Cambridge Shakespeare: The Early Quartos (Cambridge, 1998).

The First Part of King Henry IV, ed. by Herbert Weil and Judith Weil, The New Cambridge Shakespeare (Cambridge, 1997).

Henry IV Part 2, ed. by René Weis, Oxford Shakespeare (Oxford, 1998).

Julius Caesar, ed. by David Daniell, Arden 3 (Walton-on-Thames, 1998).

Love's Labour's Lost, ed. by H. R. Woudhuysen, Arden 3 (Walton-on-Thames, 1998).

The Merry Wives of Windsor, ed. by David Crane, The New Cambridge Shakespeare (Cambridge, 1997).

Œuvres Complètes, Édition bilingue, Histoires I & II, ed. by Michel Grivelet and Gilles Monsarrat (Paris, 1997).

Pericles, ed. by Doreen DelVecchio and Antony Hammond, The New Cambridge Shakespeare (Cambridge, 1998).

Poems: Written by Wil. Shake-speare. Gent, ed. by Arthur Freeman (Octavo Digital Rare Books, 1998).

Shakespeare's Sonnets, ed. by Katherine Duncan-Jones, Arden 3 (Walton-on-Thames, 1997).

Troilus and Cressida, ed. by David Bevington, Arden 3 (Walton-on-Thames, 1998.

Wells, Stanley, 'Multiple Texts and the Oxford Shakespeare', in *Textus: English Studies in Italy*, 9 (1996), 375–92.

BOOKS RECEIVED

This list includes all books received between September 1997 and September 1998 which are not reviewed in this volume of *Shakespeare Survey*. The appearance of a book in this list does not preclude its review in a subsequent volume.

Aligarh Critical Miscellany, vol. 9 (1996), no. 1 (Aligarh, 1996).

Ara, Iffat, *The Concepts of Nature and Art in the Last Plays of Shakespeare* (New Delhi, 1997).

Bretzius, Stephen, *Shakespeare in Theory: The Postmodern Academy and the Early Modern Theatre* (Michigan, 1997).

Gill, Richard, *Mastering Shakespeare* (Basingstoke, 1998).

Halasz, Alexandra, *The Marketplace of Print* (Cambridge, 1997).

Kolin, Philip C., ed., *Venus and Adonis: Critical Essays* (New York, 1997).

Le forme del teatro, vols. 5 and 6 (Rome, 1997).

Marlowe, Christopher, *Complete Works of Christopher Marlowe*, vol. 5: *Tamburlaine the Great Parts 1 and 2*, ed. by David Fuller and *The Massacre at Paris with the Death of the Duke of Guise*, ed. by Edward J. Esche (Oxford, 1998).

Mr William Shakespeare's Comedies, Histories and Tragedies, a facsimile of the First Folio in paperback (London, 1998).

Spevack, Marvin, *James Orchard Halliwell-Phillipps: A Classified Bibliography* (Hildesheim, Zurich, New York, 1997).

INDEX

INDEX

INDEX

INDEX

INDEX

INDEX

INDEX